2000
America's
Top-Rated Cities:
A Statistical Handbook

Volume 3: Central Region

Grey House
Publishing

LAKEVILLE, CT 06039

PUBLISHER: Leslie Mackenzie
EDITOR: David Garoogian
EDITORIAL DIRECTOR: Laura Mars
EDITORIAL ASSISTANT: Robin Williams
PRODUCTION MANAGER: Timothy Cushman
MARKET RESEARCH: Jessica Moody
GRAPHIC DESIGNER: Deb Fletcher

Grey House Publishing, Inc.
Pocket Knife Square
Lakeville, CT 06039
860.435.0868
FAX 860.435.6613
http://www.greyhouse.com

First edition published 1992
Seventh edition published 1999

Printed in the USA

Library of Congress Cataloging in Publication Data available

4-Volume Set	ISBN 1-891482-50-5
Volume 1	ISBN 1-891482-51-3
Volume 2	ISBN 1-891482-52-1
Volume 3	**ISBN 1-891482-53-X**
Volume 4	ISBN 1-891482-54-8

Table of Contents

Ann Arbor, Michigan

Chicago, Illinois

Des Moines, Iowa

Detroit, Michigan

Fort Wayne, Indiana

Gary, Indiana

Grand Rapids, Michigan

Indianapolis, Indiana

Kansas City, Missouri

Lansing, Michigan

Little Rock, Arkansas

Madison, Wisconsin

Milwaukee, Wisconsin

Minneapolis, Minnesota

Oklahoma City, Oklahoma

Omaha, Nebraska

Saint Louis, Missouri

Springfield, Missouri

Wichita, Kansas

Introduction

Welcome to *America's Top-Rated Cities, A Statistical Handbook, 2000,* a current and concise statistical profile of 76 cities that have received high marks for their business and living environment. This 7th edition of *ATRC*, previously published by Universal Reference Publications, incorporates information from hundreds of resources into one, easy-to-use format. It combines magazine rankings (*Money, Fortune, Entrepreneur, Sales & Marketing Management, Working Woman*, etc.) latest Federal, state and local statistics, published newspaper and magazine reports, and web site data to fill more than 60 charts and tables for each city.

Each of the four volumes is approximately 400 pages, and comprises a different region of the country – Southern, Western, Central and Eastern, and each region includes 19 cities, all with populations over 100,000.

Every year, our editors review hundreds of sources to develop the list of top cities in each region, invariably dropping some and adding others. This year's edition has 17 new cities not included last year – five Southern (**Birmingham, Chattanooga, Columbia, Jackson, Memphis**), five Eastern (**Akron, Louisville, Manchester, Providence, Rochester**), four Central (**Gary, Lansing, Omaha, Wichita**), and three Western (**Albuquerque, Reno, Spokane**). Plus, the cities from last year that made this year's cut have been revised and refreshed with new and updated data.

Within each volume, city chapters are arranged alphabetically, and each is divided into two sections: Business Environment and Living Environment. Each chapter begins with a background about the city, and narrative comments about changes in its environmental, political, or employment atmosphere that occurred in the past year. You'll learn, for example, that Las Vegas is cleaning up its image, how Chicago's mayor – an avid cyclist – supports his fellow riders, and the Y2K-ready measures the cities are taking.

There is data on cost of living, finances, taxes, population, employment and earnings, commercial real estate, education, major employers, media, crime, climate, professional sports teams and more. In most cases, you'll find comparisons between Metropolitan Statistical Areas (MSA) and U.S. census figures.

In addition to the comprehensive chapters, each volume contains four appendices: **Appendix A, Comparative Statistics:** City by city comparison of more than 50 categories that gives not just an overview of the city, but a broad profile of each geographic region of the country.

Appendix B, Metropolitan Statistical Areas (MSA): Includes the counties (and in some cases, state) that combine to form each city's MSA – an official designation used to define the area in terms of population, finance, economy, etc.

Appendix C, Chambers of Commerce and Economic Development Organizations: Includes address, phone numbers and fax numbers of these additional resources to help the readers to get further, more detailed information on each city.

Appendix D, State Departments of Labor and Employment: Another source of additional, more specific economic and employment data for each city, with address and phone numbers for easy access.

As in all previous editions, the material provided by public and private agencies and organizations was supplemented by numerous library sources and Internet sites. The editors thank everyone who responded to our requests for information, especially the Chambers of Commerce, Economic Development Organizations and Labor Market Information groups.

America's Top-Rated Cities is designed for a wide range of readers: private individuals considering relocating a residence or business; professionals considering expanding their business or changing careers; corporations considering relocation, opening up additional offices or creating new divisions; government agencies; general and market researchers; real estate consultants; human resource personnel; urban planners; investors; and urban government students.

Grey House Publishing has also acquired from Universal Reference Publications the following titles: *America's Top-Rated Smaller Cities, Health & Environment in America's Top-Rated Cities* and *Crime in America's Top-Rated Cities*, developed in the spirit of offering a series of comprehensive statistical reference books about America's top cities. Grey House is revising and updating each of these and will offer the *Smaller Cities* and *Crime* titles in the Spring of 2000, and *Environment* in the Fall of that year.

As always, we welcome your comments and suggestions for continuous improvement.

Ann Arbor, Michigan

Background

Ann Arbor is located on the Huron River, 36 miles west of Detroit. It was founded in 1824 by John Allen and Elisha W. Rumsey, two East Coast entrepreneurs who named the settlement for their wives—both Ann—and for the community's location which was within natural groves. In 1851, Ann Arbor was chartered as a city.

After the arrival of the Michigan Central Railroad in 1839, the settlement developed as an agriculture trading center, and continues to be the trading center for the rich agricultural area surrounding it.

Before the arrival of settlers, the Ojibwa tribe roamed the area, which they called Washtenaw—the land beyond—which now serves for the county of which Ann Arbor is the seat.

The University of Michigan has played a prominent role in Ann Arbor's development as a major Midwest center for aeronautical, space, nuclear, chemical, and metallurgical research. The city manufactures include machinery, tools, steel ball bearing, scientific instruments, doors and blinds, cameras, and coil springs.

Located in the humid continental climate zone, Ann Arbor's summers are hot, winters are cold, and there is an above-average occurrence of snow and rain. Proximity to the Great Lakes cause extreme temperatures to be moderated, along with high humidity and cloud cover two-thirds of the time.

General Rankings and Evaluative Comments

- Ann Arbor was ranked #6 out of 24 mid-sized, midwestern metropolitan areas in *Money's* 1998 survey of "The Best Places to Live in America." The survey was conducted by first contacting 512 representative households nationwide and asking them to rank 37 quality-of-life factors on a scale of 1 to 10. Next, a demographic profile was compiled on the 300 largest metropolitan statistical areas in the U.S. The numbers were crunched together to arrive at an overall ranking (things Americans consider most important, like clean air and water, low crime and good schools, received extra weight). Unlike previous years, the 1998 rankings were broken down by region (northeast, midwest, south, west) and population size (100,000 to 249,999; 250,000 to 999,999; 1 million plus). The city had a nationwide ranking of #68 out of 300 in 1997 and #5 out of 300 in 1996. *Money, July 1998; Money, July 1997; Money, September 1996*

- *Ladies Home Journal* ranked America's 200 largest cities based on the qualities women care about most. Ann Arbor ranked #1 out of 200. Criteria: low crime rate, well-paying jobs, quality health and child care, good public schools, the presence of women in government, size of the gender wage gap, number of sexual-harassment and discrimination complaints filed, unemployment and divorce rates, commute times, population density, number of houses of worship, parks and cultural offerings, number of women's health specialists, how well a community's women cared for themselves, complexion kindness index based on UV radiation levels, odds of finding affordable fashions, rental rates for romance movies, champagne sales and other matters of the heart. *Ladies Home Journal, November 1998*

- Zero Population Growth ranked 229 cities in terms of children's health, safety, and economic well-being. Ann Arbor was ranked #4 out of 92 suburbs and outer cities (incorporated areas of more than 100,000 within the MSA of a major city) and was given a grade of A. Criteria: total population, percent of population under 18 years of age, household language, percent population change, percent of births to teens, infant mortality rate, percent of low birth weights, dropout rate, enrollment in preprimary school, violent and property crime rates, unemployment rate, percent of children in poverty, percent of owner occupied units, number of bad air days, percent of public transportation commuters, and average travel time to work. *Zero Population Growth, Children's Environmental Index, Fall 1999*

- Reliastar Financial Corp. ranked the 125 largest metropolitan areas according to the general financial security of residents. Ann Arbor was ranked #1 out of 125 with a score of 18.3. The score indicates the percentage a metropolitan area is above or below the metropolitan norm. A metro area with a score of 10.6 is 10.6% above the metro average. Criteria: Earnings and Wealth Potential (household income, education, net assets, cost of living); Safety Net (health insurance, retirement savings, life insurance, income support programs); Personal Threats (unemployment rate, low-income households, crime rate); Community Economic Vitality (cost of community services, job quality, job creation, housing costs). *Reliastar Financial Corp., "The Best Cities to Earn and Save Money," 1999 Edition*

Business Environment

STATE ECONOMY

State Economic Profile

"Although the Michigan economy bounced back quickly from the GM strike, it is losing much of its mid-1990s momentum. Strong auto sales have not translated into employment gains in the auto industry. Canada's weak economy has caused a drop in MI's exports. And what constrains MI the most is its demographic situation. The next several years should see a slowing economy.

In spite of the GM strike and booming automobile sales, GM has not increased employment and is currently planning to close plants in Kalamazoo and Flint. In addition, some 1,000 office jobs are targeted for elimination at the Detroit headquarters; Ford is currently planning to cut jobs within the state. Auto sales for 1999 and 2000 should fall below 1998, only adding to Detroit's need for employment reductions.

Construction activity added significantly to job growth in 1998, with construction employment growing 2.5% for the state and 8.3% for Detroit. Almost 1,800 commercial/industrial developments were undertaken in 1998. With the slowing economy, construction activity is likely to contract in 1999, undermining one of MI's bright spots. Residential starts, up 7% in 1998, should decline 6.2% in 1999.

Michigan's tight labor markets have helped to absorb downsizing in the auto industry, keeping the unemployment rate manageable. Labor availability has, however, started to become a problem for the state's information technology firms. The state's weak population growth, especially its continuing loss of young households, will dampen the high home price appreciation witnessed in recent years, as well as limit job entry-level job growth." *National Association of Realtors, Economic Profiles: The Fifty States and the District of Columbia, http://nar.realtor.com/databank/profiles.htm*

IMPORTS/EXPORTS

Total Export Sales

Area	1994 ($000)	1995 ($000)	1996 ($000)	1997 ($000)	% Chg. 1994-97	% Chg. 1996-97
MSA[1]	2,075,769	1,157,910	1,311,134	1,520,885	-26.7	16.0
U.S.	512,415,609	583,030,524	622,827,063	687,597,999	34.2	10.4

Note: (1) Metropolitan Statistical Area - see Appendix A for areas included
Source: U.S. Department of Commerce, International Trade Association, Metropolitan Area Exports: An Export Performance Report on Over 250 U.S. Cities, November 10, 1998

CITY FINANCES

City Government Finances

Component	FY92 ($000)	FY92 (per capita $)
Revenue	134,280	1,214.65
Expenditure	135,573	1,226.35
Debt Outstanding	96,769	875.34
Cash & Securities	207,034	1,872.76

Source: U.S. Bureau of the Census, City Government Finances: 1991-92

City Government Revenue by Source

Source	FY92 ($000)	FY92 (per capita $)	FY92 (%)
From Federal Government	8,252	74.64	6.1
From State Governments	21,084	190.72	15.7
From Local Governments	984	8.90	0.7
Property Taxes	41,831	378.39	31.2
General Sales Taxes	0	0.00	0.0
Selective Sales Taxes	0	0.00	0.0
Income Taxes	0	0.00	0.0
Current Charges	20,592	186.27	15.3
Utility/Liquor Store	11,119	100.58	8.3
Employee Retirement[1]	16,596	150.12	12.4
Other	13,822	125.03	10.3

Note: (1) Excludes "city contributions," classified as "nonrevenue," intragovernmental transfers.
Source: U.S. Bureau of the Census, City Government Finances: 1991-92

City Government Expenditures by Function

Function	FY92 ($000)	FY92 (per capita $)	FY92 (%)
Educational Services	0	0.00	0.0
Employee Retirement[1]	9,823	88.86	7.2
Environment/Housing	21,287	192.56	15.7
Government Administration	8,715	78.83	6.4
Interest on General Debt	4,120	37.27	3.0
Public Safety	19,628	177.55	14.5
Social Services	721	6.52	0.5
Transportation	13,888	125.63	10.2
Utility/Liquor Store	25,188	227.84	18.6
Other	32,203	291.30	23.8

Note: (1) Payments to beneficiaries including withdrawal of contributions.
Source: U.S. Bureau of the Census, City Government Finances: 1991-92

Municipal Bond Ratings

Area	Moody's	S & P
Ann Arbor	A1	n/a

Note: n/a not available; n/r not rated
Source: Moody's Bond Record, 6/99

POPULATION

Population Growth

Area	1980	1990	% Chg. 1980-90	July 1998 Estimate	% Chg. 1990-98
City	107,960	109,592	1.5	109,967	0.3
MSA[1]	264,740	282,937	6.9	543,178	92.0
U.S.	226,545,805	248,765,170	9.8	270,299,000	8.7

Note: (1) Metropolitan Statistical Area - see Appendix A for areas included;
July 1998 MSA population estimate was calculated by the editors
Source: 1980/1990 Census of Housing and Population, Summary Tape File 3C;
Census Bureau Population Estimates 1998

Population Characteristics

Race	City 1980 Population	%	City 1990 Population	%	% Chg. 1980-90	MSA[1] 1990 Population	%
White	92,517	85.7	90,196	82.3	-2.5	237,109	83.8
Black	10,186	9.4	9,785	8.9	-3.9	31,468	11.1
Amer Indian/Esk/Aleut	240	0.2	263	0.2	9.6	851	0.3
Asian/Pacific Islander	4,062	3.8	8,513	7.8	109.6	11,764	4.2
Other	955	0.9	835	0.8	-12.6	1,745	0.6
Hispanic Origin[2]	2,096	1.9	2,629	2.4	25.4	5,526	2.0

Note: (1) Metropolitan Statistical Area - see Appendix A for areas included;
(2) people of Hispanic origin can be of any race
Source: 1980/1990 Census of Housing and Population, Summary Tape File 3C

Ancestry

Area	German	Irish	English	Italian	U.S.	French	Polish	Dutch
City	28.5	13.6	17.4	4.5	1.9	4.1	7.2	3.0
MSA[1]	31.5	14.8	16.7	3.9	3.2	5.0	6.8	3.3
U.S.	23.3	15.6	13.1	5.9	5.3	4.2	3.8	2.5

Note: Figures are percentages and include persons that reported multiple ancestry (eg. if a person reported being Irish and Italian, they were included in both columns); (1) Metropolitan Statistical Area - see Appendix A for areas included
Source: 1990 Census of Population and Housing, Summary Tape File 3C

Age

Area	Median Age (Years)	Under 5	Under 18	18-24	25-44	45-64	65+	80+
City	27.1	5.7	17.1	27.1	35.7	12.8	7.3	1.8
MSA[1]	29.2	6.7	21.5	19.4	36.1	15.5	7.5	1.7
U.S.	32.9	7.3	25.6	10.5	32.6	18.7	12.5	2.8

Note: (1) Metropolitan Statistical Area - see Appendix A for areas included
Source: 1990 Census of Population and Housing, Summary Tape File 3C

Male/Female Ratio

Area	Number of males per 100 females (all ages)	Number of males per 100 females (18 years old+)
City	97.4	96.2
MSA[1]	97.3	95.8
U.S.	95.0	91.9

Note: (1) Metropolitan Statistical Area - see Appendix A for areas included
Source: 1990 Census of Population, General Population Characteristics

INCOME

Per Capita/Median/Average Income

Area	Per Capita ($)	Median Household ($)	Average Household ($)
City	17,786	33,344	44,963
MSA[1]	17,115	36,307	45,105
U.S.	14,420	30,056	38,453

Note: All figures are for 1989; (1) Metropolitan Statistical Area - see Appendix A for areas included
Source: 1990 Census of Population and Housing, Summary Tape File 3C

Household Income Distribution by Race

Income ($)	City (%)					U.S. (%)				
	Total	White	Black	Other	Hisp.[1]	Total	White	Black	Other	Hisp.[1]
Less than 5,000	5.6	4.2	10.4	16.0	11.2	6.2	4.8	15.2	8.6	8.8
5,000 - 9,999	7.9	7.1	13.8	11.0	6.9	9.3	8.6	14.2	9.9	11.1
10,000 - 14,999	8.4	7.9	8.7	14.6	7.7	8.8	8.5	11.0	9.8	11.0
15,000 - 24,999	15.7	15.3	18.9	16.7	26.1	17.5	17.3	18.9	18.5	20.5
25,000 - 34,999	14.6	14.7	16.9	10.6	13.3	15.8	16.1	14.2	15.4	16.4
35,000 - 49,999	15.3	16.1	11.6	9.3	14.3	17.9	18.6	13.3	16.1	16.0
50,000 - 74,999	17.3	18.4	13.1	9.8	10.9	15.0	15.8	9.3	13.4	11.1
75,000 - 99,999	7.5	8.0	3.1	7.0	1.7	5.1	5.5	2.6	4.7	3.1
100,000+	7.8	8.4	3.5	4.9	7.7	4.4	4.8	1.3	3.7	1.9

Note: All figures are for 1989; (1) people of Hispanic origin can be of any race
Source: 1990 Census of Population and Housing, Summary Tape File 3C

Effective Buying Income

Area	Per Capita ($)	Median Household ($)	Average Household ($)
City	20,629	39,589	53,397
MSA[1]	19,305	43,600	53,479
U.S.	16,803	34,536	45,243

Note: Data as of 1/1/99; (1) Metropolitan Statistical Area - see Appendix A for areas included
Source: Standard Rate & Data Service, Newspaper Advertising Source, 9/99

Effective Household Buying Income Distribution

Area	% of Households Earning						
	$10,000 -$19,999	$20,000 -$34,999	$35,000 -$49,999	$50,000 -$74,999	$75,000 -$99,000	$100,000 -$124,999	$125,000 and up
City	14.2	20.0	15.4	19.6	10.6	4.7	5.3
MSA[1]	12.2	19.2	18.1	23.8	11.2	3.8	3.6
U.S.	16.0	22.6	18.2	18.9	7.2	2.4	2.7

Note: Data as of 1/1/99; (1) Metropolitan Statistical Area - see Appendix A for areas included
Source: Standard Rate & Data Service, Newspaper Advertising Source, 9/99

Poverty Rates by Race and Age

Area	Total (%)	By Race (%)				By Age (%)		
		White	Black	Other	Hisp.[2]	Under 5 years old	Under 18 years old	65 years and over
City	16.1	14.4	20.8	27.2	21.5	9.8	8.4	7.4
MSA[1]	12.2	10.0	23.0	25.8	18.9	12.6	10.8	8.0
U.S.	13.1	9.8	29.5	23.1	25.3	20.1	18.3	12.8

Note: Figures show the percent of people living below the poverty line in 1989. The average poverty threshold was $12,674 for a family of four in 1989; (1) Metropolitan Statistical Area - see Appendix A for areas included; (2) people of Hispanic origin can be of any race
Source: 1990 Census of Population and Housing, Summary Tape File 3C

EMPLOYMENT

Labor Force and Employment

Area	Civilian Labor Force			Workers Employed		
	Jun. 1998	Jun. 1999	% Chg.	Jun. 1998	Jun. 1999	% Chg.
City	67,390	68,234	1.3	66,312	67,092	1.2
MSA[1]	296,042	299,888	1.3	289,780	293,190	1.2
U.S.	138,798,000	140,666,000	1.3	132,265,000	134,395,000	1.6

Note: Data is not seasonally adjusted and covers workers 16 years of age and older; (1) Metropolitan Statistical Area - see Appendix A for areas included
Source: Bureau of Labor Statistics, http://stats.bls.gov

Unemployment Rate

Area	1998						1999					
	Jul.	Aug.	Sep.	Oct.	Nov.	Dec.	Jan.	Feb.	Mar.	Apr.	May.	Jun.
City	2.2	1.4	1.9	1.4	1.3	1.3	1.8	1.9	1.7	1.5	1.6	1.7
MSA[1]	3.3	2.0	2.2	1.8	1.7	1.8	3.0	2.8	2.5	2.0	2.0	2.2
U.S.	4.7	4.5	4.4	4.2	4.1	4.0	4.8	4.7	4.4	4.1	4.0	4.5

Note: Data is not seasonally adjusted and covers workers 16 years of age and older; all figures are percentages; (1) Metropolitan Statistical Area - see Appendix A for areas included
Source: Bureau of Labor Statistics, http://stats.bls.gov

Employment by Industry

Sector	MSA[1] Number of Employees	MSA[1] Percent of Total	U.S. Percent of Total
Services	70,000	25.3	30.4
Retail Trade	46,400	16.8	17.7
Government	69,400	25.1	15.6
Manufacturing	52,900	19.1	14.3
Finance/Insurance/Real Estate	10,400	3.8	5.9
Wholesale Trade	9,600	3.5	5.4
Transportation/Public Utilities	6,600	2.4	5.3
Construction	n/a	n/a	5.0
Mining	n/a	n/a	0.4

Note: Figures cover non-farm employment as of 6/99 and are not seasonally adjusted; (1) Metropolitan Statistical Area - see Appendix A for areas included; n/a not available
Source: Bureau of Labor Statistics, http://stats.bls.gov

Employment by Occupation

Occupation Category	City (%)	MSA[1] (%)	U.S. (%)
White Collar	79.3	68.1	58.1
Executive/Admin./Management	13.9	12.8	12.3
Professional	33.7	24.4	14.1
Technical & Related Support	7.6	5.8	3.7
Sales	9.7	10.0	11.8
Administrative Support/Clerical	14.3	15.2	16.3
Blue Collar	8.3	17.6	26.2
Precision Production/Craft/Repair	3.7	7.7	11.3
Machine Operators/Assem./Insp.	2.1	5.7	6.8
Transportation/Material Movers	1.1	2.1	4.1
Cleaners/Helpers/Laborers	1.4	2.1	3.9
Services	12.0	13.2	13.2
Farming/Forestry/Fishing	0.5	1.1	2.5

Note: Figures cover employed persons 16 years old and over; (1) Metropolitan Statistical Area - see Appendix A for areas included
Source: 1990 Census of Population and Housing, Summary Tape File 3C

Occupational Employment Projections: 1994 - 2005

Occupations Expected to Have the Largest Job Growth (ranked by numerical growth)	Fast-Growing Occupations[1] (ranked by percent growth)
1. Waiters & waitresses	1. Computer engineers
2. Cashiers	2. Home health aides
3. All other helper, laborer, mover	3. Systems analysts
4. Systems analysts	4. Personal and home care aides
5. Home health aides	5. Electronic pagination systems workers
6. General managers & top executives	6. All other computer scientists
7. All other profess., paraprofess., tech.	7. Physical therapists
8. Registered nurses	8. All other therapists
9. All other sales reps. & services	9. Electronics repairers, comm. & indust.
10. Salespersons, retail	10. Occupational therapists

Note: Projections cover Michigan; (1) Excludes occupations with total job growth less than 300
Source: Office of Labor Market Information, Occupational Employment Forecasts, 1994-2005

TAXES

Major State and Local Tax Rates

State Corp. Income (%)	State Personal Income (%)	Residential Property (effective rate per $100)	Sales & Use State (%)	Sales & Use Local (%)	State Gasoline (cents/ gallon)	State Cigarette (cents/ pack)
2.3[a]	4.4	n/a	6.0	None	19.0	75.0

Note: Personal/corporate income, sales, gasoline and cigarette tax rates as of January 1999. Property tax rates as of 1997; (a) Value added tax imposed on the sum of federal taxable income of the business, compensation paid to employees, dividends, interest, royalties paid and other items
Source: Federation of Tax Administrators, www.taxadmin.org; Washington D.C. Department of Finance and Revenue, Tax Rates and Tax Burdens in the District of Columbia: A Nationwide Comparison, July 1998; Chamber of Commerce, 1999

Total Taxes Per Capita and as a Percent of Income

Area	Per Capita Income ($)	Per Capita Taxes ($) Total	Per Capita Taxes ($) Federal	Per Capita Taxes ($) State/ Local	Percent of Income (%) Total	Percent of Income (%) Federal	Percent of Income (%) State/ Local
Michigan	28,565	10,361	7,221	3,139	36.3	25.3	11.0
U.S.	27,876	9,881	6,690	3,191	35.4	24.0	11.4

Note: Figures are for 1998
Source: Tax Foundation, www.taxfoundation.org

COMMERCIAL REAL ESTATE

Data not available at time of publication.

COMMERCIAL UTILITIES

Typical Monthly Electric Bills

Area	Commercial Service ($/month) 12 kW demand 1,500 kWh	Commercial Service ($/month) 100 kW demand 30,000 kWh	Industrial Service ($/month) 1,000 kW demand 400,000 kWh	Industrial Service ($/month) 20,000 kW demand 10,000,000 kWh
City	n/a	n/a	n/a	n/a
U.S.	150	2,174	23,995	508,569

Note: Based on rates in effect January 1, 1999; n/a not available
Source: Edison Electric Institute, Typical Residential, Commercial and Industrial Bills, Winter 1999

TRANSPORTATION

Transportation Statistics

Average minutes to work	17.0
Interstate highways	I-94
Bus lines	
In-city	Ann Arbor Transportation Authority
Inter-city	4
Passenger air service	
Airport	Detroit-Wayne County Airport (25 miles east)
Airlines	14
Aircraft departures	n/a
Enplaned passengers	n/a
Rail service	Amtrak
Motor freight carriers	6
Major waterways/ports	None

Source: Editor & Publisher Market Guide, 1999; FAA Airport Activity Statistics, 1997; Amtrak National Time Table, Northeast Timetable, Spring/Summer 1999; 1990 Census of Population and Housing, STF 3C; Chamber of Commerce/Economic Development 1999; Jane's Urban Transport Systems 1999-2000

Means of Transportation to Work

Area	Car/Truck/Van		Public Transportation			Bicycle	Walked	Other Means	Worked at Home
	Drove Alone	Car-pooled	Bus	Subway	Railroad				
City	61.8	9.2	5.4	0.0	0.0	2.1	17.1	0.5	3.9
MSA[1]	73.5	9.6	2.9	0.0	0.0	1.0	9.2	0.5	3.2
U.S.	73.2	13.4	3.0	1.5	0.5	0.4	3.9	1.2	3.0

Note: Figures shown are percentages and only include workers 16 years old and over;
(1) Metropolitan Statistical Area - see Appendix A for areas included
Source: 1990 Census of Population and Housing, Summary Tape File 3C

BUSINESSES

Major Business Headquarters

Company Name	1999 Rankings	
	Fortune 500	Forbes 500
Domino's Pizza	-	185
Flint Ink	-	144

Note: Companies listed are located in the city; dashes indicate no ranking
Fortune 500: Companies that produce a 10-K are ranked 1 to 500 based on 1998 revenue
Forbes 500: Private companies are ranked 1 to 500 based on 1997 revenue
Source: Forbes, November 30, 1998; Fortune, April 26, 1999

Fast-Growing Businesses

Ann Arbor is home to one of *Business Week's* "hot growth" companies: Kaydon. Criteria: increase in sales and profits, return on capital and stock price. *Business Week, 5/31/99*

Minority Business Opportunity

Ann Arbor is home to one company which is on the Black Enterprise Auto Dealer 100 list (largest based on gross sales): Bradley Automitive Group (GMC, Saturn, Pontiac, Buick) . Criteria: 1) operational in previous calendar year; 2) at least 51% black-owned. *Black Enterprise, www.blackenterprise.com*

One of the 500 largest Hispanic-owned companies in the U.S. are located in Ann Arbor. *Hispanic Business, June 1999*

HOTELS & MOTELS

Hotels/Motels

Area	Hotels/ Motels	Rooms	Luxury-Level Hotels/Motels		Average Minimum Rates ($)		
			♦♦♦♦	♦♦♦♦♦	♦♦	♦♦♦	♦♦♦♦
City	20	2,553	0	0	n/a	n/a	n/a

Note: n/a not available; classifications range from one diamond (budget properties with basic amenities) to five diamond (luxury properties with the finest service, rooms and facilities).
Source: OAG, Business Travel Planner, Winter 1998-99

CONVENTION CENTERS

Major Convention Centers

Center Name	Meeting Rooms	Exhibit Space (sq. ft.)
Clarion Hotel Atrium & Conference CEnter	15	7,000

Source: Trade Shows Worldwide, 1998; Meetings & Conventions, 4/15/99; Sucessful Meetings, 3/31/98

Living Environment

COST OF LIVING

Cost of Living Index

Composite Index	Groceries	Housing	Utilities	Trans-portation	Health Care	Misc. Goods/ Services
113.5	105.8	123.9	97.0	125.3	118.0	108.4

Note: U.S. = 100
Source: ACCRA, Cost of Living Index, 2nd Quarter 1996

HOUSING

Median Home Prices and Housing Affordability

Area	Median Price[2] 1st Qtr. 1999 ($)	HOI[3] 1st Qtr. 1999	Afford-ability Rank[4]
MSA[1]	157,000	63.4	144
U.S.	134,000	69.6	–

Note: (1) Metropolitan Statistical Area - see Appendix A for areas included; (2) U.S. figures calculated from the sales of 524,324 new and existing homes in 181 markets; (3) Housing Opportunity Index - percent of homes sold that were within the reach of the median income household at the prevailing mortgage interest rate; (4) Rank is from 1-181 with 1 being most affordable
Source: National Association of Home Builders, Housing Opportunity Index, 1st Quarter 1999

Median Home Price Projection

It is projected that the median price of existing single-family homes in the metro area will increase by 3.2% in 1999. Nationwide, home prices are projected to increase 3.8%.
Kiplinger's Personal Finance Magazine, January 1999

Average New Home Price

Area	Price ($)
City	155,000
U.S.	132,005

Note: Figures are based on a new home with 1,800 sq. ft. of living area on an 8,000 sq. ft. lot.
Source: ACCRA, Cost of Living Index, 2nd Quarter 1996

Average Apartment Rent

Area	Rent ($/mth)
City	807
U.S.	553

Note: Figures are based on an unfurnished two bedroom, 1-1/2 or 2 bath apartment, approximately 950 sq. ft. in size, excluding all utilities except water
Source: ACCRA, Cost of Living Index, 2nd Quarter 1996

RESIDENTIAL UTILITIES

Average Residential Utility Costs

Area	All Electric ($/mth)	Part Electric ($/mth)	Other Energy ($/mth)	Phone ($/mth)
City	–	57.85	39.99	22.53
U.S.	112.48	57.49	42.55	19.50

Source: ACCRA, Cost of Living Index, 2nd Quarter 1996

HEALTH CARE

Average Health Care Costs

Area	Hospital ($/day)	Doctor ($/visit)	Dentist ($/visit)
City	535.00	48.80	71.00
U.S.	378.47	45.86	57.32

Note: Hospital—based on a semi-private room; Doctor—based on a general practitioner's routine exam of an established patient; Dentist—based on adult teeth cleaning and periodic oral exam.
Source: ACCRA, Cost of Living Index, 2nd Quarter 1996

Distribution of Office-Based Physicians

Area	Family/Gen. Practitioners	Specialists		
		Medical	Surgical	Other
MSA[1]	111	545	354	541

Note: Data as of 12/31/97; (1) Metropolitan Statistical Area - see Appendix A for areas included
Source: American Medical Assn., Physician Characteristics & Distribution in the U.S., 1999

Hospitals

Ann Arbor has 3 general medical and surgical hospitals. *AHA Guide to the Healthcare Field, 1998-99*

According to *U.S. News and World Report,* Ann Arbor has 2 of the best hospitals in the U.S.: **University of Michigan Medical Center**, noted for cancer, cardiology, endocrinology, gastroenterology, geriatrics, gynecology, neurology, orthopedics, otolaryngology, psychiatry, pulmonology, rehabilitation, rheumatology, urology; **St. Joseph Mercy Health System**, noted for orthopedics. *U.S. News Online, "America's Best Hospitals," 10th Edition, www.usnews.com*

EDUCATION

Public School District Statistics

District Name	Num. Sch.	Enroll.	Classroom Teachers	Pupils per Teacher	Minority Pupils (%)	Current Exp.[1] ($/pupil)
Ann Arbor Public Schools	33	15,801	n/a	n/a	n/a	n/a
Wash ISD-Honey Creek Comm Scho	1	76	5	15.2	n/a	n/a
Washtenaw CC-Wash. Tech Mid Co	1	147	5	29.4	n/a	n/a
Washtenaw ISD	3	n/a	15	0.0	n/a	n/a

Note: Data covers the 1997-1998 school year unless otherwise noted; (1) Data covers fiscal year 1996; SD = School District; ISD = Independent School District; n/a not available
Source: National Center for Education Statistics, Common Core of Data Public Education Agency Universe 1997-98; National Center for Education Statistics, Characteristics of the 100 Largest Public Elementary and Secondary School Districts in the United States: 1997-98, July 1999

Educational Quality

School District	Education Quotient[1]	Graduate Outcome[2]	Community Index[3]	Resource Index[4]
Ann Arbor Public Schools	133.0	146.0	144.0	106.0

Note: Nearly 1,000 secondary school districts were rated in terms of educational quality. The scores range from a low of 50 to a high of 150; (1) Average of the Graduate Outcome, Community and Resource indexes; (2) Based on graduation rates and college board scores (SAT/ACT); (3) Based on the surrounding community's average level of education and the area's average income level; (4) Based on teacher salaries, per-pupil expenditures and student-teacher ratios.
Source: Expansion Management, Ratings Issue, 1998

Educational Attainment by Race

Area	High School Graduate (%)					Bachelor's Degree (%)				
	Total	White	Black	Other	Hisp.[2]	Total	White	Black	Other	Hisp.[2]
City	93.9	95.4	77.6	95.2	94.1	64.2	65.9	33.4	78.7	74.0
MSA[1]	87.2	88.5	74.3	92.1	82.0	41.9	43.0	21.5	67.0	44.9
U.S.	75.2	77.9	63.1	60.4	49.8	20.3	21.5	11.4	19.4	9.2

Note: Figures shown cover persons 25 years old and over; (1) Metropolitan Statistical Area - see Appendix A for areas included; (2) people of Hispanic origin can be of any race
Source: 1990 Census of Population and Housing, Summary Tape File 3C

School Enrollment by Type

| Area | Preprimary | | | | Elementary/High School | | | |
| | Public | | Private | | Public | | Private | |
	Enrollment	%	Enrollment	%	Enrollment	%	Enrollment	%
City	1,151	55.4	928	44.6	9,948	88.5	1,299	11.5
MSA[1]	3,711	62.5	2,225	37.5	35,078	91.0	3,490	9.0
U.S.	2,679,029	59.5	1,824,256	40.5	38,379,689	90.2	4,187,099	9.8

Note: Figures shown cover persons 3 years old and over;
(1) Metropolitan Statistical Area - see Appendix A for areas included
Source: 1990 Census of Population and Housing, Summary Tape File 3C

School Enrollment by Race

| Area | Preprimary (%) | | | | Elementary/High School (%) | | | |
	White	Black	Other	Hisp.[1]	White	Black	Other	Hisp.[1]
City	82.9	9.4	7.7	3.6	72.4	17.0	10.6	2.5
MSA[2]	83.4	12.4	4.1	1.9	78.3	16.6	5.1	2.4
U.S.	80.4	12.5	7.1	7.8	74.1	15.6	10.3	12.5

Note: Figures shown cover persons 3 years old and over; (1) people of Hispanic origin can be of any race; (2) Metropolitan Statistical Area - see Appendix A for areas included
Source: 1990 Census of Population and Housing, Summary Tape File 3C

Classroom Teacher Salaries in Public Schools

| District | B.A. Degree | | M.A. Degree | | Maximum | |
	Min. ($)	Rank[1]	Max. ($)	Rank[1]	Max. ($)	Rank[1]
	n/a	n/a	n/a	n/a	n/a	n/a
Average	26,980	-	46,065	-	51,435	-

Note: Salaries are for 1997-1998; (1) Rank ranges from 1 to 100; n/a not available
Source: American Federation of Teachers, Survey & Analysis of Salary Trends, 1998

Higher Education

| Two-Year Colleges | | Four-Year Colleges | | Medical Schools | Law Schools | Voc/Tech |
Public	Private	Public	Private			
1	0	1	1	1	1	15

Source: College Blue Book, Occupational Education, 1997; Medical School Admission Requirements, 1999-2000; Peterson's Guide to Two-Year Colleges, 1999; Peterson's Guide to Four-Year Colleges, 2000; Barron's Guide to Law Schools, 1999

MAJOR EMPLOYERS

Major Employers

Performance Personnel
Prestolite Electric
Dominos Pizza
TISM Inc. (eating places)
Walden Book Co.

Edwards Brothers (book printing)
Gelman Sciences (laboratory apparatus)
T&N Industries (motor vehicle parts)
Borders
Trimas Corp. (transportation equipment)

Note: Companies listed are located in the city
Source: Dun's Business Rankings, 1999; Ward's Business Directory, 1998

PUBLIC SAFETY

Crime Rate

| Area | All Crimes | Violent Crimes | | | | Property Crimes | | |
		Murder	Forcible Rape	Robbery	Aggrav. Assault	Burglary	Larceny -Theft	Motor Vehicle Theft
City	4,090.1	0.0	30.4	94.6	233.0	717.0	2,822.3	192.9
Suburbs[1]	3,566.2	3.9	44.1	70.4	207.7	603.3	2,363.7	273.2
MSA[2]	3,677.5	3.0	41.2	75.5	213.1	627.5	2,461.1	256.1
U.S.	4,922.7	6.8	35.9	186.1	382.0	919.6	2,886.5	505.8

Note: Crime rate is the number of crimes per 100,000 pop.; (1) defined as all areas within the MSA but located outside the central city; (2) Metropolitan Statistical Area - see Appendix A for areas incl.
Source: FBI Uniform Crime Reports, 1997

RECREATION

Culture and Recreation

Museums	Symphony Orchestras	Opera Companies	Dance Companies	Professional Theatres	Zoos	Pro Sports Teams
7	1	1	2	1	0	0

Source: International Directory of the Performing Arts, 1997; Official Museum Directory, 1999; Stern's Performing Arts Directory, 1997; USA Today Four Sport Stadium Guide, 1997; Chamber of Commerce/Economic Development, 1999

Library System

The Ann Arbor District Library has three branches, holdings of 403,687 volumes, and a budget of $7,451,869 (1996-1997). *American Library Directory, 1998-1999*

MEDIA

Newspapers

Name	Type	Freq.	Distribution	Circulation
The Ann Arbor News	n/a	7x/wk	Area	58,172
The Michigan Daily	n/a	5x/wk	Camp/Comm	18,000

Note: Includes newspapers with circulations of 500 or more located in the city; n/a not available
Source: Burrelle's Media Directory, 1999 Edition

Television Stations

Name	Ch.	Affiliation	Type	Owner
WPXD	31	PAXTV	Commercial	Paxson Communications Corporation

Note: Stations included broadcast in the Ann Arbor metro area; n/a not available
Source: Burrelle's Media Directory, 1999 Edition

AM Radio Stations

Call Letters	Freq. (kHz)	Target Audience	Station Format	Music Format
WWCM	990	General	M	Christian
WTKA	1050	General	N/S	n/a
WDEO	1290	General	M/T	Classic Rock
WSDS	1480	General	M/N/S	Country
WAAM	1600	General	M/N/T	Adult Standards

Note: Stations included broadcast in the Ann Arbor metro area; n/a not available
Target Audience: A=Asian; B=Black; C=Christian; E=Ethnic; F=French; G=General; H=Hispanic; M=Men; N=Native American; R=Religious; S=Senior Citizen; W=Women; Y=Young Adult; Z=Children
Station Format: E=Educational; M=Music; N=News; S=Sports; T=Talk
Source: Burrelle's Media Directory, 1999 Edition

FM Radio Stations

Call Letters	Freq. (mHz)	Target Audience	Station Format	Music Format
WCBN	88.3	General	M/N/S	Big Band/Classical/Country/Jazz
WEMU	89.1	General	M/N	Jazz/R&B
WFUM	91.1	General	N/T	n/a
WUOM	91.7	General	N/T	n/a
WIQB	102.9	General	M	Alternative
WVGR	104.1	General	M/N/S	Classical/Jazz
WQKL	107.1	General	M/N	Oldies

Note: Stations included broadcast in the Ann Arbor metro area; n/a not available
Station Format: E=Educational; M=Music; N=News; S=Sports; T=Talk
Target Audience: A=Asian; B=Black; C=Christian; E=Ethnic; F=French; G=General; H=Hispanic; M=Men; N=Native American; R=Religious; S=Senior Citizen; W=Women; Y=Young Adult; Z=Children
Source: Burrelle's Media Directory, 1999 Edition

CLIMATE

Average and Extreme Temperatures

Temperature	Jan	Feb	Mar	Apr	May	Jun	Jul	Aug	Sep	Oct	Nov	Dec	Yr.
Extreme High (°F)	62	65	81	89	93	104	102	100	98	91	77	68	104
Average High (°F)	30	33	44	58	70	79	83	81	74	61	48	35	58
Average Temp. (°F)	23	26	36	48	59	68	72	71	64	52	40	29	49
Average Low (°F)	16	18	27	37	47	56	61	60	53	41	32	21	39
Extreme Low (°F)	-21	-15	-4	10	25	36	41	38	29	17	9	-10	-21

Note: Figures cover the years 1958-1990
Source: National Climatic Data Center, International Station Meteorological Climate Summary, 3/95

Average Precipitation/Snowfall/Humidity

Precip./Humidity	Jan	Feb	Mar	Apr	May	Jun	Jul	Aug	Sep	Oct	Nov	Dec	Yr.
Avg. Precip. (in.)	1.8	1.8	2.5	3.0	2.9	3.6	3.1	3.4	2.8	2.2	2.6	2.7	32.4
Avg. Snowfall (in.)	10	9	7	2	Tr	0	0	0	0	Tr	3	11	41
Avg. Rel. Hum. 7am (%)	80	79	79	78	78	79	82	86	87	84	82	81	81
Avg. Rel. Hum. 4pm (%)	67	63	59	53	51	52	52	54	55	55	64	70	58

Note: Figures cover the years 1958-1990; Tr = Trace amounts (<0.05 in. of rain; <0.5 in. of snow)
Source: National Climatic Data Center, International Station Meteorological Climate Summary, 3/95

Weather Conditions

Temperature			Daytime Sky			Precipitation		
5°F & below	32°F & below	90°F & above	Clear	Partly cloudy	Cloudy	0.01 inch or more precip.	0.1 inch or more snow/ice	Thunder-storms
15	136	12	74	134	157	135	38	32

Note: Figures are average number of days per year and covers the years 1958-1990
Source: National Climatic Data Center, International Station Meteorological Climate Summary, 3/95

AIR & WATER QUALITY

Maximum Pollutant Concentrations

	Particulate Matter (ug/m³)	Carbon Monoxide (ppm)	Sulfur Dioxide (ppm)	Nitrogen Dioxide (ppm)	Ozone (ppm)	Lead (ug/m³)
MSA[1] Level	n/a	n/a	n/a	n/a	0.09	n/a
NAAQS[2]	150	9	0.140	0.053	0.12	1.50
Met NAAQS?	n/a	n/a	n/a	n/a	Yes	n/a

Note: (1) Metropolitan Statistical Area - see Appendix A for areas included; (2) National Ambient Air Quality Standards; ppm = parts per million; ug/m³ = micrograms per cubic meter; n/a not available
Source: EPA, National Air Quality and Emissions Trends Report, 1997

Drinking Water

Water System Name	Pop. Served	Primary Water Source Type	Number of Violations in 1998	Type of Violation/Contaminants
Ann Arbor	109,592	Surface	None	None

Note: Data as of July 10, 1999
Source: EPA, Office of Ground Water and Drinking Water, Safe Drinking Water Information System

Ann Arbor tap water is alkaline, soft and fluoridated.
Editor & Publisher Market Guide, 1999

Chicago, Illinois

Background

Chicago, from its very inception, has been colorful. It was a booming frontier trade town that welcomed the brawn of immigration from around the world to help build the city. Those workers lent themselves to the major industries of the times—steel and meat packing—that eventually provided fodder for Upton Sinclair's attack on the plants' labor abuses in his book "The Jungle."

Chicago's past also witnessed the Haymarket Riot, where anarchists threw a bomb upon a congregation of policemen, in order to protest the city's unemployment rate.

Chicago continues to live up to its Native American namesake, Chicagou, meaning "strong" or "powerful." As the third most populous city in the United States, Chicago has no reason to slow down. The city is home to some of the best institutions in the world— the Art Institute of Chicago, the University of Chicago, and Northwestern University. You can also find architectural wonders such as the Federal Center Plaza, designed by Mies Van Der Rohe, and the Robie House, designed by Frank Lloyd Wright.

Recent events in Chicago include the construction of The Museum of Contemporary Art, hosting the 1996 Democratic National Convention, and the 6th championship win for the 1998 Chicago Bulls.

Located along the southwest shore of Lake Michigan, Chicago's weather changes frequently. Summers can be quite hot and winters are often quite cold. Although it may seem that the winds off the lake are stronger than normal, Chicago's Windy City nickname is misleading, as the city's average wind speed is not greater than many other areas of the country.

General Rankings and Evaluative Comments

- Chicago was ranked #3 out of 11 large, midwestern metropolitan areas in *Money's* 1998 survey of "The Best Places to Live in America." The survey was conducted by first contacting 512 representative households nationwide and asking them to rank 37 quality-of-life factors on a scale of 1 to 10. Next, a demographic profile was compiled on the 300 largest metropolitan statistical areas in the U.S. The numbers were crunched together to arrive at an overall ranking (things Americans consider most important, like clean air and water, low crime and good schools, received extra weight). Unlike previous years, the 1998 rankings were broken down by region (northeast, midwest, south, west) and population size (100,000 to 249,999; 250,000 to 999,999; 1 million plus). The city had a nationwide ranking of #201 out of 300 in 1997 and #196 out of 300 in 1996. *Money, July 1998; Money, July 1997; Money, September 1996*

- *Ladies Home Journal* ranked America's 200 largest cities based on the qualities women care about most. Chicago ranked #185 out of 200. Criteria: low crime rate, well-paying jobs, quality health and child care, good public schools, the presence of women in government, size of the gender wage gap, number of sexual-harassment and discrimination complaints filed, unemployment and divorce rates, commute times, population density, number of houses of worship, parks and cultural offerings, number of women's health specialists, how well a community's women cared for themselves, complexion kindness index based on UV radiation levels, odds of finding affordable fashions, rental rates for romance movies, champagne sales and other matters of the heart. *Ladies Home Journal, November 1998*

- Zero Population Growth ranked 229 cities in terms of children's health, safety, and economic well-being. Chicago was ranked #18 out of 25 major cities (main city in a metro area with population of greater than 2 million) and was given a grade of C-. Criteria: total population, percent of population under 18 years of age, household language, percent population change, percent of births to teens, infant mortality rate, percent of low birth weights, dropout rate, enrollment in preprimary school, violent and property crime rates, unemployment rate, percent of children in poverty, percent of owner occupied units, number of bad air days, percent of public transportation commuters, and average travel time to work. *Zero Population Growth, Children's Environmental Index, Fall 1999*

- Chicago was ranked #50 out of 59 metro areas in *The Regional Economist's* "Rational Livability Ranking of 59 Large Metro Areas." The rankings were based on the metro area's total population change over the period 1990-97 divided by the number of people moving in from elsewhere in the United States (net domestic in-migration). *St. Louis Federal Reserve Bank of St. Louis, The Regional Economist, April 1999*

- Chicago appeared on *Travel & Leisure's* list of the world's 100 best cities. It was ranked #5 in the U.S. and #16 in the world. Criteria: activities/attractions, culture/arts, people, restaurants/food, and value. *Travel & Leisure, 1998 World's Best Awards*

- *Conde Nast Traveler* polled 37,293 readers for travel satisfaction. Cities were ranked based on the following criteria: people/friendliness, environment/ambiance, cultural enrichment, restaurants and fun/energy. Chicago appeared in the top 25, ranking number 13, with an overall rating of 66.3 out of 100. *Conde Nast Traveler, Readers' Choice Poll 1998*

- Chicago was selected by *Yahoo! Internet Life* as one of "America's Most Wired Cities & Towns." The city ranked #14 out of 50. Criteria: home and work net use, domain density, hosts per capita, directory density and content quality. *Yahoo! Internet Life, March 1999*

- Chicago was chosen as one of "America's 10 Best Bike Towns." Rank: #10 out of 10. Criteria: marked bike lanes, municipal bike racks, bicycle access to bridges and public transportation, employment of a local government bicycle coordinator, area cycling advocacy efforts, bike-safety programs, budget for cycling programs, and local cycling culture.

  "This lakefront metropolis has been home to the Chicagoland Bicycle Federation (CBF)—a strong cycling advocacy group; with Chicago Mayor Daley himself a cyclist, things really get done. Bike Plan 2000 is a list of 29 recommendations whose goal is to have bicycles account

for 10% of all one-person trips under 5 miles by 2000. 'Significant action has happened on 28 of the 29 points,' says Ben Gomberg, coordinator for Chicago's city bicycle program."
Bicycling, March 1999

■ Cognetics studied 273 metro areas in the United States, ranking them by entrepreneurial activity. Chicago was ranked #35 out of the 50 largest metro areas. Criteria: Significant Starts (firms started in the last 10 years that still employ at least 5 people) and Young Growers (percent of firms 10 years old or less that grew significantly during the last 4 years).
Cognetics, "Entrepreneurial Hot Spots: The Best Places in America to Start and Grow a Company," 1998

■ Chicago was selected as one of the "Best American Cities to Start a Business" by *Point of View* magazine. Criteria: coolness, quality-of-life, and business concerns. The city was ranked #20 out of 75. *Point of View, November 1998*

■ *Computerworld* selected the best markets for IT job seekers based on their annual salary, skills, and hiring surveys. Chicago ranked #2 out of 10.

"The number of IT help-wanted ads in the city have doubled in the past six months."
Computerworld, January 11, 1999

■ Reliastar Financial Corp. ranked the 125 largest metropolitan areas according to the general financial security of residents. Chicago was ranked #58 (tie) out of 125 with a score of 2.5. The score indicates the percentage a metropolitan area is above or below the metropolitan norm. A metro area with a score of 10.6 is 10.6% above the metro average. Criteria: Earnings and Wealth Potential (household income, education, net assets, cost of living); Safety Net (health insurance, retirement savings, life insurance, income support programs); Personal Threats (unemployment rate, low-income households, crime rate); Community Economic Vitality (cost of community services, job quality, job creation, housing costs).
Reliastar Financial Corp., "The Best Cities to Earn and Save Money," 1999 Edition

Business Environment

STATE ECONOMY

State Economic Profile

"Illinois' economy has lagged the nation as it continues to shift from a manufacturing to service-based economy. Its low unemployment rate and rising per capita income mask a major restructuring occurring within its economy. Growth will be weak over the next two years but start to show some rebounding in 2001 as important structural changes now underway take affect.

Over half of the new jobs created in 1998 were in the services sector, and the bulk of those are located in Chicago. Job gains will come from the high-tech and financial services sectors. Manufacturing concerns continued to shed jobs as the state lost some 8,300 manufacturing jobs in 1998. More manufacturing job losses are likely for 1999. Both Mitsubishi and Goodyear are in the process of either laying off workers or planning to do so.

IL's farm sector has also been hit particularly hard by low commodity prices and weak foreign demand. Farm income was down more than 20% in 1998. Soybean and corn producers will continue to see their financial health erode in 1999. Although foreign demand will pick up in 1999, oversupply will guarantee weak prices for bulk commodities.

Although the volume of home sales in 1998 was the highest level in over a decade, price appreciation has continued to lag the nation. Stagnant population growth continues to plague the housing market. Illinois lost over 20,000 residents on net in 1998, many of these are in the "typical buyer" age group of 25 to 44. Unsurprisingly, housing starts have been at their lowest levels in years, rising only 2% in 1998, with most of these taking place in the Chicago area." *National Association of Realtors, Economic Profiles: The Fifty States and the District of Columbia, http://nar.realtor.com/databank/profiles.htm*

IMPORTS/EXPORTS

Total Export Sales

Area	1994 ($000)	1995 ($000)	1996 ($000)	1997 ($000)	% Chg. 1994-97	% Chg. 1996-97
MSA[1]	17,333,603	21,083,418	22,030,068	23,209,949	33.9	5.4
U.S.	512,415,609	583,030,524	622,827,063	687,597,999	34.2	10.4

Note: (1) Metropolitan Statistical Area - see Appendix A for areas included
Source: U.S. Department of Commerce, International Trade Association, Metropolitan Area Exports: An Export Performance Report on Over 250 U.S. Cities, November 10, 1998

CITY FINANCES

City Government Finances

Component	FY94 ($000)	FY94 (per capita $)
Revenue	4,383,723	1,593.57
Expenditure	4,201,070	1,527.17
Debt Outstanding	6,965,521	2,532.11
Cash & Securities	9,655,076	3,509.81

Source: U.S. Bureau of the Census, City Government Finances: 1993-94

City Government Revenue by Source

Source	FY94 ($000)	FY94 (per capita $)	FY94 (%)
From Federal Government	242,316	88.09	5.5
From State Governments	707,812	257.30	16.1
From Local Governments	171	0.06	0.0
Property Taxes	624,252	226.93	14.2
General Sales Taxes	140,209	50.97	3.2
Selective Sales Taxes	634,223	230.55	14.5
Income Taxes	0	0.00	0.0
Current Charges	578,423	210.27	13.2
Utility/Liquor Store	260,214	94.59	5.9
Employee Retirement[1]	687,439	249.90	15.7
Other	508,664	184.91	11.6

Note: (1) Excludes "city contributions," classified as "nonrevenue," intragovernmental transfers.
Source: U.S. Bureau of the Census, City Government Finances: 1993-94

City Government Expenditures by Function

Function	FY94 ($000)	FY94 (per capita $)	FY94 (%)
Educational Services	56,630	20.59	1.3
Employee Retirement[1]	500,000	181.76	11.9
Environment/Housing	454,421	165.19	10.8
Government Administration	145,097	52.75	3.5
Interest on General Debt	395,997	143.95	9.4
Public Safety	1,004,058	365.00	23.9
Social Services	234,296	85.17	5.6
Transportation	716,944	260.62	17.1
Utility/Liquor Store	210,453	76.50	5.0
Other	483,174	175.64	11.5

Note: (1) Payments to beneficiaries including withdrawal of contributions.
Source: U.S. Bureau of the Census, City Government Finances: 1993-94

Municipal Bond Ratings

Area	Moody's	S & P
Chicago	Aaa	n/a

Note: n/a not available; n/r not rated
Source: Moody's Bond Record, 6/99

POPULATION

Population Growth

Area	1980	1990	% Chg. 1980-90	July 1998 Estimate	% Chg. 1990-98
City	3,005,072	2,783,726	-7.4	2,802,079	0.7
MSA[1]	6,060,387	6,069,974	0.2	7,841,548	29.2
U.S.	226,545,805	248,765,170	9.8	270,299,000	8.7

Note: (1) Metropolitan Statistical Area - see Appendix A for areas included;
July 1998 MSA population estimate was calculated by the editors
Source: 1980/1990 Census of Housing and Population, Summary Tape File 3C;
Census Bureau Population Estimates 1998

Population Characteristics

Race	City 1980 Population	%	City 1990 Population	%	% Chg. 1980-90	MSA[1] 1990 Population	%
White	1,512,405	50.3	1,265,953	45.5	-16.3	4,102,292	67.6
Black	1,197,174	39.8	1,086,389	39.0	-9.3	1,330,636	21.9
Amer Indian/Esk/Aleut	6,804	0.2	6,761	0.2	-0.6	11,755	0.2
Asian/Pacific Islander	73,745	2.5	104,141	3.7	41.2	229,475	3.8
Other	214,944	7.2	320,482	11.5	49.1	395,816	6.5
Hispanic Origin[2]	422,063	14.0	535,315	19.2	26.8	716,644	11.8

Note: (1) Metropolitan Statistical Area - see Appendix A for areas included;
(2) people of Hispanic origin can be of any race
Source: 1980/1990 Census of Housing and Population, Summary Tape File 3C

Ancestry

Area	German	Irish	English	Italian	U.S.	French	Polish	Dutch
City	9.7	8.5	2.5	4.3	1.2	1.0	9.4	0.5
MSA[1]	20.2	14.1	5.9	8.1	1.3	2.0	12.2	1.5
U.S.	23.3	15.6	13.1	5.9	5.3	4.2	3.8	2.5

Note: Figures are percentages and include persons that reported multiple ancestry (eg. if a person reported being Irish and Italian, they were included in both columns); (1) Metropolitan Statistical Area - see Appendix A for areas included
Source: 1990 Census of Population and Housing, Summary Tape File 3C

Age

Area	Median Age (Years)	Under 5	Under 18	18-24	25-44	45-64	65+	80+
City	31.1	7.7	26.0	11.3	33.3	17.7	11.8	2.5
MSA[1]	32.5	7.5	25.4	10.2	33.7	18.9	11.8	2.5
U.S.	32.9	7.3	25.6	10.5	32.6	18.7	12.5	2.8

Note: (1) Metropolitan Statistical Area - see Appendix A for areas included
Source: 1990 Census of Population and Housing, Summary Tape File 3C

Male/Female Ratio

Area	Number of males per 100 females (all ages)	Number of males per 100 females (18 years old+)
City	91.8	88.4
MSA[1]	93.3	89.9
U.S.	95.0	91.9

Note: (1) Metropolitan Statistical Area - see Appendix A for areas included
Source: 1990 Census of Population, General Population Characteristics

INCOME

Per Capita/Median/Average Income

Area	Per Capita ($)	Median Household ($)	Average Household ($)
City	12,899	26,301	34,682
MSA[1]	16,447	35,265	44,583
U.S.	14,420	30,056	38,453

Note: All figures are for 1989; (1) Metropolitan Statistical Area - see Appendix A for areas included
Source: 1990 Census of Population and Housing, Summary Tape File 3C

Household Income Distribution by Race

Income ($)	City (%)					U.S. (%)				
	Total	White	Black	Other	Hisp.[1]	Total	White	Black	Other	Hisp.[1]
Less than 5,000	10.6	5.6	18.5	10.5	9.9	6.2	4.8	15.2	8.6	8.8
5,000 - 9,999	10.2	8.5	13.4	8.3	8.5	9.3	8.6	14.2	9.9	11.1
10,000 - 14,999	8.9	8.4	9.3	9.8	9.8	8.8	8.5	11.0	9.8	11.0
15,000 - 24,999	18.0	17.3	18.0	21.1	22.1	17.5	17.3	18.9	18.5	20.5
25,000 - 34,999	15.4	15.9	13.9	18.0	18.2	15.8	16.1	14.2	15.4	16.4
35,000 - 49,999	16.6	18.4	13.5	17.6	17.9	17.9	18.6	13.3	16.1	16.0
50,000 - 74,999	12.8	15.2	9.8	10.7	10.3	15.0	15.8	9.3	13.4	11.1
75,000 - 99,999	4.0	5.4	2.4	2.5	2.2	5.1	5.5	2.6	4.7	3.1
100,000+	3.5	5.4	1.2	1.5	1.1	4.4	4.8	1.3	3.7	1.9

Note: All figures are for 1989; (1) people of Hispanic origin can be of any race
Source: 1990 Census of Population and Housing, Summary Tape File 3C

Effective Buying Income

Area	Per Capita ($)	Median Household ($)	Average Household ($)
City	15,271	32,292	41,840
MSA[1]	20,152	44,166	56,087
U.S.	16,803	34,536	45,243

Note: Data as of 1/1/99; (1) Metropolitan Statistical Area - see Appendix A for areas included
Source: Standard Rate & Data Service, Newspaper Advertising Source, 9/99

Effective Household Buying Income Distribution

Area	% of Households Earning						
	$10,000 -$19,999	$20,000 -$34,999	$35,000 -$49,999	$50,000 -$74,999	$75,000 -$99,000	$100,000 -$124,999	$125,000 and up
City	15.5	21.8	17.0	17.4	7.0	2.4	2.7
MSA[1]	11.2	18.4	17.8	23.2	11.0	4.2	4.7
U.S.	16.0	22.6	18.2	18.9	7.2	2.4	2.7

Note: Data as of 1/1/99; (1) Metropolitan Statistical Area - see Appendix A for areas included
Source: Standard Rate & Data Service, Newspaper Advertising Source, 9/99

Poverty Rates by Race and Age

Area	Total (%)	By Race (%)				By Age (%)		
		White	Black	Other	Hisp.[2]	Under 5 years old	Under 18 years old	65 years and over
City	21.6	11.0	33.2	23.7	24.2	35.6	33.9	15.9
MSA[1]	12.4	5.8	30.0	18.4	20.7	19.9	19.1	10.5
U.S.	13.1	9.8	29.5	23.1	25.3	20.1	18.3	12.8

Note: Figures show the percent of people living below the poverty line in 1989. The average poverty
threshold was $12,674 for a family of four in 1989; (1) Metropolitan Statistical Area - see Appendix A
for areas included; (2) people of Hispanic origin can be of any race
Source: 1990 Census of Population and Housing, Summary Tape File 3C

EMPLOYMENT

Labor Force and Employment

Area	Civilian Labor Force			Workers Employed		
	Jun. 1998	Jun. 1999	% Chg.	Jun. 1998	Jun. 1999	% Chg.
City	1,322,758	1,360,840	2.9	1,241,949	1,278,196	2.9
MSA[1]	4,211,674	4,334,896	2.9	4,024,141	4,141,588	2.9
U.S.	138,798,000	140,666,000	1.3	132,265,000	134,395,000	1.6

Note: Data is not seasonally adjusted and covers workers 16 years of age and older;
(1) Metropolitan Statistical Area - see Appendix A for areas included
Source: Bureau of Labor Statistics, http://stats.bls.gov

Unemployment Rate

Area	1998						1999					
	Jul.	Aug.	Sep.	Oct.	Nov.	Dec.	Jan.	Feb.	Mar.	Apr.	May.	Jun.
City	5.8	5.8	5.9	5.7	5.5	5.2	5.2	5.1	4.7	4.8	5.4	6.1
MSA[1]	4.2	4.2	4.2	4.0	4.0	4.0	4.3	4.2	3.8	3.6	3.9	4.5
U.S.	4.7	4.5	4.4	4.2	4.1	4.0	4.8	4.7	4.4	4.1	4.0	4.5

Note: Data is not seasonally adjusted and covers workers 16 years of age and older; all figures are percentages; (1) Metropolitan Statistical Area - see Appendix A for areas included
Source: Bureau of Labor Statistics, http://stats.bls.gov

Employment by Industry

Sector	MSA[1]		U.S.
	Number of Employees	Percent of Total	Percent of Total
Services	1,389,800	32.6	30.4
Retail Trade	683,000	16.0	17.7
Government	491,000	11.5	15.6
Manufacturing	654,600	15.4	14.3
Finance/Insurance/Real Estate	323,700	7.6	5.9
Wholesale Trade	277,400	6.5	5.4
Transportation/Public Utilities	260,800	6.1	5.3
Construction	180,300	4.2	5.0
Mining	1,700	<0.1	0.4

Note: Figures cover non-farm employment as of 6/99 and are not seasonally adjusted;
(1) Metropolitan Statistical Area - see Appendix A for areas included
Source: Bureau of Labor Statistics, http://stats.bls.gov

Employment by Occupation

Occupation Category	City (%)	MSA[1] (%)	U.S. (%)
White Collar	57.9	64.0	58.1
Executive/Admin./Management	11.3	14.2	12.3
Professional	13.6	14.6	14.1
Technical & Related Support	3.2	3.5	3.7
Sales	10.1	12.5	11.8
Administrative Support/Clerical	19.7	19.2	16.3
Blue Collar	26.5	23.7	26.2
Precision Production/Craft/Repair	8.9	9.7	11.3
Machine Operators/Assem./Insp.	8.7	6.4	6.8
Transportation/Material Movers	4.0	3.6	4.1
Cleaners/Helpers/Laborers	4.9	4.0	3.9
Services	15.1	11.8	13.2
Farming/Forestry/Fishing	0.5	0.6	2.5

Note: Figures cover employed persons 16 years old and over;
(1) Metropolitan Statistical Area - see Appendix A for areas included
Source: 1990 Census of Population and Housing, Summary Tape File 3C

Occupational Employment Projections: 1996 - 2006

Occupations Expected to Have the Largest Job Growth (ranked by numerical growth)	Fast-Growing Occupations[1] (ranked by percent growth)
1. General managers & top executives	1. Personal and home care aides
2. Cashiers	2. Desktop publishers
3. Salespersons, retail	3. Home health aides
4. Systems analysts	4. Physical therapy assistants and aides
5. Truck drivers, light	5. Medical assistants
6. Registered nurses	6. Physical therapists
7. Food service workers	7. Data processing equipment repairers
8. Hand packers & packagers	8. Occupational therapy assistants
9. Guards	9. Occupational therapists
10. Receptionists and information clerks	10. Human services workers

Note: Projections cover Illinois; (1) Excludes occupations with total job growth less than 300
Source: U.S. Department of Labor, Employment and Training Administration, America's Labor Market Information System (ALMIS)

TAXES

Major State and Local Tax Rates

State Corp. Income (%)	State Personal Income (%)	Residential Property (effective rate per $100)	Sales & Use State (%)	Sales & Use Local (%)	State Gasoline (cents/ gallon)	State Cigarette (cents/ pack)
7.3[a]	3.0	1.92	6.25	2.5	19.3[b]	58.0[c]

Note: Personal/corporate income, sales, gasoline and cigarette tax rates as of January 1999. Property tax rates as of 1997; (a) Includes a 2.5% personal property replacement tax; (b) Rate is comprised of 19 cents excise and 0.3 cent motor carrier tax. Carriers pay an additional surcharge of 6.3 cents. Rate does not include a 5 cent local option tax in Chicago.; (c) Counties and cities may impose an additional tax of 10 - 15 cents per pack
Source: Federation of Tax Administrators, www.taxadmin.org; Washington D.C. Department of Finance and Revenue, Tax Rates and Tax Burdens in the District of Columbia: A Nationwide Comparison, July 1998; Chamber of Commerce, 1999

Total Taxes Per Capita and as a Percent of Income

Area	Per Capita Income ($)	Per Capita Taxes ($) Total	Federal	State/ Local	Percent of Income (%) Total	Federal	State/ Local
Illinois	30,839	11,229	7,838	3,391	36.4	25.4	11.0
U.S.	27,876	9,881	6,690	3,191	35.4	24.0	11.4

Note: Figures are for 1998
Source: Tax Foundation, www.taxfoundation.org

Estimated Tax Burden

Area	State Income	Local Income	Property	Sales	Total
Chicago	2,130	0	3,750	905	6,785

Note: The numbers are estimates of taxes paid by a married couple with two children and annual earnings of $75,000. Sales tax estimates assume they spend average amounts on food, clothing, household goods and gasoline. Property tax estimates assume they live in a $250,000 home.
Source: Kiplinger's Personal Finance Magazine, October 1998

**COMMERCIAL
REAL ESTATE**

Office Market

Class/ Location	Total Space (sq. ft.)	Vacant Space (sq. ft.)	Vac. Rate (%)	Under Constr. (sq. ft.)	Net Absorp. (sq. ft.)	Rental Rates ($/sq.ft./yr.)
Class A						
CBD	43,012,896	2,879,053	6.7	0	605,778	20.33-38.99
Outside CBD	26,459,046	2,847,006	10.8	2,017,470	1,836,777	16.50-31.73
Class B						
CBD	47,171,468	7,804,085	16.5	332,608	1,269,757	15.00-34.65
Outside CBD	31,960,631	3,986,535	12.5	463,570	135,809	11.00-27.16

Note: Data as of 10/98 and covers Chicago; CBD = Central Business District; n/a not available;
Source: Society of Industrial and Office Realtors, 1999 Comparative Statistics of Industrial and Office
Real Estate Markets

"Growth in demand for space may decrease as the labor markets continue to tighten. If absorption declines, the skyline of Chicago will see little change as we approach 2000. There is approximately 17.5 million sq. ft. of vacant space available in the CBD and suburban markets, some of which is expected to be leased before the construction of an additional three million sq. ft. of office space. The downtown market is likely to experience continued reduction of available space and increases in rental rates. As a result of concerns over continued uncertainty in the financial markets, office property sales prices are expected to decrease by one to five percent. The Chicago MSA is expected to grow at a slower pace than other comparable regions in the nation." *Society of Industrial and Office Realtors, 1999 Comparative Statistics of Industrial and Office Real Estate Markets*

Industrial Market

Location	Total Space (sq. ft.)	Vacant Space (sq. ft.)	Vac. Rate (%)	Under Constr. (sq. ft.)	Net Absorp. (sq. ft.)	Lease ($/sq.ft./yr.)
Central City	217,838,035	15,753,959	7.2	308,018	-4,012,470	3.00-5.00
Suburban	655,350,317	16,214,861	2.5	9,422,916	31,663,560	3.65-6.14

Note: Data as of 10/98 and covers Chicago; n/a not available
Source: Society of Industrial and Office Realtors, 1999 Comparative Statistics of Industrial and Office
Real Estate Markets

"User demand is expected to remain strong. There is some concern about the impact of the world economy on Chicago. This will discourage some speculative development. Speculative developers are expected to turn their sights on smaller user groups through the development of smaller facilities. These buildings will typically be 75,000 to 125,000 sq. ft. with a higher parking ratio and ceiling height of 18 to 24 feet. Infill development will be the pattern in Cook County. The County witnessed the leveling of the former American National Can building, leaving 18 acres available for industrial development. In Melrose Park a 420,300 sq. ft. building was leveled to make way for a 501,000 sq. ft. speculative bulk warehouse distribution facility, and a PepsiCola bottling storage facility will occupy a 475,000 sq. ft. property which replaced a 501,000 sq. ft. building." *Society of Industrial and Office Realtors, 1999 Comparative Statistics of Industrial and Office Real Estate Markets*

Retail Market

Shopping Center Inventory (sq. ft.)	Shopping Center Construction (sq. ft.)	Construction as a Percent of Inventory (%)	Torto Wheaton Rent Index[1] ($/sq. ft.)
130,211,000	469,000	0.4	13.64

Note: Data as of 1997 and covers the Metropolitan Statistical Area - see Appendix A for areas
included; (1) Index is based on a model that predicts what the average rent should be for leases with
certain characteristics, in certain locations during certain years.
Source: National Association of Realtors, 1997-1998 Market Conditions Report

"Like the nation, economic growth in Chicago has slowed somewhat from the brisk pace set from 1994 through 1996. Per-capita income levels remain among the highest in the nation;

however, sluggish population growth in the area continues to burden local retailers. The vacancy rate rose slightly last year, particularly due to a rise in vacancies in older, medium to large size shopping centers. Much of the new space under development is already pre-leased, with very little speculative development. Chicago's retail market is likely to remain flat over the next few years as the area's slowing economy struggles to fill the large supply of older space." *National Association of Realtors, 1997-1998 Market Conditions Report*

COMMERCIAL UTILITIES

Typical Monthly Electric Bills

Area	Commercial Service ($/month)		Industrial Service ($/month)	
	12 kW demand 1,500 kWh	100 kW demand 30,000 kWh	1,000 kW demand 400,000 kWh	20,000 kW demand 10,000,000 kWh
City[1]	n/a	n/a[a]	n/a	n/a
U.S.[2]	150	2,174	23,995	508,569

Note: Based on rates in effect ; n/a not available
Source: Memphis Light, Gas and Water, 1998 Utility Bill Comparisons for Selected U.S. Cities; Edison Electric Institute, Typical Residential, Commercial and Industrial Bills, Winter 1999

TRANSPORTATION

Transportation Statistics

Average minutes to work	31.5
Interstate highways	I-55; I-57; I-80; I-88; I-90
Bus lines	
In-city	Chicago TA, 1,872 vehicles
Inter-city	1
Passenger air service	
Airport	O'Hare International; Midway
Airlines	27
Aircraft departures	434,665 (1996)
Enplaned passengers	34,937,810 (1996)
Rail service	Amtrak; Metro; Commuter Rail
Motor freight carriers	750 (local trucking)
Major waterways/ports	Port of Chicago (St. Lawrence Seaway)

Source: Editor & Publisher Market Guide, 1999; FAA Airport Activity Statistics, 1997; Amtrak National Time Table, Northeast Timetable, Spring/Summer 1999; 1990 Census of Population and Housing, STF 3C; Chamber of Commerce/Economic Development 1999; Jane's Urban Transport Systems 1999-2000

Means of Transportation to Work

Area	Car/Truck/Van		Public Transportation			Bicycle	Walked	Other Means	Worked at Home
	Drove Alone	Car-pooled	Bus	Subway	Railroad				
City	46.3	14.8	19.3	7.9	1.5	0.3	6.4	1.7	1.7
MSA[1]	63.8	12.0	8.7	4.1	3.9	0.2	4.2	1.1	2.0
U.S.	73.2	13.4	3.0	1.5	0.5	0.4	3.9	1.2	3.0

Note: Figures shown are percentages and only include workers 16 years old and over;
(1) Metropolitan Statistical Area - see Appendix A for areas included
Source: 1990 Census of Population and Housing, Summary Tape File 3C

BUSINESSES

Major Business Headquarters

Company Name	1999 Rankings	
	Fortune 500	Forbes 500
AON	259	-
Ameritech	87	-
Amsted Industries	-	137
BDO Seidman	-	115
Baker & McKenzie	-	283
Bank One Corp.	44	-
CC Industries	-	206
FMC	355	-
Grant Thornton	-	108
H Group Holding	-	122
Leo Burnett	-	246
Marmon Group	-	20
Montgomery Ward & Co	-	23
Navistar International	211	-
Pepper Cos	-	362
Quaker Oats	325	-
R.R. Donnelley & Sons	277	-
Ryerson Tull	376	-
Sara Lee	64	-
Smurfit-Stone Container	400	-
Tribune	491	-
Truserv	360	-
USG	466	-
Unicom	233	-
Walsh Group	-	212
Wirtz	-	273

Note: Companies listed are located in the city; dashes indicate no ranking
Fortune 500: Companies that produce a 10-K are ranked 1 to 500 based on 1998 revenue
Forbes 500: Private companies are ranked 1 to 500 based on 1997 revenue
Source: Forbes, November 30, 1998; Fortune, April 26, 1999

Best Companies to Work For

Amoco, First Chicago NDB Corp., Northern Trust Corp. and Sara Lee Corp., headquartered in Chicago, are among the "100 Best Companies for Working Mothers." Criteria: fair wages, opportunities for women to advance, support for child care, flexible work schedules, family-friendly benefits, and work/life supports. *Working Mother, October 1998*

Andersen Consulting (professional services/consulting), First Chicago NDB Corp. (banking), Navistar International Corp. (motor vehicles and parts) and Stone Container Corp. (forest/paper products), headquartered in Chicago, are among the "100 Best Places to Work in IS." Criteria: compensation, turnover and training. *Computerworld, May 25, 1998*

Amoco Corp. and Northern Trust, headquartered in Chicago, are among the best companies for women. Criteria: salary, benefits, opportunities for advancement and work/family policies. *www.womenswire.com*

Fast-Growing Businesses

According to *Inc.*, Chicago is home to one of America's 100 fastest-growing private companies: ThoughtWorks. Criteria for inclusion: must be an independent, privately-held, U.S. corporation, proprietorship or partnership; sales of at least $200,000 in 1995; five-year operating/sales history; increase in 1999 sales over 1998 sales; holding companies, regulated banks, and utilities were excluded. *Inc. 500, 1999*

Chicago is home to one of *Business Week's* "hot growth" companies: Duff & Phelps Credit Rating. Criteria: increase in sales and profits, return on capital and stock price. *Business Week, 5/31/99*

According to *Fortune*, Chicago is home to one of America's 100 fastest-growing companies: Whittman-Hart. Companies were ranked based on earnings-per-share growth, revenue growth and total return over the previous three years. Criteria for inclusion: public companies with sales of least $50 million. Companies that lost money in the most recent quarter, or ended in the red for the past four quarters as a whole, were not eligible. Limited partnerships and REITs were also not considered. *Fortune, "America's Fastest-Growing Companies," 1999*

According to Deloitte & Touche LLP, Chicago is home to one of America's 100 fastest-growing high-technology companies: AccuMed International. Companies are ranked by percentage growth in revenue over a five-year period. Criteria for inclusion: must be a U.S. company developing and/or providing technology products or services; company must have been in business for five years with 1993 revenues of at least $50,000. *Deloitte & Touche LLP, November 17, 1998*

Women-Owned Firms: Number, Employment and Sales

Area	Number of Firms	Employ-ment	Sales ($000)	Rank[2]
MSA[1]	260,200	1,108,800	161,200,900	3

Note: (1) Metropolitan Statistical Area - see Appendix A for areas included;
(2) Calculated on an averaging of the number of businesses, employment and sales
Source: The National Foundation for Women Business Owners, 1999 Facts on Women-Owned Businesses: Trends in the Top 50 Metropolitan Areas

Women-Owned Firms: Growth

Area	% change from 1992 to 1999			Rank[2]
	Number of Firms	Employ-ment	Sales	
MSA[1]	46.0	126.6	148.5	18

Note: (1) Metropolitan Statistical Area - see Appendix A for areas included; (2) Calculated on an averaging of the percent growth of number of businesses, employment and sales
Source: The National Foundation for Women Business Owners, 1999 Facts on Women-Owned Businesses: Trends in the Top 50 Metropolitan Areas

Minority Business Opportunity

Chicago is home to two companies which are on the Black Enterprise Industrial/Service 100 list (largest based on gross sales): Johnson Publishing Co. Inc. (publishing, broadcasting, TV prod., cosmetics, hair care); Luster Products Co. (hair care products mfg. and distrib.) . Criteria: operational in previous calendar year, at least 51% black-owned and manufactures/owns the product it sells or provides industrial or consumer services. Brokerages, real estate firms and firms that provide professional services are not eligible. *Black Enterprise, www.blackenterprise.com*

Chicago is home to one company which is on the Black Enterprise Auto Dealer 100 list (largest based on gross sales): Chicago Truck Center Inc. (GMC, Volvo truck, Nissan truck) . Criteria: 1) operational in previous calendar year; 2) at least 51% black-owned. *Black Enterprise, www.blackenterprise.com*

Four of the 500 largest Hispanic-owned companies in the U.S. are located in Chicago. *Hispanic Business, June 1999*

Chicago is home to three companies which are on the Hispanic Business Fastest-Growing 100 list (greatest sales growth from 1994 to 1998): Chicago Contract Cleaning & Supply Co. (janitorial svcs.); Suarez Elecric Co. (telecommunication/electrical construction contracting); David Gomez & Associates Inc. (executive search svcs.). *Hispanic Business, July/August 1999*

Small Business Opportunity

According to *Forbes*, Chicago is home to three of America's 200 best small companies: Duff & Phelps Credit Rating, First Commonwealth and Whittman-Hart. Criteria: companies included must be publicly traded since November 1997 with a stock price of at least $5 per share and an average daily float of 1,000 shares. The company's latest 12-month sales must be between $5 and $350 million, return on equity (ROE) must be a minimum of 12% for both the past 5 years and the most recent four quarters, and five-year sales and EPS growth must average at least 10%. Companies with declining sales or earnings during the past year were dropped as well as businesses with debt/equity ratios over 1.25. Companies with negative operating cash flow in each of the past two years were also excluded. *Forbes, November 2, 1998*

HOTELS & MOTELS

Hotels/Motels

Area	Hotels/ Motels	Rooms	Luxury-Level Hotels/Motels		Average Minimum Rates ($)		
			♦♦♦♦	♦♦♦♦♦	♦♦	♦♦♦	♦♦♦♦
City	75	26,291	10	2	97	165	209
Airport	44	10,291	0	0	n/a	n/a	n/a
Suburbs	197	28,944	1	0	n/a	n/a	n/a
Total	316	65,526	11	2	n/a	n/a	n/a

Note: n/a not available; classifications range from one diamond (budget properties with basic amenities) to five diamond (luxury properties with the finest service, rooms and facilities).
Source: OAG, Business Travel Planner, Winter 1998-99

Chicago is home to two of the top 100 hotels in the world according to *Travel & Leisure*: Ritz-Carlton (#11) and Four Seasons (#41) . Criteria: value, rooms/ambience, location, facilities/activities and service. *Travel & Leisure, 1998 World's Best Awards, Best Hotels and Resorts*

CONVENTION CENTERS

Major Convention Centers

Center Name	Meeting Rooms	Exhibit Space (sq. ft.)
Chicago Hilton and Towers	43	120,000
Forum Hotel-Chicago	17	8,085
Hyatt Regency Chicago	87	180,000
Inland Meeting & Exhibition Center	15	15,000
KPMG Center for Leadership Development	15	20,000
McCormick Place on the Lake	51	1,300,000
Merchandise Mart Expocenter	14	105,000
Navy Pier	n/a	n/a

Note: n/a not available
Source: Trade Shows Worldwide, 1998; Meetings & Conventions, 4/15/99; Sucessful Meetings, 3/31/98

Living Environment

COST OF LIVING

Cost of Living Index

Composite Index	Groceries	Housing	Utilities	Trans-portation	Health Care	Misc. Goods/Services
n/a	n/a	n/a	n/a	n/a	n/a	n/a

Note: U.S. = 100; n/a not available
Source: ACCRA, Cost of Living Index, 1st Quarter 1999

HOUSING

Median Home Prices and Housing Affordability

Area	Median Price[2] 1st Qtr. 1999 ($)	HOI[3] 1st Qtr. 1999	Afford-ability Rank[4]
MSA[1]	153,000	70.1	117
U.S.	134,000	69.6	–

Note: (1) Metropolitan Statistical Area - see Appendix A for areas included; (2) U.S. figures calculated from the sales of 524,324 new and existing homes in 181 markets; (3) Housing Opportunity Index - percent of homes sold that were within the reach of the median income household at the prevailing mortgage interest rate; (4) Rank is from 1-181 with 1 being most affordable
Source: National Association of Home Builders, Housing Opportunity Index, 1st Quarter 1999

Median Home Price Projection

It is projected that the median price of existing single-family homes in the metro area will increase by 2.8% in 1999. Nationwide, home prices are projected to increase 3.8%.
Kiplinger's Personal Finance Magazine, January 1999

Average New Home Price

Area	Price ($)
City	n/a
U.S.	142,735

Note: n/a not available
Source: ACCRA, Cost of Living Index, 1st Quarter 1999

Average Apartment Rent

Area	Rent ($/mth)
City	n/a
U.S.	601

Note: n/a not available
Source: ACCRA, Cost of Living Index, 1st Quarter 1999

RESIDENTIAL UTILITIES

Average Residential Utility Costs

Area	All Electric ($/mth)	Part Electric ($/mth)	Other Energy ($/mth)	Phone ($/mth)
City	–	–	–	n/a
U.S.	100.02	55.73	43.33	19.71

Note: n/a not available
Source: ACCRA, Cost of Living Index, 1st Quarter 1999

HEALTH CARE

Average Health Care Costs

Area	Hospital ($/day)	Doctor ($/visit)	Dentist ($/visit)
City	n/a	n/a	n/a
U.S.	430.43	52.45	66.35

Note: n/a not available
Source: ACCRA, Cost of Living Index, 1st Quarter 1999

Distribution of Office-Based Physicians

Area	Family/Gen. Practitioners	Specialists		
		Medical	Surgical	Other
MSA[1]	1,628	5,879	3,593	3,968

Note: Data as of 12/31/97; (1) Metropolitan Statistical Area - see Appendix A for areas included
Source: American Medical Assn., Physician Characteristics & Distribution in the U.S., 1999

Hospitals

Chicago has 38 general medical and surgical hospitals, 4 psychiatric, 2 rehabilitation, 1 other specialty, 1 children's general, 1 children's chronic disease, 1 children's orthopedic. *AHA Guide to the Healthcare Field, 1998-99*

According to *U.S. News and World Report,* Chicago has 6 of the best hospitals in the U.S.: **Northwestern Memorial Hospital**, noted for endocrinology, gastroenterology, geriatrics, gynecology, neurology, orthopedics, otolaryngology, pulmonology, rheumatology, urology; **Rush-Presbyterian-St. Luke's Medical Center**, noted for cancer, cardiology, endocrinology, geriatrics, gynecology, neurology, orthopedics, otolaryngology, pulmonology, rheumatology; **University of Chicago Hospitals**, noted for cancer, cardiology, endocrinology, gastroenterology, geriatrics, gynecology, neurology, orthopedics, otolaryngology, pulmonology, rheumatology, urology; **University of Illinois Hospital and Clinics**, noted for otolaryngology; **Children's Memorial Hospital**, noted for pediatrics; **Rehabilitation Institute of Chicago**, noted for rehabilitation. *U.S. News Online, "America's Best Hospitals," 10th Edition, www.usnews.com*

EDUCATION

Public School District Statistics

District Name	Num. Sch.	Enroll.	Classroom Teachers	Pupils per Teacher	Minority Pupils (%)	Current Exp.[1] ($/pupil)
Central Stickney Sch Dist 110	1	457	20	22.9	n/a	n/a
City of Chicago School Dist 29	585	477,610	23,326	20.5	89.7	6,040

Note: Data covers the 1997-1998 school year unless otherwise noted; (1) Data covers fiscal year 1996; SD = School District; ISD = Independent School District; n/a not available
Source: National Center for Education Statistics, Common Core of Data Public Education Agency Universe 1997-98; National Center for Education Statistics, Characteristics of the 100 Largest Public Elementary and Secondary School Districts in the United States: 1997-98, July 1999

Educational Quality

School District	Education Quotient[1]	Graduate Outcome[2]	Community Index[3]	Resource Index[4]
City of Chicago	84.0	52.0	85.0	147.0

Note: Nearly 1,000 secondary school districts were rated in terms of educational quality. The scores range from a low of 50 to a high of 150; (1) Average of the Graduate Outcome, Community and Resource indexes; (2) Based on graduation rates and college board scores (SAT/ACT); (3) Based on the surrounding community's average level of education and the area's average income level; (4) Based on teacher salaries, per-pupil expenditures and student-teacher ratios.
Source: Expansion Management, Ratings Issue, 1998

Educational Attainment by Race

Area	High School Graduate (%)					Bachelor's Degree (%)				
	Total	White	Black	Other	Hisp.[2]	Total	White	Black	Other	Hisp.[2]
City	66.0	72.2	63.1	49.2	40.8	19.5	26.6	10.5	15.5	6.6
MSA[1]	75.7	80.5	65.6	58.0	44.2	24.4	27.9	11.8	24.0	8.0
U.S.	75.2	77.9	63.1	60.4	49.8	20.3	21.5	11.4	19.4	9.2

Note: Figures shown cover persons 25 years old and over; (1) Metropolitan Statistical Area - see Appendix A for areas included; (2) people of Hispanic origin can be of any race
Source: 1990 Census of Population and Housing, Summary Tape File 3C

School Enrollment by Type

Area	Preprimary				Elementary/High School			
	Public		Private		Public		Private	
	Enrollment	%	Enrollment	%	Enrollment	%	Enrollment	%
City	27,249	61.1	17,333	38.9	391,046	79.5	101,138	20.5
MSA[1]	70,174	57.4	52,166	42.6	837,481	82.5	178,237	17.5
U.S.	2,679,029	59.5	1,824,256	40.5	38,379,689	90.2	4,187,099	9.8

Note: Figures shown cover persons 3 years old and over;
(1) Metropolitan Statistical Area - see Appendix A for areas included
Source: 1990 Census of Population and Housing, Summary Tape File 3C

School Enrollment by Race

Area	Preprimary (%)				Elementary/High School (%)			
	White	Black	Other	Hisp.[1]	White	Black	Other	Hisp.[1]
City	36.1	50.5	13.5	17.5	30.7	48.4	20.9	27.8
MSA[2]	68.6	23.0	8.4	9.4	56.2	29.0	14.8	17.5
U.S.	80.4	12.5	7.1	7.8	74.1	15.6	10.3	12.5

Note: Figures shown cover persons 3 years old and over; (1) people of Hispanic origin can be of any race; (2) Metropolitan Statistical Area - see Appendix A for areas included
Source: 1990 Census of Population and Housing, Summary Tape File 3C

Classroom Teacher Salaries in Public Schools

District	B.A. Degree		M.A. Degree		Maximum	
	Min. ($)	Rank[1]	Max. ($)	Rank[1]	Max. ($)	Rank[1]
Chicago	30,567	14	50,151	22	54,385	27
Average	26,980	-	46,065	-	51,435	-

Note: Salaries are for 1997-1998; (1) Rank ranges from 1 to 100
Source: American Federation of Teachers, Survey & Analysis of Salary Trends, 1998

Higher Education

Two-Year Colleges		Four-Year Colleges		Medical Schools	Law Schools	Voc/Tech
Public	Private	Public	Private			
7	5	3	22	5	6	33

Source: College Blue Book, Occupational Education, 1997; Medical School Admission Requirements, 1999-2000; Peterson's Guide to Two-Year Colleges, 1999; Peterson's Guide to Four-Year Colleges, 2000; Barron's Guide to Law Schools, 1999

MAJOR EMPLOYERS

Major Employers

Transportation Insurance
Zell/Chilmark Fund
Harris Bankcorp.
Stone-Consolidated Paper Sales Corp.

Rush-Presbyterian St. Lukes Medical Center

Stargate Systems
Northwestern Memorial Hospital
Northern Trust Co.
University of Chicago Hospitals & Health System
Continental Casualty

Note: Companies listed are located in the city
Source: Dun's Business Rankings, 1999; Ward's Business Directory, 1998

PUBLIC SAFETY

Crime Rate

Area	All Crimes	Violent Crimes				Property Crimes		
		Murder	Forcible Rape	Robbery	Aggrav. Assault	Burglary	Larceny -Theft	Motor Vehicle Theft
City	n/a	27.4	n/a	914.3	1,320.4	1,469.1	4,324.5	1,215.1
Suburbs[1]	n/a	n/a	n/a	n/a	n/a	n/a	n/a	n/a
MSA[2]	n/a	n/a	n/a	n/a	n/a	n/a	n/a	n/a
U.S.	4,922.7	6.8	35.9	186.1	382.0	919.6	2,886.5	505.8

Note: Crime rate is the number of crimes per 100,000 pop.; (1) defined as all areas within the MSA but located outside the central city; (2) Metropolitan Statistical Area - see Appendix A for areas incl.
Source: FBI Uniform Crime Reports, 1997

RECREATION

Culture and Recreation

Museums	Symphony Orchestras	Opera Companies	Dance Companies	Professional Theatres	Zoos	Pro Sports Teams
30	7	3	13	36	1	5

Source: International Directory of the Performing Arts, 1997; Official Museum Directory, 1999; Stern's Performing Arts Directory, 1997; USA Today Four Sport Stadium Guide, 1997; Chamber of Commerce/Economic Development, 1999

Library System

The Chicago Public Library has 79 branches, holdings of 11,463,011 volumes, and a budget of $92,553,591 (1996). *American Library Directory, 1998-1999*

MEDIA

Newspapers

Name	Type	Freq.	Distribution	Circulation
Back of the Yards Journal and El Periodico	General	1x/wk	Local	44,000
Bridgeport News	General	1x/wk	Local	25,300
Brighton Park Life-McKinley Park Life	General	1x/wk	Local	30,500
Chatham Citizen	General	1x/wk	Local	29,962
The Chicago Crusader	Black	1x/wk	Local	70,000
Chicago Defender	Black	6x/wk	Area	33,314
The Chicago Post	General	2x/mo	Local	38,000
Chicago Sun-Times	General	7x/wk	Area	494,146
Chicago Tribune	General	7x/wk	Area	655,522
Clear-Ridge Reporter	n/a	1x/wk	Local	35,000
Dziennik Chicagowski (Chicago Daily)	n/a	5x/wk	Local	25,000
EXITO	Hispanic	1x/wk	Area	85,000
The Extra	Hispanic	1x/wk	Area	68,000
Independent Bulletin	Black	1x/wk	Area	61,000
La Raza Newspaper	Hispanic	1x/wk	Local	150,000
New Metro News	Black	1x/wk	Area	80,000
Polish Daily News	General	7x/wk	U.S./Int'l.	28,400
Southeast Extra	Hispanic	1x/wk	Local	71,205
South End Citizen	General	1x/wk	Local	28,707
Southwest News-Herald	General	1x/wk	Area	25,000
Southwest Shopper	General	1x/wk	Local	52,000

Note: Includes newspapers with circulations of 25,000 or more located in the city; n/a not available
Source: Burrelle's Media Directory, 1999 Edition

Television Stations

Name	Ch.	Affiliation	Type	Owner
WBBM	n/a	CBST	Commercial	Westinghouse Broadcasting Company
WMAQ	n/a	NBCT	Commercial	General Electric Corporation
WLS	n/a	ABCT	Commercial	ABC Inc.
WGN	n/a	WB	Commercial	Tribune Company
WTTW	11	PBS	Public	Windows to the World Communications Inc.
WYCC	20	n/a	Public	City Colleges of Chicago
WFBT	23	n/a	Commercial	Weigel Broadcasting Company
WCIU	26	n/a	Commercial	Weigel Broadcasting Company
WFLD	32	FBC	Commercial	Fox Television Stations Inc.
WCPX	38	PAXTV	Commercial	Paxson Communications Corporation
WSNS	44	TMUN	Commercial	Telemundo Group Inc.
WPWR	50	UPN	Commercial	Channel 50 TV Corporation
WJYS	62	n/a	Commercial	Jovon Broadcasting Corporation
WGBO	66	UNIN	Commercial	Univision Inc.

Note: Stations included broadcast in the Chicago metro area; n/a not available
Source: Burrelle's Media Directory, 1999 Edition

AM Radio Stations

Call Letters	Freq. (kHz)	Target Audience	Station Format	Music Format
WIDB	95	General	S/T	n/a
WIND	560	Hispanic	M/N/T	Latin
WJWR	620	G/M	S	n/a
WMAQ	670	General	N/S/T	n/a
WGN	720	General	N/S/T	n/a
WBBM	780	General	N	n/a
WLS	890	General	N/T	n/a
WMVP	1000	General	S/T	n/a
WNVR	1030	General	M	n/a
WMBI	1110	H/R	M/T	Christian
WSCR	1160	General	S	n/a
WSBC	1240	General	M	n/a
WTAQ	1300	Hispanic	M/N/S/T	n/a
WGCI	1390	C/G	M/N	Gospel
WVON	1450	Black	E/M/N/S/T	Christian/R&B
WPNA	1490	General	E/M/N/S/T	n/a
WJJG	1530	General	M/N/S/T	Adult Standards/Big Band/MOR
WBEE	1570	G/S	M/N	Christian/Jazz/R&B
WONX	1590	H/M	M/N/T	AOR/Christian/Latin
WCGO	1600	General	M/N/T	Adult Standards

Note: Stations included broadcast in the Chicago metro area; n/a not available
Target Audience: A=Asian; B=Black; C=Christian; E=Ethnic; F=French; G=General; H=Hispanic;
M=Men; N=Native American; R=Religious; S=Senior Citizen; W=Women; Y=Young Adult; Z=Children
Station Format: E=Educational; M=Music; N=News; S=Sports; T=Talk
Music Format: AOR=Album Oriented Rock; MOR=Middle-of-the-Road
Source: Burrelle's Media Directory, 1999 Edition

FM Radio Stations

Call Letters	Freq. (mHz)	Target Audience	Station Format	Music Format
WCRX	88.1	General	M	Urban Contemporary
WSSD	88.1	B/G	M/T	R&B
WLTL	88.1	General	M/N/S	Alternative/Classic Rock/Oldies
WNTH	88.1	General	E/M/N/S/T	n/a
WZRD	88.3	General	E/M/N	n/a
WHPK	88.5	General	E/M/T	n/a
WHFH	88.5	General	E/M/N/S	n/a
WGBK	88.5	General	E/M/N/S/T	Alternative
WLUW	88.7	G/H	E/M/N/S/T	Alternative
WOUI	88.9	General	M/N/S	AOR/Classic Rock/Country/Jazz/Oldies
WRRG	88.9	n/a	M/N/S	Alternative
WARG	88.9	General	E/M/N/S	Alternative/Classical/Jazz
WKKC	89.3	B/G/R	E/M/N/S/T	Adult Contemporary/Big Band/Jazz/Oldies/R&B/Urban Contemporary
WNUR	89.3	n/a	M/N/S	n/a
WMBI	90.1	General	M	Christian
WRTE	90.5	Hispanic	E/M	Alternative/Latin/Modern Rock/World Music
WMTH	90.5	General	M/N/S	Classic Rock/Easy Listening
WBEZ	91.5	General	M/N/T	Big Band/Jazz/Latin
WKIE	92.7	General	M	Top 40
WXRT	93.1	General	M/N/T	Alternative
WLIT	93.9	General	M/N/T	Adult Contemporary
WXCD	94.7	General	N/T	n/a
WNUA	95.5	General	M/N/T	Jazz
WCRC	95.7	General	M/S	Country
WBBM	96.3	General	M/N/T	n/a
WNIB	97.1	General	M	Classical
WLUP	97.9	Men	M/N/T	Classic Rock
WFMT	98.7	General	E/M/N	Classical/Jazz
WUSN	99.5	General	M	Country
WNND	100.3	General	M/N	Adult Contemporary
WKQX	101.1	General	M	Alternative
WTMX	101.9	General	M	Easy Listening
WVAZ	102.7	Black	Women	M/N/T
WUBT	103.5	General	M	Classic Rock/Oldies/R&B
WJMK	104.3	General	M	Oldies
WOJO	105.1	Hispanic	E/M/N/T	Adult Contemporary
WCKG	105.9	General	N/S	n/a
WYLL	106.7	Religious	T	n/a
WGCI	107.5	General	M	Urban Contemporary
WLEY	107.9	Hispanic	M	Latin

Note: Stations included broadcast in the Chicago metro area; n/a not available
Station Format: E=Educational; M=Music; N=News; S=Sports; T=Talk
Target Audience: A=Asian; B=Black; C=Christian; E=Ethnic; F=French; G=General; H=Hispanic; M=Men; N=Native American; R=Religious; S=Senior Citizen; W=Women; Y=Young Adult; Z=Children
Music Format: AOR=Album Oriented Rock; MOR=Middle-of-the-Road
Source: Burrelle's Media Directory, 1999 Edition

CLIMATE

Average and Extreme Temperatures

Temperature	Jan	Feb	Mar	Apr	May	Jun	Jul	Aug	Sep	Oct	Nov	Dec	Yr.
Extreme High (°F)	65	71	88	91	93	104	102	100	99	91	78	71	104
Average High (°F)	29	33	45	59	70	79	84	82	75	63	48	34	59
Average Temp. (°F)	21	26	37	49	59	69	73	72	65	53	40	27	49
Average Low (°F)	13	17	28	39	48	57	63	62	54	42	32	19	40
Extreme Low (°F)	-27	-17	-8	7	24	36	40	41	28	17	1	-25	-27

Note: Figures cover the years 1958-1990
Source: National Climatic Data Center, International Station Meteorological Climate Summary, 3/95

Average Precipitation/Snowfall/Humidity

Precip./Humidity	Jan	Feb	Mar	Apr	May	Jun	Jul	Aug	Sep	Oct	Nov	Dec	Yr.
Avg. Precip. (in.)	1.6	1.4	2.7	3.6	3.3	3.7	3.7	4.1	3.7	2.4	2.8	2.3	35.4
Avg. Snowfall (in.)	11	8	7	2	Tr	0	0	0	0	1	2	9	39
Avg. Rel. Hum. 6am (%)	76	77	79	77	77	78	82	85	85	82	80	80	80
Avg. Rel. Hum. 3pm (%)	65	63	59	53	51	52	54	55	55	53	61	68	57

Note: Figures cover the years 1958-1990; Tr = Trace amounts (<0.05 in. of rain; <0.5 in. of snow)
Source: National Climatic Data Center, International Station Meteorological Climate Summary, 3/95

Weather Conditions

Temperature			Daytime Sky			Precipitation		
5°F & below	32°F & below	90°F & above	Clear	Partly cloudy	Cloudy	0.01 inch or more precip.	0.1 inch or more snow/ice	Thunder-storms
21	132	17	83	136	146	125	31	38

Note: Figures are average number of days per year and covers the years 1958-1990
Source: National Climatic Data Center, International Station Meteorological Climate Summary, 3/95

AIR & WATER QUALITY

Maximum Pollutant Concentrations

	Particulate Matter (ug/m^3)	Carbon Monoxide (ppm)	Sulfur Dioxide (ppm)	Nitrogen Dioxide (ppm)	Ozone (ppm)	Lead (ug/m^3)
MSA[1] Level	99	5	0.041	0.034	0.11	0.08
NAAQS[2]	150	9	0.140	0.053	0.12	1.50
Met NAAQS?	Yes	Yes	Yes	Yes	Yes	Yes

Note: (1) Metropolitan Statistical Area - see Appendix A for areas included; (2) National Ambient Air Quality Standards; ppm = parts per million; ug/m^3 = micrograms per cubic meter; n/a not available
Source: EPA, National Air Quality and Emissions Trends Report, 1997

Pollutant Standards Index

In the Chicago MSA (see Appendix A for areas included), the Pollutant Standards Index (PSI) exceeded 100 on 10 days in 1997. A PSI value greater than 100 indicates that air quality would be in the unhealthful range on that day. *EPA, National Air Quality and Emissions Trends Report, 1997*

Drinking Water

Water System Name	Pop. Served	Primary Water Source Type	Number of Violations in 1998	Type of Violation/ Contaminants
Chicago	3,000,000	Surface	None	None

Note: Data as of July 10, 1999
Source: EPA, Office of Ground Water and Drinking Water, Safe Drinking Water Information System

Chicago tap water is alkaline (Lake Michigan) and fluoridated.
Editor & Publisher Market Guide, 1999

Des Moines, Iowa

Background

In 1843, Fort Des Moines was founded at the confluence of the Des Moines and Raccoon Rivers. Though the fort was initially established to protect local Native American populations, within two years the area was opened to white settlers. By 1857, the state capital was moved from Iowa City to Des Moines. Today, Des Moines remains the capital of Iowa and is its largest city.

Des Moines is one of the top cities in the country for job seekers. Ranking third in the country for insurance activities, Des Moines has more than 50 insurance companies located in its environs. The city also has approximately 385 factories, producing a broad-based spectrum of goods ranging from grain drills to tires.

In addition to its great job market, Des Moines ranks high in areas such as education and the family. *Iowa Parent and Family Magazine*, located in Des Moines, is one of the oldest Midwest parenting publications. The monthly newspaper provides valuable information for families in central Iowa reporting on summer camps, local parenting groups, and kid's activities.

Throughout the city one can see the evidence of Des Moines' progressive state of mind. The Des Moines Art Center was designed in 1944 by Eliel Saarinen, a Finnish architect and then President of the reknown Cranbrook Academy of Art in Detroit. In 1968, I.M. Pei, architect of the John F. Kennedy International Airport in New York and the east wing of the National Gallery of Art in Washington DC, designed a gallery addition to the main Art Center structure. Finally, in 1985, Richard Meier, who had designed the Museum of Modern Art in Florence, Italy, designed an addition to the Art Center's north wing. The Home Federal Savings and Loan Building was designed by Mies van der Rohe, of the famous German Bauhaus School of Design, and a sculpture called the Crusoe Umbrella, designed by Pop artist Claes Oldenberg, stands in the middle of Nollen Plaza, a wooded park and popular gathering place.

Another gathering place is The Des Moines Botanical Center which boasts a 150 foot wide and 80 foot tall tropical dome with gardens both inside and outside. The Botanical Center maintains a permanent collection of more than 15,000 plants and an ornamental plant collection that changes six times a year.

Just 25 miles southwest of Des Moines is the locale in the film "Bridges of Madison County" starring Clint Eastwood and Meryl Streep. In the film you can see Iowa's flat and fertile fields and how the land yielded easily to growing crops. Today, much of Des Moines' political and economic concerns still rally around agriculture.

Located in the heart of North America, Des Moines has a climate which is continental in character. This results in a marked seasonal contrast in both temperature and precipitation. The winter is a season of cold dry air, interrupted by occasional storms of short duration. The autumn is characteristically sunny with diminishing precipitation.

General Rankings and Evaluative Comments

■ Des Moines was ranked #22 out of 24 mid-sized, midwestern metropolitan areas in *Money's* 1998 survey of "The Best Places to Live in America." The survey was conducted by first contacting 512 representative households nationwide and asking them to rank 37 quality-of-life factors on a scale of 1 to 10. Next, a demographic profile was compiled on the 300 largest metropolitan statistical areas in the U.S. The numbers were crunched together to arrive at an overall ranking (things Americans consider most important, like clean air and water, low crime and good schools, received extra weight). Unlike previous years, the 1998 rankings were broken down by region (northeast, midwest, south, west) and population size (100,000 to 249,999; 250,000 to 999,999; 1 million plus). The city had a nationwide ranking of #218 out of 300 in 1997 and #219 out of 300 in 1996. *Money, July 1998; Money, July 1997; Money, September 1996*

■ *Ladies Home Journal* ranked America's 200 largest cities based on the qualities women care about most. Des Moines ranked #112 out of 200. Criteria: low crime rate, well-paying jobs, quality health and child care, good public schools, the presence of women in government, size of the gender wage gap, number of sexual-harassment and discrimination complaints filed, unemployment and divorce rates, commute times, population density, number of houses of worship, parks and cultural offerings, number of women's health specialists, how well a community's women cared for themselves, complexion kindness index based on UV radiation levels, odds of finding affordable fashions, rental rates for romance movies, champagne sales and other matters of the heart. *Ladies Home Journal, November 1998*

■ Zero Population Growth ranked 229 cities in terms of children's health, safety, and economic well-being. Des Moines was ranked #18 out of 112 independent cities (cities with populations greater than 100,000 which were neither Major Cities nor Suburbs/Outer Cities) and was given a grade of B. Criteria: total population, percent of population under 18 years of age, household language, percent population change, percent of births to teens, infant mortality rate, percent of low birth weights, dropout rate, enrollment in preprimary school, violent and property crime rates, unemployment rate, percent of children in poverty, percent of owner occupied units, number of bad air days, percent of public transportation commuters, and average travel time to work. *Zero Population Growth, Children's Environmental Index, Fall 1999*

■ Cognetics studied 273 metro areas in the United States, ranking them by entrepreneurial activity. Des Moines was ranked #36 out of 134 smaller metro areas. Criteria: Significant Starts (firms started in the last 10 years that still employ at least 5 people) and Young Growers (percent of firms 10 years old or less that grew significantly during the last 4 years). *Cognetics, "Entrepreneurial Hot Spots: The Best Places in America to Start and Grow a Company," 1998*

■ Des Moines was selected as one of the "Best American Cities to Start a Business" by *Point of View* magazine. Criteria: coolness, quality-of-life, and business concerns. The city was ranked #68 out of 75. *Point of View, November 1998*

■ Des Moines appeared on *Sales & Marketing Management's* list of the "20 Hottest Cities for Selling." Rank: #2 out of 20. *S&MM* editors looked at Metropolitan Statistical Areas with populations of more than 150,000. The areas were ranked based on population increases, retail sales increases, effective buying income, increase in both residential and commercial building permits issued, unemployment rates, job growth, mix of industries, tax rates, number of corporate relocations, and the number of new corporations. *Sales & Marketing Management, April 1999*

■ Reliastar Financial Corp. ranked the 125 largest metropolitan areas according to the general financial security of residents. Des Moines was ranked #5 out of 125 with a score of 15.1. The score indicates the percentage a metropolitan area is above or below the metropolitan norm. A metro area with a score of 10.6 is 10.6% above the metro average. Criteria: Earnings and Wealth Potential (household income, education, net assets, cost of living); Safety Net (health insurance, retirement savings, life insurance, income support programs); Personal Threats (unemployment rate, low-income households, crime rate); Community Economic Vitality (cost of community services, job quality, job creation, housing costs). *Reliastar Financial Corp., "The Best Cities to Earn and Save Money," 1999 Edition*

Business Environment

STATE ECONOMY

State Economic Profile

"Iowa's economy has seen impressive growth in the last several years. A tight labor market and a softening in both the manufacturing and agriculture sectors will, however, slow Iowa's growth over the next few years.

While low food prices have helped to tame inflation, they have hurt farm income. Depressed commodity prices have hit Iowa's Gross State Product (GSP) particularly hard. Given the current oversupply in many food markets and the weak foreign demand, Iowa's farm economy will remain a drag on its economy in 1999.

Services, manufacturing and construction have all provided significant growth, helping to offset the declining farm sector. Business services and high-tech manufacturing, as well as a construction boom, largely contribute to this growth.

Des Moines, the traditional engine of Iowa's non-farm sector employment growth, has actually been growing at a rate below the rest of the state. This is partly due to Des Moines' tight labor market (1.9% unemployment rate) at the end of 1998. Economic growth has instead shifted to Cedar Rapids and Ames, both centers of university-high tech partnerships. Des Moines did, however, witness a building boom in 1998, with single-family permits jumping 35% and construction employment growing almost 12% in 1998.

There have been many bright spots to offset Iowa's hurting farm sector. Unfortunately the continued loss of population and tight labor markets will be a hurdle to companies that want to create jobs." *National Association of Realtors, Economic Profiles: The Fifty States and the District of Columbia, http://nar.realtor.com/databank/profiles.htm*

IMPORTS/EXPORTS

Total Export Sales

Area	1994 ($000)	1995 ($000)	1996 ($000)	1997 ($000)	% Chg. 1994-97	% Chg. 1996-97
MSA[1]	348,931	378,549	426,017	450,544	29.1	5.8
U.S.	512,415,609	583,030,524	622,827,063	687,597,999	34.2	10.4

Note: (1) Metropolitan Statistical Area - see Appendix A for areas included
Source: U.S. Department of Commerce, International Trade Association, Metropolitan Area Exports: An Export Performance Report on Over 250 U.S. Cities, November 10, 1998

CITY FINANCES

City Government Finances

Component	FY92 ($000)	FY92 (per capita $)
Revenue	214,189	1,097.84
Expenditure	241,536	1,238.00
Debt Outstanding	308,724	1,582.38
Cash & Securities	166,123	851.47

Source: U.S. Bureau of the Census, City Government Finances: 1991-92

City Government Revenue by Source

Source	FY92 ($000)	FY92 (per capita $)	FY92 (%)
From Federal Government	12,202	62.54	5.7
From State Governments	17,449	89.44	8.1
From Local Governments	113	0.58	0.1
Property Taxes	78,827	404.03	36.8
General Sales Taxes	0	0.00	0.0
Selective Sales Taxes	5,427	27.82	2.5
Income Taxes	0	0.00	0.0
Current Charges	42,098	215.78	19.7
Utility/Liquor Store	21,451	109.95	10.0
Employee Retirement[1]	0	0.00	0.0
Other	36,622	187.71	17.1

Note: (1) Excludes "city contributions," classified as "nonrevenue," intragovernmental transfers.
Source: U.S. Bureau of the Census, City Government Finances: 1991-92

City Government Expenditures by Function

Function	FY92 ($000)	FY92 (per capita $)	FY92 (%)
Educational Services	4,383	22.47	1.8
Employee Retirement[1]	0	0.00	0.0
Environment/Housing	80,109	410.60	33.2
Government Administration	10,751	55.10	4.5
Interest on General Debt	24,319	124.65	10.1
Public Safety	38,241	196.01	15.8
Social Services	5,146	26.38	2.1
Transportation	43,996	225.50	18.2
Utility/Liquor Store	22,732	116.51	9.4
Other	11,859	60.78	4.9

Note: (1) Payments to beneficiaries including withdrawal of contributions.
Source: U.S. Bureau of the Census, City Government Finances: 1991-92

Municipal Bond Ratings

Area	Moody's	S & P
Des Moines	Aa3	n/a

Note: n/a not available; n/r not rated
Source: Moody's Bond Record, 6/99

POPULATION

Population Growth

Area	1980	1990	% Chg. 1980-90	July 1998 Estimate	% Chg. 1990-98
City	191,003	193,187	1.1	191,293	-1.0
MSA[1]	367,561	392,928	6.9	438,938	11.7
U.S.	226,545,805	248,765,170	9.8	270,299,000	8.7

Note: (1) Metropolitan Statistical Area - see Appendix A for areas included;
July 1998 MSA population estimate was calculated by the editors
Source: 1980/1990 Census of Housing and Population, Summary Tape File 3C;
Census Bureau Population Estimates 1998

Population Characteristics

Race	City					MSA[1]	
	1980		1990		% Chg. 1980-90	1990	
	Population	%	Population	%		Population	%
White	173,032	90.6	172,426	89.3	-0.4	368,765	93.9
Black	13,164	6.9	13,667	7.1	3.8	14,598	3.7
Amer Indian/Esk/Aleut	603	0.3	800	0.4	32.7	1,063	0.3
Asian/Pacific Islander	2,498	1.3	4,437	2.3	77.6	5,886	1.5
Other	1,706	0.9	1,857	1.0	8.9	2,616	0.7
Hispanic Origin[2]	3,523	1.8	4,550	2.4	29.2	6,892	1.8

Note: (1) Metropolitan Statistical Area - see Appendix A for areas included;
(2) people of Hispanic origin can be of any race
Source: 1980/1990 Census of Housing and Population, Summary Tape File 3C

Ancestry

Area	German	Irish	English	Italian	U.S.	French	Polish	Dutch
City	35.0	20.1	16.0	4.2	4.1	4.0	1.2	5.8
MSA[1]	39.5	20.2	17.7	3.6	3.8	4.2	1.4	6.1
U.S.	23.3	15.6	13.1	5.9	5.3	4.2	3.8	2.5

Note: Figures are percentages and include persons that reported multiple ancestry (eg. if a person reported being Irish and Italian, they were included in both columns); (1) Metropolitan Statistical Area - see Appendix A for areas included
Source: 1990 Census of Population and Housing, Summary Tape File 3C

Age

Area	Median Age (Years)	Age Distribution (%)						
		Under 5	Under 18	18-24	25-44	45-64	65+	80+
City	32.2	7.8	24.2	11.9	33.3	17.2	13.3	3.4
MSA[1]	32.5	7.5	25.5	10.7	33.8	18.4	11.7	2.9
U.S.	32.9	7.3	25.6	10.5	32.6	18.7	12.5	2.8

Note: (1) Metropolitan Statistical Area - see Appendix A for areas included
Source: 1990 Census of Population and Housing, Summary Tape File 3C

Male/Female Ratio

Area	Number of males per 100 females (all ages)	Number of males per 100 females (18 years old+)
City	89.0	85.0
MSA[1]	91.7	87.4
U.S.	95.0	91.9

Note: (1) Metropolitan Statistical Area - see Appendix A for areas included
Source: 1990 Census of Population, General Population Characteristics

INCOME

Per Capita/Median/Average Income

Area	Per Capita ($)	Median Household ($)	Average Household ($)
City	13,710	26,703	33,199
MSA[1]	14,972	31,182	37,958
U.S.	14,420	30,056	38,453

Note: All figures are for 1989; (1) Metropolitan Statistical Area - see Appendix A for areas included
Source: 1990 Census of Population and Housing, Summary Tape File 3C

Household Income Distribution by Race

Income ($)	City (%)					U.S. (%)				
	Total	White	Black	Other	Hisp.[1]	Total	White	Black	Other	Hisp.[1]
Less than 5,000	6.0	5.3	12.9	10.2	6.9	6.2	4.8	15.2	8.6	8.8
5,000 - 9,999	10.2	9.5	20.5	6.7	6.0	9.3	8.6	14.2	9.9	11.1
10,000 - 14,999	10.2	10.0	13.3	12.2	16.0	8.8	8.5	11.0	9.8	11.0
15,000 - 24,999	20.2	20.1	20.7	22.8	18.3	17.5	17.3	18.9	18.5	20.5
25,000 - 34,999	18.7	19.1	11.8	22.2	19.7	15.8	16.1	14.2	15.4	16.4
35,000 - 49,999	18.1	18.8	10.1	15.4	19.0	17.9	18.6	13.3	16.1	16.0
50,000 - 74,999	11.5	11.9	8.3	7.4	11.4	15.0	15.8	9.3	13.4	11.1
75,000 - 99,999	2.7	2.8	1.8	2.8	2.2	5.1	5.5	2.6	4.7	3.1
100,000+	2.3	2.5	0.7	0.2	0.5	4.4	4.8	1.3	3.7	1.9

Note: All figures are for 1989; (1) people of Hispanic origin can be of any race
Source: 1990 Census of Population and Housing, Summary Tape File 3C

Effective Buying Income

Area	Per Capita ($)	Median Household ($)	Average Household ($)
City	16,755	33,255	41,072
MSA[1]	18,930	38,813	48,148
U.S.	16,803	34,536	45,243

Note: Data as of 1/1/99; (1) Metropolitan Statistical Area - see Appendix A for areas included
Source: Standard Rate & Data Service, Newspaper Advertising Source, 9/99

Effective Household Buying Income Distribution

Area	% of Households Earning						
	$10,000 -$19,999	$20,000 -$34,999	$35,000 -$49,999	$50,000 -$74,999	$75,000 -$99,000	$100,000 -$124,999	$125,000 and up
City	16.7	25.1	20.1	18.1	5.5	1.6	1.8
MSA[1]	13.9	22.7	20.2	22.2	8.0	2.5	2.4
U.S.	16.0	22.6	18.2	18.9	7.2	2.4	2.7

Note: Data as of 1/1/99; (1) Metropolitan Statistical Area - see Appendix A for areas included
Source: Standard Rate & Data Service, Newspaper Advertising Source, 9/99

Poverty Rates by Race and Age

Area	Total (%)	By Race (%)				By Age (%)		
		White	Black	Other	Hisp.[2]	Under 5 years old	Under 18 years old	65 years and over
City	12.9	11.0	30.8	23.5	18.3	21.8	19.3	9.1
MSA[1]	8.8	7.7	29.6	19.9	14.3	14.4	11.7	8.5
U.S.	13.1	9.8	29.5	23.1	25.3	20.1	18.3	12.8

Note: Figures show the percent of people living below the poverty line in 1989. The average poverty threshold was $12,674 for a family of four in 1989; (1) Metropolitan Statistical Area - see Appendix A for areas included; (2) people of Hispanic origin can be of any race
Source: 1990 Census of Population and Housing, Summary Tape File 3C

EMPLOYMENT

Labor Force and Employment

Area	Civilian Labor Force			Workers Employed		
	Jun. 1998	Jun. 1999	% Chg.	Jun. 1998	Jun. 1999	% Chg.
City	122,089	125,470	2.8	118,904	122,294	2.9
MSA[1]	258,433	265,535	2.7	253,131	260,348	2.9
U.S.	138,798,000	140,666,000	1.3	132,265,000	134,395,000	1.6

Note: Data is not seasonally adjusted and covers workers 16 years of age and older;
(1) Metropolitan Statistical Area - see Appendix A for areas included
Source: Bureau of Labor Statistics, http://stats.bls.gov

Unemployment Rate

Area	1998						1999					
	Jul.	Aug.	Sep.	Oct.	Nov.	Dec.	Jan.	Feb.	Mar.	Apr.	May.	Jun.
City	2.1	2.5	2.6	2.3	2.5	2.4	3.1	2.9	3.0	2.5	2.2	2.5
MSA[1]	1.6	1.9	2.0	1.8	1.9	1.9	2.4	2.3	2.3	1.9	1.7	2.0
U.S.	4.7	4.5	4.4	4.2	4.1	4.0	4.8	4.7	4.4	4.1	4.0	4.5

Note: Data is not seasonally adjusted and covers workers 16 years of age and older; all figures are percentages; (1) Metropolitan Statistical Area - see Appendix A for areas included
Source: Bureau of Labor Statistics, http://stats.bls.gov

Employment by Industry

Sector	MSA[1]		U.S.
	Number of Employees	Percent of Total	Percent of Total
Services	87,800	30.2	30.4
Retail Trade	52,200	17.9	17.7
Government	34,600	11.9	15.6
Manufacturing	24,800	8.5	14.3
Finance/Insurance/Real Estate	40,400	13.9	5.9
Wholesale Trade	22,100	7.6	5.4
Transportation/Public Utilities	15,400	5.3	5.3
Construction	n/a	n/a	5.0
Mining	n/a	n/a	0.4

Note: Figures cover non-farm employment as of 6/99 and are not seasonally adjusted; (1) Metropolitan Statistical Area - see Appendix A for areas included; n/a not available
Source: Bureau of Labor Statistics, http://stats.bls.gov

Employment by Occupation

Occupation Category	City (%)	MSA[1] (%)	U.S. (%)
White Collar	61.6	65.0	58.1
Executive/Admin./Management	11.3	13.5	12.3
Professional	12.1	13.2	14.1
Technical & Related Support	3.6	3.7	3.7
Sales	11.6	13.3	11.8
Administrative Support/Clerical	23.1	21.4	16.3
Blue Collar	22.9	20.5	26.2
Precision Production/Craft/Repair	9.2	8.6	11.3
Machine Operators/Assem./Insp.	5.9	4.8	6.8
Transportation/Material Movers	3.9	3.5	4.1
Cleaners/Helpers/Laborers	3.9	3.7	3.9
Services	14.8	12.8	13.2
Farming/Forestry/Fishing	0.7	1.7	2.5

Note: Figures cover employed persons 16 years old and over; (1) Metropolitan Statistical Area - see Appendix A for areas included
Source: 1990 Census of Population and Housing, Summary Tape File 3C

Occupational Employment Projections: 1996 - 2006

Occupations Expected to Have the Largest Job Growth (ranked by numerical growth)	Fast-Growing Occupations[1] (ranked by percent growth)
1. Truck drivers, light	1. Systems analysts
2. Salespersons, retail	2. Desktop publishers
3. Cashiers	3. Computer engineers
4. General managers & top executives	4. Database administrators
5. Janitors/cleaners/maids, ex. priv. hshld.	5. Emergency medical technicians
6. Registered nurses	6. Respiratory therapists
7. Nursing aides/orderlies/attendants	7. Adjustment clerks
8. Marketing & sales, supervisors	8. Home health aides
9. Hand packers & packagers	9. Human services workers
10. Systems analysts	10. Guards

Note: Projections cover Iowa; (1) Excludes occupations with total job growth less than 300
Source: U.S. Department of Labor, Employment and Training Administration, America's Labor Market Information System (ALMIS)

TAXES

Major State and Local Tax Rates

State Corp. Income (%)	State Personal Income (%)	Residential Property (effective rate per $100)	Sales & Use State (%)	Sales & Use Local (%)	State Gasoline (cents/ gallon)	State Cigarette (cents/ pack)
6.0 - 12.0	0.36 - 8.98	2.36	5.0	None	20.0	36.0

Note: Personal/corporate income, sales, gasoline and cigarette tax rates as of January 1999. Property tax rates as of 1997.
Source: Federation of Tax Administrators, www.taxadmin.org; Washington D.C. Department of Finance and Revenue, Tax Rates and Tax Burdens in the District of Columbia: A Nationwide Comparison, July 1998; Chamber of Commerce, 1999

Total Taxes Per Capita and as a Percent of Income

Area	Per Capita Income ($)	Per Capita Taxes ($) Total	Per Capita Taxes ($) Federal	Per Capita Taxes ($) State/ Local	Percent of Income (%) Total	Percent of Income (%) Federal	Percent of Income (%) State/ Local
Iowa	25,850	8,700	5,776	2,924	33.7	22.5	11.3
U.S.	27,876	9,881	6,690	3,191	35.4	24.0	11.4

Note: Figures are for 1998
Source: Tax Foundation, www.taxfoundation.org

Estimated Tax Burden

Area	State Income	Local Income	Property	Sales	Total
Des Moines	3,525	0	4,500	488	8,513

Note: The numbers are estimates of taxes paid by a married couple with two children and annual earnings of $75,000. Sales tax estimates assume they spend average amounts on food, clothing, household goods and gasoline. Property tax estimates assume they live in a $250,000 home.
Source: Kiplinger's Personal Finance Magazine, October 1998

**COMMERCIAL
REAL ESTATE**

Office Market

Class/ Location	Total Space (sq. ft.)	Vacant Space (sq. ft.)	Vac. Rate (%)	Under Constr. (sq. ft.)	Net Absorp. (sq. ft.)	Rental Rates ($/sq.ft./yr.)
Class A						
CBD	2,789,624	170,908	6.1	n/a	-17,155	16.00-24.50
Outside CBD	3,071,137	230,576	7.5	38,000	152,402	13.95-18.50
Class B						
CBD	2,093,141	403,370	19.3	50,000	2,794	9.50-16.50
Outside CBD	1,274,482	79,319	6.2	n/a	29,740	9.00-16.50

Note: Data as of 10/98 and covers Greater Des Moines; CBD = Central Business District; n/a not available;
Source: Society of Industrial and Office Realtors, 1999 Comparative Statistics of Industrial and Office Real Estate Markets

"The local and regional economies are expected to remain stable in Des Moines. Unemployment, currently at two percent, may create a shortage of qualified people for business growth. In turn, this shortage could cause a slowdown in demand for new office space. Two 100,000+ sq. ft. built-to-suit projects are underway in the western suburbs. Those sites are being built for John Deere Credit and Sears Credit Card and should be substantially complete within the year. Attention from REITs and outside investors has created a demand for investment properties both inside and outside of the CBD, a situation which is expected to perpetuate the trend of increased sales prices. Our SIOR reporter estimates that sales prices will increase between six and 10 percent." *Society of Industrial and Office Realtors, 1999 Comparative Statistics of Industrial and Office Real Estate Markets*

Industrial Market

Location	Total Space (sq. ft.)	Vacant Space (sq. ft.)	Vac. Rate (%)	Under Constr. (sq. ft.)	Net Absorp. (sq. ft.)	Lease ($/sq.ft./yr.)
Central City	14,361,000	574,983	4.0	n/a	142,090	2.75-5.00
Suburban	6,818,000	75,000	1.1	646,000	502,386	2.75-4.50

Note: Data as of 10/98 and covers Des Moines; n/a not available
Source: Society of Industrial and Office Realtors, 1999 Comparative Statistics of Industrial and Office Real Estate Markets

"It is the judgement of our local SIOR reporters that sales prices will remain stable whereas lease prices for all but High- Tech/R&D spaces will increase slightly. Increases in absorption should occur for warehouse/distribution space. Site prices are expected to increase by up to 10 percent. Development is expected to be concentrated in the areas near the Des Moines Airport. Color Converting Company purchased 10 acres in Airport Commerce Park West and will have a new facility completed next year. The publisher of the Des Moines Register, the local newspaper, purchased land at the Airport Business Park. During 1999, it will build a 120,000 sq. ft. facility that will house all of its presses and printing operations." *Society of Industrial and Office Realtors, 1999 Comparative Statistics of Industrial and Office Real Estate Markets*

COMMERCIAL UTILITIES

Typical Monthly Electric Bills

Area	Commercial Service ($/month)		Industrial Service ($/month)	
	12 kW demand 1,500 kWh	100 kW demand 30,000 kWh	1,000 kW demand 400,000 kWh	20,000 kW demand 10,000,000 kWh
City	n/a	n/a	n/a	n/a
U.S.	150	2,174	23,995	508,569

Note: Based on rates in effect January 1, 1999; n/a not available
Source: Edison Electric Institute, Typical Residential, Commercial and Industrial Bills, Winter 1999

TRANSPORTATION

Transportation Statistics

Average minutes to work	16.4
Interstate highways	I-35; I-80
Bus lines	
In-city	Des Moines Metropolitan TA
Inter-city	2
Passenger air service	
Airport	Des Moines Municipal
Airlines	14
Aircraft departures	16,924 (1996)
Enplaned passengers	800,024 (1996)
Rail service	No Amtrak Service
Motor freight carriers	82
Major waterways/ports	None

Source: Editor & Publisher Market Guide, 1999; FAA Airport Activity Statistics, 1997; Amtrak National Time Table, Northeast Timetable, Spring/Summer 1999; 1990 Census of Population and Housing, STF 3C; Chamber of Commerce/Economic Development 1999; Jane's Urban Transport Systems 1999-2000

Means of Transportation to Work

Area	Car/Truck/Van		Public Transportation			Bicycle	Walked	Other Means	Worked at Home
	Drove Alone	Car-pooled	Bus	Subway	Railroad				
City	74.4	15.1	3.5	0.0	0.0	0.2	3.6	0.7	2.5
MSA[1]	77.3	13.7	2.1	0.0	0.0	0.1	2.9	0.6	3.4
U.S.	73.2	13.4	3.0	1.5	0.5	0.4	3.9	1.2	3.0

Note: Figures shown are percentages and only include workers 16 years old and over;
(1) Metropolitan Statistical Area - see Appendix A for areas included
Source: 1990 Census of Population and Housing, Summary Tape File 3C

BUSINESSES

Major Business Headquarters

Company Name	1999 Rankings	
	Fortune 500	Forbes 500
Principal Financial	213	-

Note: Companies listed are located in the city; dashes indicate no ranking
Fortune 500: Companies that produce a 10-K are ranked 1 to 500 based on 1998 revenue
Forbes 500: Private companies are ranked 1 to 500 based on 1997 revenue
Source: Forbes, November 30, 1998; Fortune, April 26, 1999

Best Companies to Work For

Principal Financial Group, headquartered in Des Moines, is among the "100 Best Companies for Working Mothers." Criteria: fair wages, opportunities for women to advance, support for child care, flexible work schedules, family-friendly benefits, and work/life supports. *Working Mother, October 1998*

The Principal Financial Group (financial services), headquartered in Des Moines, is among the "100 Best Places to Work in IS." Criteria: compensation, turnover and training. *Computerworld, May 25, 1998*

HOTELS & MOTELS

Hotels/Motels

Area	Hotels/ Motels	Rooms	Luxury-Level Hotels/Motels		Average Minimum Rates ($)		
			♦♦♦♦	♦♦♦♦♦	♦♦	♦♦♦	♦♦♦♦
City	19	2,738	0	0	57	88	n/a
Airport	5	636	0	0	n/a	n/a	n/a
Suburbs	24	2,739	0	0	n/a	n/a	n/a
Total	48	6,113	0	0	n/a	n/a	n/a

Note: n/a not available; classifications range from one diamond (budget properties with basic amenities) to five diamond (luxury properties with the finest service, rooms and facilities).
Source: OAG, Business Travel Planner, Winter 1998-99

CONVENTION CENTERS

Major Convention Centers

Center Name	Meeting Rooms	Exhibit Space (sq. ft.)
Des Moines Convention Center	33	46,100
Veterans Memorial Auditorium	9	98,000

Source: Trade Shows Worldwide, 1998; Meetings & Conventions, 4/15/99; Sucessful Meetings, 3/31/98

Living Environment

COST OF LIVING

Cost of Living Index

Composite Index	Groceries	Housing	Utilities	Trans-portation	Health Care	Misc. Goods/ Services
97.3	95.6	90.2	104.4	96.8	100.8	101.9

Note: U.S. = 100
Source: ACCRA, Cost of Living Index, 1st Quarter 1999

HOUSING

Median Home Prices and Housing Affordability

Area	Median Price[2] 1st Qtr. 1999 ($)	HOI[3] 1st Qtr. 1999	Afford-ability Rank[4]
MSA[1]	94,000	90.6	4
U.S.	134,000	69.6	–

Note: (1) Metropolitan Statistical Area - see Appendix A for areas included; (2) U.S. figures calculated from the sales of 524,324 new and existing homes in 181 markets; (3) Housing Opportunity Index - percent of homes sold that were within the reach of the median income household at the prevailing mortgage interest rate; (4) Rank is from 1-181 with 1 being most affordable
Source: National Association of Home Builders, Housing Opportunity Index, 1st Quarter 1999

Median Home Price Projection

It is projected that the median price of existing single-family homes in the metro area will increase by 3.2% in 1999. Nationwide, home prices are projected to increase 3.8%.
Kiplinger's Personal Finance Magazine, January 1999

Average New Home Price

Area	Price ($)
City	127,833
U.S.	142,735

Note: Figures are based on a new home with 1,800 sq. ft. of living area on an 8,000 sq. ft. lot.
Source: ACCRA, Cost of Living Index, 1st Quarter 1999

Average Apartment Rent

Area	Rent ($/mth)
City	557
U.S.	601

Note: Figures are based on an unfurnished two bedroom, 1-1/2 or 2 bath apartment, approximately 950 sq. ft. in size, excluding all utilities except water
Source: ACCRA, Cost of Living Index, 1st Quarter 1999

RESIDENTIAL UTILITIES

Average Residential Utility Costs

Area	All Electric ($/mth)	Part Electric ($/mth)	Other Energy ($/mth)	Phone ($/mth)
City	–	48.84	55.50	19.76
U.S.	100.02	55.73	43.33	19.71

Source: ACCRA, Cost of Living Index, 1st Quarter 1999

HEALTH CARE

Average Health Care Costs

Area	Hospital ($/day)	Doctor ($/visit)	Dentist ($/visit)
City	473.50	47.40	70.00
U.S.	430.43	52.45	66.35

Note: Hospital—based on a semi-private room; Doctor—based on a general practitioner's routine exam of an established patient; Dentist—based on adult teeth cleaning and periodic oral exam.
Source: ACCRA, Cost of Living Index, 1st Quarter 1999

Distribution of Office-Based Physicians

Area	Family/Gen. Practitioners	Specialists		
		Medical	Surgical	Other
MSA[1]	76	174	171	170

Note: Data as of 12/31/97; (1) Metropolitan Statistical Area - see Appendix A for areas included
Source: American Medical Assn., Physician Characteristics & Distribution in the U.S., 1999

Hospitals

Des Moines has 5 general medical and surgical hospitals, 1 psychiatric. *AHA Guide to the Healthcare Field, 1998-99*

EDUCATION

Public School District Statistics

District Name	Num. Sch.	Enroll.	Classroom Teachers	Pupils per Teacher	Minority Pupils (%)	Current Exp.[1] ($/pupil)
Des Moines Ind Comm Sch	65	31,600	2,106	15.0	n/a	n/a
Saydel Consolidated School Dis	4	1,565	115	13.6	n/a	n/a

Note: Data covers the 1997-1998 school year unless otherwise noted; (1) Data covers fiscal year 1996; SD = School District; ISD = Independent School District; n/a not available
Source: National Center for Education Statistics, Common Core of Data Public Education Agency Universe 1997-98; National Center for Education Statistics, Characteristics of the 100 Largest Public Elementary and Secondary School Districts in the United States: 1997-98, July 1999

Educational Quality

School District	Education Quotient[1]	Graduate Outcome[2]	Community Index[3]	Resource Index[4]
Des Moines Ind.	108.0	103.0	138.0	113.0

Note: Nearly 1,000 secondary school districts were rated in terms of educational quality. The scores range from a low of 50 to a high of 150; (1) Average of the Graduate Outcome, Community and Resource indexes; (2) Based on graduation rates and college board scores (SAT/ACT); (3) Based on the surrounding community's average level of education and the area's average income level; (4) Based on teacher salaries, per-pupil expenditures and student-teacher ratios.
Source: Expansion Management, Ratings Issue, 1998

Educational Attainment by Race

Area	High School Graduate (%)					Bachelor's Degree (%)				
	Total	White	Black	Other	Hisp.[2]	Total	White	Black	Other	Hisp.[2]
City	81.0	82.4	70.7	58.2	61.7	18.9	19.6	10.8	13.6	10.5
MSA[1]	85.4	86.2	71.7	66.8	68.9	22.6	23.0	12.1	21.9	12.6
U.S.	75.2	77.9	63.1	60.4	49.8	20.3	21.5	11.4	19.4	9.2

Note: Figures shown cover persons 25 years old and over; (1) Metropolitan Statistical Area - see Appendix A for areas included; (2) people of Hispanic origin can be of any race
Source: 1990 Census of Population and Housing, Summary Tape File 3C

School Enrollment by Type

Area	Preprimary				Elementary/High School			
	Public		Private		Public		Private	
	Enrollment	%	Enrollment	%	Enrollment	%	Enrollment	%
City	2,441	67.2	1,194	32.8	26,321	91.6	2,402	8.4
MSA[1]	5,840	67.4	2,829	32.6	59,903	93.4	4,230	6.6
U.S.	2,679,029	59.5	1,824,256	40.5	38,379,689	90.2	4,187,099	9.8

Note: Figures shown cover persons 3 years old and over;
(1) Metropolitan Statistical Area - see Appendix A for areas included
Source: 1990 Census of Population and Housing, Summary Tape File 3C

School Enrollment by Race

Area	Preprimary (%)				Elementary/High School (%)			
	White	Black	Other	Hisp.[1]	White	Black	Other	Hisp.[1]
City	92.2	4.7	3.1	3.0	83.5	11.0	5.5	3.7
MSA[2]	95.8	2.2	2.1	1.7	91.2	5.3	3.5	2.7
U.S.	80.4	12.5	7.1	7.8	74.1	15.6	10.3	12.5

Note: Figures shown cover persons 3 years old and over; (1) people of Hispanic origin can be of any race; (2) Metropolitan Statistical Area - see Appendix A for areas included
Source: 1990 Census of Population and Housing, Summary Tape File 3C

Classroom Teacher Salaries in Public Schools

District	B.A. Degree		M.A. Degree		Maximum	
	Min. ($)	Rank[1]	Max. ($)	Rank[1]	Max. ($)	Rank[1]
Des Moines	22,300	95	42,983	71	47,217	74
Average	26,980	-	46,065	-	51,435	-

Note: Salaries are for 1997-1998; (1) Rank ranges from 1 to 100
Source: American Federation of Teachers, Survey & Analysis of Salary Trends, 1998

Higher Education

Two-Year Colleges		Four-Year Colleges		Medical Schools	Law Schools	Voc/ Tech
Public	Private	Public	Private			
0	1	0	3	0	1	8

Source: College Blue Book, Occupational Education, 1997; Medical School Admission Requirements, 1999-2000; Peterson's Guide to Two-Year Colleges, 1999; Peterson's Guide to Four-Year Colleges, 2000; Barron's Guide to Law Schools, 1999

MAJOR EMPLOYERS

Major Employers

Principal Financial Group
Central Iowa Hospital Corp.
Communications Data Services
Integra Health
Employers Mutual Casualty

Mercy Hospital Medical Center
Allied Group (insurance)
Norwest Mortgage
Annett Holdings (trucking)
Wellmark (hospital plans)

Note: Companies listed are located in the city
Source: Dun's Business Rankings, 1999; Ward's Business Directory, 1998

PUBLIC SAFETY

Crime Rate

Area	All Crimes	Violent Crimes				Property Crimes		
		Murder	Forcible Rape	Robbery	Aggrav. Assault	Burglary	Larceny -Theft	Motor Vehicle Theft
City	8,627.6	6.1	43.5	192.4	251.2	1,257.6	6,167.7	709.1
Suburbs[1]	3,764.8	0.9	10.7	28.1	138.2	645.1	2,707.4	234.5
MSA[2]	6,029.0	3.3	26.0	104.6	190.8	930.3	4,318.6	455.5
U.S.	4,922.7	6.8	35.9	186.1	382.0	919.6	2,886.5	505.8

Note: Crime rate is the number of crimes per 100,000 pop.; (1) defined as all areas within the MSA but located outside the central city; (2) Metropolitan Statistical Area - see Appendix A for areas incl.
Source: FBI Uniform Crime Reports, 1997

RECREATION

Culture and Recreation

Museums	Symphony Orchestras	Opera Companies	Dance Companies	Professional Theatres	Zoos	Pro Sports Teams
4	3	1	1	0	1	0

Source: International Directory of the Performing Arts, 1997; Official Museum Directory, 1999; Stern's Performing Arts Directory, 1997; USA Today Four Sport Stadium Guide, 1997; Chamber of Commerce/Economic Development, 1999

Library System

The Public Library of Des Moines has five branches, holdings of 474,140 volumes, and a budget of $4,504,075 (1995-1996). *American Library Directory, 1998-1999*

MEDIA

Newspapers

Name	Type	Freq.	Distribution	Circulation
Ankeny Press Citizen	General	1x/wk	Local	17,500
Central Shopper	General	1x/wk	Local	20,400
Cityview	General	1x/wk	Local	36,000
The Des Moines Register	General	7x/wk	Area	162,000
Lee Town Shopper	General	1x/wk	Local	20,400
North Central Shopper	General	1x/wk	Local	20,400
Northeast Shopper	General	1x/wk	Local	20,400
Northwest Shopper	General	1x/wk	Local	20,129
Southside Shopper	General	1x/wk	Local	20,400
Valley Shopper	General	1x/wk	Local	21,333

Note: Includes newspapers with circulations of 1,000 or more located in the city;
Source: Burrelle's Media Directory, 1999 Edition

Television Stations

Name	Ch.	Affiliation	Type	Owner
WOI	n/a	ABCT	Commercial	Citadel Communications Corporation
KCCI	n/a	CBST	Commercial	Pulitzer Broadcasting Company
KDIN	11	PBS	Public	State of Iowa
KIIN	12	PBS	Public	State of Iowa
WHO	13	NBCT	Commercial	The New York Times Co. Broadcast Group
KDSM	17	FBC	Commercial	Sinclair Communications Inc.
KTIN	21	PBS	Public	State of Iowa
KYIN	24	PBS	Public	State of Iowa
KSIN	27	PBS	Public	State of Iowa
KBIN	32	PBS	Public	State of Iowa
KRIN	32	PBS	Public	State of Iowa
KHIN	36	PBS	Public	State of Iowa

Note: Stations included broadcast in the Des Moines metro area; n/a not available
Source: Burrelle's Media Directory, 1999 Edition

AM Radio Stations

Call Letters	Freq. (kHz)	Target Audience	Station Format	Music Format
KIOA	940	General	M/N	Oldies
WHO	1040	General	N/T	n/a
KWKY	1150	Religious	M/N/S/T	Christian
KRNT	1350	General	M/S	Adult Standards/Big Band/Jazz/MOR
KDMI	1460	H/M/R	M/S/T	Christian/Latin
KBGG	1700	General	E/N/T	n/a

Note: Stations included broadcast in the Des Moines metro area; n/a not available
Target Audience: A=Asian; B=Black; C=Christian; E=Ethnic; F=French; G=General; H=Hispanic;
M=Men; N=Native American; R=Religious; S=Senior Citizen; W=Women; Y=Young Adult; Z=Children
Station Format: E=Educational; M=Music; N=News; S=Sports; T=Talk
Music Format: AOR=Album Oriented Rock; MOR=Middle-of-the-Road
Source: Burrelle's Media Directory, 1999 Edition

FM Radio Stations

Call Letters	Freq. (mHz)	Target Audience	Station Format	Music Format
KDPS	88.1	General	E/M/N	Adult Contemporary/Alternative/Oldies/R&B/ Top 40/Urban Contemporary
KWDM	88.7	General	E/M/S	Alternative/Top 40
KUCB	89.3	n/a	M/S	Christian/Jazz
KDFR	91.3	Religious	E/M/N/T	Christian
KJJY	92.5	General	M	Country
KIOA	93.3	General	M/N/S	Oldies
KGGO	94.9	General	M	Classic Rock
KHKI	97.3	General	M	Country
KRKQ	98.3	General	M	Classic Rock
KZZQ	99.5	Religious	M	Adult Contemporary/Christian
KLYF	100.3	n/a	M	Adult Contemporary
KMXD	100.3	General	M/N	Adult Contemporary
KSTZ	102.5	General	M	Adult Contemporary
KAZR	103.3	General	M	Classic Rock
KLTI	104.1	General	M	Adult Contemporary
KJJC	107.1	General	S	n/a
KKDM	107.5	General	M	Alternative/Modern Rock

Note: Stations included broadcast in the Des Moines metro area; n/a not available
Station Format: E=Educational; M=Music; N=News; S=Sports; T=Talk
Target Audience: A=Asian; B=Black; C=Christian; E=Ethnic; F=French; G=General; H=Hispanic; M=Men; N=Native American; R=Religious; S=Senior Citizen; W=Women; Y=Young Adult; Z=Children
Source: Burrelle's Media Directory, 1999 Edition

CLIMATE

Average and Extreme Temperatures

Temperature	Jan	Feb	Mar	Apr	May	Jun	Jul	Aug	Sep	Oct	Nov	Dec	Yr.
Extreme High (°F)	65	70	91	93	98	103	105	108	99	95	76	69	108
Average High (°F)	29	34	45	61	72	82	86	84	76	65	48	33	60
Average Temp. (°F)	20	25	36	51	62	72	76	74	65	54	39	25	50
Average Low (°F)	11	16	27	40	51	61	66	64	54	43	29	17	40
Extreme Low (°F)	-24	-20	-22	9	28	42	47	40	28	14	-3	-22	-24

Note: Figures cover the years 1945-1990
Source: National Climatic Data Center, International Station Meteorological Climate Summary, 3/95

Average Precipitation/Snowfall/Humidity

Precip./Humidity	Jan	Feb	Mar	Apr	May	Jun	Jul	Aug	Sep	Oct	Nov	Dec	Yr.
Avg. Precip. (in.)	1.1	1.1	2.3	3.1	3.8	4.4	3.5	3.9	3.1	2.4	1.7	1.2	31.8
Avg. Snowfall (in.)	8	7	7	2	Tr	0	0	0	Tr	Tr	3	7	33
Avg. Rel. Hum. 6am (%)	77	79	79	78	78	81	83	86	85	80	79	80	80
Avg. Rel. Hum. 3pm (%)	65	63	57	50	51	52	52	54	52	50	58	66	56

Note: Figures cover the years 1945-1990; Tr = Trace amounts (<0.05 in. of rain; <0.5 in. of snow)
Source: National Climatic Data Center, International Station Meteorological Climate Summary, 3/95

Weather Conditions

Temperature			Daytime Sky			Precipitation		
5°F & below	32°F & below	90°F & above	Clear	Partly cloudy	Cloudy	0.01 inch or more precip.	0.1 inch or more snow/ice	Thunder-storms
25	137	26	99	129	137	106	25	46

Note: Figures are average number of days per year and covers the years 1945-1990
Source: National Climatic Data Center, International Station Meteorological Climate Summary, 3/95

AIR & WATER QUALITY

Maximum Pollutant Concentrations

	Particulate Matter (ug/m^3)	Carbon Monoxide (ppm)	Sulfur Dioxide (ppm)	Nitrogen Dioxide (ppm)	Ozone (ppm)	Lead (ug/m^3)
MSA[1] Level	126	4	n/a	n/a	0.08	n/a
NAAQS[2]	150	9	0.140	0.053	0.12	1.50
Met NAAQS?	Yes	Yes	n/a	n/a	Yes	n/a

Note: (1) Metropolitan Statistical Area - see Appendix A for areas included; (2) National Ambient Air Quality Standards; ppm = parts per million; ug/m^3 = micrograms per cubic meter; n/a not available
Source: EPA, National Air Quality and Emissions Trends Report, 1997

Drinking Water

Water System Name	Pop. Served	Primary Water Source Type	Number of Violations in 1998	Type of Violation/ Contaminants
Des Moines Water Works	193,189	Surface	None	None

Note: Data as of July 10, 1999
Source: EPA, Office of Ground Water and Drinking Water, Safe Drinking Water Information System

Des Moines tap water is alkaline, soft and fluoridated.
Editor & Publisher Market Guide, 1999

Detroit, Michigan

Background

If Los Angeles is the city of driving cars, Detroit is the city of making cars, a legacy that began early in its founding.

Thanks to the power of advertising, we do not think twice about Ford, Pontiac, and Cadillac being names of cars. However, it bears remembering that Henry Ford was the inventor of the Model T, the car that was "propelled by power generated from within itself"; Pontiac was an Ottawa Chieftain who led an attack against the British in 1763; and Antoine de la Mothe Cadillac was a French Colonial administrator who founded the city of Detroit with a flotilla of 25 canoes, 50 French soldiers, 50 artisans, and 100 friendly Native Americans.

When Detroit finally fell into American hands, the city's economy already showed the signs of what its industrial might was to become. During the 1820s, Detroit prospered in fur trading, shipbuilding, and flour and grain distribution. During the 1860s, the city added steam engine, railroad car, stove, and furnace manufacturing to its economy as well. Finally, at the turn of the twentieth century, Henry Ford, Ransom E. Olds, and John and Horace Dodge changed the nature of Detroit's economy forever. With a history of skilled and semi-skilled workers in its carriage bicycle industries, it was not hard for these industrialists to transfer the laborers' skills onto their products. Thus Detroit was allowed an early lead in the automobile market.

Despite the omnipresence of the automobile industry in Detroit, the city leads in inland river trade along the upper Great Lakes, of steel, rubber products, and garden seeds.

Since 1994, when 18.35 square miles of Detroit was designated as an urban empowerment zone, nearly 30 companies have announced plans to spend over $2 billion opening, expanding, or relocating their operations in the economic development area. Altogether the businesses will create thousands of new jobs paying anywhere from $6 to $18 an hour. The Big Three American Auto Makers are the biggest investors expecting to spend over a billion dollars buying auto parts. Chrysler alone has about 20 minority-owned suppliers in the zone. *New York Times, April 11, 1997*

On the international economic scene, Detroit has benefited greatly from increased trade activity. With annual increases in exports of more than 10 percent per year since 1990, the area boasts the nation's third largest custom district behind Los Angeles and New York.

Detroit is undergoing a downtown housing boom with more than 360 building permits issued for single-family homes since 1990. Many of the buyers are black professionals who are moving into luxury homes in inner-city neighborhoods that were formerly areas of abandonment. *New York Times, May 5, 1997*

Downtown Detroit got an economic boost in 1996 when the Detroit Lions football team (owned by a branch of the Ford family) announced plans to move back to the city from the Silverdome in nearby Pontiac. The new domed Lions' stadium will be near a new open-air Detroit Tigers' baseball stadium scheduled to open for the 2000 season. Together, the two stadiums will form one of the largest entertainment complexes in the United States.

More expansion is currently underway by Northwest Airlines, of Wayne County's Detroit Metropolitan Airport. The $1.2 billion expansion is scheduled to open by end of year, 2001.

The climate of Detroit is influenced by its proximity to major storm tracks and to the Great Lakes. Winter storms can bring combinations of rain, freezing rain, sleet, or snow with heavy snowfall accumulations possible. In summer, most storms pass to the north. Intervals of warm, humid, sunny skies with occasional thunderstorms are followed by days of mild, dry, fair weather.

General Rankings and Evaluative Comments

- Detroit was ranked #4 out of 11 large, midwestern metropolitan areas in *Money's* 1998 survey of "The Best Places to Live in America." The survey was conducted by first contacting 512 representative households nationwide and asking them to rank 37 quality-of-life factors on a scale of 1 to 10. Next, a demographic profile was compiled on the 300 largest metropolitan statistical areas in the U.S. The numbers were crunched together to arrive at an overall ranking (things Americans consider most important, like clean air and water, low crime and good schools, received extra weight). Unlike previous years, the 1998 rankings were broken down by region (northeast, midwest, south, west) and population size (100,000 to 249,999; 250,000 to 999,999; 1 million plus). The city had a nationwide ranking of #117 out of 300 in 1997 and #86 out of 300 in 1996. *Money, July 1998; Money, July 1997; Money, September 1996*

- Ladies Home Journal ranked America's 200 largest cities based on the qualities women care about most. Detroit ranked #158 out of 200. Criteria: low crime rate, well-paying jobs, quality health and child care, good public schools, the presence of women in government, size of the gender wage gap, number of sexual-harassment and discrimination complaints filed, unemployment and divorce rates, commute times, population density, number of houses of worship, parks and cultural offerings, number of women's health specialists, how well a community's women cared for themselves, complexion kindness index based on UV radiation levels, odds of finding affordable fashions, rental rates for romance movies, champagne sales and other matters of the heart. Ladies Home Journal, November 1998

- Zero Population Growth ranked 229 cities in terms of children's health, safety, and economic well-being. Detroit was ranked #23 out of 25 major cities (main city in a metro area with population of greater than 2 million) and was given a grade of D. Criteria: total population, percent of population under 18 years of age, household language, percent population change, percent of births to teens, infant mortality rate, percent of low birth weights, dropout rate, enrollment in preprimary school, violent and property crime rates, unemployment rate, percent of children in poverty, percent of owner occupied units, number of bad air days, percent of public transportation commuters, and average travel time to work. *Zero Population Growth, Children's Environmental Index, Fall 1999*

- Detroit was ranked #34 out of 59 metro areas in *The Regional Economist's* "Rational Livability Ranking of 59 Large Metro Areas." The rankings were based on the metro area's total population change over the period 1990-97 divided by the number of people moving in from elsewhere in the United States (net domestic in-migration). *St. Louis Federal Reserve Bank of St. Louis, The Regional Economist, April 1999*

- Detroit was selected by *Yahoo! Internet Life* as one of "America's Most Wired Cities & Towns." The city ranked #27 out of 50. Criteria: home and work net use, domain density, hosts per capita, directory density and content quality. *Yahoo! Internet Life, March 1999*

- Cognetics studied 273 metro areas in the United States, ranking them by entrepreneurial activity. Detroit was ranked #38 out of the 50 largest metro areas. Criteria: Significant Starts (firms started in the last 10 years that still employ at least 5 people) and Young Growers (percent of firms 10 years old or less that grew significantly during the last 4 years). *Cognetics, "Entrepreneurial Hot Spots: The Best Places in America to Start and Grow a Company," 1998*

- Detroit was selected as one of the "Best American Cities to Start a Business" by *Point of View* magazine. Criteria: coolness, quality-of-life, and business concerns. The city was ranked #73 out of 75. *Point of View, November 1998*

- Reliastar Financial Corp. ranked the 125 largest metropolitan areas according to the general financial security of residents. Detroit was ranked #30 out of 125 with a score of 6.6. The score indicates the percentage a metropolitan area is above or below the metropolitan norm. A metro area with a score of 10.6 is 10.6% above the metro average. Criteria: Earnings and Wealth Potential (household income, education, net assets, cost of living); Safety Net (health insurance, retirement savings, life insurance, income support programs); Personal Threats (unemployment rate, low-income households, crime rate); Community Economic Vitality (cost of community services, job quality, job creation, housing costs). *Reliastar Financial Corp., "The Best Cities to Earn and Save Money," 1999 Edition*

Business Environment

STATE ECONOMY

State Economic Profile

"Although the Michigan economy bounced back quickly from the GM strike, it is losing much of its mid-1990s momentum. Strong auto sales have not translated into employment gains in the auto industry. Canada's weak economy has caused a drop in MI's exports. And what constrains MI the most is its demographic situation. The next several years should see a slowing economy.

In spite of the GM strike and booming automobile sales, GM has not increased employment and is currently planning to close plants in Kalamazoo and Flint. In addition, some 1,000 office jobs are targeted for elimination at the Detroit headquarters; Ford is currently planning to cut jobs within the state. Auto sales for 1999 and 2000 should fall below 1998, only adding to Detroit's need for employment reductions.

Construction activity added significantly to job growth in 1998, with construction employment growing 2.5% for the state and 8.3% for Detroit. Almost 1,800 commercial/industrial developments were undertaken in 1998. With the slowing economy, construction activity is likely to contract in 1999, undermining one of MI's bright spots. Residential starts, up 7% in 1998, should decline 6.2% in 1999.

Michigan's tight labor markets have helped to absorb downsizing in the auto industry, keeping the unemployment rate manageable. Labor availability has, however, started to become a problem for the state's information technology firms. The state's weak population growth, especially its continuing loss of young households, will dampen the high home price appreciation witnessed in recent years, as well as limit job entry-level job growth." *National Association of Realtors, Economic Profiles: The Fifty States and the District of Columbia, http://nar.realtor.com/databank/profiles.htm*

IMPORTS/EXPORTS

Total Export Sales

Area	1994 ($000)	1995 ($000)	1996 ($000)	1997 ($000)	% Chg. 1994-97	% Chg. 1996-97
MSA[1]	27,469,655	27,314,657	27,531,231	25,967,413	-5.5	-5.7
U.S.	512,415,609	583,030,524	622,827,063	687,597,999	34.2	10.4

Note: (1) Metropolitan Statistical Area - see Appendix A for areas included
Source: U.S. Department of Commerce, International Trade Association, Metropolitan Area Exports: An Export Performance Report on Over 250 U.S. Cities, November 10, 1998

CITY FINANCES

City Government Finances

Component	FY94 ($000)	FY94 (per capita $)
Revenue	2,138,073	2,125.47
Expenditure	2,070,447	2,058.24
Debt Outstanding	2,016,123	2,004.24
Cash & Securities	5,383,564	5,351.82

Source: U.S. Bureau of the Census, City Government Finances: 1993-94

City Government Revenue by Source

Source	FY94 ($000)	FY94 (per capita $)	FY94 (%)
From Federal Government	150,859	149.97	7.1
From State Governments	509,528	506.52	23.8
From Local Governments	33,082	32.89	1.5
Property Taxes	226,435	225.10	10.6
General Sales Taxes	0	0.00	0.0
Selective Sales Taxes	53,255	52.94	2.5
Income Taxes	293,323	291.59	13.7
Current Charges	240,370	238.95	11.2
Utility/Liquor Store	169,766	168.77	7.9
Employee Retirement[1]	344,470	342.44	16.1
Other	116,985	116.30	5.5

Note: (1) Excludes "city contributions," classified as "nonrevenue," intragovernmental transfers.
Source: U.S. Bureau of the Census, City Government Finances: 1993-94

City Government Expenditures by Function

Function	FY94 ($000)	FY94 (per capita $)	FY94 (%)
Educational Services	27,925	27.76	1.3
Employee Retirement[1]	303,097	301.31	14.6
Environment/Housing	419,433	416.96	20.3
Government Administration	146,384	145.52	7.1
Interest on General Debt	90,885	90.35	4.4
Public Safety	393,217	390.90	19.0
Social Services	101,648	101.05	4.9
Transportation	94,056	93.50	4.5
Utility/Liquor Store	260,958	259.42	12.6
Other	232,844	231.47	11.2

Note: (1) Payments to beneficiaries including withdrawal of contributions.
Source: U.S. Bureau of the Census, City Government Finances: 1993-94

Municipal Bond Ratings

Area	Moody's	S & P
Detroit	Baa2	n/a

Note: n/a not available; n/r not rated
Source: Moody's Bond Record, 6/99

POPULATION

Population Growth

Area	1980	1990	% Chg. 1980-90	July 1998 Estimate	% Chg. 1990-98
City	1,203,339	1,027,974	-14.6	970,196	-5.6
MSA[1]	4,488,072	4,382,299	-2.4	4,335,309	-1.1
U.S.	226,545,805	248,765,170	9.8	270,299,000	8.7

Note: (1) Metropolitan Statistical Area - see Appendix A for areas included;
July 1998 MSA population estimate was calculated by the editors
Source: 1980/1990 Census of Housing and Population, Summary Tape File 3C;
Census Bureau Population Estimates 1998

Population Characteristics

Race	City 1980 Population	%	City 1990 Population	%	% Chg. 1980-90	MSA[1] 1990 Population	%
White	420,529	34.9	221,932	21.6	-47.2	3,334,082	76.1
Black	758,468	63.0	778,456	75.7	2.6	942,450	21.5
Amer Indian/Esk/Aleut	3,846	0.3	3,511	0.3	-8.7	18,480	0.4
Asian/Pacific Islander	7,614	0.6	8,354	0.8	9.7	56,122	1.3
Other	12,882	1.1	15,721	1.5	22.0	31,165	0.7
Hispanic Origin[2]	28,970	2.4	27,157	2.6	-6.3	79,389	1.8

Note: (1) Metropolitan Statistical Area - see Appendix A for areas included;
(2) people of Hispanic origin can be of any race
Source: 1980/1990 Census of Housing and Population, Summary Tape File 3C

Ancestry

Area	German	Irish	English	Italian	U.S.	French	Polish	Dutch
City	5.0	3.7	2.1	1.5	1.8	1.4	4.7	0.4
MSA[1]	24.3	13.9	11.6	6.4	2.9	6.4	12.3	1.9
U.S.	23.3	15.6	13.1	5.9	5.3	4.2	3.8	2.5

Note: Figures are percentages and include persons that reported multiple ancestry (eg. if a person reported being Irish and Italian, they were included in both columns); (1) Metropolitan Statistical Area - see Appendix A for areas included
Source: 1990 Census of Population and Housing, Summary Tape File 3C

Age

Area	Median Age (Years)	Age Distribution (%) Under 5	Under 18	18-24	25-44	45-64	65+	80+
City	30.7	9.0	29.4	11.0	30.7	16.7	12.1	2.5
MSA[1]	33.0	7.6	26.1	9.8	33.0	19.2	11.8	2.4
U.S.	32.9	7.3	25.6	10.5	32.6	18.7	12.5	2.8

Note: (1) Metropolitan Statistical Area - see Appendix A for areas included
Source: 1990 Census of Population and Housing, Summary Tape File 3C

Male/Female Ratio

Area	Number of males per 100 females (all ages)	Number of males per 100 females (18 years old+)
City	86.3	80.7
MSA[1]	92.7	88.9
U.S.	95.0	91.9

Note: (1) Metropolitan Statistical Area - see Appendix A for areas included
Source: 1990 Census of Population, General Population Characteristics

INCOME

Per Capita/Median/Average Income

Area	Per Capita ($)	Median Household ($)	Average Household ($)
City	9,443	18,742	25,601
MSA[1]	15,694	34,612	42,218
U.S.	14,420	30,056	38,453

Note: All figures are for 1989; (1) Metropolitan Statistical Area - see Appendix A for areas included
Source: 1990 Census of Population and Housing, Summary Tape File 3C

Household Income Distribution by Race

Income ($)	City (%)					U.S. (%)				
	Total	White	Black	Other	Hisp.[1]	Total	White	Black	Other	Hisp.[1]
Less than 5,000	16.1	10.9	17.8	19.4	19.2	6.2	4.8	15.2	8.6	8.8
5,000 - 9,999	16.2	15.3	16.6	15.5	15.5	9.3	8.6	14.2	9.9	11.1
10,000 - 14,999	10.9	11.9	10.6	10.9	10.9	8.8	8.5	11.0	9.8	11.0
15,000 - 24,999	16.5	18.8	15.7	15.5	15.9	17.5	17.3	18.9	18.5	20.5
25,000 - 34,999	13.0	14.5	12.4	13.6	13.6	15.8	16.1	14.2	15.4	16.4
35,000 - 49,999	13.6	14.5	13.3	14.4	13.3	17.9	18.6	13.3	16.1	16.0
50,000 - 74,999	9.7	9.9	9.6	8.4	8.6	15.0	15.8	9.3	13.4	11.1
75,000 - 99,999	2.8	2.7	2.9	1.3	2.0	5.1	5.5	2.6	4.7	3.1
100,000+	1.2	1.5	1.2	1.0	1.0	4.4	4.8	1.3	3.7	1.9

Note: All figures are for 1989; (1) people of Hispanic origin can be of any race
Source: 1990 Census of Population and Housing, Summary Tape File 3C

Effective Buying Income

Area	Per Capita ($)	Median Household ($)	Average Household ($)
City	10,539	21,290	28,770
MSA[1]	17,649	38,496	46,990
U.S.	16,803	34,536	45,243

Note: Data as of 1/1/99; (1) Metropolitan Statistical Area - see Appendix A for areas included
Source: Standard Rate & Data Service, Newspaper Advertising Source, 9/99

Effective Household Buying Income Distribution

Area	% of Households Earning						
	$10,000 -$19,999	$20,000 -$34,999	$35,000 -$49,999	$50,000 -$74,999	$75,000 -$99,000	$100,000 -$124,999	$125,000 and up
City	20.6	20.1	14.5	12.2	3.8	1.0	0.5
MSA[1]	13.9	19.4	18.1	21.6	9.0	2.8	2.7
U.S.	16.0	22.6	18.2	18.9	7.2	2.4	2.7

Note: Data as of 1/1/99; (1) Metropolitan Statistical Area - see Appendix A for areas included
Source: Standard Rate & Data Service, Newspaper Advertising Source, 9/99

Poverty Rates by Race and Age

Area	Total (%)	By Race (%)				By Age (%)		
		White	Black	Other	Hisp.[2]	Under 5 years old	Under 18 years old	65 years and over
City	32.4	21.9	35.2	36.7	35.7	52.7	46.6	20.1
MSA[1]	12.9	7.1	33.0	17.7	20.6	22.9	19.6	10.5
U.S.	13.1	9.8	29.5	23.1	25.3	20.1	18.3	12.8

Note: Figures show the percent of people living below the poverty line in 1989. The average poverty threshold was $12,674 for a family of four in 1989; (1) Metropolitan Statistical Area - see Appendix A for areas included; (2) people of Hispanic origin can be of any race
Source: 1990 Census of Population and Housing, Summary Tape File 3C

EMPLOYMENT

Labor Force and Employment

Area	Civilian Labor Force			Workers Employed		
	Jun. 1998	Jun. 1999	% Chg.	Jun. 1998	Jun. 1999	% Chg.
City	400,740	403,504	0.7	369,908	372,866	0.8
MSA[1]	2,288,959	2,304,934	0.7	2,201,080	2,218,676	0.8
U.S.	138,798,000	140,666,000	1.3	132,265,000	134,395,000	1.6

Note: Data is not seasonally adjusted and covers workers 16 years of age and older;
(1) Metropolitan Statistical Area - see Appendix A for areas included
Source: Bureau of Labor Statistics, http://stats.bls.gov

Unemployment Rate

Area	1998						1999					
	Jul.	Aug.	Sep.	Oct.	Nov.	Dec.	Jan.	Feb.	Mar.	Apr.	May.	Jun.
City	9.8	6.6	7.8	6.8	6.2	5.9	7.7	8.0	7.3	6.7	6.8	7.6
MSA[1]	4.8	3.3	3.5	3.1	3.0	3.0	4.0	4.1	3.8	3.4	3.2	3.7
U.S.	4.7	4.5	4.4	4.2	4.1	4.0	4.8	4.7	4.4	4.1	4.0	4.5

Note: Data is not seasonally adjusted and covers workers 16 years of age and older; all figures are percentages; (1) Metropolitan Statistical Area - see Appendix A for areas included
Source: Bureau of Labor Statistics, http://stats.bls.gov

Employment by Industry

Sector	MSA[1]		U.S.
	Number of Employees	Percent of Total	Percent of Total
Services	676,400	31.2	30.4
Retail Trade	376,200	17.4	17.7
Government	238,900	11.0	15.6
Manufacturing	439,100	20.3	14.3
Finance/Insurance/Real Estate	113,700	5.2	5.9
Wholesale Trade	131,700	6.1	5.4
Transportation/Public Utilities	96,800	4.5	5.3
Construction	94,200	4.3	5.0
Mining	1,000	<0.1	0.4

Note: Figures cover non-farm employment as of 6/99 and are not seasonally adjusted; (1) Metropolitan Statistical Area - see Appendix A for areas included
Source: Bureau of Labor Statistics, http://stats.bls.gov

Employment by Occupation

Occupation Category	City (%)	MSA[1] (%)	U.S. (%)
White Collar	50.1	58.8	58.1
Executive/Admin./Management	7.8	12.0	12.3
Professional	11.0	14.1	14.1
Technical & Related Support	3.3	3.9	3.7
Sales	8.5	11.8	11.8
Administrative Support/Clerical	19.5	17.0	16.3
Blue Collar	29.3	27.6	26.2
Precision Production/Craft/Repair	8.8	11.9	11.3
Machine Operators/Assem./Insp.	11.5	8.5	6.8
Transportation/Material Movers	4.4	3.6	4.1
Cleaners/Helpers/Laborers	4.6	3.5	3.9
Services	20.0	12.9	13.2
Farming/Forestry/Fishing	0.5	0.8	2.5

Note: Figures cover employed persons 16 years old and over; (1) Metropolitan Statistical Area - see Appendix A for areas included
Source: 1990 Census of Population and Housing, Summary Tape File 3C

Occupational Employment Projections: 1994 - 2005

Occupations Expected to Have the Largest Job Growth (ranked by numerical growth)	Fast-Growing Occupations[1] (ranked by percent growth)
1. Waiters & waitresses	1. Computer engineers
2. Cashiers	2. Home health aides
3. All other helper, laborer, mover	3. Systems analysts
4. Systems analysts	4. Personal and home care aides
5. Home health aides	5. Electronic pagination systems workers
6. General managers & top executives	6. All other computer scientists
7. All other profess., paraprofess., tech.	7. Physical therapists
8. Registered nurses	8. All other therapists
9. All other sales reps. & services	9. Electronics repairers, comm. & indust.
10. Salespersons, retail	10. Occupational therapists

Note: Projections cover Michigan; (1) Excludes occupations with total job growth less than 300
Source: Office of Labor Market Information, Occupational Employment Forecasts, 1994-2005

TAXES

Major State and Local Tax Rates

| State Corp. Income (%) | State Personal Income (%) | Residential Property (effective rate per $100) | Sales & Use | | State Gasoline (cents/gallon) | State Cigarette (cents/pack) |
			State (%)	Local (%)		
2.3[a]	4.4	2.58	6.0	None	19.0	75.0

Note: Personal/corporate income, sales, gasoline and cigarette tax rates as of January 1999.
Property tax rates as of 1997; (a) Value added tax imposed on the sum of federal taxable income of the business, compensation paid to employees, dividends, interest, royalties paid and other items
Source: Federation of Tax Administrators, www.taxadmin.org; Washington D.C. Department of Finance and Revenue, Tax Rates and Tax Burdens in the District of Columbia: A Nationwide Comparison, July 1998; Chamber of Commerce, 1999

Total Taxes Per Capita and as a Percent of Income

| Area | Per Capita Income ($) | Per Capita Taxes ($) | | | Percent of Income (%) | | |
		Total	Federal	State/Local	Total	Federal	State/Local
Michigan	28,565	10,361	7,221	3,139	36.3	25.3	11.0
U.S.	27,876	9,881	6,690	3,191	35.4	24.0	11.4

Note: Figures are for 1998
Source: Tax Foundation, www.taxfoundation.org

Estimated Tax Burden

Area	State Income	Local Income	Property	Sales	Total
Detroit	2,695	2,250	3,500	585	9,030

Note: The numbers are estimates of taxes paid by a married couple with two children and annual earnings of $75,000. Sales tax estimates assume they spend average amounts on food, clothing, household goods and gasoline. Property tax estimates assume they live in a $250,000 home.
Source: Kiplinger's Personal Finance Magazine, October 1998

COMMERCIAL REAL ESTATE

Office Market

Class/ Location	Total Space (sq. ft.)	Vacant Space (sq. ft.)	Vac. Rate (%)	Under Constr. (sq. ft.)	Net Absorp. (sq. ft.)	Rental Rates ($/sq.ft./yr.)
Class A						
CBD	8,027,033	1,004,943	12.5	n/a	222,090	19.85-26.50
Outside CBD	24,186,210	1,168,752	4.8	870,000	1,249,458	18.00-31.00
Class B						
CBD	12,668,763	941,780	7.4	n/a	n/a	15.50-19.60
Outside CBD	27,994,126	1,105,778	4.0	n/a	n/a	14.00-18.50

Note: Data as of 10/98 and covers Detroit; CBD = Central Business District; n/a not available;
Source: Society of Industrial and Office Realtors, 1999 Comparative Statistics of Industrial and Office Real Estate Markets

"New construction should command rental rates of $26.00 per sq. ft. and up during 1999. Many projects are expected to change hands from international investors to local buyers. Global expansion and NAFTA should continue to bode well for the Big Three and their supply firms. Detroit should experience an influx of national and international firms. Expansions to the Metro Detroit Airport, the Daimler-Chrysler merger, and Ford Motor's operations should continue to add to the strength of the market. Our SIOR reporter feels that between the uncertainty created by the 1998 financial market turmoil and the pressure on the automotive, health care, and engineering firms to focus on the bottom line, 1999 should be a healthy year of slow and steady growth." *Society of Industrial and Office Realtors, 1999 Comparative Statistics of Industrial and Office Real Estate Markets*

Industrial Market

Location	Total Space (sq. ft.)	Vacant Space (sq. ft.)	Vac. Rate (%)	Under Constr. (sq. ft.)	Net Absorp. (sq. ft.)	Net Lease ($/sq.ft./yr.)
Central City	23,600,000	5,300,000	22.5	200,000	1,100,000	1.25-3.50
Suburban	175,700,000	9,700,000	5.5	2,100,000	4,200,000	3.75-7.00

Note: Data as of 10/98 and covers Detroit; n/a not available
Source: Society of Industrial and Office Realtors, 1999 Comparative Statistics of Industrial and Office Real Estate Markets

"The auto industry still the major driver in the Detroit industrial market, should remain fundamentally sound over the next year. This will be the leading source of demand and growth for Detroit in 1999. With 2.4 million sq. ft. of new space in development, total inventory will increase at a healthy rate. Development of 1.5 million sq. ft. of warehouse space near the airport may relieve some of the upward pressures lease prices are experiencing. Absorption is expected to be moderate, but should be more than 2.5 million sq. ft. for the year, leading to somewhat higher sales and lease prices. The substantial shortages of High- Tech/R&D space may spur some development in this property type. Shortage in all size categories of space may be alleviated by an increase in construction activity." *Society of Industrial and Office Realtors, 1999 Comparative Statistics of Industrial and Office Real Estate Markets*

Retail Market

Shopping Center Inventory (sq. ft.)	Shopping Center Construction (sq. ft.)	Construction as a Percent of Inventory (%)	Torto Wheaton Rent Index[1] ($/sq. ft.)
51,996,000	302,000	0.6	14.30

Note: Data as of 1997 and covers the Metropolitan Statistical Area - see Appendix A for areas included; (1) Index is based on a model that predicts what the average rent should be for leases with certain characteristics, in certain locations during certain years.
Source: National Association of Realtors, 1997-1998 Market Conditions Report

"Manufacturing, particularly auto-related, accounts for over 21% of total non-farm employment in Detroit. The area's economy has been boosted by strong auto sales in recent years. Solid real personal income growth has buoyed the area's retail sector. The rent index has soared 41% over the past two years. Downtown revitalization efforts have spurred retail projects such as the 55,000 square foot Chene Square development, which opened this year. However, Detroit's retail sector is highly subject to the cyclical nature of the auto industry. The area's economy is expected to proceed at a much slower pace over the next five years. That, coupled with sluggish population growth, will dampen retail activity." *National Association of Realtors, 1997-1998 Market Conditions Report*

COMMERCIAL UTILITIES

Typical Monthly Electric Bills

Area	Commercial Service ($/month)		Industrial Service ($/month)	
	12 kW demand 1,500 kWh	100 kW demand 30,000 kWh	1,000 kW demand 400,000 kWh	20,000 kW demand 10,000,000 kWh
City	156	2,741	27,746	448,435
U.S.	150	2,174	23,995	508,569

Note: Based on rates in effect January 1, 1999
Source: Edison Electric Institute, Typical Residential, Commercial and Industrial Bills, Winter 1999

TRANSPORTATION

Transportation Statistics

Average minutes to work	24.7
Interstate highways	I-75; I-96; I-94
Bus lines	
In-city	D-DOT (Department of Transportation, City of Detroit), 487 vehicles
Inter-city	5
Passenger air service	
Airport	Detroit-Wayne County Airport
Airlines	19
Aircraft departures	170,980 (1996)
Enplaned passengers	14,117,157 (1996)
Rail service	Amtrak; Light Rail planned
Motor freight carriers	200
Major waterways/ports	Detroit River

Source: Editor & Publisher Market Guide, 1999; FAA Airport Activity Statistics, 1997; Amtrak National Time Table, Northeast Timetable, Spring/Summer 1999; 1990 Census of Population and Housing, STF 3C; Chamber of Commerce/Economic Development 1999; Jane's Urban Transport Systems 1999-2000

Means of Transportation to Work

Area	Car/Truck/Van		Public Transportation			Bicycle	Walked	Other Means	Worked at Home
	Drove Alone	Car-pooled	Bus	Subway	Railroad				
City	67.8	16.1	10.2	0.0	0.0	0.1	3.4	1.3	1.1
MSA[1]	83.4	10.1	2.2	0.0	0.0	0.1	1.9	0.6	1.6
U.S.	73.2	13.4	3.0	1.5	0.5	0.4	3.9	1.2	3.0

Note: Figures shown are percentages and only include workers 16 years old and over;
(1) Metropolitan Statistical Area - see Appendix A for areas included
Source: 1990 Census of Population and Housing, Summary Tape File 3C

BUSINESSES

Major Business Headquarters

Company Name	1999 Rankings	
	Fortune 500	Forbes 500
American Axle & Manufacturing	-	69
Comerica	460	-
DTE Energy	368	-
General Motors	1	-
Little Caesar Enterprises	-	372
Sherwood Food Distributors	-	319
Soave Enterprises	-	430
Stroh Brewery	-	126
Walbridge Aldinger	-	358

Note: Companies listed are located in the city; dashes indicate no ranking
Fortune 500: Companies that produce a 10-K are ranked 1 to 500 based on 1998 revenue
Forbes 500: Private companies are ranked 1 to 500 based on 1997 revenue
Source: Forbes, November 30, 1998; Fortune, April 26, 1999

Best Companies to Work For

Comerica (financial services), headquartered in Detroit, is among the "100 Best Places to Work in IS." Criteria: compensation, turnover and training. *Computerworld, May 25, 1998*

Brogan & Partners (ad agency), Compuware Corp. (software), Little Caesars Pizza and Mexican Industries (auto parts), headquartered in Detroit, are among the best companies for women. Criteria: salary, benefits, opportunities for advancement and work/family policies. *www.womenswire.com*

Women-Owned Firms: Number, Employment and Sales

Area	Number of Firms	Employ-ment	Sales ($000)	Rank[2]
MSA[1]	123,600	371,400	50,060,700	12

Note: (1) Metropolitan Statistical Area - see Appendix A for areas included;
(2) Calculated on an averaging of the number of businesses, employment and sales
Source: The National Foundation for Women Business Owners, 1999 Facts on Women-Owned Businesses: Trends in the Top 50 Metropolitan Areas

Women-Owned Firms: Growth

Area	% change from 1992 to 1999			Rank[2]
	Number of Firms	Employ-ment	Sales	
MSA[1]	40.8	100.4	124.1	38

Note: (1) Metropolitan Statistical Area - see Appendix A for areas included; (2) Calculated on an averaging of the percent growth of number of businesses, employment and sales
Source: The National Foundation for Women Business Owners, 1999 Facts on Women-Owned Businesses: Trends in the Top 50 Metropolitan Areas

Minority Business Opportunity

Detroit is home to five companies which are on the Black Enterprise Industrial/Service 100 list (largest based on gross sales): The Bing Group (steel processing, metal stamping distribution); Barden Companies Inc. (radio broadcasting, real estate devel., casino gaming); Thomas Madison Inc. (automotive metal stamping, steel sales and procesing); The O-J Group (transportation services); Hawkins Food Group (retail restaurant operations) . Criteria: operational in previous calendar year, at least 51% black-owned and manufactures/owns the product it sells or provides industrial or consumer services. Brokerages, real estate firms and firms that provide professional services are not eligible. *Black Enterprise, www.blackenterprise.com*

Detroit is home to one company which is on the Black Enterprise Auto Dealer 100 list (largest based on gross sales): Conyers Riverside Ford Sales Inc. (Ford) . Criteria: 1) operational in previous calendar year; 2) at least 51% black-owned. *Black Enterprise, www.blackenterprise.com*

One of the 500 largest Hispanic-owned companies in the U.S. are located in Detroit. *Hispanic Business, June 1999*

HOTELS & MOTELS

Hotels/Motels

Area	Hotels/ Motels	Rooms	Luxury-Level Hotels/Motels		Average Minimum Rates ($)		
			♦♦♦♦	♦♦♦♦♦	♦♦	♦♦♦	♦♦♦♦
City	12	3,229	0	0	117	129	n/a
Airport	22	3,499	0	0	n/a	n/a	n/a
Suburbs	123	17,233	2	0	n/a	n/a	n/a
Total	157	23,961	2	0	n/a	n/a	n/a

Note: n/a not available; classifications range from one diamond (budget properties with basic amenities) to five diamond (luxury properties with the finest service, rooms and facilities).
Source: OAG, Business Travel Planner, Winter 1998-99

CONVENTION CENTERS

Major Convention Centers

Center Name	Meeting Rooms	Exhibit Space (sq. ft.)
Cobo Conference and Exposition Center	84	700,000
Detroit Light Guard Armory	n/a	48,000
Joe Louis Arena	n/a	22,000
Michigan State Fair and Exposition Center	n/a	52,800
The Westin Hotel Renaissance Center	30	24,950

Note: n/a not available
Source: Trade Shows Worldwide, 1998; Meetings & Conventions, 4/15/99; Sucessful Meetings, 3/31/98

Living Environment

COST OF LIVING

Cost of Living Index

Composite Index	Groceries	Housing	Utilities	Trans- portation	Health Care	Misc. Goods/ Services
110.9	104.7	133.9	110.5	101.7	112.4	97.2

Note: U.S. = 100
Source: ACCRA, Cost of Living Index, 1st Quarter 1999

HOUSING

Median Home Prices and Housing Affordability

Area	Median Price[2] 1st Qtr. 1999 ($)	HOI[3] 1st Qtr. 1999	Afford- ability Rank[4]
MSA[1]	134,000	65.6	137
U.S.	134,000	69.6	–

Note: (1) Metropolitan Statistical Area - see Appendix A for areas included; (2) U.S. figures calculated from the sales of 524,324 new and existing homes in 181 markets; (3) Housing Opportunity Index - percent of homes sold that were within the reach of the median income household at the prevailing mortgage interest rate; (4) Rank is from 1-181 with 1 being most affordable
Source: National Association of Home Builders, Housing Opportunity Index, 1st Quarter 1999

Median Home Price Projection

It is projected that the median price of existing single-family homes in the metro area will increase by 2.5% in 1999. Nationwide, home prices are projected to increase 3.8%.
Kiplinger's Personal Finance Magazine, January 1999

Average New Home Price

Area	Price ($)
City	199,140
U.S.	142,735

Note: Figures are based on a new home with 1,800 sq. ft. of living area on an 8,000 sq. ft. lot.
Source: ACCRA, Cost of Living Index, 1st Quarter 1999

Average Apartment Rent

Area	Rent ($/mth)
City	773
U.S.	601

Note: Figures are based on an unfurnished two bedroom, 1-1/2 or 2 bath apartment, approximately 950 sq. ft. in size, excluding all utilities except water
Source: ACCRA, Cost of Living Index, 1st Quarter 1999

RESIDENTIAL UTILITIES

Average Residential Utility Costs

Area	All Electric ($/mth)	Part Electric ($/mth)	Other Energy ($/mth)	Phone ($/mth)
City	–	66.67	41.13	23.88
U.S.	100.02	55.73	43.33	19.71

Source: ACCRA, Cost of Living Index, 1st Quarter 1999

HEALTH CARE

Average Health Care Costs

Area	Hospital ($/day)	Doctor ($/visit)	Dentist ($/visit)
City	550.41	52.80	81.90
U.S.	430.43	52.45	66.35

Note: Hospital—based on a semi-private room; Doctor—based on a general practitioner's routine exam of an established patient; Dentist—based on adult teeth cleaning and periodic oral exam.
Source: ACCRA, Cost of Living Index, 1st Quarter 1999

Distribution of Office-Based Physicians

Area	Family/Gen. Practitioners	Specialists		
		Medical	Surgical	Other
MSA[1]	601	2,688	1,751	1,797

Note: Data as of 12/31/97; (1) Metropolitan Statistical Area - see Appendix A for areas included
Source: American Medical Assn., Physician Characteristics & Distribution in the U.S., 1999

Hospitals

Detroit has 1 general medical and surgical hospital, 1 rehabilitation, 1 children's general. *AHA Guide to the Healthcare Field, 1998-99*

According to *U.S. News and World Report,* Detroit has 3 of the best hospitals in the U.S.: **Henry Ford Hospital**, noted for cardiology, endocrinology, gastroenterology, neurology, orthopedics, otolaryngology, pulmonology, urology; **Harper Hospital**, noted for cancer; **Sinai Hospital**, noted for gynecology. *U.S. News Online, "America's Best Hospitals," 10th Edition, www.usnews.com*

EDUCATION

Public School District Statistics

District Name	Num. Sch.	Enroll.	Classroom Teachers	Pupils per Teacher	Minority Pupils (%)	Current Exp.[1] ($/pupil)
Det Board of Ed—Web Dubois Pr	1	193	10	19.3	n/a	n/a
Det Publ Schs-Mlk Jr. Ed. Cent	1	134	9	14.9	n/a	n/a
Detroit City School District	271	174,730	8,658	20.2	95.1	7,424
Detroit Pub. Schs.-Timbuktu	1	n/a	n/a	n/a	n/a	n/a
University Public School	1	460	28	16.4	n/a	n/a

Note: Data covers the 1997-1998 school year unless otherwise noted; (1) Data covers fiscal year 1996; SD = School District; ISD = Independent School District; n/a not available
Source: National Center for Education Statistics, Common Core of Data Public Education Agency Universe 1997-98; National Center for Education Statistics, Characteristics of the 100 Largest Public Elementary and Secondary School Districts in the United States: 1997-98, July 1999

Educational Quality

School District	Education Quotient[1]	Graduate Outcome[2]	Community Index[3]	Resource Index[4]
Detroit City	54.0	50.0	63.0	60.0

Note: Nearly 1,000 secondary school districts were rated in terms of educational quality. The scores range from a low of 50 to a high of 150; (1) Average of the Graduate Outcome, Community and Resource indexes; (2) Based on graduation rates and college board scores (SAT/ACT); (3) Based on the surrounding community's average level of education and the area's average income level; (4) Based on teacher salaries, per-pupil expenditures and student-teacher ratios.
Source: Expansion Management, Ratings Issue, 1998

Educational Attainment by Race

Area	High School Graduate (%)					Bachelor's Degree (%)				
	Total	White	Black	Other	Hisp.[2]	Total	White	Black	Other	Hisp.[2]
City	62.1	61.3	62.6	55.8	45.3	9.6	12.1	8.4	18.7	7.2
MSA[1]	75.7	78.5	64.4	73.2	62.9	17.7	19.2	9.9	34.1	13.1
U.S.	75.2	77.9	63.1	60.4	49.8	20.3	21.5	11.4	19.4	9.2

Note: Figures shown cover persons 25 years old and over; (1) Metropolitan Statistical Area - see Appendix A for areas included; (2) people of Hispanic origin can be of any race
Source: 1990 Census of Population and Housing, Summary Tape File 3C

School Enrollment by Type

Area	Preprimary				Elementary/High School			
	Public		Private		Public		Private	
	Enrollment	%	Enrollment	%	Enrollment	%	Enrollment	%
City	13,196	72.4	5,027	27.6	180,245	87.3	26,179	12.7
MSA[1]	63,323	68.3	29,435	31.7	685,077	88.7	87,455	11.3
U.S.	2,679,029	59.5	1,824,256	40.5	38,379,689	90.2	4,187,099	9.8

Note: Figures shown cover persons 3 years old and over;
(1) Metropolitan Statistical Area - see Appendix A for areas included
Source: 1990 Census of Population and Housing, Summary Tape File 3C

School Enrollment by Race

Area	Preprimary (%)				Elementary/High School (%)			
	White	Black	Other	Hisp.[1]	White	Black	Other	Hisp.[1]
City	18.1	78.5	3.4	3.5	13.5	83.3	3.1	3.3
MSA[2]	77.6	19.5	2.9	2.3	69.8	26.9	3.3	2.6
U.S.	80.4	12.5	7.1	7.8	74.1	15.6	10.3	12.5

Note: Figures shown cover persons 3 years old and over; (1) people of Hispanic origin can be of any race; (2) Metropolitan Statistical Area - see Appendix A for areas included
Source: 1990 Census of Population and Housing, Summary Tape File 3C

Classroom Teacher Salaries in Public Schools

District	B.A. Degree		M.A. Degree		Maximum	
	Min. ($)	Rank[1]	Max. ($)	Rank[1]	Max. ($)	Rank[1]
Detroit	30,537	15	55,408	8	56,408	19
Average	26,980	-	46,065	-	51,435	-

Note: Salaries are for 1997-1998; (1) Rank ranges from 1 to 100
Source: American Federation of Teachers, Survey & Analysis of Salary Trends, 1998

Higher Education

Two-Year Colleges		Four-Year Colleges		Medical Schools	Law Schools	Voc/ Tech
Public	Private	Public	Private			
1	1	1	4	1	2	17

Source: College Blue Book, Occupational Education, 1997; Medical School Admission Requirements, 1999-2000; Peterson's Guide to Two-Year Colleges, 1999; Peterson's Guide to Four-Year Colleges, 2000; Barron's Guide to Law Schools, 1999

MAJOR EMPLOYERS

Major Employers

Blue Cross & Blue Shield of Michigan
Detroit Diesel Corp.
Detroit Newspapers
Harpers Hospital
Sinai Hospital

Children's Hospital of Michigan
Detroit Edison
General Motors Corp.
Michigan Bell Telephone
St. John Hospital & Medical Ctr.

Note: Companies listed are located in the city
Source: Dun's Business Rankings, 1999; Ward's Business Directory, 1998

PUBLIC SAFETY

Crime Rate

Area	All Crimes	Violent Crimes				Property Crimes		
		Murder	Forcible Rape	Robbery	Aggrav. Assault	Burglary	Larceny -Theft	Motor Vehicle Theft
City	11,669.1	45.9	94.8	803.6	1,207.3	1,891.9	4,351.9	3,273.8
Suburbs[1]	4,215.1	2.5	31.3	78.0	264.0	541.1	2,819.8	478.4
MSA[2]	5,931.5	12.5	45.9	245.1	481.2	852.2	3,172.6	1,122.1
U.S.	4,922.7	6.8	35.9	186.1	382.0	919.6	2,886.5	505.8

Note: Crime rate is the number of crimes per 100,000 pop.; (1) defined as all areas within the MSA but located outside the central city; (2) Metropolitan Statistical Area - see Appendix A for areas incl.
Source: FBI Uniform Crime Reports, 1997

RECREATION

Culture and Recreation

Museums	Symphony Orchestras	Opera Companies	Dance Companies	Professional Theatres	Zoos	Pro Sports Teams
9	1	1	2	6	1	3

Source: International Directory of the Performing Arts, 1997; Official Museum Directory, 1999; Stern's Performing Arts Directory, 1997; USA Today Four Sport Stadium Guide, 1997; Chamber of Commerce/Economic Development, 1999

Library System

The Detroit Public Library has 24 branches, holdings of 2,781,000 volumes, and a budget of $25,832,422 (1996-1997). *American Library Directory, 1998-1999*

MEDIA

Newspapers

Name	Type	Freq.	Distribution	Circulation
Detroit Free Press	General	7x/wk	State	381,599
The Detroit News	General	7x/wk	State	246,638
The Metro Times	n/a	1x/wk	Area	110,000
Michigan Chronicle	Black	1x/wk	Local	41,436
Michigan Chronicle-Pontiac Edition	General	1x/wk	State	47,428

Note: Includes newspapers with circulations of 25,000 or more located in the city; n/a not available
Source: Burrelle's Media Directory, 1999 Edition

Television Stations

Name	Ch.	Affiliation	Type	Owner
WDIV	n/a	NBCT	Commercial	Post-Newsweek Business Information Inc.
WDWB	20	WB	Commercial	Granite Broadcasting Corporation
WTVS	56	PBS	Public	Detroit Educational Television Foundation
WWJ	62	CBST	Commercial	Westinghouse Broadcasting Company
WCH	68	n/a	Commercial	Metro Detroit Broadcasting

Note: Stations included broadcast in the Detroit metro area; n/a not available
Source: Burrelle's Media Directory, 1999 Edition

AM Radio Stations

Call Letters	Freq. (kHz)	Target Audience	Station Format	Music Format
WLLZ	560	n/a	M	Christian
WJR	760	General	N/S/T	n/a
WCAR	1090	General	E/M/N/T	Christian/Classical
WDFN	1130	General	N/S/T	n/a
WCHB	1200	General	N/S/T	n/a
WQBH	1400	B/G	M/N/S	Christian/Jazz/Oldies/R&B

Note: Stations included broadcast in the Detroit metro area; n/a not available
Target Audience: A=Asian; B=Black; C=Christian; E=Ethnic; F=French; G=General; H=Hispanic; M=Men; N=Native American; R=Religious; S=Senior Citizen; W=Women; Y=Young Adult; Z=Children
Station Format: E=Educational; M=Music; N=News; S=Sports; T=Talk
Source: Burrelle's Media Directory, 1999 Edition

FM Radio Stations

Call Letters	Freq. (mHz)	Target Audience	Station Format	Music Format
WSDP	88.1	General	E/M/N/S	Alternative
WHPR	88.1	General	M/T	Jazz/R&B
WHFR	89.3	General	E/M/N/S/T	Alternative/Big Band/Classical/Country/ Jazz/Urban Contemporary
WDTR	90.9	General	E/M	Christian/Classic Rock/Classical/Gospel/Jazz/ Latin/Oldies/R&B/Urban Contemporary
WMXD	92.3	Black	Women	M/N/T
WCSX	94.7	General	M	Classic Rock
WPLT	96.3	Young Adult	M/N/T	Alternative
WKRK	97.1	Men	N/S/T	n/a
WJLB	97.9	B/G	M	Urban Contemporary
WVMV	98.7	General	M	Adult Contemporary/Jazz/R&B
WNIC	100.3	Women	M/N/T	Adult Contemporary
WRIF	101.1	General	M	AOR
WDET	101.9	General	M/N	Alternative/Jazz/R&B
WMUZ	103.5	General	E/M/T	Christian
WXDG	105.1	General	M/N/T	Classic Rock/R&B
WDTJ	105.9	General	M/N/T	Urban Contemporary
WWWW	106.7	General	M/N	Country
WGPR	107.5	General	Men	Religious

Note: Stations included broadcast in the Detroit metro area; n/a not available
Station Format: E=Educational; M=Music; N=News; S=Sports; T=Talk
Target Audience: A=Asian; B=Black; C=Christian; E=Ethnic; F=French; G=General; H=Hispanic;
M=Men; N=Native American; R=Religious; S=Senior Citizen; W=Women; Y=Young Adult; Z=Children
Music Format: AOR=Album Oriented Rock; MOR=Middle-of-the-Road
Source: Burrelle's Media Directory, 1999 Edition

CLIMATE

Average and Extreme Temperatures

Temperature	Jan	Feb	Mar	Apr	May	Jun	Jul	Aug	Sep	Oct	Nov	Dec	Yr.
Extreme High (°F)	62	65	81	89	93	104	102	100	98	91	77	68	104
Average High (°F)	30	33	44	58	70	79	83	81	74	61	48	35	58
Average Temp. (°F)	23	26	36	48	59	68	72	71	64	52	40	29	49
Average Low (°F)	16	18	27	37	47	56	61	60	53	41	32	21	39
Extreme Low (°F)	-21	-15	-4	10	25	36	41	38	29	17	9	-10	-21

Note: Figures cover the years 1958-1990
Source: National Climatic Data Center, International Station Meteorological Climate Summary, 3/95

Average Precipitation/Snowfall/Humidity

Precip./Humidity	Jan	Feb	Mar	Apr	May	Jun	Jul	Aug	Sep	Oct	Nov	Dec	Yr.
Avg. Precip. (in.)	1.8	1.8	2.5	3.0	2.9	3.6	3.1	3.4	2.8	2.2	2.6	2.7	32.4
Avg. Snowfall (in.)	10	9	7	2	Tr	0	0	0	0	Tr	3	11	41
Avg. Rel. Hum. 7am (%)	80	79	79	78	78	79	82	86	87	84	82	81	81
Avg. Rel. Hum. 4pm (%)	67	63	59	53	51	52	52	54	55	55	64	70	58

Note: Figures cover the years 1958-1990; Tr = Trace amounts (<0.05 in. of rain; <0.5 in. of snow)
Source: National Climatic Data Center, International Station Meteorological Climate Summary, 3/95

Weather Conditions

Temperature			Daytime Sky			Precipitation		
5°F & below	32°F & below	90°F & above	Clear	Partly cloudy	Cloudy	0.01 inch or more precip.	0.1 inch or more snow/ice	Thunder-storms
15	136	12	74	134	157	135	38	32

Note: Figures are average number of days per year and covers the years 1958-1990
Source: National Climatic Data Center, International Station Meteorological Climate Summary, 3/95

AIR & WATER QUALITY

Maximum Pollutant Concentrations

	Particulate Matter (ug/m³)	Carbon Monoxide (ppm)	Sulfur Dioxide (ppm)	Nitrogen Dioxide (ppm)	Ozone (ppm)	Lead (ug/m³)
MSA[1] Level	106	5	0.044	0.026	0.12	0.09
NAAQS[2]	150	9	0.140	0.053	0.12	1.50
Met NAAQS?	Yes	Yes	Yes	Yes	Yes	Yes

Note: (1) Metropolitan Statistical Area - see Appendix A for areas included; (2) National Ambient Air Quality Standards; ppm = parts per million; ug/m³ = micrograms per cubic meter; n/a not available
Source: EPA, National Air Quality and Emissions Trends Report, 1997

Pollutant Standards Index

In the Detroit MSA (see Appendix A for areas included), the Pollutant Standards Index (PSI) exceeded 100 on 12 days in 1997. A PSI value greater than 100 indicates that air quality would be in the unhealthful range on that day. *EPA, National Air Quality and Emissions Trends Report, 1997*

Drinking Water

Water System Name	Pop. Served	Primary Water Source Type	Number of Violations in 1998	Type of Violation/ Contaminants
Detroit	1,027,974	Surface	None	None

Note: Data as of July 10, 1999
Source: EPA, Office of Ground Water and Drinking Water, Safe Drinking Water Information System

Detroit tap water is alkaline, soft.
Editor & Publisher Market Guide, 1999

Fort Wayne, Indiana

Background

Fort Wayne lies 100 miles northeast of Indianapolis, at the confluence of the St. Mary and St. Joseph Rivers, which form the Maumee River. The waters, spanned by 21 bridges, divide the town into three parts.

Once the stronghold of the Miami tribe, the area was prominent in frontier history. The Miami Native Americans ruled the lower peninsula region, fighting against the Iroquois who had been armed by the English colonists. Later, the tribe established itself in the Wabash Valley and built a village at the Lakeside district in Fort Wayne. They continued to side with the British during the American Revolution. After the revolution, President Washington ordered armies into the center of the Miami Territory to stop the Miami War Parties, which had been encouraged to attack the new nation by the British. After Chief Little Turtle, one of the most feared and respected tribal leaders, defeated the army of General Arthur St. Clair, Washington sought the help of General "Mad" Anthony Wayne who succeeded in defeating the rebellious tribes. Wayne marched on Miamitown and built the first American fort there. When the fort was turned over to Colonel John Hamtramck on October 21, 1794, the Colonel immediately changed the name to Fort Wayne.

Fort Wayne's industrial growth began with the building of the Wabash and Erie Canal in the 1830s and was further stimulated in the 1850s when the railway came.

Although the city is in an area rich in dairy, livestock, and vegetable farming, it is primarily a diversified industrial center, with heavy truck, copper wire, and diamond dies its primary manufactures. Fort Wayne's economy has also benefited from a General Motors' Truck & Bus group plant, with more than 2,000 employes, which has attracted manufacturer's of auto fans, piston, gas pumps, and weatherstripping.

In 1998, Fort Wayne was awarded as an All-America City.

The land surrounding the city is generally level to the south and east, rolling to the west and southwest, and quite hilly to the north and northwest.

The climate is influenced to a certain extent by the Great Lakes, and does not differ greatly from the climates of other midwestern cities on the same general latitude. Rain is fairly constant throughout the warmer months, with somewhat larger amounts falling in late spring and early summer. Damaging hailstorms occur approximately twice a year, and severe flooding has also occurred in the area. While snow generally covers the ground for about 30 days during the winter months, heavy snowstorms are infrequent. With the exception of considerable cloudiness during the winter, Fort Wayne enjoys a good Midwestern average for sunshine.

General Rankings and Evaluative Comments

- Fort Wayne was ranked #4 out of 24 mid-sized, midwestern metropolitan areas in *Money's* 1998 survey of "The Best Places to Live in America." The survey was conducted by first contacting 512 representative households nationwide and asking them to rank 37 quality-of-life factors on a scale of 1 to 10. Next, a demographic profile was compiled on the 300 largest metropolitan statistical areas in the U.S. The numbers were crunched together to arrive at an overall ranking (things Americans consider most important, like clean air and water, low crime and good schools, received extra weight). Unlike previous years, the 1998 rankings were broken down by region (northeast, midwest, south, west) and population size (100,000 to 249,999; 250,000 to 999,999; 1 million plus). The city had a nationwide ranking of #75 out of 300 in 1997 and #125 out of 300 in 1996. *Money, July 1998; Money, July 1997; Money, September 1996*

- *Ladies Home Journal* ranked America's 200 largest cities based on the qualities women care about most. Fort Wayne ranked #153 out of 200. Criteria: low crime rate, well-paying jobs, quality health and child care, good public schools, the presence of women in government, size of the gender wage gap, number of sexual-harassment and discrimination complaints filed, unemployment and divorce rates, commute times, population density, number of houses of worship, parks and cultural offerings, number of women's health specialists, how well a community's women cared for themselves, complexion kindness index based on UV radiation levels, odds of finding affordable fashions, rental rates for romance movies, champagne sales and other matters of the heart. *Ladies Home Journal, November 1998*

- Zero Population Growth ranked 229 cities in terms of children's health, safety, and economic well-being. Fort Wayne was ranked #30 out of 112 independent cities (cities with populations greater than 100,000 which were neither Major Cities nor Suburbs/Outer Cities) and was given a grade of B-. Criteria: total population, percent of population under 18 years of age, household language, percent population change, percent of births to teens, infant mortality rate, percent of low birth weights, dropout rate, enrollment in preprimary school, violent and property crime rates, unemployment rate, percent of children in poverty, percent of owner occupied units, number of bad air days, percent of public transportation commuters, and average travel time to work. *Zero Population Growth, Children's Environmental Index, Fall 1999*

- Cognetics studied 273 metro areas in the United States, ranking them by entrepreneurial activity. Fort Wayne was ranked #15 out of 134 smaller metro areas. Criteria: Significant Starts (firms started in the last 10 years that still employ at least 5 people) and Young Growers (percent of firms 10 years old or less that grew significantly during the last 4 years). *Cognetics, "Entrepreneurial Hot Spots: The Best Places in America to Start and Grow a Company," 1998*

- Reliastar Financial Corp. ranked the 125 largest metropolitan areas according to the general financial security of residents. Fort Wayne was ranked #2 out of 125 with a score of 16.5. The score indicates the percentage a metropolitan area is above or below the metropolitan norm. A metro area with a score of 10.6 is 10.6% above the metro average. Criteria: Earnings and Wealth Potential (household income, education, net assets, cost of living); Safety Net (health insurance, retirement savings, life insurance, income support programs); Personal Threats (unemployment rate, low-income households, crime rate); Community Economic Vitality (cost of community services, job quality, job creation, housing costs). *Reliastar Financial Corp., "The Best Cities to Earn and Save Money," 1999 Edition*

Business Environment

STATE ECONOMY

State Economic Profile

"Indiana is lagging the nation in both job and Gross State Product (GSP) growth. While US job growth in 1998 was 2.0%, IN's was only 0.4%. Indiana's primary obstacle to growth is its lack of workers. The state unemployment rate is below the national, and its population growth rate is barely above zero.

IN's manufacturing base is much stronger than its neighbors, actually adding manufacturing jobs in 1998. The recent surge in automobile sales has helped boost employment in IN's auto sector, with some gains projected in 1999. Even if auto sales continue at the current pace, which is unlikely, Indiana auto plants would have a hard time finding workers to fill those jobs.

Demographic forces have restrained IN's housing and construction markets. Construction employment was down 2% in 1998, even though residential permits were up 15%. Home sales have been at the highest level in years, although new construction and slow population growth have kept price appreciation below the national.

Much of Indiana's economic strength has been in Indianapolis. Job growth in Indianapolis was 2.7% in 1998, almost 8 times the state average. Construction employment was up 7% in Indianapolis, while down for the state as a whole. Indianapolis' housing market has also witnessed price appreciation and new construction above the rest of the state.

While low foreign demand for manufacturing goods has hit IN as hard as other states in the region, its tight labor markets and a surge in auto sales have minimized job losses. These same tight labor markets, however, constrain IN to a moderate to slow growth path." *National Association of Realtors, Economic Profiles: The Fifty States and the District of Columbia, http://nar.realtor.com/databank/profiles.htm*

IMPORTS/EXPORTS

Total Export Sales

Area	1994 ($000)	1995 ($000)	1996 ($000)	1997 ($000)	% Chg. 1994-97	% Chg. 1996-97
MSA[1]	770,882	1,029,423	991,375	1,078,161	39.9	8.8
U.S.	512,415,609	583,030,524	622,827,063	687,597,999	34.2	10.4

Note: (1) Metropolitan Statistical Area - see Appendix A for areas included
Source: U.S. Department of Commerce, International Trade Association, Metropolitan Area Exports: An Export Performance Report on Over 250 U.S. Cities, November 10, 1998

CITY FINANCES

City Government Finances

Component	FY92 ($000)	FY92 (per capita $)
Revenue	112,214	589.57
Expenditure	113,447	596.04
Debt Outstanding	80,260	421.68
Cash & Securities	34,599	181.78

Source: U.S. Bureau of the Census, City Government Finances: 1991-92

City Government Revenue by Source

Source	FY92 ($000)	FY92 (per capita $)	FY92 (%)
From Federal Government	2,470	12.98	2.2
From State Governments	16,001	84.07	14.3
From Local Governments	1,219	6.40	1.1
Property Taxes	39,478	207.42	35.2
General Sales Taxes	0	0.00	0.0
Selective Sales Taxes	0	0.00	0.0
Income Taxes	4,655	24.46	4.1
Current Charges	16,945	89.03	15.1
Utility/Liquor Store	19,482	102.36	17.4
Employee Retirement[1]	4,633	24.34	4.1
Other	7,331	38.52	6.5

Note: (1) Excludes "city contributions," classified as "nonrevenue," intragovernmental transfers.
Source: U.S. Bureau of the Census, City Government Finances: 1991-92

City Government Expenditures by Function

Function	FY92 ($000)	FY92 (per capita $)	FY92 (%)
Educational Services	0	0.00	0.0
Employee Retirement[1]	8,217	43.17	7.2
Environment/Housing	23,909	125.62	21.1
Government Administration	5,149	27.05	4.5
Interest on General Debt	4,048	21.27	3.6
Public Safety	23,407	122.98	20.6
Social Services	777	4.08	0.7
Transportation	11,888	62.46	10.5
Utility/Liquor Store	13,296	69.86	11.7
Other	22,756	119.56	20.1

Note: (1) Payments to beneficiaries including withdrawal of contributions.
Source: U.S. Bureau of the Census, City Government Finances: 1991-92

Municipal Bond Ratings

Area	Moody's	S & P
Fort Wayne	Aa2	n/a

Note: n/a not available; n/r not rated
Source: Moody's Bond Record, 6/99

POPULATION

Population Growth

Area	1980	1990	% Chg. 1980-90	July 1998 Estimate	% Chg. 1990-98
City	172,196	173,072	0.5	185,716	7.3
MSA[1]	354,156	363,811	2.7	481,639	32.4
U.S.	226,545,805	248,765,170	9.8	270,299,000	8.7

Note: (1) Metropolitan Statistical Area - see Appendix A for areas included;
July 1998 MSA population estimate was calculated by the editors
Source: 1980/1990 Census of Housing and Population, Summary Tape File 3C;
Census Bureau Population Estimates 1998

Population Characteristics

Race	City 1980 Population	%	City 1990 Population	%	% Chg. 1980-90	MSA[1] 1990 Population	%
White	144,255	83.8	139,005	80.3	-3.6	326,568	89.8
Black	24,644	14.3	28,915	16.7	17.3	30,141	8.3
Amer Indian/Esk/Aleut	431	0.3	665	0.4	54.3	1,133	0.3
Asian/Pacific Islander	1,158	0.7	1,733	1.0	49.7	2,640	0.7
Other	1,708	1.0	2,754	1.6	61.2	3,329	0.9
Hispanic Origin[2]	3,506	2.0	4,394	2.5	25.3	6,105	1.7

Note: (1) Metropolitan Statistical Area - see Appendix A for areas included;
(2) people of Hispanic origin can be of any race
Source: 1980/1990 Census of Housing and Population, Summary Tape File 3C

Ancestry

Area	German	Irish	English	Italian	U.S.	French	Polish	Dutch
City	43.7	14.5	11.6	2.4	3.9	5.8	1.9	2.9
MSA[1]	50.6	15.0	12.7	2.4	4.1	6.3	2.3	3.1
U.S.	23.3	15.6	13.1	5.9	5.3	4.2	3.8	2.5

Note: Figures are percentages and include persons that reported multiple ancestry (eg. if a person reported being Irish and Italian, they were included in both columns); (1) Metropolitan Statistical Area - see Appendix A for areas included
Source: 1990 Census of Population and Housing, Summary Tape File 3C

Age

Area	Median Age (Years)	Under 5	Under 18	18-24	25-44	45-64	65+	80+
City	31.5	8.0	26.4	10.9	33.1	16.2	13.4	3.4
MSA[1]	32.1	7.8	27.9	9.7	33.2	17.6	11.6	2.6
U.S.	32.9	7.3	25.6	10.5	32.6	18.7	12.5	2.8

Note: (1) Metropolitan Statistical Area - see Appendix A for areas included
Source: 1990 Census of Population and Housing, Summary Tape File 3C

Male/Female Ratio

Area	Number of males per 100 females (all ages)	Number of males per 100 females (18 years old+)
City	91.2	86.3
MSA[1]	94.6	90.7
U.S.	95.0	91.9

Note: (1) Metropolitan Statistical Area - see Appendix A for areas included
Source: 1990 Census of Population, General Population Characteristics

INCOME

Per Capita/Median/Average Income

Area	Per Capita ($)	Median Household ($)	Average Household ($)
City	12,726	26,344	31,336
MSA[1]	14,287	31,689	37,952
U.S.	14,420	30,056	38,453

Note: All figures are for 1989; (1) Metropolitan Statistical Area - see Appendix A for areas included
Source: 1990 Census of Population and Housing, Summary Tape File 3C

Household Income Distribution by Race

Income ($)	City (%)					U.S. (%)				
	Total	White	Black	Other	Hisp.[1]	Total	White	Black	Other	Hisp.[1]
Less than 5,000	5.0	4.0	11.1	5.9	6.3	6.2	4.8	15.2	8.6	8.8
5,000 - 9,999	9.9	9.3	13.7	9.0	11.8	9.3	8.6	14.2	9.9	11.1
10,000 - 14,999	10.1	10.0	11.0	9.0	11.3	8.8	8.5	11.0	9.8	11.0
15,000 - 24,999	22.1	21.9	23.0	22.8	23.6	17.5	17.3	18.9	18.5	20.5
25,000 - 34,999	18.6	19.2	14.5	21.0	17.5	15.8	16.1	14.2	15.4	16.4
35,000 - 49,999	18.9	19.4	15.3	21.1	18.6	17.9	18.6	13.3	16.1	16.0
50,000 - 74,999	11.5	12.0	9.1	7.3	8.7	15.0	15.8	9.3	13.4	11.1
75,000 - 99,999	2.3	2.4	2.0	2.6	1.3	5.1	5.5	2.6	4.7	3.1
100,000+	1.5	1.7	0.2	1.3	0.7	4.4	4.8	1.3	3.7	1.9

Note: All figures are for 1989; (1) people of Hispanic origin can be of any race
Source: 1990 Census of Population and Housing, Summary Tape File 3C

Effective Buying Income

Area	Per Capita ($)	Median Household ($)	Average Household ($)
City	15,578	32,136	38,149
MSA[1]	17,407	37,702	45,983
U.S.	16,803	34,536	45,243

Note: Data as of 1/1/99; (1) Metropolitan Statistical Area - see Appendix A for areas included
Source: Standard Rate & Data Service, Newspaper Advertising Source, 9/99

Effective Household Buying Income Distribution

Area	% of Households Earning						
	$10,000 -$19,999	$20,000 -$34,999	$35,000 -$49,999	$50,000 -$74,999	$75,000 -$99,000	$100,000 -$124,999	$125,000 and up
City	17.3	26.8	20.3	17.7	5.1	1.1	1.1
MSA[1]	14.2	24.0	21.1	22.1	7.0	1.9	1.8
U.S.	16.0	22.6	18.2	18.9	7.2	2.4	2.7

Note: Data as of 1/1/99; (1) Metropolitan Statistical Area - see Appendix A for areas included
Source: Standard Rate & Data Service, Newspaper Advertising Source, 9/99

Poverty Rates by Race and Age

Area	Total (%)	By Race (%)				By Age (%)		
		White	Black	Other	Hisp.[2]	Under 5 years old	Under 18 years old	65 years and over
City	11.5	8.4	25.8	16.4	11.9	18.6	16.5	9.0
MSA[1]	7.6	5.8	24.9	15.7	10.6	12.3	10.0	8.3
U.S.	13.1	9.8	29.5	23.1	25.3	20.1	18.3	12.8

Note: Figures show the percent of people living below the poverty line in 1989. The average poverty
threshold was $12,674 for a family of four in 1989; (1) Metropolitan Statistical Area - see Appendix A
for areas included; (2) people of Hispanic origin can be of any race
Source: 1990 Census of Population and Housing, Summary Tape File 3C

EMPLOYMENT

Labor Force and Employment

Area	Civilian Labor Force			Workers Employed		
	Jun. 1998	Jun. 1999	% Chg.	Jun. 1998	Jun. 1999	% Chg.
City	99,785	100,427	0.6	96,836	96,677	-0.2
MSA[1]	268,670	269,482	0.3	262,399	261,966	-0.2
U.S.	138,798,000	140,666,000	1.3	132,265,000	134,395,000	1.6

Note: Data is not seasonally adjusted and covers workers 16 years of age and older;
(1) Metropolitan Statistical Area - see Appendix A for areas included
Source: Bureau of Labor Statistics, http://stats.bls.gov

Unemployment Rate

Area	1998						1999					
	Jul.	Aug.	Sep.	Oct.	Nov.	Dec.	Jan.	Feb.	Mar.	Apr.	May.	Jun.
City	4.3	3.0	4.4	3.1	3.2	3.6	4.2	4.2	3.7	3.3	3.5	3.7
MSA[1]	3.5	2.4	3.3	2.4	2.5	2.7	3.2	3.2	2.8	2.4	2.6	2.8
U.S.	4.7	4.5	4.4	4.2	4.1	4.0	4.8	4.7	4.4	4.1	4.0	4.5

Note: Data is not seasonally adjusted and covers workers 16 years of age and older; all figures are percentages; (1) Metropolitan Statistical Area - see Appendix A for areas included
Source: Bureau of Labor Statistics, http://stats.bls.gov

Employment by Industry

Sector	MSA[1]		U.S.
	Number of Employees	Percent of Total	Percent of Total
Services	69,100	25.0	30.4
Retail Trade	47,300	17.1	17.7
Government	25,100	9.1	15.6
Manufacturing	75,100	27.2	14.3
Finance/Insurance/Real Estate	15,200	5.5	5.9
Wholesale Trade	16,900	6.1	5.4
Transportation/Public Utilities	13,200	4.8	5.3
Construction	n/a	n/a	5.0
Mining	n/a	n/a	0.4

Note: Figures cover non-farm employment as of 6/99 and are not seasonally adjusted; (1) Metropolitan Statistical Area - see Appendix A for areas included; n/a not available
Source: Bureau of Labor Statistics, http://stats.bls.gov

Employment by Occupation

Occupation Category	City (%)	MSA[1] (%)	U.S. (%)
White Collar	56.0	55.6	58.1
Executive/Admin./Management	10.7	11.7	12.3
Professional	12.4	12.8	14.1
Technical & Related Support	3.7	3.4	3.7
Sales	12.1	11.9	11.8
Administrative Support/Clerical	17.1	15.9	16.3
Blue Collar	29.1	31.1	26.2
Precision Production/Craft/Repair	10.9	12.1	11.3
Machine Operators/Assem./Insp.	9.6	10.1	6.8
Transportation/Material Movers	4.1	4.4	4.1
Cleaners/Helpers/Laborers	4.5	4.5	3.9
Services	14.5	12.1	13.2
Farming/Forestry/Fishing	0.5	1.2	2.5

Note: Figures cover employed persons 16 years old and over; (1) Metropolitan Statistical Area - see Appendix A for areas included
Source: 1990 Census of Population and Housing, Summary Tape File 3C

Occupational Employment Projections: 1994 - 2005

Projections not available at time of publication.

TAXES

Major State and Local Tax Rates

State Corp. Income (%)	State Personal Income (%)	Residential Property (effective rate per $100)	Sales & Use		State Gasoline (cents/ gallon)	State Cigarette (cents/ pack)
			State (%)	Local (%)		
7.9[a]	3.4	n/a	5.0	None	15.0[b]	15.5

Note: Personal/corporate income, sales, gasoline and cigarette tax rates as of January 1999. Property tax rates as of 1997; (a) Consists of 3.4% on income from sources within the state plus a 4.5% supplemental income tax; (b) Carriers pay an additional surcharge of 11 cents
Source: Federation of Tax Administrators, www.taxadmin.org; Washington D.C. Department of Finance and Revenue, Tax Rates and Tax Burdens in the District of Columbia: A Nationwide Comparison, July 1998; Chamber of Commerce, 1999

Total Taxes Per Capita and as a Percent of Income

Area	Per Capita Income ($)	Per Capita Taxes ($)			Percent of Income (%)		
		Total	Federal	State/ Local	Total	Federal	State/ Local
Indiana	25,444	8,864	6,055	2,809	34.8	23.8	11.0
U.S.	27,876	9,881	6,690	3,191	35.4	24.0	11.4

Note: Figures are for 1998
Source: Tax Foundation, www.taxfoundation.org

Estimated Tax Burden

Area	State Income	Local Income	Property	Sales	Total
Fort Wayne	2,380	560	3,250	488	6,678

Note: The numbers are estimates of taxes paid by a married couple with two children and annual earnings of $75,000. Sales tax estimates assume they spend average amounts on food, clothing, household goods and gasoline. Property tax estimates assume they live in a $250,000 home.
Source: Kiplinger's Personal Finance Magazine, October 1998

COMMERCIAL REAL ESTATE

Office Market

Class/ Location	Total Space (sq. ft.)	Vacant Space (sq. ft.)	Vac. Rate (%)	Under Constr. (sq. ft.)	Net Absorp. (sq. ft.)	Rental Rates ($/sq.ft./yr.)
Class A						
CBD	1,813,173	72,200	4.0	0	6,906	13.75-19.00
Outside CBD	2,029,600	57,752	2.8	0	58,363	13.75-17.50
Class B						
CBD	670,110	111,791	16.7	0	11,833	11.25-13.00
Outside CBD	993,517	140,110	14.1	0	8,064	11.25-13.00

Note: Data as of 10/98 and covers Ft. Wayne; CBD = Central Business District; n/a not available; Source: Society of Industrial and Office Realtors, 1999 Comparative Statistics of Industrial and Office Real Estate Markets

"The local economy will be robust during 1999. Development will be strongest in the 1-69 corridor near the airport. The continued lack of properly zoned commercial and industrial land will restrict the area's growth and focus new construction only on specific areas. The expansion of existing tenants will be the greatest source of absorption. There is concern that the consolidation of banks may lead to a flight to larger office spaces. Our SIOR reporter foresees slight increases in construction and rental rates. Sales prices should remain constant. The increase in the area's population will result in increased prorata shares of state and federal aid. These funds may be used in part to improve the area's aging infrastructure." *Society of Industrial and Office Realtors, 1999 Comparative Statistics of Industrial and Office Real Estate Markets*

Industrial Market

Location	Total Space (sq. ft.)	Vacant Space (sq. ft.)	Vac. Rate (%)	Under Constr. (sq. ft.)	Net Absorp. (sq. ft.)	Net Lease ($/sq.ft./yr.)
Central City	n/a	n/a	n/a	n/a	n/a	1.50-4.00
Suburban	34,540,000	3,950,000	11.4	775,000	-685,000	2.00-4.50

Note: Data as of 10/98 and covers Fort Wayne; n/a not available
Source: Society of Industrial and Office Realtors, 1999 Comparative Statistics of Industrial and Office Real Estate Markets

"Our local SIOR reporter foresees a reduction in demand for industrial space over the next year in combination with modest speculative development. Further new construction will slow, except for build-to-suits and other specialty space. As some employers leave the market, buildings will become available for recycling to growing companies seeking large buildings. Sales prices of industrial buildings are expected to decrease slightly, although absorption is expected to increase by six to 10 percent. Construction, although up one to five percent, will still be considered modest for the area. Oversupply of space 100,000 sq. ft. and larger should be systematically absorbed. Dollar volume-sales and dollar volume-leases will increase moderately." *Society of Industrial and Office Realtors, 1999 Comparative Statistics of Industrial and Office Real Estate Markets*

COMMERCIAL UTILITIES

Typical Monthly Electric Bills

Area	Commercial Service ($/month)		Industrial Service ($/month)	
	12 kW demand 1,500 kWh	100 kW demand 30,000 kWh	1,000 kW demand 400,000 kWh	20,000 kW demand 10,000,000 kWh
City	153	2,005	23,749	363,979
U.S.	150	2,174	23,995	508,569

Note: Based on rates in effect January 1, 1999
Source: Edison Electric Institute, Typical Residential, Commercial and Industrial Bills, Winter 1999

TRANSPORTATION

Transportation Statistics

Average minutes to work	18.0
Interstate highways	I-69
Bus lines	
In-city	Ft. Wayne Public Transportation Commission
Inter-city	1
Passenger air service	
Airport	Ft. Wayne International
Airlines	9
Aircraft departures	n/a
Enplaned passengers	n/a
Rail service	No Amtrak service
Motor freight carriers	73
Major waterways/ports	None

Source: Editor & Publisher Market Guide, 1999; FAA Airport Activity Statistics, 1997; Amtrak National Time Table, Northeast Timetable, Spring/Summer 1999; 1990 Census of Population and Housing, STF 3C; Chamber of Commerce/Economic Development 1999; Jane's Urban Transport Systems 1999-2000

Means of Transportation to Work

Area	Car/Truck/Van		Public Transportation			Bicycle	Walked	Other Means	Worked at Home
	Drove Alone	Car-pooled	Bus	Subway	Railroad				
City	79.9	12.1	2.0	0.0	0.0	0.3	3.1	0.7	1.8
MSA[1]	82.3	11.0	1.1	0.0	0.0	0.2	2.3	0.6	2.5
U.S.	73.2	13.4	3.0	1.5	0.5	0.4	3.9	1.2	3.0

Note: Figures shown are percentages and only include workers 16 years old and over;
(1) Metropolitan Statistical Area - see Appendix A for areas included
Source: 1990 Census of Population and Housing, Summary Tape File 3C

BUSINESSES

Major Business Headquarters

Company Name	1999 Rankings	
	Fortune 500	Forbes 500
Kelley Automotive Group	-	217
Lincoln National	270	-
OmniSource	-	331

Note: Companies listed are located in the city; dashes indicate no ranking
Fortune 500: Companies that produce a 10-K are ranked 1 to 500 based on 1998 revenue
Forbes 500: Private companies are ranked 1 to 500 based on 1997 revenue
Source: Forbes, November 30, 1998; Fortune, April 26, 1999

Best Companies to Work For

Lincoln Financial Group, headquartered in Fort Wayne, is among the "100 Best Companies for Working Mothers." Criteria: fair wages, opportunities for women to advance, support for child care, flexible work schedules, family-friendly benefits, and work/life supports. *Working Mother, October 1998*

Essex Group (metal products), headquartered in Fort Wayne, is among the "100 Best Places to Work in IS." Criteria: compensation, turnover and training. *Computerworld, May 25, 1998*

HOTELS & MOTELS

Hotels/Motels

Area	Hotels/ Motels	Rooms	Luxury-Level Hotels/Motels		Average Minimum Rates ($)		
			♦♦♦♦	♦♦♦♦♦	♦♦	♦♦♦	♦♦♦♦
City	24	2,768	0	0	68	80	n/a
Airport	1	148	0	0	n/a	n/a	n/a
Total	25	2,916	0	0	n/a	n/a	n/a

Note: n/a not available; classifications range from one diamond (budget properties with basic amenities) to five diamond (luxury properties with the finest service, rooms and facilities).
Source: OAG, Business Travel Planner, Winter 1998-99

CONVENTION CENTERS

Major Convention Centers

Center Name	Meeting Rooms	Exhibit Space (sq. ft.)
Allen Co. War Memorial Coliseum & Expo Ctr.	11	180,000
Allen County War Memorial Coliseum and Exposition Center	11	180,000
Grand Wayne Center	7	25,000
Grand Wayne Center	7	25,000

Source: Trade Shows Worldwide, 1998; Meetings & Conventions, 4/15/99; Sucessful Meetings, 3/31/98

Living Environment

COST OF LIVING

Cost of Living Index

Composite Index	Groceries	Housing	Utilities	Trans- portation	Health Care	Misc. Goods/ Services
94.3	101.3	90.5	100.7	91.7	89.9	93.9

Note: U.S. = 100; Figures are for Fort Wayne/Allen County
Source: ACCRA, Cost of Living Index, 1st Quarter 1999

HOUSING

Median Home Prices and Housing Affordability

Area	Median Price[2] 1st Qtr. 1999 ($)	HOI[3] 1st Qtr. 1999	Afford- ability Rank[4]
MSA[1]	n/a	n/a	n/a
U.S.	134,000	69.6	—

Note: (1) Metropolitan Statistical Area - see Appendix A for areas included; (2) U.S. figures calculated from the sales of 524,324 new and existing homes in 181 markets; (3) Housing Opportunity Index - percent of homes sold that were within the reach of the median income household at the prevailing mortgage interest rate; (4) Rank is from 1-181 with 1 being most affordable; n/a not available
Source: National Association of Home Builders, Housing Opportunity Index, 1st Quarter 1999

Median Home Price Projection

It is projected that the median price of existing single-family homes in the metro area will increase by 2.5% in 1999. Nationwide, home prices are projected to increase 3.8%. *Kiplinger's Personal Finance Magazine, January 1999*

Average New Home Price

Area	Price ($)
City[1]	128,425
U.S.	142,735

Note: Figures are based on a new home with 1,800 sq. ft. of living area on an 8,000 sq. ft. lot;
(1) Fort Wayne/Allen County
Source: ACCRA, Cost of Living Index, 1st Quarter 1999

Average Apartment Rent

Area	Rent ($/mth)
City[1]	523
U.S.	601

Note: Figures are based on an unfurnished two bedroom, 1-1/2 or 2 bath apartment, approximately 950 sq. ft. in size, excluding all utilities except water; (1) Fort Wayne/Allen County
Source: ACCRA, Cost of Living Index, 1st Quarter 1999

RESIDENTIAL UTILITIES

Average Residential Utility Costs

Area	All Electric ($/mth)	Part Electric ($/mth)	Other Energy ($/mth)	Phone ($/mth)
City[1]	—	49.04	47.87	23.83
U.S.	100.02	55.73	43.33	19.71

Note: (1) Fort Wayne/Allen County
Source: ACCRA, Cost of Living Index, 1st Quarter 1999

HEALTH CARE

Average Health Care Costs

Area	Hospital ($/day)	Doctor ($/visit)	Dentist ($/visit)
City[1]	510.00	43.80	54.60
U.S.	430.43	52.45	66.35

Note: Hospital—based on a semi-private room; Doctor—based on a general practitioner's routine exam of an established patient; Dentist—based on adult teeth cleaning and periodic oral exam; (1) (1) Fort Wayne/Allen County
Source: ACCRA, Cost of Living Index, 1st Quarter 1999

Distribution of Office-Based Physicians

Area	Family/Gen. Practitioners	Specialists		
		Medical	Surgical	Other
MSA[1]	141	178	191	190

Note: Data as of 12/31/97; (1) Metropolitan Statistical Area - see Appendix A for areas included
Source: American Medical Assn., Physician Characteristics & Distribution in the U.S., 1999

Hospitals

Fort Wayne has 4 general medical and surgical hospitals, 1 psychiatric. *AHA Guide to the Healthcare Field, 1998-99*

EDUCATION

Public School District Statistics

District Name	Num. Sch.	Enroll.	Classroom Teachers	Pupils per Teacher	Minority Pupils (%)	Current Exp.[1] ($/pupil)
Fort Wayne Community Schools	53	31,727	1,665	19.1	n/a	n/a
M S D Southwest Allen County	9	5,374	324	16.6	n/a	n/a
Northwest Allen County Schools	8	3,781	197	19.2	n/a	n/a

Note: Data covers the 1997-1998 school year unless otherwise noted; (1) Data covers fiscal year 1996; SD = School District; ISD = Independent School District; n/a not available
Source: National Center for Education Statistics, Common Core of Data Public Education Agency Universe 1997-98; National Center for Education Statistics, Characteristics of the 100 Largest Public Elementary and Secondary School Districts in the United States: 1997-98, July 1999

Educational Quality

School District	Education Quotient[1]	Graduate Outcome[2]	Community Index[3]	Resource Index[4]
Fort Wayne Community Sch.	88.0	89.0	129.0	79.0

Note: Nearly 1,000 secondary school districts were rated in terms of educational quality. The scores range from a low of 50 to a high of 150; (1) Average of the Graduate Outcome, Community and Resource indexes; (2) Based on graduation rates and college board scores (SAT/ACT); (3) Based on the surrounding community's average level of education and the area's average income level; (4) Based on teacher salaries, per-pupil expenditures and student-teacher ratios.
Source: Expansion Management, Ratings Issue, 1998

Educational Attainment by Race

Area	High School Graduate (%)					Bachelor's Degree (%)				
	Total	White	Black	Other	Hisp.[2]	Total	White	Black	Other	Hisp.[2]
City	77.1	79.6	64.4	61.4	60.0	15.7	17.1	6.9	15.3	7.2
MSA[1]	80.6	82.0	65.6	65.5	63.0	17.3	18.0	8.0	17.7	9.3
U.S.	75.2	77.9	63.1	60.4	49.8	20.3	21.5	11.4	19.4	9.2

Note: Figures shown cover persons 25 years old and over; (1) Metropolitan Statistical Area - see Appendix A for areas included; (2) people of Hispanic origin can be of any race
Source: 1990 Census of Population and Housing, Summary Tape File 3C

School Enrollment by Type

Area	Preprimary Public Enrollment	%	Private Enrollment	%	Elementary/High School Public Enrollment	%	Private Enrollment	%
City	1,880	53.2	1,652	46.8	24,519	83.7	4,783	16.3
MSA[1]	4,397	54.1	3,726	45.9	56,218	84.7	10,137	15.3
U.S.	2,679,029	59.5	1,824,256	40.5	38,379,689	90.2	4,187,099	9.8

Note: Figures shown cover persons 3 years old and over;
(1) Metropolitan Statistical Area - see Appendix A for areas included
Source: 1990 Census of Population and Housing, Summary Tape File 3C

School Enrollment by Race

Area	Preprimary (%) White	Black	Other	Hisp.[1]	Elementary/High School (%) White	Black	Other	Hisp.[1]
City	74.6	21.5	3.9	3.4	69.8	26.0	4.2	4.3
MSA[2]	88.1	9.6	2.3	2.4	85.5	11.9	2.6	2.7
U.S.	80.4	12.5	7.1	7.8	74.1	15.6	10.3	12.5

Note: Figures shown cover persons 3 years old and over; (1) people of Hispanic origin can be of any race; (2) Metropolitan Statistical Area - see Appendix A for areas included
Source: 1990 Census of Population and Housing, Summary Tape File 3C

Classroom Teacher Salaries in Public Schools

District	B.A. Degree Min. ($)	Rank[1]	M.A. Degree Max. ($)	Rank[1]	Maximum Max. ($)	Rank[1]
Fort Wayne	24,425	78	45,919	45	49,583	59
Average	26,980	-	46,065	-	51,435	-

Note: Salaries are for 1997-1998; (1) Rank ranges from 1 to 100
Source: American Federation of Teachers, Survey & Analysis of Salary Trends, 1998

Higher Education

Two-Year Colleges Public	Private	Four-Year Colleges Public	Private	Medical Schools	Law Schools	Voc/Tech
1	3	1	5	0	0	8

Source: College Blue Book, Occupational Education, 1997; Medical School Admission Requirements, 1999-2000; Peterson's Guide to Two-Year Colleges, 1999; Peterson's Guide to Four-Year Colleges, 2000; Barron's Guide to Law Schools, 1999

MAJOR EMPLOYERS

Major Employers

IOM Health System
Xolox Corp. (computer equipment)
Parkview Hospital
Slaters Steels Corp.
Zollner Pistons (auto parts)

QHG of Indiana (management services)
Poly Hi Solidur Inc. (plastic products)
H.R. America (help supply)
St. Joseph Health System
Lincoln National Investment Companies

Note: Companies listed are located in the city
Source: Dun's Business Rankings, 1999; Ward's Business Directory, 1998

PUBLIC SAFETY

Crime Rate

Area	All Crimes	Violent Crimes Murder	Forcible Rape	Robbery	Aggrav. Assault	Property Crimes Burglary	Larceny -Theft	Motor Vehicle Theft
City	8,199.4	19.3	60.5	268.6	194.2	1,312.8	5,544.9	799.2
Suburbs[1]	2,633.1	2.4	16.1	33.6	144.5	451.5	1,791.2	193.6
MSA[2]	4,809.1	9.0	33.5	125.5	164.0	788.2	3,258.6	430.4
U.S.	4,922.7	6.8	35.9	186.1	382.0	919.6	2,886.5	505.8

Note: Crime rate is the number of crimes per 100,000 pop.; (1) defined as all areas within the MSA but located outside the central city; (2) Metropolitan Statistical Area - see Appendix A for areas incl.
Source: FBI Uniform Crime Reports, 1997

RECREATION

Culture and Recreation

Museums	Symphony Orchestras	Opera Companies	Dance Companies	Professional Theatres	Zoos	Pro Sports Teams
3	1	0	2	0	1	0

Source: International Directory of the Performing Arts, 1997; Official Museum Directory, 1999; Stern's Performing Arts Directory, 1997; USA Today Four Sport Stadium Guide, 1997; Chamber of Commerce/Economic Development, 1999

Library System

The Allen County Public Library has 13 branches, holdings of 2,527,059 volumes, and a budget of $15,316,488 (1996). *American Library Directory, 1998-1999*

MEDIA

Newspapers

Name	Type	Freq.	Distribution	Circulation
Frost Illustrated	Black	1x/wk	Local	9,000
The Journal Gazette	General	7x/wk	Regional	62,000
The News-Sentinel	n/a	6x/wk	Local	55,000

Note: Includes newspapers with circulations of 1,000 or more located in the city; n/a not available
Source: Burrelle's Media Directory, 1999 Edition

Television Stations

Name	Ch.	Affiliation	Type	Owner
WANE	15	CBST	Commercial	LIN Television
WPTA	21	ABCT	Commercial	Granite Broadcasting Corporation
WKJG	33	NBCT	Commercial	Corporation for General Trade
WFWA	39	PBS	Public	Fort Wayne Public Television
WFFT	55	FBC/UPN	Commercial	Great Trails Broadcasting Co.

Note: Stations included broadcast in the Fort Wayne metro area; n/a not available
Source: Burrelle's Media Directory, 1999 Edition

FM Radio Stations

Call Letters	Freq. (mHz)	Target Audience	Station Format	Music Format
WLAB	88.3	Religious	M	Christian
WBNI	89.1	General	M/N	Classical/Jazz
WBCL	90.3	General	M/N/T	Christian
WFWI	92.3	General	M	Classic Rock
WBTU	93.3	General	M/N/T	Country
WYSR	94.1	General	M	Adult Top 40
WAJI	95.1	General	M	Adult Contemporary
WEJE	96.3	General	M	Alternative
WMEE	97.3	General	M	n/a
WBYR	98.9	General	M/N/T	AOR
WLDE	101.7	General	M/N/S	Oldies
WCKZ	102.3	General	M	Top 40
WEXI	102.9	General	M/S/T	Adult Contemporary
WXKE	103.9	General	M/S	AOR
WQHK	105.1	General	M	Country
WJFX	107.9	General	M/N/T	R&B/Top 40

Note: Stations included broadcast in the Fort Wayne metro area; n/a not available
Station Format: E=Educational; M=Music; N=News; S=Sports; T=Talk
Target Audience: A=Asian; B=Black; C=Christian; E=Ethnic; F=French; G=General; H=Hispanic; M=Men; N=Native American; R=Religious; S=Senior Citizen; W=Women; Y=Young Adult; Z=Children
Music Format: AOR=Album Oriented Rock; MOR=Middle-of-the-Road
Source: Burrelle's Media Directory, 1999 Edition

AM Radio Stations

Call Letters	Freq. (kHz)	Target Audience	Station Format	Music Format
WFCV	1090	Religious	N/T	n/a
WOWO	1190	General	N/S/T	n/a
WGL	1250	General	T	n/a
WHWD	1380	General	M	Big Band
WGLL	1570	General	T	n/a

Note: Stations included broadcast in the Fort Wayne metro area; n/a not available
Target Audience: A=Asian; B=Black; C=Christian; E=Ethnic; F=French; G=General; H=Hispanic; M=Men; N=Native American; R=Religious; S=Senior Citizen; W=Women; Y=Young Adult; Z=Children
Station Format: E=Educational; M=Music; N=News; S=Sports; T=Talk
Source: Burrelle's Media Directory, 1999 Edition

CLIMATE

Average and Extreme Temperatures

Temperature	Jan	Feb	Mar	Apr	May	Jun	Jul	Aug	Sep	Oct	Nov	Dec	Yr.
Extreme High (°F)	69	69	82	88	94	106	103	101	100	90	79	71	106
Average High (°F)	31	35	46	60	71	81	84	82	76	64	49	36	60
Average Temp. (°F)	24	27	37	49	60	70	74	72	65	53	41	29	50
Average Low (°F)	16	19	28	39	49	59	63	61	53	42	32	22	40
Extreme Low (°F)	-22	-18	-10	7	27	38	44	38	29	19	-1	-18	-22

Note: Figures cover the years 1948-1990
Source: National Climatic Data Center, International Station Meteorological Climate Summary, 3/95

Average Precipitation/Snowfall/Humidity

Precip./Humidity	Jan	Feb	Mar	Apr	May	Jun	Jul	Aug	Sep	Oct	Nov	Dec	Yr.
Avg. Precip. (in.)	2.3	2.1	2.9	3.4	3.6	3.8	3.6	3.4	2.6	2.7	2.8	2.7	35.9
Avg. Snowfall (in.)	8	8	5	2	Tr	0	0	0	0	Tr	3	7	33
Avg. Rel. Hum. 7am (%)	81	81	80	77	76	78	81	86	86	84	83	83	81
Avg. Rel. Hum. 4pm (%)	71	68	62	54	52	52	53	55	53	55	67	74	59

Note: Figures cover the years 1948-1990; Tr = Trace amounts (<0.05 in. of rain; <0.5 in. of snow)
Source: National Climatic Data Center, International Station Meteorological Climate Summary, 3/95

Weather Conditions

Temperature			Daytime Sky			Precipitation		
5°F & below	32°F & below	90°F & above	Clear	Partly cloudy	Cloudy	0.01 inch or more precip.	0.1 inch or more snow/ice	Thunder-storms
16	131	16	75	140	150	131	31	39

Note: Figures are average number of days per year and covers the years 1948-1990
Source: National Climatic Data Center, International Station Meteorological Climate Summary, 3/95

AIR & WATER QUALITY

Maximum Pollutant Concentrations

	Particulate Matter (ug/m³)	Carbon Monoxide (ppm)	Sulfur Dioxide (ppm)	Nitrogen Dioxide (ppm)	Ozone (ppm)	Lead (ug/m³)
MSA[1] Level	77	6	n/a	n/a	0.10	0.03
NAAQS[2]	150	9	0.140	0.053	0.12	1.50
Met NAAQS?	Yes	Yes	n/a	n/a	Yes	Yes

Note: (1) Metropolitan Statistical Area - see Appendix A for areas included; (2) National Ambient Air Quality Standards; ppm = parts per million; ug/m³ = micrograms per cubic meter; n/a not available
Source: EPA, National Air Quality and Emissions Trends Report, 1997

Drinking Water

Water System Name	Pop. Served	Primary Water Source Type	Number of Violations in 1998	Type of Violation/ Contaminants
Ft. Wayne-3 Rivers Filtration Plant	180,000	Surface	None	None

Note: Data as of July 10, 1999
Source: EPA, Office of Ground Water and Drinking Water, Safe Drinking Water Information System

Fort Wayne tap water is alkaline, soft and fluoridated.
Editor & Publisher Market Guide, 1999

Gary, Indiana

Background

Gary, or Steel City, was the vision of a turn-of-the-century business magnate. Originally the area was a place of marshes and dunes, inhabited by the Miamis and Potawatomis from the seventeenth to nineteenth centuries. French Jesuits (perhaps even the famed Father Jacques Marquette) wandered through the area, and an ingenious French inventor, Octave Chanute, came to the area in 1896, climbed aboard a glider and launched himself into the air and the record books.

The city itself did not come into being until 1906. Judge Elbert H. Gary, the chairman of United States Steel, had decided that the perfect place for a new mammoth steel mill would be near Lake Michigan, where barges could easily ship iron ore and limestone. Trains would haul coal from the mines of southern Indiana to the new mill. Quickly the city was built on the dunes of northwestern Indiana, and it was named after Judge Gary.

In 1909, steel production began at USS's Gary Works, the largest steel mill in the world at that time. The city became a magnet for immigrants from Eastern and Southern Europe; later African Americans and Mexicans flooded to the city to work.

Gary's steel mills suffered much during the Great Depression, as business slumped. Unions made inroads in the mills in the 1930s, with USS recognizing the group that would later become the United Steel Workers. The steel works and Gary made a dramatic comeback during World War II. The 1950s and 1960s were boom times for the mills, but the 1970s were a difficult time and many jobs were eliminated in the city's steel industry.

The industry made somewhat of a comeback in the late 1980s and early 1990s and today, steel manufacturing is still critical to the city's economic life. Finished steel goods, such as sheet metal, tubing, bridges, tinplate are naturally produced in abundance. Food processing and clothing manufacturing are also important local industries.

In recent years, due to the legalization of riverboat gambling in Indiana, casinos have made their appearance in Gary, attracting tourists.

The healthcare industry and educational institutions also employs substantial numbers. The largest such employers are Methodist Hospital Northlake, Indiana University, and a technical college.

The city offers various incentives to businesses. These include an Urban Enterprise Zone and an Airport Development Zone. Certain tax exemptions are granted to businesses that build in these zones.

The climate in Gary is greatly affected by nearby Lake Michigan. The lake's warmth helps keep Gary relatively cool in the summer and warm in the winter. Temperatures range from the fifties to the eighties in the summer and from the teens to the forties in the winter. Rainfall averages thirty-six inches per year. Being so close to Lake Michigan, however, causes about forty inches of lake effect snow annually.

General Rankings and Evaluative Comments

- Gary was ranked #5 out of 24 mid-sized, midwestern metropolitan areas in *Money's* 1998 survey of "The Best Places to Live in America." The survey was conducted by first contacting 512 representative households nationwide and asking them to rank 37 quality-of-life factors on a scale of 1 to 10. Next, a demographic profile was compiled on the 300 largest metropolitan statistical areas in the U.S. The numbers were crunched together to arrive at an overall ranking (things Americans consider most important, like clean air and water, low crime and good schools, received extra weight). Unlike previous years, the 1998 rankings were broken down by region (northeast, midwest, south, west) and population size (100,000 to 249,999; 250,000 to 999,999; 1 million plus). The city had a nationwide ranking of #60 out of 300 in 1997 and #163 out of 300 in 1996. *Money, July 1998; Money, July 1997; Money, September 1996*

- *Ladies Home Journal* ranked America's 200 largest cities based on the qualities women care about most. Gary ranked #192 out of 200. Criteria: low crime rate, well-paying jobs, quality health and child care, good public schools, the presence of women in government, size of the gender wage gap, number of sexual-harassment and discrimination complaints filed, unemployment and divorce rates, commute times, population density, number of houses of worship, parks and cultural offerings, number of women's health specialists, how well a community's women cared for themselves, complexion kindness index based on UV radiation levels, odds of finding affordable fashions, rental rates for romance movies, champagne sales and other matters of the heart. *Ladies Home Journal, November 1998*

- Zero Population Growth ranked 229 cities in terms of children's health, safety, and economic well-being. Gary was ranked #110 out of 112 independent cities (cities with populations greater than 100,000 which were neither Major Cities nor Suburbs/Outer Cities) and was given a grade of F. Criteria: total population, percent of population under 18 years of age, household language, percent population change, percent of births to teens, infant mortality rate, percent of low birth weights, dropout rate, enrollment in preprimary school, violent and property crime rates, unemployment rate, percent of children in poverty, percent of owner occupied units, number of bad air days, percent of public transportation commuters, and average travel time to work. *Zero Population Growth, Children's Environmental Index, Fall 1999*

- Reliastar Financial Corp. ranked the 125 largest metropolitan areas according to the general financial security of residents. Gary was ranked #97 out of 125 with a score of -5.0. The score indicates the percentage a metropolitan area is above or below the metropolitan norm. A metro area with a score of 10.6 is 10.6% above the metro average. Criteria: Earnings and Wealth Potential (household income, education, net assets, cost of living); Safety Net (health insurance, retirement savings, life insurance, income support programs); Personal Threats (unemployment rate, low-income households, crime rate); Community Economic Vitality (cost of community services, job quality, job creation, housing costs). *Reliastar Financial Corp., "The Best Cities to Earn and Save Money," 1999 Edition*

Business Environment

STATE ECONOMY

State Economic Profile

"Indiana is lagging the nation in both job and Gross State Product (GSP) growth. While US job growth in 1998 was 2.0%, IN's was only 0.4%. Indiana's primary obstacle to growth is its lack of workers. The state unemployment rate is below the national, and its population growth rate is barely above zero.

IN's manufacturing base is much stronger than its neighbors, actually adding manufacturing jobs in 1998. The recent surge in automobile sales has helped boost employment in IN's auto sector, with some gains projected in 1999. Even if auto sales continue at the current pace, which is unlikely, Indiana auto plants would have a hard time finding workers to fill those jobs.

Demographic forces have restrained IN's housing and construction markets. Construction employment was down 2% in 1998, even though residential permits were up 15%. Home sales have been at the highest level in years, although new construction and slow population growth have kept price appreciation below the national.

Much of Indiana's economic strength has been in Indianapolis. Job growth in Indianapolis was 2.7% in 1998, almost 8 times the state average. Construction employment was up 7% in Indianapolis, while down for the state as a whole. Indianapolis' housing market has also witnessed price appreciation and new construction above the rest of the state.

While low foreign demand for manufacturing goods has hit IN as hard as other states in the region, its tight labor markets and a surge in auto sales have minimized job losses. These same tight labor markets, however, constrain IN to a moderate to slow growth path." *National Association of Realtors, Economic Profiles: The Fifty States and the District of Columbia, http://nar.realtor.com/databank/profiles.htm*

IMPORTS/EXPORTS

Total Export Sales

Area	1994 ($000)	1995 ($000)	1996 ($000)	1997 ($000)	% Chg. 1994-97	% Chg. 1996-97
MSA[1]	267,481	310,599	303,193	336,851	25.9	11.1
U.S.	512,415,609	583,030,524	622,827,063	687,597,999	34.2	10.4

Note: (1) Metropolitan Statistical Area - see Appendix A for areas included
Source: U.S. Department of Commerce, International Trade Association, Metropolitan Area Exports: An Export Performance Report on Over 250 U.S. Cities, November 10, 1998

CITY FINANCES

City Government Finances

Component	FY92 ($000)	FY92 (per capita $)
Revenue	97,732	847.59
Expenditure	109,795	952.21
Debt Outstanding	116,774	1,012.73
Cash & Securities	100,813	874.31

Source: U.S. Bureau of the Census, City Government Finances: 1991-92

City Government Revenue by Source

Source	FY92 ($000)	FY92 (per capita $)	FY92 (%)
From Federal Government	8,141	70.60	8.3
From State Governments	17,434	151.20	17.8
From Local Governments	66	0.57	0.1
Property Taxes	37,649	326.51	38.5
General Sales Taxes	0	0.00	0.0
Selective Sales Taxes	0	0.00	0.0
Income Taxes	0	0.00	0.0
Current Charges	21,313	184.84	21.8
Utility/Liquor Store	0	0.00	0.0
Employee Retirement[1]	2,076	18.00	2.1
Other	11,053	95.86	11.3

Note: (1) Excludes "city contributions," classified as "nonrevenue," intragovernmental transfers.
Source: U.S. Bureau of the Census, City Government Finances: 1991-92

City Government Expenditures by Function

Function	FY92 ($000)	FY92 (per capita $)	FY92 (%)
Educational Services	0	0.00	0.0
Employee Retirement[1]	3,222	27.94	2.9
Environment/Housing	20,961	181.79	19.1
Government Administration	22,702	196.88	20.7
Interest on General Debt	9,890	85.77	9.0
Public Safety	16,448	142.65	15.0
Social Services	5,776	50.09	5.3
Transportation	10,456	90.68	9.5
Utility/Liquor Store	0	0.00	0.0
Other	20,340	176.40	18.5

Note: (1) Payments to beneficiaries including withdrawal of contributions.
Source: U.S. Bureau of the Census, City Government Finances: 1991-92

Municipal Bond Ratings

Area	Moody's	S & P
Gary	n/a	n/a

Note: n/a not available; n/r not rated
Source: Moody's Bond Record, 6/99

POPULATION

Population Growth

Area	1980	1990	% Chg. 1980-90	July 1998 Estimate	% Chg. 1990-98
City	151,953	116,646	-23.2	108,469	-7.0
MSA[1]	642,733	604,526	-5.9	628,229	3.9
U.S.	226,545,805	248,765,170	9.8	270,299,000	8.7

Note: (1) Metropolitan Statistical Area - see Appendix A for areas included;
July 1998 MSA population estimate was calculated by the editors
Source: 1980/1990 Census of Housing and Population, Summary Tape File 3C;
Census Bureau Population Estimates 1998

Population Characteristics

Race	City 1980 Population	%	City 1990 Population	%	% Chg. 1980-90	MSA[1] 1990 Population	%
White	38,564	25.4	18,995	16.3	-50.7	460,933	76.2
Black	107,539	70.8	94,013	80.6	-12.6	117,003	19.4
Amer Indian/Esk/Aleut	221	0.1	207	0.2	-6.3	1,377	0.2
Asian/Pacific Islander	366	0.2	145	0.1	-60.4	3,366	0.6
Other	5,263	3.5	3,286	2.8	-37.6	21,847	3.6
Hispanic Origin[2]	10,971	7.2	6,282	5.4	-42.7	47,116	7.8

Note: (1) Metropolitan Statistical Area - see Appendix A for areas included;
(2) people of Hispanic origin can be of any race
Source: 1980/1990 Census of Housing and Population, Summary Tape File 3C

Ancestry

Area	German	Irish	English	Italian	U.S.	French	Polish	Dutch
City	3.6	3.3	1.7	0.8	2.3	0.3	1.8	0.5
MSA[1]	25.5	15.4	9.6	4.1	2.9	2.8	10.7	3.3
U.S.	23.3	15.6	13.1	5.9	5.3	4.2	3.8	2.5

Note: Figures are percentages and include persons that reported multiple ancestry (eg. if a person
reported being Irish and Italian, they were included in both columns); (1) Metropolitan Statistical Area -
see Appendix A for areas included
Source: 1990 Census of Population and Housing, Summary Tape File 3C

Age

Area	Median Age (Years)	Age Distribution (%) Under 5	Under 18	18-24	25-44	45-64	65+	80+
City	31.2	8.0	31.7	9.4	27.9	19.6	11.4	1.9
MSA[1]	32.9	7.0	27.8	9.6	31.0	19.8	11.8	2.1
U.S.	32.9	7.3	25.6	10.5	32.6	18.7	12.5	2.8

Note: (1) Metropolitan Statistical Area - see Appendix A for areas included
Source: 1990 Census of Population and Housing, Summary Tape File 3C

Male/Female Ratio

Area	Number of males per 100 females (all ages)	Number of males per 100 females (18 years old+)
City	84.4	78.3
MSA[1]	92.8	88.9
U.S.	95.0	91.9

Note: (1) Metropolitan Statistical Area - see Appendix A for areas included
Source: 1990 Census of Population, General Population Characteristics

INCOME

Per Capita/Median/Average Income

Area	Per Capita ($)	Median Household ($)	Average Household ($)
City	8,994	19,390	25,447
MSA[1]	13,174	31,629	36,665
U.S.	14,420	30,056	38,453

Note: All figures are for 1989; (1) Metropolitan Statistical Area - see Appendix A for areas included
Source: 1990 Census of Population and Housing, Summary Tape File 3C

Household Income Distribution by Race

Income ($)	City (%)					U.S. (%)				
	Total	White	Black	Other	Hisp.[1]	Total	White	Black	Other	Hisp.[1]
Less than 5,000	16.4	10.0	18.0	17.6	15.8	6.2	4.8	15.2	8.6	8.8
5,000 - 9,999	13.9	13.2	14.2	11.9	9.1	9.3	8.6	14.2	9.9	11.1
10,000 - 14,999	10.7	11.3	10.6	10.1	9.3	8.8	8.5	11.0	9.8	11.0
15,000 - 24,999	18.0	22.4	17.0	15.5	19.1	17.5	17.3	18.9	18.5	20.5
25,000 - 34,999	13.1	15.9	12.3	17.9	20.3	15.8	16.1	14.2	15.4	16.4
35,000 - 49,999	13.8	12.7	14.0	14.2	12.5	17.9	18.6	13.3	16.1	16.0
50,000 - 74,999	10.6	11.9	10.4	9.7	11.7	15.0	15.8	9.3	13.4	11.1
75,000 - 99,999	2.7	1.4	3.1	3.0	2.2	5.1	5.5	2.6	4.7	3.1
100,000+	0.7	1.2	0.6	0.0	0.0	4.4	4.8	1.3	3.7	1.9

Note: All figures are for 1989; (1) people of Hispanic origin can be of any race
Source: 1990 Census of Population and Housing, Summary Tape File 3C

Effective Buying Income

Area	Per Capita ($)	Median Household ($)	Average Household ($)
City	10,519	22,810	29,699
MSA[1]	15,996	37,088	43,754
U.S.	16,803	34,536	45,243

Note: Data as of 1/1/99; (1) Metropolitan Statistical Area - see Appendix A for areas included
Source: Standard Rate & Data Service, Newspaper Advertising Source, 9/99

Effective Household Buying Income Distribution

Area	% of Households Earning						
	$10,000 -$19,999	$20,000 -$34,999	$35,000 -$49,999	$50,000 -$74,999	$75,000 -$99,000	$100,000 -$124,999	$125,000 and up
City	19.8	21.0	14.3	13.9	4.5	0.7	0.4
MSA[1]	14.4	20.9	19.1	22.7	7.5	1.7	1.6
U.S.	16.0	22.6	18.2	18.9	7.2	2.4	2.7

Note: Data as of 1/1/99; (1) Metropolitan Statistical Area - see Appendix A for areas included
Source: Standard Rate & Data Service, Newspaper Advertising Source, 9/99

Poverty Rates by Race and Age

Area	Total (%)	By Race (%)				By Age (%)		
		White	Black	Other	Hisp.[2]	Under 5 years old	Under 18 years old	65 years and over
City	29.4	16.4	32.0	32.2	27.9	49.1	43.0	19.1
MSA[1]	12.2	6.6	32.3	19.9	16.5	21.2	18.5	9.3
U.S.	13.1	9.8	29.5	23.1	25.3	20.1	18.3	12.8

Note: Figures show the percent of people living below the poverty line in 1989. The average poverty threshold was $12,674 for a family of four in 1989; (1) Metropolitan Statistical Area - see Appendix A for areas included; (2) people of Hispanic origin can be of any race
Source: 1990 Census of Population and Housing, Summary Tape File 3C

EMPLOYMENT

Labor Force and Employment

Area	Civilian Labor Force			Workers Employed		
	Jun. 1998	Jun. 1999	% Chg.	Jun. 1998	Jun. 1999	% Chg.
City	47,051	47,133	0.2	43,511	43,144	-0.8
MSA[1]	309,637	308,679	-0.3	299,306	296,780	-0.8
U.S.	138,798,000	140,666,000	1.3	132,265,000	134,395,000	1.6

Note: Data is not seasonally adjusted and covers workers 16 years of age and older;
(1) Metropolitan Statistical Area - see Appendix A for areas included
Source: Bureau of Labor Statistics, http://stats.bls.gov

Unemployment Rate

Area	1998						1999					
	Jul.	Aug.	Sep.	Oct.	Nov.	Dec.	Jan.	Feb.	Mar.	Apr.	May.	Jun.
City	7.1	8.0	7.9	7.9	8.2	8.5	9.2	9.0	8.7	7.6	8.2	8.5
MSA[1]	3.1	3.6	3.6	3.5	3.7	3.9	4.2	4.2	4.0	3.4	3.7	3.9
U.S.	4.7	4.5	4.4	4.2	4.1	4.0	4.8	4.7	4.4	4.1	4.0	4.5

Note: Data is not seasonally adjusted and covers workers 16 years of age and older; all figures are percentages; (1) Metropolitan Statistical Area - see Appendix A for areas included
Source: Bureau of Labor Statistics, http://stats.bls.gov

Employment by Industry

Sector	MSA[1]		U.S.
	Number of Employees	Percent of Total	Percent of Total
Services	74,900	27.3	30.4
Retail Trade	52,400	19.1	17.7
Government	38,400	14.0	15.6
Manufacturing	49,800	18.2	14.3
Finance/Insurance/Real Estate	9,300	3.4	5.9
Wholesale Trade	11,100	4.1	5.4
Transportation/Public Utilities	14,800	5.4	5.3
Construction	n/a	n/a	5.0
Mining	n/a	n/a	0.4

Note: Figures cover non-farm employment as of 6/99 and are not seasonally adjusted; (1) Metropolitan Statistical Area - see Appendix A for areas included; n/a not available
Source: Bureau of Labor Statistics, http://stats.bls.gov

Employment by Occupation

Occupation Category	City (%)	MSA[1] (%)	U.S. (%)
White Collar	48.0	53.1	58.1
Executive/Admin./Management	6.4	9.6	12.3
Professional	11.5	12.5	14.1
Technical & Related Support	3.3	3.2	3.7
Sales	9.9	11.6	11.8
Administrative Support/Clerical	16.7	16.2	16.3
Blue Collar	32.0	32.7	26.2
Precision Production/Craft/Repair	9.6	14.5	11.3
Machine Operators/Assem./Insp.	9.8	7.8	6.8
Transportation/Material Movers	7.1	5.7	4.1
Cleaners/Helpers/Laborers	5.5	4.8	3.9
Services	19.7	13.4	13.2
Farming/Forestry/Fishing	0.4	0.7	2.5

Note: Figures cover employed persons 16 years old and over; (1) Metropolitan Statistical Area - see Appendix A for areas included
Source: 1990 Census of Population and Housing, Summary Tape File 3C

Occupational Employment Projections: 1994 - 2005

Projections not available at time of publication.

TAXES

Major State and Local Tax Rates

State Corp. Income (%)	State Personal Income (%)	Residential Property (effective rate per $100)	Sales & Use State (%)	Sales & Use Local (%)	State Gasoline (cents/ gallon)	State Cigarette (cents/ pack)
7.9[a]	3.4	n/a	5.0	None	15.0[b]	15.5

Note: Personal/corporate income, sales, gasoline and cigarette tax rates as of January 1999.
Property tax rates as of 1997; (a) Consists of 3.4% on income from sources within the state plus a
4.5% supplemental income tax; (b) Carriers pay an additional surcharge of 11 cents
Source: Federation of Tax Administrators, www.taxadmin.org; Washington D.C. Department of
Finance and Revenue, Tax Rates and Tax Burdens in the District of Columbia: A Nationwide
Comparison, July 1998; Chamber of Commerce, 1999

Total Taxes Per Capita and as a Percent of Income

Area	Per Capita Income ($)	Per Capita Taxes ($) Total	Per Capita Taxes ($) Federal	Per Capita Taxes ($) State/ Local	Percent of Income (%) Total	Percent of Income (%) Federal	Percent of Income (%) State/ Local
Indiana	25,444	8,864	6,055	2,809	34.8	23.8	11.0
U.S.	27,876	9,881	6,690	3,191	35.4	24.0	11.4

Note: Figures are for 1998
Source: Tax Foundation, www.taxfoundation.org

COMMERCIAL REAL ESTATE

Office Market

Class/ Location	Total Space (sq. ft.)	Vacant Space (sq. ft.)	Vac. Rate (%)	Under Constr. (sq. ft.)	Net Absorp. (sq. ft.)	Rental Rates ($/sq.ft./yr.)
Class A						
CBD	n/a	n/a	n/a	n/a	n/a	n/a
Outside CBD	775,000	38,750	5.0	30,000	28,250	15.00-18.00
Class B						
CBD	575,000	46,000	8.0	5,000	23,000	6.00-9.00
Outside CBD	1,898,000	94,900	5.0	20,000	43,100	10.00-15.00

Note: Data as of 10/98 and covers Gary-Hammond-East Chicago; CBD = Central Business District;
n/a not available;
Source: Society of Industrial and Office Realtors, 1999 Comparative Statistics of Industrial and Office
Real Estate Markets

"Limited rehabilitation of older high-rise buildings in the city of Gary is taking place and is
expected to continue. The redevelopment of the older urban center should continue with
marginal success. The outdated office stock underscores the need for significant public
incentives to encourage investors. Most new construction is expected to occur in suburban
areas. Our SIOR reporters estimate that there will be small increases in rental rates and sales
prices for all markets. Medical and health-related services are considered the fastest growing
sector. In 1999, service industries and non-manufacturing industries are expected to grow,
whereas the importance of manufacturing, particularly steel, is expected to diminish slightly."
*Society of Industrial and Office Realtors, 1999 Comparative Statistics of Industrial and Office
Real Estate Markets*

Industrial Market

Location	Total Space (sq. ft.)	Vacant Space (sq. ft.)	Vac. Rate (%)	Under Constr. (sq. ft.)	Net Absorp. (sq. ft.)	Gross Lease ($/sq.ft./yr.)
Central City	31,875,000	3,187,500	10.0	150,000	762,500	1.90-3.50
Suburban	17,300,000	1,297,500	7.5	350,000	277,500	2.00-6.00

Note: Data as of 10/98 and covers Gary; n/a not available
Source: Society of Industrial and Office Realtors, 1999 Comparative Statistics of Industrial and Office
Real Estate Markets

"Demand will increase by as much as five percent. Relatively little new speculative space is
planned or expected, a result of lender discipline that requires pre-leasing or pre-sale

agreements. The area's population is expected to grow, but it will grow away from the older urban areas in favor of the suburban markets. Disadvantageous inventory tax constraints will dissuade many distributors from pursuing new construction in this area. In spite of substantial shortages that have plagued the market for years in all size categories, the existing constraints will allow for only moderate increases in construction activity. The prime interstate corridors will realize growth as infrastructure continues to improve. Site prices are expected to increase between one and five percent. Expansions of the casinos will continue. The importance of steel and manufacturing will decrease." *Society of Industrial and Office Realtors, 1999 Comparative Statistics of Industrial and Office Real Estate Markets*

COMMERCIAL UTILITIES

Typical Monthly Electric Bills

Area	Commercial Service ($/month)		Industrial Service ($/month)	
	12 kW demand 1,500 kWh	100 kW demand 30,000 kWh	1,000 kW demand 400,000 kWh	20,000 kW demand 10,000,000 kWh
City	n/a	n/a	n/a	n/a
U.S.	150	2,174	23,995	508,569

Note: Based on rates in effect January 1, 1999; n/a not available
Source: Edison Electric Institute, Typical Residential, Commercial and Industrial Bills, Winter 1999

TRANSPORTATION

Transportation Statistics

Average minutes to work	23.9
Interstate highways	I-65; I-80; I-90; I-94
Bus lines	
In-city	Gary Public Transportation Corp.
Inter-city	2
Passenger air service	
Airport	O'Hare International (Chicago, 58 miles NW)
Airlines	n/a
Aircraft departures	n/a
Enplaned passengers	n/a
Rail service	No Amtrak Service
Motor freight carriers	279
Major waterways/ports	Lake Michigan

Source: Editor & Publisher Market Guide, 1999; FAA Airport Activity Statistics, 1997; Amtrak National Time Table, Northeast Timetable, Spring/Summer 1999; 1990 Census of Population and Housing, STF 3C; Chamber of Commerce/Economic Development 1999; Jane's Urban Transport Systems 1999-2000

Means of Transportation to Work

Area	Car/Truck/Van		Public Transportation			Bicycle	Walked	Other Means	Worked at Home
	Drove Alone	Car-pooled	Bus	Subway	Railroad				
City	72.8	16.5	3.5	0.1	2.3	0.1	3.0	0.9	0.8
MSA[1]	79.9	12.0	1.3	0.1	1.8	0.1	2.7	0.6	1.6
U.S.	73.2	13.4	3.0	1.5	0.5	0.4	3.9	1.2	3.0

Note: Figures shown are percentages and only include workers 16 years old and over;
(1) Metropolitan Statistical Area - see Appendix A for areas included
Source: 1990 Census of Population and Housing, Summary Tape File 3C

BUSINESSES

Major Business Headquarters

Company Name	1999 Rankings	
	Fortune 500	Forbes 500

No companies listed.

Note: Companies listed are located in the city; dashes indicate no ranking
Fortune 500: Companies that produce a 10-K are ranked 1 to 500 based on 1998 revenue
Forbes 500: Private companies are ranked 1 to 500 based on 1997 revenue
Source: Forbes, November 30, 1998; Fortune, April 26, 1999

Minority Business Opportunity

Gary is home to one company which is on the Black Enterprise Industrial/Service 100 list (largest based on gross sales): Powersco Inc. & Sons Construction (general construction, demolition, excavation, carpentry, masonry) . Criteria: operational in previous calendar year, at least 51% black-owned and manufactures/owns the product it sells or provides industrial or consumer services. Brokerages, real estate firms and firms that provide professional services are not eligible. *Black Enterprise, www.blackenterprise.com*

HOTELS & MOTELS

Hotels/Motels

Area	Hotels/ Motels	Rooms	Luxury-Level Hotels/Motels		Average Minimum Rates ($)		
			♦♦♦♦	♦♦♦♦♦	♦♦	♦♦♦	♦♦♦♦
City	0	0	0	0	n/a	n/a	n/a

Note: n/a not available; classifications range from one diamond (budget properties with basic amenities) to five diamond (luxury properties with the finest service, rooms and facilities). Source: OAG, Business Travel Planner, Winter 1998-99

CONVENTION CENTERS

Major Convention Centers

Center Name	Meeting Rooms	Exhibit Space (sq. ft.)
Genesis Convention Center	11	70,000

Source: Trade Shows Worldwide, 1998; Meetings & Conventions, 4/15/99; Sucessful Meetings, 3/31/98

Living Environment

COST OF LIVING

Cost of Living Index

Composite Index	Groceries	Housing	Utilities	Trans-portation	Health Care	Misc. Goods/Services
n/a	n/a	n/a	n/a	n/a	n/a	n/a

Note: U.S. = 100; n/a not available
Source: ACCRA, Cost of Living Index, 1st Quarter 1999

HOUSING

Median Home Prices and Housing Affordability

Area	Median Price[2] 1st Qtr. 1999 ($)	HOI[3] 1st Qtr. 1999	Afford-ability Rank[4]
MSA[1]	n/a	n/a	n/a
U.S.	134,000	69.6	—

Note: (1) Metropolitan Statistical Area - see Appendix A for areas included; (2) U.S. figures calculated from the sales of 524,324 new and existing homes in 181 markets; (3) Housing Opportunity Index - percent of homes sold that were within the reach of the median income household at the prevailing mortgage interest rate; (4) Rank is from 1-181 with 1 being most affordable; n/a not available
Source: National Association of Home Builders, Housing Opportunity Index, 1st Quarter 1999

Median Home Price Projection

It is projected that the median price of existing single-family homes in the metro area will increase by 2.6% in 1999. Nationwide, home prices are projected to increase 3.8%.
Kiplinger's Personal Finance Magazine, January 1999

Average New Home Price

Area	Price ($)
City	n/a
U.S.	142,735

Note: n/a not available
Source: ACCRA, Cost of Living Index, 1st Quarter 1999

Average Apartment Rent

Area	Rent ($/mth)
City	n/a
U.S.	601

Note: n/a not available
Source: ACCRA, Cost of Living Index, 1st Quarter 1999

RESIDENTIAL UTILITIES

Average Residential Utility Costs

Area	All Electric ($/mth)	Part Electric ($/mth)	Other Energy ($/mth)	Phone ($/mth)
City	—	—	—	n/a
U.S.	100.02	55.73	43.33	19.71

Note: n/a not available
Source: ACCRA, Cost of Living Index, 1st Quarter 1999

HEALTH CARE

Average Health Care Costs

Area	Hospital ($/day)	Doctor ($/visit)	Dentist ($/visit)
City	n/a	n/a	n/a
U.S.	430.43	52.45	66.35

Note: n/a not available
Source: ACCRA, Cost of Living Index, 1st Quarter 1999

Distribution of Office-Based Physicians

Area	Family/Gen. Practitioners	Specialists		
		Medical	Surgical	Other
MSA[1]	160	262	244	207

Note: Data as of 12/31/97; (1) Metropolitan Statistical Area - see Appendix A for areas included
Source: American Medical Assn., Physician Characteristics & Distribution in the U.S., 1999

Hospitals

Gary has 1 general medical and surgical hospital. *AHA Guide to the Healthcare Field, 1998-99*

EDUCATION

Public School District Statistics

District Name	Num. Sch.	Enroll.	Classroom Teachers	Pupils per Teacher	Minority Pupils (%)	Current Exp.[1] ($/pupil)
Gary Community School Corp	39	21,679	1,116	19.4	n/a	n/a
Lake Ridge Schools	6	2,621	132	19.9	n/a	n/a

Note: Data covers the 1997-1998 school year unless otherwise noted; (1) Data covers fiscal year 1996; SD = School District; ISD = Independent School District; n/a not available
Source: National Center for Education Statistics, Common Core of Data Public Education Agency Universe 1997-98; National Center for Education Statistics, Characteristics of the 100 Largest Public Elementary and Secondary School Districts in the United States: 1997-98, July 1999

Educational Quality

School District	Education Quotient[1]	Graduate Outcome[2]	Community Index[3]	Resource Index[4]
Gary Community Sch.	62.0	54.0	82.0	74.0

Note: Nearly 1,000 secondary school districts were rated in terms of educational quality. The scores range from a low of 50 to a high of 150; (1) Average of the Graduate Outcome, Community and Resource indexes; (2) Based on graduation rates and college board scores (SAT/ACT); (3) Based on the surrounding community's average level of education and the area's average income level; (4) Based on teacher salaries, per-pupil expenditures and student-teacher ratios.
Source: Expansion Management, Ratings Issue, 1998

Educational Attainment by Race

Area	High School Graduate (%)					Bachelor's Degree (%)				
	Total	White	Black	Other	Hisp.[2]	Total	White	Black	Other	Hisp.[2]
City	64.8	57.6	67.1	50.2	50.7	8.8	9.1	9.0	2.2	3.7
MSA[1]	75.4	77.9	67.1	60.5	59.3	14.0	15.1	9.7	11.4	6.2
U.S.	75.2	77.9	63.1	60.4	49.8	20.3	21.5	11.4	19.4	9.2

Note: Figures shown cover persons 25 years old and over; (1) Metropolitan Statistical Area - see Appendix A for areas included; (2) people of Hispanic origin can be of any race
Source: 1990 Census of Population and Housing, Summary Tape File 3C

School Enrollment by Type

Area	Preprimary				Elementary/High School			
	Public		Private		Public		Private	
	Enrollment	%	Enrollment	%	Enrollment	%	Enrollment	%
City	1,560	79.8	396	20.2	25,315	93.7	1,700	6.3
MSA[1]	6,173	58.8	4,317	41.2	106,474	89.5	12,519	10.5
U.S.	2,679,029	59.5	1,824,256	40.5	38,379,689	90.2	4,187,099	9.8

Note: Figures shown cover persons 3 years old and over;
(1) Metropolitan Statistical Area - see Appendix A for areas included
Source: 1990 Census of Population and Housing, Summary Tape File 3C

School Enrollment by Race

Area	Preprimary (%)				Elementary/High School (%)			
	White	Black	Other	Hisp.[1]	White	Black	Other	Hisp.[1]
City	9.6	88.6	1.8	5.5	9.4	87.3	3.3	5.2
MSA[2]	74.9	20.7	4.4	8.0	69.7	24.6	5.7	10.5
U.S.	80.4	12.5	7.1	7.8	74.1	15.6	10.3	12.5

Note: Figures shown cover persons 3 years old and over; (1) people of Hispanic origin can be of any race; (2) Metropolitan Statistical Area - see Appendix A for areas included
Source: 1990 Census of Population and Housing, Summary Tape File 3C

Classroom Teacher Salaries in Public Schools

District	B.A. Degree		M.A. Degree		Maximum	
	Min. ($)	Rank[1]	Max. ($)	Rank[1]	Max. ($)	Rank[1]
	n/a	n/a	n/a	n/a	n/a	n/a
Average	26,980	-	46,065	-	51,435	-

Note: Salaries are for 1997-1998; (1) Rank ranges from 1 to 100; n/a not available
Source: American Federation of Teachers, Survey & Analysis of Salary Trends, 1998

Higher Education

Two-Year Colleges		Four-Year Colleges		Medical Schools	Law Schools	Voc/ Tech
Public	Private	Public	Private			
1	0	1	0	0	0	2

Source: College Blue Book, Occupational Education, 1997; Medical School Admission Requirements, 1999-2000; Peterson's Guide to Two-Year Colleges, 1999; Peterson's Guide to Four-Year Colleges, 2000; Barron's Guide to Law Schools, 1999

MAJOR EMPLOYERS

Major Employers

Trump Indiana
JM Foster (heavy construction)
Pangere Corp. (roofing)
Garlup Construction Co.

Methodist Hospitals
Dixie Dairy
Gary Steel Products
USX Corporation

Note: Companies listed are located in the city
Source: Dun's Business Rankings, 1999; Ward's Business Directory, 1998

PUBLIC SAFETY

Crime Rate

Area	All Crimes	Violent Crimes				Property Crimes		
		Murder	Forcible Rape	Robbery	Aggrav. Assault	Burglary	Larceny -Theft	Motor Vehicle Theft
City	8,703.6	84.1	137.4	635.3	797.6	2,394.4	2,664.0	1,990.9
Suburbs[1]	5,178.6	2.9	18.8	128.2	868.6	676.1	2,905.5	578.3
MSA[2]	5,828.3	17.9	40.7	221.7	855.5	992.9	2,861.0	838.7
U.S.	4,922.7	6.8	35.9	186.1	382.0	919.6	2,886.5	505.8

Note: Crime rate is the number of crimes per 100,000 pop.; (1) defined as all areas within the MSA but located outside the central city; (2) Metropolitan Statistical Area - see Appendix A for areas incl.
Source: FBI Uniform Crime Reports, 1997

RECREATION

Culture and Recreation

Museums	Symphony Orchestras	Opera Companies	Dance Companies	Professional Theatres	Zoos	Pro Sports Teams
0	0	0	0	0	0	0

Source: International Directory of the Performing Arts, 1997; Official Museum Directory, 1999; Stern's Performing Arts Directory, 1997; USA Today Four Sport Stadium Guide, 1997; Chamber of Commerce/Economic Development, 1999

Library System

The Gary Public Library has four branches, holdings of 567,101 volumes, and a budget of $4,650,259 (1995-1996). *American Library Directory, 1998-1999*

MEDIA

Newspapers

Name	Type	Freq.	Distribution	Circulation
The Gary Crusader	Black	1x/wk	Local	36,000
Gary Info	Black	1x/wk	Local	33,000
Post-Tribune	General	7x/wk	Area	69,561

Note: Includes newspapers with circulations of 500 or more located in the city;
Source: Burrelle's Media Directory, 1999 Edition

Television Stations

Name	Ch.	Affiliation	Type	Owner

No stations listed.

Note: Stations included broadcast in the Gary metro area; n/a not available
Source: Burrelle's Media Directory, 1999 Edition

AM Radio Stations

Call Letters	Freq. (kHz)	Target Audience	Station Format	Music Format
WWCA	1270	General	M	Latin
WLTH	1370	General	M/N/S/T	Adult Contemporary/Christian/R&B/Urban Contemp.

Note: Stations included broadcast in the Gary metro area
Target Audience: A=Asian; B=Black; C=Christian; E=Ethnic; F=French; G=General; H=Hispanic; M=Men; N=Native American; R=Religious; S=Senior Citizen; W=Women; Y=Young Adult; Z=Children
Station Format: E=Educational; M=Music; N=News; S=Sports; T=Talk
Source: Burrelle's Media Directory, 1999 Edition

FM Radio Stations

Call Letters	Freq. (mHz)	Target Audience	Station Format	Music Format
WGVE	88.7	General	E/M/N/T	Adult Contemporary/Jazz

Note: Stations included broadcast in the Gary metro area
Station Format: E=Educational; M=Music; N=News; S=Sports; T=Talk
Target Audience: A=Asian; B=Black; C=Christian; E=Ethnic; F=French; G=General; H=Hispanic; M=Men; N=Native American; R=Religious; S=Senior Citizen; W=Women; Y=Young Adult; Z=Children
Source: Burrelle's Media Directory, 1999 Edition

CLIMATE

Average and Extreme Temperatures

Temperature	Jan	Feb	Mar	Apr	May	Jun	Jul	Aug	Sep	Oct	Nov	Dec	Yr.
Extreme High (°F)	65	71	88	91	93	104	102	100	99	91	78	71	104
Average High (°F)	29	33	45	59	70	79	84	82	75	63	48	34	59
Average Temp. (°F)	21	26	37	49	59	69	73	72	65	53	40	27	49
Average Low (°F)	13	17	28	39	48	57	63	62	54	42	32	19	40
Extreme Low (°F)	-27	-17	-8	7	24	36	40	41	28	17	1	-25	-27

Note: Figures cover the years 1958-1900
Source: National Climatic Data Center, International Station Meteorological Climate Summary, 3/95

Average Precipitation/Snowfall/Humidity

Precip./Humidity	Jan	Feb	Mar	Apr	May	Jun	Jul	Aug	Sep	Oct	Nov	Dec	Yr.
Avg. Precip. (in.)	1.6	1.4	2.7	3.6	3.3	3.7	3.7	4.1	3.7	2.4	2.8	2.3	35.4
Avg. Snowfall (in.)	11	8	7	2	Tr	0	0	0	0	1	2	9	39
Avg. Rel. Hum. 0am (%)	76	77	79	77	77	78	82	85	85	82	80	80	80
Avg. Rel. Hum. 0pm (%)	65	63	59	53	51	52	54	55	55	53	61	68	57

Note: Figures cover the years 1958-1900; Tr = Trace amounts (<0.05 in. of rain; <0.5 in. of snow)
Source: National Climatic Data Center, International Station Meteorological Climate Summary, 3/95

Weather Conditions

Temperature			Daytime Sky			Precipitation		
0°F & below	0°F & below	0°F & above	Clear	Partly cloudy	Cloudy	0.01 inch or more precip.	0.1 inch or more snow/ice	Thunder-storms
21	132	17	83	136	146	125	31	38

Note: Figures are average number of days per year and covers the years 1958-1900
Source: National Climatic Data Center, International Station Meteorological Climate Summary, 3/95

AIR & WATER QUALITY

Maximum Pollutant Concentrations

	Particulate Matter (ug/m^3)	Carbon Monoxide (ppm)	Sulfur Dioxide (ppm)	Nitrogen Dioxide (ppm)	Ozone (ppm)	Lead (ug/m^3)
MSA[1] Level	138	4	0.032	n/a	0.12	0.04
NAAQS[2]	150	9	0.140	0.053	0.12	1.50
Met NAAQS?	Yes	Yes	Yes	n/a	Yes	Yes

Note: (1) Metropolitan Statistical Area - see Appendix A for areas included; (2) National Ambient Air Quality Standards; ppm = parts per million; ug/m^3 = micrograms per cubic meter; n/a not available
Source: EPA, National Air Quality and Emissions Trends Report, 1997

Pollutant Standards Index

In the Gary MSA (see Appendix A for areas included), the Pollutant Standards Index (PSI) exceeded 100 on 12 days in 1997. A PSI value greater than 100 indicates that air quality would be in the unhealthful range on that day. *EPA, National Air Quality and Emissions Trends Report, 1997*

Drinking Water

Water System Name	Pop. Served	Primary Water Source Type	Number of Violations in 1998	Type of Violation/ Contaminants
Northwest Indiana Water Co.	230,000	Surface	None	None

Note: Data as of July 10, 1999
Source: EPA, Office of Ground Water and Drinking Water, Safe Drinking Water Information System

Gary tap water is soft, filtered and fluoridated.
Editor & Publisher Market Guide, 1999

Grand Rapids, Michigan

Background

The city of Grand Rapids, Michigan is perhaps best known for its fine furniture making. The presence of an abundant forest, as well as the hydropower and trade afforded by a powerful river, contributed to the reputation of an industry that is known worldwide.

However, before Grand Rapids became involved in making seats for churches, buses, and schools, the site was a Native American settlement of the Ottawa, Chippewa, and Potawatomi tribes. The earliest white presence in the area were fur traders who bought furs from the Native American tribes in the early 19th century. One by one, more white settlers found their way into the area on the rapids of the Grand River. A Baptist Mission was established in 1825, and a year after that, Louis Campau erected a trading post. In 1833, the area's first permanent white settlement appeared, led by Samuel Dexter of Herkimer County, New York.

The Grand Rapids metro area has been cited as the only one in the midwest to recover all of the manufacturing jobs it lost in the recessions of the early 1980s. Its 2,200 manufacturers employ nearly 15 percent more than they did in 1990, according to the Grand Rapids Areas Chamber of Commerce. The main industries are office furniture, auto components, fabricated metals, and food processing. *Industry Week, 4/7/97*

Grand Rapids is located in the westcentral part of Kent County in the picturesque Grand River Valley, about 30 miles east of Lake Michigan.Fall is a very colorful time of year in western Michigan, perhaps compensating for the late spring.

During the winter, excessive cloudiness and numerous snow flurries occur with strong westerly winds. Lake Michigan has a tempering effect on cold waves coming in from the west in the winter. Prolonged severe cold waves with temperatures below zero are infrequent. The snowfall season extends from mid-November to mid-March and some winters have had continuous snow cover throughout this period.

General Rankings and Evaluative Comments

■ Grand Rapids was ranked #7 out of 11 large, midwestern metropolitan areas in *Money's* 1998 survey of "The Best Places to Live in America." The survey was conducted by first contacting 512 representative households nationwide and asking them to rank 37 quality-of-life factors on a scale of 1 to 10. Next, a demographic profile was compiled on the 300 largest metropolitan statistical areas in the U.S. The numbers were crunched together to arrive at an overall ranking (things Americans consider most important, like clean air and water, low crime and good schools, received extra weight). Unlike previous years, the 1998 rankings were broken down by region (northeast, midwest, south, west) and population size (100,000 to 249,999; 250,000 to 999,999; 1 million plus). The city had a nationwide ranking of #150 out of 300 in 1997 and #71 out of 300 in 1996. *Money, 7/98; Money, 7/97; Money, 9/96*

■ Grand Rapids appeared on *Fortune's* list of "The Best Cities for Business." Rank: #10 out of 10. One hundred and sixty cities worldwide were analyzed by Arthur Andersen's Business Location Service. The North American research focused on cities creating new wealth and opportunities. *Fortune* made the final selection of the top 10 cities in the U.S. *Fortune, 11/98*

■ *Ladies Home Journal* ranked America's 200 largest cities based on the qualities women care about most. Grand Rapids ranked #79 out of 200. Criteria: low crime rate, well-paying jobs, quality health and child care, good public schools, the presence of women in government, size of the gender wage gap, number of sexual-harassment and discrimination complaints filed, unemployment and divorce rates, commute times, population density, number of houses of worship, parks and cultural offerings, number of women's health specialists, how well a community's women cared for themselves, complexion kindness index based on UV radiation levels, odds of finding affordable fashions, rental rates for romance movies, champagne sales and other matters of the heart. *Ladies Home Journal, November 1998*

■ Zero Population Growth ranked 229 cities in terms of children's health, safety, and economic well-being. Grand Rapids was ranked #40 out of 112 independent cities (cities with populations greater than 100,000 which were neither Major Cities nor Suburbs/Outer Cities) and was given a grade of C+. Criteria: total population, percent of population under 18 years of age, household language, percent population change, percent of births to teens, infant mortality rate, percent of low birth weights, dropout rate, enrollment in preprimary school, violent and property crime rates, unemployment rate, percent of children in poverty, percent of owner occupied units, number of bad air days, percent of public transportation commuters, and average travel time to work. *ZPG, Children's Environmental Index, Fall 1999*

■ Grand Rapids was ranked #29 out of 59 metro areas in *The Regional Economist's* "Rational Livability Ranking of 59 Large Metro Areas." The rankings were based on the metro area's total population change over the period 1990-97 divided by the number of people moving in from elsewhere in the United States (net domestic in-migration). *St. Louis Federal Reserve Bank of St. Louis, The Regional Economist, April 1999*

■ Cognetics studied 273 metro areas in the United States, ranking them by entrepreneurial activity. Grand Rapids was ranked #13 out of the 50 largest metro areas. Criteria: Significant Starts (firms started in the last 10 years that still employ at least 5 people) and Young Growers (percent of firms 10 years old or less that grew significantly during the last 4 years). *Cognetics, "Entrepreneurial Hot Spots: The Best Places in America to Start and Grow a Company," 1998*

■ Grand Rapids was selected as one of the "Best American Cities to Start a Business" by *Point of View* magazine. Criteria: coolness, quality-of-life, and business concerns. The city was ranked #62 out of 75. *Point of View, November 1998*

■ Reliastar Financial Corp. ranked the 125 largest metropolitan areas according to the general financial security of residents. Grand Rapids was ranked #4 out of 125 with a score of 16.1. The score indicates the percentage a metropolitan area is above or below the metropolitan norm. A metro area with a score of 10.6 is 10.6% above the metro average. Criteria: Earnings and Wealth Potential (household income, education, net assets, cost of living); Safety Net (health insurance, retirement savings, life insurance, income support programs); Personal Threats (unemployment rate, low-income households, crime rate); Community Economic Vitality (cost of community services, job quality, job creation, housing costs). *Reliastar Financial Corp., "The Best Cities to Earn and Save Money," 1999 Edition*

Business Environment

STATE ECONOMY

State Economic Profile

" Although the Michigan economy bounced back quickly from the GM strike, it is losing much of its mid-1990s momentum. Strong auto sales have not translated into employment gains in the auto industry. Canada's weak economy has caused a drop in MI's exports. And what constrains MI the most is its demographic situation. The next several years should see a slowing economy.

In spite of the GM strike and booming automobile sales, GM has not increased employment and is currently planning to close plants in Kalamazoo and Flint. In addition, some 1,000 office jobs are targeted for elimination at the Detroit headquarters; Ford is currently planning to cut jobs within the state. Auto sales for 1999 and 2000 should fall below 1998, only adding to Detroit's need for employment reductions.

Construction activity added significantly to job growth in 1998, with construction employment growing 2.5% for the state and 8.3% for Detroit. Almost 1,800 commercial/industrial developments were undertaken in 1998. With the slowing economy, construction activity is likely to contract in 1999, undermining one of MI's bright spots. Residential starts, up 7% in 1998, should decline 6.2% in 1999.

Michigan's tight labor markets have helped to absorb downsizing in the auto industry, keeping the unemployment rate manageable. Labor availability has, however, started to become a problem for the state's information technology firms. The state's weak population growth, especially its continuing loss of young households, will dampen the high home price appreciation witnessed in recent years, as well as limit job entry-level job growth." *National Association of Realtors, Economic Profiles: The Fifty States and the District of Columbia, http://nar.realtor.com/databank/profiles.htm*

IMPORTS/EXPORTS

Total Export Sales

Area	1994 ($000)	1995 ($000)	1996 ($000)	1997 ($000)	% Chg. 1994-97	% Chg. 1996-97
MSA[1]	1,993,494	2,304,077	2,656,497	2,933,117	47.1	10.4
U.S.	512,415,609	583,030,524	622,827,063	687,597,999	34.2	10.4

Note: (1) Metropolitan Statistical Area - see Appendix A for areas included
Source: U.S. Department of Commerce, International Trade Association, Metropolitan Area Exports: An Export Performance Report on Over 250 U.S. Cities, November 10, 1998

CITY FINANCES

City Government Finances

Component	FY92 ($000)	FY92 (per capita $)
Revenue	222,109	1,178.01
Expenditure	247,324	1,311.74
Debt Outstanding	278,306	1,476.06
Cash & Securities	472,958	2,508.45

Source: U.S. Bureau of the Census, City Government Finances: 1991-92

City Government Revenue by Source

Source	FY92 ($000)	FY92 (per capita $)	FY92 (%)
From Federal Government	14,665	77.78	6.6
From State Governments	28,235	149.75	12.7
From Local Governments	5,053	26.80	2.3
Property Taxes	29,312	155.46	13.2
General Sales Taxes	0	0.00	0.0
Selective Sales Taxes	0	0.00	0.0
Income Taxes	26,525	140.68	11.9
Current Charges	42,878	227.41	19.3
Utility/Liquor Store	31,240	165.69	14.1
Employee Retirement[1]	26,161	138.75	11.8
Other	18,040	95.68	8.1

Note: (1) Excludes "city contributions," classified as "nonrevenue," intragovernmental transfers.
Source: U.S. Bureau of the Census, City Government Finances: 1991-92

City Government Expenditures by Function

Function	FY92 ($000)	FY92 (per capita $)	FY92 (%)
Educational Services	3,808	20.20	1.5
Employee Retirement[1]	11,611	61.58	4.7
Environment/Housing	64,149	340.23	25.9
Government Administration	14,885	78.95	6.0
Interest on General Debt	5,232	27.75	2.1
Public Safety	36,264	192.34	14.7
Social Services	0	0.00	0.0
Transportation	22,447	119.05	9.1
Utility/Liquor Store	71,654	380.03	29.0
Other	17,274	91.62	7.0

Note: (1) Payments to beneficiaries including withdrawal of contributions.
Source: U.S. Bureau of the Census, City Government Finances: 1991-92

Municipal Bond Ratings

Area	Moody's	S & P
Grand Rapids	Aa3	n/a

Note: n/a not available; n/r not rated
Source: Moody's Bond Record, 6/99

POPULATION

Population Growth

Area	1980	1990	% Chg. 1980-90	July 1998 Estimate	% Chg. 1990-98
City	181,843	189,126	4.0	185,437	-2.0
MSA[1]	601,680	688,399	14.4	1,040,835	51.2
U.S.	226,545,805	248,765,170	9.8	270,299,000	8.7

Note: (1) Metropolitan Statistical Area - see Appendix A for areas included;
July 1998 MSA population estimate was calculated by the editors
Source: 1980/1990 Census of Housing and Population, Summary Tape File 3C;
Census Bureau Population Estimates 1998

Population Characteristics

Race	City 1980 Population	1980 %	City 1990 Population	1990 %	% Chg. 1980-90	MSA[1] 1990 Population	1990 %
White	147,220	81.0	145,123	76.7	-1.4	624,739	90.8
Black	28,811	15.8	35,134	18.6	21.9	40,858	5.9
Amer Indian/Esk/Aleut	1,346	0.7	1,501	0.8	11.5	3,555	0.5
Asian/Pacific Islander	1,415	0.8	1,968	1.0	39.1	7,509	1.1
Other	3,051	1.7	5,400	2.9	77.0	11,738	1.7
Hispanic Origin[2]	5,751	3.2	8,447	4.5	46.9	21,151	3.1

Note: (1) Metropolitan Statistical Area - see Appendix A for areas included;
(2) people of Hispanic origin can be of any race
Source: 1980/1990 Census of Housing and Population, Summary Tape File 3C

Ancestry

Area	German	Irish	English	Italian	U.S.	French	Polish	Dutch
City	21.4	12.3	10.4	2.5	2.2	4.5	10.4	21.4
MSA[1]	27.5	13.2	13.5	2.5	2.8	5.0	7.9	30.5
U.S.	23.3	15.6	13.1	5.9	5.3	4.2	3.8	2.5

Note: Figures are percentages and include persons that reported multiple ancestry (eg. if a person
reported being Irish and Italian, they were included in both columns); (1) Metropolitan Statistical Area -
see Appendix A for areas included
Source: 1990 Census of Population and Housing, Summary Tape File 3C

Age

Area	Median Age (Years)	Age Distribution (%) Under 5	Under 18	18-24	25-44	45-64	65+	80+
City	29.8	9.4	27.6	12.5	32.9	14.0	13.0	3.8
MSA[1]	30.6	8.7	28.6	11.0	33.3	16.6	10.5	2.6
U.S.	32.9	7.3	25.6	10.5	32.6	18.7	12.5	2.8

Note: (1) Metropolitan Statistical Area - see Appendix A for areas included
Source: 1990 Census of Population and Housing, Summary Tape File 3C

Male/Female Ratio

Area	Number of males per 100 females (all ages)	Number of males per 100 females (18 years old+)
City	90.2	85.6
MSA[1]	94.8	91.1
U.S.	95.0	91.9

Note: (1) Metropolitan Statistical Area - see Appendix A for areas included
Source: 1990 Census of Population, General Population Characteristics

INCOME

Per Capita/Median/Average Income

Area	Per Capita ($)	Median Household ($)	Average Household ($)
City	12,070	26,809	32,106
MSA[1]	14,370	33,515	39,827
U.S.	14,420	30,056	38,453

Note: All figures are for 1989; (1) Metropolitan Statistical Area - see Appendix A for areas included
Source: 1990 Census of Population and Housing, Summary Tape File 3C

Household Income Distribution by Race

Income ($)	City (%)					U.S. (%)				
	Total	White	Black	Other	Hisp.[1]	Total	White	Black	Other	Hisp.[1]
Less than 5,000	6.1	4.4	13.8	9.5	6.8	6.2	4.8	15.2	8.6	8.8
5,000 - 9,999	11.2	9.7	18.1	16.7	17.6	9.3	8.6	14.2	9.9	11.1
10,000 - 14,999	10.0	9.2	13.3	12.6	14.4	8.8	8.5	11.0	9.8	11.0
15,000 - 24,999	19.3	19.2	18.8	23.4	19.0	17.5	17.3	18.9	18.5	20.5
25,000 - 34,999	17.9	19.2	12.1	13.2	17.5	15.8	16.1	14.2	15.4	16.4
35,000 - 49,999	18.4	19.8	12.3	14.7	13.1	17.9	18.6	13.3	16.1	16.0
50,000 - 74,999	12.4	13.1	9.1	8.5	7.3	15.0	15.8	9.3	13.4	11.1
75,000 - 99,999	2.9	3.2	1.9	1.5	3.1	5.1	5.5	2.6	4.7	3.1
100,000+	1.9	2.3	0.6	0.0	1.1	4.4	4.8	1.3	3.7	1.9

Note: All figures are for 1989; (1) people of Hispanic origin can be of any race
Source: 1990 Census of Population and Housing, Summary Tape File 3C

Effective Buying Income

Area	Per Capita ($)	Median Household ($)	Average Household ($)
City	14,959	33,044	40,220
MSA[1]	17,013	38,583	47,166
U.S.	16,803	34,536	45,243

Note: Data as of 1/1/99; (1) Metropolitan Statistical Area - see Appendix A for areas included
Source: Standard Rate & Data Service, Newspaper Advertising Source, 9/99

Effective Household Buying Income Distribution

Area	% of Households Earning						
	$10,000 -$19,999	$20,000 -$34,999	$35,000 -$49,999	$50,000 -$74,999	$75,000 -$99,000	$100,000 -$124,999	$125,000 and up
City	17.0	24.1	19.4	18.7	5.8	1.7	1.4
MSA[1]	13.9	22.4	20.9	22.6	7.2	2.1	2.2
U.S.	16.0	22.6	18.2	18.9	7.2	2.4	2.7

Note: Data as of 1/1/99; (1) Metropolitan Statistical Area - see Appendix A for areas included
Source: Standard Rate & Data Service, Newspaper Advertising Source, 9/99

Poverty Rates by Race and Age

Area	Total (%)	By Race (%)				By Age (%)		
		White	Black	Other	Hisp.[2]	Under 5 years old	Under 18 years old	65 years and over
City	16.1	10.8	33.8	31.1	33.3	24.6	23.2	10.0
MSA[1]	8.3	6.4	31.4	20.0	22.9	12.5	10.7	8.1
U.S.	13.1	9.8	29.5	23.1	25.3	20.1	18.3	12.8

Note: Figures show the percent of people living below the poverty line in 1989. The average poverty threshold was $12,674 for a family of four in 1989; (1) Metropolitan Statistical Area - see Appendix A for areas included; (2) people of Hispanic origin can be of any race
Source: 1990 Census of Population and Housing, Summary Tape File 3C

EMPLOYMENT

Labor Force and Employment

Area	Civilian Labor Force			Workers Employed		
	Jun. 1998	Jun. 1999	% Chg.	Jun. 1998	Jun. 1999	% Chg.
City	114,362	117,902	3.1	109,258	111,925	2.4
MSA[1]	603,513	620,984	2.9	584,012	598,270	2.4
U.S.	138,798,000	140,666,000	1.3	132,265,000	134,395,000	1.6

Note: Data is not seasonally adjusted and covers workers 16 years of age and older; (1) Metropolitan Statistical Area - see Appendix A for areas included
Source: Bureau of Labor Statistics, http://stats.bls.gov

Unemployment Rate

Area	1998						1999					
	Jul.	Aug.	Sep.	Oct.	Nov.	Dec.	Jan.	Feb.	Mar.	Apr.	May.	Jun.
City	5.3	4.0	3.9	3.5	3.5	3.6	4.9	4.9	4.8	4.1	4.0	5.1
MSA[1]	3.7	2.9	2.7	2.6	2.7	2.7	3.7	3.7	3.6	3.0	2.9	3.7
U.S.	4.7	4.5	4.4	4.2	4.1	4.0	4.8	4.7	4.4	4.1	4.0	4.5

Note: Data is not seasonally adjusted and covers workers 16 years of age and older; all figures are percentages; (1) Metropolitan Statistical Area - see Appendix A for areas included
Source: Bureau of Labor Statistics, http://stats.bls.gov

Employment by Industry

Sector	MSA[1]		U.S.
	Number of Employees	Percent of Total	Percent of Total
Services	148,900	25.3	30.4
Retail Trade	107,800	18.3	17.7
Government	55,500	9.4	15.6
Manufacturing	161,600	27.4	14.3
Finance/Insurance/Real Estate	25,300	4.3	5.9
Wholesale Trade	39,900	6.8	5.4
Transportation/Public Utilities	19,800	3.4	5.3
Construction	n/a	n/a	5.0
Mining	n/a	n/a	0.4

Note: Figures cover non-farm employment as of 6/99 and are not seasonally adjusted;
(1) Metropolitan Statistical Area - see Appendix A for areas included; n/a not available
Source: Bureau of Labor Statistics, http://stats.bls.gov

Employment by Occupation

Occupation Category	City (%)	MSA[1] (%)	U.S. (%)
White Collar	54.8	54.9	58.1
Executive/Admin./Management	10.2	11.7	12.3
Professional	14.0	12.4	14.1
Technical & Related Support	3.0	3.0	3.7
Sales	11.6	12.3	11.8
Administrative Support/Clerical	16.0	15.5	16.3
Blue Collar	28.6	30.9	26.2
Precision Production/Craft/Repair	9.6	11.7	11.3
Machine Operators/Assem./Insp.	10.9	10.8	6.8
Transportation/Material Movers	3.3	4.1	4.1
Cleaners/Helpers/Laborers	4.8	4.4	3.9
Services	15.7	12.6	13.2
Farming/Forestry/Fishing	0.9	1.6	2.5

Note: Figures cover employed persons 16 years old and over;
(1) Metropolitan Statistical Area - see Appendix A for areas included
Source: 1990 Census of Population and Housing, Summary Tape File 3C

Occupational Employment Projections: 1994 - 2005

Occupations Expected to Have the Largest Job Growth (ranked by numerical growth)	Fast-Growing Occupations[1] (ranked by percent growth)
1. Waiters & waitresses	1. Computer engineers
2. Cashiers	2. Home health aides
3. All other helper, laborer, mover	3. Systems analysts
4. Systems analysts	4. Personal and home care aides
5. Home health aides	5. Electronic pagination systems workers
6. General managers & top executives	6. All other computer scientists
7. All other profess., paraprofess., tech.	7. Physical therapists
8. Registered nurses	8. All other therapists
9. All other sales reps. & services	9. Electronics repairers, comm. & indust.
10. Salespersons, retail	10. Occupational therapists

Note: Projections cover Michigan; (1) Excludes occupations with total job growth less than 300
Source: Office of Labor Market Information, Occupational Employment Forecasts, 1994-2005

TAXES

Major State and Local Tax Rates

State Corp. Income (%)	State Personal Income (%)	Residential Property (effective rate per $100)	Sales & Use		State Gasoline (cents/ gallon)	State Cigarette (cents/ pack)
			State (%)	Local (%)		
2.3[a]	4.4	n/a	6.0	None	19.0	75.0

Note: Personal/corporate income, sales, gasoline and cigarette tax rates as of January 1999.
Property tax rates as of 1997; (a) Value added tax imposed on the sum of federal taxable income of
the business, compensation paid to employees, dividends, interest, royalties paid and other items
Source: Federation of Tax Administrators, www.taxadmin.org; Washington D.C. Department of
Finance and Revenue, Tax Rates and Tax Burdens in the District of Columbia: A Nationwide
Comparison, July 1998; Chamber of Commerce, 1999

Total Taxes Per Capita and as a Percent of Income

Area	Per Capita Income ($)	Per Capita Taxes ($)			Percent of Income (%)		
		Total	Federal	State/ Local	Total	Federal	State/ Local
Michigan	28,565	10,361	7,221	3,139	36.3	25.3	11.0
U.S.	27,876	9,881	6,690	3,191	35.4	24.0	11.4

Note: Figures are for 1998
Source: Tax Foundation, www.taxfoundation.org

Estimated Tax Burden

Area	State Income	Local Income	Property	Sales	Total
Grand Rapids	2,770	750	3,250	585	7,355

Note: The numbers are estimates of taxes paid by a married couple with two children and annual
earnings of $75,000. Sales tax estimates assume they spend average amounts on food, clothing,
household goods and gasoline. Property tax estimates assume they live in a $250,000 home.
Source: Kiplinger's Personal Finance Magazine, October 1998

COMMERCIAL REAL ESTATE

Office Market

Class/ Location	Total Space (sq. ft.)	Vacant Space (sq. ft.)	Vac. Rate (%)	Under Constr. (sq. ft.)	Net Absorp. (sq. ft.)	Rental Rates ($/sq.ft./yr.)
Class A						
CBD	1,795,000	69,000	3.8	0	-17,600	15.50-22.50
Outside CBD	4,178,300	321,900	7.7	120,000	298,000	12.00-19.00
Class B						
CBD	2,109,000	231,935	11.0	295,000	126,465	10.00-17.00
Outside CBD	2,107,500	336,000	15.9	0	40,080	8.00-14.50

Note: Data as of 10/98 and covers Grand Rapids; CBD = Central Business District; n/a not available;
Source: Society of Industrial and Office Realtors, 1999 Comparative Statistics of Industrial and Office Real Estate Markets

"Expansions in local medical, educational, and research organizations will fuel Grand Rapids' 1999 growth. Construction will start for the new courthouse, consisting of 375,000 sq. ft. of space, sometime this year. Occupancy of this structure isn't expected until the year 2002. As capacity is reached for Class A office space, new Class A CBD construction is anticipated. Our local SIOR reporter forecasts a dramatic 20 percent increase in absorption. This is in conjunction with up to a 10 percent increase in construction and up to a 10 percent decrease in vacancy rates. Much of the construction will be in Class A office space. Sales prices are expected to increase slightly over the year." *Society of Industrial and Office Realtors, 1999 Comparative Statistics of Industrial and Office Real Estate Markets*

Industrial Market

Location	Total Space (sq. ft.)	Vacant Space (sq. ft.)	Vac. Rate (%)	Under Constr. (sq. ft.)	Net Absorp. (sq. ft.)	Net Lease ($/sq.ft./yr.)
Central City	80,000,000	4,000,000	5.0	2,000,000	1,800,000	1.50-4.50
Suburban	n/a	n/a	n/a	n/a	n/a	2.50-4.75

Note: Data as of 10/98 and covers Grand Rapids. Inventory figures are combined; n/a not available
Source: Society of Industrial and Office Realtors, 1999 Comparative Statistics of Industrial and Office Real Estate Markets

"The local economy is expected to grow at a healthy pace. The manufacturing, automotive, and office furniture sectors of the economy will perform nicely. According to our SIOR reporters, investors should see a moderate increase in sales and lease prices in all categories and sizes of prime industrial space. Tax-free renaissance zones, considered among the largest in the nation, will encourage revitalization of development in the older downtown areas. Low interest rates, in combination with ample money from local banks, will help fuel construction. Substantial shortages exist for prime industrial space less than 60,000 sq. ft. Increases in construction may help reduce this shortage, because absorption is expected to remain near the 1 million sq. ft. level. The total dollar volume of sales is expected to increase moderately." *Society of Industrial and Office Realtors, 1999 Comparative Statistics of Industrial and Office Real Estate Markets*

COMMERCIAL UTILITIES

Typical Monthly Electric Bills

Area	Commercial Service ($/month)		Industrial Service ($/month)	
	12 kW demand 1,500 kWh	100 kW demand 30,000 kWh	1,000 kW demand 400,000 kWh	20,000 kW demand 10,000,000 kWh
City	153	2,081	23,525	396,252
U.S.	150	2,174	23,995	508,569

Note: Based on rates in effect January 1, 1999
Source: Edison Electric Institute, Typical Residential, Commercial and Industrial Bills, Winter 1999

TRANSPORTATION

Transportation Statistics

Average minutes to work	16.7
Interstate highways	I-96
Bus lines	
In-city	Grand Rapids Area TA
Inter-city	2
Passenger air service	
Airport	Kent County International
Airlines	9
Aircraft departures	18,081 (1996)
Enplaned passengers	777,649 (1996)
Rail service	Amtrak
Motor freight carriers	32
Major waterways/ports	Grand River

Source: Editor & Publisher Market Guide, 1999; FAA Airport Activity Statistics, 1997; Amtrak National Time Table, Northeast Timetable, Spring/Summer 1999; 1990 Census of Population and Housing, STF 3C; Chamber of Commerce/Economic Development 1999; Jane's Urban Transport Systems 1999-2000

Means of Transportation to Work

Area	Car/Truck/Van		Public Transportation			Bicycle	Walked	Other Means	Worked at Home
	Drove Alone	Car-pooled	Bus	Subway	Railroad				
City	76.8	11.7	3.2	0.0	0.0	0.3	4.3	1.0	2.7
MSA[1]	82.7	9.8	1.1	0.0	0.0	0.2	2.8	0.6	2.8
U.S.	73.2	13.4	3.0	1.5	0.5	0.4	3.9	1.2	3.0

Note: Figures shown are percentages and only include workers 16 years old and over;
(1) Metropolitan Statistical Area - see Appendix A for areas included
Source: 1990 Census of Population and Housing, Summary Tape File 3C

BUSINESSES

Major Business Headquarters

Company Name	1999 Rankings	
	Fortune 500	Forbes 500
Gordon Food Service	-	97
Meijer	-	15

Note: Companies listed are located in the city; dashes indicate no ranking
Fortune 500: Companies that produce a 10-K are ranked 1 to 500 based on 1998 revenue
Forbes 500: Private companies are ranked 1 to 500 based on 1997 revenue
Source: Forbes, November 30, 1998; Fortune, April 26, 1999

Fast-Growing Businesses

Grand Rapids is home to one of *Business Week's* "hot growth" companies: A.S.V.. Criteria: increase in sales and profits, return on capital and stock price. *Business Week, 5/31/99*

HOTELS & MOTELS

Hotels/Motels

Area	Hotels/ Motels	Rooms	Luxury-Level Hotels/Motels		Average Minimum Rates ($)		
			♦♦♦♦	♦♦♦♦♦	♦♦	♦♦♦	♦♦♦♦
City	14	2,159	1	0	67	77	165
Airport	15	1,924	0	0	n/a	n/a	n/a
Suburbs	9	401	0	0	n/a	n/a	n/a
Total	38	4,484	1	0	n/a	n/a	n/a

Note: n/a not available; classifications range from one diamond (budget properties with basic amenities) to five diamond (luxury properties with the finest service, rooms and facilities).
Source: OAG, Business Travel Planner, Winter 1998-99

CONVENTION CENTERS

Major Convention Centers

Center Name	Meeting Rooms	Exhibit Space (sq. ft.)
Amway Grand Plaza Hotel	52	155,000
Grand Center	7	118,518

Source: Trade Shows Worldwide, 1998; Meetings & Conventions, 4/15/99; Sucessful Meetings, 3/31/98

Living Environment

COST OF LIVING

Cost of Living Index

Composite Index	Groceries	Housing	Utilities	Trans-portation	Health Care	Misc. Goods/ Services
107.6	111.8	115.0	102.9	102.6	102.5	102.6

Note: U.S. = 100
Source: ACCRA, Cost of Living Index, 4th Quarter 1998

HOUSING

Median Home Prices and Housing Affordability

Area	Median Price[2] 1st Qtr. 1999 ($)	HOI[3] 1st Qtr. 1999	Afford-ability Rank[4]
MSA[1]	100,000	80.2	55
U.S.	134,000	69.6	–

Note: (1) Metropolitan Statistical Area - see Appendix A for areas included; (2) U.S. figures calculated from the sales of 524,324 new and existing homes in 181 markets; (3) Housing Opportunity Index - percent of homes sold that were within the reach of the median income household at the prevailing mortgage interest rate; (4) Rank is from 1-181 with 1 being most affordable
Source: National Association of Home Builders, Housing Opportunity Index, 1st Quarter 1999

Median Home Price Projection

It is projected that the median price of existing single-family homes in the metro area will increase by 4.4% in 1999. Nationwide, home prices are projected to increase 3.8%.
Kiplinger's Personal Finance Magazine, January 1999

Average New Home Price

Area	Price ($)
City	163,663
U.S.	141,438

Note: Figures are based on a new home with 1,800 sq. ft. of living area on an 8,000 sq. ft. lot.
Source: ACCRA, Cost of Living Index, 4th Quarter 1998

Average Apartment Rent

Area	Rent ($/mth)
City	616
U.S.	593

Note: Figures are based on an unfurnished two bedroom, 1-1/2 or 2 bath apartment, approximately 950 sq. ft. in size, excluding all utilities except water
Source: ACCRA, Cost of Living Index, 4th Quarter 1998

RESIDENTIAL UTILITIES

Average Residential Utility Costs

Area	All Electric ($/mth)	Part Electric ($/mth)	Other Energy ($/mth)	Phone ($/mth)
City	–	52.73	52.33	17.44
U.S.	101.64	55.45	43.56	19.81

Source: ACCRA, Cost of Living Index, 4th Quarter 1998

HEALTH CARE

Average Health Care Costs

Area	Hospital ($/day)	Doctor ($/visit)	Dentist ($/visit)
City	449.50	55.00	62.80
U.S.	417.46	51.94	64.89

Note: Hospital—based on a semi-private room; Doctor—based on a general practitioner's routine exam of an established patient; Dentist—based on adult teeth cleaning and periodic oral exam.
Source: ACCRA, Cost of Living Index, 4th Quarter 1998

Distribution of Office-Based Physicians

| Area | Family/Gen. Practitioners | Specialists | | |
		Medical	Surgical	Other
MSA[1]	192	389	355	346

Note: Data as of 12/31/97; (1) Metropolitan Statistical Area - see Appendix A for areas included
Source: American Medical Assn., Physician Characteristics & Distribution in the U.S., 1999

Hospitals

Grand Rapids has 4 general medical and surgical hospitals, 2 psychiatric, 1 rehabilitation, 1 other specialty. *AHA Guide to the Healthcare Field, 1998-99*

According to *U.S. News and World Report,* Grand Rapids has 2 of the best hospitals in the U.S.:
Spectrum Health-Downtown Campus, noted for orthopedics, pulmonology; **St. Mary's Health Services**, noted for orthopedics. *U.S. News Online, "America's Best Hospitals," 10th Edition, www.usnews.com*

EDUCATION

Public School District Statistics

District Name	Num. Sch.	Enroll.	Classroom Teachers	Pupils per Teacher	Minority Pupils (%)	Current Exp.[1] ($/pupil)
East Grand Rapids Public Sch	5	2,623	155	16.9	n/a	n/a
Forest Hills Public Schools	12	7,545	438	17.2	n/a	n/a
Grand Rapids Public Schools	100	26,727	1,435	18.6	n/a	n/a
Kelloggsville Public Schools	7	2,222	116	19.2	n/a	n/a
Kenowa Hills Public Schools	7	3,189	157	20.3	n/a	n/a
Kent ISD	1	n/a	74	0.0	n/a	n/a
Northview Public School Distri	6	3,334	168	19.8	n/a	n/a

Note: Data covers the 1997-1998 school year unless otherwise noted; (1) Data covers fiscal year 1996; SD = School District; ISD = Independent School District; n/a not available
Source: National Center for Education Statistics, Common Core of Data Public Education Agency Universe 1997-98; National Center for Education Statistics, Characteristics of the 100 Largest Public Elementary and Secondary School Districts in the United States: 1997-98, July 1999

Educational Quality

School District	Education Quotient[1]	Graduate Outcome[2]	Community Index[3]	Resource Index[4]
Grand Rapids City	77.0	80.0	82.0	69.0

Note: Nearly 1,000 secondary school districts were rated in terms of educational quality. The scores range from a low of 50 to a high of 150; (1) Average of the Graduate Outcome, Community and Resource indexes; (2) Based on graduation rates and college board scores (SAT/ACT); (3) Based on the surrounding community's average level of education and the area's average income level; (4) Based on teacher salaries, per-pupil expenditures and student-teacher ratios.
Source: Expansion Management, Ratings Issue, 1998

Educational Attainment by Race

| Area | High School Graduate (%) | | | | | Bachelor's Degree (%) | | | | |
	Total	White	Black	Other	Hisp.[2]	Total	White	Black	Other	Hisp.[2]
City	76.4	80.0	63.8	46.9	41.0	20.8	23.7	7.7	10.7	8.2
MSA[1]	80.2	81.6	65.9	54.1	48.0	20.2	21.0	8.4	12.4	7.7
U.S.	75.2	77.9	63.1	60.4	49.8	20.3	21.5	11.4	19.4	9.2

Note: Figures shown cover persons 25 years old and over; (1) Metropolitan Statistical Area - see Appendix A for areas included; (2) people of Hispanic origin can be of any race
Source: 1990 Census of Population and Housing, Summary Tape File 3C

School Enrollment by Type

Area	Preprimary				Elementary/High School			
	Public		Private		Public		Private	
	Enrollment	%	Enrollment	%	Enrollment	%	Enrollment	%
City	3,105	60.8	2,004	39.2	24,319	76.0	7,660	24.0
MSA[1]	12,129	66.4	6,136	33.6	103,726	81.8	23,081	18.2
U.S.	2,679,029	59.5	1,824,256	40.5	38,379,689	90.2	4,187,099	9.8

Note: Figures shown cover persons 3 years old and over;
(1) Metropolitan Statistical Area - see Appendix A for areas included
Source: 1990 Census of Population and Housing, Summary Tape File 3C

School Enrollment by Race

Area	Preprimary (%)				Elementary/High School (%)			
	White	Black	Other	Hisp.[1]	White	Black	Other	Hisp.[1]
City	73.4	20.5	6.1	5.5	62.8	29.6	7.6	7.3
MSA[2]	89.6	6.5	3.9	2.6	86.5	8.4	5.1	4.5
U.S.	80.4	12.5	7.1	7.8	74.1	15.6	10.3	12.5

Note: Figures shown cover persons 3 years old and over; (1) people of Hispanic origin can be of any
race; (2) Metropolitan Statistical Area - see Appendix A for areas included
Source: 1990 Census of Population and Housing, Summary Tape File 3C

Classroom Teacher Salaries in Public Schools

District	B.A. Degree		M.A. Degree		Maximum	
	Min. ($)	Rank[1]	Max. ($)	Rank[1]	Max. ($)	Rank[1]
Grand Rapids	28,878	24	51,371	14	52,825	38
Average	26,980	-	46,065	-	51,435	-

Note: Salaries are for 1997-1998; (1) Rank ranges from 1 to 100
Source: American Federation of Teachers, Survey & Analysis of Salary Trends, 1998

Higher Education

Two-Year Colleges		Four-Year Colleges		Medical Schools	Law Schools	Voc/ Tech
Public	Private	Public	Private			
1	0	0	7	0	0	5

Source: College Blue Book, Occupational Education, 1997; Medical School Admission Requirements,
1999-2000; Peterson's Guide to Two-Year Colleges, 1999; Peterson's Guide to Four-Year Colleges,
2000; Barron's Guide to Law Schools, 1999

MAJOR EMPLOYERS

Major Employers

Autodie International	Gordon Food Service
Diesel Technology (auto parts)	Mannesmann Dematic Rapistan Corp. (conveyors)
Pridgeon & Clay (automotive stampings)	Metropolitan Hospital
Old Kent Financial Corp.	Spectrum Health-Downtown Campus
Steelcase	Lacks Exterior Systems (plastic products)

Note: Companies listed are located in the city
Source: Dun's Business Rankings, 1999; Ward's Business Directory, 1998

PUBLIC SAFETY

Crime Rate

Area	All Crimes	Violent Crimes				Property Crimes		
		Murder	Forcible Rape	Robbery	Aggrav. Assault	Burglary	Larceny -Theft	Motor Vehicle Theft
City	7,182.4	12.8	20.9	294.9	841.5	1,440.0	3,988.4	583.8
Suburbs[1]	3,807.5	1.7	41.5	44.4	204.1	727.9	2,554.2	233.8
MSA[2]	4,459.9	3.8	37.5	92.8	327.3	865.6	2,831.4	301.4
U.S.	4,922.7	6.8	35.9	186.1	382.0	919.6	2,886.5	505.8

Note: Crime rate is the number of crimes per 100,000 pop.; (1) defined as all areas within the MSA but located outside the central city; (2) Metropolitan Statistical Area - see Appendix A for areas incl.
Source: FBI Uniform Crime Reports, 1997

RECREATION

Culture and Recreation

Museums	Symphony Orchestras	Opera Companies	Dance Companies	Professional Theatres	Zoos	Pro Sports Teams
4	2	1	0	0	1	0

Source: International Directory of the Performing Arts, 1997; Official Museum Directory, 1999; Stern's Performing Arts Directory, 1997; USA Today Four Sport Stadium Guide, 1997; Chamber of Commerce/Economic Development, 1999

Library System

The Kent District Library has 18 branches, holdings of 773,533 volumes, and a budget of $7,167,664 (1996). *American Library Directory, 1998-1999*

MEDIA

Newspapers

Name	Type	Freq.	Distribution	Circulation
The Grand Rapids Press	General	7x/wk	Area	153,061
Grand Rapids Times	Black	1x/wk	Local	6,000

Note: Includes newspapers with circulations of 1,000 or more located in the city;
Source: Burrelle's Media Directory, 1999 Edition

Television Stations

Name	Ch.	Affiliation	Type	Owner
WOOD	n/a	NBCT	Commercial	LCH Communications
WZZM	13	ABCT	Commercial	Gannett Broadcasting
WXMI	17	FBC	Commercial	Tribune Broadcasting Company
WGVU	35	PBS	Public	Grand Valley State University
WZPX	43	PAXTV	Commercial	DP Media Inc.
WGVK	52	PBS	Public	Grand Valley State University

Note: Stations included broadcast in the Grand Rapids metro area; n/a not available
Source: Burrelle's Media Directory, 1999 Edition

AM Radio Stations

Call Letters	Freq. (kHz)	Target Audience	Station Format	Music Format
WMFN	640	Men	S	n/a
WMJH	810	General	M/N	Adult Standards
WTKG	1230	General	N/S/T	n/a
WOOD	1300	General	N/S/T	n/a
WBBL	1340	Men	N/S/T	n/a
WNWZ	1410	General	M/N/S	Country
WGVU	1480	General	M/N/T	Jazz/R&B
WYGR	1530	Hispanic	M	Big Band
WFUR	1570	R/W	M/N	Christian
WJNZ	1680	Black	M/N/T	R&B/Urban Contemporary

Note: Stations included broadcast in the Grand Rapids metro area; n/a not available
Target Audience: A=Asian; B=Black; C=Christian; E=Ethnic; F=French; G=General; H=Hispanic; M=Men; N=Native American; R=Religious; S=Senior Citizen; W=Women; Y=Young Adult; Z=Children
Station Format: E=Educational; M=Music; N=News; S=Sports; T=Talk
Source: Burrelle's Media Directory, 1999 Edition

FM Radio Stations

Call Letters	Freq. (mHz)	Target Audience	Station Format	Music Format
WYCE	88.1	General	M	AOR/Jazz/R&B
WGVU	88.5	General	M	Jazz
WCSG	91.3	General	M/N/S	Christian
WBCT	93.7	General	M	Country
WKLQ	94.5	General	M/N/T	Alternative
WLHT	95.7	General	M/N/S	Adult Contemporary
WVTI	96.1	G/W	M	Adult Contemporary/Top 40
WLAV	96.9	General	M/N/T	Classic Rock
WGRD	97.9	General	M/N/S/T	Alternative/Modern Rock
WFGR	98.7	General	M/N	Country
WCUZ	101.3	General	M	Country
WFUR	102.9	R/W	M/N/S	Christian/MOR
WSNX	104.5	General	M	R&B
WOOD	105.7	General	M	Adult Contemporary
WODJ	107.3	General	M/N	Oldies

Note: Stations included broadcast in the Grand Rapids metro area
Station Format: E=Educational; M=Music; N=News; S=Sports; T=Talk
Target Audience: A=Asian; B=Black; C=Christian; E=Ethnic; F=French; G=General; H=Hispanic; M=Men; N=Native American; R=Religious; S=Senior Citizen; W=Women; Y=Young Adult; Z=Children
Music Format: AOR=Album Oriented Rock; MOR=Middle-of-the-Road
Source: Burrelle's Media Directory, 1999 Edition

CLIMATE

Average and Extreme Temperatures

Temperature	Jan	Feb	Mar	Apr	May	Jun	Jul	Aug	Sep	Oct	Nov	Dec	Yr.
Extreme High (°F)	66	67	80	88	92	102	100	100	97	87	81	67	102
Average High (°F)	30	32	42	57	69	79	83	81	73	61	46	34	57
Average Temp. (°F)	23	25	34	47	58	67	72	70	62	51	39	28	48
Average Low (°F)	15	16	25	36	46	56	60	59	51	41	31	21	38
Extreme Low (°F)	-22	-19	-8	3	22	33	41	39	28	18	-10	-18	-22

Note: Figures cover the years 1948-1990
Source: National Climatic Data Center, International Station Meteorological Climate Summary, 3/95

Average Precipitation/Snowfall/Humidity

Precip./Humidity	Jan	Feb	Mar	Apr	May	Jun	Jul	Aug	Sep	Oct	Nov	Dec	Yr.
Avg. Precip. (in.)	1.9	1.6	2.6	3.5	3.0	3.5	3.2	3.2	3.7	2.7	3.1	2.7	34.7
Avg. Snowfall (in.)	21	12	11	3	Tr	0	0	0	Tr	1	8	18	73
Avg. Rel. Hum. 7am (%)	81	80	80	79	79	81	84	88	89	85	83	83	83
Avg. Rel. Hum. 4pm (%)	71	66	61	54	50	52	52	55	58	60	68	74	60

Note: Figures cover the years 1948-1990; Tr = Trace amounts (<0.05 in. of rain; <0.5 in. of snow)
Source: National Climatic Data Center, International Station Meteorological Climate Summary, 3/95

Weather Conditions

Temperature			Daytime Sky			Precipitation		
5°F & below	32°F & below	90°F & above	Clear	Partly cloudy	Cloudy	0.01 inch or more precip.	0.1 inch or more snow/ice	Thunder-storms
15	146	11	67	119	179	142	57	34

Note: Figures are average number of days per year and covers the years 1948-1990
Source: National Climatic Data Center, International Station Meteorological Climate Summary, 3/95

AIR & WATER QUALITY

Maximum Pollutant Concentrations

	Particulate Matter (ug/m^3)	Carbon Monoxide (ppm)	Sulfur Dioxide (ppm)	Nitrogen Dioxide (ppm)	Ozone (ppm)	Lead (ug/m^3)
MSA[1] Level	60	2	0.008	n/a	0.12	0.01
NAAQS[2]	150	9	0.140	0.053	0.12	1.50
Met NAAQS?	Yes	Yes	Yes	n/a	Yes	Yes

Note: (1) Metropolitan Statistical Area - see Appendix A for areas included; (2) National Ambient Air Quality Standards; ppm = parts per million; ug/m^3 = micrograms per cubic meter; n/a not available
Source: EPA, National Air Quality and Emissions Trends Report, 1997

Pollutant Standards Index

In the Grand Rapids MSA (see Appendix A for areas included), the Pollutant Standards Index (PSI) exceeded 100 on 10 days in 1997. A PSI value greater than 100 indicates that air quality would be in the unhealthful range on that day. *EPA, National Air Quality and Emissions Trends Report, 1997*

Drinking Water

Water System Name	Pop. Served	Primary Water Source Type	Number of Violations in 1998	Type of Violation/ Contaminants
Grand Rapids	197,649	Surface	None	None

Note: Data as of July 10, 1999
Source: EPA, Office of Ground Water and Drinking Water, Safe Drinking Water Information System

Grand Rapids tap water is alkaline, hard and fluoridated.
Editor & Publisher Market Guide, 1999

Indianapolis, Indiana

Background

Indianapolis sits within the boundaries of the Northern manufacturing belt and the Midwestern corn belt, and its economy reflects both influences. On one side lies Indianapolis' industrial sector: transportation, airplane and truck parts, paper and rubber products, and computer software. Approximately 1,400 firms employs one-fourth of the total Indianapolis workforce. On the other side lies agriculture. Indianapolis is a leading grain market, as well as the largest meat processing center outside of Chicago.

All this economic activity, however, led to pollution and other problems of urban decay. In the 1960s, the city was rated one of the dirtiest cities in America. During the 1970s, Unigov, a city and county agency, and the Indiana Redevelopment Commission, sought to actively combat urban blight. Today, Indianapolis can boast of one of the lowest crime rates for a major U.S. city, usually indicative of equitable living standards and wages.

Since 1995 there have been several recent and major business expansions in Indianapolis. As part of its downtown revitalization, Circle Centre, a $319 million retail and entertainment complex opened in September 1995, and United Airlines is investing nearly $1 billion for a 7,500-employee maintenance center. Federal Express is expanding its sorting capabilities at the Indianapolis hub, spending $250 million and creating 1,000 jobs. Indianapolis is also a national leader in saving costs through the privatization of services previously provided by the public sector, namely the Indianapolis International Airport and the city's wastewater treatment plants. *Site Selection, April/May 1997*

In addition to trying to improve its living conditions, the city promotes its cultural, recreational, and educational scene. Indianapolis possesses one of the finest children's museums in the United States. The city's 85 parks offer many outdoor activities, and the Indianapolis 500 draws thousands of car racing fans. And the city's university quarter, housing divisions of Indiana and Purdue Universities, make for a lively learning center.

Indianapolis has a temperate climate, with very warm summers and no dry season. Very cold winter weather may be produced by the invasion of continental polar air from northern latitudes. In the summer, tropical air from the Gulf of Mexico brings warm temperatures and moderate humidity.

General Rankings and Evaluative Comments

- Indianapolis was ranked #8 out of 11 large, midwestern metropolitan areas in *Money's* 1998 survey of "The Best Places to Live in America." The survey was conducted by first contacting 512 representative households nationwide and asking them to rank 37 quality-of-life factors on a scale of 1 to 10. Next, a demographic profile was compiled on the 300 largest metropolitan statistical areas in the U.S. The numbers were crunched together to arrive at an overall ranking (things Americans consider most important, like clean air and water, low crime and good schools, received extra weight). Unlike previous years, the 1998 rankings were broken down by region (northeast, midwest, south, west) and population size (100,000 to 249,999; 250,000 to 999,999; 1 million plus). The city had a nationwide ranking of #141 out of 300 in 1997 and #72 out of 300 in 1996. *Money, July 1998; Money, July 1997; Money, September 1996*

- *Ladies Home Journal* ranked America's 200 largest cities based on the qualities women care about most. Indianapolis ranked #139 out of 200. Criteria: low crime rate, well-paying jobs, quality health and child care, good public schools, the presence of women in government, size of the gender wage gap, number of sexual-harassment and discrimination complaints filed, unemployment and divorce rates, commute times, population density, number of houses of worship, parks and cultural offerings, number of women's health specialists, how well a community's women cared for themselves, complexion kindness index based on UV radiation levels, odds of finding affordable fashions, rental rates for romance movies, champagne sales and other matters of the heart. *Ladies Home Journal, November 1998*

- Zero Population Growth ranked 229 cities in terms of children's health, safety, and economic well-being. Indianapolis was ranked #50 out of 112 independent cities (cities with populations greater than 100,000 which were neither Major Cities nor Suburbs/Outer Cities) and was given a grade of C. Criteria: total population, percent of population under 18 years of age, household language, percent population change, percent of births to teens, infant mortality rate, percent of low birth weights, dropout rate, enrollment in preprimary school, violent and property crime rates, unemployment rate, percent of children in poverty, percent of owner occupied units, number of bad air days, percent of public transportation commuters, and average travel time to work. *Zero Population Growth, Children's Environmental Index, Fall 1999*

- Indianapolis was ranked #23 out of 59 metro areas in *The Regional Economist's* "Rational Livability Ranking of 59 Large Metro Areas." The rankings were based on the metro area's total population change over the period 1990-97 divided by the number of people moving in from elsewhere in the United States (net domestic in-migration). *St. Louis Federal Reserve Bank of St. Louis, The Regional Economist, April 1999*

- Indianapolis was selected by *Yahoo! Internet Life* as one of "America's Most Wired Cities & Towns." The city ranked #32 out of 50. Criteria: home and work net use, domain density, hosts per capita, directory density and content quality. *Yahoo! Internet Life, March 1999*

- Cognetics studied 273 metro areas in the United States, ranking them by entrepreneurial activity. Indianapolis was ranked #5 out of the 50 largest metro areas. Criteria: Significant Starts (firms started in the last 10 years that still employ at least 5 people) and Young Growers (percent of firms 10 years old or less that grew significantly during the last 4 years). *Cognetics, "Entrepreneurial Hot Spots: The Best Places in America to Start and Grow a Company," 1998*

- Indianapolis was included among *Entrepreneur* magazine's listing of the "20 Best Cities for Small Business." It was ranked #11 among large metro areas and #1 among central metro areas. Criteria: entrepreneurial activity, small-business growth, economic growth, and risk of failure. *Entrepreneur, October 1999*

- Indianapolis was selected as one of the "Best American Cities to Start a Business" by *Point of View* magazine. Criteria: coolness, quality-of-life, and business concerns. The city was ranked #43 out of 75. *Point of View, November 1998*

■ Reliastar Financial Corp. ranked the 125 largest metropolitan areas according to the general financial security of residents. Indianapolis was ranked #14 (tie) out of 125 with a score of 9.8. The score indicates the percentage a metropolitan area is above or below the metropolitan norm. A metro area with a score of 10.6 is 10.6% above the metro average. Criteria: Earnings and Wealth Potential (household income, education, net assets, cost of living); Safety Net (health insurance, retirement savings, life insurance, income support programs); Personal Threats (unemployment rate, low-income households, crime rate); Community Economic Vitality (cost of community services, job quality, job creation, housing costs).
Reliastar Financial Corp., "The Best Cities to Earn and Save Money," 1999 Edition

Business Environment

STATE ECONOMY

State Economic Profile

"Indiana is lagging the nation in both job and Gross State Product (GSP) growth. While US job growth in 1998 was 2.0%, IN's was only 0.4%. Indiana's primary obstacle to growth is its lack of workers. The state unemployment rate is below the national, and its population growth rate is barely above zero.

IN's manufacturing base is much stronger than its neighbors, actually adding manufacturing jobs in 1998. The recent surge in automobile sales has helped boost employment in IN's auto sector, with some gains projected in 1999. Even if auto sales continue at the current pace, which is unlikely, Indiana auto plants would have a hard time finding workers to fill those jobs.

Demographic forces have restrained IN's housing and construction markets. Construction employment was down 2% in 1998, even though residential permits were up 15%. Home sales have been at the highest level in years, although new construction and slow population growth have kept price appreciation below the national.

Much of Indiana's economic strength has been in Indianapolis. Job growth in Indianapolis was 2.7% in 1998, almost 8 times the state average. Construction employment was up 7% in Indianapolis, while down for the state as a whole. Indianapolis' housing market has also witnessed price appreciation and new construction above the rest of the state.

While low foreign demand for manufacturing goods has hit IN as hard as other states in the region, its tight labor markets and a surge in auto sales have minimized job losses. These same tight labor markets, however, constrain IN to a moderate to slow growth path." *National Association of Realtors, Economic Profiles: The Fifty States and the District of Columbia, http://nar.realtor.com/databank/profiles.htm*

IMPORTS/EXPORTS

Total Export Sales

Area	1994 ($000)	1995 ($000)	1996 ($000)	1997 ($000)	% Chg. 1994-97	% Chg. 1996-97
MSA[1]	3,003,834	3,555,925	4,012,775	4,301,806	43.2	7.2
U.S.	512,415,609	583,030,524	622,827,063	687,597,999	34.2	10.4

Note: (1) Metropolitan Statistical Area - see Appendix A for areas included
Source: U.S. Department of Commerce, International Trade Association, Metropolitan Area Exports: An Export Performance Report on Over 250 U.S. Cities, November 10, 1998

CITY FINANCES

City Government Finances

Component	FY94 ($000)	FY94 (per capita $)
Revenue	1,068,586	1,429.97
Expenditure	1,316,567	1,761.81
Debt Outstanding	1,559,942	2,087.49
Cash & Securities	972,527	1,301.42

Source: U.S. Bureau of the Census, City Government Finances: 1993-94

City Government Revenue by Source

Source	FY94 ($000)	FY94 (per capita $)	FY94 (%)
From Federal Government	51,854	69.39	4.9
From State Governments	250,916	335.77	23.5
From Local Governments	1,468	1.96	0.1
Property Taxes	413,336	553.12	38.7
General Sales Taxes	0	0.00	0.0
Selective Sales Taxes	22,423	30.01	2.1
Income Taxes	53,875	72.09	5.0
Current Charges	191,303	256.00	17.9
Utility/Liquor Store	6,652	8.90	0.6
Employee Retirement[1]	26,068	34.88	2.4
Other	50,691	67.83	4.7

Note: (1) Excludes "city contributions," classified as "nonrevenue," intragovernmental transfers.
Source: U.S. Bureau of the Census, City Government Finances: 1993-94

City Government Expenditures by Function

Function	FY94 ($000)	FY94 (per capita $)	FY94 (%)
Educational Services	738	0.99	0.1
Employee Retirement[1]	35,459	47.45	2.7
Environment/Housing	424,340	567.85	32.2
Government Administration	95,941	128.39	7.3
Interest on General Debt	58,963	78.90	4.5
Public Safety	166,244	222.47	12.6
Social Services	286,385	383.24	21.8
Transportation	128,907	172.50	9.8
Utility/Liquor Store	24,022	32.15	1.8
Other	95,568	127.89	7.3

Note: (1) Payments to beneficiaries including withdrawal of contributions.
Source: U.S. Bureau of the Census, City Government Finances: 1993-94

Municipal Bond Ratings

Area	Moody's	S & P
Indianapolis	Aaa	n/a

Note: n/a not available; n/r not rated
Source: Moody's Bond Record, 6/99

POPULATION

Population Growth

Area	1980	1990	% Chg. 1980-90	July 1998 Estimate	% Chg. 1990-98
City	700,807	731,321	4.4	741,304	1.4
MSA[1]	1,166,575	1,249,822	7.1	1,529,565	22.4
U.S.	226,545,805	248,765,170	9.8	270,299,000	8.7

Note: (1) Metropolitan Statistical Area - see Appendix A for areas included;
July 1998 MSA population estimate was calculated by the editors
Source: 1980/1990 Census of Housing and Population, Summary Tape File 3C;
Census Bureau Population Estimates 1998

Population Characteristics

Race	City 1980 Population	%	City 1990 Population	%	% Chg. 1980-90	MSA[1] 1990 Population	%
White	540,584	77.1	555,216	75.9	2.7	1,061,822	85.0
Black	152,590	21.8	164,861	22.5	8.0	171,545	13.7
Amer Indian/Esk/Aleut	1,356	0.2	1,758	0.2	29.6	2,695	0.2
Asian/Pacific Islander	4,539	0.6	6,656	0.9	46.6	10,001	0.8
Other	1,738	0.2	2,830	0.4	62.8	3,759	0.3
Hispanic Origin[2]	6,143	0.9	7,463	1.0	21.5	11,114	0.9

Note: (1) Metropolitan Statistical Area - see Appendix A for areas included;
(2) people of Hispanic origin can be of any race
Source: 1980/1990 Census of Housing and Population, Summary Tape File 3C

Ancestry

Area	German	Irish	English	Italian	U.S.	French	Polish	Dutch
City	28.7	15.9	12.8	2.3	6.7	3.1	1.4	2.4
MSA[1]	32.5	17.5	15.2	2.3	7.5	3.4	1.5	3.0
U.S.	23.3	15.6	13.1	5.9	5.3	4.2	3.8	2.5

Note: Figures are percentages and include persons that reported multiple ancestry (eg. if a person
reported being Irish and Italian, they were included in both columns); (1) Metropolitan Statistical Area -
see Appendix A for areas included
Source: 1990 Census of Population and Housing, Summary Tape File 3C

Age

Area	Median Age (Years)	Age Distribution (%) Under 5	Under 18	18-24	25-44	45-64	65+	80+
City	31.6	8.0	25.6	10.4	34.9	17.6	11.4	2.6
MSA[1]	32.3	7.7	26.4	9.8	34.4	18.4	11.1	2.5
U.S.	32.9	7.3	25.6	10.5	32.6	18.7	12.5	2.8

Note: (1) Metropolitan Statistical Area - see Appendix A for areas included
Source: 1990 Census of Population and Housing, Summary Tape File 3C

Male/Female Ratio

Area	Number of males per 100 females (all ages)	Number of males per 100 females (18 years old+)
City	90.4	86.1
MSA[1]	92.4	88.4
U.S.	95.0	91.9

Note: (1) Metropolitan Statistical Area - see Appendix A for areas included
Source: 1990 Census of Population, General Population Characteristics

INCOME

Per Capita/Median/Average Income

Area	Per Capita ($)	Median Household ($)	Average Household ($)
City	14,478	29,006	35,946
MSA[1]	15,159	31,655	39,103
U.S.	14,420	30,056	38,453

Note: All figures are for 1989; (1) Metropolitan Statistical Area - see Appendix A for areas included
Source: 1990 Census of Population and Housing, Summary Tape File 3C

Household Income Distribution by Race

Income ($)	City (%)					U.S. (%)				
	Total	White	Black	Other	Hisp.[1]	Total	White	Black	Other	Hisp.[1]
Less than 5,000	5.9	3.8	13.7	8.1	8.3	6.2	4.8	15.2	8.6	8.8
5,000 - 9,999	8.6	7.3	13.9	7.3	7.9	9.3	8.6	14.2	9.9	11.1
10,000 - 14,999	9.0	8.2	12.0	9.9	13.4	8.8	8.5	11.0	9.8	11.0
15,000 - 24,999	19.1	18.9	20.1	17.6	21.3	17.5	17.3	18.9	18.5	20.5
25,000 - 34,999	17.0	17.7	14.3	15.2	17.8	15.8	16.1	14.2	15.4	16.4
35,000 - 49,999	18.8	20.1	13.9	17.6	19.5	17.9	18.6	13.3	16.1	16.0
50,000 - 74,999	14.4	15.8	8.8	16.5	6.8	15.0	15.8	9.3	13.4	11.1
75,000 - 99,999	4.0	4.5	2.5	3.2	2.5	5.1	5.5	2.6	4.7	3.1
100,000+	3.2	3.7	0.9	4.7	2.6	4.4	4.8	1.3	3.7	1.9

Note: All figures are for 1989; (1) people of Hispanic origin can be of any race
Source: 1990 Census of Population and Housing, Summary Tape File 3C

Effective Buying Income

Area	Per Capita ($)	Median Household ($)	Average Household ($)
City	17,522	35,279	43,100
MSA[1]	19,042	38,764	48,792
U.S.	16,803	34,536	45,243

Note: Data as of 1/1/99; (1) Metropolitan Statistical Area - see Appendix A for areas included
Source: Standard Rate & Data Service, Newspaper Advertising Source, 9/99

Effective Household Buying Income Distribution

Area	% of Households Earning						
	$10,000 -$19,999	$20,000 -$34,999	$35,000 -$49,999	$50,000 -$74,999	$75,000 -$99,000	$100,000 -$124,999	$125,000 and up
City	15.2	23.7	18.9	19.7	7.3	2.2	2.3
MSA[1]	14.0	22.2	18.8	21.9	8.7	2.7	2.7
U.S.	16.0	22.6	18.2	18.9	7.2	2.4	2.7

Note: Data as of 1/1/99; (1) Metropolitan Statistical Area - see Appendix A for areas included
Source: Standard Rate & Data Service, Newspaper Advertising Source, 9/99

Poverty Rates by Race and Age

Area	Total (%)	By Race (%)				By Age (%)		
		White	Black	Other	Hisp.[2]	Under 5 years old	Under 18 years old	65 years and over
City	12.5	8.4	26.4	13.8	13.0	20.1	18.9	11.7
MSA[1]	9.6	6.9	26.2	12.1	11.5	15.1	13.7	10.3
U.S.	13.1	9.8	29.5	23.1	25.3	20.1	18.3	12.8

Note: Figures show the percent of people living below the poverty line in 1989. The average poverty threshold was $12,674 for a family of four in 1989; (1) Metropolitan Statistical Area - see Appendix A for areas included; (2) people of Hispanic origin can be of any race
Source: 1990 Census of Population and Housing, Summary Tape File 3C

EMPLOYMENT

Labor Force and Employment

Area	Civilian Labor Force			Workers Employed		
	Jun. 1998	Jun. 1999	% Chg.	Jun. 1998	Jun. 1999	% Chg.
City	419,771	424,291	1.1	408,532	412,763	1.0
MSA[1]	842,064	851,783	1.2	823,116	831,641	1.0
U.S.	138,798,000	140,666,000	1.3	132,265,000	134,395,000	1.6

Note: Data is not seasonally adjusted and covers workers 16 years of age and older;
(1) Metropolitan Statistical Area - see Appendix A for areas included
Source: Bureau of Labor Statistics, http://stats.bls.gov

Unemployment Rate

Area	1998						1999					
	Jul.	Aug.	Sep.	Oct.	Nov.	Dec.	Jan.	Feb.	Mar.	Apr.	May.	Jun.
City	2.8	2.8	2.8	2.6	2.8	2.8	3.0	2.8	2.6	2.4	2.6	2.7
MSA[1]	2.9	2.3	2.3	2.2	2.3	2.4	2.7	2.6	2.3	2.0	2.3	2.4
U.S.	4.7	4.5	4.4	4.2	4.1	4.0	4.8	4.7	4.4	4.1	4.0	4.5

Note: Data is not seasonally adjusted and covers workers 16 years of age and older; all figures are percentages; (1) Metropolitan Statistical Area - see Appendix A for areas included
Source: Bureau of Labor Statistics, http://stats.bls.gov

Employment by Industry

Sector	MSA[1]		U.S.
	Number of Employees	Percent of Total	Percent of Total
Services	238,400	27.4	30.4
Retail Trade	168,600	19.4	17.7
Government	105,800	12.1	15.6
Manufacturing	130,800	15.0	14.3
Finance/Insurance/Real Estate	65,900	7.6	5.9
Wholesale Trade	56,200	6.5	5.4
Transportation/Public Utilities	54,500	6.3	5.3
Construction	50,300	5.8	5.0
Mining	800	0.1	0.4

Note: Figures cover non-farm employment as of 6/99 and are not seasonally adjusted; (1) Metropolitan Statistical Area - see Appendix A for areas included
Source: Bureau of Labor Statistics, http://stats.bls.gov

Employment by Occupation

Occupation Category	City (%)	MSA[1] (%)	U.S. (%)
White Collar	62.1	60.9	58.1
Executive/Admin./Management	12.7	12.9	12.3
Professional	14.4	13.6	14.1
Technical & Related Support	3.9	3.8	3.7
Sales	12.5	12.8	11.8
Administrative Support/Clerical	18.6	17.8	16.3
Blue Collar	23.6	25.4	26.2
Precision Production/Craft/Repair	9.8	11.2	11.3
Machine Operators/Assem./Insp.	5.9	6.3	6.8
Transportation/Material Movers	3.9	4.0	4.1
Cleaners/Helpers/Laborers	4.0	3.9	3.9
Services	13.6	12.5	13.2
Farming/Forestry/Fishing	0.7	1.3	2.5

Note: Figures cover employed persons 16 years old and over; (1) Metropolitan Statistical Area - see Appendix A for areas included
Source: 1990 Census of Population and Housing, Summary Tape File 3C

Occupational Employment Projections: 1994 - 2005

Projections not available at time of publication.

TAXES

Major State and Local Tax Rates

State Corp. Income (%)	State Personal Income (%)	Residential Property (effective rate per $100)	Sales & Use		State Gasoline (cents/ gallon)	State Cigarette (cents/ pack)
			State (%)	Local (%)		
7.9[a]	3.4	1.53	5.0	None	15.0[b]	15.5

Note: Personal/corporate income, sales, gasoline and cigarette tax rates as of January 1999. Property tax rates as of 1997; (a) Consists of 3.4% on income from sources within the state plus a 4.5% supplemental income tax; (b) Carriers pay an additional surcharge of 11 cents Source: Federation of Tax Administrators, www.taxadmin.org; Washington D.C. Department of Finance and Revenue, Tax Rates and Tax Burdens in the District of Columbia: A Nationwide Comparison, July 1998; Chamber of Commerce, 1999

Total Taxes Per Capita and as a Percent of Income

Area	Per Capita Income ($)	Per Capita Taxes ($)			Percent of Income (%)		
		Total	Federal	State/ Local	Total	Federal	State/ Local
Indiana	25,444	8,864	6,055	2,809	34.8	23.8	11.0
U.S.	27,876	9,881	6,690	3,191	35.4	24.0	11.4

Note: Figures are for 1998 Source: Tax Foundation, www.taxfoundation.org

Estimated Tax Burden

Area	State Income	Local Income	Property	Sales	Total
Indianapolis	2,380	490	3,500	488	6,858

Note: The numbers are estimates of taxes paid by a married couple with two children and annual earnings of $75,000. Sales tax estimates assume they spend average amounts on food, clothing, household goods and gasoline. Property tax estimates assume they live in a $250,000 home. Source: Kiplinger's Personal Finance Magazine, October 1998

COMMERCIAL REAL ESTATE

Office Market

Class/ Location	Total Space (sq. ft.)	Vacant Space (sq. ft.)	Vac. Rate (%)	Under Constr. (sq. ft.)	Net Absorp. (sq. ft.)	Rental Rates ($/sq.ft./yr.)
Class A						
CBD	6,624,529	683,742	10.3	0	138,292	16.00-25.00
Outside CBD	5,169,774	479,713	9.3	790,625	303,097	14.75-22.00
Class B						
CBD	1,854,765	364,014	19.6	0	76,230	11.50-17.50
Outside CBD	6,110,323	790,182	12.9	0	82,505	12.00-17.50

Note: Data as of 10/98 and covers Indianapolis; CBD = Central Business District; n/a not available; Source: Society of Industrial and Office Realtors, 1999 Comparative Statistics of Industrial and Office Real Estate Markets

"Tight labor markets and the slowdown of exports to Asia will crimp Indianapolis' expansion. Strong absorption is expected to continue as a result of the pro-business approach of the local government and the growing desirability of downtown. With quality space in high demand, development of Class A space will continue, including speculative suburban office projects. The demand for large blocks of space is also expected to increase development over the next year. The mayor and the Indianapolis and Central Indiana Technology Partnership are expected to propel the local economy and encourage high-technology businesses to move to the area. Moderate increases are expected in vacancy and rental rates. Sales prices are expected to increase between one and five percent." *Society of Industrial and Office Realtors, 1999 Comparative Statistics of Industrial and Office Real Estate Markets*

Industrial Market

Location	Total Space (sq. ft.)	Vacant Space (sq. ft.)	Vac. Rate (%)	Under Constr. (sq. ft.)	Net Absorp. (sq. ft.)	Gross Lease ($/sq.ft./yr.)
Central City	184,500,000	13,763,700	7.5	2,658,580	6,548,805	1.75-6.00
Suburban	n/a	n/a	n/a	n/a	n/a	2.75-7.00

Note: Data as of 10/98 and covers Indianapolis; n/a not available
Source: Society of Industrial and Office Realtors, 1999 Comparative Statistics of Industrial and Office Real Estate Markets

"Significant additional speculative construction will occur in the marketplace over 1999 and will be concentrated throughout the tax abatement areas. It is estimated that construction will include more than 2.5 million sq. ft. of bulk space and 350,000 sq. ft. of mid-size distribution space. The primary buyers will continue to be REITs and merchant builders. Most new businesses moving into the market will be distribution related, partly because of a shift away from manufacturing in the Indianapolis market. The area's primary concern in 1999 will be the availability of labor for distribution-related employment. Our local SIOR reporter predicts demand growth and healthy absorption for 1999. Sales prices are expected to rise for all categories of industrial space with up to a 10 percent increase in High-Tech/R&D facilities." *Society of Industrial and Office Realtors, 1999 Comparative Statistics of Industrial and Office Real Estate Markets*

Retail Market

Shopping Center Inventory (sq. ft.)	Shopping Center Construction (sq. ft.)	Construction as a Percent of Inventory (%)	Torto Wheaton Rent Index[1] ($/sq. ft.)
31,989,000	1,109,000	3.5	9.69

Note: Data as of 1997 and covers the Metropolitan Statistical Area - see Appendix A for areas included; (1) Index is based on a model that predicts what the average rent should be for leases with certain characteristics, in certain locations during certain years.
Source: National Association of Realtors, 1997-1998 Market Conditions Report

"The Indianapolis area has experienced healthy economic growth throughout the 90s. Its population has grown faster than the national average, while real income growth has consistently been strong. The retail rent index has risen steadily over the past four years, including 1.9% in 1997. Indianapolis' success has many national retailers considering it a favorable place for expansion. However, like elsewhere in the nation, many small, independent retailers have fallen prey to the large, national chains. Indianapolis' current labor shortage should improve over the next few years. Retail rents in the area are expected to remain relatively steady." *National Association of Realtors, 1997-1998 Market Conditions Report*

COMMERCIAL UTILITIES

Typical Monthly Electric Bills

Area	Commercial Service ($/month)		Industrial Service ($/month)	
	12 kW demand 1,500 kWh	100 kW demand 30,000 kWh	1,000 kW demand 400,000 kWh	20,000 kW demand 10,000,000 kWh
City	120	1,933	19,483	332,263
U.S.	150	2,174	23,995	508,569

Note: Based on rates in effect January 1, 1999
Source: Edison Electric Institute, Typical Residential, Commercial and Industrial Bills, Winter 1999

TRANSPORTATION

Transportation Statistics

Average minutes to work	20.8
Interstate highways	I-65; I-69; I-70; I-74
Bus lines	
In-city	Indianapolis Public Transportation (METRO), 191 vehicles
Inter-city	1
Passenger air service	
Airport	Indianapolis International
Airlines	17
Aircraft departures	62,140 (1996)
Enplaned passengers	3,326,430 (1996)
Rail service	Amtrak
Motor freight carriers	n/a
Major waterways/ports	White River

Source: Editor & Publisher Market Guide, 1999; FAA Airport Activity Statistics, 1997; Amtrak National Time Table, Northeast Timetable, Spring/Summer 1999; 1990 Census of Population and Housing, STF 3C; Chamber of Commerce/Economic Development 1999; Jane's Urban Transport Systems 1999-2000

Means of Transportation to Work

Area	Car/Truck/Van		Public Transportation			Bicycle	Walked	Other Means	Worked at Home
	Drove Alone	Car-pooled	Bus	Subway	Railroad				
City	78.0	13.4	3.1	0.0	0.0	0.2	2.4	0.8	2.0
MSA[1]	79.7	12.9	1.9	0.0	0.0	0.1	2.2	0.7	2.4
U.S.	73.2	13.4	3.0	1.5	0.5	0.4	3.9	1.2	3.0

Note: Figures shown are percentages and only include workers 16 years old and over;
(1) Metropolitan Statistical Area - see Appendix A for areas included
Source: 1990 Census of Population and Housing, Summary Tape File 3C

BUSINESSES

Major Business Headquarters

Company Name	1999 Rankings	
	Fortune 500	Forbes 500
Anthem Insurance	278	-
Bindley Western	217	-
Eli Lilly	160	-
Huber Hunt & Nichols	-	191
LDI	-	242
National Wine & Spirits	-	445

Note: Companies listed are located in the city; dashes indicate no ranking
Fortune 500: Companies that produce a 10-K are ranked 1 to 500 based on 1998 revenue
Forbes 500: Private companies are ranked 1 to 500 based on 1997 revenue
Source: Forbes, November 30, 1998; Fortune, April 26, 1999

Best Companies to Work For

Guidant (products for treating heart disease), headquartered in Indianapolis, is among the "100 Best Companies to Work for in America." Criteria: trust in management, pride in work/company, camaraderie, company responses to the Hewitt People Practices Inventory, and employee responses to their Great Place to Work survey. The companies also had to be at least 10 years old and have a minimum of 500 employees. *Fortune, January 11, 1999*

Eli Lilly, headquartered in Indianapolis, is among the "100 Best Companies for Working Mothers." Criteria: fair wages, opportunities for women to advance, support for child care, flexible work schedules, family-friendly benefits, and work/life supports. *Working Mother, October 1998*

Bindley Western Industries, Inc. (wholesale), headquartered in Indianapolis, is among the "100 Best Places to Work in IS." Criteria: compensation, turnover and training. *Computerworld, May 25, 1998*

Fast-Growing Businesses

According to *Fortune*, Indianapolis is home to one of America's 100 fastest-growing companies: Analytical Surveys. Companies were ranked based on earnings-per-share growth, revenue growth and total return over the previous three years. Criteria for inclusion: public companies with sales of least $50 million. Companies that lost money in the most recent quarter, or ended in the red for the past four quarters as a whole, were not eligible. Limited partnerships and REITs were also not considered. *Fortune, "America's Fastest-Growing Companies," 1999*

Women-Owned Firms: Number, Employment and Sales

Area	Number of Firms	Employ-ment	Sales ($000)	Rank[2]
MSA[1]	55,200	216,600	25,908,000	29

Note: (1) Metropolitan Statistical Area - see Appendix A for areas included;
(2) Calculated on an averaging of the number of businesses, employment and sales
Source: The National Foundation for Women Business Owners, 1999 Facts on Women-Owned Businesses: Trends in the Top 50 Metropolitan Areas

Women-Owned Firms: Growth

Area	% change from 1992 to 1999			Rank[2]
	Number of Firms	Employ-ment	Sales	
MSA[1]	43.8	92.7	123.2	37

Note: (1) Metropolitan Statistical Area - see Appendix A for areas included; (2) Calculated on an averaging of the percent growth of number of businesses, employment and sales
Source: The National Foundation for Women Business Owners, 1999 Facts on Women-Owned Businesses: Trends in the Top 50 Metropolitan Areas

Minority Business Opportunity

Indianapolis is home to one company which is on the Black Enterprise Industrial/Service 100 list (largest based on gross sales): Mays Chemical Co. Inc. (industrial chemical distributor) . Criteria: operational in previous calendar year, at least 51% black-owned and manufactures/owns the product it sells or provides industrial or consumer services. Brokerages, real estate firms and firms that provide professional services are not eligible. *Black Enterprise, www.blackenterprise.com*

Three of the 500 largest Hispanic-owned companies in the U.S. are located in Indianapolis. *Hispanic Business, June 1999*

Indianapolis is home to two companies which are on the Hispanic Business Fastest-Growing 100 list (greatest sales growth from 1994 to 1998): Charlier Clark & Linard PC (engineering, architectural, & surveying svcs.); Communications Products Inc. (telecom. svcs.). *Hispanic Business, July/August 1999*

Small Business Opportunity

According to *Forbes*, Indianapolis is home to four of America's 200 best small companies: Analytical Surveys, Consolidated Products, Crossman Communities and ITT Educational Services. Criteria: companies included must be publicly traded since November 1997 with a stock price of at least $5 per share and an average daily float of 1,000 shares. The company's latest 12-month sales must be between $5 and $350 million, return on equity (ROE) must be a minimum of 12% for both the past 5 years and the most recent four quarters, and five-year sales and EPS growth must average at least 10%. Companies with declining sales or earnings during the past year were dropped as well as businesses with debt/equity ratios over 1.25. Companies with negative operating cash flow in each of the past two years were also excluded. *Forbes, November 2, 1998*

HOTELS & MOTELS

Hotels/Motels

Area	Hotels/ Motels	Rooms	Luxury-Level Hotels/Motels		Average Minimum Rates ($)		
			♦♦♦♦	♦♦♦♦♦	♦♦	♦♦♦	♦♦♦♦
City	80	12,119	1	0	67	123	195
Airport	10	1,893	0	0	n/a	n/a	n/a
Suburbs	21	1,517	0	0	n/a	n/a	n/a
Total	111	15,529	1	0	n/a	n/a	n/a

Note: n/a not available; classifications range from one diamond (budget properties with basic amenities) to five diamond (luxury properties with the finest service, rooms and facilities).
Source: OAG, Business Travel Planner, Winter 1998-99

CONVENTION CENTERS

Major Convention Centers

Center Name	Meeting Rooms	Exhibit Space (sq. ft.)
Indiana Convention Center and RCA Dome	55	300,000
Indiana State Fairgrounds Event Center	15	1,000,000
University Place Conference Center and Hotel	30	10,504

Source: Trade Shows Worldwide, 1998; Meetings & Conventions, 4/15/99; Sucessful Meetings, 3/31/98

Living Environment

COST OF LIVING

Cost of Living Index

Composite Index	Groceries	Housing	Utilities	Trans-portation	Health Care	Misc. Goods/Services
96.0	100.7	88.8	98.7	93.8	95.4	100.0

Note: U.S. = 100
Source: ACCRA, Cost of Living Index, 1st Quarter 1999

HOUSING

Median Home Prices and Housing Affordability

Area	Median Price[2] 1st Qtr. 1999 ($)	HOI[3] 1st Qtr. 1999	Afford-ability Rank[4]
MSA[1]	132,000	78.0	72
U.S.	134,000	69.6	–

Note: (1) Metropolitan Statistical Area - see Appendix A for areas included; (2) U.S. figures calculated from the sales of 524,324 new and existing homes in 181 markets; (3) Housing Opportunity Index - percent of homes sold that were within the reach of the median income household at the prevailing mortgage interest rate; (4) Rank is from 1-181 with 1 being most affordable
Source: National Association of Home Builders, Housing Opportunity Index, 1st Quarter 1999

Median Home Price Projection

It is projected that the median price of existing single-family homes in the metro area will increase by 2.7% in 1999. Nationwide, home prices are projected to increase 3.8%.
Kiplinger's Personal Finance Magazine, January 1999

Average New Home Price

Area	Price ($)
City	125,307
U.S.	142,735

Note: Figures are based on a new home with 1,800 sq. ft. of living area on an 8,000 sq. ft. lot.
Source: ACCRA, Cost of Living Index, 1st Quarter 1999

Average Apartment Rent

Area	Rent ($/mth)
City	617
U.S.	601

Note: Figures are based on an unfurnished two bedroom, 1-1/2 or 2 bath apartment, approximately 950 sq. ft. in size, excluding all utilities except water
Source: ACCRA, Cost of Living Index, 1st Quarter 1999

RESIDENTIAL UTILITIES

Average Residential Utility Costs

Area	All Electric ($/mth)	Part Electric ($/mth)	Other Energy ($/mth)	Phone ($/mth)
City	–	50.52	48.63	18.00
U.S.	100.02	55.73	43.33	19.71

Source: ACCRA, Cost of Living Index, 1st Quarter 1999

HEALTH CARE

Average Health Care Costs

Area	Hospital ($/day)	Doctor ($/visit)	Dentist ($/visit)
City	427.19	49.10	62.50
U.S.	430.43	52.45	66.35

Note: Hospital—based on a semi-private room; Doctor—based on a general practitioner's routine exam of an established patient; Dentist—based on adult teeth cleaning and periodic oral exam.
Source: ACCRA, Cost of Living Index, 1st Quarter 1999

Distribution of Office-Based Physicians

Area	Family/Gen. Practitioners	Specialists		
		Medical	Surgical	Other
MSA[1]	458	968	772	866

Note: Data as of 12/31/97; (1) Metropolitan Statistical Area - see Appendix A for areas included
Source: American Medical Assn., Physician Characteristics & Distribution in the U.S., 1999

Hospitals

Indianapolis has 8 general medical and surgical hospitals, 2 psychiatric, 1 rehabilitation, 1 alcoholism and other chemical dependency. *AHA Guide to the Healthcare Field, 1998-99*

According to *U.S. News and World Report,* Indianapolis has 2 of the best hospitals in the U.S.: **Clarian Health Partners**, noted for cancer, cardiology, endocrinology, gastroenterology, geriatrics, gynecology, neurology, otolaryngology, pulmonology, rheumatology, urology; **St. Vincent Hospital and Health Center**, noted for cardiology. *U.S. News Online, "America's Best Hospitals," 10th Edition, www.usnews.com*

EDUCATION

Public School District Statistics

District Name	Num. Sch.	Enroll.	Classroom Teachers	Pupils per Teacher	Minority Pupils (%)	Current Exp.[1] ($/pupil)
Central IN Educational Srv Ctr	n/a	n/a	n/a	n/a	n/a	n/a
Franklin Township Com Sch Corp	7	4,976	251	19.8	n/a	n/a
IN Department of Correction	2	n/a	n/a	n/a	n/a	n/a
IN Department of Mental Health	1	40	7	5.7	n/a	n/a
IN State Department of Health	4	619	153	4.0	n/a	n/a
Indianapolis Public Schools	83	44,434	2,644	16.8	n/a	6,252
M S D Decatur Township	6	5,063	255	19.9	n/a	n/a
M S D Lawrence Township	16	14,319	839	17.1	n/a	n/a
M S D Perry Township	15	11,831	690	17.1	n/a	n/a
M S D Pike Township	10	7,595	440	17.3	n/a	n/a
M S D Warren Township	18	9,888	657	15.1	n/a	n/a
M S D Washington Township	14	10,093	557	18.1	n/a	n/a
M S D Wayne Township	15	12,644	724	17.5	n/a	n/a

Note: Data covers the 1997-1998 school year unless otherwise noted; (1) Data covers fiscal year 1996; SD = School District; ISD = Independent School District; n/a not available
Source: National Center for Education Statistics, Common Core of Data Public Education Agency Universe 1997-98; National Center for Education Statistics, Characteristics of the 100 Largest Public Elementary and Secondary School Districts in the United States: 1997-98, July 1999

Educational Quality

School District	Education Quotient[1]	Graduate Outcome[2]	Community Index[3]	Resource Index[4]
Indianapolis Public Sch.	71.0	55.0	105.0	97.0

Note: Nearly 1,000 secondary school districts were rated in terms of educational quality. The scores range from a low of 50 to a high of 150; (1) Average of the Graduate Outcome, Community and Resource indexes; (2) Based on graduation rates and college board scores (SAT/ACT); (3) Based on the surrounding community's average level of education and the area's average income level; (4) Based on teacher salaries, per-pupil expenditures and student-teacher ratios.
Source: Expansion Management, Ratings Issue, 1998

Educational Attainment by Race

Area	High School Graduate (%)					Bachelor's Degree (%)				
	Total	White	Black	Other	Hisp.[2]	Total	White	Black	Other	Hisp.[2]
City	76.4	79.2	65.2	79.8	75.2	21.7	24.5	9.6	39.4	20.2
MSA[1]	78.6	80.4	65.6	79.9	76.3	21.1	22.4	9.9	37.9	21.6
U.S.	75.2	77.9	63.1	60.4	49.8	20.3	21.5	11.4	19.4	9.2

Note: Figures shown cover persons 25 years old and over; (1) Metropolitan Statistical Area - see Appendix A for areas included; (2) people of Hispanic origin can be of any race
Source: 1990 Census of Population and Housing, Summary Tape File 3C

School Enrollment by Type

Area	Preprimary				Elementary/High School			
	Public		Private		Public		Private	
	Enrollment	%	Enrollment	%	Enrollment	%	Enrollment	%
City	6,699	51.1	6,414	48.9	101,922	87.2	14,951	12.8
MSA[1]	12,635	53.2	11,125	46.8	191,105	90.0	21,252	10.0
U.S.	2,679,029	59.5	1,824,256	40.5	38,379,689	90.2	4,187,099	9.8

Note: Figures shown cover persons 3 years old and over;
(1) Metropolitan Statistical Area - see Appendix A for areas included
Source: 1990 Census of Population and Housing, Summary Tape File 3C

School Enrollment by Race

Area	Preprimary (%)				Elementary/High School (%)			
	White	Black	Other	Hisp.[1]	White	Black	Other	Hisp.[1]
City	76.0	22.5	1.5	1.2	67.8	30.4	1.8	1.3
MSA[2]	85.9	12.8	1.4	1.1	81.0	17.5	1.5	1.2
U.S.	80.4	12.5	7.1	7.8	74.1	15.6	10.3	12.5

Note: Figures shown cover persons 3 years old and over; (1) people of Hispanic origin can be of any race; (2) Metropolitan Statistical Area - see Appendix A for areas included
Source: 1990 Census of Population and Housing, Summary Tape File 3C

Classroom Teacher Salaries in Public Schools

District	B.A. Degree		M.A. Degree		Maximum	
	Min. ($)	Rank[1]	Max. ($)	Rank[1]	Max. ($)	Rank[1]
Indianapolis	26,351	50	51,053	17	54,518	26
Average	26,980	-	46,065	-	51,435	-

Note: Salaries are for 1997-1998; (1) Rank ranges from 1 to 100
Source: American Federation of Teachers, Survey & Analysis of Salary Trends, 1998

Higher Education

Two-Year Colleges		Four-Year Colleges		Medical Schools	Law Schools	Voc/ Tech
Public	Private	Public	Private			
1	3	1	5	1	1	17

Source: College Blue Book, Occupational Education, 1997; Medical School Admission Requirements, 1999-2000; Peterson's Guide to Two-Year Colleges, 1999; Peterson's Guide to Four-Year Colleges, 2000; Barron's Guide to Law Schools, 1999

MAJOR EMPLOYERS

Major Employers

Allison Engine Co.
Celadon Trucking Services
Eli Lilly International
Resort Condominiums International
St. Vincent Hospital & Health Care Center

BankOne Indiana
Community Hospitals of Indiana
Indiana Bell Telephone
USA Group (management services)
Indianapolis Newspapers

Note: Companies listed are located in the city
Source: Dun's Business Rankings, 1999; Ward's Business Directory, 1998

PUBLIC SAFETY

Crime Rate

Area	All Crimes	Violent Crimes				Property Crimes		
		Murder	Forcible Rape	Robbery	Aggrav. Assault	Burglary	Larceny -Theft	Motor Vehicle Theft
City	6,743.4	18.7	71.0	427.9	614.8	1,474.2	3,146.9	990.0
Suburbs[1]	3,630.7	3.4	22.1	68.9	188.0	588.0	2,455.8	304.6
MSA[2]	5,260.6	11.4	47.7	256.8	411.5	1,052.0	2,817.7	663.5
U.S.	4,922.7	6.8	35.9	186.1	382.0	919.6	2,886.5	505.8

Note: Crime rate is the number of crimes per 100,000 pop.; (1) defined as all areas within the MSA but located outside the central city; (2) Metropolitan Statistical Area - see Appendix A for areas incl.
Source: FBI Uniform Crime Reports, 1997

RECREATION

Culture and Recreation

Museums	Symphony Orchestras	Opera Companies	Dance Companies	Professional Theatres	Zoos	Pro Sports Teams
12	1	1	2	2	1	2

Source: International Directory of the Performing Arts, 1997; Official Museum Directory, 1999; Stern's Performing Arts Directory, 1997; USA Today Four Sport Stadium Guide, 1997; Chamber of Commerce/Economic Development, 1999

Library System

The Indianapolis-Marion County Public Library has 21 branches, holdings of 1,951,804 volumes, and a budget of $26,742,241 (1996). *American Library Directory, 1998-1999*

MEDIA

Newspapers

Name	Type	Freq.	Distribution	Circulation
Indiana Herald	Black	1x/wk	Local	25,000
The Indianapolis News	General	6x/wk	Area	54,423
Indianapolis Recorder	Black	1x/wk	Area	10,000
The Indianapolis Star	General	7x/wk	Local	230,932
National Jewish Post and Opinion	General	1x/wk	U.S.	24,000
The Spotlight	General	1x/wk	Local	25,000

Note: Includes newspapers with circulations of 10,000 or more located in the city;
Source: Burrelle's Media Directory, 1999 Edition

Television Stations

Name	Ch.	Affiliation	Type	Owner
WTTV	n/a	WB	Commercial	Sinclair Communications Inc.
WRTV	n/a	ABCT	Commercial	McGraw-Hill
WISH	n/a	CBST	Commercial	LIN Television
WTHR	13	NBCT	Commercial	Dispatch Printing Company
WFYI	20	n/a	Public	Metropolitan Indianapolis Public Broadcasting
WNDY	23	UPN	Commercial	Paramount Communications Inc.
WTTK	29	WB	Commercial	Sinclair Communications Inc.
WHMB	40	n/a	Commercial	Le Sea Broadcasting Corporation
WXIN	59	FBC	Commercial	Tribune Broadcasting Company
WTBU	69	PBS	Public	Butler University

Note: Stations included broadcast in the Indianapolis metro area; n/a not available
Source: Burrelle's Media Directory, 1999 Edition

AM Radio Stations

Call Letters	Freq. (kHz)	Target Audience	Station Format	Music Format
WSYW	810	General	M	n/a
WXLW	950	Religious	M/N/S/T	Christian
WIBC	1070	General	N/S/T	n/a
WNDE	1260	General	S	n/a
WTLC	1310	General	M/N/T	Gospel/Jazz/Oldies/R&B
WBAT	1400	General	M/N/S	Adult Contemporary/Oldies
WMYS	1430	General	M/N/S	Adult Standards/MOR
WBRI	1500	Religious	M/N/T	Christian
WNTS	1590	Religious	M/T	Gospel

Note: Stations included broadcast in the Indianapolis metro area; n/a not available
Target Audience: A=Asian; B=Black; C=Christian; E=Ethnic; F=French; G=General; H=Hispanic; M=Men; N=Native American; R=Religious; S=Senior Citizen; W=Women; Y=Young Adult; Z=Children
Station Format: E=Educational; M=Music; N=News; S=Sports; T=Talk
Music Format: AOR=Album Oriented Rock; MOR=Middle-of-the-Road
Source: Burrelle's Media Directory, 1999 Edition

FM Radio Stations

Call Letters	Freq. (mHz)	Target Audience	Station Format	Music Format
WICR	88.7	General	M/N/S	Alternative/Big Band/Classical/Jazz
WJEL	89.3	General	M/N/S	Classic Rock
WFYI	90.1	General	M/N/T	Adult Contemporary/Adult Standards/ Classic Rock/Classical/Oldies/R&B
WBDG	90.9	n/a	M/N/S	Adult Contemporary/Alternative/AOR
WEDM	91.1	General	M/N/S	n/a
WRFT	91.5	General	E/M	n/a
WNAP	93.1	General	M	Classic Rock
WGRL	93.9	General	M	Country
WFBQ	94.7	General	M/N	AOR
WFMS	95.5	General	M	Country
WPZZ	95.9	General	M/N/S	Christian
WHHH	96.3	General	M	Urban Contemporary
WENS	97.1	General	M	Adult Contemporary
WXIR	98.3	General	Religious	Senior Citizen
WCJC	99.3	General	M/N/S	Country
WZPL	99.5	General	M	Adult Contemporary
WYJZ	100.9	G/M/W	M/N/S	Country/Jazz
WRZX	103.3	General	M/N/T	Alternative
WGLD	104.5	General	M	Adult Contemporary/Jazz
WTLC	105.7	Black	M/N/S	R&B/Urban Contemporary
WGGR	106.7	General	M/N/S/T	Urban Contemporary
WSYW	107.1	General	M	Jazz
WTPI	107.9	General	M	Adult Contemporary/Jazz

Note: Stations included broadcast in the Indianapolis metro area; n/a not available
Station Format: E=Educational; M=Music; N=News; S=Sports; T=Talk
Target Audience: A=Asian; B=Black; C=Christian; E=Ethnic; F=French; G=General; H=Hispanic;
M=Men; N=Native American; R=Religious; S=Senior Citizen; W=Women; Y=Young Adult; Z=Children
Music Format: AOR=Album Oriented Rock; MOR=Middle-of-the-Road
Source: Burrelle's Media Directory, 1999 Edition

CLIMATE

Average and Extreme Temperatures

Temperature	Jan	Feb	Mar	Apr	May	Jun	Jul	Aug	Sep	Oct	Nov	Dec	Yr.
Extreme High (°F)	71	72	85	89	93	102	104	102	100	90	81	74	104
Average High (°F)	35	39	50	63	73	82	85	84	78	66	51	39	62
Average Temp. (°F)	27	31	41	52	63	72	76	73	67	55	43	31	53
Average Low (°F)	18	22	31	41	52	61	65	63	55	44	33	23	42
Extreme Low (°F)	-22	-21	-7	18	28	39	48	41	34	20	-2	-23	-23

Note: Figures cover the years 1948-1990
Source: National Climatic Data Center, International Station Meteorological Climate Summary, 3/95

Average Precipitation/Snowfall/Humidity

Precip./Humidity	Jan	Feb	Mar	Apr	May	Jun	Jul	Aug	Sep	Oct	Nov	Dec	Yr.
Avg. Precip. (in.)	2.8	2.5	3.6	3.6	4.0	3.9	4.3	3.4	2.9	2.6	3.3	3.3	40.2
Avg. Snowfall (in.)	7	6	4	1	Tr	0	0	0	0	Tr	2	5	25
Avg. Rel. Hum. 7am (%)	81	81	79	77	79	80	84	87	87	85	83	83	82
Avg. Rel. Hum. 4pm (%)	68	64	59	53	53	53	56	56	53	53	63	70	59

Note: Figures cover the years 1948-1990; Tr = Trace amounts (<0.05 in. of rain; <0.5 in. of snow)
Source: National Climatic Data Center, International Station Meteorological Climate Summary, 3/95

Weather Conditions

Temperature			Daytime Sky			Precipitation		
10°F & below	32°F & below	90°F & above	Clear	Partly cloudy	Cloudy	0.01 inch or more precip.	0.1 inch or more snow/ice	Thunder-storms
19	119	19	83	128	154	127	24	43

Note: Figures are average number of days per year and covers the years 1948-1990
Source: National Climatic Data Center, International Station Meteorological Climate Summary, 3/95

AIR & WATER QUALITY

Maximum Pollutant Concentrations

	Particulate Matter (ug/m^3)	Carbon Monoxide (ppm)	Sulfur Dioxide (ppm)	Nitrogen Dioxide (ppm)	Ozone (ppm)	Lead (ug/m^3)
MSA[1] Level	54	4	0.030	0.015	0.11	0.08
NAAQS[2]	150	9	0.140	0.053	0.12	1.50
Met NAAQS?	Yes	Yes	Yes	Yes	Yes	Yes

Note: (1) Metropolitan Statistical Area - see Appendix A for areas included; (2) National Ambient Air Quality Standards; ppm = parts per million; ug/m^3 = micrograms per cubic meter; n/a not available
Source: EPA, National Air Quality and Emissions Trends Report, 1997

Pollutant Standards Index

In the Indianapolis MSA (see Appendix A for areas included), the Pollutant Standards Index (PSI) exceeded 100 on 12 days in 1997. A PSI value greater than 100 indicates that air quality would be in the unhealthful range on that day. *EPA, National Air Quality and Emissions Trends Report, 1997*

Drinking Water

Water System Name	Pop. Served	Primary Water Source Type	Number of Violations in 1998	Type of Violation/ Contaminants
Indianapolis Water Company	801,000	Surface	None	None

Note: Data as of July 10, 1999
Source: EPA, Office of Ground Water and Drinking Water, Safe Drinking Water Information System

Indianapolis tap water is alkaline, hard and fluoridated. Three separate systems with separate sources and purification plants.
Editor & Publisher Market Guide, 1999

Kansas City, Missouri

Background

Kansas City lies on the western boundary of the state. With its sister city of the same name on the other side of the Kansas/Missouri border, both Kansas Cities make up the greater Kansas City metropolitan area.

As one might expect from the Heartland of America, Kansas City's major industries are hard wheat and cattle. However, do not be lulled into painting this picture for all of Kansas City. It is a modern urban institution with over 100 parks and playgrounds, suburban areas with an above average living standard, European statues that line wide stretching boulevards, and a foreign trade zone where foreign countries can store their goods free of import duties.

Downtown Kansas City is in the midst of a major renovation and restoration project which is transforming the landscape by blending 19th century buildings with modern skyscrapers. Planned, under construction, or completed are corporate headquarters for DST Systems (a processor of mutual fund accounts), a Federal Court complex, and an AMC entertainment center with a 30-screen movie theater. Historic Union Station is presently undergoing a $234 million major renovation which will not only restore the grand hall with its 95-foot ceilings, but will also be home to the new Science City Museum. The expected completion date is November 1999. *New York Times, 2/8/98*

The territory of the Kansa (or Kaw) tribe received intermittent visits from white settlers during the 18th and 19th centuries. In 1724, Etienne Venyard, Sieur de Bougmont built a fort in the general vicinity, and in 1804, Meriwether Lewis and William Clark explored the area on behalf of President Jefferson for the Louisiana Purchase. In 1821, the site was a trading post established by Francois Chouteau.

A combination of gold prospectors passing through on their way to California, steamboat, rail, and overland trade, and the migration of would be settlers to California and the Southwest stimulated economic activity in Kansas City during the 1800s.

It was in this solid Midwestern city that the jazz clubs on 18th Street and Vine gave birth to the careers of Charlie Parker and Count Basie.

The National Weather Service office at Kansas City is very near the geographical center of the United States. The gently rolling terrain with no topographic impediments allows a free sweep of air from all directions, often with conflict between warm moist air from the Gulf of Mexico and cold polar air from the north. The summer season is characterized by warm days, mild nights, and moderate humidity. Winters are not severely cold, and snowfalls of 10 inches or more are comparatively rare.

General Rankings and Evaluative Comments

■ Kansas City was ranked #11 out of 11 large, midwestern metropolitan areas in *Money's* 1998 survey of "The Best Places to Live in America." The survey was conducted by first contacting 512 representative households nationwide and asking them to rank 37 quality-of-life factors on a scale of 1 to 10. Next, a demographic profile was compiled on the 300 largest metropolitan statistical areas in the U.S. The numbers were crunched together to arrive at an overall ranking (things Americans consider most important, like clean air and water, low crime and good schools, received extra weight). Unlike previous years, the 1998 rankings were broken down by region (northeast, midwest, south, west) and population size (100,000 to 249,999; 250,000 to 999,999; 1 million plus). The city had a nationwide ranking of #221 out of 300 in 1997 and #172 out of 300 in 1996. *Money, July 1998; Money, July 1997; Money, September 1996*

■ *Ladies Home Journal* ranked America's 200 largest cities based on the qualities women care about most. Kansas City ranked #178 out of 200. Criteria: low crime rate, well-paying jobs, quality health and child care, good public schools, the presence of women in government, size of the gender wage gap, number of sexual-harassment and discrimination complaints filed, unemployment and divorce rates, commute times, population density, number of houses of worship, parks and cultural offerings, number of women's health specialists, how well a community's women cared for themselves, complexion kindness index based on UV radiation levels, odds of finding affordable fashions, rental rates for romance movies, champagne sales and other matters of the heart. *Ladies Home Journal, November 1998*

■ Zero Population Growth ranked 229 cities in terms of children's health, safety, and economic well-being. Kansas City was ranked #66 out of 112 independent cities (cities with populations greater than 100,000 which were neither Major Cities nor Suburbs/Outer Cities) and was given a grade of C. Criteria: total population, percent of population under 18 years of age, household language, percent population change, percent of births to teens, infant mortality rate, percent of low birth weights, dropout rate, enrollment in preprimary school, violent and property crime rates, unemployment rate, percent of children in poverty, percent of owner occupied units, number of bad air days, percent of public transportation commuters, and average travel time to work. *Zero Population Growth, Children's Environmental Index, Fall 1999*

■ Kansas City was ranked #26 out of 59 metro areas in *The Regional Economist's* "Rational Livability Ranking of 59 Large Metro Areas." The rankings were based on the metro area's total population change over the period 1990-97 divided by the number of people moving in from elsewhere in the United States (net domestic in-migration). *St. Louis Federal Reserve Bank of St. Louis, The Regional Economist, April 1999*

■ Kansas City appeared on *Travel & Leisure's* list of the world's 100 best cities. It was ranked #47 in the U.S. Criteria: activities/attractions, culture/arts, people, restaurants/food, and value. *Travel & Leisure, 1998 World's Best Awards*

■ Kansas City was selected by *Yahoo! Internet Life* as one of "America's Most Wired Cities & Towns." The city ranked #36 out of 50. Criteria: home and work net use, domain density, hosts per capita, directory density and content quality. *Yahoo! Internet Life, March 1999*

■ Cognetics studied 273 metro areas in the United States, ranking them by entrepreneurial activity. Kansas City was ranked #14 out of the 50 largest metro areas. Criteria: Significant Starts (firms started in the last 10 years that still employ at least 5 people) and Young Growers (percent of firms 10 years old or less that grew significantly during the last 4 years). *Cognetics, "Entrepreneurial Hot Spots: The Best Places in America to Start and Grow a Company," 1998*

■ Kansas City was selected as one of the "Best American Cities to Start a Business" by *Point of View* magazine. Criteria: coolness, quality-of-life, and business concerns. The city was ranked #36 out of 75. *Point of View, November 1998*

■ Reliastar Financial Corp. ranked the 125 largest metropolitan areas according to the general financial security of residents. Kansas City was ranked #38 out of 125 with a score of 5.5. The score indicates the percentage a metropolitan area is above or below the metropolitan norm. A metro area with a score of 10.6 is 10.6% above the metro average. Criteria: Earnings and Wealth Potential (household income, education, net assets, cost of living); Safety Net (health insurance, retirement savings, life insurance, income support programs); Personal Threats (unemployment rate, low-income households, crime rate); Community Economic Vitality (cost of community services, job quality, job creation, housing costs).
Reliastar Financial Corp., "The Best Cities to Earn and Save Money," 1999 Edition

Business Environment

STATE ECONOMY

State Economic Profile

"St. Louis' weak economy and a slowdown in Kansas City are placing a drag on the Missouri economy. Gross State Product and job growth, after matching or surpassing the national for several years, has slowed. After strong home sales in 1998, MO's housing and construction markets will likely slow considerably in 1999.

Like most Plains states, MO's significant farm sector has been a drag on the economy. Farm income was down over 20% in 1998 as commodity prices and foreign demand remained weak. With overcapacity in MO's beef and grain sectors, a major restructing is in store. Even with a resurgence in Asian demand, the current trend in commodity prices is not likely to reverse.

Manufacturing employment shrank 0.5% in 1998. St. Louis witnessed an even greater decline of 0.9%. With the prospect of job cuts at Boeing's St. Louis facilities, Missouri will likely witness further contraction in manufacturing employment in 1999.

An increase in building activity in St. Louis, fueled by corporate relocations, helped to offset declining activity elsewhere in the state. Almost half of the new construction jobs created in MO were in St. Louis.

MO's relatively high unemployment rate has in some ways been a bonus, helping to attract some corporate relocations. MasterCard and Convergys, for instance, have moved operations to St. Louis to take advantage of the available labor. In spite of these moves, St. Louis should still add little to state GSP and job growth. Gains in Kansas City, Columbia and Springfield will help to offset the weakness in St. Louis and the soft farm economy." *National Association of Realtors, Economic Profiles: The Fifty States and the District of Columbia, http://nar.realtor.com/databank/profiles.htm*

IMPORTS/EXPORTS

Total Export Sales

Area	1994 ($000)	1995 ($000)	1996 ($000)	1997 ($000)	% Chg. 1994-97	% Chg. 1996-97
MSA[1]	2,578,560	3,350,170	3,985,073	3,817,637	48.1	-4.2
U.S.	512,415,609	583,030,524	622,827,063	687,597,999	34.2	10.4

Note: (1) Metropolitan Statistical Area - see Appendix A for areas included
Source: U.S. Department of Commerce, International Trade Association, Metropolitan Area Exports: An Export Performance Report on Over 250 U.S. Cities, November 10, 1998

CITY FINANCES

City Government Finances

Component	FY92 ($000)	FY92 (per capita $)
Revenue	670,837	1,542.36
Expenditure	662,313	1,522.76
Debt Outstanding	905,332	2,081.50
Cash & Securities	1,542,753	3,547.02

Source: U.S. Bureau of the Census, City Government Finances: 1991-92

City Government Revenue by Source

Source	FY92 ($000)	FY92 (per capita $)	FY92 (%)
From Federal Government	27,663	63.60	4.1
From State Governments	24,249	55.75	3.6
From Local Governments	4,657	10.71	0.7
Property Taxes	62,233	143.08	9.3
General Sales Taxes	69,121	158.92	10.3
Selective Sales Taxes	77,908	179.12	11.6
Income Taxes	103,750	238.54	15.5
Current Charges	83,447	191.86	12.4
Utility/Liquor Store	46,960	107.97	7.0
Employee Retirement[1]	82,514	189.71	12.3
Other	88,335	203.10	13.2

Note: (1) Excludes "city contributions," classified as "nonrevenue," intragovernmental transfers.
Source: U.S. Bureau of the Census, City Government Finances: 1991-92

City Government Expenditures by Function

Function	FY92 ($000)	FY92 (per capita $)	FY92 (%)
Educational Services	23,559	54.17	3.6
Employee Retirement[1]	30,310	69.69	4.6
Environment/Housing	128,522	295.49	19.4
Government Administration	40,484	93.08	6.1
Interest on General Debt	45,672	105.01	6.9
Public Safety	125,914	289.50	19.0
Social Services	41,212	94.75	6.2
Transportation	132,189	303.92	20.0
Utility/Liquor Store	62,030	142.62	9.4
Other	32,421	74.54	4.9

Note: (1) Payments to beneficiaries including withdrawal of contributions.
Source: U.S. Bureau of the Census, City Government Finances: 1991-92

Municipal Bond Ratings

Area	Moody's	S & P
Kansas City	Aa3	n/a

Note: n/a not available; n/r not rated
Source: Moody's Bond Record, 6/99

POPULATION

Population Growth

Area	1980	1990	% Chg. 1980-90	July 1998 Estimate	% Chg. 1990-98
City	448,159	435,141	-2.9	441,574	1.5
MSA[1]	1,433,458	1,566,280	9.3	1,726,167	10.2
U.S.	226,545,805	248,765,170	9.8	270,299,000	8.7

Note: (1) Metropolitan Statistical Area - see Appendix A for areas included;
July 1998 MSA population estimate was calculated by the editors
Source: 1980/1990 Census of Housing and Population, Summary Tape File 3C;
Census Bureau Population Estimates 1998

Population Characteristics

Race	City 1980 Population	%	City 1990 Population	%	% Chg. 1980-90	MSA[1] 1990 Population	%
White	313,840	70.0	290,898	66.9	-7.3	1,321,680	84.4
Black	122,336	27.3	128,843	29.6	5.3	200,436	12.8
Amer Indian/Esk/Aleut	2,115	0.5	2,240	0.5	5.9	8,178	0.5
Asian/Pacific Islander	3,591	0.8	4,903	1.1	36.5	15,908	1.0
Other	6,277	1.4	8,257	1.9	31.5	20,078	1.3
Hispanic Origin[2]	14,703	3.3	16,819	3.9	14.4	45,092	2.9

Note: (1) Metropolitan Statistical Area - see Appendix A for areas included;
(2) people of Hispanic origin can be of any race
Source: 1980/1990 Census of Housing and Population, Summary Tape File 3C

Ancestry

Area	German	Irish	English	Italian	U.S.	French	Polish	Dutch
City	23.9	16.6	12.5	3.6	3.7	3.4	1.4	2.3
MSA[1]	32.3	19.7	16.4	3.1	4.9	4.3	1.9	3.2
U.S.	23.3	15.6	13.1	5.9	5.3	4.2	3.8	2.5

Note: Figures are percentages and include persons that reported multiple ancestry (eg. if a person reported being Irish and Italian, they were included in both columns); (1) Metropolitan Statistical Area - see Appendix A for areas included
Source: 1990 Census of Population and Housing, Summary Tape File 3C

Age

Area	Median Age (Years)	Under 5	Under 18	18-24	25-44	45-64	65+	80+
City	32.7	7.7	24.7	9.8	34.2	18.4	12.9	3.2
MSA[1]	32.9	7.7	26.4	9.1	34.2	18.7	11.6	2.8
U.S.	32.9	7.3	25.6	10.5	32.6	18.7	12.5	2.8

Note: (1) Metropolitan Statistical Area - see Appendix A for areas included
Source: 1990 Census of Population and Housing, Summary Tape File 3C

Male/Female Ratio

Area	Number of males per 100 females (all ages)	Number of males per 100 females (18 years old+)
City	90.3	86.6
MSA[1]	93.5	89.9
U.S.	95.0	91.9

Note: (1) Metropolitan Statistical Area - see Appendix A for areas included
Source: 1990 Census of Population, General Population Characteristics

INCOME

Per Capita/Median/Average Income

Area	Per Capita ($)	Median Household ($)	Average Household ($)
City	13,799	26,713	33,510
MSA[1]	15,067	31,613	38,701
U.S.	14,420	30,056	38,453

Note: All figures are for 1989; (1) Metropolitan Statistical Area - see Appendix A for areas included
Source: 1990 Census of Population and Housing, Summary Tape File 3C

Household Income Distribution by Race

Income ($)	City (%)					U.S. (%)				
	Total	White	Black	Other	Hisp.[1]	Total	White	Black	Other	Hisp.[1]
Less than 5,000	8.4	5.0	17.4	11.2	7.5	6.2	4.8	15.2	8.6	8.8
5,000 - 9,999	9.5	7.7	14.0	12.3	10.8	9.3	8.6	14.2	9.9	11.1
10,000 - 14,999	9.5	8.7	11.9	7.5	8.6	8.8	8.5	11.0	9.8	11.0
15,000 - 24,999	19.2	18.9	20.0	19.8	20.6	17.5	17.3	18.9	18.5	20.5
25,000 - 34,999	16.8	17.6	14.6	19.2	18.5	15.8	16.1	14.2	15.4	16.4
35,000 - 49,999	17.3	19.1	12.3	16.4	17.9	17.9	18.6	13.3	16.1	16.0
50,000 - 74,999	12.9	14.9	7.8	9.8	14.1	15.0	15.8	9.3	13.4	11.1
75,000 - 99,999	3.5	4.4	1.3	2.4	1.5	5.1	5.5	2.6	4.7	3.1
100,000+	2.9	3.7	0.8	1.4	0.5	4.4	4.8	1.3	3.7	1.9

Note: All figures are for 1989; (1) people of Hispanic origin can be of any race
Source: 1990 Census of Population and Housing, Summary Tape File 3C

Effective Buying Income

Area	Per Capita ($)	Median Household ($)	Average Household ($)
City	16,316	32,318	39,976
MSA[1]	18,388	38,137	47,475
U.S.	16,803	34,536	45,243

Note: Data as of 1/1/99; (1) Metropolitan Statistical Area - see Appendix A for areas included
Source: Standard Rate & Data Service, Newspaper Advertising Source, 9/99

Effective Household Buying Income Distribution

Area	% of Households Earning						
	$10,000 -$19,999	$20,000 -$34,999	$35,000 -$49,999	$50,000 -$74,999	$75,000 -$99,000	$100,000 -$124,999	$125,000 and up
City	16.3	23.7	18.2	17.7	6.2	2.0	2.0
MSA[1]	13.9	22.3	19.5	21.4	8.2	2.6	2.7
U.S.	16.0	22.6	18.2	18.9	7.2	2.4	2.7

Note: Data as of 1/1/99; (1) Metropolitan Statistical Area - see Appendix A for areas included
Source: Standard Rate & Data Service, Newspaper Advertising Source, 9/99

Poverty Rates by Race and Age

Area	Total (%)	By Race (%)				By Age (%)		
		White	Black	Other	Hisp.[2]	Under 5 years old	Under 18 years old	65 years and over
City	15.3	8.7	29.6	21.8	18.4	26.2	22.8	14.6
MSA[1]	9.8	6.9	28.1	16.1	14.9	15.9	13.7	11.2
U.S.	13.1	9.8	29.5	23.1	25.3	20.1	18.3	12.8

Note: Figures show the percent of people living below the poverty line in 1989. The average poverty threshold was $12,674 for a family of four in 1989; (1) Metropolitan Statistical Area - see Appendix A for areas included; (2) people of Hispanic origin can be of any race
Source: 1990 Census of Population and Housing, Summary Tape File 3C

EMPLOYMENT

Labor Force and Employment

Area	Civilian Labor Force			Workers Employed		
	Jun. 1998	Jun. 1999	% Chg.	Jun. 1998	Jun. 1999	% Chg.
City	258,277	269,066	4.2	244,863	256,996	5.0
MSA[1]	978,605	1,016,072	3.8	936,816	981,512	4.8
U.S.	138,798,000	140,666,000	1.3	132,265,000	134,395,000	1.6

Note: Data is not seasonally adjusted and covers workers 16 years of age and older;
(1) Metropolitan Statistical Area - see Appendix A for areas included
Source: Bureau of Labor Statistics, http://stats.bls.gov

Unemployment Rate

Area	1998						1999					
	Jul.	Aug.	Sep.	Oct.	Nov.	Dec.	Jan.	Feb.	Mar.	Apr.	May.	Jun.
City	5.6	5.0	4.2	3.7	3.7	3.5	3.1	3.4	3.4	3.4	3.5	4.5
MSA[1]	4.5	3.8	3.4	3.2	3.2	2.9	3.0	3.1	3.0	2.8	2.9	3.4
U.S.	4.7	4.5	4.4	4.2	4.1	4.0	4.8	4.7	4.4	4.1	4.0	4.5

Note: Data is not seasonally adjusted and covers workers 16 years of age and older; all figures are percentages; (1) Metropolitan Statistical Area - see Appendix A for areas included
Source: Bureau of Labor Statistics, http://stats.bls.gov

Employment by Industry

Sector	MSA[1]		U.S.
	Number of Employees	Percent of Total	Percent of Total
Services	287,500	29.5	30.4
Retail Trade	169,300	17.4	17.7
Government	138,700	14.3	15.6
Manufacturing	109,700	11.3	14.3
Finance/Insurance/Real Estate	69,800	7.2	5.9
Wholesale Trade	66,200	6.8	5.4
Transportation/Public Utilities	78,600	8.1	5.3
Construction	n/a	n/a	5.0
Mining	n/a	n/a	0.4

Note: Figures cover non-farm employment as of 6/99 and are not seasonally adjusted; (1) Metropolitan Statistical Area - see Appendix A for areas included; n/a not available
Source: Bureau of Labor Statistics, http://stats.bls.gov

Employment by Occupation

Occupation Category	City (%)	MSA[1] (%)	U.S. (%)
White Collar	62.0	63.0	58.1
Executive/Admin./Management	12.2	13.2	12.3
Professional	14.3	14.1	14.1
Technical & Related Support	3.9	3.9	3.7
Sales	11.3	12.8	11.8
Administrative Support/Clerical	20.3	19.0	16.3
Blue Collar	22.1	23.4	26.2
Precision Production/Craft/Repair	8.5	10.0	11.3
Machine Operators/Assem./Insp.	5.8	5.6	6.8
Transportation/Material Movers	3.8	3.9	4.1
Cleaners/Helpers/Laborers	4.1	3.9	3.9
Services	15.1	12.4	13.2
Farming/Forestry/Fishing	0.7	1.3	2.5

Note: Figures cover employed persons 16 years old and over; (1) Metropolitan Statistical Area - see Appendix A for areas included
Source: 1990 Census of Population and Housing, Summary Tape File 3C

Occupational Employment Projections: 1996 - 2006

Occupations Expected to Have the Largest Job Growth (ranked by numerical growth)	Fast-Growing Occupations[1] (ranked by percent growth)
1. Salespersons, retail	1. Computer engineers
2. Teachers, secondary school	2. Systems analysts
3. Truck drivers, light	3. Desktop publishers
4. General managers & top executives	4. Home health aides
5. Cashiers	5. Teachers, special education
6. Nursing aides/orderlies/attendants	6. Personal and home care aides
7. Child care workers, private household	7. Speech-language pathologists/audiologists
8. Teachers aides, clerical & paraprofess.	8. Paralegals
9. Systems analysts	9. Occupational therapists
10. Marketing & sales, supervisors	10. Physical therapy assistants and aides

Note: Projections cover Missouri; (1) Excludes occupations with total job growth less than 300
Source: U.S. Department of Labor, Employment and Training Administration, America's Labor Market Information System (ALMIS)

TAXES

Major State and Local Tax Rates

State Corp. Income (%)	State Personal Income (%)	Residential Property (effective rate per $100)	Sales & Use		State Gasoline (cents/ gallon)	State Cigarette (cents/ pack)
			State (%)	Local (%)		
6.25	1.5 - 6.0	1.20	4.225	2.375	17.05[a]	17.0[b]

Note: Personal/corporate income, sales, gasoline and cigarette tax rates as of January 1999. Property tax rates as of 1997; (a) Rate is comprised of 17 cents excise and 0.05 cents motor carrier tax; (b) Counties and cities may impose an additional tax of 4 - 7 cents per pack
Source: Federation of Tax Administrators, www.taxadmin.org; Washington D.C. Department of Finance and Revenue, Tax Rates and Tax Burdens in the District of Columbia: A Nationwide Comparison, July 1998; Chamber of Commerce, 1999

Total Taxes Per Capita and as a Percent of Income

Area	Per Capita Income ($)	Per Capita Taxes ($)			Percent of Income (%)		
		Total	Federal	State/ Local	Total	Federal	State/ Local
Missouri	26,334	9,207	6,136	3,072	35.0	23.3	11.7
U.S.	27,876	9,881	6,690	3,191	35.4	24.0	11.4

Note: Figures are for 1998
Source: Tax Foundation, www.taxfoundation.org

Estimated Tax Burden

Area	State Income	Local Income	Property	Sales	Total
Kansas City	2,338	750	3,500	1,024	7,612

Note: The numbers are estimates of taxes paid by a married couple with two children and annual earnings of $75,000. Sales tax estimates assume they spend average amounts on food, clothing, household goods and gasoline. Property tax estimates assume they live in a $250,000 home.
Source: Kiplinger's Personal Finance Magazine, October 1998

**COMMERCIAL
REAL ESTATE**

Office Market

Class/ Location	Total Space (sq. ft.)	Vacant Space (sq. ft.)	Vac. Rate (%)	Under Constr. (sq. ft.)	Net Absorp. (sq. ft.)	Rental Rates ($/sq.ft./yr.)
Class A						
CBD	4,976,390	270,814	5.4	212,000	110,000	16.25-25.00
Outside CBD	9,265,369	515,818	5.6	722,000	460,000	18.75-23.50
Class B						
CBD	8,859,858	906,907	10.2	204,000	n/a	12.00-14.50
Outside CBD	21,544,230	1,305,221	6.1	1,734,000	n/a	14.00-19.75

Note: Data as of 10/98 and covers Kansas City; CBD = Central Business District; n/a not available;
Source: Society of Industrial and Office Realtors, 1999 Comparative Statistics of Industrial and Office Real Estate Markets

"Among larger U.S. cities, Kansas City is rated as fourth in new job creation and has become one of the top choices of locations in which to operate a business. Job growth and favorable demographic trends are expected to continue and should benefit the office market. Kansas City's diversified business base is expected to thrive even under the uncertainty of the foreign markets and domestic financial markets. New development, primarily Class B space, will be focused in the suburban markets, especially South Johnson County. Phases of the Sprint campus are expected to be completed over the next five years, with one million sq. ft. finished by the end of 1999. This is touted as 'the largest office building development in the world.' Investment sales are expected to slow in 1999." *Society of Industrial and Office Realtors, 1999 Comparative Statistics of Industrial and Office Real Estate Markets*

Industrial Market

Location	Total Space (sq. ft.)	Vacant Space (sq. ft.)	Vac. Rate (%)	Under Constr. (sq. ft.)	Net Absorp. (sq. ft.)	Gross Lease ($/sq.ft./yr.)
Central City	87,858,073	4,837,194	5.5	530,000	827,679	3.95-5.00
Suburban	46,691,000	3,268,920	7.0	925,000	846,486	4.50-9.25

Note: Data as of 10/98 and covers Kansas City; n/a not available
Source: Society of Industrial and Office Realtors, 1999 Comparative Statistics of Industrial and Office Real Estate Markets

"More than 1.3 million sq. ft. of new speculative construction will reach the Kansas City market by mid-1999. The depth of demand will actually be tested over the next few months, particularly in the warehouse/distribution sub-market. It is expected that competition for tenants will become very active as the space is delivered. There is a 2 to 2.5-year supply predicted by mid-year, once the new construction has been completed. The vacancy rate for the metropolitan area will probably rise during the second and third quarters in response to the availability of the new space. Next year will see a 20 percent rise in warehouse- distribution space, six to 10 percent in High Tech/R&D and one to five percent in manufacturing space. Lease prices are expected go up 11 to 15 percent for High Tech/R&D and six to 10 percent for warehouse/distribution space." *Society of Industrial and Office Realtors, 1999 Comparative Statistics of Industrial and Office Real Estate Markets*

Retail Market

Shopping Center Inventory (sq. ft.)	Shopping Center Construction (sq. ft.)	Construction as a Percent of Inventory (%)	Torto Wheaton Rent Index[1] ($/sq. ft.)
35,751,000	1,083,000	3.0	11.19

Note: Data as of 1997 and covers the Metropolitan Statistical Area - see Appendix A for areas included; (1) Index is based on a model that predicts what the average rent should be for leases with certain characteristics, in certain locations during certain years.
Source: National Association of Realtors, 1997-1998 Market Conditions Report

"Population growth in Kansas City has exceeded the national average during the past two years. That, combined with solid personal income growth, has helped expand the area's retail sector. The retail rent index erased a sharp decline in 1995, rising 18.3% in 1996 and 2.6% last year. Kansas City's suburban areas have experienced robust growth. Strong demographics and increased traffic activity near Independence Center have set off a restaurant boom. While the majority of stores are doing well, some local analysts feel the market may be reaching a saturation point. Shopping center completions are expected to slow substantially over the next two years." *National Association of Realtors, 1997-1998 Market Conditions Report*

COMMERCIAL UTILITIES

Typical Monthly Electric Bills

Area	Commercial Service ($/month)		Industrial Service ($/month)	
	12 kW demand 1,500 kWh	100 kW demand 30,000 kWh	1,000 kW demand 400,000 kWh	20,000 kW demand 10,000,000 kWh
City	133	1,851	20,685	301,857
U.S.	150	2,174	23,995	508,569

Note: Based on rates in effect January 1, 1999
Source: Edison Electric Institute, Typical Residential, Commercial and Industrial Bills, Winter 1999

TRANSPORTATION

Transportation Statistics

Average minutes to work	20.5
Interstate highways	I-29; I-35; I-70
Bus lines	
In-city	Kansas City Area TA, 290 vehicles
Inter-city	2
Passenger air service	
Airport	Kansas City International
Airlines	14
Aircraft departures	66,243 (1996)
Enplaned passengers	4,819,759 (1996)
Rail service	Amtrak; Light Rail planned
Motor freight carriers	225
Major waterways/ports	Kansas/Missouri Rivers

Source: Editor & Publisher Market Guide, 1999; FAA Airport Activity Statistics, 1997; Amtrak National Time Table, Northeast Timetable, Spring/Summer 1999; 1990 Census of Population and Housing, STF 3C; Chamber of Commerce/Economic Development 1999; Jane's Urban Transport Systems 1999-2000

Means of Transportation to Work

Area	Car/Truck/Van		Public Transportation			Bicycle	Walked	Other Means	Worked at Home
	Drove Alone	Car-pooled	Bus	Subway	Railroad				
City	74.7	13.6	5.6	0.0	0.0	0.1	2.8	1.0	2.2
MSA[1]	79.9	12.5	2.0	0.0	0.0	0.1	1.9	0.8	2.8
U.S.	73.2	13.4	3.0	1.5	0.5	0.4	3.9	1.2	3.0

Note: Figures shown are percentages and only include workers 16 years old and over;
(1) Metropolitan Statistical Area - see Appendix A for areas included
Source: 1990 Census of Population and Housing, Summary Tape File 3C

BUSINESSES

Major Business Headquarters

Company Name	1999 Rankings	
	Fortune 500	Forbes 500
American Century Investments	-	363
Bartlett and Co	-	316
Black & Veatch	-	85
Dunn Industries	-	336
Farmland Industries	184	-
Hallmark Cards	-	32
Interstate Bakeries	451	-
Russel Stover Candies	-	458
Sutherland Lumber	-	310
Utilicorp United	132	-

Note: Companies listed are located in the city; dashes indicate no ranking
Fortune 500: Companies that produce a 10-K are ranked 1 to 500 based on 1998 revenue
Forbes 500: Private companies are ranked 1 to 500 based on 1997 revenue
Source: Forbes, November 30, 1998; Fortune, April 26, 1999

Best Companies to Work For

Cerner (clinical information systems), headquartered in Kansas City, is among the " 100 Best Companies to Work for in America." Criteria: trust in management, pride in work/company, camaraderie, company responses to the Hewitt People Practices Inventory, and employee responses to their Great Place to Work survey. The companies also had to be at least 10 years old and have a minimum of 500 employees. *Fortune, January 11, 1999*

Hallmark Cards and St. Lukes Hospital of Kansas City, headquartered in Kansas City, are among the " 100 Best Companies for Working Mothers." Criteria: fair wages, opportunities for women to advance, support for child care, flexible work schedules, family-friendly benefits, and work/life supports. *Working Mother, October 1998*

Women-Owned Firms: Number, Employment and Sales

Area	Number of Firms	Employment	Sales ($000)	Rank[2]
MSA[1]	58,500	123,200	26,040,000	34

Note: (1) Metropolitan Statistical Area - see Appendix A for areas included;
(2) Calculated on an averaging of the number of businesses, employment and sales
Source: The National Foundation for Women Business Owners, 1999 Facts on Women-Owned Businesses: Trends in the Top 50 Metropolitan Areas

Women-Owned Firms: Growth

Area	% change from 1992 to 1999			Rank[2]
	Number of Firms	Employment	Sales	
MSA[1]	33.7	75.8	129.7	46

Note: (1) Metropolitan Statistical Area - see Appendix A for areas included; (2) Calculated on an averaging of the percent growth of number of businesses, employment and sales
Source: The National Foundation for Women Business Owners, 1999 Facts on Women-Owned Businesses: Trends in the Top 50 Metropolitan Areas

Minority Business Opportunity

Kansas City is home to one company which is on the Hispanic Business Fastest-Growing 100 list (greatest sales growth from 1994 to 1998): Rafael Architects Inc. (architecture, design and planning svcs.). *Hispanic Business, July/August 1999*

HOTELS & MOTELS

Hotels/Motels

Area	Hotels/ Motels	Rooms	Luxury-Level Hotels/Motels		Average Minimum Rates ($)		
			♦♦♦♦	♦♦♦♦♦	♦♦	♦♦♦	♦♦♦♦
City	46	8,816	1	0	77	100	151
Airport	12	1,945	0	0	n/a	n/a	n/a
Suburbs	58	6,022	0	0	n/a	n/a	n/a
Total	116	16,783	1	0	n/a	n/a	n/a

Note: n/a not available; classifications range from one diamond (budget properties with basic amenities) to five diamond (luxury properties with the finest service, rooms and facilities).
Source: OAG, Business Travel Planner, Winter 1998-99

CONVENTION CENTERS

Major Convention Centers

Center Name	Meeting Rooms	Exhibit Space (sq. ft.)
American Royal Center	2	372,000
Hyatt Regency Crown Center	21	15,360
Kansas City Convention Center	58	388,000
Kansas City Market Center/Convention Center	20	59,000
Kansas City Marriott Downtown	23	22,380
Radisson Suites, Kansas City	9	6,500
The Ritz-Carlton, Kansas City	22	19,250
Westin Crown Center	25	16,000

Source: Trade Shows Worldwide, 1998; Meetings & Conventions, 4/15/99;
Sucessful Meetings, 3/31/98

Living Environment

COST OF LIVING

Cost of Living Index

Composite Index	Groceries	Housing	Utilities	Trans-portation	Health Care	Misc. Goods/ Services
98.2	95.5	90.4	102.0	94.3	107.0	105.0

Note: U.S. = 100; Figures are for the Metropolitan Statistical Area - see Appendix A for areas included
Source: ACCRA, Cost of Living Index, 1st Quarter 1999

HOUSING

Median Home Prices and Housing Affordability

Area	Median Price[2] 1st Qtr. 1999 ($)	HOI[3] 1st Qtr. 1999	Afford-ability Rank[4]
MSA[1]	n/a	n/a	n/a
U.S.	134,000	69.6	—

Note: (1) Metropolitan Statistical Area - see Appendix A for areas included; (2) U.S. figures calculated from the sales of 524,324 new and existing homes in 181 markets; (3) Housing Opportunity Index - percent of homes sold that were within the reach of the median income household at the prevailing mortgage interest rate; (4) Rank is from 1-181 with 1 being most affordable; n/a not available
Source: National Association of Home Builders, Housing Opportunity Index, 1st Quarter 1999

Median Home Price Projection

It is projected that the median price of existing single-family homes in the metro area will increase by 4.0% in 1999. Nationwide, home prices are projected to increase 3.8%.
Kiplinger's Personal Finance Magazine, January 1999

Average New Home Price

Area	Price ($)
MSA[1]	123,168
U.S.	142,735

Note: Figures are based on a new home with 1,800 sq. ft. of living area on an 8,000 sq. ft. lot; (1) Metropolitan Statistical Area - see Appendix A for areas included
Source: ACCRA, Cost of Living Index, 1st Quarter 1999

Average Apartment Rent

Area	Rent ($/mth)
MSA[1]	566
U.S.	601

Note: Figures are based on an unfurnished two bedroom, 1-1/2 or 2 bath apartment, approximately 950 sq. ft. in size, excluding all utilities except water; (1) Metropolitan Statistical Area - see Appendix A for areas included
Source: ACCRA, Cost of Living Index, 1st Quarter 1999

RESIDENTIAL UTILITIES

Average Residential Utility Costs

Area	All Electric ($/mth)	Part Electric ($/mth)	Other Energy ($/mth)	Phone ($/mth)
MSA[1]	–	55.17	43.06	24.04
U.S.	100.02	55.73	43.33	19.71

Note: (1) (1) Metropolitan Statistical Area - see Appendix A for areas included
Source: ACCRA, Cost of Living Index, 1st Quarter 1999

HEALTH CARE

Average Health Care Costs

Area	Hospital ($/day)	Doctor ($/visit)	Dentist ($/visit)
MSA[1]	555.80	54.00	65.71
U.S.	430.43	52.45	66.35

Note: Hospital—based on a semi-private room; Doctor—based on a general practitioner's routine exam of an established patient; Dentist—based on adult teeth cleaning and periodic oral exam; (1) Metropolitan Statistical Area - see Appendix A for areas included
Source: ACCRA, Cost of Living Index, 1st Quarter 1999

Distribution of Office-Based Physicians

Area	Family/Gen. Practitioners	Specialists		
		Medical	Surgical	Other
MSA[1]	162	510	428	351

Note: Data as of 12/31/97; (1) Metropolitan Statistical Area - see Appendix A for areas included
Source: American Medical Assn., Physician Characteristics & Distribution in the U.S., 1999

Hospitals

Kansas City has 3 general medical and surgical hospitals. *AHA Guide to the Healthcare Field, 1998-99*

EDUCATION

Public School District Statistics

District Name	Num. Sch.	Enroll.	Classroom Teachers	Pupils per Teacher	Minority Pupils (%)	Current Exp.[1] ($/pupil)
Center 58	6	2,622	195	13.4	n/a	n/a
Hickman Mills C-1	14	7,421	504	14.7	n/a	n/a
Kansas City 33	79	38,711	2,537	15.3	n/a	n/a
North Kansas City 74	29	17,017	1,082	15.7	n/a	n/a
Park Hill	12	8,508	509	16.7	n/a	n/a

Note: Data covers the 1997-1998 school year unless otherwise noted; (1) Data covers fiscal year 1996; SD = School District; ISD = Independent School District; n/a not available
Source: National Center for Education Statistics, Common Core of Data Public Education Agency Universe 1997-98; National Center for Education Statistics, Characteristics of the 100 Largest Public Elementary and Secondary School Districts in the United States: 1997-98, July 1999

Educational Quality

School District	Education Quotient[1]	Graduate Outcome[2]	Community Index[3]	Resource Index[4]
Kansas City SD	86.0	52.0	103.0	149.0

Note: Nearly 1,000 secondary school districts were rated in terms of educational quality. The scores range from a low of 50 to a high of 150; (1) Average of the Graduate Outcome, Community and Resource indexes; (2) Based on graduation rates and college board scores (SAT/ACT); (3) Based on the surrounding community's average level of education and the area's average income level; (4) Based on teacher salaries, per-pupil expenditures and student-teacher ratios.
Source: Expansion Management, Ratings Issue, 1998

Educational Attainment by Race

Area	High School Graduate (%)					Bachelor's Degree (%)				
	Total	White	Black	Other	Hisp.[2]	Total	White	Black	Other	Hisp.[2]
City	78.8	82.9	68.5	68.6	62.4	22.0	26.5	10.0	18.5	11.4
MSA[1]	82.3	84.2	70.3	71.8	67.3	23.4	24.9	11.7	22.0	13.3
U.S.	75.2	77.9	63.1	60.4	49.8	20.3	21.5	11.4	19.4	9.2

Note: Figures shown cover persons 25 years old and over; (1) Metropolitan Statistical Area - see Appendix A for areas included; (2) people of Hispanic origin can be of any race
Source: 1990 Census of Population and Housing, Summary Tape File 3C

School Enrollment by Type

| Area | Preprimary | | | | Elementary/High School | | | |
| | Public | | Private | | Public | | Private | |
	Enrollment	%	Enrollment	%	Enrollment	%	Enrollment	%
City	4,496	55.5	3,601	44.5	57,590	85.6	9,712	14.4
MSA[1]	18,724	56.8	14,261	43.2	236,921	89.4	28,033	10.6
U.S.	2,679,029	59.5	1,824,256	40.5	38,379,689	90.2	4,187,099	9.8

Note: Figures shown cover persons 3 years old and over;
(1) Metropolitan Statistical Area - see Appendix A for areas included
Source: 1990 Census of Population and Housing, Summary Tape File 3C

School Enrollment by Race

| Area | Preprimary (%) | | | | Elementary/High School (%) | | | |
	White	Black	Other	Hisp.[1]	White	Black	Other	Hisp.[1]
City	65.3	31.4	3.3	4.2	55.4	40.0	4.6	5.5
MSA[2]	85.4	12.3	2.3	3.3	80.0	16.3	3.7	4.0
U.S.	80.4	12.5	7.1	7.8	74.1	15.6	10.3	12.5

Note: Figures shown cover persons 3 years old and over; (1) people of Hispanic origin can be of any
race; (2) Metropolitan Statistical Area - see Appendix A for areas included
Source: 1990 Census of Population and Housing, Summary Tape File 3C

Classroom Teacher Salaries in Public Schools

| District | B.A. Degree | | M.A. Degree | | Maximum | |
	Min. ($)	Rank[1]	Max. ($)	Rank[1]	Max. ($)	Rank[1]
Kansas City	25,275	62	42,644	72	47,851	68
Average	26,980	-	46,065	-	51,435	-

Note: Salaries are for 1997-1998; (1) Rank ranges from 1 to 100
Source: American Federation of Teachers, Survey & Analysis of Salary Trends, 1998

Higher Education

| Two-Year Colleges | | Four-Year Colleges | | Medical Schools | Law Schools | Voc/Tech |
Public	Private	Public	Private			
2	0	1	8	1	1	17

Source: College Blue Book, Occupational Education, 1997; Medical School Admission Requirements,
1999-2000; Peterson's Guide to Two-Year Colleges, 1999; Peterson's Guide to Four-Year Colleges,
2000; Barron's Guide to Law Schools, 1999

MAJOR EMPLOYERS

Major Employers

Kansas City Station Corp. (amusement services)

BGM Industries (building maintenance)

Black & Veatch (engineering services)

Children's Mercy Hospital

DST Systems (data processing)

Hallmark Cards

American Century Services (data processing)

Research Medical Center

Sprint Communications

St. Luke's Hospital of Kansas City

Note: Companies listed are located in the city
Source: Dun's Business Rankings, 1999; Ward's Business Directory, 1998

PUBLIC SAFETY

Crime Rate

Area	All Crimes	Violent Crimes				Property Crimes		
		Murder	Forcible Rape	Robbery	Aggrav. Assault	Burglary	Larceny -Theft	Motor Vehicle Theft
City	10,952.1	22.1	92.2	599.7	1,181.5	1,911.4	5,502.2	1,642.9
Suburbs[1]	n/a	n/a	n/a	n/a	n/a	n/a	n/a	n/a
MSA[2]	n/a	n/a	n/a	n/a	n/a	n/a	n/a	n/a
U.S.	4,922.7	6.8	35.9	186.1	382.0	919.6	2,886.5	505.8

Note: Crime rate is the number of crimes per 100,000 pop.; (1) defined as all areas within the MSA but located outside the central city; (2) Metropolitan Statistical Area - see Appendix A for areas incl.
Source: FBI Uniform Crime Reports, 1997

RECREATION

Culture and Recreation

Museums	Symphony Orchestras	Opera Companies	Dance Companies	Professional Theatres	Zoos	Pro Sports Teams
10	1	1	1	5	1	2

Source: International Directory of the Performing Arts, 1997; Official Museum Directory, 1999; Stern's Performing Arts Directory, 1997; USA Today Four Sport Stadium Guide, 1997; Chamber of Commerce/Economic Development, 1999

Library System

The Kansas City Public Library has eight branches, holdings of 1,895,264 volumes, and a budget of $10,314,502 (1995-1996). *American Library Directory, 1998-1999*

MEDIA

Newspapers

Name	Type	Freq.	Distribution	Circulation
The Call	Black	1x/wk	Local	17,999
Dos Mundos	Hispanic	2x/mo	Local	20,000
Kansas City Globe	Black	1x/wk	Local	10,500
The Kansas City Star	General	7x/wk	Regional	278,852
Missouri State Post	n/a	1x/wk	State	30,600
The New Times	Alternative	1x/wk	Regional	40,000
Penny Shopper	General	1x/wk	Local	3,000
Wednesday Magazine	General	1x/wk	Local	33,723

Note: Includes newspapers with circulations of 1,000 or more located in the city; n/a not available
Source: Burrelle's Media Directory, 1999 Edition

Television Stations

Name	Ch.	Affiliation	Type	Owner
WDAF	n/a	FBC	Commercial	New World Communications
KMBC	n/a	ABCT	Commercial	Hearst-Argyle Broadcasting
KCPT	19	PBS	Public	Public Television 19
KCWB	29	UPN	Commercial	KCWB-TV Inc.
KMCI	38	n/a	Commercial	Miller Broadcasting Company
KSHB	41	NBCT	Commercial	Scripps Howard Broadcasting
KPXE	50	PAXTV	Commercial	Paxson Communications Corporation

Note: Stations included broadcast in the Kansas City metro area; n/a not available
Source: Burrelle's Media Directory, 1999 Edition

AM Radio Stations

Call Letters	Freq. (kHz)	Target Audience	Station Format	Music Format
WHB	810	General	M/N/S/T	Country
KUGT	1170	General	M/T	Adult Contemporary/Christian
KCTE	1510	General	S	n/a
KPRT	1590	Religious	M/T	Christian

Note: Stations included broadcast in the Kansas City metro area; n/a not available
Target Audience: A=Asian; B=Black; C=Christian; E=Ethnic; F=French; G=General; H=Hispanic; M=Men; N=Native American; R=Religious; S=Senior Citizen; W=Women; Y=Young Adult; Z=Children
Station Format: E=Educational; M=Music; N=News; S=Sports; T=Talk
Source: Burrelle's Media Directory, 1999 Edition

FM Radio Stations

Call Letters	Freq. (mHz)	Target Audience	Station Format	Music Format
KLJC	88.5	Religious	E/M	Christian
KCUR	89.3	General	M/N/T	Big Band/Jazz/Latin
KKFI	90.1	General	n/a	n/a
KMXV	93.3	General	M	Adult Contemporary/Top 40
KFKF	94.1	General	M	Country
KSRC	102.1	Women	M	Adult Contemporary
KPRS	103.3	General	E/M/N/S/T	Urban Contemporary
KBEQ	104.3	General	M	Top 40
KNRX	107.3	General	M/N/S/T	Oldies/R&B

Note: Stations included broadcast in the Kansas City metro area; n/a not available
Station Format: E=Educational; M=Music; N=News; S=Sports; T=Talk
Target Audience: A=Asian; B=Black; C=Christian; E=Ethnic; F=French; G=General; H=Hispanic; M=Men; N=Native American; R=Religious; S=Senior Citizen; W=Women; Y=Young Adult; Z=Children
Source: Burrelle's Media Directory, 1999 Edition

CLIMATE

Average and Extreme Temperatures

Temperature	Jan	Feb	Mar	Apr	May	Jun	Jul	Aug	Sep	Oct	Nov	Dec	Yr.
Extreme High (°F)	69	76	86	93	92	105	107	109	102	92	82	70	109
Average High (°F)	35	40	54	65	74	84	90	87	79	66	52	39	64
Average Temp. (°F)	26	31	44	55	64	74	79	77	68	56	43	30	54
Average Low (°F)	17	22	34	44	54	63	69	66	58	45	34	21	44
Extreme Low (°F)	-17	-19	-10	12	30	42	54	43	33	21	1	-23	-23

Note: Figures cover the years 1972-1990
Source: National Climatic Data Center, International Station Meteorological Climate Summary, 3/95

Average Precipitation/Snowfall/Humidity

Precip./Humidity	Jan	Feb	Mar	Apr	May	Jun	Jul	Aug	Sep	Oct	Nov	Dec	Yr.
Avg. Precip. (in.)	1.1	1.2	2.8	3.0	5.5	4.1	3.8	4.1	4.9	3.6	2.1	1.6	38.1
Avg. Snowfall (in.)	6	5	3	1	0	0	0	0	0	Tr	1	5	21
Avg. Rel. Hum. 6am (%)	76	77	78	77	82	84	84	86	86	80	79	78	80
Avg. Rel. Hum. 3pm (%)	58	59	54	50	54	54	51	53	53	51	57	60	54

Note: Figures cover the years 1972-1990; Tr = Trace amounts (<0.05 in. of rain; <0.5 in. of snow)
Source: National Climatic Data Center, International Station Meteorological Climate Summary, 3/95

Weather Conditions

Temperature			Daytime Sky			Precipitation		
10°F & below	32°F & below	90°F & above	Clear	Partly cloudy	Cloudy	0.01 inch or more precip.	0.1 inch or more snow/ice	Thunder-storms
22	110	39	112	134	119	103	17	51

Note: Figures are average number of days per year and covers the years 1972-1990
Source: National Climatic Data Center, International Station Meteorological Climate Summary, 3/95

AIR & WATER QUALITY

Maximum Pollutant Concentrations

	Particulate Matter (ug/m^3)	Carbon Monoxide (ppm)	Sulfur Dioxide (ppm)	Nitrogen Dioxide (ppm)	Ozone (ppm)	Lead (ug/m^3)
MSA[1] Level	75	7	0.021	0.020	0.12	0.45
NAAQS[2]	150	9	0.140	0.053	0.12	1.50
Met NAAQS?	Yes	Yes	Yes	Yes	Yes	Yes

Note: (1) Metropolitan Statistical Area - see Appendix A for areas included; (2) National Ambient Air Quality Standards; ppm = parts per million; ug/m^3 = micrograms per cubic meter; n/a not available
Source: EPA, National Air Quality and Emissions Trends Report, 1997

Pollutant Standards Index

In the Kansas City MSA (see Appendix A for areas included), the Pollutant Standards Index (PSI) exceeded 100 on 18 days in 1997. A PSI value greater than 100 indicates that air quality would be in the unhealthful range on that day. *EPA, National Air Quality and Emissions Trends Report, 1997*

Drinking Water

Water System Name	Pop. Served	Primary Water Source Type	Number of Violations in 1998	Type of Violation/ Contaminants
Kansas City	450,000	Surface	None	None

Note: Data as of July 10, 1999
Source: EPA, Office of Ground Water and Drinking Water, Safe Drinking Water Information System

Kansas City tap water is neutral, soft and fluoridated.
Editor & Publisher Market Guide, 1999

Lansing, Michigan

Background

Ottawas, Potawatomis and Chippewas lived and hunted in a wide area that included what would become the city of Lansing, which itself began as a scam. Two men sold land to citizens of Lansing, New York. The salesmen said the land would be located in the city of Biddle, Michigan. When the New Yorkers arrived in the late 1830s they found no city, just woodlands. They settled anyway and named the town after their old home. In 1847 the state legislature moved the capital from Detroit to the still sparsely settled town of Lansing. Workers laid a wooden plank road from Detroit to Lansing in 1852, and the village began to grow.

The town was promoted to a city in 1859, and after the coming of the railroad in 1871, Lansing's industries began to expand. Early commercial concerns included the making of wagons, carriages, and wheels. However, the city would soon become famous for the manufacture of horseless carriages. In the 1890s, Ransom E. Olds and Frank G. Clark established an automobile manufacturing plant there that would produce the Oldsmobile. The city has been an important center for auto products ever since.

Since it is Michigan's capital, the state government employs the most people in the city. Another large public sector employer is Michigan State University, offering many areas of educational advancement.

Of course, the largest private sector employer is General Motors. The auto giant has its small car division headquarters in Lansing. Auto parts and engine production are also vital sectors of the local economy.

Both the state government and General Motors have reduced their number of workers in recent years, with the university's workforce remaining roughly the same. Today, service businesses take up a large and growing percentage of Lansing's economy—nearly forty percent. Pharmaceutical and software research businesses are new additions to the city's economy.

The medical industry is also important. Sparrow Hospital and the Ingham Regional Medical Center provide healthcare to the community, and thousands of people work at both facilities. High finance is also a part of the Lansing's commercial scene. Banking and insurance concerns also employ thousands.

To rejuvenate parts of the city, the state government established two Renaissance Zones. State and local taxes, except those on sales, have been lifted to encourage economic growth.

The metropolitan area's weather conditions are typical for this part of the North American continent, with cold winters and warm summers. The Great Lakes affect the climate; their drifting winds keep Lansing from experiencing excessive heat or cold. Temperatures range from the teens to the forties in the winter, while the mean temperature in the summer is in the upper eighties. The Great Lake causes the area to be overcast much of the time. Average annual rainfall is thirty inches, while snowfall tends to be slightly less than fifty inches per year.

General Rankings and Evaluative Comments

- Lansing was ranked #8 out of 24 mid-sized, midwestern metropolitan areas in *Money's* 1998 survey of "The Best Places to Live in America." The survey was conducted by first contacting 512 representative households nationwide and asking them to rank 37 quality-of-life factors on a scale of 1 to 10. Next, a demographic profile was compiled on the 300 largest metropolitan statistical areas in the U.S. The numbers were crunched together to arrive at an overall ranking (things Americans consider most important, like clean air and water, low crime and good schools, received extra weight). Unlike previous years, the 1998 rankings were broken down by region (northeast, midwest, south, west) and population size (100,000 to 249,999; 250,000 to 999,999; 1 million plus). The city had a nationwide ranking of #237 out of 300 in 1997 and #111 out of 300 in 1996. *Money, July 1998; Money, July 1997; Money, September 1996*

- *Ladies Home Journal* ranked America's 200 largest cities based on the qualities women care about most. Lansing ranked #166 out of 200. Criteria: low crime rate, well-paying jobs, quality health and child care, good public schools, the presence of women in government, size of the gender wage gap, number of sexual-harassment and discrimination complaints filed, unemployment and divorce rates, commute times, population density, number of houses of worship, parks and cultural offerings, number of women's health specialists, how well a community's women cared for themselves, complexion kindness index based on UV radiation levels, odds of finding affordable fashions, rental rates for romance movies, champagne sales and other matters of the heart. *Ladies Home Journal, November 1998*

- Zero Population Growth ranked 229 cities in terms of children's health, safety, and economic well-being. Lansing was ranked #60 out of 112 independent cities (cities with populations greater than 100,000 which were neither Major Cities nor Suburbs/Outer Cities) and was given a grade of C. Criteria: total population, percent of population under 18 years of age, household language, percent population change, percent of births to teens, infant mortality rate, percent of low birth weights, dropout rate, enrollment in preprimary school, violent and property crime rates, unemployment rate, percent of children in poverty, percent of owner occupied units, number of bad air days, percent of public transportation commuters, and average travel time to work. *Zero Population Growth, Children's Environmental Index, Fall 1999*

- Reliastar Financial Corp. ranked the 125 largest metropolitan areas according to the general financial security of residents. Lansing was ranked #34 out of 125 with a score of 6.0. The score indicates the percentage a metropolitan area is above or below the metropolitan norm. A metro area with a score of 10.6 is 10.6% above the metro average. Criteria: Earnings and Wealth Potential (household income, education, net assets, cost of living); Safety Net (health insurance, retirement savings, life insurance, income support programs); Personal Threats (unemployment rate, low-income households, crime rate); Community Economic Vitality (cost of community services, job quality, job creation, housing costs).
Reliastar Financial Corp., "The Best Cities to Earn and Save Money," 1999 Edition

Business Environment

STATE ECONOMY

State Economic Profile

"Although the Michigan economy bounced back quickly from the GM strike, it is losing much of its mid-1990s momentum. Strong auto sales have not translated into employment gains in the auto industry. Canada's weak economy has caused a drop in MI's exports. And what constrains MI the most is its demographic situation. The next several years should see a slowing economy.

In spite of the GM strike and booming automobile sales, GM has not increased employment and is currently planning to close plants in Kalamazoo and Flint. In addition, some 1,000 office jobs are targeted for elimination at the Detroit headquarters; Ford is currently planning to cut jobs within the state. Auto sales for 1999 and 2000 should fall below 1998, only adding to Detroit's need for employment reductions.

Construction activity added significantly to job growth in 1998, with construction employment growing 2.5% for the state and 8.3% for Detroit. Almost 1,800 commercial/industrial developments were undertaken in 1998. With the slowing economy, construction activity is likely to contract in 1999, undermining one of MI's bright spots. Residential starts, up 7% in 1998, should decline 6.2% in 1999.

Michigan's tight labor markets have helped to absorb downsizing in the auto industry, keeping the unemployment rate manageable. Labor availability has, however, started to become a problem for the state's information technology firms. The state's weak population growth, especially its continuing loss of young households, will dampen the high home price appreciation witnessed in recent years, as well as limit job entry-level job growth." *National Association of Realtors, Economic Profiles: The Fifty States and the District of Columbia, http://nar.realtor.com/databank/profiles.htm*

IMPORTS/EXPORTS

Total Export Sales

Area	1994 ($000)	1995 ($000)	1996 ($000)	1997 ($000)	% Chg. 1994-97	% Chg. 1996-97
MSA[1]	208,627	224,039	202,209	217,475	4.2	7.5
U.S.	512,415,609	583,030,524	622,827,063	687,597,999	34.2	10.4

Note: (1) Metropolitan Statistical Area - see Appendix A for areas included
Source: U.S. Department of Commerce, International Trade Association, Metropolitan Area Exports: An Export Performance Report on Over 250 U.S. Cities, November 10, 1998

CITY FINANCES

City Government Finances

Component	FY92 ($000)	FY92 (per capita $)
Revenue	310,981	2,457.26
Expenditure	290,223	2,293.24
Debt Outstanding	130,142	1,028.34
Cash & Securities	449,121	3,548.79

Source: U.S. Bureau of the Census, City Government Finances: 1991-92

City Government Revenue by Source

Source	FY92 ($000)	FY92 (per capita $)	FY92 (%)
From Federal Government	3,776	29.84	1.2
From State Governments	25,449	201.09	8.2
From Local Governments	0	0.00	0.0
Property Taxes	29,540	233.41	9.5
General Sales Taxes	0	0.00	0.0
Selective Sales Taxes	0	0.00	0.0
Income Taxes	20,023	158.21	6.4
Current Charges	30,460	240.68	9.8
Utility/Liquor Store	139,321	1,100.86	44.8
Employee Retirement[1]	39,326	310.74	12.6
Other	23,086	182.42	7.4

Note: (1) Excludes "city contributions," classified as "nonrevenue," intragovernmental transfers.
Source: U.S. Bureau of the Census, City Government Finances: 1991-92

City Government Expenditures by Function

Function	FY92 ($000)	FY92 (per capita $)	FY92 (%)
Educational Services	0	0.00	0.0
Employee Retirement[1]	10,116	79.93	3.5
Environment/Housing	22,623	178.76	7.8
Government Administration	10,423	82.36	3.6
Interest on General Debt	5,747	45.41	2.0
Public Safety	26,533	209.65	9.1
Social Services	1,315	10.39	0.5
Transportation	11,276	89.10	3.9
Utility/Liquor Store	143,690	1,135.39	49.5
Other	58,500	462.25	20.2

Note: (1) Payments to beneficiaries including withdrawal of contributions.
Source: U.S. Bureau of the Census, City Government Finances: 1991-92

Municipal Bond Ratings

Area	Moody's	S & P
Lansing	Aa3	n/a

Note: n/a not available; n/r not rated
Source: Moody's Bond Record, 6/99

POPULATION

Population Growth

Area	1980	1990	% Chg. 1980-90	July 1998 Estimate	% Chg. 1990-98
City	130,414	127,321	-2.4	127,825	0.4
MSA[1]	419,750	432,674	3.1	452,490	4.6
U.S.	226,545,805	248,765,170	9.8	270,299,000	8.7

Note: (1) Metropolitan Statistical Area - see Appendix A for areas included;
July 1998 MSA population estimate was calculated by the editors
Source: 1980/1990 Census of Housing and Population, Summary Tape File 3C;
Census Bureau Population Estimates 1998

Population Characteristics

Race	City 1980 Population	%	City 1990 Population	%	% Chg. 1980-90	MSA[1] 1990 Population	%
White	105,646	81.0	94,218	74.0	-10.8	381,729	88.2
Black	18,081	13.9	23,639	18.6	30.7	31,224	7.2
Amer Indian/Esk/Aleut	1,212	0.9	1,595	1.3	31.6	2,896	0.7
Asian/Pacific Islander	1,144	0.9	2,148	1.7	87.8	8,138	1.9
Other	4,331	3.3	5,721	4.5	32.1	8,687	2.0
Hispanic Origin[2]	7,968	6.1	10,156	8.0	27.5	16,571	3.8

Note: (1) Metropolitan Statistical Area - see Appendix A for areas included;
(2) people of Hispanic origin can be of any race
Source: 1980/1990 Census of Housing and Population, Summary Tape File 3C

Ancestry

Area	German	Irish	English	Italian	U.S.	French	Polish	Dutch
City	27.9	13.7	15.2	2.4	3.3	5.3	3.8	3.9
MSA[1]	35.6	15.5	20.0	2.9	3.5	5.9	5.0	5.0
U.S.	23.3	15.6	13.1	5.9	5.3	4.2	3.8	2.5

Note: Figures are percentages and include persons that reported multiple ancestry (eg. if a person reported being Irish and Italian, they were included in both columns); (1) Metropolitan Statistical Area - see Appendix A for areas included
Source: 1990 Census of Population and Housing, Summary Tape File 3C

Age

Area	Median Age (Years)	Under 5	Under 18	18-24	25-44	45-64	65+	80+
City	29.7	9.2	27.6	11.7	36.4	14.6	9.6	2.1
MSA[1]	29.8	7.3	25.7	15.9	33.1	16.4	9.0	2.1
U.S.	32.9	7.3	25.6	10.5	32.6	18.7	12.5	2.8

Note: (1) Metropolitan Statistical Area - see Appendix A for areas included
Source: 1990 Census of Population and Housing, Summary Tape File 3C

Male/Female Ratio

Area	Number of males per 100 females (all ages)	Number of males per 100 females (18 years old+)
City	90.0	86.1
MSA[1]	93.6	90.6
U.S.	95.0	91.9

Note: (1) Metropolitan Statistical Area - see Appendix A for areas included
Source: 1990 Census of Population, General Population Characteristics

INCOME

Per Capita/Median/Average Income

Area	Per Capita ($)	Median Household ($)	Average Household ($)
City	12,232	26,398	30,458
MSA[1]	14,044	32,156	38,027
U.S.	14,420	30,056	38,453

Note: All figures are for 1989; (1) Metropolitan Statistical Area - see Appendix A for areas included
Source: 1990 Census of Population and Housing, Summary Tape File 3C

Household Income Distribution by Race

Income ($)	City (%)					U.S. (%)				
	Total	White	Black	Other	Hisp.[1]	Total	White	Black	Other	Hisp.[1]
Less than 5,000	7.8	5.7	15.5	15.8	13.3	6.2	4.8	15.2	8.6	8.8
5,000 - 9,999	10.9	9.8	16.4	10.9	12.0	9.3	8.6	14.2	9.9	11.1
10,000 - 14,999	9.6	9.9	7.9	10.8	9.0	8.8	8.5	11.0	9.8	11.0
15,000 - 24,999	18.8	19.9	14.3	16.4	17.3	17.5	17.3	18.9	18.5	20.5
25,000 - 34,999	17.3	18.4	12.4	15.6	12.7	15.8	16.1	14.2	15.4	16.4
35,000 - 49,999	19.0	19.7	16.2	16.5	20.2	17.9	18.6	13.3	16.1	16.0
50,000 - 74,999	12.3	12.4	12.2	11.8	12.9	15.0	15.8	9.3	13.4	11.1
75,000 - 99,999	3.0	2.8	3.9	1.7	1.4	5.1	5.5	2.6	4.7	3.1
100,000+	1.2	1.3	1.1	0.6	1.2	4.4	4.8	1.3	3.7	1.9

Note: All figures are for 1989; (1) people of Hispanic origin can be of any race
Source: 1990 Census of Population and Housing, Summary Tape File 3C

Effective Buying Income

Area	Per Capita ($)	Median Household ($)	Average Household ($)
City	13,717	29,409	33,909
MSA[1]	16,004	36,025	43,423
U.S.	16,803	34,536	45,243

Note: Data as of 1/1/99; (1) Metropolitan Statistical Area - see Appendix A for areas included
Source: Standard Rate & Data Service, Newspaper Advertising Source, 9/99

Effective Household Buying Income Distribution

Area	% of Households Earning						
	$10,000 -$19,999	$20,000 -$34,999	$35,000 -$49,999	$50,000 -$74,999	$75,000 -$99,000	$100,000 -$124,999	$125,000 and up
City	18.2	25.0	19.6	16.2	4.0	1.0	0.4
MSA[1]	14.9	22.7	19.7	20.9	7.3	1.9	1.6
U.S.	16.0	22.6	18.2	18.9	7.2	2.4	2.7

Note: Data as of 1/1/99; (1) Metropolitan Statistical Area - see Appendix A for areas included
Source: Standard Rate & Data Service, Newspaper Advertising Source, 9/99

Poverty Rates by Race and Age

Area	Total (%)	By Race (%)				By Age (%)		
		White	Black	Other	Hisp.[2]	Under 5 years old	Under 18 years old	65 years and over
City	19.4	14.2	33.6	35.5	31.1	30.8	28.5	11.4
MSA[1]	12.9	10.6	30.5	32.0	26.3	18.3	14.9	9.5
U.S.	13.1	9.8	29.5	23.1	25.3	20.1	18.3	12.8

Note: Figures show the percent of people living below the poverty line in 1989. The average poverty threshold was $12,674 for a family of four in 1989; (1) Metropolitan Statistical Area - see Appendix A for areas included; (2) people of Hispanic origin can be of any race
Source: 1990 Census of Population and Housing, Summary Tape File 3C

EMPLOYMENT

Labor Force and Employment

Area	Civilian Labor Force			Workers Employed		
	Jun. 1998	Jun. 1999	% Chg.	Jun. 1998	Jun. 1999	% Chg.
City	65,832	65,702	-0.2	63,314	63,164	-0.2
MSA[1]	240,498	240,072	-0.2	233,784	233,229	-0.2
U.S.	138,798,000	140,666,000	1.3	132,265,000	134,395,000	1.6

Note: Data is not seasonally adjusted and covers workers 16 years of age and older;
(1) Metropolitan Statistical Area - see Appendix A for areas included
Source: Bureau of Labor Statistics, http://stats.bls.gov

Unemployment Rate

Area	1998						1999					
	Jul.	Aug.	Sep.	Oct.	Nov.	Dec.	Jan.	Feb.	Mar.	Apr.	May.	Jun.
City	7.5	3.3	3.0	2.9	2.9	3.3	4.1	4.0	3.9	3.4	3.2	3.9
MSA[1]	6.4	2.4	2.2	2.1	2.2	2.5	3.2	3.1	3.0	2.5	2.4	2.9
U.S.	4.7	4.5	4.4	4.2	4.1	4.0	4.8	4.7	4.4	4.1	4.0	4.5

Note: Data is not seasonally adjusted and covers workers 16 years of age and older; all figures are percentages; (1) Metropolitan Statistical Area - see Appendix A for areas included
Source: Bureau of Labor Statistics, http://stats.bls.gov

Employment by Industry

Sector	MSA[1]		U.S.
	Number of Employees	Percent of Total	Percent of Total
Services	58,900	25.4	30.4
Retail Trade	44,200	19.1	17.7
Government	60,800	26.3	15.6
Manufacturing	28,600	12.3	14.3
Finance/Insurance/Real Estate	14,800	6.4	5.9
Wholesale Trade	8,600	3.7	5.4
Transportation/Public Utilities	6,000	2.6	5.3
Construction	n/a	n/a	5.0
Mining	n/a	n/a	0.4

Note: Figures cover non-farm employment as of 6/99 and are not seasonally adjusted; (1) Metropolitan Statistical Area - see Appendix A for areas included; n/a not available
Source: Bureau of Labor Statistics, http://stats.bls.gov

Employment by Occupation

Occupation Category	City (%)	MSA[1] (%)	U.S. (%)
White Collar	58.2	60.9	58.1
Executive/Admin./Management	11.1	12.1	12.3
Professional	12.7	15.5	14.1
Technical & Related Support	4.0	4.1	3.7
Sales	10.8	11.2	11.8
Administrative Support/Clerical	19.5	18.1	16.3
Blue Collar	24.0	22.6	26.2
Precision Production/Craft/Repair	9.2	9.6	11.3
Machine Operators/Assem./Insp.	7.1	6.1	6.8
Transportation/Material Movers	3.7	3.3	4.1
Cleaners/Helpers/Laborers	4.0	3.6	3.9
Services	16.9	14.8	13.2
Farming/Forestry/Fishing	0.9	1.7	2.5

Note: Figures cover employed persons 16 years old and over; (1) Metropolitan Statistical Area - see Appendix A for areas included
Source: 1990 Census of Population and Housing, Summary Tape File 3C

Occupational Employment Projections: 1994 - 2005

Occupations Expected to Have the Largest Job Growth (ranked by numerical growth)	Fast-Growing Occupations[1] (ranked by percent growth)
1. Waiters & waitresses	1. Computer engineers
2. Cashiers	2. Home health aides
3. All other helper, laborer, mover	3. Systems analysts
4. Systems analysts	4. Personal and home care aides
5. Home health aides	5. Electronic pagination systems workers
6. General managers & top executives	6. All other computer scientists
7. All other profess., paraprofess., tech.	7. Physical therapists
8. Registered nurses	8. All other therapists
9. All other sales reps. & services	9. Electronics repairers, comm. & indust.
10. Salespersons, retail	10. Occupational therapists

Note: Projections cover Michigan; (1) Excludes occupations with total job growth less than 300
Source: Office of Labor Market Information, Occupational Employment Forecasts, 1994-2005

TAXES

Major State and Local Tax Rates

State Corp. Income (%)	State Personal Income (%)	Residential Property (effective rate per $100)	Sales & Use State (%)	Sales & Use Local (%)	State Gasoline (cents/ gallon)	State Cigarette (cents/ pack)
2.3[a]	4.4	n/a	6.0	None	19.0	75.0

Note: Personal/corporate income, sales, gasoline and cigarette tax rates as of January 1999.
Property tax rates as of 1997; (a) Value added tax imposed on the sum of federal taxable income of
the business, compensation paid to employees, dividends, interest, royalties paid and other items
Source: Federation of Tax Administrators, www.taxadmin.org; Washington D.C. Department of
Finance and Revenue, Tax Rates and Tax Burdens in the District of Columbia: A Nationwide
Comparison, July 1998; Chamber of Commerce, 1999

Total Taxes Per Capita and as a Percent of Income

Area	Per Capita Income ($)	Per Capita Taxes ($) Total	Per Capita Taxes ($) Federal	Per Capita Taxes ($) State/ Local	Percent of Income (%) Total	Percent of Income (%) Federal	Percent of Income (%) State/ Local
Michigan	28,565	10,361	7,221	3,139	36.3	25.3	11.0
U.S.	27,876	9,881	6,690	3,191	35.4	24.0	11.4

Note: Figures are for 1998
Source: Tax Foundation, www.taxfoundation.org

**COMMERCIAL
REAL ESTATE**

Office Market

Class/ Location	Total Space (sq. ft.)	Vacant Space (sq. ft.)	Vac. Rate (%)	Under Constr. (sq. ft.)	Net Absorp. (sq. ft.)	Rental Rates ($/sq.ft./yr.)
Class A						
CBD	1,589,794	22,258	1.4	n/a	153,290	n/a
Outside CBD	1,423,975	146,101	10.3	n/a	377,911	n/a
Class B						
CBD	692,236	35,304	5.1	n/a	-168,576	n/a
Outside CBD	3,164,040	329,522	10.4	n/a	500,709	n/a

Note: Data as of 10/98 and covers Lansing; CBD = Central Business District; n/a not available;
Source: Society of Industrial and Office Realtors, 1999 Comparative Statistics of Industrial and Office
Real Estate Markets

"The populations of Ingham, Eaton, and Clinton total 432,700 people, and they are expected
to reach 446,500 by the year 2000. General Motors employs 16,000 people in the Oldsmobile
and Small Car divisions here. However, greater Lansing's economy is becoming more diverse
and is no longer solely dependent on the automobile industry, a trend that is expected to
persist. Office conversions in the CBD of Class C space into Class B space are expected to run
at a moderate pace. Construction is expected to increase by up to 10 percent in 1999.

Increases in absorption should be between one and five percent. Rental rates are also expected to increase moderately." *Society of Industrial and Office Realtors, 1999 Comparative Statistics of Industrial and Office Real Estate Markets*

Industrial Market

Location	Total Space (sq. ft.)	Vacant Space (sq. ft.)	Vac. Rate (%)	Under Constr. (sq. ft.)	Net Absorp. (sq. ft.)	Lease ($/sq.ft./yr.)
Central City	984,990	36,175	3.7	n/a	125,371	4.00-5.75
Suburban	2,831,434	535,840	18.9	36,000	146,847	3.50-5.75

Note: Data as of 10/98 and covers Lansing; n/a not available
Source: Society of Industrial and Office Realtors, 1999 Comparative Statistics of Industrial and Office Real Estate Markets

"Although there is a shortage of quality industrial space throughout Greater Lansing, investors remain reluctant to shoulder escalated construction prices to accommodate sporadic demand. This coming year few speculative buildings will be developed. Any activity is likely to be in the form of buildings less than 50,000 sq. ft. and confined to the north and west sub-markets. Our local SIOR reporter feels that there are substantial shortages in all spaces above 5,000 sq. ft. Sales prices are expected to remain constant. The demand for large blocks of quality space is increasing with build-to-suit and expansions prevalent. Lease prices for warehouse/distribution and manufacturing space is expected to rise slightly. Absorption increases should help reduce vacancies in warehouse/distribution and manufacturing space in the suburban markets." *Society of Industrial and Office Realtors, 1999 Comparative Statistics of Industrial and Office Real Estate Markets*

COMMERCIAL UTILITIES

Typical Monthly Electric Bills

Area	Commercial Service ($/month)		Industrial Service ($/month)	
	12 kW demand 1,500 kWh	100 kW demand 30,000 kWh	1,000 kW demand 400,000 kWh	20,000 kW demand 10,000,000 kWh
City[1]	n/a	n/a[a]	n/a	n/a
U.S.[2]	150	2,174	23,995	508,569

Note: Based on rates in effect ; n/a not available
Source: Memphis Light, Gas and Water, 1998 Utility Bill Comparisons for Selected U.S. Cities; Edison Electric Institute, Typical Residential, Commercial and Industrial Bills, Winter 1999

TRANSPORTATION

Transportation Statistics

Average minutes to work	17.3
Interstate highways	I-69; I-96
Bus lines	
In-city	Capital Area Transportation Authority
Inter-city	2
Passenger air service	
Airport	Capital City Airport
Airlines	6
Aircraft departures	n/a
Enplaned passengers	n/a
Rail service	Amtrak service to East Lansing
Motor freight carriers	26
Major waterways/ports	None

Source: Editor & Publisher Market Guide, 1999; FAA Airport Activity Statistics, 1997; Amtrak National Time Table, Northeast Timetable, Spring/Summer 1999; 1990 Census of Population and Housing, STF 3C; Chamber of Commerce/Economic Development 1999; Jane's Urban Transport Systems 1999-2000

Means of Transportation to Work

Area	Car/Truck/Van		Public Transportation			Bicycle	Walked	Other Means	Worked at Home
	Drove Alone	Car-pooled	Bus	Subway	Railroad				
City	77.3	12.4	2.8	0.0	0.0	0.4	4.0	0.8	2.3
MSA[1]	77.0	11.3	1.5	0.0	0.0	0.8	5.7	0.7	3.0
U.S.	73.2	13.4	3.0	1.5	0.5	0.4	3.9	1.2	3.0

Note: Figures shown are percentages and only include workers 16 years old and over;
(1) Metropolitan Statistical Area - see Appendix A for areas included
Source: 1990 Census of Population and Housing, Summary Tape File 3C

BUSINESSES

Major Business Headquarters

Company Name	1999 Rankings	
	Fortune 500	Forbes 500

No companies listed.

Note: Companies listed are located in the city; dashes indicate no ranking
Fortune 500: Companies that produce a 10-K are ranked 1 to 500 based on 1998 revenue
Forbes 500: Private companies are ranked 1 to 500 based on 1997 revenue
Source: Forbes, November 30, 1998; Fortune, April 26, 1999

Minority Business Opportunity

Lansing is home to one company which is on the Black Enterprise Industrial/Service 100 list (largest based on gross sales): Trumark Inc. (automotive metal stampings and welded assemblies) . Criteria: operational in previous calendar year, at least 51% black-owned and manufactures/owns the product it sells or provides industrial or consumer services. Brokerages, real estate firms and firms that provide professional services are not eligible. *Black Enterprise, www.blackenterprise.com*

HOTELS & MOTELS

Hotels/Motels

Area	Hotels/ Motels	Rooms	Luxury-Level Hotels/Motels		Average Minimum Rates ($)		
			♦♦♦♦	♦♦♦♦♦	♦♦	♦♦♦	♦♦♦♦
City	17	2,339	0	0	75	96	n/a

Note: n/a not available; classifications range from one diamond (budget properties with basic amenities) to five diamond (luxury properties with the finest service, rooms and facilities).
Source: OAG, Business Travel Planner, Winter 1998-99

CONVENTION CENTERS

Major Convention Centers

Center Name	Meeting Rooms	Exhibit Space (sq. ft.)
Lansing Center	10	72,000

Source: Trade Shows Worldwide, 1998; Meetings & Conventions, 4/15/99;
Sucessful Meetings, 3/31/98

Living Environment

COST OF LIVING

Cost of Living Index

Composite Index	Groceries	Housing	Utilities	Trans-portation	Health Care	Misc. Goods/Services
106.2	104.1	129.9	81.2	97.3	97.1	97.2

Note: U.S. = 100
Source: ACCRA, Cost of Living Index, 1st Quarter 1999

HOUSING

Median Home Prices and Housing Affordability

Area	Median Price[2] 1st Qtr. 1999 ($)	HOI[3] 1st Qtr. 1999	Affordability Rank[4]
MSA[1]	101,000	75.6	90
U.S.	134,000	69.6	–

Note: (1) Metropolitan Statistical Area - see Appendix A for areas included; (2) U.S. figures calculated from the sales of 524,324 new and existing homes in 181 markets; (3) Housing Opportunity Index - percent of homes sold that were within the reach of the median income household at the prevailing mortgage interest rate; (4) Rank is from 1-181 with 1 being most affordable
Source: National Association of Home Builders, Housing Opportunity Index, 1st Quarter 1999

Median Home Price Projection

It is projected that the median price of existing single-family homes in the metro area will decrease by -1.0% in 1999. Nationwide, home prices are projected to increase 3.8%.
Kiplinger's Personal Finance Magazine, January 1999

Average New Home Price

Area	Price ($)
City	189,500
U.S.	142,735

Note: Figures are based on a new home with 1,800 sq. ft. of living area on an 8,000 sq. ft. lot.
Source: ACCRA, Cost of Living Index, 1st Quarter 1999

Average Apartment Rent

Area	Rent ($/mth)
City	645
U.S.	601

Note: Figures are based on an unfurnished two bedroom, 1-1/2 or 2 bath apartment, approximately 950 sq. ft. in size, excluding all utilities except water
Source: ACCRA, Cost of Living Index, 1st Quarter 1999

RESIDENTIAL UTILITIES

Average Residential Utility Costs

Area	All Electric ($/mth)	Part Electric ($/mth)	Other Energy ($/mth)	Phone ($/mth)
City	–	37.06	41.59	18.59
U.S.	100.02	55.73	43.33	19.71

Source: ACCRA, Cost of Living Index, 1st Quarter 1999

HEALTH CARE

Average Health Care Costs

Area	Hospital ($/day)	Doctor ($/visit)	Dentist ($/visit)
City	479.00	42.75	71.33
U.S.	430.43	52.45	66.35

Note: Hospital—based on a semi-private room; Doctor—based on a general practitioner's routine exam of an established patient; Dentist—based on adult teeth cleaning and periodic oral exam.
Source: ACCRA, Cost of Living Index, 1st Quarter 1999

Distribution of Office-Based Physicians

Area	Family/Gen. Practitioners	Specialists		
		Medical	Surgical	Other
MSA[1]	93	201	130	154

Note: Data as of 12/31/97; (1) Metropolitan Statistical Area - see Appendix A for areas included
Source: American Medical Assn., Physician Characteristics & Distribution in the U.S., 1999

Hospitals

Lansing has 3 general medical and surgical hospitals. *AHA Guide to the Healthcare Field, 1998-99*

EDUCATION

Public School District Statistics

District Name	Num. Sch.	Enroll.	Classroom Teachers	Pupils per Teacher	Minority Pupils (%)	Current Exp.[1] ($/pupil)
Community Health Agency	n/a	n/a	n/a	n/a	n/a	n/a
Department of Corrections	n/a	n/a	n/a	n/a	n/a	n/a
Department of Education	n/a	n/a	n/a	n/a	n/a	n/a
Family Independence Agency	n/a	n/a	n/a	n/a	n/a	n/a
Lansing Public School District	45	19,060	1,134	16.8	n/a	n/a
Waverly Community Schools	8	3,321	192	17.3	n/a	n/a

Note: Data covers the 1997-1998 school year unless otherwise noted; (1) Data covers fiscal year 1996; SD = School District; ISD = Independent School District; n/a not available
Source: National Center for Education Statistics, Common Core of Data Public Education Agency Universe 1997-98; National Center for Education Statistics, Characteristics of the 100 Largest Public Elementary and Secondary School Districts in the United States: 1997-98, July 1999

Educational Quality

School District	Education Quotient[1]	Graduate Outcome[2]	Community Index[3]	Resource Index[4]
Lansing Public	74.0	72.0	86.0	75.0

Note: Nearly 1,000 secondary school districts were rated in terms of educational quality. The scores range from a low of 50 to a high of 150; (1) Average of the Graduate Outcome, Community and Resource indexes; (2) Based on graduation rates and college board scores (SAT/ACT); (3) Based on the surrounding community's average level of education and the area's average income level; (4) Based on teacher salaries, per-pupil expenditures and student-teacher ratios.
Source: Expansion Management, Ratings Issue, 1998

Educational Attainment by Race

Area	High School Graduate (%)					Bachelor's Degree (%)				
	Total	White	Black	Other	Hisp.[2]	Total	White	Black	Other	Hisp.[2]
City	78.3	80.9	72.0	60.1	54.6	18.3	19.9	13.6	9.8	6.4
MSA[1]	84.2	85.3	75.8	73.2	61.0	24.7	24.5	21.0	33.4	12.5
U.S.	75.2	77.9	63.1	60.4	49.8	20.3	21.5	11.4	19.4	9.2

Note: Figures shown cover persons 25 years old and over; (1) Metropolitan Statistical Area - see Appendix A for areas included; (2) people of Hispanic origin can be of any race
Source: 1990 Census of Population and Housing, Summary Tape File 3C

School Enrollment by Type

Area	Preprimary				Elementary/High School			
	Public		Private		Public		Private	
	Enrollment	%	Enrollment	%	Enrollment	%	Enrollment	%
City	1,707	65.2	911	34.8	20,001	90.4	2,118	9.6
MSA[1]	5,761	67.9	2,718	32.1	68,193	91.6	6,215	8.4
U.S.	2,679,029	59.5	1,824,256	40.5	38,379,689	90.2	4,187,099	9.8

Note: Figures shown cover persons 3 years old and over;
(1) Metropolitan Statistical Area - see Appendix A for areas included
Source: 1990 Census of Population and Housing, Summary Tape File 3C

School Enrollment by Race

Area	Preprimary (%)				Elementary/High School (%)			
	White	Black	Other	Hisp.[1]	White	Black	Other	Hisp.[1]
City	71.7	18.9	9.4	9.7	61.1	27.1	11.8	12.9
MSA[2]	88.0	6.7	5.4	4.7	84.1	9.7	6.2	5.9
U.S.	80.4	12.5	7.1	7.8	74.1	15.6	10.3	12.5

Note: Figures shown cover persons 3 years old and over; (1) people of Hispanic origin can be of any race; (2) Metropolitan Statistical Area - see Appendix A for areas included
Source: 1990 Census of Population and Housing, Summary Tape File 3C

Classroom Teacher Salaries in Public Schools

District	B.A. Degree		M.A. Degree		Maximum	
	Min. ($)	Rank[1]	Max. ($)	Rank[1]	Max. ($)	Rank[1]
	n/a	n/a	n/a	n/a	n/a	n/a
Average	26,980	-	46,065	-	51,435	-

Note: Salaries are for 1997-1998; (1) Rank ranges from 1 to 100; n/a not available
Source: American Federation of Teachers, Survey & Analysis of Salary Trends, 1998

Higher Education

Two-Year Colleges		Four-Year Colleges		Medical Schools	Law Schools	Voc/ Tech
Public	Private	Public	Private			
1	0	0	2	0	2	7

Source: College Blue Book, Occupational Education, 1997; Medical School Admission Requirements, 1999-2000; Peterson's Guide to Two-Year Colleges, 1999; Peterson's Guide to Four-Year Colleges, 2000; Barron's Guide to Law Schools, 1999

MAJOR EMPLOYERS

Major Employers

Auto Owners Insurance	Edward W. Sparrow Hospital Assn.
Guthrie Investment Group	Brooke Life Insurance
Jackson National Life Insurance	Oldsmobile Division
Trumark Inc. (automotive stampings)	Wohlert Corp. (motor vehicle parts)
Ingham Regional Medical Center	Maxco (construction materials)

Note: Companies listed are located in the city
Source: Dun's Business Rankings, 1999; Ward's Business Directory, 1998

PUBLIC SAFETY

Crime Rate

Area	All Crimes	Violent Crimes				Property Crimes		
		Murder	Forcible Rape	Robbery	Aggrav. Assault	Burglary	Larceny -Theft	Motor Vehicle Theft
City	7,713.3	13.0	130.0	215.3	804.3	1,379.5	4,760.1	411.1
Suburbs[1]	n/a	n/a	n/a	n/a	n/a	n/a	n/a	n/a
MSA[2]	n/a	n/a	n/a	n/a	n/a	n/a	n/a	n/a
U.S.	4,922.7	6.8	35.9	186.1	382.0	919.6	2,886.5	505.8

Note: Crime rate is the number of crimes per 100,000 pop.; (1) defined as all areas within the MSA but located outside the central city; (2) Metropolitan Statistical Area - see Appendix A for areas incl.
Source: FBI Uniform Crime Reports, 1997

RECREATION

Culture and Recreation

Museums	Symphony Orchestras	Opera Companies	Dance Companies	Professional Theatres	Zoos	Pro Sports Teams
4	1	1	0	1	1	0

Source: International Directory of the Performing Arts, 1997; Official Museum Directory, 1999; Stern's Performing Arts Directory, 1997; USA Today Four Sport Stadium Guide, 1997; Chamber of Commerce/Economic Development, 1999

Library System

The Library of Michigan has holdings of 5,626,581 volumes and a budget of $7,190,600 (1995-1996). *American Library Directory, 1998-1999*

MEDIA

Newspapers

Name	Type	Freq.	Distribution	Circulation
Lansing State Journal	General	7x/wk	Area	70,000
The State News	General	5x/wk	Camp/Comm	30,500

Note: Includes newspapers with circulations of 500 or more located in the city;
Source: Burrelle's Media Directory, 1999 Edition

Television Stations

Name	Ch.	Affiliation	Type	Owner
WLNS	n/a	CBST	Commercial	Young Broadcasting Inc.
WILX	10	NBCT	Commercial	Benedek Broadcasting Corporation
WKAR	23	PBS	Public	Michigan State University
WSYM	47	FBC	Commercial	Journal Broadcast Group
WLAJ	53	ABCT	Commercial	Freedom Broadcasting

Note: Stations included broadcast in the Lansing metro area; n/a not available
Source: Burrelle's Media Directory, 1999 Edition

AM Radio Stations

Call Letters	Freq. (kHz)	Target Audience	Station Format	Music Format
WVFN	730	G/M	S	n/a
WKAR	870	General	N/S/T	n/a
WUNN	1110	General	M/N/S	Christian/MOR
WXLA	1180	B/G	M/N	Adult Contemporary/Urban Contemporary
WJIM	1240	General	N/T	n/a
WILS	1320	General	M/N	Adult Contemporary/Adult Standards

Note: Stations included broadcast in the Lansing metro area; n/a not available
Target Audience: A=Asian; B=Black; C=Christian; E=Ethnic; F=French; G=General; H=Hispanic;
M=Men; N=Native American; R=Religious; S=Senior Citizen; W=Women; Y=Young Adult; Z=Children
Station Format: E=Educational; M=Music; N=News; S=Sports; T=Talk
Music Format: AOR=Album Oriented Rock; MOR=Middle-of-the-Road
Source: Burrelle's Media Directory, 1999 Edition

FM Radio Stations

Call Letters	Freq. (mHz)	Target Audience	Station Format	Music Format
WDBM	88.9	n/a	M/S	Alternative
WLNZ	89.7	General	M	Jazz
WKAR	90.5	General	M/N/S	Classical
WWDX	92.1	General	M/N/T	Alternative
WMMQ	92.7	General	M	Classic Rock
WXIK	94.1	General	M/N	Country
WQHH	96.5	General	M	Urban Contemporary
WJIM	97.5	General	M	Oldies
WFMK	99.1	General	M	Adult Contemporary
WITL	100.7	General	M/N	Country
WILS	101.7	General	M/N/S	n/a
WJXQ	106.1	General	M/N/T	AOR

Note: Stations included broadcast in the Lansing metro area; n/a not available
Station Format: E=Educational; M=Music; N=News; S=Sports; T=Talk
Target Audience: A=Asian; B=Black; C=Christian; E=Ethnic; F=French; G=General; H=Hispanic;
M=Men; N=Native American; R=Religious; S=Senior Citizen; W=Women; Y=Young Adult; Z=Children
Music Format: AOR=Album Oriented Rock; MOR=Middle-of-the-Road
Source: Burrelle's Media Directory, 1999 Edition

CLIMATE

Average and Extreme Temperatures

Temperature	Jan	Feb	Mar	Apr	May	Jun	Jul	Aug	Sep	Oct	Nov	Dec	Yr.
Extreme High (°F)	66	64	78	86	94	99	100	100	97	89	79	66	100
Average High (°F)	29	32	42	56	69	78	83	81	73	60	46	34	57
Average Temp. (°F)	22	24	33	46	57	67	71	69	62	50	39	27	48
Average Low (°F)	14	15	24	35	45	55	59	57	50	39	31	20	37
Extreme Low (°F)	-18	-24	-15	-2	19	30	37	35	26	15	-5	-17	-24

Note: Figures cover the years 1948-1990
Source: National Climatic Data Center, International Station Meteorological Climate Summary, 3/95

Average Precipitation/Snowfall/Humidity

Precip./Humidity	Jan	Feb	Mar	Apr	May	Jun	Jul	Aug	Sep	Oct	Nov	Dec	Yr.
Avg. Precip. (in.)	1.7	1.6	2.3	2.8	2.7	3.6	2.6	3.1	3.2	2.1	2.6	2.3	30.6
Avg. Snowfall (in.)	12	10	8	3	Tr	0	0	0	Tr	Tr	5	12	51
Avg. Rel. Hum. 7am (%)	83	82	82	80	79	81	84	89	90	87	85	84	84
Avg. Rel. Hum. 4pm (%)	72	68	62	54	52	53	53	55	58	59	68	74	61

Note: Figures cover the years 1948-1990; Tr = Trace amounts (<0.05 in. of rain; <0.5 in. of snow)
Source: National Climatic Data Center, International Station Meteorological Climate Summary, 3/95

Weather Conditions

Temperature			Daytime Sky			Precipitation		
5°F & below	32°F & below	90°F & above	Clear	Partly cloudy	Cloudy	0.01 inch or more precip.	0.1 inch or more snow/ice	Thunder-storms
20	149	11	71	131	163	142	47	32

Note: Figures are average number of days per year and covers the years 1948-1990
Source: National Climatic Data Center, International Station Meteorological Climate Summary, 3/95

AIR & WATER QUALITY

Maximum Pollutant Concentrations

	Particulate Matter (ug/m³)	Carbon Monoxide (ppm)	Sulfur Dioxide (ppm)	Nitrogen Dioxide (ppm)	Ozone (ppm)	Lead (ug/m³)
MSA[1] Level	n/a	n/a	n/a	n/a	0.09	n/a
NAAQS[2]	150	9	0.140	0.053	0.12	1.50
Met NAAQS?	n/a	n/a	n/a	n/a	Yes	n/a

Note: (1) Metropolitan Statistical Area - see Appendix A for areas included; (2) National Ambient Air Quality Standards; ppm = parts per million; ug/m³ = micrograms per cubic meter; n/a not available
Source: EPA, National Air Quality and Emissions Trends Report, 1997

Drinking Water

Water System Name	Pop. Served	Primary Water Source Type	Number of Violations in 1998	Type of Violation/ Contaminants
Lansing	131,546	Ground	None	None

Note: Data as of July 10, 1999
Source: EPA, Office of Ground Water and Drinking Water, Safe Drinking Water Information System

Lansing tap water is alkaline, soft and fluoridated.
Editor & Publisher Market Guide, 1999

Little Rock, Arkansas

Background

In 1722, Bernard de la Harpe paddled his canoe along what would become known as the Arkansas River. On the southern bank of the river, near the site of an Arkansas tribal village and a mossy boulder which de la Harpe called La Petit Roche—Little Rock, he built a trading post. Ninety years later a trapper by the name of William Lewis built his home at the "little rock." In 1819, Arkansas became a territory, and in 1821 Little Rock was chosen as the territorial capital. The river became the lifeline of the town and steamboats docked to load bales of cotton and other products of the Arkansas land.

In 1861, Arkansas withdrew from the Union. But by 1863 it became the second Confederate capital to fall to the Yankees, who occupied the city for the remainder of the war. The post-war period was a time of rapid growth for the town. By 1888 Little Rock had telephones, waterworks, electric trolleys, and streetlights.

By the 1890s, Little Rock had become an important transportation center with the expansion of the railways. Industry in the metropolitan area grew rapidly due to nearby oil, gas, coal timber, and bauxite reserves. In 1969, the city became a river port with the opening of locks on the Arkansas River. The city remains the chief market for the surrounding agricultural region.

In 1957, the city became the center of attention for the Civil Rights Movement when the Arkansas governor ordered the state militia to prevent nine black students from being the first to integrate a local high school. U.S. President Dwight D. Eisenhower sent federal troops to maintain order and the black students began to attend classes. Within ten years, all of the Little Rock schools were desegregated.

Today, the city's higher education institutions include the University of Arkansas at Little Rock, Philander Smith College, the University of Arkansas for Medical Sciences, Arkansas Baptist College, and the state schools for the blind and deaf.

Little Rock is one of the most agreeable cities in the South. The town has lovingly restored the original Pulaski County Courthouse from Little Rock's earliest years, as well as the Old State House, which now serves as an Arkansas state history museum. The oldest part of Little Rock is called the Quapaw Quarter, a neighborhood of shady trees and beautifully restored Victorian homes. The nearby MacArthur Park reminds the city of one of it's most famous sons, General Douglas MacArthur. The General was born in the Old Arsenal in Little Rock, where his father was the commanding officer. That 1836 building now houses the Museum of Science and History, which looks across the park to Arkansas Art Center. Of course, another famous son of Little Rock is the 42nd President of the United States, Bill Clinton.

Little Rock is located on the Arkansas River near the geographical center of the state. The modified continental climate includes exposure to all of the North American air mass types. However, with its proximity to the Gulf of Mexico, the summer season is marked by prolonged periods of warm and humid weather. Precipitation is fairly well distributed throughout the year. Snow is almost negligible. Glaze and ice storms, although infrequent, are at times severe.

General Rankings and Evaluative Comments

- Little Rock was ranked #17 out of 44 mid-sized, southern metropolitan areas in *Money's* 1998 survey of "The Best Places to Live in America." The survey was conducted by first contacting 512 representative households nationwide and asking them to rank 37 quality-of-life factors on a scale of 1 to 10. Next, a demographic profile was compiled on the 300 largest metropolitan statistical areas in the U.S. The numbers were crunched together to arrive at an overall ranking (things Americans consider most important, like clean air and water, low crime and good schools, received extra weight). Unlike previous years, the 1998 rankings were broken down by region (northeast, midwest, south, west) and population size (100,000 to 249,999; 250,000 to 999,999; 1 million plus). The city had a nationwide ranking of #142 out of 300 in 1997 and #195 out of 300 in 1996. *Money, July 1998; Money, July 1997; Money, September 1996*

- *Ladies Home Journal* ranked America's 200 largest cities based on the qualities women care about most. Little Rock ranked #137 out of 200. Criteria: low crime rate, well-paying jobs, quality health and child care, good public schools, the presence of women in government, size of the gender wage gap, number of sexual-harassment and discrimination complaints filed, unemployment and divorce rates, commute times, population density, number of houses of worship, parks and cultural offerings, number of women's health specialists, how well a community's women cared for themselves, complexion kindness index based on UV radiation levels, odds of finding affordable fashions, rental rates for romance movies, champagne sales and other matters of the heart. *Ladies Home Journal, November 1998*

- Zero Population Growth ranked 229 cities in terms of children's health, safety, and economic well-being. Little Rock was ranked #44 out of 112 independent cities (cities with populations greater than 100,000 which were neither Major Cities nor Suburbs/Outer Cities) and was given a grade of C+. Criteria: total population, percent of population under 18 years of age, household language, percent population change, percent of births to teens, infant mortality rate, percent of low birth weights, dropout rate, enrollment in preprimary school, violent and property crime rates, unemployment rate, percent of children in poverty, percent of owner occupied units, number of bad air days, percent of public transportation commuters, and average travel time to work. *Zero Population Growth, Children's Environmental Index, Fall 1999*

- Cognetics studied 273 metro areas in the United States, ranking them by entrepreneurial activity. Little Rock was ranked #53 out of 134 smaller metro areas. Criteria: Significant Starts (firms started in the last 10 years that still employ at least 5 people) and Young Growers (percent of firms 10 years old or less that grew significantly during the last 4 years). *Cognetics, "Entrepreneurial Hot Spots: The Best Places in America to Start and Grow a Company," 1998*

- Little Rock was selected as one of the "Best American Cities to Start a Business" by *Point of View* magazine. Criteria: coolness, quality-of-life, and business concerns. The city was ranked #56 out of 75. *Point of View, November 1998*

- Reliastar Financial Corp. ranked the 125 largest metropolitan areas according to the general financial security of residents. Little Rock was ranked #71 out of 125 with a score of -0.3. The score indicates the percentage a metropolitan area is above or below the metropolitan norm. A metro area with a score of 10.6 is 10.6% above the metro average. Criteria: Earnings and Wealth Potential (household income, education, net assets, cost of living); Safety Net (health insurance, retirement savings, life insurance, income support programs); Personal Threats (unemployment rate, low-income households, crime rate); Community Economic Vitality (cost of community services, job quality, job creation, housing costs). *Reliastar Financial Corp., "The Best Cities to Earn and Save Money," 1999 Edition*

Business Environment

STATE ECONOMY

State Economic Profile

"Arkansas' economy has trailed the nation's over the last several years. This trend should not change in the near future. A heavy dependence on manufacturing and agriculture leaves Arkansas with a fragile economy. Although its cost structure is very favorable, its shortage of an educated and skilled labor force hampers its potential for growth.

Low foreign demand and a shortage of skilled workers are currently hampering Arkansas' manufacturing sector. The apparel industry is suffering from both foreign competition and a decline in foreign demand. Even with a rebound in demand, its future looks dim. While several food processors, one of Arkansas key industries, increased payrolls in 1998, their long-term future remains uncertain.

While 1998 was a banner year for many industries, agriculture was not one of them. Commodity prices have continued to soften in the face of weak foreign demand. Arkansas' rice, hog and soybean producers have been hit particularly hard by falling prices. However, its poultry industry has not suffered as hard as others and still faces strong domestic demand. Consolidation among producers in both the poultry and hog industries, however, makes it unlikely that these sectors will provide much, if any, employment growth in the near term.

Home sales have been strong in recent years with some rebound in price appreciation in 1998. However, population growth among the "typical buyers" of housing will be negative over the next few years, raising some concern over the future strength of Arkansas' housing market." *National Association of Realtors, Economic Profiles: The Fifty States and the District of Columbia, http://nar.realtor.com/databank/profiles.htm*

IMPORTS/EXPORTS

Total Export Sales

Area	1994 ($000)	1995 ($000)	1996 ($000)	1997 ($000)	% Chg. 1994-97	% Chg. 1996-97
MSA[1]	218,994	193,609	210,392	349,367	59.5	66.1
U.S.	512,415,609	583,030,524	622,827,063	687,597,999	34.2	10.4

Note: (1) Metropolitan Statistical Area - see Appendix A for areas included
Source: U.S. Department of Commerce, International Trade Association, Metropolitan Area Exports: An Export Performance Report on Over 250 U.S. Cities, November 10, 1998

CITY FINANCES

City Government Finances

Component	FY92 ($000)	FY92 (per capita $)
Revenue	159,689	902.64
Expenditure	159,085	899.23
Debt Outstanding	295,176	1,668.48
Cash & Securities	337,306	1,906.62

Source: U.S. Bureau of the Census, City Government Finances: 1991-92

City Government Revenue by Source

Source	FY92 ($000)	FY92 (per capita $)	FY92 (%)
From Federal Government	5,315	30.04	3.3
From State Governments	11,338	64.09	7.1
From Local Governments	19,425	109.80	12.2
Property Taxes	12,960	73.26	8.1
General Sales Taxes	0	0.00	0.0
Selective Sales Taxes	15,971	90.28	10.0
Income Taxes	0	0.00	0.0
Current Charges	43,749	247.29	27.4
Utility/Liquor Store	16,377	92.57	10.3
Employee Retirement[1]	5,872	33.19	3.7
Other	28,682	162.12	18.0

Note: (1) Excludes "city contributions," classified as "nonrevenue," intragovernmental transfers.
Source: U.S. Bureau of the Census, City Government Finances: 1991-92

City Government Expenditures by Function

Function	FY92 ($000)	FY92 (per capita $)	FY92 (%)
Educational Services	3,820	21.59	2.4
Employee Retirement[1]	3,503	19.80	2.2
Environment/Housing	27,615	156.09	17.4
Government Administration	8,908	50.35	5.6
Interest on General Debt	19,551	110.51	12.3
Public Safety	34,094	192.72	21.4
Social Services	4,462	25.22	2.8
Transportation	32,689	184.77	20.5
Utility/Liquor Store	12,862	72.70	8.1
Other	11,581	65.46	7.3

Note: (1) Payments to beneficiaries including withdrawal of contributions.
Source: U.S. Bureau of the Census, City Government Finances: 1991-92

Municipal Bond Ratings

Area	Moody's	S & P
Little Rock	n/a	n/a

Note: n/a not available; n/r not rated
Source: Moody's Bond Record, 6/99

POPULATION

Population Growth

Area	1980	1990	% Chg. 1980-90	July 1998 Estimate	% Chg. 1990-98
City	158,461	175,781	10.9	175,303	-0.3
MSA[1]	474,464	513,117	8.1	560,128	9.2
U.S.	226,545,805	248,765,170	9.8	270,299,000	8.7

Note: (1) Metropolitan Statistical Area - see Appendix A for areas included;
July 1998 MSA population estimate was calculated by the editors
Source: 1980/1990 Census of Housing and Population, Summary Tape File 3C;
Census Bureau Population Estimates 1998

Population Characteristics

Race	City 1980 Population	%	City 1990 Population	%	% Chg. 1980-90	MSA[1] 1990 Population	%
White	105,504	66.6	113,723	64.7	7.8	404,696	78.9
Black	51,093	32.2	59,864	34.1	17.2	101,877	19.9
Amer Indian/Esk/Aleut	379	0.2	460	0.3	21.4	2,048	0.4
Asian/Pacific Islander	1,099	0.7	1,475	0.8	34.2	3,176	0.6
Other	386	0.2	259	0.1	-32.9	1,320	0.3
Hispanic Origin[2]	1,331	0.8	1,427	0.8	7.2	4,741	0.9

Note: (1) Metropolitan Statistical Area - see Appendix A for areas included;
(2) people of Hispanic origin can be of any race
Source: 1980/1990 Census of Housing and Population, Summary Tape File 3C

Ancestry

Area	German	Irish	English	Italian	U.S.	French	Polish	Dutch
City	15.6	14.5	14.2	1.4	6.3	3.5	1.1	1.9
MSA[1]	18.0	18.3	13.6	1.5	10.2	3.5	1.1	2.6
U.S.	23.3	15.6	13.1	5.9	5.3	4.2	3.8	2.5

Note: Figures are percentages and include persons that reported multiple ancestry (eg. if a person reported being Irish and Italian, they were included in both columns); (1) Metropolitan Statistical Area - see Appendix A for areas included
Source: 1990 Census of Population and Housing, Summary Tape File 3C

Age

Area	Median Age (Years)	Age Distribution (%) Under 5	Under 18	18-24	25-44	45-64	65+	80+
City	32.7	7.3	24.9	10.3	34.9	17.4	12.5	3.1
MSA[1]	32.2	7.3	26.5	10.5	33.4	18.2	11.3	2.6
U.S.	32.9	7.3	25.6	10.5	32.6	18.7	12.5	2.8

Note: (1) Metropolitan Statistical Area - see Appendix A for areas included
Source: 1990 Census of Population and Housing, Summary Tape File 3C

Male/Female Ratio

Area	Number of males per 100 females (all ages)	Number of males per 100 females (18 years old+)
City	85.3	81.6
MSA[1]	92.0	88.2
U.S.	95.0	91.9

Note: (1) Metropolitan Statistical Area - see Appendix A for areas included
Source: 1990 Census of Population, General Population Characteristics

INCOME

Per Capita/Median/Average Income

Area	Per Capita ($)	Median Household ($)	Average Household ($)
City	15,307	26,889	36,897
MSA[1]	12,809	26,501	33,336
U.S.	14,420	30,056	38,453

Note: All figures are for 1989; (1) Metropolitan Statistical Area - see Appendix A for areas included
Source: 1990 Census of Population and Housing, Summary Tape File 3C

Household Income Distribution by Race

Income ($)	City (%)					U.S. (%)				
	Total	White	Black	Other	Hisp.[1]	Total	White	Black	Other	Hisp.[1]
Less than 5,000	7.1	4.4	13.9	9.5	5.7	6.2	4.8	15.2	8.6	8.8
5,000 - 9,999	9.7	7.7	14.9	6.8	12.2	9.3	8.6	14.2	9.9	11.1
10,000 - 14,999	10.1	8.3	14.6	12.8	11.5	8.8	8.5	11.0	9.8	11.0
15,000 - 24,999	19.3	18.8	21.0	8.0	12.0	17.5	17.3	18.9	18.5	20.5
25,000 - 34,999	16.0	16.7	14.2	18.2	22.0	15.8	16.1	14.2	15.4	16.4
35,000 - 49,999	15.6	16.9	12.1	18.7	15.9	17.9	18.6	13.3	16.1	16.0
50,000 - 74,999	13.7	16.1	7.5	15.8	19.3	15.0	15.8	9.3	13.4	11.1
75,000 - 99,999	4.1	5.1	1.3	5.2	1.3	5.1	5.5	2.6	4.7	3.1
100,000+	4.4	6.0	0.4	5.0	0.0	4.4	4.8	1.3	3.7	1.9

Note: All figures are for 1989; (1) people of Hispanic origin can be of any race
Source: 1990 Census of Population and Housing, Summary Tape File 3C

Effective Buying Income

Area	Per Capita ($)	Median Household ($)	Average Household ($)
City	19,973	36,205	48,119
MSA[1]	17,365	34,657	45,315
U.S.	16,803	34,536	45,243

Note: Data as of 1/1/99; (1) Metropolitan Statistical Area - see Appendix A for areas included
Source: Standard Rate & Data Service, Newspaper Advertising Source, 9/99

Effective Household Buying Income Distribution

Area	% of Households Earning						
	$10,000 -$19,999	$20,000 -$34,999	$35,000 -$49,999	$50,000 -$74,999	$75,000 -$99,000	$100,000 -$124,999	$125,000 and up
City	15.1	22.3	17.0	18.6	8.6	3.1	4.2
MSA[1]	15.5	23.6	18.4	19.4	7.1	2.1	2.4
U.S.	16.0	22.6	18.2	18.9	7.2	2.4	2.7

Note: Data as of 1/1/99; (1) Metropolitan Statistical Area - see Appendix A for areas included
Source: Standard Rate & Data Service, Newspaper Advertising Source, 9/99

Poverty Rates by Race and Age

Area	Total (%)	By Race (%)				By Age (%)		
		White	Black	Other	Hisp.[2]	Under 5 years old	Under 18 years old	65 years and over
City	14.6	7.2	28.9	12.4	19.8	23.6	21.7	13.5
MSA[1]	13.5	9.2	30.8	12.2	17.4	19.8	18.2	16.8
U.S.	13.1	9.8	29.5	23.1	25.3	20.1	18.3	12.8

Note: Figures show the percent of people living below the poverty line in 1989. The average poverty threshold was $12,674 for a family of four in 1989; (1) Metropolitan Statistical Area - see Appendix A for areas included; (2) people of Hispanic origin can be of any race
Source: 1990 Census of Population and Housing, Summary Tape File 3C

EMPLOYMENT

Labor Force and Employment

Area	Civilian Labor Force			Workers Employed		
	Jun. 1998	Jun. 1999	% Chg.	Jun. 1998	Jun. 1999	% Chg.
City	100,745	105,148	4.4	96,556	101,464	5.1
MSA[1]	298,209	310,958	4.3	286,072	300,613	5.1
U.S.	138,798,000	140,666,000	1.3	132,265,000	134,395,000	1.6

Note: Data is not seasonally adjusted and covers workers 16 years of age and older;
(1) Metropolitan Statistical Area - see Appendix A for areas included
Source: Bureau of Labor Statistics, http://stats.bls.gov

Unemployment Rate

Area	1998						1999					
	Jul.	Aug.	Sep.	Oct.	Nov.	Dec.	Jan.	Feb.	Mar.	Apr.	May.	Jun.
City	4.3	4.3	3.9	3.5	3.4	3.4	3.8	3.5	3.1	2.8	2.9	3.5
MSA[1]	4.2	4.1	3.8	3.5	3.4	3.4	3.8	3.5	3.0	2.8	2.8	3.3
U.S.	4.7	4.5	4.4	4.2	4.1	4.0	4.8	4.7	4.4	4.1	4.0	4.5

Note: Data is not seasonally adjusted and covers workers 16 years of age and older; all figures are percentages; (1) Metropolitan Statistical Area - see Appendix A for areas included
Source: Bureau of Labor Statistics, http://stats.bls.gov

Employment by Industry

Sector	MSA[1]		U.S.
	Number of Employees	Percent of Total	Percent of Total
Services	91,300	29.4	30.4
Retail Trade	54,100	17.4	17.7
Government	59,000	19.0	15.6
Manufacturing	33,600	10.8	14.3
Finance/Insurance/Real Estate	17,900	5.8	5.9
Wholesale Trade	18,200	5.9	5.4
Transportation/Public Utilities	21,700	7.0	5.3
Construction	n/a	n/a	5.0
Mining	n/a	n/a	0.4

Note: Figures cover non-farm employment as of 6/99 and are not seasonally adjusted; (1) Metropolitan Statistical Area - see Appendix A for areas included; n/a not available
Source: Bureau of Labor Statistics, http://stats.bls.gov

Employment by Occupation

Occupation Category	City (%)	MSA[1] (%)	U.S. (%)
White Collar	69.6	60.7	58.1
Executive/Admin./Management	14.8	12.3	12.3
Professional	18.9	14.1	14.1
Technical & Related Support	4.0	3.6	3.7
Sales	14.2	13.6	11.8
Administrative Support/Clerical	17.7	17.1	16.3
Blue Collar	17.0	25.3	26.2
Precision Production/Craft/Repair	6.5	10.6	11.3
Machine Operators/Assem./Insp.	4.2	6.2	6.8
Transportation/Material Movers	3.1	4.6	4.1
Cleaners/Helpers/Laborers	3.1	3.9	3.9
Services	12.6	12.4	13.2
Farming/Forestry/Fishing	0.8	1.5	2.5

Note: Figures cover employed persons 16 years old and over; (1) Metropolitan Statistical Area - see Appendix A for areas included
Source: 1990 Census of Population and Housing, Summary Tape File 3C

Occupational Employment Projections: 1996 - 2006

Occupations Expected to Have the Largest Job Growth (ranked by numerical growth)	Fast-Growing Occupations[1] (ranked by percent growth)
1. Truck drivers, light	1. Database administrators
2. Salespersons, retail	2. Systems analysts
3. Cashiers	3. Personal and home care aides
4. Nursing aides/orderlies/attendants	4. Occupational therapists
5. Registered nurses	5. Physical therapy assistants and aides
6. General managers & top executives	6. Home health aides
7. Child care workers, private household	7. Computer engineers
8. Home health aides	8. Respiratory therapists
9. Marketing & sales, supervisors	9. Physical therapists
10. Teachers, secondary school	10. Medical records technicians

Note: Projections cover Arkansas; (1) Excludes occupations with total job growth less than 300
Source: U.S. Department of Labor, Employment and Training Administration, America's Labor Market Information System (ALMIS)

TAXES

Major State and Local Tax Rates

State Corp. Income (%)	State Personal Income (%)	Residential Property (effective rate per $100)	Sales & Use		State Gasoline (cents/ gallon)	State Cigarette (cents/ pack)
			State (%)	Local (%)		
1.0 - 6.5	1.0 - 7.0[a]	1.19	4.625	1.5	18.7[b]	31.5

Note: Personal/corporate income, sales, gasoline and cigarette tax rates as of January 1999. Property tax rates as of 1997; (a) A special tax table is available for low income taxpayers reducing their tax payments; (b) Rate is comprised of 18.5 cents excise plus 0.2 cent motor carrier tax
Source: Federation of Tax Administrators, www.taxadmin.org; Washington D.C. Department of Finance and Revenue, Tax Rates and Tax Burdens in the District of Columbia: A Nationwide Comparison, July 1998; Chamber of Commerce, 1999

Total Taxes Per Capita and as a Percent of Income

Area	Per Capita Income ($)	Per Capita Taxes ($)			Percent of Income (%)		
		Total	Federal	State/ Local	Total	Federal	State/ Local
Arkansas	21,586	7,352	4,842	2,510	34.1	22.4	11.6
U.S.	27,876	9,881	6,690	3,191	35.4	24.0	11.4

Note: Figures are for 1998
Source: Tax Foundation, www.taxfoundation.org

Estimated Tax Burden

Area	State Income	Local Income	Property	Sales	Total
Little Rock	3,660	0	3,000	916	7,576

Note: The numbers are estimates of taxes paid by a married couple with two children and annual earnings of $75,000. Sales tax estimates assume they spend average amounts on food, clothing, household goods and gasoline. Property tax estimates assume they live in a $250,000 home.
Source: Kiplinger's Personal Finance Magazine, October 1998

**COMMERCIAL
REAL ESTATE**

Office Market

Class/ Location	Total Space (sq. ft.)	Vacant Space (sq. ft.)	Vac. Rate (%)	Under Constr. (sq. ft.)	Net Absorp. (sq. ft.)	Rental Rates ($/sq.ft./yr.)
Class A						
CBD	2,297,771	277,517	12.1	n/a	82,556	9.90-15.00
Outside CBD	2,609,142	80,244	3.1	206,000	65,835	15.75-17.50
Class B						
CBD	2,443,510	243,888	10.0	n/a	34,173	7.75-11.50
Outside CBD	3,029,471	316,501	10.4	34,000	55,470	8.00-13.50

Note: Data as of 10/98 and covers Little Rock; CBD = Central Business District; n/a not available;
Source: Society of Industrial and Office Realtors, 1999 Comparative Statistics of Industrial and Office
Real Estate Markets

"Nearly $300 million will be spent on civic improvements during 1999, including a new arena, an expanded convention center, and the presidential library. None of this will affect the office market much. Bank consolidations will, however, make a difference. Regions Bank acquired First Commercial Bank in 1998 and is planning to downsize and release about 60,000 sq. ft. of space into the downtown market during 1999. Our SIOR reporter anticipates a stable market in 1999 with few changes. Despite the prospect of a solid economy and citywide office vacancy of around 11 percent, little speculative or build-to-suit office development is on the horizon." *Society of Industrial and Office Realtors, 1999 Comparative Statistics of Industrial and Office Real Estate Markets*

Industrial Market

Location	Total Space (sq. ft.)	Vacant Space (sq. ft.)	Vac. Rate (%)	Under Constr. (sq. ft.)	Net Absorp. (sq. ft.)	Gross Lease ($/sq.ft./yr.)
Central City	8,835,000	383,291	4.3	n/a	199,000	3.00-3.75
Suburban	21,947,700	662,000	3.0	433,800	283,397	1.75-5.00

Note: Data as of 10/98 and covers Little Rock; n/a not available
Source: Society of Industrial and Office Realtors, 1999 Comparative Statistics of Industrial and Office
Real Estate Markets

"Prospects for continued growth in the Little Rock market are excellent. The community added 2,300 new jobs during 1998, a trend which is expected to continue. Anticipated civic developments are also huge in number for a city the size of Little Rock. Nearly $300 million will be spent on the new arena, expanded Convention Center, and River Market District. The site selected for the new Clinton Library in the River Market area will, in fact, affect the industrial market causing many displacements. Growing industries, such as Ailtel, Axiom, Molex, Sysco, and Leisure Arts should also add to the market momentum in 1999. In short, our SIOR reporter anticipates both construction and absorption of manufacturing and High Tech/R&D space will rise from six to 10 percent during 1999, and lease prices will increase by one to five percent for warehouse/distribution and High Tech/R&D space. The dollar volume of sales and leases should remain about the same." *Society of Industrial and Office Realtors, 1999 Comparative Statistics of Industrial and Office Real Estate Markets*

COMMERCIAL UTILITIES

Typical Monthly Electric Bills

Area	Commercial Service ($/month)		Industrial Service ($/month)	
	12 kW demand 1,500 kWh	100 kW demand 30,000 kWh	1,000 kW demand 400,000 kWh	20,000 kW demand 10,000,000 kWh
City	118	1,750	19,147	312,140
U.S.	150	2,174	23,995	508,569

Note: Based on rates in effect January 1, 1999
Source: Edison Electric Institute, Typical Residential, Commercial and Industrial Bills, Winter 1999

TRANSPORTATION

Transportation Statistics

Average minutes to work	17.1
Interstate highways	I-30; I-40
Bus lines	
In-city	Central Arkansas Transit
Inter-city	2
Passenger air service	
Airport	Little Rock National Airport (Adams Field)
Airlines	11
Aircraft departures	21,065 (1996)
Enplaned passengers	1,252,312 (1996)
Rail service	Amtrak
Motor freight carriers	70
Major waterways/ports	Arkansas River

Source: Editor & Publisher Market Guide, 1999; FAA Airport Activity Statistics, 1997; Amtrak National Time Table, Northeast Timetable, Spring/Summer 1999; 1990 Census of Population and Housing, STF 3C; Chamber of Commerce/Economic Development 1999; Jane's Urban Transport Systems 1999-2000

Means of Transportation to Work

Area	Car/Truck/Van		Public Transportation			Bicycle	Walked	Other Means	Worked at Home
	Drove Alone	Car-pooled	Bus	Subway	Railroad				
City	80.5	13.5	1.4	0.0	0.0	0.1	1.9	1.0	1.7
MSA[1]	79.8	14.4	0.8	0.0	0.0	0.1	1.9	1.0	2.0
U.S.	73.2	13.4	3.0	1.5	0.5	0.4	3.9	1.2	3.0

Note: Figures shown are percentages and only include workers 16 years old and over;
(1) Metropolitan Statistical Area - see Appendix A for areas included
Source: 1990 Census of Population and Housing, Summary Tape File 3C

BUSINESSES

Major Business Headquarters

Company Name	1999 Rankings	
	Fortune 500	Forbes 500
Alltel	311	-
Dillard's	203	-

Note: Companies listed are located in the city; dashes indicate no ranking
Fortune 500: Companies that produce a 10-K are ranked 1 to 500 based on 1998 revenue
Forbes 500: Private companies are ranked 1 to 500 based on 1997 revenue
Source: Forbes, November 30, 1998; Fortune, April 26, 1999

HOTELS & MOTELS

Hotels/Motels

Area	Hotels/ Motels	Rooms	Luxury-Level Hotels/Motels		Average Minimum Rates ($)		
			♦♦♦♦	♦♦♦♦♦	♦♦	♦♦♦	♦♦♦♦
City	26	3,666	0	0	n/a	n/a	n/a
Airport	4	622	0	0	n/a	n/a	n/a
Suburbs	19	1,861	0	0	n/a	n/a	n/a
Total	49	6,149	0	0	n/a	n/a	n/a

Note: n/a not available; classifications range from one diamond (budget properties with basic amenities) to five diamond (luxury properties with the finest service, rooms and facilities).
Source: OAG, Business Travel Planner, Winter 1998-99

CONVENTION CENTERS

Major Convention Centers

Center Name	Meeting Rooms	Exhibit Space (sq. ft.)
Arkansas State Fair Grounds	5	86,000
Camelot Hotel	9	8,720
Statehouse Convention Center	8	62,125
University Conference Center	9	11,000

Source: Trade Shows Worldwide, 1998; Meetings & Conventions, 4/15/99; Sucessful Meetings, 3/31/98

Living Environment

COST OF LIVING

Cost of Living Index

Composite Index	Groceries	Housing	Utilities	Trans-portation	Health Care	Misc. Goods/ Services
95.5	106.7	83.1	116.2	103.6	98.7	92.6

Note: U.S. = 100; Figures are for Little Rock-N. Little Rock
Source: ACCRA, Cost of Living Index, 1st Quarter 1999

HOUSING

Median Home Prices and Housing Affordability

Area	Median Price[2] 1st Qtr. 1999 ($)	HOI[3] 1st Qtr. 1999	Afford-ability Rank[4]
MSA[1]	n/a	n/a	n/a
U.S.	134,000	69.6	–

Note: (1) Metropolitan Statistical Area - see Appendix A for areas included; (2) U.S. figures calculated from the sales of 524,324 new and existing homes in 181 markets; (3) Housing Opportunity Index - percent of homes sold that were within the reach of the median income household at the prevailing mortgage interest rate; (4) Rank is from 1-181 with 1 being most affordable; n/a not available
Source: National Association of Home Builders, Housing Opportunity Index, 1st Quarter 1999

Median Home Price Projection

It is projected that the median price of existing single-family homes in the metro area will increase by 3.0% in 1999. Nationwide, home prices are projected to increase 3.8%.
Kiplinger's Personal Finance Magazine, January 1999

Average New Home Price

Area	Price ($)
City[1]	114,450
U.S.	142,735

Note: Figures are based on a new home with 1,800 sq. ft. of living area on an 8,000 sq. ft. lot;
(1) Little Rock-N. Little Rock
Source: ACCRA, Cost of Living Index, 1st Quarter 1999

Average Apartment Rent

Area	Rent ($/mth)
City[1]	588
U.S.	601

Note: Figures are based on an unfurnished two bedroom, 1-1/2 or 2 bath apartment, approximately 950 sq. ft. in size, excluding all utilities except water; (1) Little Rock-N. Little Rock
Source: ACCRA, Cost of Living Index, 1st Quarter 1999

RESIDENTIAL UTILITIES

Average Residential Utility Costs

Area	All Electric ($/mth)	Part Electric ($/mth)	Other Energy ($/mth)	Phone ($/mth)
City[1]	–	75.02	36.30	28.10
U.S.	100.02	55.73	43.33	19.71

Note: (1) Little Rock-N. Little Rock
Source: ACCRA, Cost of Living Index, 1st Quarter 1999

HEALTH CARE

Average Health Care Costs

Area	Hospital ($/day)	Doctor ($/visit)	Dentist ($/visit)
City[1]	285.80	51.40	77.40
U.S.	430.43	52.45	66.35

Note: Hospital—based on a semi-private room; Doctor—based on a general practitioner's routine exam of an established patient; Dentist—based on adult teeth cleaning and periodic oral exam; (1) (1) Little Rock-N. Little Rock
Source: ACCRA, Cost of Living Index, 1st Quarter 1999

Distribution of Office-Based Physicians

Area	Family/Gen. Practitioners	Specialists Medical	Surgical	Other
MSA[1]	183	424	367	406

Note: Data as of 12/31/97; (1) Metropolitan Statistical Area - see Appendix A for areas included
Source: American Medical Assn., Physician Characteristics & Distribution in the U.S., 1999

Hospitals

Little Rock has 6 general medical and surgical hospitals, 2 psychiatric, 1 rehabilitation, 1 children's general. *AHA Guide to the Healthcare Field, 1998-99*

According to *U.S. News and World Report,* Little Rock has 1 of the best hospitals in the U.S.: **University Hospital of Arkansas,** noted for orthopedics, otolaryngology, urology. *U.S. News Online, "America's Best Hospitals," 10th Edition, www.usnews.com*

EDUCATION

Public School District Statistics

District Name	Num. Sch.	Enroll.	Classroom Teachers	Pupils per Teacher	Minority Pupils (%)	Current Exp.[1] ($/pupil)
Ark. School For The Blind	2	91	32	2.8	n/a	n/a
Ark. School For The Deaf	2	192	44	4.4	n/a	n/a
Ark. Youth Servs. School Syst.	1	136	17	8.0	n/a	n/a
Little Rock School District	48	24,889	1,585	15.7	n/a	n/a
Pulaski Co. Spec. School Dist.	37	20,029	1,210	16.6	n/a	n/a

Note: Data covers the 1997-1998 school year unless otherwise noted; (1) Data covers fiscal year 1996; SD = School District; ISD = Independent School District; n/a not available
Source: National Center for Education Statistics, Common Core of Data Public Education Agency Universe 1997-98; National Center for Education Statistics, Characteristics of the 100 Largest Public Elementary and Secondary School Districts in the United States: 1997-98, July 1999

Educational Quality

School District	Education Quotient[1]	Graduate Outcome[2]	Community Index[3]	Resource Index[4]
Little Rock SD	92.0	64.0	119.0	143.0

Note: Nearly 1,000 secondary school districts were rated in terms of educational quality. The scores range from a low of 50 to a high of 150; (1) Average of the Graduate Outcome, Community and Resource indexes; (2) Based on graduation rates and college board scores (SAT/ACT); (3) Based on the surrounding community's average level of education and the area's average income level; (4) Based on teacher salaries, per-pupil expenditures and student-teacher ratios.
Source: Expansion Management, Ratings Issue, 1998

Educational Attainment by Race

Area	High School Graduate (%)					Bachelor's Degree (%)				
	Total	White	Black	Other	Hisp.[2]	Total	White	Black	Other	Hisp.[2]
City	82.0	87.0	68.9	80.5	78.6	30.3	35.4	16.5	45.5	34.7
MSA[1]	76.6	79.0	64.8	74.8	76.0	20.4	21.8	13.1	24.7	19.3
U.S.	75.2	77.9	63.1	60.4	49.8	20.3	21.5	11.4	19.4	9.2

Note: Figures shown cover persons 25 years old and over; (1) Metropolitan Statistical Area - see Appendix A for areas included; (2) people of Hispanic origin can be of any race
Source: 1990 Census of Population and Housing, Summary Tape File 3C

School Enrollment by Type

Area	Preprimary				Elementary/High School			
	Public		Private		Public		Private	
	Enrollment	%	Enrollment	%	Enrollment	%	Enrollment	%
City	1,427	40.4	2,108	59.6	22,873	79.7	5,818	20.3
MSA[1]	4,862	53.5	4,231	46.5	80,860	88.7	10,321	11.3
U.S.	2,679,029	59.5	1,824,256	40.5	38,379,689	90.2	4,187,099	9.8

Note: Figures shown cover persons 3 years old and over;
(1) Metropolitan Statistical Area - see Appendix A for areas included
Source: 1990 Census of Population and Housing, Summary Tape File 3C

School Enrollment by Race

Area	Preprimary (%)				Elementary/High School (%)			
	White	Black	Other	Hisp.[1]	White	Black	Other	Hisp.[1]
City	65.5	34.1	0.4	1.0	45.6	53.0	1.4	0.6
MSA[2]	77.6	21.9	0.5	1.1	69.4	29.0	1.6	1.3
U.S.	80.4	12.5	7.1	7.8	74.1	15.6	10.3	12.5

Note: Figures shown cover persons 3 years old and over; (1) people of Hispanic origin can be of any race; (2) Metropolitan Statistical Area - see Appendix A for areas included
Source: 1990 Census of Population and Housing, Summary Tape File 3C

Classroom Teacher Salaries in Public Schools

District	B.A. Degree		M.A. Degree		Maximum	
	Min. ($)	Rank[1]	Max. ($)	Rank[1]	Max. ($)	Rank[1]
Little Rock	21,020	99	38,614	87	42,246	92
Average	26,980	-	46,065	-	51,435	-

Note: Salaries are for 1997-1998; (1) Rank ranges from 1 to 100
Source: American Federation of Teachers, Survey & Analysis of Salary Trends, 1998

Higher Education

Two-Year Colleges		Four-Year Colleges		Medical Schools	Law Schools	Voc/ Tech
Public	Private	Public	Private			
0	1	2	1	1	1	20

Source: College Blue Book, Occupational Education, 1997; Medical School Admission Requirements, 1999-2000; Peterson's Guide to Two-Year Colleges, 1999; Peterson's Guide to Four-Year Colleges, 2000; Barron's Guide to Law Schools, 1999

Major Employers

Alltel Information Services (computer processing)
Arkansas Children's Hospital
Little Rock Newspapers
Affiliated Foods Southwest
Dillards

Mercantile Stores

Arkansas Blue Cross & Blue Shield
Stephens Group (oil & gas)
St. Vincent Health System
Quality Foods

Note: Companies listed are located in the city
Source: Dun's Business Rankings, 1999; Ward's Business Directory, 1998

PUBLIC SAFETY

Crime Rate

Area	All Crimes	Violent Crimes				Property Crimes		
		Murder	Forcible Rape	Robbery	Aggrav. Assault	Burglary	Larceny -Theft	Motor Vehicle Theft
City	11,865.8	18.5	89.8	471.6	705.5	2,224.2	7,516.3	839.9
Suburbs[1]	5,537.8	11.9	57.6	112.0	386.1	981.0	3,597.3	392.0
MSA[2]	7,639.7	14.1	68.3	231.4	492.2	1,393.9	4,899.0	540.8
U.S.	4,922.7	6.8	35.9	186.1	382.0	919.6	2,886.5	505.8

Note: Crime rate is the number of crimes per 100,000 pop.; (1) defined as all areas within the MSA but located outside the central city; (2) Metropolitan Statistical Area - see Appendix A for areas incl.
Source: FBI Uniform Crime Reports, 1997

RECREATION

Culture and Recreation

Museums	Symphony Orchestras	Opera Companies	Dance Companies	Professional Theatres	Zoos	Pro Sports Teams
4	1	0	1	2	1	0

Source: International Directory of the Performing Arts, 1997; Official Museum Directory, 1999; Stern's Performing Arts Directory, 1997; USA Today Four Sport Stadium Guide, 1997; Chamber of Commerce/Economic Development, 1999

Library System

The Central Arkansas Library System has six branches and holdings of 494,573 volumes.
American Library Directory, 1998-1999

MEDIA

Newspapers

Name	Type	Freq.	Distribution	Circulation
Arkansas Democrat-Gazette	General	7x/wk	State	176,683
Arkansas State Press	Black	1x/wk	Local	5,000
Arkansas Times	General	1x/wk	Local	38,000
The Arkansas Tribune	Black	1x/wk	State	3,000
The Daily Record	n/a	5x/wk	Local	6,000

Note: Includes newspapers with circulations of 1,000 or more located in the city; n/a not available
Source: Burrelle's Media Directory, 1999 Edition

Television Stations

Name	Ch.	Affiliation	Type	Owner
KARK	n/a	NBCT	Commercial	n/a
KATV	n/a	ABCT	Commercial	Allbritton Communications Company
KTHV	11	CBST	Commercial	Gannett Broadcasting
KLRT	16	FBC	Commercial	Clear Channel Broadcasting Inc.
KVTN	25	n/a	Commercial	Agape Church Inc.
KASN	38	UPN	Commercial	MMC Television Corporation
KVTJ	48	n/a	n/a	Agape Church Inc.

Note: Stations included broadcast in the Little Rock metro area; n/a not available
Source: Burrelle's Media Directory, 1999 Edition

AM Radio Stations

Call Letters	Freq. (kHz)	Target Audience	Station Format	Music Format
KMTL	760	General	M	Christian
KGHT	880	General	M	Christian
KARN	920	General	N/S/T	n/a
KJBN	1050	Religious	M/T	Christian
KAAY	1090	Religious	M/N/T	Christian/Gospel
KLRG	1150	B/R	M/N	Gospel
KLIH	1250	General	M	Gospel
KRNN	1380	General	N/T	n/a
KITA	1440	Black	M	Christian/Gospel

Note: Stations included broadcast in the Little Rock metro area; n/a not available
Target Audience: A=Asian; B=Black; C=Christian; E=Ethnic; F=French; G=General; H=Hispanic; M=Men; N=Native American; R=Religious; S=Senior Citizen; W=Women; Y=Young Adult; Z=Children
Station Format: E=Educational; M=Music; N=News; S=Sports; T=Talk
Source: Burrelle's Media Directory, 1999 Edition

FM Radio Stations

Call Letters	Freq. (mHz)	Target Audience	Station Format	Music Format
KABF	88.3	Black	M/N/S/T	Alternative/Blues/Classical/Gospel/Jazz/Latin/World Music
KUAR	89.1	General	E/M/N	Big Band/Classical/Jazz
KLRE	90.5	General	M	Classical
KIPR	92.3	Black	M/N/S	Urban Contemporary
KKPT	94.1	General	M	Classic Rock
KOLL	94.9	General	M/N/T	Oldies
KSSN	95.7	General	M/N/T	Country
KURB	98.5	General	M	Adult Contemporary/Adult Top 40
KYFX	99.5	n/a	M/N	Adult Contemporary/Jazz
KQAR	100.3	General	M	Adult Contemporary
KDRE	101.1	General	M	n/a
KARN	101.7	General	N/S/T	n/a
KOKY	102.1	General	M	Urban Contemporary
KKRN	102.5	n/a	n/a	n/a
KVLO	102.9	General	M	Adult Contemporary
KSYG	103.7	General	T	n/a
KMJX	105.1	General	M/N/S	AOR/Classic Rock
KHTE	106.3	General	M/N/S	Country
KDDK	106.7	General	M/N/T	Country

Note: Stations included broadcast in the Little Rock metro area; n/a not available
Station Format: E=Educational; M=Music; N=News; S=Sports; T=Talk
Target Audience: A=Asian; B=Black; C=Christian; E=Ethnic; F=French; G=General; H=Hispanic; M=Men; N=Native American; R=Religious; S=Senior Citizen; W=Women; Y=Young Adult; Z=Children
Music Format: AOR=Album Oriented Rock; MOR=Middle-of-the-Road
Source: Burrelle's Media Directory, 1999 Edition

CLIMATE

Average and Extreme Temperatures

Temperature	Jan	Feb	Mar	Apr	May	Jun	Jul	Aug	Sep	Oct	Nov	Dec	Yr.
Extreme High (°F)	83	85	91	95	98	105	112	108	103	97	86	80	112
Average High (°F)	50	54	63	73	81	89	92	91	85	75	62	53	73
Average Temp. (°F)	40	45	53	63	71	79	82	81	74	63	52	43	62
Average Low (°F)	30	34	42	51	60	68	72	70	63	51	41	34	51
Extreme Low (°F)	-4	-5	17	28	40	46	54	52	38	29	17	-1	-5

Note: Figures cover the years 1948-1990
Source: National Climatic Data Center, International Station Meteorological Climate Summary, 3/95

Average Precipitation/Snowfall/Humidity

Precip./Humidity	Jan	Feb	Mar	Apr	May	Jun	Jul	Aug	Sep	Oct	Nov	Dec	Yr.
Avg. Precip. (in.)	4.1	4.2	4.9	5.2	5.4	3.6	3.5	3.2	3.8	3.5	4.8	4.5	50.7
Avg. Snowfall (in.)	3	2	1	Tr	0	0	0	0	0	0	Tr	1	5
Avg. Rel. Hum. 6am (%)	80	80	78	81	86	86	87	88	87	86	82	80	84
Avg. Rel. Hum. 3pm (%)	57	54	50	50	53	52	54	52	52	48	52	57	53

Note: Figures cover the years 1948-1990; Tr = Trace amounts (<0.05 in. of rain; <0.5 in. of snow)
Source: National Climatic Data Center, International Station Meteorological Climate Summary, 3/95

Weather Conditions

Temperature			Daytime Sky			Precipitation		
10°F & below	32°F & below	90°F & above	Clear	Partly cloudy	Cloudy	0.01 inch or more precip.	0.1 inch or more snow/ice	Thunder-storms
1	57	73	110	142	113	104	4	57

Note: Figures are average number of days per year and covers the years 1948-1990
Source: National Climatic Data Center, International Station Meteorological Climate Summary, 3/95

AIR & WATER QUALITY

Maximum Pollutant Concentrations

	Particulate Matter (ug/m^3)	Carbon Monoxide (ppm)	Sulfur Dioxide (ppm)	Nitrogen Dioxide (ppm)	Ozone (ppm)	Lead (ug/m^3)
MSA[1] Level	61	5	0.006	0.010	0.10	n/a
NAAQS[2]	150	9	0.140	0.053	0.12	1.50
Met NAAQS?	Yes	Yes	Yes	Yes	Yes	n/a

Note: (1) Metropolitan Statistical Area - see Appendix A for areas included; (2) National Ambient Air Quality Standards; ppm = parts per million; ug/m^3 = micrograms per cubic meter; n/a not available
Source: EPA, National Air Quality and Emissions Trends Report, 1997

Pollutant Standards Index

In the Little Rock MSA (see Appendix A for areas included), the Pollutant Standards Index (PSI) exceeded 100 on 1 day in 1997. A PSI value greater than 100 indicates that air quality would be in the unhealthful range on that day. *EPA, National Air Quality and Emissions Trends Report, 1997*

Drinking Water

Water System Name	Pop. Served	Primary Water Source Type	Number of Violations in 1998	Type of Violation/ Contaminants
Little Rock Muni Water Works	204,543	Surface	None	None

Note: Data as of July 10, 1999
Source: EPA, Office of Ground Water and Drinking Water, Safe Drinking Water Information System

Little Rock tap water is neutral, soft and fluoridated.
Editor & Publisher Market Guide, 1999

Madison, Wisconsin

Background

Madison was selected as the territorial capital in 1836 before construction of the city was even begun in 1838. Despite repeated threats to move the capital elsewhere by the members of the legislature, it has maintained its status. It was named for President James Madison in 1836, and incorporated into a village in 1856. When Wisconsin attained statehood in 1848, the University of Wisconsin (one of the largest in the country) was established.

Most of the city, including its business center, is situated on an isthmus between Lake Mendota and Lake Minona in the southcentral part of the state. Two other lakes, Kengonsa and Waubesa lie to the south. By ordinance, the city's skyline is dominated by the capitol dome, which weighs 2,500 tons.

Madison serves as the trade center of a rich agricultural and dairy region. Food processing is a major industry. Batteries, dairy equipment, medical supplies, and machine tools are produced there as well.

Madison has the typical continental climate of interior North America with a large annual temperature range and frequent short period temperature changes. The range of extreme temperatures is from about 110 to -40 degrees. The city lies in the path of the frequent cyclones and anticyclones which move eastward over this area during fall, winter, and spring. The most frequent air masses are of polar origin. Occasional influxes of arctic air affect this area during the winter months. Summers are pleasant, with only occasional periods of extreme heat or high humidity.

General Rankings and Evaluative Comments

■ Madison was ranked #1 out of 24 mid-sized, midwestern metropolitan areas in *Money's* 1998 survey of "The Best Places to Live in America." The survey was conducted by first contacting 512 representative households nationwide and asking them to rank 37 quality-of-life factors on a scale of 1 to 10. Next, a demographic profile was compiled on the 300 largest metropolitan statistical areas in the U.S. The numbers were crunched together to arrive at an overall ranking (things Americans consider most important, like clean air and water, low crime and good schools, received extra weight). Unlike previous years, the 1998 rankings were broken down by region (northeast, midwest, south, west) and population size (100,000 to 249,999; 250,000 to 999,999; 1 million plus). The city had a nationwide ranking of #7 out of 300 in 1997 and #1 out of 300 in 1996. *Money, July 1998; Money, July 1997; Money, September 1996*

■ *Ladies Home Journal* ranked America's 200 largest cities based on the qualities women care about most. Madison ranked #2 out of 200. Criteria: low crime rate, well-paying jobs, quality health and child care, good public schools, the presence of women in government, size of the gender wage gap, number of sexual-harassment and discrimination complaints filed, unemployment and divorce rates, commute times, population density, number of houses of worship, parks and cultural offerings, number of women's health specialists, how well a community's women cared for themselves, complexion kindness index based on UV radiation levels, odds of finding affordable fashions, rental rates for romance movies, champagne sales and other matters of the heart. *Ladies Home Journal, November 1998*

■ Madison was selected as one of the 10 healthiest cities for women by *American Health*. It was ranked #10 out of America's 120 most populous metro areas. Criteria: number and quality of doctors and hospitals, quality of women's health centers, number of recreational opportunities, rate of violent crimes, cleanliness of air and water, percentage of women-owned businesses, and the number of family-friendly employers.

"Madison has an impressively low unemployment rate; in 1997, it was just 1.7%—one of the lowest in the U.S. Madison also boasts a high interest in fitness, as it was named the 'best bike town in the Midwest' by *Bicycling* magazine." *American Health, 1998*

■ Zero Population Growth ranked 229 cities in terms of children's health, safety, and economic well-being. Madison was ranked #2 out of 112 independent cities (cities with populations greater than 100,000 which were neither Major Cities nor Suburbs/Outer Cities) and was given a grade of A+. Criteria: total population, percent of population under 18 years of age, household language, percent population change, percent of births to teens, infant mortality rate, percent of low birth weights, dropout rate, enrollment in preprimary school, violent and property crime rates, unemployment rate, percent of children in poverty, percent of owner occupied units, number of bad air days, percent of public transportation commuters, and average travel time to work. *Zero Population Growth, Children's Environmental Index, Fall 1999*

■ Madison was selected as one of "America's Best Towns to Raise an Outdoor Family" by *Outdoor Explorer* magazine. Criteria: easy access to the outdoors, quality education, affordable housing, good health care, decent employment opportunities and low crime rates. The city was ranked #2 out of 25.

"With lakes covering more than 4,500 acres, 92 miles of shoreline for swimming, 40 launching sites for boats and an additional 1,500 acres of parks and conservation land, it is easy to see why [Madison scored so high]." *Outdoor Explorer, Summer 1999*

■ Madison appeared on *New Mobility's* list of "10 Disability Friendly Cities." Rank: #9 out of 10. Criteria: affordable and accessible housing, transportation, quality medical care, personal assistance services and strong advocacy.

"All Madison's fixed-route buses are 100 percent accessible on weekends and holidays, and mostly accessible during the week. All of the city's numerous parks have accessible parking and paved pathways. Major employer Oscar Mayer has an open hiring policy." *New Mobility, December 1997*

■ Cognetics studied 273 metro areas in the United States, ranking them by entrepreneurial activity. Madison was ranked #17 out of 134 smaller metro areas. Criteria: Significant Starts (firms started in the last 10 years that still employ at least 5 people) and Young Growers (percent of firms 10 years old or less that grew significantly during the last 4 years). *Cognetics, "Entrepreneurial Hot Spots: The Best Places in America to Start and Grow a Company," 1998*

■ Madison was selected as one of the "Best American Cities to Start a Business" by *Point of View* magazine. Criteria: coolness, quality-of-life, and business concerns. The city was ranked #16 out of 75. *Point of View, November 1998*

■ Reliastar Financial Corp. ranked the 125 largest metropolitan areas according to the general financial security of residents. Madison was ranked #36 out of 125 with a score of 5.7. The score indicates the percentage a metropolitan area is above or below the metropolitan norm. A metro area with a score of 10.6 is 10.6% above the metro average. Criteria: Earnings and Wealth Potential (household income, education, net assets, cost of living); Safety Net (health insurance, retirement savings, life insurance, income support programs); Personal Threats (unemployment rate, low-income households, crime rate); Community Economic Vitality (cost of community services, job quality, job creation, housing costs). *Reliastar Financial Corp., "The Best Cities to Earn and Save Money," 1999 Edition*

Business Environment

STATE ECONOMY

State Economic Profile

Wisconsin's expansion has begun to slow. For the first time in some years, 1998 saw WI grow at a rate below the national. WI's manufacturing sector remains stagnant and its farm sector struggling. WI's tight labor market will help to absorb some of these declines. An unsustainable increase in construction has driven job growth. WI's economy should trail the nation for some years before rebounding in 2001.

WI's construction industry remains a lone bright spot. Several commercial projects are under way in Milwaukee, such as the new convention center and baseball park. In addition, industrial and office construction is picking up in the suburbs. Public construction is also set to rise as the new federal transportation regulation raised WI's federal transportation funding by 48% to $520 million.

WI's residential market remains healthy with residential permits growing at a torrid pace in 1998. Existing home sales along with house prices are rising. Despite recent price appreciation, affordability still exceeds the national average. In the long run, however, the fast pace of construction will slow as residential construction is outpacing household formation in the state.

WI exports a large share of its manufacturing and agricultural output. Weak export demand is resulting in cutbacks to its papermaking, pulp, and equipment manufacturing industries. Farm income also dropped by over 90% in 1998 as commodity prices tumbled and export demand shrank. Commodity prices will remain weak, leaving little promise of a resurgence in WI's farm sector (outside of dairy, which is performing well). Slowing population growth, especially among younger households, will slow long-run growth. WI's high exposure to manufacturing and agriculture will continue to create downside risks for the state. WI will moderately underperform the nation in the near term." *National Association of Realtors, Economic Profiles: The Fifty States and the District of Columbia, http://nar.realtor.com/databank/profiles.htm*

IMPORTS/EXPORTS

Total Export Sales

Area	1994 ($000)	1995 ($000)	1996 ($000)	1997 ($000)	% Chg. 1994-97	% Chg. 1996-97
MSA[1]	417,083	497,462	522,408	602,973	44.6	15.4
U.S.	512,415,609	583,030,524	622,827,063	687,597,999	34.2	10.4

Note: (1) Metropolitan Statistical Area - see Appendix A for areas included
Source: U.S. Department of Commerce, International Trade Association, Metropolitan Area Exports: An Export Performance Report on Over 250 U.S. Cities, November 10, 1998

CITY FINANCES

City Government Finances

Component	FY92 ($000)	FY92 (per capita $)
Revenue	169,564	869.39
Expenditure	177,805	911.64
Debt Outstanding	136,760	701.19
Cash & Securities	158,687	813.62

Source: U.S. Bureau of the Census, City Government Finances: 1991-92

City Government Revenue by Source

Source	FY92 ($000)	FY92 (per capita $)	FY92 (%)
From Federal Government	7,581	38.87	4.5
From State Governments	47,559	243.84	28.0
From Local Governments	2,410	12.36	1.4
Property Taxes	53,793	275.81	31.7
General Sales Taxes	3	0.02	0.0
Selective Sales Taxes	2,630	13.48	1.6
Income Taxes	0	0.00	0.0
Current Charges	19,659	100.80	11.6
Utility/Liquor Store	14,382	73.74	8.5
Employee Retirement[1]	0	0.00	0.0
Other	21,547	110.48	12.7

Note: (1) Excludes "city contributions," classified as "nonrevenue," intragovernmental transfers.
Source: U.S. Bureau of the Census, City Government Finances: 1991-92

City Government Expenditures by Function

Function	FY92 ($000)	FY92 (per capita $)	FY92 (%)
Educational Services	5,754	29.50	3.2
Employee Retirement[1]	0	0.00	0.0
Environment/Housing	51,246	262.75	28.8
Government Administration	8,209	42.09	4.6
Interest on General Debt	7,409	37.99	4.2
Public Safety	45,252	232.02	25.5
Social Services	6,339	32.50	3.6
Transportation	20,435	104.77	11.5
Utility/Liquor Store	31,062	159.26	17.5
Other	2,099	10.76	1.2

Note: (1) Payments to beneficiaries including withdrawal of contributions.
Source: U.S. Bureau of the Census, City Government Finances: 1991-92

Municipal Bond Ratings

Area	Moody's	S & P
Madison	Aaa	n/a

Note: n/a not available; n/r not rated
Source: Moody's Bond Record, 6/99

POPULATION

Population Growth

Area	1980	1990	% Chg. 1980-90	July 1998 Estimate	% Chg. 1990-98
City	170,616	191,262	12.1	209,306	9.4
MSA[1]	323,545	367,085	13.5	404,794	10.3
U.S.	226,545,805	248,765,170	9.8	270,299,000	8.7

Note: (1) Metropolitan Statistical Area - see Appendix A for areas included;
July 1998 MSA population estimate was calculated by the editors
Source: 1980/1990 Census of Housing and Population, Summary Tape File 3C;
Census Bureau Population Estimates 1998

Population Characteristics

Race	City 1980 Population	%	City 1990 Population	%	% Chg. 1980-90	MSA[1] 1990 Population	%
White	161,333	94.6	173,690	90.8	7.7	344,682	93.9
Black	4,557	2.7	7,925	4.1	73.9	10,414	2.8
Amer Indian/Esk/Aleut	454	0.3	778	0.4	71.4	1,326	0.4
Asian/Pacific Islander	3,176	1.9	7,406	3.9	133.2	8,582	2.3
Other	1,096	0.6	1,463	0.8	33.5	2,081	0.6
Hispanic Origin[2]	2,451	1.4	3,614	1.9	47.5	5,204	1.4

Note: (1) Metropolitan Statistical Area - see Appendix A for areas included;
(2) people of Hispanic origin can be of any race
Source: 1980/1990 Census of Housing and Population, Summary Tape File 3C

Ancestry

Area	German	Irish	English	Italian	U.S.	French	Polish	Dutch
City	44.2	16.7	12.9	3.7	1.4	3.9	5.1	2.4
MSA[1]	49.3	16.5	12.9	3.1	1.5	3.9	4.7	2.3
U.S.	23.3	15.6	13.1	5.9	5.3	4.2	3.8	2.5

Note: Figures are percentages and include persons that reported multiple ancestry (eg. if a person reported being Irish and Italian, they were included in both columns); (1) Metropolitan Statistical Area - see Appendix A for areas included
Source: 1990 Census of Population and Housing, Summary Tape File 3C

Age

Area	Median Age (Years)	Age Distribution (%) Under 5	Under 18	18-24	25-44	45-64	65+	80+
City	29.3	6.2	18.5	22.2	35.5	14.6	9.2	2.3
MSA[1]	30.7	7.0	22.7	15.7	36.3	16.0	9.2	2.3
U.S.	32.9	7.3	25.6	10.5	32.6	18.7	12.5	2.8

Note: (1) Metropolitan Statistical Area - see Appendix A for areas included
Source: 1990 Census of Population and Housing, Summary Tape File 3C

Male/Female Ratio

Area	Number of males per 100 females (all ages)	Number of males per 100 females (18 years old+)
City	96.5	92.9
MSA[1]	97.4	94.4
U.S.	95.0	91.9

Note: (1) Metropolitan Statistical Area - see Appendix A for areas included
Source: 1990 Census of Population, General Population Characteristics

INCOME

Per Capita/Median/Average Income

Area	Per Capita ($)	Median Household ($)	Average Household ($)
City	15,143	29,420	36,977
MSA[1]	15,542	32,703	39,589
U.S.	14,420	30,056	38,453

Note: All figures are for 1989; (1) Metropolitan Statistical Area - see Appendix A for areas included
Source: 1990 Census of Population and Housing, Summary Tape File 3C

Household Income Distribution by Race

Income ($)	City (%)					U.S. (%)				
	Total	White	Black	Other	Hisp.[1]	Total	White	Black	Other	Hisp.[1]
Less than 5,000	5.8	4.9	12.1	22.2	8.7	6.2	4.8	15.2	8.6	8.8
5,000 - 9,999	9.2	8.7	17.0	14.4	6.4	9.3	8.6	14.2	9.9	11.1
10,000 - 14,999	9.1	8.8	11.5	13.8	10.8	8.8	8.5	11.0	9.8	11.0
15,000 - 24,999	18.0	17.9	20.9	16.7	26.7	17.5	17.3	18.9	18.5	20.5
25,000 - 34,999	16.5	16.8	15.5	11.6	20.0	15.8	16.1	14.2	15.4	16.4
35,000 - 49,999	18.1	18.7	13.6	9.5	10.5	17.9	18.6	13.3	16.1	16.0
50,000 - 74,999	14.7	15.3	7.3	7.0	11.6	15.0	15.8	9.3	13.4	11.1
75,000 - 99,999	4.8	5.1	1.5	2.7	3.2	5.1	5.5	2.6	4.7	3.1
100,000+	3.7	3.9	0.7	1.9	2.0	4.4	4.8	1.3	3.7	1.9

Note: All figures are for 1989; (1) people of Hispanic origin can be of any race
Source: 1990 Census of Population and Housing, Summary Tape File 3C

Effective Buying Income

Area	Per Capita ($)	Median Household ($)	Average Household ($)
City	18,780	37,228	46,592
MSA[1]	20,037	41,240	51,092
U.S.	16,803	34,536	45,243

Note: Data as of 1/1/99; (1) Metropolitan Statistical Area - see Appendix A for areas included
Source: Standard Rate & Data Service, Newspaper Advertising Source, 9/99

Effective Household Buying Income Distribution

Area	% of Households Earning						
	$10,000 -$19,999	$20,000 -$34,999	$35,000 -$49,999	$50,000 -$74,999	$75,000 -$99,000	$100,000 -$124,999	$125,000 and up
City	14.6	22.3	17.8	20.6	8.5	3.0	2.9
MSA[1]	12.7	21.6	19.1	24.0	9.0	2.9	3.0
U.S.	16.0	22.6	18.2	18.9	7.2	2.4	2.7

Note: Data as of 1/1/99; (1) Metropolitan Statistical Area - see Appendix A for areas included
Source: Standard Rate & Data Service, Newspaper Advertising Source, 9/99

Poverty Rates by Race and Age

Area	Total (%)	By Race (%)				By Age (%)		
		White	Black	Other	Hisp.[2]	Under 5 years old	Under 18 years old	65 years and over
City	16.1	13.8	35.2	42.2	22.9	15.7	13.2	4.8
MSA[1]	10.5	8.9	35.0	37.6	21.3	10.6	8.8	5.0
U.S.	13.1	9.8	29.5	23.1	25.3	20.1	18.3	12.8

Note: Figures show the percent of people living below the poverty line in 1989. The average poverty threshold was $12,674 for a family of four in 1989; (1) Metropolitan Statistical Area - see Appendix A for areas included; (2) people of Hispanic origin can be of any race
Source: 1990 Census of Population and Housing, Summary Tape File 3C

EMPLOYMENT

Labor Force and Employment

Area	Civilian Labor Force			Workers Employed		
	Jun. 1998	Jun. 1999	% Chg.	Jun. 1998	Jun. 1999	% Chg.
City	132,796	134,318	1.1	130,334	132,147	1.4
MSA[1]	264,691	267,827	1.2	260,364	263,987	1.4
U.S.	138,798,000	140,666,000	1.3	132,265,000	134,395,000	1.6

Note: Data is not seasonally adjusted and covers workers 16 years of age and older; (1) Metropolitan Statistical Area - see Appendix A for areas included
Source: Bureau of Labor Statistics, http://stats.bls.gov

Unemployment Rate

Area	1998						1999					
	Jul.	Aug.	Sep.	Oct.	Nov.	Dec.	Jan.	Feb.	Mar.	Apr.	May.	Jun.
City	1.7	1.6	1.6	1.6	1.6	1.4	1.7	1.8	1.7	1.5	1.6	1.6
MSA[1]	1.6	1.4	1.4	1.4	1.4	1.3	1.8	1.9	1.7	1.4	1.4	1.4
U.S.	4.7	4.5	4.4	4.2	4.1	4.0	4.8	4.7	4.4	4.1	4.0	4.5

Note: Data is not seasonally adjusted and covers workers 16 years of age and older; all figures are percentages; (1) Metropolitan Statistical Area - see Appendix A for areas included
Source: Bureau of Labor Statistics, http://stats.bls.gov

Employment by Industry

Sector	MSA[1] Number of Employees	MSA[1] Percent of Total	U.S. Percent of Total
Services	73,900	26.0	30.4
Retail Trade	47,600	16.8	17.7
Government	72,700	25.6	15.6
Manufacturing	30,000	10.6	14.3
Finance/Insurance/Real Estate	22,600	8.0	5.9
Wholesale Trade	13,100	4.6	5.4
Transportation/Public Utilities	9,600	3.4	5.3
Construction	n/a	n/a	5.0
Mining	n/a	n/a	0.4

Note: Figures cover non-farm employment as of 6/99 and are not seasonally adjusted; (1) Metropolitan Statistical Area - see Appendix A for areas included; n/a not available
Source: Bureau of Labor Statistics, http://stats.bls.gov

Employment by Occupation

Occupation Category	City (%)	MSA[1] (%)	U.S. (%)
White Collar	71.1	67.3	58.1
Executive/Admin./Management	13.3	13.6	12.3
Professional	22.0	18.5	14.1
Technical & Related Support	7.0	5.9	3.7
Sales	11.0	10.9	11.8
Administrative Support/Clerical	17.8	18.3	16.3
Blue Collar	13.4	17.5	26.2
Precision Production/Craft/Repair	5.5	7.7	11.3
Machine Operators/Assem./Insp.	3.4	4.3	6.8
Transportation/Material Movers	2.3	2.8	4.1
Cleaners/Helpers/Laborers	2.1	2.6	3.9
Services	14.6	13.0	13.2
Farming/Forestry/Fishing	0.9	2.2	2.5

Note: Figures cover employed persons 16 years old and over; (1) Metropolitan Statistical Area - see Appendix A for areas included
Source: 1990 Census of Population and Housing, Summary Tape File 3C

Occupational Employment Projections: 1996 - 2006

Occupations Expected to Have the Largest Job Growth (ranked by numerical growth)	Fast-Growing Occupations[1] (ranked by percent growth)
1. Janitors/cleaners/maids, ex. priv. hshld.	1. Systems analysts
2. General managers & top executives	2. Desktop publishers
3. Cashiers	3. Personal and home care aides
4. Truck drivers, light	4. Database administrators
5. Salespersons, retail	5. Paralegals
6. Systems analysts	6. Securities, financial services sales
7. Home health aides	7. Occupational therapists
8. Teachers aides, clerical & paraprofess.	8. Home health aides
9. Registered nurses	9. Teachers, special education
10. Waiters & waitresses	10. Medical assistants

Note: Projections cover Wisconsin; (1) Excludes occupations with total job growth less than 300
Source: U.S. Department of Labor, Employment and Training Administration, America's Labor Market Information System (ALMIS)

TAXES

Major State and Local Tax Rates

State Corp. Income (%)	State Personal Income (%)	Residential Property (effective rate per $100)	Sales & Use State (%)	Sales & Use Local (%)	State Gasoline (cents/ gallon)	State Cigarette (cents/ pack)
7.9	4.77 - 6.77	n/a	5.0	0.5	25.4	59.0

Note: Personal/corporate income, sales, gasoline and cigarette tax rates as of January 1999.
Property tax rates as of 1997.
Source: Federation of Tax Administrators, www.taxadmin.org; Washington D.C. Department of Finance and Revenue, Tax Rates and Tax Burdens in the District of Columbia: A Nationwide Comparison, July 1998; Chamber of Commerce, 1999

Total Taxes Per Capita and as a Percent of Income

Area	Per Capita Income ($)	Per Capita Taxes ($) Total	Per Capita Taxes ($) Federal	Per Capita Taxes ($) State/ Local	Percent of Income (%) Total	Percent of Income (%) Federal	Percent of Income (%) State/ Local
Wisconsin	26,499	9,897	6,313	3,584	37.3	23.8	13.5
U.S.	27,876	9,881	6,690	3,191	35.4	24.0	11.4

Note: Figures are for 1998
Source: Tax Foundation, www.taxfoundation.org

Estimated Tax Burden

Area	State Income	Local Income	Property	Sales	Total
Madison	4,612	0	6,000	536	11,148

Note: The numbers are estimates of taxes paid by a married couple with two children and annual earnings of $75,000. Sales tax estimates assume they spend average amounts on food, clothing, household goods and gasoline. Property tax estimates assume they live in a $250,000 home.
Source: Kiplinger's Personal Finance Magazine, October 1998

COMMERCIAL REAL ESTATE

Data not available at time of publication.

COMMERCIAL UTILITIES

Typical Monthly Electric Bills

Area	Commercial Service ($/month) 12 kW demand 1,500 kWh	Commercial Service ($/month) 100 kW demand 30,000 kWh	Industrial Service ($/month) 1,000 kW demand 400,000 kWh	Industrial Service ($/month) 20,000 kW demand 10,000,000 kWh
City	99	1,641	19,137	315,745
U.S.	150	2,174	23,995	508,569

Note: Based on rates in effect January 1, 1999
Source: Edison Electric Institute, Typical Residential, Commercial and Industrial Bills, Winter 1999

TRANSPORTATION

Transportation Statistics

Average minutes to work	16.9
Interstate highways	I-90; I-94
Bus lines	
In-city	Madison Metro Transit
Inter-city	4
Passenger air service	
Airport	Dane County Regional
Airlines	8
Aircraft departures	11,473 (1996)
Enplaned passengers	518,393 (1996)
Rail service	Amtrak Thruway Motorcoach Connection
Motor freight carriers	40
Major waterways/ports	None

Source: Editor & Publisher Market Guide, 1999; FAA Airport Activity Statistics, 1997; Amtrak National Time Table, Northeast Timetable, Spring/Summer 1999; 1990 Census of Population and Housing, STF 3C; Chamber of Commerce/Economic Development 1999; Jane's Urban Transport Systems 1999-2000

Means of Transportation to Work

Area	Car/Truck/Van		Public Transportation			Bicycle	Walked	Other Means	Worked at Home
	Drove Alone	Car-pooled	Bus	Subway	Railroad				
City	61.2	11.6	7.4	0.0	0.0	3.3	12.7	1.0	2.7
MSA[1]	68.5	12.5	4.4	0.0	0.0	1.9	8.2	0.8	3.6
U.S.	73.2	13.4	3.0	1.5	0.5	0.4	3.9	1.2	3.0

Note: Figures shown are percentages and only include workers 16 years old and over; (1) Metropolitan Statistical Area - see Appendix A for areas included
Source: 1990 Census of Population and Housing, Summary Tape File 3C

BUSINESSES

Major Business Headquarters

Company Name	1999 Rankings	
	Fortune 500	Forbes 500
American Family Ins. Group	384	-

Note: Companies listed are located in the city; dashes indicate no ranking
Fortune 500: Companies that produce a 10-K are ranked 1 to 500 based on 1998 revenue
Forbes 500: Private companies are ranked 1 to 500 based on 1997 revenue
Source: Forbes, November 30, 1998; Fortune, April 26, 1999

Best Companies to Work For

American Family Insurance Group (insurance), headquartered in Madison, is among the " 100 Best Places to Work in IS." Criteria: compensation, turnover and training. *Computerworld, May 25, 1998*

HOTELS & MOTELS

Hotels/Motels

Area	Hotels/ Motels	Rooms	Luxury-Level Hotels/Motels		Average Minimum Rates ($)		
			♦♦♦♦	♦♦♦♦♦	♦♦	♦♦♦	♦♦♦♦
City	40	4,427	0	0	64	95	n/a
Airport	1	40	0	0	n/a	n/a	n/a
Total	41	4,467	0	0	n/a	n/a	n/a

Note: n/a not available; classifications range from one diamond (budget properties with basic amenities) to five diamond (luxury properties with the finest service, rooms and facilities).
Source: OAG, Business Travel Planner, Winter 1998-99

CONVENTION CENTERS

Major Convention Centers

Center Name	Meeting Rooms	Exhibit Space (sq. ft.)
Dane County Expo Center	13	100,000
Madison Civic Center	n/a	n/a
Monona Terrace Convention Center	24	250,000
University of Wisconsin Extension Conference Centers	34	n/a

Note: n/a not available
Source: Trade Shows Worldwide, 1998; Meetings & Conventions, 4/15/99;
Sucessful Meetings, 3/31/98

Living Environment

COST OF LIVING

Cost of Living Index

Composite Index	Groceries	Housing	Utilities	Trans-portation	Health Care	Misc. Goods/Services
106.0	103.1	120.0	89.6	109.6	109.1	97.9

Note: U.S. = 100
Source: ACCRA, Cost of Living Index, 3rd Quarter 1998

HOUSING

Median Home Prices and Housing Affordability

Area	Median Price[2] 1st Qtr. 1999 ($)	HOI[3] 1st Qtr. 1999	Afford-ability Rank[4]
MSA[1]	n/a	n/a	n/a
U.S.	134,000	69.6	–

Note: (1) Metropolitan Statistical Area - see Appendix A for areas included; (2) U.S. figures calculated from the sales of 524,324 new and existing homes in 181 markets; (3) Housing Opportunity Index - percent of homes sold that were within the reach of the median income household at the prevailing mortgage interest rate; (4) Rank is from 1-181 with 1 being most affordable; n/a not available
Source: National Association of Home Builders, Housing Opportunity Index, 1st Quarter 1999

Median Home Price Projection

It is projected that the median price of existing single-family homes in the metro area will decrease by -1.0% in 1999. Nationwide, home prices are projected to increase 3.8%.
Kiplinger's Personal Finance Magazine, January 1999

Average New Home Price

Area	Price ($)
City	166,687
U.S.	138,988

Note: Figures are based on a new home with 1,800 sq. ft. of living area on an 8,000 sq. ft. lot.
Source: ACCRA, Cost of Living Index, 3rd Quarter 1998

Average Apartment Rent

Area	Rent ($/mth)
City	656
U.S.	586

Note: Figures are based on an unfurnished two bedroom, 1-1/2 or 2 bath apartment, approximately 950 sq. ft. in size, excluding all utilities except water
Source: ACCRA, Cost of Living Index, 3rd Quarter 1998

RESIDENTIAL UTILITIES

Average Residential Utility Costs

Area	All Electric ($/mth)	Part Electric ($/mth)	Other Energy ($/mth)	Phone ($/mth)
City	–	48.47	41.91	17.65
U.S.	103.76	55.93	43.48	19.86

Source: ACCRA, Cost of Living Index, 3rd Quarter 1998

HEALTH CARE

Average Health Care Costs

Area	Hospital ($/day)	Doctor ($/visit)	Dentist ($/visit)
City	314.75	67.50	66.50
U.S.	405.11	50.96	63.88

Note: Hospital—based on a semi-private room; Doctor—based on a general practitioner's routine exam of an established patient; Dentist—based on adult teeth cleaning and periodic oral exam.
Source: ACCRA, Cost of Living Index, 3rd Quarter 1998

Distribution of Office-Based Physicians

Area	Family/Gen. Practitioners	Specialists		
		Medical	Surgical	Other
MSA[1]	157	387	239	363

Note: Data as of 12/31/97; (1) Metropolitan Statistical Area - see Appendix A for areas included
Source: American Medical Assn., Physician Characteristics & Distribution in the U.S., 1999

Hospitals

Madison has 4 general medical and surgical hospitals, 1 psychiatric. *AHA Guide to the Healthcare Field, 1998-99*

According to *U.S. News and World Report,* Madison has 1 of the best hospitals in the U.S.: **University of Wisconsin Hospital & Clinics**, noted for cancer, cardiology, endocrinology, gastroenterology, geriatrics, ophthalmology, orthopedics, otolaryngology, rheumatology, urology. *U.S. News Online, "America's Best Hospitals," 10th Edition, www.usnews.com*

EDUCATION

Public School District Statistics

District Name	Num. Sch.	Enroll.	Classroom Teachers	Pupils per Teacher	Minority Pupils (%)	Current Exp.[1] ($/pupil)
Madison Metropolitan Sch Dist	50	25,327	n/a	n/a	n/a	n/a

Note: Data covers the 1997-1998 school year unless otherwise noted; (1) Data covers fiscal year 1996; SD = School District; ISD = Independent School District; n/a not available
Source: National Center for Education Statistics, Common Core of Data Public Education Agency Universe 1997-98; National Center for Education Statistics, Characteristics of the 100 Largest Public Elementary and Secondary School Districts in the United States: 1997-98, July 1999

Educational Quality

School District	Education Quotient[1]	Graduate Outcome[2]	Community Index[3]	Resource Index[4]
Madison Metropolitan	128.0	150.0	143.0	81.0

Note: Nearly 1,000 secondary school districts were rated in terms of educational quality. The scores range from a low of 50 to a high of 150; (1) Average of the Graduate Outcome, Community and Resource indexes; (2) Based on graduation rates and college board scores (SAT/ACT); (3) Based on the surrounding community's average level of education and the area's average income level; (4) Based on teacher salaries, per-pupil expenditures and student-teacher ratios.
Source: Expansion Management, Ratings Issue, 1998

Educational Attainment by Race

Area	High School Graduate (%)					Bachelor's Degree (%)				
	Total	White	Black	Other	Hisp.[2]	Total	White	Black	Other	Hisp.[2]
City	90.6	91.0	80.6	89.3	87.2	42.0	41.7	24.8	62.8	48.4
MSA[1]	88.9	89.2	80.1	87.0	82.9	34.2	33.8	24.0	57.6	41.5
U.S.	75.2	77.9	63.1	60.4	49.8	20.3	21.5	11.4	19.4	9.2

Note: Figures shown cover persons 25 years old and over; (1) Metropolitan Statistical Area - see Appendix A for areas included; (2) people of Hispanic origin can be of any race
Source: 1990 Census of Population and Housing, Summary Tape File 3C

School Enrollment by Type

Area	Preprimary				Elementary/High School			
	Public		Private		Public		Private	
	Enrollment	%	Enrollment	%	Enrollment	%	Enrollment	%
City	2,039	54.5	1,705	45.5	19,043	90.4	2,023	9.6
MSA[1]	4,454	59.1	3,077	40.9	47,805	92.0	4,184	8.0
U.S.	2,679,029	59.5	1,824,256	40.5	38,379,689	90.2	4,187,099	9.8

Note: Figures shown cover persons 3 years old and over;
(1) Metropolitan Statistical Area - see Appendix A for areas included
Source: 1990 Census of Population and Housing, Summary Tape File 3C

School Enrollment by Race

Area	Preprimary (%)				Elementary/High School (%)			
	White	Black	Other	Hisp.[1]	White	Black	Other	Hisp.[1]
City	84.8	7.7	7.5	3.0	84.7	9.1	6.3	2.3
MSA[2]	89.7	5.0	5.2	2.3	91.3	5.0	3.8	2.1
U.S.	80.4	12.5	7.1	7.8	74.1	15.6	10.3	12.5

Note: Figures shown cover persons 3 years old and over; (1) people of Hispanic origin can be of any race; (2) Metropolitan Statistical Area - see Appendix A for areas included
Source: 1990 Census of Population and Housing, Summary Tape File 3C

Classroom Teacher Salaries in Public Schools

District	B.A. Degree		M.A. Degree		Maximum	
	Min. ($)	Rank[1]	Max. ($)	Rank[1]	Max. ($)	Rank[1]
Madison	25,449	60	45,808	47	53,443	36
Average	26,980	-	46,065	-	51,435	-

Note: Salaries are for 1997-1998; (1) Rank ranges from 1 to 100
Source: American Federation of Teachers, Survey & Analysis of Salary Trends, 1998

Higher Education

Two-Year Colleges		Four-Year Colleges		Medical Schools	Law Schools	Voc/Tech
Public	Private	Public	Private			
1	2	1	1	1	1	8

Source: College Blue Book, Occupational Education, 1997; Medical School Admission Requirements, 1999-2000; Peterson's Guide to Two-Year Colleges, 1999; Peterson's Guide to Four-Year Colleges, 2000; Barron's Guide to Law Schools, 1999

MAJOR EMPLOYERS

Major Employers

CUNA Mutual Insurance Society
Famous Footwear
Madison-Kipp Corp. (aluminum die-casting)
University of Wisconsin Hospital & Clinics
Webcrafters (book printing)

Interstate Energy Corp.
Quality Environmental Services
Meriter Hospital
WPL Holdings (electric services)
Wisconsin Power & Light

Note: Companies listed are located in the city
Source: Dun's Business Rankings, 1999; Ward's Business Directory, 1998

PUBLIC SAFETY

Crime Rate

Area	All Crimes	Violent Crimes				Property Crimes		
		Murder	Forcible Rape	Robbery	Aggrav. Assault	Burglary	Larceny -Theft	Motor Vehicle Theft
City	4,460.6	1.5	40.9	171.8	218.7	705.7	2,991.6	330.4
Suburbs[1]	3,275.1	2.1	18.8	17.7	194.5	453.6	2,460.2	128.3
MSA[2]	3,877.2	1.8	30.0	96.0	206.8	581.6	2,730.1	230.9
U.S.	4,922.7	6.8	35.9	186.1	382.0	919.6	2,886.5	505.8

Note: Crime rate is the number of crimes per 100,000 pop.; (1) defined as all areas within the MSA but located outside the central city; (2) Metropolitan Statistical Area - see Appendix A for areas incl.
Source: FBI Uniform Crime Reports, 1997

RECREATION

Culture and Recreation

Museums	Symphony Orchestras	Opera Companies	Dance Companies	Professional Theatres	Zoos	Pro Sports Teams
4	2	1	3	3	1	0

Source: International Directory of the Performing Arts, 1997; Official Museum Directory, 1999; Stern's Performing Arts Directory, 1997; USA Today Four Sport Stadium Guide, 1997; Chamber of Commerce/Economic Development, 1999

Library System

The Madison Public Library has seven branches, holdings of 696,188 volumes, and a budget of $7,523,171 (1997). *American Library Directory, 1998-1999*

MEDIA

Newspapers

Name	Type	Freq.	Distribution	Circulation
Badger Herald	n/a	5x/wk	Campus	16,000
The Capital Times	General	6x/wk	Area	22,000
Daily Cardinal	General	5x/wk	Camp/Comm	10,000
The Madison Times	Black/Hisp	1x/wk	Local	7,000
Wisconsin State Journal	General	7x/wk	Area	86,000

Note: Includes newspapers with circulations of 1,000 or more located in the city; n/a not available
Source: Burrelle's Media Directory, 1999 Edition

Television Stations

Name	Ch.	Affiliation	Type	Owner
WISC	n/a	CBST	Commercial	Evening Telegram Company
WMTV	15	NBCT	Commercial	Benedek Broadcasting Corporation
WHRM	20	PBS	Public	State of WI Educational Communications Board
WHA	21	PBS	Public	University of Wisconsin Board of Regents
WKOW	27	ABCT	Commercial	Shockley Communications Corporation
WHWC	28	PBS	Public	State of WI Educational Communications Board
WHLA	31	PBS	Public	State of WI Educational Communications Board
WLEF	36	PBS	Public	State of WI Educational Communications Board
WPNE	38	PBS	Public	State of WI Educational Communications Board
WMSN	47	FBC	Commercial	Sullivan Broadcasting
WHPN	57	UPN	Commercial	n/a

Note: Stations included broadcast in the Madison metro area; n/a not available
Source: Burrelle's Media Directory, 1999 Edition

FM Radio Stations

Call Letters	Freq. (mHz)	Target Audience	Station Format	Music Format
WERN	88.7	General	E/M/T	Classical
WPNE	89.3	General	E/M	Classical
WORT	89.9	G/H	M/N/T	Alternative/Big Band/Classic Rock/Classical
WHLA	90.3	General	E/T	n/a
WHBM	90.3	General	E/T	n/a
WHHI	91.3	General	E/T	n/a
WMAD	92.1	General	M	Alternative
WJJO	94.1	General	M/N/S	AOR
WOLX	94.9	General	M/N	Oldies
WMLI	96.3	General	M/N/S	Easy Listening
WMGN	98.1	General	M	Adult Contemporary/Jazz
WIBA	101.5	General	M	Classic Rock
WNWC	102.5	Religious	M/N/S/T	Christian
WZEE	104.1	General	M/N	Top 40
WMMM	105.5	General	M/N/S	Adult Top 40/Alternative/AOR
WWQM	106.3	General	M	Country

Note: Stations included broadcast in the Madison metro area; n/a not available
Station Format: E=Educational; M=Music; N=News; S=Sports; T=Talk
Target Audience: A=Asian; B=Black; C=Christian; E=Ethnic; F=French; G=General; H=Hispanic; M=Men; N=Native American; R=Religious; S=Senior Citizen; W=Women; Y=Young Adult; Z=Children
Music Format: AOR=Album Oriented Rock; MOR=Middle-of-the-Road
Source: Burrelle's Media Directory, 1999 Edition

AM Radio Stations

Call Letters	Freq. (kHz)	Target Audience	Station Format	Music Format
WLBL	930	General	E/M/N/T	n/a
WHA	970	General	E/T	n/a
WTSO	1070	General	M/N/S/T	Adult Standards/Oldies
WNWC	1190	Religious	M/N/T	Christian
WIBA	1310	General	N/T	n/a
WHIT	1550	General	S	n/a
WTDY	1670	General	N/T	n/a

Note: Stations included broadcast in the Madison metro area; n/a not available
Target Audience: A=Asian; B=Black; C=Christian; E=Ethnic; F=French; G=General; H=Hispanic; M=Men; N=Native American; R=Religious; S=Senior Citizen; W=Women; Y=Young Adult; Z=Children
Station Format: E=Educational; M=Music; N=News; S=Sports; T=Talk
Source: Burrelle's Media Directory, 1999 Edition

CLIMATE

Average and Extreme Temperatures

Temperature	Jan	Feb	Mar	Apr	May	Jun	Jul	Aug	Sep	Oct	Nov	Dec	Yr.
Extreme High (°F)	56	61	82	94	93	101	104	102	99	90	76	62	104
Average High (°F)	26	30	42	58	70	79	84	81	72	61	44	30	57
Average Temp. (°F)	17	21	32	46	57	67	72	69	61	50	36	23	46
Average Low (°F)	8	12	22	35	45	54	59	57	49	38	27	14	35
Extreme Low (°F)	-37	-28	-29	0	19	31	36	35	25	13	-8	-25	-37

Note: Figures cover the years 1948-1990
Source: National Climatic Data Center, International Station Meteorological Climate Summary, 3/95

Average Precipitation/Snowfall/Humidity

Precip./Humidity	Jan	Feb	Mar	Apr	May	Jun	Jul	Aug	Sep	Oct	Nov	Dec	Yr.
Avg. Precip. (in.)	1.1	1.1	2.1	2.9	3.2	3.8	3.9	3.9	3.0	2.3	2.0	1.7	31.1
Avg. Snowfall (in.)	10	7	9	2	Tr	0	0	0	Tr	Tr	4	11	42
Avg. Rel. Hum. 6am (%)	78	80	81	80	79	81	85	89	90	85	84	82	83
Avg. Rel. Hum. 3pm (%)	66	63	59	50	50	51	53	55	55	54	64	69	57

Note: Figures cover the years 1948-1990; Tr = Trace amounts (<0.05 in. of rain; <0.5 in. of snow)
Source: National Climatic Data Center, International Station Meteorological Climate Summary, 3/95

Weather Conditions

Temperature			Daytime Sky			Precipitation		
5°F & below	32°F & below	90°F & above	Clear	Partly cloudy	Cloudy	0.01 inch or more precip.	0.1 inch or more snow/ice	Thunderstorms
35	161	14	88	119	158	118	38	40

Note: Figures are average number of days per year and covers the years 1948-1990
Source: National Climatic Data Center, International Station Meteorological Climate Summary, 3/95

AIR & WATER QUALITY

Maximum Pollutant Concentrations

	Particulate Matter (ug/m^3)	Carbon Monoxide (ppm)	Sulfur Dioxide (ppm)	Nitrogen Dioxide (ppm)	Ozone (ppm)	Lead (ug/m^3)
MSA[1] Level	42	4	0.017	n/a	0.09	n/a
NAAQS[2]	150	9	0.140	0.053	0.12	1.50
Met NAAQS?	Yes	Yes	Yes	n/a	Yes	n/a

Note: (1) Metropolitan Statistical Area - see Appendix A for areas included; (2) National Ambient Air Quality Standards; ppm = parts per million; ug/m^3 = micrograms per cubic meter; n/a not available
Source: EPA, National Air Quality and Emissions Trends Report, 1997

Drinking Water

Water System Name	Pop. Served	Primary Water Source Type	Number of Violations in 1998	Type of Violation/ Contaminants
Madison Water Utility	200,814	Ground	None	None

Note: Data as of July 10, 1999
Source: EPA, Office of Ground Water and Drinking Water, Safe Drinking Water Information System

Madison tap water is alkaline, hard and fluoridated.
Editor & Publisher Market Guide, 1999

Milwaukee, Wisconsin

Background

Many people associate Milwaukee with beer, perhaps due to the 1970s television show, Laverne and Shirley, where the main characters worked in a brewery, or to the large influx of German immigrants during the 1840s, who left an indelible mark upon the city.

Milwaukee originally began as a trading post for French fur traders. Its favorable location on the western shore of Lake Michigan, and at the confluence of the Milwaukee, Menomonee, and Kinnickinnic Rivers made the site a natural meeting place. In 1818, Solomon Laurent Juneau, a son-in-law of a French fur trader, became Milwaukee's first founder and permanent white settler.

During the 1840s, Milwaukee saw a wave of German immigrants hit its shores. Many of these exiles were unsuccessful revolutionaries in the overthrow of German monarchies. Despite their lack of success back home, these immigrants managed to impart considerable influences in the new country, including: political, with three Socialist mayors; economical, with Pabst and Schlitz Breweries being in Milwaukee; and cultural, with the Goethe House cultural resource center located in the central library of the Milwaukee Public Library System.

Today, Milwaukee includes many nationalities, such as Irish, Serbian, Scandinavian, Polish, Italian, and German. In 1996, Milwaukee opened its $17.3 million Museum Center, featuring science, technology, and natural history, and the first IMAX theater in Wisconsin. Also, its economy depends on not only the beer industry, but on meat packing, farm equipment, education, fabricated metal, and river trade. And after a hard day's work, it's nice to know an ice cold beer is just a reach away.

Milwaukee's weather is quite changeable. Arctic air masses from Canada bring the coldest winter temperatures, zero degrees or lower. Summer temperatures reach into the 90s but rarely exceed 100 degrees.

General Rankings and Evaluative Comments

- Milwaukee was ranked #6 out of 11 large, midwestern metropolitan areas in *Money's* 1998 survey of "The Best Places to Live in America." The survey was conducted by first contacting 512 representative households nationwide and asking them to rank 37 quality-of-life factors on a scale of 1 to 10. Next, a demographic profile was compiled on the 300 largest metropolitan statistical areas in the U.S. The numbers were crunched together to arrive at an overall ranking (things Americans consider most important, like clean air and water, low crime and good schools, received extra weight). Unlike previous years, the 1998 rankings were broken down by region (northeast, midwest, south, west) and population size (100,000 to 249,999; 250,000 to 999,999; 1 million plus). The city had a nationwide ranking of #175 out of 300 in 1997 and #177 out of 300 in 1996. *Money, July 1998; Money, July 1997; Money, September 1996*

- *Ladies Home Journal* ranked America's 200 largest cities based on the qualities women care about most. Milwaukee ranked #128 out of 200. Criteria: low crime rate, well-paying jobs, quality health and child care, good public schools, the presence of women in government, size of the gender wage gap, number of sexual-harassment and discrimination complaints filed, unemployment and divorce rates, commute times, population density, number of houses of worship, parks and cultural offerings, number of women's health specialists, how well a community's women cared for themselves, complexion kindness index based on UV radiation levels, odds of finding affordable fashions, rental rates for romance movies, champagne sales and other matters of the heart. Ladies Home Journal, November 1998

- Zero Population Growth ranked 229 cities in terms of children's health, safety, and economic well-being. Milwaukee was ranked #95 out of 112 independent cities (cities with populations greater than 100,000 which were neither Major Cities nor Suburbs/Outer Cities) and was given a grade of D. Criteria: total population, percent of population under 18 years of age, household language, percent population change, percent of births to teens, infant mortality rate, percent of low birth weights, dropout rate, enrollment in preprimary school, violent and property crime rates, unemployment rate, percent of children in poverty, percent of owner occupied units, number of bad air days, percent of public transportation commuters, and average travel time to work. *Zero Population Growth, Children's Environmental Index, Fall 1999*

- Milwaukee was ranked #45 out of 59 metro areas in *The Regional Economist's* "Rational Livability Ranking of 59 Large Metro Areas." The rankings were based on the metro area's total population change over the period 1990-97 divided by the number of people moving in from elsewhere in the United States (net domestic in-migration). *St. Louis Federal Reserve Bank of St. Louis, The Regional Economist, April 1999*

- Milwaukee was selected by *Yahoo! Internet Life* as one of "America's Most Wired Cities & Towns." The city ranked #31 out of 50. Criteria: home and work net use, domain density, hosts per capita, directory density and content quality. *Yahoo! Internet Life, March 1999*

- Cognetics studied 273 metro areas in the United States, ranking them by entrepreneurial activity. Milwaukee was ranked #18 out of the 50 largest metro areas. Criteria: Significant Starts (firms started in the last 10 years that still employ at least 5 people) and Young Growers (percent of firms 10 years old or less that grew significantly during the last 4 years). *Cognetics, "Entrepreneurial Hot Spots: The Best Places in America to Start and Grow a Company," 1998*

- Milwaukee was selected as one of the "Best American Cities to Start a Business" by *Point of View* magazine. Criteria: coolness, quality-of-life, and business concerns. The city was ranked #60 out of 75. *Point of View, November 1998*

- Reliastar Financial Corp. ranked the 125 largest metropolitan areas according to the general financial security of residents. Milwaukee was ranked #62 out of 125 with a score of 2.0. The score indicates the percentage a metropolitan area is above or below the metropolitan norm. A metro area with a score of 10.6 is 10.6% above the metro average. Criteria: Earnings and Wealth Potential (household income, education, net assets, cost of living); Safety Net (health insurance, retirement savings, life insurance, income support programs); Personal Threats (unemployment rate, low-income households, crime rate); Community Economic Vitality (cost of community services, job quality, job creation, housing costs). *Reliastar Financial Corp., "The Best Cities to Earn and Save Money," 1999 Edition*

Business Environment

STATE ECONOMY

State Economic Profile

Wisconsin's expansion has begun to slow. For the first time in some years, 1998 saw WI grow at a rate below the national. WI's manufacturing sector remains stagnant and its farm sector struggling. WI's tight labor market will help to absorb some of these declines. An unsustainable increase in construction has driven job growth. WI's economy should trail the nation for some years before rebounding in 2001.

WI's construction industry remains a lone bright spot. Several commercial projects are under way in Milwaukee, such as the new convention center and baseball park. In addition, industrial and office construction is picking up in the suburbs. Public construction is also set to rise as the new federal transportation regulation raised WI's federal transportation funding by 48% to $520 million.

WI's residential market remains healthy with residential permits growing at a torrid pace in 1998. Existing home sales along with house prices are rising. Despite recent price appreciation, affordability still exceeds the national average. In the long run, however, the fast pace of construction will slow as residential construction is outpacing household formation in the state.

WI exports a large share of its manufacturing and agricultural output. Weak export demand is resulting in cutbacks to its papermaking, pulp, and equipment manufacturing industries. Farm income also dropped by over 90% in 1998 as commodity prices tumbled and export demand shrank. Commodity prices will remain weak, leaving little promise of a resurgence in WI's farm sector (outside of dairy, which is performing well). Slowing population growth, especially among younger households, will slow long-run growth. WI's high exposure to manufacturing and agriculture will continue to create downside risks for the state. WI will moderately underperform the nation in the near term." *National Association of Realtors, Economic Profiles: The Fifty States and the District of Columbia, http://nar.realtor.com/databank/profiles.htm*

IMPORTS/EXPORTS

Total Export Sales

Area	1994 ($000)	1995 ($000)	1996 ($000)	1997 ($000)	% Chg. 1994-97	% Chg. 1996-97
MSA[1]	2,913,545	3,506,904	3,717,211	3,837,641	31.7	3.2
U.S.	512,415,609	583,030,524	622,827,063	687,597,999	34.2	10.4

Note: (1) Metropolitan Statistical Area - see Appendix A for areas included
Source: U.S. Department of Commerce, International Trade Association, Metropolitan Area Exports: An Export Performance Report on Over 250 U.S. Cities, November 10, 1998

CITY FINANCES

City Government Finances

Component	FY94 ($000)	FY94 (per capita $)
Revenue	895,259	1,484.10
Expenditure	761,126	1,261.75
Debt Outstanding	559,363	927.28
Cash & Securities	2,406,458	3,989.27

Source: U.S. Bureau of the Census, City Government Finances: 1993-94

City Government Revenue by Source

Source	FY94 ($000)	FY94 (per capita $)	FY94 (%)
From Federal Government	59,792	99.12	6.7
From State Governments	277,946	460.76	31.0
From Local Governments	958	1.59	0.1
Property Taxes	157,585	261.23	17.6
General Sales Taxes	0	0.00	0.0
Selective Sales Taxes	5,175	8.58	0.6
Income Taxes	0	0.00	0.0
Current Charges	83,021	137.63	9.3
Utility/Liquor Store	47,425	78.62	5.3
Employee Retirement[1]	207,087	343.30	23.1
Other	56,270	93.28	6.3

Note: (1) Excludes "city contributions," classified as "nonrevenue," intragovernmental transfers.
Source: U.S. Bureau of the Census, City Government Finances: 1993-94

City Government Expenditures by Function

Function	FY94 ($000)	FY94 (per capita $)	FY94 (%)
Educational Services	21,764	36.08	2.9
Employee Retirement[1]	86,583	143.53	11.4
Environment/Housing	190,029	315.02	25.0
Government Administration	48,523	80.44	6.4
Interest on General Debt	35,057	58.12	4.6
Public Safety	213,156	353.36	28.0
Social Services	14,273	23.66	1.9
Transportation	55,920	92.70	7.3
Utility/Liquor Store	30,296	50.22	4.0
Other	65,525	108.62	8.6

Note: (1) Payments to beneficiaries including withdrawal of contributions.
Source: U.S. Bureau of the Census, City Government Finances: 1993-94

Municipal Bond Ratings

Area	Moody's	S & P
Milwaukee	Aaa	n/a

Note: n/a not available; n/r not rated
Source: Moody's Bond Record, 6/99

POPULATION

Population Growth

Area	1980	1990	% Chg. 1980-90	July 1998 Estimate	% Chg. 1990-98
City	636,212	628,088	-1.3	578,364	-7.9
MSA[1]	1,397,143	1,432,149	2.5	1,466,157	2.4
U.S.	226,545,805	248,765,170	9.8	270,299,000	8.7

Note: (1) Metropolitan Statistical Area - see Appendix A for areas included;
July 1998 MSA population estimate was calculated by the editors
Source: 1980/1990 Census of Housing and Population, Summary Tape File 3C;
Census Bureau Population Estimates 1998

Population Characteristics

Race	City 1980 Population	%	City 1990 Population	%	% Chg. 1980-90	MSA[1] 1990 Population	%
White	468,064	73.6	397,827	63.3	-15.0	1,184,263	82.7
Black	147,055	23.1	191,567	30.5	30.3	197,144	13.8
Amer Indian/Esk/Aleut	5,348	0.8	6,016	1.0	12.5	8,138	0.6
Asian/Pacific Islander	4,451	0.7	11,831	1.9	165.8	18,384	1.3
Other	11,294	1.8	20,847	3.3	84.6	24,220	1.7
Hispanic Origin[2]	26,111	4.1	37,420	6.0	43.3	48,276	3.4

Note: (1) Metropolitan Statistical Area - see Appendix A for areas included;
(2) people of Hispanic origin can be of any race
Source: 1980/1990 Census of Housing and Population, Summary Tape File 3C

Ancestry

Area	German	Irish	English	Italian	U.S.	French	Polish	Dutch
City	33.7	8.4	4.1	3.5	1.0	3.1	14.3	1.0
MSA[1]	48.4	11.4	6.7	4.3	1.1	3.9	15.0	1.6
U.S.	23.3	15.6	13.1	5.9	5.3	4.2	3.8	2.5

Note: Figures are percentages and include persons that reported multiple ancestry (eg. if a person reported being Irish and Italian, they were included in both columns); (1) Metropolitan Statistical Area - see Appendix A for areas included
Source: 1990 Census of Population and Housing, Summary Tape File 3C

Age

Area	Median Age (Years)	Age Distribution (%) Under 5	Under 18	18-24	25-44	45-64	65+	80+
City	30.3	8.6	27.5	12.0	32.6	15.5	12.4	3.1
MSA[1]	32.7	7.7	26.3	9.9	32.9	18.4	12.5	3.0
U.S.	32.9	7.3	25.6	10.5	32.6	18.7	12.5	2.8

Note: (1) Metropolitan Statistical Area - see Appendix A for areas included
Source: 1990 Census of Population and Housing, Summary Tape File 3C

Male/Female Ratio

Area	Number of males per 100 females (all ages)	Number of males per 100 females (18 years old+)
City	89.6	84.8
MSA[1]	92.9	88.8
U.S.	95.0	91.9

Note: (1) Metropolitan Statistical Area - see Appendix A for areas included
Source: 1990 Census of Population, General Population Characteristics

INCOME

Per Capita/Median/Average Income

Area	Per Capita ($)	Median Household ($)	Average Household ($)
City	11,106	23,627	28,415
MSA[1]	14,785	32,316	38,958
U.S.	14,420	30,056	38,453

Note: All figures are for 1989; (1) Metropolitan Statistical Area - see Appendix A for areas included
Source: 1990 Census of Population and Housing, Summary Tape File 3C

Household Income Distribution by Race

Income ($)	City (%)					U.S. (%)				
	Total	White	Black	Other	Hisp.[1]	Total	White	Black	Other	Hisp.[1]
Less than 5,000	6.3	4.1	12.0	10.2	10.1	6.2	4.8	15.2	8.6	8.8
5,000 - 9,999	14.9	11.4	24.1	20.1	19.0	9.3	8.6	14.2	9.9	11.1
10,000 - 14,999	11.2	10.6	12.5	13.2	11.8	8.8	8.5	11.0	9.8	11.0
15,000 - 24,999	20.0	20.4	18.8	19.7	18.9	17.5	17.3	18.9	18.5	20.5
25,000 - 34,999	16.6	18.1	12.4	15.7	15.5	15.8	16.1	14.2	15.4	16.4
35,000 - 49,999	17.5	19.9	11.3	13.7	16.5	17.9	18.6	13.3	16.1	16.0
50,000 - 74,999	10.6	12.0	7.3	5.8	6.4	15.0	15.8	9.3	13.4	11.1
75,000 - 99,999	2.1	2.4	1.2	1.1	1.2	5.1	5.5	2.6	4.7	3.1
100,000+	1.0	1.2	0.4	0.5	0.5	4.4	4.8	1.3	3.7	1.9

Note: All figures are for 1989; (1) people of Hispanic origin can be of any race
Source: 1990 Census of Population and Housing, Summary Tape File 3C

Effective Buying Income

Area	Per Capita ($)	Median Household ($)	Average Household ($)
City	13,219	28,470	34,271
MSA[1]	17,808	38,781	47,035
U.S.	16,803	34,536	45,243

Note: Data as of 1/1/99; (1) Metropolitan Statistical Area - see Appendix A for areas included
Source: Standard Rate & Data Service, Newspaper Advertising Source, 9/99

Effective Household Buying Income Distribution

Area	% of Households Earning						
	$10,000 -$19,999	$20,000 -$34,999	$35,000 -$49,999	$50,000 -$74,999	$75,000 -$99,000	$100,000 -$124,999	$125,000 and up
City	20.6	24.6	18.3	16.3	3.9	0.8	0.6
MSA[1]	14.6	21.3	19.6	22.8	7.8	2.2	2.4
U.S.	16.0	22.6	18.2	18.9	7.2	2.4	2.7

Note: Data as of 1/1/99; (1) Metropolitan Statistical Area - see Appendix A for areas included
Source: Standard Rate & Data Service, Newspaper Advertising Source, 9/99

Poverty Rates by Race and Age

Area	Total (%)	By Race (%)				By Age (%)		
		White	Black	Other	Hisp.[2]	Under 5 years old	Under 18 years old	65 years and over
City	22.2	10.8	41.9	40.2	35.5	41.5	37.8	10.0
MSA[1]	11.6	5.8	41.3	32.8	30.3	22.5	19.4	7.1
U.S.	13.1	9.8	29.5	23.1	25.3	20.1	18.3	12.8

Note: Figures show the percent of people living below the poverty line in 1989. The average poverty threshold was $12,674 for a family of four in 1989; (1) Metropolitan Statistical Area - see Appendix A for areas included; (2) people of Hispanic origin can be of any race
Source: 1990 Census of Population and Housing, Summary Tape File 3C

EMPLOYMENT

Labor Force and Employment

Area	Civilian Labor Force			Workers Employed		
	Jun. 1998	Jun. 1999	% Chg.	Jun. 1998	Jun. 1999	% Chg.
City	299,340	297,583	-0.6	282,160	281,729	-0.2
MSA[1]	823,838	819,482	-0.5	793,434	792,220	-0.2
U.S.	138,798,000	140,666,000	1.3	132,265,000	134,395,000	1.6

Note: Data is not seasonally adjusted and covers workers 16 years of age and older;
(1) Metropolitan Statistical Area - see Appendix A for areas included
Source: Bureau of Labor Statistics, http://stats.bls.gov

Unemployment Rate

Area	1998						1999					
	Jul.	Aug.	Sep.	Oct.	Nov.	Dec.	Jan.	Feb.	Mar.	Apr.	May.	Jun.
City	6.0	6.0	5.4	5.6	5.3	4.6	5.3	5.5	5.3	5.2	5.4	5.3
MSA[1]	3.7	3.7	3.4	3.5	3.4	2.9	3.6	3.6	3.4	3.2	3.3	3.3
U.S.	4.7	4.5	4.4	4.2	4.1	4.0	4.8	4.7	4.4	4.1	4.0	4.5

Note: Data is not seasonally adjusted and covers workers 16 years of age and older; all figures are percentages; (1) Metropolitan Statistical Area - see Appendix A for areas included
Source: Bureau of Labor Statistics, http://stats.bls.gov

Employment by Industry

Sector	MSA[1]		U.S.
	Number of Employees	Percent of Total	Percent of Total
Services	274,200	31.7	30.4
Retail Trade	133,000	15.4	17.7
Government	93,000	10.8	15.6
Manufacturing	178,000	20.6	14.3
Finance/Insurance/Real Estate	59,100	6.8	5.9
Wholesale Trade	51,200	5.9	5.4
Transportation/Public Utilities	41,600	4.8	5.3
Construction	n/a	n/a	5.0
Mining	n/a	n/a	0.4

Note: Figures cover non-farm employment as of 6/99 and are not seasonally adjusted; (1) Metropolitan Statistical Area - see Appendix A for areas included; n/a not available
Source: Bureau of Labor Statistics, http://stats.bls.gov

Employment by Occupation

Occupation Category	City (%)	MSA[1] (%)	U.S. (%)
White Collar	53.9	59.7	58.1
Executive/Admin./Management	9.2	12.3	12.3
Professional	12.1	14.3	14.1
Technical & Related Support	3.5	3.6	3.7
Sales	10.3	12.0	11.8
Administrative Support/Clerical	18.8	17.5	16.3
Blue Collar	29.1	26.9	26.2
Precision Production/Craft/Repair	10.2	11.2	11.3
Machine Operators/Assem./Insp.	10.2	8.6	6.8
Transportation/Material Movers	4.3	3.6	4.1
Cleaners/Helpers/Laborers	4.4	3.5	3.9
Services	16.4	12.5	13.2
Farming/Forestry/Fishing	0.6	0.8	2.5

Note: Figures cover employed persons 16 years old and over; (1) Metropolitan Statistical Area - see Appendix A for areas included
Source: 1990 Census of Population and Housing, Summary Tape File 3C

Occupational Employment Projections: 1996 - 2006

Occupations Expected to Have the Largest Job Growth (ranked by numerical growth)	Fast-Growing Occupations[1] (ranked by percent growth)
1. Janitors/cleaners/maids, ex. priv. hshld.	1. Systems analysts
2. General managers & top executives	2. Desktop publishers
3. Cashiers	3. Personal and home care aides
4. Truck drivers, light	4. Database administrators
5. Salespersons, retail	5. Paralegals
6. Systems analysts	6. Securities, financial services sales
7. Home health aides	7. Occupational therapists
8. Teachers aides, clerical & paraprofess.	8. Home health aides
9. Registered nurses	9. Teachers, special education
10. Waiters & waitresses	10. Medical assistants

Note: Projections cover Wisconsin; (1) Excludes occupations with total job growth less than 300
Source: U.S. Department of Labor, Employment and Training Administration, America's Labor Market Information System (ALMIS)

TAXES

Major State and Local Tax Rates

State Corp. Income (%)	State Personal Income (%)	Residential Property (effective rate per $100)	Sales & Use State (%)	Local (%)	State Gasoline (cents/gallon)	State Cigarette (cents/pack)
7.9	4.77 - 6.77	2.97	5.0	0.6	25.4	59.0

Note: Personal/corporate income, sales, gasoline and cigarette tax rates as of January 1999. Property tax rates as of 1997.
Source: Federation of Tax Administrators, www.taxadmin.org; Washington D.C. Department of Finance and Revenue, Tax Rates and Tax Burdens in the District of Columbia: A Nationwide Comparison, July 1998; Chamber of Commerce, 1999

Total Taxes Per Capita and as a Percent of Income

Area	Per Capita Income ($)	Per Capita Taxes ($) Total	Federal	State/Local	Percent of Income (%) Total	Federal	State/Local
Wisconsin	26,499	9,897	6,313	3,584	37.3	23.8	13.5
U.S.	27,876	9,881	6,690	3,191	35.4	24.0	11.4

Note: Figures are for 1998
Source: Tax Foundation, www.taxfoundation.org

Estimated Tax Burden

Area	State Income	Local Income	Property	Sales	Total
Milwaukee	4,612	0	6,500	536	11,648

Note: The numbers are estimates of taxes paid by a married couple with two children and annual earnings of $75,000. Sales tax estimates assume they spend average amounts on food, clothing, household goods and gasoline. Property tax estimates assume they live in a $250,000 home.
Source: Kiplinger's Personal Finance Magazine, October 1998

**COMMERCIAL
REAL ESTATE**

Office Market

Class/ Location	Total Space (sq. ft.)	Vacant Space (sq. ft.)	Vac. Rate (%)	Under Constr. (sq. ft.)	Net Absorp. (sq. ft.)	Rental Rates ($/sq.ft./yr.)
Class A						
CBD	4,450,600	267,036	6.0	n/a	159,576	19.00-22.00
Outside CBD	7,430,650	378,963	5.1	165,000	141,814	17.50-21.00
Class B						
CBD	8,820,440	1,430,385	16.2	n/a	69,089	14.00-17.00
Outside CBD	4,875,000	478,678	9.8	n/a	80,681	10.00-16.00

*Note: Data as of 10/98 and covers Milwaukee; CBD = Central Business District; n/a not available;
Source: Society of Industrial and Office Realtors, 1999 Comparative Statistics of Industrial and Office
Real Estate Markets*

"Some speculative office space is planned for Waukesha County, which is west of Milwaukee. Insurance companies and business services firms lead the rental activity in Milwaukee. Absorption, construction, rental rates, and sale prices for Class A buildings are all expected to increase as much as five percent in 1999. A University of Wisconsin study indicates service sector employment growing much faster in the suburbs than in the CBD. Recent balance in absorption show downtown in good stride, but older Class B space remains at a disadvantage." *Society of Industrial and Office Realtors, 1999 Comparative Statistics of Industrial and Office Real Estate Markets*

Industrial Market

Location	Total Space (sq. ft.)	Vacant Space (sq. ft.)	Vac. Rate (%)	Under Constr. (sq. ft.)	Net Absorp. (sq. ft.)	Net Lease ($/sq.ft./yr.)
Central City	n/a	n/a	n/a	n/a	n/a	n/a
Suburban	201,700,000	6,000,000	3.0	750,000	1,700,000	2.50-6.50

*Note: Data as of 10/98 and covers Milwaukee; n/a not available
Source: Society of Industrial and Office Realtors, 1999 Comparative Statistics of Industrial and Office
Real Estate Markets*

"Most of the nearly one million sq. ft. of new construction scheduled to become available in Milwaukee during 1999 will be located south of the city near the airport. Approximately 70 percent of it will consist of large warehouse/distribution properties. Our SIOR reporter notes that rent wars could begin when all the new space becomes available. It is likely that 1999 will see six to 10 percent increases in sales prices, lease prices, and absorption of manufacturing spaces. There will probably be six to 10 percent growth in the construction of warehouse/distribution space as well, although sales and lease prices within that sub-market will probably rise by only one to five percent next year. Demand and supply for High-Tech/R&D space are expected to remain the same in 1999." *Society of Industrial and Office Realtors, 1999 Comparative Statistics of Industrial and Office Real Estate Markets*

COMMERCIAL UTILITIES

Typical Monthly Electric Bills

Area	Commercial Service ($/month)		Industrial Service ($/month)	
	12 kW demand 1,500 kWh	100 kW demand 30,000 kWh	1,000 kW demand 400,000 kWh	20,000 kW demand 10,000,000 kWh
City	113	1,949	19,554	330,406
U.S.	150	2,174	23,995	508,569

*Note: Based on rates in effect January 1, 1999
Source: Edison Electric Institute, Typical Residential, Commercial and Industrial Bills, Winter 1999*

TRANSPORTATION

Transportation Statistics

Average minutes to work	20.1
Interstate highways	I-43; I-94
Bus lines	
In-city	Milwaukee County Transit System, 536 vehicles
Inter-city	5
Passenger air service	
Airport	General Mitchell International
Airlines	17
Aircraft departures	46,434 (1996)
Enplaned passengers	2,499,728 (1996)
Rail service	Amtrak
Motor freight carriers	500
Major waterways/ports	Port of Milwaukee; Lake Michigan; Milwaukee River

Source: Editor & Publisher Market Guide, 1999; FAA Airport Activity Statistics, 1997; Amtrak National Time Table, Northeast Timetable, Spring/Summer 1999; 1990 Census of Population and Housing, STF 3C; Chamber of Commerce/Economic Development 1999; Jane's Urban Transport Systems 1999-2000

Means of Transportation to Work

Area	Car/Truck/Van		Public Transportation			Bicycle	Walked	Other Means	Worked at Home
	Drove Alone	Car-pooled	Bus	Subway	Railroad				
City	67.2	13.2	10.8	0.0	0.0	0.3	6.0	0.8	1.6
MSA[1]	76.7	11.0	5.1	0.0	0.0	0.3	4.0	0.6	2.2
U.S.	73.2	13.4	3.0	1.5	0.5	0.4	3.9	1.2	3.0

Note: Figures shown are percentages and only include workers 16 years old and over;
(1) Metropolitan Statistical Area - see Appendix A for areas included
Source: 1990 Census of Population and Housing, Summary Tape File 3C

BUSINESSES

Major Business Headquarters

Company Name	1999 Rankings	
	Fortune 500	Forbes 500
Firstar Corp.	427	-
Grede Foundries	-	438
Johnson Controls	131	-
Journal Communications	-	342
Manpower	183	-
Northwestern Mutual Life Ins.	107	-

Note: Companies listed are located in the city; dashes indicate no ranking
Fortune 500: Companies that produce a 10-K are ranked 1 to 500 based on 1998 revenue
Forbes 500: Private companies are ranked 1 to 500 based on 1997 revenue
Source: Forbes, November 30, 1998; Fortune, April 26, 1999

Best Companies to Work For

Harley-Davidson (motorcycles), headquartered in Milwaukee, is among the "100 Best Companies to Work for in America." Criteria: trust in management, pride in work/company, camaraderie, company responses to the Hewitt People Practices Inventory, and employee responses to their Great Place to Work survey. The companies also had to be at least 10 years old and have a minimum of 500 employees. *Fortune, January 11, 1999*

Harley-Davidson (motorcycles), Johnson Controls (manufacturing) and Wisconsin Energy Corp. (utilities), headquartered in Milwaukee, are among the "100 Best Places to Work in IS." Criteria: compensation, turnover and training. *Computerworld, May 25, 1998*

Women-Owned Firms: Number, Employment and Sales

Area	Number of Firms	Employ- ment	Sales ($000)	Rank[2]
MSA[1]	39,800	127,200	15,691,200	45

Note: (1) Metropolitan Statistical Area - see Appendix A for areas included;
(2) Calculated on an averaging of the number of businesses, employment and sales
Source: The National Foundation for Women Business Owners, 1999 Facts on Women-Owned
Businesses: Trends in the Top 50 Metropolitan Areas

Women-Owned Firms: Growth

Area	% change from 1992 to 1999			Rank[2]
	Number of Firms	Employ- ment	Sales	
MSA[1]	38.1	90.3	104.5	47

Note: (1) Metropolitan Statistical Area - see Appendix A for areas included; (2) Calculated on an
averaging of the percent growth of number of businesses, employment and sales
Source: The National Foundation for Women Business Owners, 1999 Facts on Women-Owned
Businesses: Trends in the Top 50 Metropolitan Areas

Minority Business Opportunity

Milwaukee is home to one company which is on the Black Enterprise Industrial/Service 100 list (largest based on gross sales): V and J Holding Companies Inc. (Burger King & Pizza Hut franchisee) . Criteria: operational in previous calendar year, at least 51% black-owned and manufactures/owns the product it sells or provides industrial or consumer services. Brokerages, real estate firms and firms that provide professional services are not eligible. *Black Enterprise, www.blackenterprise.com*

Small Business Opportunity

According to *Forbes*, Milwaukee is home to two of America's 200 best small companies: Badger Meter and Strattec Security. Criteria: companies included must be publicly traded since November 1997 with a stock price of at least $5 per share and an average daily float of 1,000 shares. The company's latest 12-month sales must be between $5 and $350 million, return on equity (ROE) must be a minimum of 12% for both the past 5 years and the most recent four quarters, and five-year sales and EPS growth must average at least 10%. Companies with declining sales or earnings during the past year were dropped as well as businesses with debt/equity ratios over 1.25. Companies with negative operating cash flow in each of the past two years were also excluded. *Forbes, November 2, 1998*

HOTELS & MOTELS

Hotels/Motels

Area	Hotels/ Motels	Rooms	Luxury-Level Hotels/Motels		Average Minimum Rates ($)		
			◆◆◆◆	◆◆◆◆◆	◆◆	◆◆◆	◆◆◆◆
City	20	3,177	3	0	62	90	170
Airport	13	1,928	0	0	n/a	n/a	n/a
Suburbs	39	4,384	0	0	n/a	n/a	n/a
Total	72	9,489	3	0	n/a	n/a	n/a

Note: n/a not available; classifications range from one diamond (budget properties with basic amenities) to five diamond (luxury properties with the finest service, rooms and facilities).
Source: OAG, Business Travel Planner, Winter 1998-99

CONVENTION CENTERS

Major Convention Centers

Center Name	Meeting Rooms	Exhibit Space (sq. ft.)
Hyatt Regency Milwaukee	19	16,052
Midwest Express Center, Phase I	42	250,000
Midwest Express Center, Phase II	28	125,180
Performing Arts Center	8	9,552

Source: Trade Shows Worldwide, 1998; Meetings & Conventions, 4/15/99; Sucessful Meetings, 3/31/98

Living Environment

COST OF LIVING

Cost of Living Index

Composite Index	Groceries	Housing	Utilities	Trans-portation	Health Care	Misc. Goods/ Services
107.7	100.2	121.6	101.9	104.9	100.0	103.1

Note: U.S. = 100; Figures are for the Metropolitan Statistical Area - see Appendix A for areas included
Source: ACCRA, Cost of Living Index, 1st Quarter 1999

HOUSING

Median Home Prices and Housing Affordability

Area	Median Price[2] 1st Qtr. 1999 ($)	HOI[3] 1st Qtr. 1999	Afford-ability Rank[4]
MSA[1]	108,000	79.1	65
U.S.	134,000	69.6	—

Note: (1) Metropolitan Statistical Area - see Appendix A for areas included; (2) U.S. figures calculated from the sales of 524,324 new and existing homes in 181 markets; (3) Housing Opportunity Index - percent of homes sold that were within the reach of the median income household at the prevailing mortgage interest rate; (4) Rank is from 1-181 with 1 being most affordable
Source: National Association of Home Builders, Housing Opportunity Index, 1st Quarter 1999

Median Home Price Projection

It is projected that the median price of existing single-family homes in the metro area will increase by 2.6% in 1999. Nationwide, home prices are projected to increase 3.8%.
Kiplinger's Personal Finance Magazine, January 1999

Average New Home Price

Area	Price ($)
MSA[1]	171,978
U.S.	142,735

Note: Figures are based on a new home with 1,800 sq. ft. of living area on an 8,000 sq. ft. lot; (1) Metropolitan Statistical Area - see Appendix A for areas included
Source: ACCRA, Cost of Living Index, 1st Quarter 1999

Average Apartment Rent

Area	Rent ($/mth)
MSA[1]	694
U.S.	601

Note: Figures are based on an unfurnished two bedroom, 1-1/2 or 2 bath apartment, approximately 950 sq. ft. in size, excluding all utilities except water; (1) Metropolitan Statistical Area - see Appendix A for areas included
Source: ACCRA, Cost of Living Index, 1st Quarter 1999

RESIDENTIAL UTILITIES

Average Residential Utility Costs

Area	All Electric ($/mth)	Part Electric ($/mth)	Other Energy ($/mth)	Phone ($/mth)
MSA[1]	—	46.34	57.89	16.28
U.S.	100.02	55.73	43.33	19.71

Note: (1) (1) Metropolitan Statistical Area - see Appendix A for areas included
Source: ACCRA, Cost of Living Index, 1st Quarter 1999

HEALTH CARE

Average Health Care Costs

Area	Hospital ($/day)	Doctor ($/visit)	Dentist ($/visit)
MSA[1]	411.50	55.80	65.40
U.S.	430.43	52.45	66.35

Note: Hospital—based on a semi-private room; Doctor—based on a general practitioner's routine exam of an established patient; Dentist—based on adult teeth cleaning and periodic oral exam; (1) Metropolitan Statistical Area - see Appendix A for areas included
Source: ACCRA, Cost of Living Index, 1st Quarter 1999

Distribution of Office-Based Physicians

Area	Family/Gen. Practitioners	Specialists		
		Medical	Surgical	Other
MSA[1]	364	1,061	740	953

Note: Data as of 12/31/97; (1) Metropolitan Statistical Area - see Appendix A for areas included
Source: American Medical Assn., Physician Characteristics & Distribution in the U.S., 1999

Hospitals

Milwaukee has 1 general medical and surgical hospital, 2 psychiatric, 1 eye, ear, nose and throat, 1 rehabilitation, 1 children's general. *AHA Guide to the Healthcare Field, 1998-99*

According to *U.S. News and World Report,* Milwaukee has 2 of the best hospitals in the U.S.: **Froedtert Memorial Lutheran Hospital**, noted for gastroenterology; **Sinai Samaritan Medical Center**, noted for cardiology. *U.S. News Online, "America's Best Hospitals," 10th Edition, www.usnews.com*

EDUCATION

Public School District Statistics

District Name	Num. Sch.	Enroll.	Classroom Teachers	Pupils per Teacher	Minority Pupils (%)	Current Exp.[1] ($/pupil)
Fox Point J2 Sch Dist	2	927	69	13.4	n/a	n/a
Glendale-River Hills Sch Dist	3	1,212	77	15.7	n/a	n/a
Maple Dale-Indian Hill Sch Dis	2	651	48	13.6	n/a	n/a
Milwaukee Sch Dist	206	101,253	n/a	n/a	78.9	7,353

Note: Data covers the 1997-1998 school year unless otherwise noted; (1) Data covers fiscal year 1996; SD = School District; ISD = Independent School District; n/a not available
Source: National Center for Education Statistics, Common Core of Data Public Education Agency Universe 1997-98; National Center for Education Statistics, Characteristics of the 100 Largest Public Elementary and Secondary School Districts in the United States: 1997-98, July 1999

Educational Quality

School District	Education Quotient[1]	Graduate Outcome[2]	Community Index[3]	Resource Index[4]
Milwaukee SD	73.0	64.0	83.0	88.0

Note: Nearly 1,000 secondary school districts were rated in terms of educational quality. The scores range from a low of 50 to a high of 150; (1) Average of the Graduate Outcome, Community and Resource indexes; (2) Based on graduation rates and college board scores (SAT/ACT); (3) Based on the surrounding community's average level of education and the area's average income level; (4) Based on teacher salaries, per-pupil expenditures and student-teacher ratios.
Source: Expansion Management, Ratings Issue, 1998

Educational Attainment by Race

Area	High School Graduate (%)					Bachelor's Degree (%)				
	Total	White	Black	Other	Hisp.[2]	Total	White	Black	Other	Hisp.[2]
City	71.5	76.3	60.2	54.0	46.9	14.8	17.6	6.9	13.2	6.2
MSA[1]	79.7	82.5	60.7	60.5	51.7	21.3	23.0	7.6	19.4	8.5
U.S.	75.2	77.9	63.1	60.4	49.8	20.3	21.5	11.4	19.4	9.2

Note: Figures shown cover persons 25 years old and over; (1) Metropolitan Statistical Area - see Appendix A for areas included; (2) people of Hispanic origin can be of any race
Source: 1990 Census of Population and Housing, Summary Tape File 3C

School Enrollment by Type

Area	Preprimary				Elementary/High School			
	Public		Private		Public		Private	
	Enrollment	%	Enrollment	%	Enrollment	%	Enrollment	%
City	6,616	66.3	3,359	33.7	92,372	80.6	22,277	19.4
MSA[1]	15,931	56.8	12,092	43.2	204,342	81.5	46,314	18.5
U.S.	2,679,029	59.5	1,824,256	40.5	38,379,689	90.2	4,187,099	9.8

Note: Figures shown cover persons 3 years old and over;
(1) Metropolitan Statistical Area - see Appendix A for areas included
Source: 1990 Census of Population and Housing, Summary Tape File 3C

School Enrollment by Race

Area	Preprimary (%)				Elementary/High School (%)			
	White	Black	Other	Hisp.[1]	White	Black	Other	Hisp.[1]
City	54.3	38.4	7.3	7.2	43.2	47.0	9.8	10.0
MSA[2]	82.1	14.0	3.9	3.9	72.3	22.0	5.6	5.7
U.S.	80.4	12.5	7.1	7.8	74.1	15.6	10.3	12.5

Note: Figures shown cover persons 3 years old and over; (1) people of Hispanic origin can be of any race; (2) Metropolitan Statistical Area - see Appendix A for areas included
Source: 1990 Census of Population and Housing, Summary Tape File 3C

Classroom Teacher Salaries in Public Schools

District	B.A. Degree		M.A. Degree		Maximum	
	Min. ($)	Rank[1]	Max. ($)	Rank[1]	Max. ($)	Rank[1]
Milwaukee	24,684	70	48,660	29	54,001	32
Average	26,980	-	46,065	-	51,435	-

Note: Salaries are for 1997-1998; (1) Rank ranges from 1 to 100
Source: American Federation of Teachers, Survey & Analysis of Salary Trends, 1998

Higher Education

Two-Year Colleges		Four-Year Colleges		Medical Schools	Law Schools	Voc/Tech
Public	Private	Public	Private			
1	1	1	8	1	1	19

Source: College Blue Book, Occupational Education, 1997; Medical School Admission Requirements, 1999-2000; Peterson's Guide to Two-Year Colleges, 1999; Peterson's Guide to Four-Year Colleges, 2000; Barron's Guide to Law Schools, 1999

MAJOR EMPLOYERS

Major Employers

Allen-Bradley Co. (electronic equipment)	Briggs & Stratton Corp. (internal combustion engines)
Firstar Bank Milwaukee	Germantown-45 Inc. (eating places)
Miller Brewing	Northwestern Mutual Life
St. Joseph's Hospital of the Franciscan Sisters	St. Luke's Medical Center
Staffworks	Children's Health Systems of Wisconsin

Note: Companies listed are located in the city
Source: Dun's Business Rankings, 1999; Ward's Business Directory, 1998

PUBLIC SAFETY

Crime Rate

Area	All Crimes	Violent Crimes				Property Crimes		
		Murder	Forcible Rape	Robbery	Aggrav. Assault	Burglary	Larceny -Theft	Motor Vehicle Theft
City	7,587.0	19.4	48.8	565.3	419.4	1,084.8	4,129.5	1,319.8
Suburbs[1]	3,012.6	0.9	6.8	42.8	73.9	386.5	2,339.0	162.6
MSA[2]	4,966.5	8.8	24.7	266.0	221.5	684.8	3,103.8	656.9
U.S.	4,922.7	6.8	35.9	186.1	382.0	919.6	2,886.5	505.8

Note: Crime rate is the number of crimes per 100,000 pop.; (1) defined as all areas within the MSA but located outside the central city; (2) Metropolitan Statistical Area - see Appendix A for areas incl.
Source: FBI Uniform Crime Reports, 1997

RECREATION

Culture and Recreation

Museums	Symphony Orchestras	Opera Companies	Dance Companies	Professional Theatres	Zoos	Pro Sports Teams
10	2	2	4	6	1	2

Source: International Directory of the Performing Arts, 1997; Official Museum Directory, 1999; Stern's Performing Arts Directory, 1997; USA Today Four Sport Stadium Guide, 1997; Chamber of Commerce/Economic Development, 1999

Library System

The Milwaukee Public Library has 12 branches, holdings of 2,121,280 volumes, and a budget of $19,803,557 (1996). *American Library Directory, 1998-1999*

MEDIA

Newspapers

Name	Type	Freq.	Distribution	Circulation
The Irish American Post	n/a	6x/yr	U.S.	20,000
Milwaukee Community Journal	Black	2x/wk	Local	62,000
Milwaukee Journal-Sentinel	General	7x/wk	Area	295,065
Shepherd Express	General	1x/wk	Area	58,000
The Spanish Times	Hispanic	1x/wk	Area	20,000
The Weekend	Black	1x/wk	Local	22,000

Note: Includes newspapers with circulations of 10,000 or more located in the city; n/a not available
Source: Burrelle's Media Directory, 1999 Edition

Television Stations

Name	Ch.	Affiliation	Type	Owner
WTMJ	n/a	NBCT	Commercial	Journal Communications
WITI	n/a	FBC	Commercial	Fox Television Stations Inc.
WMVS	10	n/a	Public	Milwaukee Area Technical College
WISN	12	ABCT	Commercial	Hearst-Argyle Broadcasting
WVTV	18	WB	Commercial	Glencairn Communications
WCGV	24	UPN	Commercial	Sinclair Communications Inc.
WVCY	30	n/a	Non-comm.	VCY America Inc.
WMVT	36	PBS	Public	Milwaukee Area Technical College
WJJA	49	n/a	Commercial	TV 49 Inc.
WHKE	55	PAXTV	Commercial	DP Media Inc.
WDJT	58	CBST	Commercial	Weigel Broadcasting Company

Note: Stations included broadcast in the Milwaukee metro area; n/a not available
Source: Burrelle's Media Directory, 1999 Edition

AM Radio Stations

Call Letters	Freq. (kHz)	Target Audience	Station Format	Music Format
WTMJ	620	General	N/S/T	n/a
WVCY	690	Religious	n/a	n/a
WMUR	750	General	M/N/S/T	Alternative/Classic Rock/R&B/Urban Contemporary
WNOV	860	General	M	Christian/R&B
WOKY	920	General	M/N/T	Adult Standards/Big Band
WISN	1130	Men	N/S/T	n/a
WEMP	1250	General	M	Oldies
WMCS	1290	n/a	M	Oldies
WJYI	1340	General	M	Christian
WGLB	1560	General	M/N/S/T	Adult Contemporary/Gospel

Note: Stations included broadcast in the Milwaukee metro area; n/a not available
Target Audience: A=Asian; B=Black; C=Christian; E=Ethnic; F=French; G=General; H=Hispanic; M=Men; N=Native American; R=Religious; S=Senior Citizen; W=Women; Y=Young Adult; Z=Children
Station Format: E=Educational; M=Music; N=News; S=Sports; T=Talk
Source: Burrelle's Media Directory, 1999 Edition

FM Radio Stations

Call Letters	Freq. (mHz)	Target Audience	Station Format	Music Format
WMWK	88.1	n/a	E/M/N/T	Christian
WYMS	88.9	G/H	M	Jazz
WUWM	89.7	General	M/N	Alternative
WHAD	90.7	General	E/T	n/a
WMSE	91.7	B/H	M	Alternative/Big Band/Latin/R&B/Urban Contemporary
WJZI	93.3	General	M	Jazz
WKTI	94.5	General	M	Adult Contemporary
WZTR	95.7	General	M/N/S/T	Oldies
WKLH	96.5	General	M/N/S	Classic Rock
WLTQ	97.3	General	M	Adult Contemporary
WFMR	98.3	General	M/N	Classical
WVCX	98.9	General	M/N/T	Christian
WMYX	99.1	General	M	Adult Contemporary
WKKV	100.7	General	M	Urban Contemporary
WLUM	102.1	General	M/N/S	Alternative
WLZR	102.9	General	M/N	AOR
WXSS	103.7	General	M/N	Adult Contemporary
WMIL	106.1	General	M/N	Country
WPNT	106.9	General	M/N	Oldies/R&B
WVCY	107.7	General	E/M/N/T	Christian

Note: Stations included broadcast in the Milwaukee metro area; n/a not available
Station Format: E=Educational; M=Music; N=News; S=Sports; T=Talk
Target Audience: A=Asian; B=Black; C=Christian; E=Ethnic; F=French; G=General; H=Hispanic; M=Men; N=Native American; R=Religious; S=Senior Citizen; W=Women; Y=Young Adult; Z=Children
Music Format: AOR=Album Oriented Rock; MOR=Middle-of-the-Road
Source: Burrelle's Media Directory, 1999 Edition

CLIMATE

Average and Extreme Temperatures

Temperature	Jan	Feb	Mar	Apr	May	Jun	Jul	Aug	Sep	Oct	Nov	Dec	Yr.
Extreme High (°F)	60	65	82	91	92	101	101	103	98	89	77	63	103
Average High (°F)	27	31	40	54	65	76	80	79	71	60	45	32	55
Average Temp. (°F)	20	24	33	45	55	66	71	70	62	51	38	25	47
Average Low (°F)	12	16	26	36	45	55	62	61	53	42	30	18	38
Extreme Low (°F)	-26	-19	-10	12	21	36	40	44	28	18	-5	-20	-26

Note: Figures cover the years 1948-1990
Source: National Climatic Data Center, International Station Meteorological Climate Summary, 3/95

Average Precipitation/Snowfall/Humidity

Precip./Humidity	Jan	Feb	Mar	Apr	May	Jun	Jul	Aug	Sep	Oct	Nov	Dec	Yr.
Avg. Precip. (in.)	1.6	1.4	2.6	3.3	2.9	3.4	3.6	3.4	2.9	2.3	2.3	2.2	32.0
Avg. Snowfall (in.)	13	10	9	2	Tr	0	0	0	0	Tr	3	11	49
Avg. Rel. Hum. 6am (%)	76	77	78	78	77	79	82	86	86	82	80	80	80
Avg. Rel. Hum. 3pm (%)	68	66	64	58	58	58	59	62	61	61	66	70	63

Note: Figures cover the years 1948-1990; Tr = Trace amounts (<0.05 in. of rain; <0.5 in. of snow)
Source: National Climatic Data Center, International Station Meteorological Climate Summary, 3/95

Weather Conditions

Temperature			Daytime Sky			Precipitation		
5°F & below	32°F & below	90°F & above	Clear	Partly cloudy	Cloudy	0.01 inch or more precip.	0.1 inch or more snow/ice	Thunder-storms
22	141	10	90	118	157	126	38	35

Note: Figures are average number of days per year and covers the years 1948-1990
Source: National Climatic Data Center, International Station Meteorological Climate Summary, 3/95

AIR & WATER QUALITY

Maximum Pollutant Concentrations

	Particulate Matter (ug/m³)	Carbon Monoxide (ppm)	Sulfur Dioxide (ppm)	Nitrogen Dioxide (ppm)	Ozone (ppm)	Lead (ug/m³)
MSA[1] Level	61	3	0.028	0.021	0.13	0.03
NAAQS[2]	150	9	0.140	0.053	0.12	1.50
Met NAAQS?	Yes	Yes	Yes	Yes	No	Yes

Note: (1) Metropolitan Statistical Area - see Appendix A for areas included; (2) National Ambient Air Quality Standards; ppm = parts per million; ug/m³ = micrograms per cubic meter; n/a not available
Source: EPA, National Air Quality and Emissions Trends Report, 1997

Pollutant Standards Index

In the Milwaukee MSA (see Appendix A for areas included), the Pollutant Standards Index (PSI) exceeded 100 on 5 days in 1997. A PSI value greater than 100 indicates that air quality would be in the unhealthful range on that day. *EPA, National Air Quality and Emissions Trends Report, 1997*

Drinking Water

Water System Name	Pop. Served	Primary Water Source Type	Number of Violations in 1998	Type of Violation/ Contaminants
Milwaukee Waterworks	682,332	Surface	None	None

Note: Data as of July 10, 1999
Source: EPA, Office of Ground Water and Drinking Water, Safe Drinking Water Information System

Milwaukee tap water is alkaline, medium hard and fluoridated.
Editor & Publisher Market Guide, 1999

Minneapolis, Minnesota

Background

If one were to describe the city of Minneapolis in sound bites, the two most likely words might be modern and progressive. Indeed, in addition to a reputation for brutally cold winters, Minneapolis attracts excellence in the fields of performing arts, visual arts, education, finance, advertising, and manufacturing.

In 1680, a French Franciscan priest, Father Louis Hennepin, was the area's first white man to arrive. In 1819, Fort Snelling was established to protect fur traders from the Sioux and Chippewa Tribes. In 1848, two towns, St. Anthony, which later became St. Paul, and Minneapolis, grew simultaneously, thus forming the metropolitan area known today as the Twin Cities. A tide of Swedish, German, and Norwegian immigrants came in the late 19th century, giving the city a decidedly Scandinavian flavor.

Minneapolis' traditional industries were lumber and flour milling. Today, existence of corporations such as General Mills, Cargill, and Pillsbury suggests that flour milling remains a strong economic sector. However, since the 1950s, Minneapolis had entered its "brain industry" phase, wherein electronics, computers, and other related science industries play a vital role in the city's economy.

These businesses contribute significant funds to the arts. Programs such as The Five Percent Club, and institutions such as The Guthrie Theatre and the Walker Arts Center are allowed to continue on a financially unburdened path, providing entertaining and thought-provoking works to the public.

Minneapolis is located at the confluence of the Mississippi and Minnesota Rivers. Numerous lakes mark the surrounding region, with 22 within the city park system. The climate is predominantly continental, with extreme swings in seasonal temperatures. Temperatures range from less than -30 degrees to over 100 degrees.

Blizzards, freezing rain, tornadoes, wind and hail storms do occur. Due to the spring snow melt and excessive rain, the Mississippi River sees its share of floods.

General Rankings and Evaluative Comments

■ Minneapolis was ranked #1 out of 11 large, midwestern metropolitan areas in *Money's* 1998 survey of "The Best Places to Live in America." The survey was conducted by first contacting 512 representative households nationwide and asking them to rank 37 quality-of-life factors on a scale of 1 to 10. Next, a demographic profile was compiled on the 300 largest metropolitan statistical areas in the U.S. The numbers were crunched together to arrive at an overall ranking (things Americans consider most important, like clean air and water, low crime and good schools, received extra weight). Unlike previous years, the 1998 rankings were broken down by region (northeast, midwest, south, west) and population size (100,000 to 249,999; 250,000 to 999,999; 1 million plus). The city had a nationwide ranking of #118 out of 300 in 1997 and #87 out of 300 in 1996. *Money, July 1998; Money, July 1997; Money, September 1996*

■ *Ladies Home Journal* ranked America's 200 largest cities based on the qualities women care about most. Minneapolis ranked #9 out of 200. Criteria: low crime rate, well-paying jobs, quality health and child care, good public schools, the presence of women in government, size of the gender wage gap, number of sexual-harassment and discrimination complaints filed, unemployment and divorce rates, commute times, population density, number of houses of worship, parks and cultural offerings, number of women's health specialists, how well a community's women cared for themselves, complexion kindness index based on UV radiation levels, odds of finding affordable fashions, rental rates for romance movies, champagne sales and other matters of the heart.

"64 percent of the seats in the city council [are] held by women." *Ladies Home Journal, November 1998*

■ Minneapolis was selected as one of the 10 healthiest cities for women by *American Health*. It was ranked #6 out of America's 120 most populous metro areas. Criteria: number and quality of doctors and hospitals, quality of women's health centers, number of recreational opportunities, rate of violent crimes, cleanliness of air and water, percentage of women-owned businesses, and the number of family-friendly employers. *American Health, 1998*

■ Zero Population Growth ranked 229 cities in terms of children's health, safety, and economic well-being. Minneapolis was ranked #8 out of 25 major cities (main city in a metro area with population of greater than 2 million) and was given a grade of B-. Criteria: total population, percent of population under 18 years of age, household language, percent population change, percent of births to teens, infant mortality rate, percent of low birth weights, dropout rate, enrollment in preprimary school, violent and property crime rates, unemployment rate, percent of children in poverty, percent of owner occupied units, number of bad air days, percent of public transportation commuters, and average travel time to work. *Zero Population Growth, Children's Environmental Index, Fall 1999*

■ Minneapolis was ranked #28 out of 59 metro areas in *The Regional Economist's* "Rational Livability Ranking of 59 Large Metro Areas." The rankings were based on the metro area's total population change over the period 1990-97 divided by the number of people moving in from elsewhere in the United States (net domestic in-migration). *St. Louis Federal Reserve Bank of St. Louis, The Regional Economist, April 1999*

■ Minneapolis appeared on *Travel & Leisure's* list of the world's 100 best cities. It was ranked #28 in the U.S. and #85 in the world. Criteria: activities/attractions, culture/arts, people, restaurants/food, and value. *Travel & Leisure, 1998 World's Best Awards*

■ Minneapolis was selected by *Yahoo! Internet Life* as one of "America's Most Wired Cities & Towns." The city ranked #8 out of 50. Criteria: home and work net use, domain density, hosts per capita, directory density and content quality. *Yahoo! Internet Life, March 1999*

- Cognetics studied 273 metro areas in the United States, ranking them by entrepreneurial activity. Minneapolis was ranked #12 out of the 50 largest metro areas. Criteria: Significant Starts (firms started in the last 10 years that still employ at least 5 people) and Young Growers (percent of firms 10 years old or less that grew significantly during the last 4 years). *Cognetics, "Entrepreneurial Hot Spots: The Best Places in America to Start and Grow a Company," 1998*

- Minneapolis was selected as one of the "Best American Cities to Start a Business" by *Point of View* magazine. Criteria: coolness, quality-of-life, and business concerns. The city was ranked #44 out of 75. *Point of View, November 1998*

- Minneapolis appeared on *Sales & Marketing Management's* list of the "20 Hottest Cities for Selling." Rank: #13 out of 20. *S&MM* editors looked at Metropolitan Statistical Areas with populations of more than 150,000. The areas were ranked based on population increases, retail sales increases, effective buying income, increase in both residential and commercial building permits issued, unemployment rates, job growth, mix of industries, tax rates, number of corporate relocations, and the number of new corporations. *Sales & Marketing Management, April 1999*

- Reliastar Financial Corp. ranked the 125 largest metropolitan areas according to the general financial security of residents. Minneapolis was ranked #8 out of 125 with a score of 13.4. The score indicates the percentage a metropolitan area is above or below the metropolitan norm. A metro area with a score of 10.6 is 10.6% above the metro average. Criteria: Earnings and Wealth Potential (household income, education, net assets, cost of living); Safety Net (health insurance, retirement savings, life insurance, income support programs); Personal Threats (unemployment rate, low-income households, crime rate); Community Economic Vitality (cost of community services, job quality, job creation, housing costs). *Reliastar Financial Corp., "The Best Cities to Earn and Save Money," 1999 Edition*

Business Environment

STATE ECONOMY

State Economic Profile

"Minnesota's economy has been a strong performer in recent years. Job growth has been impressive and the construction market has been booming. As the US economy slows in 1999, Minnesota's growth should decelerate.

MN's tight labor market (1.8% unemployment in Minneapolis-St. Paul) and high rate of job creation have allowed the state to weather several layoffs. 3M, Cargill, and Honeywell have all released significant numbers of workers. And while the Northwest strike temporarily hit MN's economy, other sectors have more than offset these concerns.

Minnesota, specifically Minneapolis-St. Paul, experienced a major boom in residential and commercial building in 1998. The 16,811 single-family permits issued in 1998 was the highest level in over a decade. Construction employment increased 6.8% in Minneapolis-St. Paul in 1998. Driving this boom is the impressive levels of price appreciation witnessed in 1998 and the thin inventory of homes for sale. The large volume currently being built will help to moderate price appreciation in 1999 and 2000.

Among its Midwestern neighbors, MN alone has actually attracted residents from other states. Net migration has been around 10,000 for several years, helping to ease tightness in the labor market and fuel the housing market.

Minnesota will continue to be among the strongest performing Plains state. Labor shortages and the high cost of doing business, however, will limit its growth to below the national average. Most of the action will continue to be concentrated in Minneapolis-St. Paul."
National Association of Realtors, Economic Profiles: The Fifty States and the District of Columbia, http://nar.realtor.com/databank/profiles.htm

IMPORTS/EXPORTS

Total Export Sales

Area	1994 ($000)	1995 ($000)	1996 ($000)	1997 ($000)	% Chg. 1994-97	% Chg. 1996-97
MSA[1]	8,863,531	11,071,822	12,383,979	12,006,701	35.5	-3.0
U.S.	512,415,609	583,030,524	622,827,063	687,597,999	34.2	10.4

Note: (1) Metropolitan Statistical Area - see Appendix A for areas included
Source: U.S. Department of Commerce, International Trade Association, Metropolitan Area Exports: An Export Performance Report on Over 250 U.S. Cities, November 10, 1998

CITY FINANCES

City Government Finances

Component	FY92 ($000)	FY92 (per capita $)
Revenue	750,435	2,059.56
Expenditure	795,166	2,182.32
Debt Outstanding	2,289,852	6,284.47
Cash & Securities	2,801,340	7,688.24

Source: U.S. Bureau of the Census, City Government Finances: 1991-92

City Government Revenue by Source

Source	FY92 ($000)	FY92 (per capita $)	FY92 (%)
From Federal Government	26,097	71.62	3.5
From State Governments	128,988	354.01	17.2
From Local Governments	14,917	40.94	2.0
Property Taxes	142,488	391.06	19.0
General Sales Taxes	0	0.00	0.0
Selective Sales Taxes	38,349	105.25	5.1
Income Taxes	0	0.00	0.0
Current Charges	95,360	261.71	12.7
Utility/Liquor Store	23,179	63.61	3.1
Employee Retirement[1]	107,562	295.20	14.3
Other	173,495	476.15	23.1

Note: (1) Excludes "city contributions," classified as "nonrevenue," intragovernmental transfers.
Source: U.S. Bureau of the Census, City Government Finances: 1991-92

City Government Expenditures by Function

Function	FY92 ($000)	FY92 (per capita $)	FY92 (%)
Educational Services	16,937	46.48	2.1
Employee Retirement[1]	29,689	81.48	3.7
Environment/Housing	253,725	696.34	31.9
Government Administration	30,151	82.75	3.8
Interest on General Debt	163,903	449.83	20.6
Public Safety	97,663	268.03	12.3
Social Services	9,948	27.30	1.3
Transportation	115,239	316.27	14.5
Utility/Liquor Store	29,311	80.44	3.7
Other	48,600	133.38	6.1

Note: (1) Payments to beneficiaries including withdrawal of contributions.
Source: U.S. Bureau of the Census, City Government Finances: 1991-92

Municipal Bond Ratings

Area	Moody's	S & P
Minneapolis	Aaa	n/a

Note: n/a not available; n/r not rated
Source: Moody's Bond Record, 6/99

POPULATION

Population Growth

Area	1980	1990	% Chg. 1980-90	July 1998 Estimate	% Chg. 1990-98
City	370,951	368,383	-0.7	351,731	-4.5
MSA[1]	2,137,133	2,464,124	15.3	2,840,562	15.3
U.S.	226,545,805	248,765,170	9.8	270,299,000	8.7

Note: (1) Metropolitan Statistical Area - see Appendix A for areas included;
July 1998 MSA population estimate was calculated by the editors
Source: 1980/1990 Census of Housing and Population, Summary Tape File 3C;
Census Bureau Population Estimates 1998

Population Characteristics

Race	City 1980 Population	%	City 1990 Population	%	% Chg. 1980-90	MSA[1] 1990 Population	%
White	325,415	87.7	289,246	78.5	-11.1	2,272,798	92.2
Black	28,469	7.7	48,032	13.0	68.7	89,359	3.6
Amer Indian/Esk/Aleut	9,198	2.5	12,213	3.3	32.8	23,338	0.9
Asian/Pacific Islander	5,358	1.4	15,809	4.3	195.1	64,944	2.6
Other	2,511	0.7	3,083	0.8	22.8	13,685	0.6
Hispanic Origin[2]	4,684	1.3	7,309	2.0	56.0	33,835	1.4

Note: (1) Metropolitan Statistical Area - see Appendix A for areas included;
(2) people of Hispanic origin can be of any race
Source: 1980/1990 Census of Housing and Population, Summary Tape File 3C

Ancestry

Area	German	Irish	English	Italian	U.S.	French	Polish	Dutch
City	30.2	13.3	8.5	2.1	1.2	4.8	5.2	1.5
MSA[1]	43.8	15.2	9.2	2.5	1.2	6.1	5.8	2.0
U.S.	23.3	15.6	13.1	5.9	5.3	4.2	3.8	2.5

Note: Figures are percentages and include persons that reported multiple ancestry (eg. if a person reported being Irish and Italian, they were included in both columns); (1) Metropolitan Statistical Area - see Appendix A for areas included
Source: 1990 Census of Population and Housing, Summary Tape File 3C

Age

Area	Median Age (Years)	Age Distribution (%) Under 5	Under 18	18-24	25-44	45-64	65+	80+
City	31.5	7.3	20.6	13.3	39.2	14.1	12.9	3.9
MSA[1]	31.6	8.1	26.3	10.0	36.8	17.1	9.9	2.5
U.S.	32.9	7.3	25.6	10.5	32.6	18.7	12.5	2.8

Note: (1) Metropolitan Statistical Area - see Appendix A for areas included
Source: 1990 Census of Population and Housing, Summary Tape File 3C

Male/Female Ratio

Area	Number of males per 100 females (all ages)	Number of males per 100 females (18 years old+)
City	94.1	92.2
MSA[1]	95.5	92.6
U.S.	95.0	91.9

Note: (1) Metropolitan Statistical Area - see Appendix A for areas included
Source: 1990 Census of Population, General Population Characteristics

INCOME

Per Capita/Median/Average Income

Area	Per Capita ($)	Median Household ($)	Average Household ($)
City	14,830	25,324	33,245
MSA[1]	16,842	36,565	43,942
U.S.	14,420	30,056	38,453

Note: All figures are for 1989; (1) Metropolitan Statistical Area - see Appendix A for areas included
Source: 1990 Census of Population and Housing, Summary Tape File 3C

Household Income Distribution by Race

Income ($)	City (%)					U.S. (%)				
	Total	White	Black	Other	Hisp.[1]	Total	White	Black	Other	Hisp.[1]
Less than 5,000	6.3	4.7	13.3	17.3	7.1	6.2	4.8	15.2	8.6	8.8
5,000 - 9,999	12.7	11.1	21.8	21.0	12.1	9.3	8.6	14.2	9.9	11.1
10,000 - 14,999	10.6	10.1	13.0	14.9	12.4	8.8	8.5	11.0	9.8	11.0
15,000 - 24,999	19.8	20.0	19.3	17.8	26.5	17.5	17.3	18.9	18.5	20.5
25,000 - 34,999	15.8	16.4	12.9	11.4	15.0	15.8	16.1	14.2	15.4	16.4
35,000 - 49,999	16.2	17.2	11.0	10.3	14.2	17.9	18.6	13.3	16.1	16.0
50,000 - 74,999	11.9	12.9	6.6	5.2	7.7	15.0	15.8	9.3	13.4	11.1
75,000 - 99,999	3.6	3.9	1.4	1.5	3.3	5.1	5.5	2.6	4.7	3.1
100,000+	3.2	3.7	0.7	0.6	1.7	4.4	4.8	1.3	3.7	1.9

Note: All figures are for 1989; (1) people of Hispanic origin can be of any race
Source: 1990 Census of Population and Housing, Summary Tape File 3C

Effective Buying Income

Area	Per Capita ($)	Median Household ($)	Average Household ($)
City	17,421	30,709	40,072
MSA[1]	19,457	42,629	51,403
U.S.	16,803	34,536	45,243

Note: Data as of 1/1/99; (1) Metropolitan Statistical Area - see Appendix A for areas included
Source: Standard Rate & Data Service, Newspaper Advertising Source, 9/99

Effective Household Buying Income Distribution

Area	% of Households Earning						
	$10,000 -$19,999	$20,000 -$34,999	$35,000 -$49,999	$50,000 -$74,999	$75,000 -$99,000	$100,000 -$124,999	$125,000 and up
City	18.9	24.5	16.9	16.7	5.7	2.1	2.1
MSA[1]	11.9	20.7	20.3	24.9	9.1	2.9	3.0
U.S.	16.0	22.6	18.2	18.9	7.2	2.4	2.7

Note: Data as of 1/1/99; (1) Metropolitan Statistical Area - see Appendix A for areas included
Source: Standard Rate & Data Service, Newspaper Advertising Source, 9/99

Poverty Rates by Race and Age

Area	Total (%)	By Race (%)				By Age (%)		
		White	Black	Other	Hisp.[2]	Under 5 years old	Under 18 years old	65 years and over
City	18.5	11.7	40.5	47.4	28.9	33.1	30.6	11.0
MSA[1]	8.1	5.9	37.0	32.7	19.1	13.2	11.2	8.2
U.S.	13.1	9.8	29.5	23.1	25.3	20.1	18.3	12.8

Note: Figures show the percent of people living below the poverty line in 1989. The average poverty threshold was $12,674 for a family of four in 1989; (1) Metropolitan Statistical Area - see Appendix A for areas included; (2) people of Hispanic origin can be of any race
Source: 1990 Census of Population and Housing, Summary Tape File 3C

EMPLOYMENT

Labor Force and Employment

Area	Civilian Labor Force			Workers Employed		
	Jun. 1998	Jun. 1999	% Chg.	Jun. 1998	Jun. 1999	% Chg.
City	211,608	214,370	1.3	204,556	207,440	1.4
MSA[1]	1,692,549	1,719,174	1.6	1,653,173	1,676,687	1.4
U.S.	138,798,000	140,666,000	1.3	132,265,000	134,395,000	1.6

Note: Data is not seasonally adjusted and covers workers 16 years of age and older;
(1) Metropolitan Statistical Area - see Appendix A for areas included
Source: Bureau of Labor Statistics, http://stats.bls.gov

Unemployment Rate

Area	1998						1999					
	Jul.	Aug.	Sep.	Oct.	Nov.	Dec.	Jan.	Feb.	Mar.	Apr.	May.	Jun.
City	2.5	2.4	3.3	2.6	2.2	1.9	2.3	2.1	2.0	2.0	2.1	3.2
MSA[1]	1.7	1.7	2.7	1.8	1.7	1.6	2.3	2.0	1.9	1.6	1.6	2.5
U.S.	4.7	4.5	4.4	4.2	4.1	4.0	4.8	4.7	4.4	4.1	4.0	4.5

Note: Data is not seasonally adjusted and covers workers 16 years of age and older; all figures are percentages; (1) Metropolitan Statistical Area - see Appendix A for areas included
Source: Bureau of Labor Statistics, http://stats.bls.gov

Employment by Industry

Sector	MSA[1]		U.S.
	Number of Employees	Percent of Total	Percent of Total
Services	505,700	29.4	30.4
Retail Trade	301,700	17.5	17.7
Government	223,800	13.0	15.6
Manufacturing	284,100	16.5	14.3
Finance/Insurance/Real Estate	129,500	7.5	5.9
Wholesale Trade	105,900	6.1	5.4
Transportation/Public Utilities	95,700	5.6	5.3
Construction	75,100	4.4	5.0
Mining	n/a	n/a	0.4

Note: Figures cover non-farm employment as of 6/99 and are not seasonally adjusted; (1) Metropolitan Statistical Area - see Appendix A for areas included; n/a not available
Source: Bureau of Labor Statistics, http://stats.bls.gov

Employment by Occupation

Occupation Category	City (%)	MSA[1] (%)	U.S. (%)
White Collar	65.7	65.0	58.1
Executive/Admin./Management	12.9	14.2	12.3
Professional	18.9	15.3	14.1
Technical & Related Support	4.6	4.6	3.7
Sales	11.1	12.7	11.8
Administrative Support/Clerical	18.2	18.3	16.3
Blue Collar	18.1	21.6	26.2
Precision Production/Craft/Repair	6.3	9.4	11.3
Machine Operators/Assem./Insp.	5.5	6.0	6.8
Transportation/Material Movers	3.0	3.2	4.1
Cleaners/Helpers/Laborers	3.1	3.1	3.9
Services	15.7	12.3	13.2
Farming/Forestry/Fishing	0.6	1.1	2.5

Note: Figures cover employed persons 16 years old and over; (1) Metropolitan Statistical Area - see Appendix A for areas included
Source: 1990 Census of Population and Housing, Summary Tape File 3C

Occupational Employment Projections: 1996 - 2006

Occupations Expected to Have the Largest Job Growth (ranked by numerical growth)	Fast-Growing Occupations[1] (ranked by percent growth)
1. General managers & top executives	1. Systems analysts
2. Database administrators	2. Desktop publishers
3. Salespersons, retail	3. Personal and home care aides
4. Cashiers	4. Physical therapy assistants and aides
5. Systems analysts	5. Occupational therapy assistants
6. Truck drivers, light	6. Home health aides
7. Home health aides	7. Human services workers
8. Receptionists and information clerks	8. Data processing equipment repairers
9. Computer engineers	9. Paralegals
10. Marketing & sales, supervisors	10. Surgical technologists

Note: Projections cover Minnesota; (1) Excludes occupations with total job growth less than 300
Source: U.S. Department of Labor, Employment and Training Administration, America's Labor Market Information System (ALMIS)

TAXES

Major State and Local Tax Rates

State Corp. Income (%)	State Personal Income (%)	Residential Property (effective rate per $100)	Sales & Use		State Gasoline (cents/ gallon)	State Cigarette (cents/ pack)
			State (%)	Local (%)		
9.8[a]	6.0 - 8.5	1.25	6.5	0.5	20.0	48.0

Note: Personal/corporate income, sales, gasoline and cigarette tax rates as of January 1999.
Property tax rates as of 1997; (a) Plus a 5.8% tax on any Alternative Minimum Taxable Income over the base tax
Source: Federation of Tax Administrators, www.taxadmin.org; Washington D.C. Department of Finance and Revenue, Tax Rates and Tax Burdens in the District of Columbia: A Nationwide Comparison, July 1998; Chamber of Commerce, 1999

Total Taxes Per Capita and as a Percent of Income

Area	Per Capita Income ($)	Per Capita Taxes ($)			Percent of Income (%)		
		Total	Federal	State/ Local	Total	Federal	State/ Local
Minnesota	29,799	11,081	7,168	3,913	37.2	24.1	13.1
U.S.	27,876	9,881	6,690	3,191	35.4	24.0	11.4

Note: Figures are for 1998
Source: Tax Foundation, www.taxfoundation.org

Estimated Tax Burden

Area	State Income	Local Income	Property	Sales	Total
Minneapolis	2,609	0	5,500	683	8,792

Note: The numbers are estimates of taxes paid by a married couple with two children and annual earnings of $75,000. Sales tax estimates assume they spend average amounts on food, clothing, household goods and gasoline. Property tax estimates assume they live in a $250,000 home.
Source: Kiplinger's Personal Finance Magazine, October 1998

**COMMERCIAL
REAL ESTATE**

Office Market

Class/ Location	Total Space (sq. ft.)	Vacant Space (sq. ft.)	Vac. Rate (%)	Under Constr. (sq. ft.)	Net Absorp. (sq. ft.)	Rental Rates ($/sq.ft./yr.)
Class A						
CBD	11,165,605	490,717	4.4	1,700,000	-31,680	16.00-35.00
Outside CBD	5,965,329	216,637	3.6	1,000,000	538,147	20.00-33.00
Class B						
CBD	11,082,202	822,602	7.4	n/a	353,396	13.00-25.00
Outside CBD	19,845,048	1,443,862	7.3	538,000	298,717	13.00-23.00

*Note: Data as of 10/98 and covers Minneapolis; CBD = Central Business District; n/a not available;
Source: Society of Industrial and Office Realtors, 1999 Comparative Statistics of Industrial and Office
Real Estate Markets*

"Nineteen multitenant office projects totaling four million sq. ft. are under construction in the Twin Cities. Besides that, an additional 31 projects totaling eight million sq. ft. have been proposed or planned. So far, the danger of overbuilding remains remote in Minneapolis-St. Paul. Although speculative development is occurring there, most projects coming onto the market are either pre-leased or become fully leased within a few months of completion. It is expected that 250,000 to 300,000 sq. ft. will be absorbed in the Minneapolis CBD during 1999. Rents for all classes of buildings will increase as a result of the limited amount of office space. Large blocks of space are expected to become available in Piper Tower, at 250 Marquette Avenue, in the IDS Tower, at Pillsbury Center, and at 50 South Sixth Street. Conversions of some industrial space into Class B and C office space are also expected." *Society of Industrial and Office Realtors, 1999 Comparative Statistics of Industrial and Office Real Estate Markets*

Industrial Market

Location	Total Space (sq. ft.)	Vacant Space (sq. ft.)	Vac. Rate (%)	Under Constr. (sq. ft.)	Net Absorp. (sq. ft.)	Net Lease ($/sq.ft./yr.)
Central City	84,625,000	2,636,000	3.1	308,000	6,077,298	3.50-4.75
Suburban	129,550,000	7,395,000	5.7	4,000,000	7,338,820	3.50-4.75

*Note: Data as of 10/98 and covers Minneapolis; n/a not available
Source: Society of Industrial and Office Realtors, 1999 Comparative Statistics of Industrial and Office
Real Estate Markets*

"New speculative development has continued at a strong pace in Minneapolis-St. Paul. Fifty new projects totaling 4.7 million sq. ft. have been proposed, are being planned, or are under construction. Most of the development is occurring in Dakota County and in the southwestern suburbs. More growth is expected in Scott County as well. Scarcity of land has deterred development in the cities of Minneapolis and St. Paul. Investors have remained enthusiastic about the region. Although the REITs that led the market during the early part of this year in their purchases of portfolios were later forced into inactivity, pension funds, leveraged investors, and trade buyers have continued the buying pace. Capitalization rates have shifted from 9.25-10 percent to 9.75-10.25 percent reflecting the change. Insurance companies are expected to resume their dominant role as commercial real estate lenders." *Society of Industrial and Office Realtors, 1999 Comparative Statistics of Industrial and Office Real Estate Markets*

Retail Market

Shopping Center Inventory (sq. ft.)	Shopping Center Construction (sq. ft.)	Construction as a Percent of Inventory (%)	Torto Wheaton Rent Index[1] ($/sq. ft.)
39,152,000	677,000	1.7	10.31

*Note: Data as of 1997 and covers the Metropolitan Statistical Area - see Appendix A for areas
included; (1) Index is based on a model that predicts what the average rent should be for leases with
certain characteristics, in certain locations during certain years.
Source: National Association of Realtors, 1997-1998 Market Conditions Report*

"Estimated at 2.81 million, Minneapolis' population has grown an average of 1.5% annually over the past two years, compared to 0.9% for the nation. Real personal income growth has been strong recently, which has helped push the area's retail rent index up 27% over the past three years. However, rents remain below the Midwest average of $12.30. Minneapolis, of course, is home to the 4.2 million square foot Mall of America, which boasts a multitude of bars and restaurants, a14 screen megaplex, an indoor amusement park and an aquarium. The mall typifies a trend in several areas, where entertainment is being used to attract customers to retail centers." *National Association of Realtors, 1997-1998 Market Conditions Report*

COMMERCIAL UTILITIES

Typical Monthly Electric Bills

Area	Commercial Service ($/month)		Industrial Service ($/month)	
	12 kW demand 1,500 kWh	100 kW demand 30,000 kWh	1,000 kW demand 400,000 kWh	20,000 kW demand 10,000,000 kWh
City	107	1,701	18,915	312,867
U.S.	150	2,174	23,995	508,569

Note: Based on rates in effect January 1, 1999
Source: Edison Electric Institute, Typical Residential, Commercial and Industrial Bills, Winter 1999

TRANSPORTATION

Transportation Statistics

Average minutes to work	19.6
Interstate highways	I-35; I-94
Bus lines	
In-city	Metropolitan Council, 963 vehicles
Inter-city	3
Passenger air service	
Airport	Minneapolis-St. Paul International
Airlines	23
Aircraft departures	154,956 (1996)
Enplaned passengers	12,615,766 (1996)
Rail service	Amtrak; light rail proposed
Motor freight carriers	150
Major waterways/ports	Port of Minneapolis

Source: Editor & Publisher Market Guide, 1999; FAA Airport Activity Statistics, 1997; Amtrak National Time Table, Northeast Timetable, Spring/Summer 1999; 1990 Census of Population and Housing, STF 3C; Chamber of Commerce/Economic Development 1999; Jane's Urban Transport Systems 1999-2000

Means of Transportation to Work

Area	Car/Truck/Van		Public Transportation			Bicycle	Walked	Other Means	Worked at Home
	Drove Alone	Car-pooled	Bus	Subway	Railroad				
City	60.3	10.5	15.7	0.0	0.0	1.6	7.8	0.9	3.1
MSA[1]	76.0	11.2	5.2	0.0	0.0	0.4	3.2	0.6	3.4
U.S.	73.2	13.4	3.0	1.5	0.5	0.4	3.9	1.2	3.0

Note: Figures shown are percentages and only include workers 16 years old and over;
(1) Metropolitan Statistical Area - see Appendix A for areas included
Source: 1990 Census of Population and Housing, Summary Tape File 3C

BUSINESSES

Major Business Headquarters

Company Name	1999 Rankings	
	Fortune 500	Forbes 500
Cargill	-	1
Carlson Cos	-	91
Dayton Hudson	30	-
GFI America	-	463
General Mills	272	-
Genmar Holdings	-	388
Holiday Cos	-	106
Honeywell	193	-
Lutheran Brotherhood	483	-
MA Mortenson	-	277
U.S. Bancorp	215	-

Note: Companies listed are located in the city; dashes indicate no ranking
Fortune 500: Companies that produce a 10-K are ranked 1 to 500 based on 1998 revenue
Forbes 500: Private companies are ranked 1 to 500 based on 1997 revenue
Source: Forbes, November 30, 1998; Fortune, April 26, 1999

Best Companies to Work For

Medtronic (products that treat heart disease), headquartered in Minneapolis, is among the "100 Best Companies to Work for in America." Criteria: trust in management, pride in work/company, camaraderie, company responses to the Hewitt People Practices Inventory, and employee responses to their Great Place to Work survey. The companies also had to be at least 10 years old and have a minimum of 500 employees. *Fortune, January 11, 1999*

General Mills, headquartered in Minneapolis, is among the "100 Best Companies for Working Mothers." Criteria: fair wages, opportunities for women to advance, support for child care, flexible work schedules, family-friendly benefits, and work/life supports. *Working Mother, October 1998*

Honeywell, Inc. (electronics) and Reliastar Financial Corp. (financial services), headquartered in Minneapolis, are among the "100 Best Places to Work in IS." Criteria: compensation, turnover and training. *Computerworld, May 25, 1998*

Fast-Growing Businesses

According to *Inc.*, Minneapolis is home to two of America's 100 fastest-growing private companies: Network Management Services and Systems Group. Criteria for inclusion: must be an independent, privately-held, U.S. corporation, proprietorship or partnership; sales of at least $200,000 in 1995; five-year operating/sales history; increase in 1999 sales over 1998 sales; holding companies, regulated banks, and utilities were excluded. *Inc. 500, 1999*

Minneapolis is home to one of *Business Week's* "hot growth" companies: Funco and Techne. Criteria: increase in sales and profits, return on capital and stock price. *Business Week, 5/31/99*

According to *Fortune*, Minneapolis is home to one of America's 100 fastest-growing companies: Tower Automotive. Companies were ranked based on earnings-per-share growth, revenue growth and total return over the previous three years. Criteria for inclusion: public companies with sales of least $50 million. Companies that lost money in the most recent quarter, or ended in the red for the past four quarters as a whole, were not eligible. Limited partnerships and REITs were also not considered. *Fortune, "America's Fastest-Growing Companies," 1999*

Women-Owned Firms: Number, Employment and Sales

Area	Number of Firms	Employ-ment	Sales ($000)	Rank[2]
MSA[1]	119,600	337,400	51,063,400	14

Note: (1) Metropolitan Statistical Area - see Appendix A for areas included;
(2) Calculated on an averaging of the number of businesses, employment and sales
Source: The National Foundation for Women Business Owners, 1999 Facts on Women-Owned Businesses: Trends in the Top 50 Metropolitan Areas

Women-Owned Firms: Growth

Area	% change from 1992 to 1999			Rank[2]
	Number of Firms	Employ-ment	Sales	
MSA[1]	42.3	95.1	143.4	29

Note: (1) Metropolitan Statistical Area - see Appendix A for areas included; (2) Calculated on an averaging of the percent growth of number of businesses, employment and sales
Source: The National Foundation for Women Business Owners, 1999 Facts on Women-Owned Businesses: Trends in the Top 50 Metropolitan Areas

Small Business Opportunity

According to *Forbes*, Minneapolis is home to four of America's 200 best small companies: Barbers Hairstyling, Grow Biz International, Masaba Holdings and Techne. Criteria: companies included must be publicly traded since November 1997 with a stock price of at least $5 per share and an average daily float of 1,000 shares. The company's latest 12-month sales must be between $5 and $350 million, return on equity (ROE) must be a minimum of 12% for both the past 5 years and the most recent four quarters, and five-year sales and EPS growth must average at least 10%. Companies with declining sales or earnings during the past year were dropped as well as businesses with debt/equity ratios over 1.25. Companies with negative operating cash flow in each of the past two years were also excluded. *Forbes, November 2, 1998*

HOTELS & MOTELS

Hotels/Motels

Area	Hotels/ Motels	Rooms	Luxury-Level Hotels/Motels		Average Minimum Rates ($)		
			◆◆◆◆	◆◆◆◆◆	◆◆	◆◆◆	◆◆◆◆
City	27	5,808	1	0	69	123	215
Airport	43	7,959	0	0	n/a	n/a	n/a
Suburbs	66	6,386	0	0	n/a	n/a	n/a
Total	136	20,153	1	0	n/a	n/a	n/a

Note: n/a not available; classifications range from one diamond (budget properties with basic amenities) to five diamond (luxury properties with the finest service, rooms and facilities).
Source: OAG, Business Travel Planner, Winter 1998-99

CONVENTION CENTERS

Major Convention Centers

Center Name	Meeting Rooms	Exhibit Space (sq. ft.)
Earle Brown Heritage Center	10	13,000
Minneapolis Convention Center	56	280,000

Source: Trade Shows Worldwide, 1998; Meetings & Conventions, 4/15/99; Sucessful Meetings, 3/31/98

Living Environment

COST OF LIVING

Cost of Living Index

Composite Index	Groceries	Housing	Utilities	Trans-portation	Health Care	Misc. Goods/ Services
103.5	98.1	96.0	107.1	116.9	115.3	105.8

Note: U.S. = 100
Source: ACCRA, Cost of Living Index, 1st Quarter 1999

HOUSING

Median Home Prices and Housing Affordability

Area	Median Price[2] 1st Qtr. 1999 ($)	HOI[3] 1st Qtr. 1999	Afford-ability Rank[4]
MSA[1]	129,000	82.8	32
U.S.	134,000	69.6	–

Note: (1) Metropolitan Statistical Area - see Appendix A for areas included; (2) U.S. figures calculated from the sales of 524,324 new and existing homes in 181 markets; (3) Housing Opportunity Index - percent of homes sold that were within the reach of the median income household at the prevailing mortgage interest rate; (4) Rank is from 1-181 with 1 being most affordable
Source: National Association of Home Builders, Housing Opportunity Index, 1st Quarter 1999

Median Home Price Projection

It is projected that the median price of existing single-family homes in the metro area will increase by 3.6% in 1999. Nationwide, home prices are projected to increase 3.8%.
Kiplinger's Personal Finance Magazine, January 1999

Average New Home Price

Area	Price ($)
City	135,230
U.S.	142,735

Note: Figures are based on a new home with 1,800 sq. ft. of living area on an 8,000 sq. ft. lot.
Source: ACCRA, Cost of Living Index, 1st Quarter 1999

Average Apartment Rent

Area	Rent ($/mth)
City	621
U.S.	601

Note: Figures are based on an unfurnished two bedroom, 1-1/2 or 2 bath apartment, approximately 950 sq. ft. in size, excluding all utilities except water
Source: ACCRA, Cost of Living Index, 1st Quarter 1999

RESIDENTIAL UTILITIES

Average Residential Utility Costs

Area	All Electric ($/mth)	Part Electric ($/mth)	Other Energy ($/mth)	Phone ($/mth)
City	–	50.76	54.68	22.28
U.S.	100.02	55.73	43.33	19.71

Source: ACCRA, Cost of Living Index, 1st Quarter 1999

HEALTH CARE

Average Health Care Costs

Area	Hospital ($/day)	Doctor ($/visit)	Dentist ($/visit)
City	672.00	54.80	71.20
U.S.	430.43	52.45	66.35

Note: Hospital—based on a semi-private room; Doctor—based on a general practitioner's routine exam of an established patient; Dentist—based on adult teeth cleaning and periodic oral exam.
Source: ACCRA, Cost of Living Index, 1st Quarter 1999

Distribution of Office-Based Physicians

Area	Family/Gen. Practitioners	Specialists		
		Medical	Surgical	Other
MSA[1]	1,020	1,541	1,114	1,257

Note: Data as of 12/31/97; (1) Metropolitan Statistical Area - see Appendix A for areas included
Source: American Medical Assn., Physician Characteristics & Distribution in the U.S., 1999

Hospitals

Minneapolis has 5 general medical and surgical hospitals, 1 children's general, 1 children's orthopedic. *AHA Guide to the Healthcare Field, 1998-99*

According to *U.S. News and World Report,* Minneapolis has 1 of the best hospitals in the U.S.: **Hennepin County Medical Center**, noted for endocrinology. *U.S. News Online, "America's Best Hospitals," 10th Edition, www.usnews.com*

EDUCATION

Public School District Statistics

District Name	Num. Sch.	Enroll.	Classroom Teachers	Pupils per Teacher	Minority Pupils (%)	Current Exp.[1] ($/pupil)
Cedar Riverside Community Sch	1	112	n/a	n/a	n/a	n/a
Central Mn Joint Powers Dist	3	474	n/a	n/a	n/a	n/a
Cyber Village Academy	1	n/a	n/a	n/a	n/a	n/a
Frederick Douglass Math/Sci	1	31	n/a	n/a	n/a	n/a
Higher Ground Academy	1	n/a	n/a	n/a	n/a	n/a
Minneapolis	150	49,157	n/a	n/a	67.7	7,831
Minnesota Transitions Charter	1	142	n/a	n/a	n/a	n/a
New Visions Charter School	1	180	n/a	n/a	n/a	n/a
Saint Anthony-New Brighton	3	1,325	n/a	n/a	n/a	n/a
Skills For Tomorrow Char Sch	1	74	n/a	n/a	n/a	n/a
Southwest Mn Joint Powers	1	2	n/a	n/a	n/a	n/a

Note: Data covers the 1997-1998 school year unless otherwise noted; (1) Data covers fiscal year 1996; SD = School District; ISD = Independent School District; n/a not available
Source: National Center for Education Statistics, Common Core of Data Public Education Agency Universe 1997-98; National Center for Education Statistics, Characteristics of the 100 Largest Public Elementary and Secondary School Districts in the United States: 1997-98, July 1999

Educational Quality

School District	Education Quotient[1]	Graduate Outcome[2]	Community Index[3]	Resource Index[4]
Minneapolis SD	106.0	84.0	146.0	143.0

Note: Nearly 1,000 secondary school districts were rated in terms of educational quality. The scores range from a low of 50 to a high of 150; (1) Average of the Graduate Outcome, Community and Resource indexes; (2) Based on graduation rates and college board scores (SAT/ACT); (3) Based on the surrounding community's average level of education and the area's average income level; (4) Based on teacher salaries, per-pupil expenditures and student-teacher ratios.
Source: Expansion Management, Ratings Issue, 1998

Educational Attainment by Race

Area	High School Graduate (%)					Bachelor's Degree (%)				
	Total	White	Black	Other	Hisp.[2]	Total	White	Black	Other	Hisp.[2]
City	82.6	84.9	71.9	66.3	73.1	30.3	32.8	13.8	21.4	23.8
MSA[1]	87.2	88.0	76.2	70.7	76.7	27.1	27.5	17.3	25.2	19.9
U.S.	75.2	77.9	63.1	60.4	49.8	20.3	21.5	11.4	19.4	9.2

Note: Figures shown cover persons 25 years old and over; (1) Metropolitan Statistical Area - see Appendix A for areas included; (2) people of Hispanic origin can be of any race
Source: 1990 Census of Population and Housing, Summary Tape File 3C

School Enrollment by Type

Area	Preprimary				Elementary/High School			
	Public		Private		Public		Private	
	Enrollment	%	Enrollment	%	Enrollment	%	Enrollment	%
City	3,848	59.9	2,577	40.1	38,107	84.8	6,823	15.2
MSA[1]	35,492	63.1	20,730	36.9	359,955	89.1	44,235	10.9
U.S.	2,679,029	59.5	1,824,256	40.5	38,379,689	90.2	4,187,099	9.8

Note: Figures shown cover persons 3 years old and over;
(1) Metropolitan Statistical Area - see Appendix A for areas included
Source: 1990 Census of Population and Housing, Summary Tape File 3C

School Enrollment by Race

Area	Preprimary (%)				Elementary/High School (%)			
	White	Black	Other	Hisp.[1]	White	Black	Other	Hisp.[1]
City	69.2	19.0	11.8	3.1	56.8	26.2	16.9	3.4
MSA[2]	90.7	4.3	5.0	1.9	87.8	5.3	6.9	2.1
U.S.	80.4	12.5	7.1	7.8	74.1	15.6	10.3	12.5

Note: Figures shown cover persons 3 years old and over; (1) people of Hispanic origin can be of any race; (2) Metropolitan Statistical Area - see Appendix A for areas included
Source: 1990 Census of Population and Housing, Summary Tape File 3C

Classroom Teacher Salaries in Public Schools

District	B.A. Degree		M.A. Degree		Maximum	
	Min. ($)	Rank[1]	Max. ($)	Rank[1]	Max. ($)	Rank[1]
Minneapolis	26,109	52	49,257	26	57,000	17
Average	26,980	-	46,065	-	51,435	-

Note: Salaries are for 1997-1998; (1) Rank ranges from 1 to 100
Source: American Federation of Teachers, Survey & Analysis of Salary Trends, 1998

Higher Education

Two-Year Colleges		Four-Year Colleges		Medical Schools	Law Schools	Voc/ Tech
Public	Private	Public	Private			
2	4	1	3	1	1	12

Source: College Blue Book, Occupational Education, 1997; Medical School Admission Requirements, 1999-2000; Peterson's Guide to Two-Year Colleges, 1999; Peterson's Guide to Four-Year Colleges, 2000; Barron's Guide to Law Schools, 1999

MAJOR EMPLOYERS

Major Employers

American Express Financial Corp.
Ceridian Corp. (navigation instruments)
General Mills
Methodist Hospital
Norwest Nova (mortgage bankers)

Carlson Companies (management consulting)
Fairview Hospital & Healthcare Services
Medtronic Inc. (electromedical apparatus)
North Memorial Health Care
American Yearbook Co. (publishing)

Note: Companies listed are located in the city
Source: Dun's Business Rankings, 1999; Ward's Business Directory, 1998

PUBLIC SAFETY

Crime Rate

Area	All Crimes	Violent Crimes				Property Crimes		
		Murder	Forcible Rape	Robbery	Aggrav. Assault	Burglary	Larceny -Theft	Motor Vehicle Theft
City	11,439.5	15.9	147.3	909.0	777.9	2,263.3	5,730.7	1,595.4
Suburbs[1]	4,441.7	2.0	40.3	69.2	135.2	639.1	3,202.5	353.4
MSA[2]	5,364.5	3.8	54.4	179.9	220.0	853.3	3,535.9	517.2
U.S.	4,922.7	6.8	35.9	186.1	382.0	919.6	2,886.5	505.8

Note: Crime rate is the number of crimes per 100,000 pop.; (1) defined as all areas within the MSA but located outside the central city; (2) Metropolitan Statistical Area - see Appendix A for areas incl.
Source: FBI Uniform Crime Reports, 1997

RECREATION

Culture and Recreation

Museums	Symphony Orchestras	Opera Companies	Dance Companies	Professional Theatres	Zoos	Pro Sports Teams
6	2	1	4	12	0	3

Source: International Directory of the Performing Arts, 1997; Official Museum Directory, 1999; Stern's Performing Arts Directory, 1997; USA Today Four Sport Stadium Guide, 1997; Chamber of Commerce/Economic Development, 1999

Library System

The Minneapolis Public Library has 14 branches, holdings of 2,114,887 volumes, and a budget of $16,810,778 (1996). *American Library Directory, 1998-1999*

MEDIA

Newspapers

Name	Type	Freq.	Distribution	Circulation
Apple Valley-Rosemount-Sun-Current	General	1x/wk	Local	13,741
Brooklyn Park Sun Post	General	1x/wk	Local	17,667
Burnsville-Lakeville Sun Current	General	1x/wk	Local	14,488
Crystal-Robbinsdale Sun Post	General	1x/wk	Local	11,683
East Calhoun News	n/a	1x/mo	Local	5,500
Excelsior-Shorewood Sun Sailor	General	1x/wk	Local	14,538
Finance & Commerce	General	5x/wk	U.S.	1,100
Hopkins Sun Sailor	General	1x/wk	Local	14,565
Insight News	n/a	1x/wk	Local	35,000
Minneapolis Spokesman	Black	1x/wk	Local	16,000
The Minnesota Daily	General	5x/wk	Camp/Comm	42,000
Saint Paul Recorder	Black	1x/wk	Local	10,000
Skyway News	General	1x/wk	Area	55,000
Star Tribune	General	7x/wk	Area	387,300

Note: Includes newspapers with circulations of 1,000 or more located in the city; n/a not available
Source: Burrelle's Media Directory, 1999 Edition

Television Stations

Name	Ch.	Affiliation	Type	Owner
WCCO	n/a	CBST	Commercial	Westinghouse Broadcasting Company
KMSP	n/a	UPN	Commercial	United Television Inc.
KARE	11	NBCT	Commercial	Gannett Broadcasting
WFTC	29	FBC	Commercial	Clear Channel Broadcasting Inc.

Note: Stations included broadcast in the Minneapolis metro area; n/a not available
Source: Burrelle's Media Directory, 1999 Edition

AM Radio Stations

Call Letters	Freq. (kHz)	Target Audience	Station Format	Music Format
KFXN	690	General	M/N/S	Alternative
KUOM	770	General	M/N/S	Alternative
WCCO	830	General	N/S/T	n/a
KSGS	950	Black	M	R&B/Urban Contemporary
KKMS	980	General	N/T	n/a
WCTS	1030	General	E	n/a
KFAN	1130	General	N/S/T	n/a
WWTC	1280	General	T	n/a
WMNN	1330	General	N	n/a
KDIZ	1440	General	M	n/a

Note: Stations included broadcast in the Minneapolis metro area; n/a not available
Target Audience: A=Asian; B=Black; C=Christian; E=Ethnic; F=French; G=General; H=Hispanic; M=Men; N=Native American; R=Religious; S=Senior Citizen; W=Women; Y=Young Adult; Z=Children
Station Format: E=Educational; M=Music; N=News; S=Sports; T=Talk
Source: Burrelle's Media Directory, 1999 Edition

FM Radio Stations

Call Letters	Freq. (mHz)	Target Audience	Station Format	Music Format
KBEM	88.5	General	M/N	Jazz
WCAL	89.3	General	E/M	Classical
KMOJ	89.9	General	E/M/N/T	Blues/Christian/Easy Listening/Gospel/Jazz/Oldies/ Reggae/R&B/Top 40/Urban Contemp./World Music
KFAI	90.3	Alternative	Hispanic	M/N/T
KQRS	92.5	General	M/N/T	Classic Rock
KXXR	93.7	General	M/N/T	Alternative/AOR/Modern Rock
KSTP	94.5	General	M	Adult Contemporary
KTCZ	97.1	General	M/N/T	Adult Contemporary/Alternative/AOR/Classic Rock
WRQC	100.3	General	M	AOR/Classic Rock
KDWB	101.3	General	M	n/a
KEEY	102.1	General	M/N/T	Country
WLTE	102.9	General	M	Adult Contemporary
WXPT	104.1	General	M	Alternative/Modern Rock
KZNR	105.1	General	M	Alternative
KZNT	105.3	General	M/N/T	Alternative
KZNZ	105.7	General	M/N/T	Alternative
KDXL	106.5	General	M/N/S	AOR
KQQL	107.9	General	M	Oldies

Note: Stations included broadcast in the Minneapolis metro area; n/a not available
Station Format: E=Educational; M=Music; N=News; S=Sports; T=Talk
Target Audience: A=Asian; B=Black; C=Christian; E=Ethnic; F=French; G=General; H=Hispanic; M=Men; N=Native American; R=Religious; S=Senior Citizen; W=Women; Y=Young Adult; Z=Children
Music Format: AOR=Album Oriented Rock; MOR=Middle-of-the-Road
Source: Burrelle's Media Directory, 1999 Edition

CLIMATE

Average and Extreme Temperatures

Temperature	Jan	Feb	Mar	Apr	May	Jun	Jul	Aug	Sep	Oct	Nov	Dec	Yr.
Extreme High (°F)	57	60	83	95	96	102	105	101	98	89	74	63	105
Average High (°F)	21	27	38	56	69	79	84	81	71	59	41	26	54
Average Temp. (°F)	12	18	30	46	59	69	74	71	61	50	33	19	45
Average Low (°F)	3	9	21	36	48	58	63	61	50	39	25	11	35
Extreme Low (°F)	-34	-28	-32	2	18	37	43	39	26	15	-17	-29	-34

Note: Figures cover the years 1948-1990
Source: National Climatic Data Center, International Station Meteorological Climate Summary, 3/95

Average Precipitation/Snowfall/Humidity

Precip./Humidity	Jan	Feb	Mar	Apr	May	Jun	Jul	Aug	Sep	Oct	Nov	Dec	Yr.
Avg. Precip. (in.)	0.8	0.8	1.9	2.2	3.1	4.0	3.8	3.6	2.5	1.9	1.4	1.0	27.1
Avg. Snowfall (in.)	11	9	12	3	Tr	0	0	0	Tr	Tr	7	10	52
Avg. Rel. Hum. 6am (%)	75	76	77	75	75	79	81	84	85	81	80	79	79
Avg. Rel. Hum. 3pm (%)	64	62	58	48	47	50	50	52	53	52	62	68	55

Note: Figures cover the years 1948-1990; Tr = Trace amounts (<0.05 in. of rain; <0.5 in. of snow)
Source: National Climatic Data Center, International Station Meteorological Climate Summary, 3/95

Weather Conditions

Temperature			Daytime Sky			Precipitation		
5°F & below	32°F & below	90°F & above	Clear	Partly cloudy	Cloudy	0.01 inch or more precip.	0.1 inch or more snow/ice	Thunder-storms
45	156	16	93	125	147	113	41	37

Note: Figures are average number of days per year and covers the years 1948-1990
Source: National Climatic Data Center, International Station Meteorological Climate Summary, 3/95

AIR & WATER QUALITY

Maximum Pollutant Concentrations

	Particulate Matter (ug/m^3)	Carbon Monoxide (ppm)	Sulfur Dioxide (ppm)	Nitrogen Dioxide (ppm)	Ozone (ppm)	Lead (ug/m^3)
MSA[1] Level	77	5	0.027	0.023	0.09	0.01
NAAQS[2]	150	9	0.140	0.053	0.12	1.50
Met NAAQS?	Yes	Yes	Yes	Yes	Yes	Yes

*Note: (1) Metropolitan Statistical Area - see Appendix A for areas included; (2) National Ambient Air Quality Standards; ppm = parts per million; ug/m^3 = micrograms per cubic meter; n/a not available
Source: EPA, National Air Quality and Emissions Trends Report, 1997*

Pollutant Standards Index

In the Minneapolis MSA (see Appendix A for areas included), the Pollutant Standards Index (PSI) exceeded 100 on 0 days in 1997. A PSI value greater than 100 indicates that air quality would be in the unhealthful range on that day. *EPA, National Air Quality and Emissions Trends Report, 1997*

Drinking Water

Water System Name	Pop. Served	Primary Water Source Type	Number of Violations in 1998	Type of Violation/ Contaminants
Minneapolis	480,526	Surface	None	None

*Note: Data as of July 10, 1999
Source: EPA, Office of Ground Water and Drinking Water, Safe Drinking Water Information System*

Minneapolis tap water is alkaline, soft and fluoridated. Water is hard in the suburbs.
Editor & Publisher Market Guide, 1999

Oklahoma City, Oklahoma

Background

The 1992 film "Far and Away," directed by Ron Howard, shows Tom Cruise charging away on his horse to claim land in the Oklahoma Territory. That dramatic scene depicted a true event from the great Oklahoma Land Run of 1889. A pistol was fired from the Oklahoma Station house of the Santa Fe railroad and 10,000 homesteaders raced away to stake land claims in central Oklahoma territory. Overnight Oklahoma City, "OKC" as the locals like to call their town, had been founded.

The new town grew quickly along the tracks of the Santa Fe railroad. Soon it became a distribution center for the territory's crops and livestock. Today the city still functions as a major transportation center for the state's farm produce and huge livestock industry. By 1910 the city had become the state capital, which also furthered growth. But in 1928 growth went through the ceiling when oil was discovered within the Oklahoma City limits. Oil forever changed the economic face of Oklahoma City from one of livestock and feed to one of livestock, feed, and oil.

After World War II, Oklahoma City, like many other cities, entered industry, most notably aircraft and aircraft related industries. The Tinker Air Force Base and the Federal Aviation Administration's Mike Monroney Aeronautical Center has made Oklahoma City one of the nations leading aviation centers. The city's industry includes executive aircraft, petroleum products, electronic equipment, and oil field machinery.

The area has a lot to offer those who like a Western lifestyle. The town is the home of the National Cowboy Hall of Fame and Western Heritage Center, while the Oklahoma State Museum of History has an outstanding collection of Native American artifacts. Each September the State Fair is held in Oklahoma City and each January, the International Finals Rodeo is held at the State Fair Park. If swinging a bat is more your style than trying to stay on a bronco, there's the National Softball Hall of Fame and Museum.

Don't be fooled, however, by what might appear to be the city's simple tastes. Oklahoma City is sophisticated enough to hire the famous architect I.M. Pei to redesign its downtown area. Taking inspiration from the Tivoli Gardens of Copenhagen, the downtown now boasts of the Myriad Gardens, a 12-acre recreational park with gardens, an amphitheater, and the seven-story Crystal Bridge Tropical Conservatory.

On April 19, 1995 Oklahoma City became the site of the deadliest terrorist incident ever to occur in the United States. On that day, a truck bomb destroyed part of the Alfred P. Murray Federal Building in the downtown area, leaving 168 people dead and more than 500 injured. In the face of such tragedy, the world marveled at the way in which Oklahoma City and the State of Oklahoma carried itself with dignity and generosity. The people's response to and support for each other became known as the "Oklahoma Standard." Oklahoma and its principal city has always been a place where people care for their own. Today the Oklahoma City Memorial Foundation continues in its pledge to build a fitting memorial for those people whose lives were ended or forever changed on that day.

Oklahoma City's weather is changeable. There are pronounced daily and seasonal temperature changes and considerable variation in seasonal and annual precipitation. Summers are long and usually hot. Winters are comparatively mild and short.

General Rankings and Evaluative Comments

■ Oklahoma City was ranked #16 out of 19 large, southern metropolitan areas in *Money's* 1998 survey of "The Best Places to Live in America." The survey was conducted by first contacting 512 representative households nationwide and asking them to rank 37 quality-of-life factors on a scale of 1 to 10. Next, a demographic profile was compiled on the 300 largest metropolitan statistical areas in the U.S. The numbers were crunched together to arrive at an overall ranking (things Americans consider most important, like clean air and water, low crime and good schools, received extra weight). Unlike previous years, the 1998 rankings were broken down by region (northeast, midwest, south, west) and population size (100,000 to 249,999; 250,000 to 999,999; 1 million plus). The city had a nationwide ranking of #222 out of 300 in 1997 and #185 out of 300 in 1996. *Money, July 1998; Money, July 1997; Money, September 1996*

■ *Ladies Home Journal* ranked America's 200 largest cities based on the qualities women care about most. Oklahoma City ranked #148 out of 200. Criteria: low crime rate, well-paying jobs, quality health and child care, good public schools, the presence of women in government, size of the gender wage gap, number of sexual-harassment and discrimination complaints filed, unemployment and divorce rates, commute times, population density, number of houses of worship, parks and cultural offerings, number of women's health specialists, how well a community's women cared for themselves, complexion kindness index based on UV radiation levels, odds of finding affordable fashions, rental rates for romance movies, champagne sales and other matters of the heart. *Ladies Home Journal, November 1998*

■ Zero Population Growth ranked 229 cities in terms of children's health, safety, and economic well-being. Oklahoma City was ranked #74 out of 112 independent cities (cities with populations greater than 100,000 which were neither Major Cities nor Suburbs/Outer Cities) and was given a grade of C-. Criteria: total population, percent of population under 18 years of age, household language, percent population change, percent of births to teens, infant mortality rate, percent of low birth weights, dropout rate, enrollment in preprimary school, violent and property crime rates, unemployment rate, percent of children in poverty, percent of owner occupied units, number of bad air days, percent of public transportation commuters, and average travel time to work. *ZPG, Children's Environmental Index, Fall 1999*

■ Oklahoma City was ranked #24 out of 59 metro areas in *The Regional Economist's* "Rational Livability Ranking of 59 Large Metro Areas." The rankings were based on the metro area's total population change over the period 1990-97 divided by the number of people moving in from elsewhere in the United States (net domestic in-migration). *St. Louis Federal Reserve Bank of St. Louis, The Regional Economist, April 1999*

■ Oklahoma City was selected by *Yahoo! Internet Life* as one of " America's Most Wired Cities & Towns." The city ranked #38 out of 50. Criteria: home and work net use, domain density, hosts per capita, directory density and content quality. *Yahoo! Internet Life, March 1999*

■ Cognetics studied 273 metro areas in the United States, ranking them by entrepreneurial activity. Oklahoma City was ranked #40 out of the 50 largest metro areas. Criteria: Significant Starts (firms started in the last 10 years that still employ at least 5 people) and Young Growers (percent of firms 10 years old or less that grew significantly during the last 4 years). *Cognetics, "Entrepreneurial Hot Spots: The Best Places in America to Start and Grow a Company," 1998*

■ Oklahoma City was selected as one of the "Best American Cities to Start a Business" by *Point of View* magazine. Criteria: coolness, quality-of-life, and business concerns. The city was ranked #67 out of 75. *Point of View, November 1998*

■ Reliastar Financial Corp. ranked the 125 largest metropolitan areas according to the general financial security of residents. Oklahoma City was ranked #35 out of 125 with a score of 5.9. The score indicates the percentage a metropolitan area is above or below the metropolitan norm. A metro area with a score of 10.6 is 10.6% above the metro average. Criteria: Earnings and Wealth Potential (household income, education, net assets, cost of living); Safety Net (health insurance, retirement savings, life insurance, income support programs); Personal Threats (unemployment rate, low-income households, crime rate); Community Economic Vitality (cost of community services, job quality, job creation, housing costs). *Reliastar Financial Corp., "The Best Cities to Earn and Save Money," 1999 Edition*

Business Environment

STATE ECONOMY

State Economic Profile

"Oklahoma is displaying strong employment growth. OK has diversified its economy to be less dependent upon oil, and has hence been able to absorb oil industry job losses into its services, construction and trade sectors. OK's low cost of doing business will allow it to attract new firms even as the US economy slows in 1999.

OK's oil industry is characterized by small producers and high unit costs. Weak oil prices have been particularly hard on OK as rig counts reached record lows. In spite of recent OPEC cutbacks, oil prices are expected to remain low. A continued contraction of OK's oil industry is likely in 1999 and 2000.

Although employment growth in Oklahoma City trailed the state (2.3% vs. 2.9%), home sales and construction were stronger. Retail employment should increase in Oklahoma City with the new "Defense Mega Center" outside Tinker Air Force Base.

Tulsa's employment and housing markets outpaced the rest of the state. Job growth was over 3% in 1998. Tulsa's residential construction market accounts for over 30% of OK's starts. While still strong, construction in both Tulsa and Oklahoma City should slow in 1999.

OK's competitive business environment has helped to attract a number of relocating businesses. In 1998, over 100 companies announced expansions or relocations to take place over the next 3 years. The result could be more than 12,000 jobs created. Declining oil-based tax revenues will limit the state government's ability to offer relocation incentives. While the long-term outlook is positive, near-term growth will be close to the national." *National Association of Realtors, Economic Profiles: The Fifty States and the District of Columbia, http://nar.realtor.com/databank/profiles.htm*

IMPORTS/EXPORTS

Total Export Sales

Area	1994 ($000)	1995 ($000)	1996 ($000)	1997 ($000)	% Chg. 1994-97	% Chg. 1996-97
MSA[1]	488,563	485,803	483,903	519,966	6.4	7.5
U.S.	512,415,609	583,030,524	622,827,063	687,597,999	34.2	10.4

Note: (1) Metropolitan Statistical Area - see Appendix A for areas included
Source: U.S. Department of Commerce, International Trade Association, Metropolitan Area Exports: An Export Performance Report on Over 250 U.S. Cities, November 10, 1998

CITY FINANCES

City Government Finances

Component	FY92 ($000)	FY92 (per capita $)
Revenue	407,225	896.71
Expenditure	416,887	917.98
Debt Outstanding	571,114	1,257.59
Cash & Securities	525,031	1,156.11

Source: U.S. Bureau of the Census, City Government Finances: 1991-92

City Government Revenue by Source

Source	FY92 ($000)	FY92 (per capita $)	FY92 (%)
From Federal Government	10,141	22.33	2.5
From State Governments	8,383	18.46	2.1
From Local Governments	111	0.24	0.0
Property Taxes	26,600	58.57	6.5
General Sales Taxes	136,863	301.37	33.6
Selective Sales Taxes	24,195	53.28	5.9
Income Taxes	0	0.00	0.0
Current Charges	97,264	214.17	23.9
Utility/Liquor Store	38,170	84.05	9.4
Employee Retirement[1]	14,290	31.47	3.5
Other	51,208	112.76	12.6

Note: (1) Excludes "city contributions," classified as "nonrevenue," intragovernmental transfers.
Source: U.S. Bureau of the Census, City Government Finances: 1991-92

City Government Expenditures by Function

Function	FY92 ($000)	FY92 (per capita $)	FY92 (%)
Educational Services	0	0.00	0.0
Employee Retirement[1]	5,999	13.21	1.4
Environment/Housing	95,817	210.99	23.0
Government Administration	15,699	34.57	3.8
Interest on General Debt	26,096	57.46	6.3
Public Safety	118,585	261.12	28.4
Social Services	1,125	2.48	0.3
Transportation	77,538	170.74	18.6
Utility/Liquor Store	49,109	108.14	11.8
Other	26,919	59.28	6.5

Note: (1) Payments to beneficiaries including withdrawal of contributions.
Source: U.S. Bureau of the Census, City Government Finances: 1991-92

Municipal Bond Ratings

Area	Moody's	S & P
Oklahoma City	Aa2	n/a

Note: n/a not available; n/r not rated
Source: Moody's Bond Record, 6/99

POPULATION

Population Growth

Area	1980	1990	% Chg. 1980-90	July 1998 Estimate	% Chg. 1990-98
City	403,243	444,730	10.3	472,221	6.2
MSA[1]	860,969	958,839	11.4	1,049,263	9.4
U.S.	226,545,805	248,765,170	9.8	270,299,000	8.7

Note: (1) Metropolitan Statistical Area - see Appendix A for areas included;
July 1998 MSA population estimate was calculated by the editors
Source: 1980/1990 Census of Housing and Population, Summary Tape File 3C;
Census Bureau Population Estimates 1998

Population Characteristics

Race	City 1980 Population	%	City 1990 Population	%	% Chg. 1980-90	MSA[1] 1990 Population	%
White	323,665	80.3	333,108	74.9	2.9	779,187	81.3
Black	58,550	14.5	70,887	15.9	21.1	100,587	10.5
Amer Indian/Esk/Aleut	11,199	2.8	19,099	4.3	70.5	46,111	4.8
Asian/Pacific Islander	4,610	1.1	10,182	2.3	120.9	16,867	1.8
Other	5,219	1.3	11,454	2.6	119.5	16,087	1.7
Hispanic Origin[2]	11,295	2.8	21,148	4.8	87.2	32,851	3.4

Note: (1) Metropolitan Statistical Area - see Appendix A for areas included;
(2) people of Hispanic origin can be of any race
Source: 1980/1990 Census of Housing and Population, Summary Tape File 3C

Ancestry

Area	German	Irish	English	Italian	U.S.	French	Polish	Dutch
City	21.9	18.8	14.2	1.6	6.4	3.8	1.1	3.9
MSA[1]	24.0	20.3	15.1	1.6	7.0	4.1	1.2	4.2
U.S.	23.3	15.6	13.1	5.9	5.3	4.2	3.8	2.5

Note: Figures are percentages and include persons that reported multiple ancestry (eg. if a person reported being Irish and Italian, they were included in both columns); (1) Metropolitan Statistical Area - see Appendix A for areas included
Source: 1990 Census of Population and Housing, Summary Tape File 3C

Age

Area	Median Age (Years)	Under 5	Under 18	18-24	25-44	45-64	65+	80+
City	32.3	7.7	25.9	9.9	33.8	18.6	11.8	2.6
MSA[1]	31.9	7.4	26.5	10.8	33.3	18.4	11.0	2.5
U.S.	32.9	7.3	25.6	10.5	32.6	18.7	12.5	2.8

Note: (1) Metropolitan Statistical Area - see Appendix A for areas included
Source: 1990 Census of Population and Housing, Summary Tape File 3C

Male/Female Ratio

Area	Number of males per 100 females (all ages)	Number of males per 100 females (18 years old+)
City	93.3	89.5
MSA[1]	95.0	91.3
U.S.	95.0	91.9

Note: (1) Metropolitan Statistical Area - see Appendix A for areas included
Source: 1990 Census of Population, General Population Characteristics

INCOME

Per Capita/Median/Average Income

Area	Per Capita ($)	Median Household ($)	Average Household ($)
City	13,528	25,741	33,258
MSA[1]	13,269	26,883	34,117
U.S.	14,420	30,056	38,453

Note: All figures are for 1989; (1) Metropolitan Statistical Area - see Appendix A for areas included
Source: 1990 Census of Population and Housing, Summary Tape File 3C

Household Income Distribution by Race

Income ($)	City (%)					U.S. (%)				
	Total	White	Black	Other	Hisp.[1]	Total	White	Black	Other	Hisp.[1]
Less than 5,000	6.9	5.4	13.7	10.6	6.8	6.2	4.8	15.2	8.6	8.8
5,000 - 9,999	10.6	9.4	16.9	11.1	14.7	9.3	8.6	14.2	9.9	11.1
10,000 - 14,999	10.4	10.0	12.2	12.3	14.5	8.8	8.5	11.0	9.8	11.0
15,000 - 24,999	20.7	20.4	21.0	23.6	26.2	17.5	17.3	18.9	18.5	20.5
25,000 - 34,999	16.9	17.2	15.3	16.2	17.1	15.8	16.1	14.2	15.4	16.4
35,000 - 49,999	16.1	17.0	11.9	13.9	12.3	17.9	18.6	13.3	16.1	16.0
50,000 - 74,999	12.3	13.5	7.3	9.2	5.7	15.0	15.8	9.3	13.4	11.1
75,000 - 99,999	3.3	3.8	1.2	2.1	1.2	5.1	5.5	2.6	4.7	3.1
100,000+	2.8	3.4	0.5	1.1	1.5	4.4	4.8	1.3	3.7	1.9

Note: All figures are for 1989; (1) people of Hispanic origin can be of any race
Source: 1990 Census of Population and Housing, Summary Tape File 3C

Effective Buying Income

Area	Per Capita ($)	Median Household ($)	Average Household ($)
City	15,021	29,270	37,548
MSA[1]	15,673	31,017	40,876
U.S.	16,803	34,536	45,243

Note: Data as of 1/1/99; (1) Metropolitan Statistical Area - see Appendix A for areas included
Source: Standard Rate & Data Service, Newspaper Advertising Source, 9/99

Effective Household Buying Income Distribution

Area	% of Households Earning						
	$10,000 -$19,999	$20,000 -$34,999	$35,000 -$49,999	$50,000 -$74,999	$75,000 -$99,000	$100,000 -$124,999	$125,000 and up
City	19.1	25.8	17.4	15.5	5.0	1.5	1.7
MSA[1]	18.0	25.1	18.2	17.0	5.5	1.6	1.7
U.S.	16.0	22.6	18.2	18.9	7.2	2.4	2.7

Note: Data as of 1/1/99; (1) Metropolitan Statistical Area - see Appendix A for areas included
Source: Standard Rate & Data Service, Newspaper Advertising Source, 9/99

Poverty Rates by Race and Age

Area	Total (%)	By Race (%)				By Age (%)		
		White	Black	Other	Hisp.[2]	Under 5 years old	Under 18 years old	65 years and over
City	15.9	11.2	32.4	25.6	30.7	27.4	22.9	13.1
MSA[1]	13.9	10.8	30.8	24.1	26.6	22.8	18.6	13.1
U.S.	13.1	9.8	29.5	23.1	25.3	20.1	18.3	12.8

Note: Figures show the percent of people living below the poverty line in 1989. The average poverty
threshold was $12,674 for a family of four in 1989; (1) Metropolitan Statistical Area - see Appendix A
for areas included; (2) people of Hispanic origin can be of any race
Source: 1990 Census of Population and Housing, Summary Tape File 3C

EMPLOYMENT

Labor Force and Employment

Area	Civilian Labor Force			Workers Employed		
	Jun. 1998	Jun. 1999	% Chg.	Jun. 1998	Jun. 1999	% Chg.
City	245,638	250,635	2.0	235,425	242,981	3.2
MSA[1]	533,628	544,617	2.1	512,767	529,228	3.2
U.S.	138,798,000	140,666,000	1.3	132,265,000	134,395,000	1.6

Note: Data is not seasonally adjusted and covers workers 16 years of age and older;
(1) Metropolitan Statistical Area - see Appendix A for areas included
Source: Bureau of Labor Statistics, http://stats.bls.gov

Unemployment Rate

Area	1998						1999					
	Jul.	Aug.	Sep.	Oct.	Nov.	Dec.	Jan.	Feb.	Mar.	Apr.	May.	Jun.
City	5.6	3.7	3.9	3.8	3.4	3.4	3.5	3.7	3.5	3.3	3.1	3.1
MSA[1]	5.2	3.5	3.7	3.6	3.2	3.2	3.3	3.4	3.2	3.0	2.8	2.8
U.S.	4.7	4.5	4.4	4.2	4.1	4.0	4.8	4.7	4.4	4.1	4.0	4.5

Note: Data is not seasonally adjusted and covers workers 16 years of age and older; all figures are percentages; (1) Metropolitan Statistical Area - see Appendix A for areas included
Source: Bureau of Labor Statistics, http://stats.bls.gov

Employment by Industry

Sector	MSA[1]		U.S.
	Number of Employees	Percent of Total	Percent of Total
Services	161,900	30.8	30.4
Retail Trade	98,000	18.6	17.7
Government	102,900	19.5	15.6
Manufacturing	55,000	10.4	14.3
Finance/Insurance/Real Estate	31,100	5.9	5.9
Wholesale Trade	26,000	4.9	5.4
Transportation/Public Utilities	24,600	4.7	5.3
Construction	20,300	3.9	5.0
Mining	6,700	1.3	0.4

Note: Figures cover non-farm employment as of 6/99 and are not seasonally adjusted;
(1) Metropolitan Statistical Area - see Appendix A for areas included
Source: Bureau of Labor Statistics, http://stats.bls.gov

Employment by Occupation

Occupation Category	City (%)	MSA[1] (%)	U.S. (%)
White Collar	61.7	60.9	58.1
Executive/Admin./Management	12.9	12.7	12.3
Professional	13.4	13.9	14.1
Technical & Related Support	4.4	4.2	3.7
Sales	13.6	12.7	11.8
Administrative Support/Clerical	17.5	17.4	16.3
Blue Collar	23.2	23.8	26.2
Precision Production/Craft/Repair	10.0	10.8	11.3
Machine Operators/Assem./Insp.	5.8	5.6	6.8
Transportation/Material Movers	3.8	4.0	4.1
Cleaners/Helpers/Laborers	3.6	3.4	3.9
Services	13.9	13.7	13.2
Farming/Forestry/Fishing	1.2	1.5	2.5

Note: Figures cover employed persons 16 years old and over;
(1) Metropolitan Statistical Area - see Appendix A for areas included
Source: 1990 Census of Population and Housing, Summary Tape File 3C

Occupational Employment Projections: 1996 - 2006

Occupations Expected to Have the Largest Job Growth (ranked by numerical growth)	Fast-Growing Occupations[1] (ranked by percent growth)
1. Nursing aides/orderlies/attendants	1. Home health aides
2. Salespersons, retail	2. Physical therapy assistants and aides
3. General managers & top executives	3. Systems analysts
4. Teachers, secondary school	4. Database administrators
5. Cashiers	5. Medical assistants
6. Registered nurses	6. Physical therapists
7. Truck drivers, light	7. Personal and home care aides
8. Teachers aides, clerical & paraprofess.	8. Paralegals
9. Systems analysts	9. Data processing equipment repairers
10. Waiters & waitresses	10. Teachers, special education

Note: Projections cover Oklahoma; (1) Excludes occupations with total job growth less than 300
Source: U.S. Department of Labor, Employment and Training Administration, America's Labor Market Information System (ALMIS)

TAXES

Major State and Local Tax Rates

State Corp. Income (%)	State Personal Income (%)	Residential Property (effective rate per $100)	Sales & Use		State Gasoline (cents/ gallon)	State Cigarette (cents/ pack)
			State (%)	Local (%)		
6.0	0.5 - 6.75[a]	1.13	4.5	3.875	17.0[b]	23.0

Note: Personal/corporate income, sales, gasoline and cigarette tax rates as of January 1999.
Property tax rates as of 1997; (a) Range is for persons not deducting federal income tax. Separate schedules, with rates ranging from 0.5% to 10%, apply to taxpayers deducting federal income taxes; (b) Rate is comprised of 16 cents excise and 1 cent motor carrier tax
Source: Federation of Tax Administrators, www.taxadmin.org; Washington D.C. Department of Finance and Revenue, Tax Rates and Tax Burdens in the District of Columbia: A Nationwide Comparison, July 1998; Chamber of Commerce, 1999

Total Taxes Per Capita and as a Percent of Income

Area	Per Capita Income ($)	Per Capita Taxes ($)			Percent of Income (%)		
		Total	Federal	State/ Local	Total	Federal	State/ Local
Oklahoma	22,153	7,152	4,787	2,365	32.3	21.6	10.7
U.S.	27,876	9,881	6,690	3,191	35.4	24.0	11.4

Note: Figures are for 1998
Source: Tax Foundation, www.taxfoundation.org

Estimated Tax Burden

Area	State Income	Local Income	Property	Sales	Total
Oklahoma City	3,102	0	2,750	1,252	7,104

Note: The numbers are estimates of taxes paid by a married couple with two children and annual earnings of $75,000. Sales tax estimates assume they spend average amounts on food, clothing, household goods and gasoline. Property tax estimates assume they live in a $250,000 home.
Source: Kiplinger's Personal Finance Magazine, October 1998

**COMMERCIAL
REAL ESTATE**

Office Market

Class/ Location	Total Space (sq. ft.)	Vacant Space (sq. ft.)	Vac. Rate (%)	Under Constr. (sq. ft.)	Net Absorp. (sq. ft.)	Rental Rates ($/sq.ft./yr.)
Class A						
CBD	3,450,000	869,000	25.2	n/a	-172,500	10.00-14.50
Outside CBD	5,200,000	325,000	6.3	n/a	85,000	11.50-18.00
Class B						
CBD	1,950,000	745,000	38.2	n/a	32,000	7.50-10.00
Outside CBD	3,425,000	385,000	11.2	n/a	12,500	7.50-11.50

Note: Data as of 10/98 and covers Oklahoma City; CBD = Central Business District; n/a not available; Source: Society of Industrial and Office Realtors, 1999 Comparative Statistics of Industrial and Office Real Estate Markets

"The demand for downtown Oklahoma City space is beginning to grow. Major expenditures are being made to enhance the CBD, including a new ballpark, canal, library, arena, and remodeled music hall. This $350 to $400 million project, which is about half completed, should help revitalize the city's downtown office market. Rental rates in suburban areas approaching $18 per sq. ft. open the possibility of new speculative office construction there as well. Anticipated job growth for the Oklahoma City market over the next three years is about two percent annually, or about 11,000 jobs per year. Our SIOR reporter expects a one to five percent increase in rental rates, absorption, construction, and sales prices during 1999. Vacancy should decline by the same amount." *Society of Industrial and Office Realtors, 1999 Comparative Statistics of Industrial and Office Real Estate Markets*

Industrial Market

Location	Total Space (sq. ft.)	Vacant Space (sq. ft.)	Vac. Rate (%)	Under Constr. (sq. ft.)	Net Absorp. (sq. ft.)	Gross Lease ($/sq.ft./yr.)
Central City	n/a	n/a	n/a	n/a	n/a	n/a
Suburban	72,000,000	2,600,000	3.6	1,600,000	4,400,000	2.00-6.00

*Note: Data as of 10/98 and covers Oklahoma City; n/a not available
Source: Society of Industrial and Office Realtors, 1999 Comparative Statistics of Industrial and Office Real Estate Markets*

"Oklahoma City has a moderate to substantial shortage of all types of industrial space. One problem has been low lease prices which have not supported new construction. During 1999 that barrier should be overcome for the warehouse/distribution market. Our SIOR reporter anticipates an increase of 11 to 15 percent for lease prices and a six to 10 percent increase in the amount of bulk warehouse space built. A total of about two million sq. ft. of industrial space will likely be constructed citywide in 1999. Although the demand for space will be strong, lenders still require leases before construction in most cases. The Edmond market will be very strong in 1999. Once a sleepy, residential community with little office or industrial space, many executives who live in the area are locating businesses there. Oklahoma City's southwest industrial market will also be vibrant." *Society of Industrial and Office Realtors, 1999 Comparative Statistics of Industrial and Office Real Estate Markets*

Retail Market

Shopping Center Inventory (sq. ft.)	Shopping Center Construction (sq. ft.)	Construction as a Percent of Inventory (%)	Torto Wheaton Rent Index[1] ($/sq. ft.)
23,933,000	252,000	1.1	9.06

*Note: Data as of 1997 and covers the Metropolitan Statistical Area - see Appendix A for areas included; (1) Index is based on a model that predicts what the average rent should be for leases with certain characteristics, in certain locations during certain years.
Source: National Association of Realtors, 1997-1998 Market Conditions Report*

"During the 1990s, Oklahoma City worked diligently to diversify its economy. Increased diversity has contributed to strong payroll growth in recent years. However, relatively low wage rates are a burden on the retail trade sector. The area's retail rent index has steadily increased over the last two years, edging up 3.4% in 1996 and 4.0% in 1997. Rents still remain well below the South's average of $13.79 per square foot. Oklahoma City's retail market is expected to remain stable in the near future, with upward rent movement. America On-Line and Southwest Airlines have announced plans that will bring an estimated 2,100 jobs to the area." *National Association of Realtors, 1997-1998 Market Conditions Report*

COMMERCIAL UTILITIES

Typical Monthly Electric Bills

Area	Commercial Service ($/month)		Industrial Service ($/month)	
	12 kW demand 1,500 kWh	100 kW demand 30,000 kWh	1,000 kW demand 400,000 kWh	20,000 kW demand 10,000,000 kWh
City	126	1,523	16,770	232,351
U.S.	150	2,174	23,995	508,569

Note: Based on rates in effect January 1, 1999
Source: Edison Electric Institute, Typical Residential, Commercial and Industrial Bills, Winter 1999

TRANSPORTATION

Transportation Statistics

Average minutes to work	19.3
Interstate highways	I-35; I-40; I-44;
Bus lines	
In-city	Metro Transit, 88 vehicles
Inter-city	2
Passenger air service	
Airport	Will Rogers World Airport
Airlines	11
Aircraft departures	30,710 (1996)
Enplaned passengers	1,742,844 (1996)
Rail service	No Amtrak Service
Motor freight carriers	32 regular routes; 170+ irregular
Major waterways/ports	None

Source: Editor & Publisher Market Guide, 1999; FAA Airport Activity Statistics, 1997; Amtrak National Time Table, Northeast Timetable, Spring/Summer 1999; 1990 Census of Population and Housing, STF 3C; Chamber of Commerce/Economic Development 1999; Jane's Urban Transport Systems 1999-2000

Means of Transportation to Work

Area	Car/Truck/Van		Public Transportation			Bicycle	Walked	Other Means	Worked at Home
	Drove Alone	Car-pooled	Bus	Subway	Railroad				
City	80.8	12.8	0.8	0.0	0.0	0.1	2.0	1.2	2.3
MSA[1]	80.3	13.3	0.5	0.0	0.0	0.2	2.1	1.0	2.5
U.S.	73.2	13.4	3.0	1.5	0.5	0.4	3.9	1.2	3.0

Note: Figures shown are percentages and only include workers 16 years old and over;
(1) Metropolitan Statistical Area - see Appendix A for areas included
Source: 1990 Census of Population and Housing, Summary Tape File 3C

BUSINESSES

Major Business Headquarters

Company Name	1999 Rankings	
	Fortune 500	Forbes 500
Fleming	101	-

Note: Companies listed are located in the city; dashes indicate no ranking
Fortune 500: Companies that produce a 10-K are ranked 1 to 500 based on 1998 revenue
Forbes 500: Private companies are ranked 1 to 500 based on 1997 revenue
Source: Forbes, November 30, 1998; Fortune, April 26, 1999

Fast-Growing Businesses

According to *Inc.*, Oklahoma City is home to two of America's 100 fastest-growing private companies: Accord Human Resources and DataCom Sciences. Criteria for inclusion: must be an independent, privately-held, U.S. corporation, proprietorship or partnership; sales of at least $200,000 in 1995; five-year operating/sales history; increase in 1999 sales over 1998 sales; holding companies, regulated banks, and utilities were excluded. *Inc. 500, 1999*

Women-Owned Firms: Number, Employment and Sales

Area	Number of Firms	Employ-ment	Sales ($000)	Rank[2]
MSA[1]	40,200	92,100	11,219,500	47

Note: (1) Metropolitan Statistical Area - see Appendix A for areas included;
(2) Calculated on an averaging of the number of businesses, employment and sales
Source: The National Foundation for Women Business Owners, 1999 Facts on Women-Owned Businesses: Trends in the Top 50 Metropolitan Areas

Women-Owned Firms: Growth

Area	% change from 1992 to 1999			Rank[2]
	Number of Firms	Employ-ment	Sales	
MSA[1]	33.1	100.6	130.2	42

Note: (1) Metropolitan Statistical Area - see Appendix A for areas included; (2) Calculated on an averaging of the percent growth of number of businesses, employment and sales
Source: The National Foundation for Women Business Owners, 1999 Facts on Women-Owned Businesses: Trends in the Top 50 Metropolitan Areas

Minority Business Opportunity

Two of the 500 largest Hispanic-owned companies in the U.S. are located in Oklahoma City. *Hispanic Business, June 1999*

Small Business Opportunity

According to *Forbes*, Oklahoma City is home to one of America's 200 best small companies: Sonic. Criteria: companies included must be publicly traded since November 1997 with a stock price of at least $5 per share and an average daily float of 1,000 shares. The company's latest 12-month sales must be between $5 and $350 million, return on equity (ROE) must be a minimum of 12% for both the past 5 years and the most recent four quarters, and five-year sales and EPS growth must average at least 10%. Companies with declining sales or earnings during the past year were dropped as well as businesses with debt/equity ratios over 1.25. Companies with negative operating cash flow in each of the past two years were also excluded. *Forbes, November 2, 1998*

HOTELS & MOTELS

Hotels/Motels

Area	Hotels/Motels	Rooms	Luxury-Level Hotels/Motels		Average Minimum Rates ($)		
			♦♦♦♦	♦♦♦♦♦	♦♦	♦♦♦	♦♦♦♦
City	42	5,744	1	0	52	85	149
Airport	11	1,521	0	0	n/a	n/a	n/a
Suburbs	24	2,006	0	0	n/a	n/a	n/a
Total	77	9,271	1	0	n/a	n/a	n/a

Note: n/a not available; classifications range from one diamond (budget properties with basic amenities) to five diamond (luxury properties with the finest service, rooms and facilities).
Source: OAG, Business Travel Planner, Winter 1998-99

CONVENTION CENTERS

Major Convention Centers

Center Name	Meeting Rooms	Exhibit Space (sq. ft.)
Civic Center Music Hall	4	3,500
Myriad Convention Center	24	275,000
State Fair Parks of Oklahoma	n/a	900,000
Will Rogers Center	1	6,000

Note: n/a not available
Source: Trade Shows Worldwide, 1998; Meetings & Conventions, 4/15/99;
Sucessful Meetings, 3/31/98

Living Environment

COST OF LIVING

Cost of Living Index

Composite Index	Groceries	Housing	Utilities	Trans-portation	Health Care	Misc. Goods/ Services
92.2	94.5	80.0	98.2	94.2	92.3	99.4

Note: U.S. = 100
Source: ACCRA, Cost of Living Index, 1st Quarter 1999

HOUSING

Median Home Prices and Housing Affordability

Area	Median Price[2] 1st Qtr. 1999 ($)	HOI[3] 1st Qtr. 1999	Afford-ability Rank[4]
MSA[1]	85,000	81.0	44
U.S.	134,000	69.6	—

Note: (1) Metropolitan Statistical Area - see Appendix A for areas included; (2) U.S. figures calculated from the sales of 524,324 new and existing homes in 181 markets; (3) Housing Opportunity Index - percent of homes sold that were within the reach of the median income household at the prevailing mortgage interest rate; (4) Rank is from 1-181 with 1 being most affordable
Source: National Association of Home Builders, Housing Opportunity Index, 1st Quarter 1999

Median Home Price Projection

It is projected that the median price of existing single-family homes in the metro area will increase by 2.0% in 1999. Nationwide, home prices are projected to increase 3.8%.
Kiplinger's Personal Finance Magazine, January 1999

Average New Home Price

Area	Price ($)
City	109,500
U.S.	142,735

Note: Figures are based on a new home with 1,800 sq. ft. of living area on an 8,000 sq. ft. lot.
Source: ACCRA, Cost of Living Index, 1st Quarter 1999

Average Apartment Rent

Area	Rent ($/mth)
City	537
U.S.	601

Note: Figures are based on an unfurnished two bedroom, 1-1/2 or 2 bath apartment, approximately 950 sq. ft. in size, excluding all utilities except water
Source: ACCRA, Cost of Living Index, 1st Quarter 1999

RESIDENTIAL UTILITIES

Average Residential Utility Costs

Area	All Electric ($/mth)	Part Electric ($/mth)	Other Energy ($/mth)	Phone ($/mth)
City	—	60.79	35.77	20.58
U.S.	100.02	55.73	43.33	19.71

Source: ACCRA, Cost of Living Index, 1st Quarter 1999

HEALTH CARE

Average Health Care Costs

Area	Hospital ($/day)	Doctor ($/visit)	Dentist ($/visit)
City	305.94	46.25	69.50
U.S.	430.43	52.45	66.35

Note: Hospital—based on a semi-private room; Doctor—based on a general practitioner's routine exam of an established patient; Dentist—based on adult teeth cleaning and periodic oral exam.
Source: ACCRA, Cost of Living Index, 1st Quarter 1999

Distribution of Office-Based Physicians

Area	Family/Gen. Practitioners	Specialists		
		Medical	Surgical	Other
MSA[1]	244	542	482	530

Note: Data as of 12/31/97; (1) Metropolitan Statistical Area - see Appendix A for areas included
Source: American Medical Assn., Physician Characteristics & Distribution in the U.S., 1999

Hospitals

Oklahoma City has 1 general medical and surgical hospital, 1 psychiatric, 1 rehabilitation, 1 orthopedic. AHA Guide to the Healthcare Field, 1998-99

EDUCATION

Public School District Statistics

District Name	Num. Sch.	Enroll.	Classroom Teachers	Pupils per Teacher	Minority Pupils (%)	Current Exp.[1] ($/pupil)
Crooked Oak	4	864	63	13.7	n/a	n/a
Crutcho	1	384	33	11.6	n/a	n/a
Moore	27	18,297	1,151	15.9	n/a	n/a
Oklahoma City	88	39,300	2,441	16.1	n/a	n/a
Western Heights	6	3,185	201	15.8	n/a	n/a

Note: Data covers the 1997-1998 school year unless otherwise noted; (1) Data covers fiscal year 1996; SD = School District; ISD = Independent School District; n/a not available
Source: National Center for Education Statistics, Common Core of Data Public Education Agency Universe 1997-98; National Center for Education Statistics, Characteristics of the 100 Largest Public Elementary and Secondary School Districts in the United States: 1997-98, July 1999

Educational Quality

School District	Education Quotient[1]	Graduate Outcome[2]	Community Index[3]	Resource Index[4]
Oklahoma City SD	75.0	68.0	107.0	81.0

Note: Nearly 1,000 secondary school districts were rated in terms of educational quality. The scores range from a low of 50 to a high of 150; (1) Average of the Graduate Outcome, Community and Resource indexes; (2) Based on graduation rates and college board scores (SAT/ACT); (3) Based on the surrounding community's average level of education and the area's average income level; (4) Based on teacher salaries, per-pupil expenditures and student-teacher ratios.
Source: Expansion Management, Ratings Issue, 1998

Educational Attainment by Race

Area	High School Graduate (%)					Bachelor's Degree (%)				
	Total	White	Black	Other	Hisp.[2]	Total	White	Black	Other	Hisp.[2]
City	78.2	80.8	72.6	61.9	47.5	21.6	23.7	12.9	14.9	10.3
MSA[1]	79.2	80.6	74.5	68.5	55.3	21.6	22.7	14.2	17.7	11.1
U.S.	75.2	77.9	63.1	60.4	49.8	20.3	21.5	11.4	19.4	9.2

Note: Figures shown cover persons 25 years old and over; (1) Metropolitan Statistical Area - see Appendix A for areas included; (2) people of Hispanic origin can be of any race
Source: 1990 Census of Population and Housing, Summary Tape File 3C

School Enrollment by Type

Area	Preprimary				Elementary/High School			
	Public		Private		Public		Private	
	Enrollment	%	Enrollment	%	Enrollment	%	Enrollment	%
City	4,639	60.5	3,033	39.5	66,351	90.3	7,166	9.7
MSA[1]	10,338	60.2	6,849	39.8	156,353	92.8	12,146	7.2
U.S.	2,679,029	59.5	1,824,256	40.5	38,379,689	90.2	4,187,099	9.8

Note: Figures shown cover persons 3 years old and over;
(1) Metropolitan Statistical Area - see Appendix A for areas included
Source: 1990 Census of Population and Housing, Summary Tape File 3C

School Enrollment by Race

Area	Preprimary (%)				Elementary/High School (%)			
	White	Black	Other	Hisp.[1]	White	Black	Other	Hisp.[1]
City	72.4	18.2	9.4	5.7	65.7	21.8	12.5	7.3
MSA[2]	79.1	12.1	8.8	4.3	75.6	13.7	10.7	4.9
U.S.	80.4	12.5	7.1	7.8	74.1	15.6	10.3	12.5

Note: Figures shown cover persons 3 years old and over; (1) people of Hispanic origin can be of any race; (2) Metropolitan Statistical Area - see Appendix A for areas included
Source: 1990 Census of Population and Housing, Summary Tape File 3C

Classroom Teacher Salaries in Public Schools

District	B.A. Degree		M.A. Degree		Maximum	
	Min. ($)	Rank[1]	Max. ($)	Rank[1]	Max. ($)	Rank[1]
Oklahoma City	23,170	87	34,050	98	35,200	99
Average	26,980	-	46,065	-	51,435	-

Note: Salaries are for 1997-1998; (1) Rank ranges from 1 to 100
Source: American Federation of Teachers, Survey & Analysis of Salary Trends, 1998

Higher Education

Two-Year Colleges		Four-Year Colleges		Medical Schools	Law Schools	Voc/Tech
Public	Private	Public	Private			
2	0	1	3	1	1	13

Source: College Blue Book, Occupational Education, 1997; Medical School Admission Requirements, 1999-2000; Peterson's Guide to Two-Year Colleges, 1999; Peterson's Guide to Four-Year Colleges, 2000; Barron's Guide to Law Schools, 1999

MAJOR EMPLOYERS

Major Employers

Visionquest Marketing Service
Mercy Health Center
Kerr-McGee (chemicals)
CMI Corp. (construction machinery)
American Fidelity Corp. (insurance)

St. Anthony Health Care Corp.
Unit Parts Co. (electrical equip.)
Integris Southwest Medical Center
Amerivision Communications
SSM Healthcare of Oklahoma

Note: Companies listed are located in the city
Source: Dun's Business Rankings, 1999; Ward's Business Directory, 1998

PUBLIC SAFETY

Crime Rate

Area	All Crimes	Violent Crimes				Property Crimes		
		Murder	Forcible Rape	Robbery	Aggrav. Assault	Burglary	Larceny -Theft	Motor Vehicle Theft
City	11,655.6	12.5	86.6	295.9	677.9	2,071.4	7,547.6	963.7
Suburbs[1]	4,720.1	3.4	38.6	69.3	228.1	983.3	3,065.3	332.1
MSA[2]	7,910.7	7.6	60.7	173.6	435.0	1,483.8	5,127.3	622.6
U.S.	4,922.7	6.8	35.9	186.1	382.0	919.6	2,886.5	505.8

Note: Crime rate is the number of crimes per 100,000 pop.; (1) defined as all areas within the MSA but located outside the central city; (2) Metropolitan Statistical Area - see Appendix A for areas incl.
Source: FBI Uniform Crime Reports, 1997

RECREATION

Culture and Recreation

Museums	Symphony Orchestras	Opera Companies	Dance Companies	Professional Theatres	Zoos	Pro Sports Teams
9	1	1	2	1	1	0

Source: International Directory of the Performing Arts, 1997; Official Museum Directory, 1999; Stern's Performing Arts Directory, 1997; USA Today Four Sport Stadium Guide, 1997; Chamber of Commerce/Economic Development, 1999

Library System

The Metropolitan Library System in Oklahoma County has 12 branches, holdings of 785,590 volumes, and a budget of $10,766,409 (1995-1996). *American Library Directory, 1998-1999*

MEDIA

Newspapers

Name	Type	Freq.	Distribution	Circulation
Black Chronicle	Black	1x/wk	U.S.	29,803
The Capitol Hill Beacon	General	1x/wk	Local	1,400
The Daily Oklahoman	General	7x/wk	State	210,145
El Nacional	Hispanic	2x/mo	Local	10,750
The Journal Record	General	5x/wk	State	4,100
Metro Buyer's Guide	General	1x/wk	Local	350,000
Tinker Take Off	General	1x/wk	Local	28,600

Note: Includes newspapers with circulations of 1,000 or more located in the city;
Source: Burrelle's Media Directory, 1999 Edition

Television Stations

Name	Ch.	Affiliation	Type	Owner
KOET	n/a	PBS	Public	Oklahoma Educational Television Authority
KFOR	n/a	NBCT	Commercial	New York Times Company
KOCO	n/a	ABCT	Commercial	Hearst-Argyle Broadcasting
KWTV	n/a	CBST	Commercial	Griffin Television Inc.
KWET	12	n/a	Public	Oklahoma Educational Television Authority
KETA	13	PBS	Public	Oklahoma Educational Television Authority
KTBO	14	n/a	Commercial	Trinity Broadcasting Network
KOKH	25	FBC	Commercial	Sullivan Broadcasting
KOCB	34	WB	Commercial	Sinclair Communications Inc.
KPSG	43	PBS	Commercial	Oklahoma Educational Television Authority
KSBI	52	n/a	Commercial	Locke Supply Company
KOPX	62	PAXTV	n/a	Paxson Communications Corporation

Note: Stations included broadcast in the Oklahoma City metro area; n/a not available
Source: Burrelle's Media Directory, 1999 Edition

AM Radio Stations

Call Letters	Freq. (kHz)	Target Audience	Station Format	Music Format
KQCV	800	Religious	T	n/a
KBYE	890	Religious	M	Christian
WKY	930	General	M/T	Christian
KTOK	1000	General	N/S/T	n/a
KVSP	1140	Black	M	R&B/Urban Contemporary
KTLV	1220	B/R	T	n/a
KXXY	1340	B/C/H/M	M/S/T	Latin/R&B
KOMA	1520	General	M	Oldies

Note: Stations included broadcast in the Oklahoma City metro area; n/a not available
Target Audience: A=Asian; B=Black; C=Christian; E=Ethnic; F=French; G=General; H=Hispanic;
M=Men; N=Native American; R=Religious; S=Senior Citizen; W=Women; Y=Young Adult; Z=Children
Station Format: E=Educational; M=Music; N=News; S=Sports; T=Talk
Source: Burrelle's Media Directory, 1999 Edition

FM Radio Stations

Call Letters	Freq. (mHz)	Target Audience	Station Format	Music Format
KOCC	88.9	General	M/S	Adult Contemporary/Christian/Country
KCSC	90.1	General	M/N	Classical
KOKF	90.9	General	M	Alternative/Christian/Urban Contemporary
KOMA	92.5	n/a	M/N/S	Oldies
KQSR	94.7	General	M	Alternative
KXXY	96.1	General	M/N	Country
KTNT	97.9	General	M	Adult Contemporary
KYIS	98.9	General	M/N/S	Adult Contemporary
KATT	100.5	General	M	AOR
KTST	101.9	General	M	Country
KJYO	102.7	General	M	n/a
KMGL	104.1	General	M	Adult Contemporary
KNTL	104.9	Religious	T	n/a
KRXO	107.7	General	M	Classic Rock

Note: Stations included broadcast in the Oklahoma City metro area; n/a not available
Station Format: E=Educational; M=Music; N=News; S=Sports; T=Talk
Target Audience: A=Asian; B=Black; C=Christian; E=Ethnic; F=French; G=General; H=Hispanic; M=Men; N=Native American; R=Religious; S=Senior Citizen; W=Women; Y=Young Adult; Z=Children
Music Format: AOR=Album Oriented Rock; MOR=Middle-of-the-Road
Source: Burrelle's Media Directory, 1999 Edition

CLIMATE

Average and Extreme Temperatures

Temperature	Jan	Feb	Mar	Apr	May	Jun	Jul	Aug	Sep	Oct	Nov	Dec	Yr.
Extreme High (°F)	80	84	93	100	104	105	109	110	104	96	87	86	110
Average High (°F)	47	52	61	72	79	87	93	92	84	74	60	50	71
Average Temp. (°F)	36	41	50	60	69	77	82	81	73	62	49	40	60
Average Low (°F)	26	30	38	49	58	66	71	70	62	51	38	29	49
Extreme Low (°F)	-4	-3	1	20	32	47	53	51	36	22	11	-8	-8

Note: Figures cover the years 1948-1990
Source: National Climatic Data Center, International Station Meteorological Climate Summary, 3/95

Average Precipitation/Snowfall/Humidity

Precip./Humidity	Jan	Feb	Mar	Apr	May	Jun	Jul	Aug	Sep	Oct	Nov	Dec	Yr.
Avg. Precip. (in.)	1.2	1.5	2.5	2.8	5.6	4.4	2.8	2.5	3.5	3.1	1.6	1.3	32.8
Avg. Snowfall (in.)	3	3	2	Tr	0	0	0	0	0	Tr	1	2	10
Avg. Rel. Hum. 6am (%)	78	78	76	77	84	84	81	81	82	79	78	77	80
Avg. Rel. Hum. 3pm (%)	53	52	47	46	52	51	46	44	47	46	48	52	49

Note: Figures cover the years 1948-1990; Tr = Trace amounts (<0.05 in. of rain; <0.5 in. of snow)
Source: National Climatic Data Center, International Station Meteorological Climate Summary, 3/95

Weather Conditions

Temperature			Daytime Sky			Precipitation		
10°F & below	32°F & below	90°F & above	Clear	Partly cloudy	Cloudy	0.01 inch or more precip.	0.1 inch or more snow/ice	Thunderstorms
5	79	70	124	131	110	80	8	50

Note: Figures are average number of days per year and covers the years 1948-1990
Source: National Climatic Data Center, International Station Meteorological Climate Summary, 3/95

AIR & WATER QUALITY

Maximum Pollutant Concentrations

	Particulate Matter (ug/m³)	Carbon Monoxide (ppm)	Sulfur Dioxide (ppm)	Nitrogen Dioxide (ppm)	Ozone (ppm)	Lead (ug/m³)
MSA[1] Level	58	5	n/a	0.015	0.10	0.00
NAAQS[2]	150	9	0.140	0.053	0.12	1.50
Met NAAQS?	Yes	Yes	n/a	Yes	Yes	Yes

Note: (1) Metropolitan Statistical Area - see Appendix A for areas included; (2) National Ambient Air Quality Standards; ppm = parts per million; ug/m³ = micrograms per cubic meter; n/a not available
Source: EPA, National Air Quality and Emissions Trends Report, 1997

Pollutant Standards Index

In the Oklahoma City MSA (see Appendix A for areas included), the Pollutant Standards Index (PSI) exceeded 100 on 4 days in 1997. A PSI value greater than 100 indicates that air quality would be in the unhealthful range on that day. *EPA, National Air Quality and Emissions Trends Report, 1997*

Drinking Water

Water System Name	Pop. Served	Primary Water Source Type	Number of Violations in 1998	Type of Violation/ Contaminants
Oklahoma City Draper	276,000	Surface	None	None
Oklahoma City Hefner	276,000	Surface	None	None

Note: Data as of July 10, 1999
Source: EPA, Office of Ground Water and Drinking Water, Safe Drinking Water Information System

Oklahoma City tap water is alkaline, soft and fluoridated.
Editor & Publisher Market Guide, 1999

Omaha, Nebraska

Background

The area now known as Omaha was first inhabited by the Otoe and Omaha Indians. After Thomas Jefferson acquired the area for the United States in the Louisiana Purchase of 1803, the Lewis and Clark expedition traveled through the region. Fort Atkinson was built in 1819 just north of what would become the city, and fur traders set up shop in the immediate area. Mormons, on their great trek from Illinois to the West, stayed in the area for a season in the late 1840s.

In 1854, Congress passed the infamous Kansas-Nebraska Act, which would help lead to the Civil War, making two territories out of the Great Plains. The same year the federal government negotiated a treaty with the Omahas, who gave up most their lands in Nebraska. Whites eagerly poured across the Missouri River from Council Bluff, Iowa, to settle the area. Founded in 1854, Omaha became the territorial capital a year later.

A majority of Nebraskans, who lived south of the Platte River, did not want Omaha to remain the capital, since it was north of the river. Thus, it was decided to move the capital from Omaha to Lincoln when Nebraska became a state in 1867. The reason for creating the territory of Nebraska had been to facilitate the building of a transcontinental railroad, and the Union Pacific Railroad laid the first track westward in Omaha in 1865.

Omaha was in the center of large agricultural region, and by the late nineteenth century, the city gained renown for its meatpacking industry. Cattle, which fed off the grasslands of the Plains, were driven to the slaughterhouses of Omaha. Other agricultural-related businesses that existed and grew in the city were grain storage bins and flourmills.

The city suffered disasters of biblical proportions during the 1890s as it was hit by drought, hordes of grasshoppers, and a national depression. Recovery occurred a few years later, and the city experienced good economic times for nearly thirty years. But then the economy slumped again during the Great Depression.

World War II pulled the nation and Omaha out of hard times. Early in the Cold War, the Strategic Air Command set up its headquarters at Offult Air Force Base, close to the city.

Nowadays, meatpacking is not the dominant industry it once was in the Queen of the Prairie. However, processed food production is still significant, with the presence of the cereal giant Kellogg and the frozen food company Vlasic. Other manufacturing concerns make telephone equipment, machines, and metal and printed goods.

Insurance has long been a mainstay of the local economy. Over twenty such companies, including the famed Mutual of Omaha, have their headquarters in the metropolitan area.

The service industry also makes up a large percentage of the area's businesses. Several telemarketing firms operate out of the city.

With a continental climate, winters can be somewhat frigid, temperatures dipping down to the teens normally, and rising to the upper forties. The summers are warm, with temperatures ranging from the fifties to the eighties. The average rainfall is twenty-nine inches, much of it falling from April through September. Snow also falls at an average of twenty-nine inches per year.

General Rankings and Evaluative Comments

■ Omaha was ranked #11 out of 24 mid-sized, midwestern metropolitan areas in *Money's* 1998 survey of "The Best Places to Live in America." The survey was conducted by first contacting 512 representative households nationwide and asking them to rank 37 quality-of-life factors on a scale of 1 to 10. Next, a demographic profile was compiled on the 300 largest metropolitan statistical areas in the U.S. The numbers were crunched together to arrive at an overall ranking (things Americans consider most important, like clean air and water, low crime and good schools, received extra weight). Unlike previous years, the 1998 rankings were broken down by region (northeast, midwest, south, west) and population size (100,000 to 249,999; 250,000 to 999,999; 1 million plus). The city had a nationwide ranking of #260 out of 300 in 1997 and #216 out of 300 in 1996. *Money, July 1998; Money, July 1997; Money, September 1996*

■ *Ladies Home Journal* ranked America's 200 largest cities based on the qualities women care about most. Omaha ranked #122 out of 200. Criteria: low crime rate, well-paying jobs, quality health and child care, good public schools, the presence of women in government, size of the gender wage gap, number of sexual-harassment and discrimination complaints filed, unemployment and divorce rates, commute times, population density, number of houses of worship, parks and cultural offerings, number of women's health specialists, how well a community's women cared for themselves, complexion kindness index based on UV radiation levels, odds of finding affordable fashions, rental rates for romance movies, champagne sales and other matters of the heart. *Ladies Home Journal, November 1998*

■ Zero Population Growth ranked 229 cities in terms of children's health, safety, and economic well-being. Omaha was ranked #16 out of 112 independent cities (cities with populations greater than 100,000 which were neither Major Cities nor Suburbs/Outer Cities) and was given a grade of B+. Criteria: total population, percent of population under 18 years of age, household language, percent population change, percent of births to teens, infant mortality rate, percent of low birth weights, dropout rate, enrollment in preprimary school, violent and property crime rates, unemployment rate, percent of children in poverty, percent of owner occupied units, number of bad air days, percent of public transportation commuters, and average travel time to work. *Zero Population Growth, Children's Environmental Index, Fall 1999*

■ Cognetics studied 273 metro areas in the United States, ranking them by entrepreneurial activity. Omaha was ranked #33 out of 134 smaller metro areas. Criteria: Significant Starts (firms started in the last 10 years that still employ at least 5 people) and Young Growers (percent of firms 10 years old or less that grew significantly during the last 4 years). *Cognetics, "Entrepreneurial Hot Spots: The Best Places in America to Start and Grow a Company," 1998*

■ Omaha appeared on *Forbes* list of "Best Places for Business Growth." Rank: #13 out of 162 metro areas. Criteria: average wage and salary increases, job growth rates, number of technology clusters (measures business activity in 13 different technology areas), overall concentration of technology activity relative to national average and technology output growth. *Forbes, May 31, 1999*

■ Omaha was selected as one of the "Best American Cities to Start a Business" by *Point of View* magazine. Criteria: coolness, quality-of-life, and business concerns. The city was ranked #34 out of 75. *Point of View, November 1998*

■ Omaha appeared on *Sales & Marketing Management's* list of the "20 Hottest Cities for Selling." Rank: #14 out of 20. *S&MM* editors looked at Metropolitan Statistical Areas with populations of more than 150,000. The areas were ranked based on population increases, retail sales increases, effective buying income, increase in both residential and commercial building permits issued, unemployment rates, job growth, mix of industries, tax rates, number of corporate relocations, and the number of new corporations.
Sales & Marketing Management, April 1999

■ Reliastar Financial Corp. ranked the 125 largest metropolitan areas according to the general financial security of residents. Omaha was ranked #22 out of 125 with a score of 8.0. The score indicates the percentage a metropolitan area is above or below the metropolitan norm. A metro area with a score of 10.6 is 10.6% above the metro average. Criteria: Earnings and Wealth Potential (household income, education, net assets, cost of living); Safety Net (health insurance, retirement savings, life insurance, income support programs); Personal Threats (unemployment rate, low-income households, crime rate); Community Economic Vitality (cost of community services, job quality, job creation, housing costs).
Reliastar Financial Corp., "The Best Cities to Earn and Save Money," 1999 Edition

Business Environment

STATE ECONOMY

State Economic Profile

"After several years of solid growth, the Nebraska economy has begun to slow. Farm income and employment were weak in 1998 and should not recover in 1999. NE's engine of growth in recent years, the business services sector, is no longer adding jobs at its previous pace. With an expected slowdown in the US economy, NE business services will likely add little to employment in 1999. Some strength will remain in Omaha's strong labor market.

A low-cost of doing business and an educated workforce attracted several telemarketing, customer service and data processing firms to Nebraska. For several years employment growth in these sectors averaged over 5%. Business services job growth decelerated in 1998, and with the slowing of the US economy expected in 1999, job growth in NE's business services in 1999 will only be around 2.5%.

Nebraska is one of the nation's most agriculture-dependent states. Weak global demand and over-capacity in US agriculture made 1998 a difficult year for NE's farmers and ranchers. Farm income is down, and the number of farm-related business liquidations is up. Closely related industries, such as farm equipment, are also having considerable difficulty. Beef prices should stabilize in 1999 as cuts in herd size have decreased over-capacity. Pork prices should remain soft in 1999.

Most of the strength in NE's economy is occurring in Omaha. Its economy is much more diversified than the state's as a whole. NE's job growth was twice the state rate in 1998. Its credit card processing sector is currently planning an expansion, as is its high-tech sector. Its major constraint will be its extremely tight labor market." *National Association of Realtors, Economic Profiles: The Fifty States and the District of Columbia, http://nar.realtor.com/databank/profiles.htm*

IMPORTS/EXPORTS

Total Export Sales

Area	1994 ($000)	1995 ($000)	1996 ($000)	1997 ($000)	% Chg. 1994-97	% Chg. 1996-97
MSA[1]	393,250	425,917	608,290	691,431	75.8	13.7
U.S.	512,415,609	583,030,524	622,827,063	687,597,999	34.2	10.4

Note: (1) Metropolitan Statistical Area - see Appendix A for areas included
Source: U.S. Department of Commerce, International Trade Association, Metropolitan Area Exports: An Export Performance Report on Over 250 U.S. Cities, November 10, 1998

CITY FINANCES

City Government Finances

Component	FY92 ($000)	FY92 (per capita $)
Revenue	259,373	737.60
Expenditure	222,291	632.15
Debt Outstanding	194,849	554.11
Cash & Securities	313,688	892.06

Source: U.S. Bureau of the Census, City Government Finances: 1991-92

City Government Revenue by Source

Source	FY92 ($000)	FY92 (per capita $)	FY92 (%)
From Federal Government	4,075	11.59	1.6
From State Governments	27,666	78.68	10.7
From Local Governments	4,210	11.97	1.6
Property Taxes	66,047	187.82	25.5
General Sales Taxes	56,698	161.24	21.9
Selective Sales Taxes	13,111	37.28	5.1
Income Taxes	0	0.00	0.0
Current Charges	39,311	111.79	15.2
Utility/Liquor Store	0	0.00	0.0
Employee Retirement[1]	31,671	90.07	12.2
Other	16,584	47.16	6.4

Note: (1) Excludes "city contributions," classified as "nonrevenue," intragovernmental transfers.
Source: U.S. Bureau of the Census, City Government Finances: 1991-92

City Government Expenditures by Function

Function	FY92 ($000)	FY92 (per capita $)	FY92 (%)
Educational Services	5,870	16.69	2.6
Employee Retirement[1]	13,757	39.12	6.2
Environment/Housing	59,596	169.48	26.8
Government Administration	11,542	32.82	5.2
Interest on General Debt	14,472	41.16	6.5
Public Safety	61,778	175.68	27.8
Social Services	909	2.58	0.4
Transportation	30,816	87.63	13.9
Utility/Liquor Store	0	0.00	0.0
Other	23,551	66.97	10.6

Note: (1) Payments to beneficiaries including withdrawal of contributions.
Source: U.S. Bureau of the Census, City Government Finances: 1991-92

Municipal Bond Ratings

Area	Moody's	S & P
Omaha	n/a	n/a

Note: n/a not available; n/r not rated
Source: Moody's Bond Record, 6/99

POPULATION

Population Growth

Area	1980	1990	% Chg. 1980-90	July 1998 Estimate	% Chg. 1990-98
City	314,267	335,795	6.9	371,291	10.6
MSA[1]	585,122	618,262	5.7	695,738	12.5
U.S.	226,545,805	248,765,170	9.8	270,299,000	8.7

Note: (1) Metropolitan Statistical Area - see Appendix A for areas included;
July 1998 MSA population estimate was calculated by the editors
Source: 1980/1990 Census of Housing and Population, Summary Tape File 3C;
Census Bureau Population Estimates 1998

Population Characteristics

Race	City 1980 Population	%	City 1990 Population	%	% Chg. 1980-90	MSA[1] 1990 Population	%
White	268,995	85.6	281,676	83.9	4.7	550,845	89.1
Black	37,889	12.1	43,829	13.1	15.7	51,036	8.3
Amer Indian/Esk/Aleut	1,839	0.6	2,325	0.7	26.4	3,175	0.5
Asian/Pacific Islander	2,381	0.8	3,602	1.1	51.3	6,890	1.1
Other	3,163	1.0	4,363	1.3	37.9	6,316	1.0
Hispanic Origin[2]	7,319	2.3	9,703	2.9	32.6	15,274	2.5

Note: (1) Metropolitan Statistical Area - see Appendix A for areas included;
(2) people of Hispanic origin can be of any race
Source: 1980/1990 Census of Housing and Population, Summary Tape File 3C

Ancestry

Area	German	Irish	English	Italian	U.S.	French	Polish	Dutch
City	37.6	21.1	11.5	4.8	1.3	3.5	5.8	2.2
MSA[1]	41.6	21.2	13.1	4.3	1.9	3.8	5.2	2.6
U.S.	23.3	15.6	13.1	5.9	5.3	4.2	3.8	2.5

Note: Figures are percentages and include persons that reported multiple ancestry (eg. if a person reported being Irish and Italian, they were included in both columns); (1) Metropolitan Statistical Area - see Appendix A for areas included
Source: 1990 Census of Population and Housing, Summary Tape File 3C

Age

Area	Median Age (Years)	Under 5	Under 18	18-24	25-44	45-64	65+	80+
City	32.1	7.6	25.5	10.9	32.7	18.1	12.9	3.2
MSA[1]	31.4	8.1	27.9	10.0	34.1	17.5	10.6	2.5
U.S.	32.9	7.3	25.6	10.5	32.6	18.7	12.5	2.8

Note: (1) Metropolitan Statistical Area - see Appendix A for areas included
Source: 1990 Census of Population and Housing, Summary Tape File 3C

Male/Female Ratio

Area	Number of males per 100 females (all ages)	Number of males per 100 females (18 years old+)
City	91.3	87.2
MSA[1]	94.2	90.4
U.S.	95.0	91.9

Note: (1) Metropolitan Statistical Area - see Appendix A for areas included
Source: 1990 Census of Population, General Population Characteristics

INCOME

Per Capita/Median/Average Income

Area	Per Capita ($)	Median Household ($)	Average Household ($)
City	13,957	26,927	34,675
MSA[1]	13,989	30,323	36,870
U.S.	14,420	30,056	38,453

Note: All figures are for 1989; (1) Metropolitan Statistical Area - see Appendix A for areas included
Source: 1990 Census of Population and Housing, Summary Tape File 3C

Household Income Distribution by Race

Income ($)	City (%)					U.S. (%)				
	Total	White	Black	Other	Hisp.[1]	Total	White	Black	Other	Hisp.[1]
Less than 5,000	6.2	4.5	17.2	12.7	10.1	6.2	4.8	15.2	8.6	8.8
5,000 - 9,999	9.8	8.7	17.4	13.6	10.6	9.3	8.6	14.2	9.9	11.1
10,000 - 14,999	10.0	9.4	14.5	12.2	10.3	8.8	8.5	11.0	9.8	11.0
15,000 - 24,999	20.2	20.0	21.3	19.2	18.0	17.5	17.3	18.9	18.5	20.5
25,000 - 34,999	17.0	17.7	11.9	16.5	23.8	15.8	16.1	14.2	15.4	16.4
35,000 - 49,999	17.6	18.6	10.8	15.6	17.0	17.9	18.6	13.3	16.1	16.0
50,000 - 74,999	12.5	13.6	5.6	8.1	9.1	15.0	15.8	9.3	13.4	11.1
75,000 - 99,999	3.3	3.7	0.9	0.6	1.0	5.1	5.5	2.6	4.7	3.1
100,000+	3.3	3.7	0.4	1.5	0.2	4.4	4.8	1.3	3.7	1.9

Note: All figures are for 1989; (1) people of Hispanic origin can be of any race
Source: 1990 Census of Population and Housing, Summary Tape File 3C

Effective Buying Income

Area	Per Capita ($)	Median Household ($)	Average Household ($)
City	20,477	40,682	51,388
MSA[1]	20,761	43,263	55,345
U.S.	16,803	34,536	45,243

Note: Data as of 1/1/99; (1) Metropolitan Statistical Area - see Appendix A for areas included
Source: Standard Rate & Data Service, Newspaper Advertising Source, 9/99

Effective Household Buying Income Distribution

Area	% of Households Earning						
	$10,000 -$19,999	$20,000 -$34,999	$35,000 -$49,999	$50,000 -$74,999	$75,000 -$99,000	$100,000 -$124,999	$125,000 and up
City	13.3	20.6	17.8	21.0	10.2	3.8	4.4
MSA[1]	11.8	20.4	18.6	23.0	11.2	3.8	3.8
U.S.	16.0	22.6	18.2	18.9	7.2	2.4	2.7

Note: Data as of 1/1/99; (1) Metropolitan Statistical Area - see Appendix A for areas included
Source: Standard Rate & Data Service, Newspaper Advertising Source, 9/99

Poverty Rates by Race and Age

Area	Total (%)	By Race (%)				By Age (%)		
		White	Black	Other	Hisp.[2]	Under 5 years old	Under 18 years old	65 years and over
City	12.6	8.7	34.6	27.5	19.0	24.3	18.8	10.6
MSA[1]	9.6	7.3	30.8	20.8	14.8	16.9	13.1	9.8
U.S.	13.1	9.8	29.5	23.1	25.3	20.1	18.3	12.8

Note: Figures show the percent of people living below the poverty line in 1989. The average poverty threshold was $12,674 for a family of four in 1989; (1) Metropolitan Statistical Area - see Appendix A for areas included; (2) people of Hispanic origin can be of any race
Source: 1990 Census of Population and Housing, Summary Tape File 3C

EMPLOYMENT

Labor Force and Employment

Area	Civilian Labor Force			Workers Employed		
	Jun. 1998	Jun. 1999	% Chg.	Jun. 1998	Jun. 1999	% Chg.
City	204,227	209,732	2.7	197,170	203,091	3.0
MSA[1]	388,372	398,082	2.5	377,252	387,546	2.7
U.S.	138,798,000	140,666,000	1.3	132,265,000	134,395,000	1.6

Note: Data is not seasonally adjusted and covers workers 16 years of age and older;
(1) Metropolitan Statistical Area - see Appendix A for areas included
Source: Bureau of Labor Statistics, http://stats.bls.gov

Unemployment Rate

Area	1998						1999					
	Jul.	Aug.	Sep.	Oct.	Nov.	Dec.	Jan.	Feb.	Mar.	Apr.	May.	Jun.
City	3.3	2.9	2.8	2.9	2.5	2.2	3.2	2.9	2.7	2.2	2.7	3.2
MSA[1]	2.8	2.4	2.3	2.4	2.1	1.9	2.7	2.5	2.3	1.9	2.3	2.6
U.S.	4.7	4.5	4.4	4.2	4.1	4.0	4.8	4.7	4.4	4.1	4.0	4.5

Note: Data is not seasonally adjusted and covers workers 16 years of age and older; all figures are percentages; (1) Metropolitan Statistical Area - see Appendix A for areas included
Source: Bureau of Labor Statistics, http://stats.bls.gov

Employment by Industry

Sector	MSA[1]		U.S.
	Number of Employees	Percent of Total	Percent of Total
Services	134,100	32.8	30.4
Retail Trade	72,400	17.7	17.7
Government	50,300	12.3	15.6
Manufacturing	39,400	9.6	14.3
Finance/Insurance/Real Estate	34,500	8.4	5.9
Wholesale Trade	26,200	6.4	5.4
Transportation/Public Utilities	31,300	7.7	5.3
Construction	n/a	n/a	5.0
Mining	n/a	n/a	0.4

Note: Figures cover non-farm employment as of 6/99 and are not seasonally adjusted;
(1) Metropolitan Statistical Area - see Appendix A for areas included; n/a not available
Source: Bureau of Labor Statistics, http://stats.bls.gov

Employment by Occupation

Occupation Category	City (%)	MSA[1] (%)	U.S. (%)
White Collar	63.8	63.6	58.1
Executive/Admin./Management	12.4	12.8	12.3
Professional	14.7	14.1	14.1
Technical & Related Support	3.7	3.8	3.7
Sales	13.5	13.5	11.8
Administrative Support/Clerical	19.5	19.3	16.3
Blue Collar	21.4	21.6	26.2
Precision Production/Craft/Repair	9.1	9.3	11.3
Machine Operators/Assem./Insp.	5.1	4.9	6.8
Transportation/Material Movers	3.4	3.6	4.1
Cleaners/Helpers/Laborers	3.8	3.7	3.9
Services	14.0	13.3	13.2
Farming/Forestry/Fishing	0.8	1.6	2.5

Note: Figures cover employed persons 16 years old and over;
(1) Metropolitan Statistical Area - see Appendix A for areas included
Source: 1990 Census of Population and Housing, Summary Tape File 3C

Occupational Employment Projections: 1996 - 2006

Occupations Expected to Have the Largest Job Growth (ranked by numerical growth)	Fast-Growing Occupations[1] (ranked by percent growth)
1. Truck drivers, light	1. Photographic processing machine operators
2. General managers & top executives	2. Carpet installers
3. Cashiers	3. Stenographers
4. Janitors/cleaners/maids, ex. priv. hshld.	4. Guards
5. Butchers & meatcutters	5. Travel agents
6. Marketing & sales, supervisors	6. Meat, poultry, fish cutters
7. Waiters & waitresses	7. Food service and lodging managers
8. Salespersons, retail	8. Data processing equipment repairers
9. Nursing aides/orderlies/attendants	9. Refuse collectors
10. Bookkeeping, accounting & auditing clerks	10. Butchers & meatcutters

Note: Projections cover Nebraska; (1) Excludes occupations with total job growth less than 300
Source: U.S. Department of Labor, Employment and Training Administration, America's Labor Market Information System (ALMIS)

TAXES

Major State and Local Tax Rates

State Corp. Income (%)	State Personal Income (%)	Residential Property (effective rate per $100)	Sales & Use State (%)	Local (%)	State Gasoline (cents/gallon)	State Cigarette (cents/pack)
5.58 - 7.81	2.62 - 6.99	n/a	5.0	1.5	24.4[a]	34.0

Note: Personal/corporate income, sales, gasoline and cigarette tax rates as of January 1999. Property tax rates as of 1997; (a) Rate is comprised of 23.5 cents excise and 0.9 cents motor carrier tax
Source: Federation of Tax Administrators, www.taxadmin.org; Washington D.C. Department of Finance and Revenue, Tax Rates and Tax Burdens in the District of Columbia: A Nationwide Comparison, July 1998; Chamber of Commerce, 1999

Total Taxes Per Capita and as a Percent of Income

Area	Per Capita Income ($)	Per Capita Taxes ($) Total	Federal	State/Local	Percent of Income (%) Total	Federal	State/Local
Nebraska	26,688	9,343	6,286	3,057	35.0	23.6	11.5
U.S.	27,876	9,881	6,690	3,191	35.4	24.0	11.4

Note: Figures are for 1998
Source: Tax Foundation, www.taxfoundation.org

Estimated Tax Burden

Area	State Income	Local Income	Property	Sales	Total
Omaha	2,932	0	5,500	585	9,017

Note: The numbers are estimates of taxes paid by a married couple with two children and annual earnings of $75,000. Sales tax estimates assume they spend average amounts on food, clothing, household goods and gasoline. Property tax estimates assume they live in a $250,000 home.
Source: Kiplinger's Personal Finance Magazine, October 1998

COMMERCIAL REAL ESTATE

Office Market

Class/ Location	Total Space (sq. ft.)	Vacant Space (sq. ft.)	Vac. Rate (%)	Under Constr. (sq. ft.)	Net Absorp. (sq. ft.)	Rental Rates ($/sq.ft./yr.)
Class A						
CBD	1,872,744	23,622	1.3	0	-55,322	15.00-23.00
Outside CBD	6,464,473	323,224	5.0	325,000	-57,923	18.00-24.00
Class B						
CBD	2,809,115	370,076	13.2	0	4,274	11.00-13.00
Outside CBD	3,480,870	278,470	8.0	35,000	292,246	14.50-17.00

Note: Data as of 10/98 and covers Omaha; CBD = Central Business District; n/a not available;
Source: Society of Industrial and Office Realtors, 1999 Comparative Statistics of Industrial and Office Real Estate Markets

"Construction of a 40-story, 954,000 sq. ft. building is scheduled to begin in Omaha during late 1999. Our SIOR reporter notes that while the local economy has remained strong, there is a very low unemployment rate in Omaha. This could retard economic growth and deter some companies from relocating to the area. Although increases in construction, sales, leasing, and absorption rates are expected to be at a rate of one to five percent in 1999, this rate will represent a slowdown from the trends during the past two years." *Society of Industrial and Office Realtors, 1999 Comparative Statistics of Industrial and Office Real Estate Markets*

Industrial Market

Location	Total Space (sq. ft.)	Vacant Space (sq. ft.)	Vac. Rate (%)	Under Constr. (sq. ft.)	Net Absorp. (sq. ft.)	Net Lease ($/sq.ft./yr.)
Central City	7,341,500	651,000	8.9	130,000	-124,000	1.00-3.75
Suburban	9,982,000	399,000	4.0	457,000	965,500	2.25-6.00

Note: Data as of 10/98 and covers Omaha; n/a not available
Source: Society of Industrial and Office Realtors, 1999 Comparative Statistics of Industrial and Office Real Estate Markets

"The local and regional economies have been strong and business expansions are expected to continue. Omaha's extremely low unemployment rate is, however, a threat to the city's prospects for growth in the near future. Sales prices for all types and qualities of industrial buildings have been increasing. An announcement made in early 1998 by Caterpillar Corporation of its plan to build a manufacturing plant has promoted a substantial surge in activity in Omaha. Currently, the city is experiencing a moderate shortage of industrial space 20,000-250,000 sq. ft. in size. The present inventory consists of 75 percent warehouse/distribution, 15 percent manufacturing, and 10 percent High Tech/R&D space. Absorption in 1998 included 80 percent for warehouse/distribution, 10 percent for manufacturing uses, and 10 percent for High Tech/R&D users." *Society of Industrial and Office Realtors, 1999 Comparative Statistics of Industrial and Office Real Estate Markets*

COMMERCIAL UTILITIES

Typical Monthly Electric Bills

Area	Commercial Service ($/month)		Industrial Service ($/month)	
	12 kW demand 1,500 kWh	100 kW demand 30,000 kWh	1,000 kW demand 400,000 kWh	20,000 kW demand 10,000,000 kWh
City	n/a	n/a	n/a	n/a
U.S.	150	2,174	23,995	508,569

Note: Based on rates in effect January 1, 1999; n/a not available
Source: Edison Electric Institute, Typical Residential, Commercial and Industrial Bills, Winter 1999

TRANSPORTATION

Transportation Statistics

Average minutes to work	17.3
Interstate highways	I-80
Bus lines	
In-city	Metro Area Transit, 164 vehicles
Inter-city	1
Passenger air service	
Airport	Eppley Airfield
Airlines	14
Aircraft departures	25,131 (1996)
Enplaned passengers	1,666,357 (1996)
Rail service	Amtrak
Motor freight carriers	90
Major waterways/ports	Port of Omaha (serves the Missouri River basin)

Source: Editor & Publisher Market Guide, 1999; FAA Airport Activity Statistics, 1997; Amtrak National Time Table, Northeast Timetable, Spring/Summer 1999; 1990 Census of Population and Housing, STF 3C; Chamber of Commerce/Economic Development 1999; Jane's Urban Transport Systems 1999-2000

Means of Transportation to Work

Area	Car/Truck/Van		Public Transportation			Bicycle	Walked	Other Means	Worked at Home
	Drove Alone	Car-pooled	Bus	Subway	Railroad				
City	78.0	12.2	3.1	0.0	0.0	0.1	3.3	0.8	2.5
MSA[1]	79.7	11.8	2.0	0.0	0.0	0.1	2.7	0.7	3.1
U.S.	73.2	13.4	3.0	1.5	0.5	0.4	3.9	1.2	3.0

Note: Figures shown are percentages and only include workers 16 years old and over;
(1) Metropolitan Statistical Area - see Appendix A for areas included
Source: 1990 Census of Population and Housing, Summary Tape File 3C

BUSINESSES

Major Business Headquarters

Company Name	1999 Rankings	
	Fortune 500	Forbes 500
Berkshire Hathaway	112	-
Conagra	50	-
Inacom	363	-
Mutual of Omaha Insurance	399	-
Peter Kiewit Sons'	434	44
Scoular	-	100

Note: Companies listed are located in the city; dashes indicate no ranking
Fortune 500: Companies that produce a 10-K are ranked 1 to 500 based on 1998 revenue
Forbes 500: Private companies are ranked 1 to 500 based on 1997 revenue
Source: Forbes, November 30, 1998; Fortune, April 26, 1999

Fast-Growing Businesses

Omaha is home to one of *Business Week's* "hot growth" companies: Transaction Systems Architects. Criteria: increase in sales and profits, return on capital and stock price. *Business Week, 5/31/99*

Minority Business Opportunity

One of the 500 largest Hispanic-owned companies in the U.S. are located in Omaha. *Hispanic Business, June 1999*

Small Business Opportunity

According to *Forbes*, Omaha is home to one of America's 200 best small companies: infoUSA. Criteria: companies included must be publicly traded since November 1997 with a stock price of at least $5 per share and an average daily float of 1,000 shares. The company's latest 12-month sales must be between $5 and $350 million, return on equity (ROE) must be a minimum of 12% for both the past 5 years and the most recent four quarters, and five-year sales and EPS growth must average at least 10%. Companies with declining sales or earnings during the past year were dropped as well as businesses with debt/equity ratios over 1.25. Companies with negative operating cash flow in each of the past two years were also excluded. *Forbes, November 2, 1998*

HOTELS & MOTELS

Hotels/Motels

Area	Hotels/ Motels	Rooms	Luxury-Level Hotels/Motels		Average Minimum Rates ($)		
			♦♦♦♦	♦♦♦♦♦	♦♦	♦♦♦	♦♦♦♦
City	39	5,143	0	0	66	74	n/a
Airport	2	242	0	0	n/a	n/a	n/a
Suburbs	19	1,798	0	0	n/a	n/a	n/a
Total	60	7,183	0	0	n/a	n/a	n/a

Note: n/a not available; classifications range from one diamond (budget properties with basic amenities) to five diamond (luxury properties with the finest service, rooms and facilities).
Source: OAG, Business Travel Planner, Winter 1998-99

CONVENTION CENTERS

Major Convention Centers

Center Name	Meeting Rooms	Exhibit Space (sq. ft.)
Omaha Civic Auditorium	n/a	120,000
Peter Kiewit Conference	22	2,000

Note: n/a not available
Source: Trade Shows Worldwide, 1998; Meetings & Conventions, 4/15/99;
Sucessful Meetings, 3/31/98

Living Environment

COST OF LIVING

Cost of Living Index

Composite Index	Groceries	Housing	Utilities	Trans-portation	Health Care	Misc. Goods/ Services
94.2	94.7	94.1	87.4	100.7	93.3	93.9

Note: U.S. = 100
Source: ACCRA, Cost of Living Index, 1st Quarter 1999

HOUSING

Median Home Prices and Housing Affordability

Area	Median Price[2] 1st Qtr. 1999 ($)	HOI[3] 1st Qtr. 1999	Afford-ability Rank[4]
MSA[1]	105,000	77.1	80
U.S.	134,000	69.6	—

Note: (1) Metropolitan Statistical Area - see Appendix A for areas included; (2) U.S. figures calculated from the sales of 524,324 new and existing homes in 181 markets; (3) Housing Opportunity Index - percent of homes sold that were within the reach of the median income household at the prevailing mortgage interest rate; (4) Rank is from 1-181 with 1 being most affordable
Source: National Association of Home Builders, Housing Opportunity Index, 1st Quarter 1999

Median Home Price Projection

It is projected that the median price of existing single-family homes in the metro area will increase by 3.8% in 1999. Nationwide, home prices are projected to increase 3.8%.
Kiplinger's Personal Finance Magazine, January 1999

Average New Home Price

Area	Price ($)
City	132,129
U.S.	142,735

Note: Figures are based on a new home with 1,800 sq. ft. of living area on an 8,000 sq. ft. lot.
Source: ACCRA, Cost of Living Index, 1st Quarter 1999

Average Apartment Rent

Area	Rent ($/mth)
City	594
U.S.	601

Note: Figures are based on an unfurnished two bedroom, 1-1/2 or 2 bath apartment, approximately 950 sq. ft. in size, excluding all utilities except water
Source: ACCRA, Cost of Living Index, 1st Quarter 1999

RESIDENTIAL UTILITIES

Average Residential Utility Costs

Area	All Electric ($/mth)	Part Electric ($/mth)	Other Energy ($/mth)	Phone ($/mth)
City	—	50.78	33.08	21.02
U.S.	100.02	55.73	43.33	19.71

Source: ACCRA, Cost of Living Index, 1st Quarter 1999

HEALTH CARE

Average Health Care Costs

Area	Hospital ($/day)	Doctor ($/visit)	Dentist ($/visit)
City	355.00	46.00	66.80
U.S.	430.43	52.45	66.35

Note: Hospital—based on a semi-private room; Doctor—based on a general practitioner's routine exam of an established patient; Dentist—based on adult teeth cleaning and periodic oral exam.
Source: ACCRA, Cost of Living Index, 1st Quarter 1999

Distribution of Office-Based Physicians

Area	Family/Gen. Practitioners	Specialists		
		Medical	Surgical	Other
MSA[1]	218	429	373	396

Note: Data as of 12/31/97; (1) Metropolitan Statistical Area - see Appendix A for areas included
Source: American Medical Assn., Physician Characteristics & Distribution in the U.S., 1999

Hospitals

Omaha has 6 general medical and surgical hospitals, 3 psychiatric, 2 children's general. *AHA Guide to the Healthcare Field, 1998-99*

According to *U.S. News and World Report,* Omaha has 1 of the best hospitals in the U.S.: **Nebraska Health System**, noted for cancer, rheumatology. *U.S. News Online, "America's Best Hospitals," 10th Edition, www.usnews.com*

EDUCATION

Public School District Statistics

District Name	Num. Sch.	Enroll.	Classroom Teachers	Pupils per Teacher	Minority Pupils (%)	Current Exp.[1] ($/pupil)
Educational Service Unit 19	n/a	n/a	n/a	n/a	n/a	n/a
Educational Service Unit 3	8	86	7	12.3	n/a	n/a
Millard Public Schools	29	19,027	1,111	17.1	n/a	n/a
NE School For Deaf	2	30	12	2.5	n/a	n/a
Omaha Public Schools	80	45,046	2,798	16.1	42.4	5,276
Westside Community Schools	14	5,280	361	14.6	n/a	n/a

Note: Data covers the 1997-1998 school year unless otherwise noted; (1) Data covers fiscal year 1996; SD = School District; ISD = Independent School District; n/a not available
Source: National Center for Education Statistics, Common Core of Data Public Education Agency Universe 1997-98; National Center for Education Statistics, Characteristics of the 100 Largest Public Elementary and Secondary School Districts in the United States: 1997-98, July 1999

Educational Quality

School District	Education Quotient[1]	Graduate Outcome[2]	Community Index[3]	Resource Index[4]
Omaha Public Schools	122.0	118.0	136.0	128.0

Note: Nearly 1,000 secondary school districts were rated in terms of educational quality. The scores range from a low of 50 to a high of 150; (1) Average of the Graduate Outcome, Community and Resource indexes; (2) Based on graduation rates and college board scores (SAT/ACT); (3) Based on the surrounding community's average level of education and the area's average income level; (4) Based on teacher salaries, per-pupil expenditures and student-teacher ratios.
Source: Expansion Management, Ratings Issue, 1998

Educational Attainment by Race

Area	High School Graduate (%)					Bachelor's Degree (%)				
	Total	White	Black	Other	Hisp.[2]	Total	White	Black	Other	Hisp.[2]
City	82.6	84.5	69.0	72.8	61.5	23.1	24.7	9.4	24.5	11.1
MSA[1]	84.4	85.5	72.7	75.3	68.7	22.8	23.6	12.0	24.5	13.9
U.S.	75.2	77.9	63.1	60.4	49.8	20.3	21.5	11.4	19.4	9.2

Note: Figures shown cover persons 25 years old and over; (1) Metropolitan Statistical Area - see Appendix A for areas included; (2) people of Hispanic origin can be of any race
Source: 1990 Census of Population and Housing, Summary Tape File 3C

School Enrollment by Type

| Area | Preprimary | | | | Elementary/High School | | | |
| | Public | | Private | | Public | | Private | |
	Enrollment	%	Enrollment	%	Enrollment	%	Enrollment	%
City	4,250	61.1	2,709	38.9	44,993	81.7	10,057	18.3
MSA[1]	8,461	60.9	5,425	39.1	96,810	86.3	15,363	13.7
U.S.	2,679,029	59.5	1,824,256	40.5	38,379,689	90.2	4,187,099	9.8

Note: Figures shown cover persons 3 years old and over;
(1) Metropolitan Statistical Area - see Appendix A for areas included
Source: 1990 Census of Population and Housing, Summary Tape File 3C

School Enrollment by Race

| Area | Preprimary (%) | | | | Elementary/High School (%) | | | |
	White	Black	Other	Hisp.[1]	White	Black	Other	Hisp.[1]
City	80.7	15.0	4.3	3.2	76.9	19.1	4.0	4.2
MSA[2]	87.5	9.1	3.4	2.7	85.7	11.0	3.3	3.2
U.S.	80.4	12.5	7.1	7.8	74.1	15.6	10.3	12.5

Note: Figures shown cover persons 3 years old and over; (1) people of Hispanic origin can be of any race; (2) Metropolitan Statistical Area - see Appendix A for areas included
Source: 1990 Census of Population and Housing, Summary Tape File 3C

Classroom Teacher Salaries in Public Schools

| District | B.A. Degree | | M.A. Degree | | Maximum | |
	Min. ($)	Rank[1]	Max. ($)	Rank[1]	Max. ($)	Rank[1]
Omaha	22,464	93	43,200	68	47,520	72
Average	26,980	-	46,065	-	51,435	-

Note: Salaries are for 1997-1998; (1) Rank ranges from 1 to 100
Source: American Federation of Teachers, Survey & Analysis of Salary Trends, 1998

Higher Education

| Two-Year Colleges | | Four-Year Colleges | | Medical Schools | Law Schools | Voc/ Tech |
Public	Private	Public	Private			
1	2	2	5	2	1	19

Source: College Blue Book, Occupational Education, 1997; Medical School Admission Requirements, 1999-2000; Peterson's Guide to Two-Year Colleges, 1999; Peterson's Guide to Four-Year Colleges, 2000; Barron's Guide to Law Schools, 1999

MAJOR EMPLOYERS

Major Employers

Alegent Health-Bergan Mercy Medical Center
Drivers Management
Inacom Corp. (computers)
Mutual of Omaha
Oriental Trading Co.

First National Bank of Omaha
First Data Resources
United of Omaha Life Insurance
Union Pacific Railroad
West Telemarketing Corp.

Note: Companies listed are located in the city
Source: Dun's Business Rankings, 1999; Ward's Business Directory, 1998

PUBLIC SAFETY

Crime Rate

| Area | All Crimes | Violent Crimes | | | | Property Crimes | | |
		Murder	Forcible Rape	Robbery	Aggrav. Assault	Burglary	Larceny -Theft	Motor Vehicle Theft
City	7,236.2	8.8	50.0	232.6	1,094.0	899.8	3,964.8	986.2
Suburbs[1]	3,033.3	1.5	14.2	48.9	147.2	539.7	2,031.9	249.9
MSA[2]	5,223.1	5.3	32.9	144.6	640.5	727.3	3,039.0	633.5
U.S.	4,922.7	6.8	35.9	186.1	382.0	919.6	2,886.5	505.8

Note: Crime rate is the number of crimes per 100,000 pop.; (1) defined as all areas within the MSA but located outside the central city; (2) Metropolitan Statistical Area - see Appendix A for areas incl.
Source: FBI Uniform Crime Reports, 1997

RECREATION

Culture and Recreation

Museums	Symphony Orchestras	Opera Companies	Dance Companies	Professional Theatres	Zoos	Pro Sports Teams
6	1	1	1	5	1	0

Source: International Directory of the Performing Arts, 1997; Official Museum Directory, 1999; Stern's Performing Arts Directory, 1997; USA Today Four Sport Stadium Guide, 1997; Chamber of Commerce/Economic Development, 1999

Library System

The Omaha Public Library has nine branches, holdings of 728,235 volumes, and a budget of $9,146,123 (1996). *American Library Directory, 1998-1999*

MEDIA

Newspapers

Name	Type	Freq.	Distribution	Circulation
Catholic Voice	Religious	2x/mo	Area	69,000
Daily Record	n/a	5x/wk	Area	1,500
Nuestro Mundo	Hispanic	1x/mo	State	7,500
Omaha Shopper	n/a	1x/wk	Area	58,000
Omaha Star	General	1x/wk	Area	30,500
Omaha World-Herald	General	7x/wk	Regional	238,462

Note: Includes newspapers with circulations of 1,000 or more located in the city; n/a not available
Source: Burrelle's Media Directory, 1999 Edition

Television Stations

Name	Ch.	Affiliation	Type	Owner
KMTV	n/a	CBST	Commercial	Lee Enterprises Inc.
WOWT	n/a	NBCT	Commercial	Chronicle Broadcasting Inc.
KETV	n/a	ABCT	Commercial	Hearst-Argyle Broadcasting
KXVO	15	WB	Commercial	Cocola Broadcasting Inc.
KPTM	42	FBC	Commercial	Pappas Telecasting Companies

Note: Stations included broadcast in the Omaha metro area; n/a not available
Source: Burrelle's Media Directory, 1999 Edition

AM Radio Stations

Call Letters	Freq. (kHz)	Target Audience	Station Format	Music Format
WOW	590	General	M/N/S	Country
KCRO	660	G/R	M/T	Christian
KFAB	1110	General	N/T	n/a
KOIL	1180	General	S	n/a
KKAR	1290	General	N/S/T	n/a
KBBX	1420	G/H	M	Latin
KOSR	1490	General	M	AOR

Note: Stations included broadcast in the Omaha metro area; n/a not available
Target Audience: A=Asian; B=Black; C=Christian; E=Ethnic; F=French; G=General; H=Hispanic; M=Men; N=Native American; R=Religious; S=Senior Citizen; W=Women; Y=Young Adult; Z=Children
Station Format: E=Educational; M=Music; N=News; S=Sports; T=Talk
Music Format: AOR=Album Oriented Rock; MOR=Middle-of-the-Road
Source: Burrelle's Media Directory, 1999 Edition

FM Radio Stations

Call Letters	Freq. (mHz)	Target Audience	Station Format	Music Format
KESY	n/a	Women	M	Adult Contemporary
KNOS	88.9	Black	E/M/N/S/T	Blues/Gospel/Jazz/Oldies/Reggae/ R&B/Urban Contemporary
KVSS	89.9	General	M/T	Christian
KVNO	90.7	General	M/N/T	Classical/Jazz/Latin
KIOS	91.5	General	M/N	Classical/Jazz
KEZO	92.3	General	M	AOR
KTNP	93.3	General	M/N/S	Adult Contemporary
WOW	94.1	General	M/N/S	Country
KEFM	96.1	General	M	Adult Contemporary
KQKQ	98.5	General	M/N/S	Top 40
KGOR	99.9	General	M	Oldies
KGBI	100.7	Religious	M/N/T	Christian
KZFX	101.9	General	M	Classic Rock
KXKT	103.7	General	M	Country
KSRZ	104.5	Women	M	Adult Contemporary
KKCD	105.9	General	M/N	Classic Rock

Note: Stations included broadcast in the Omaha metro area; n/a not available
Station Format: E=Educational; M=Music; N=News; S=Sports; T=Talk
Target Audience: A=Asian; B=Black; C=Christian; E=Ethnic; F=French; G=General; H=Hispanic; M=Men; N=Native American; R=Religious; S=Senior Citizen; W=Women; Y=Young Adult; Z=Children
Music Format: AOR=Album Oriented Rock; MOR=Middle-of-the-Road
Source: Burrelle's Media Directory, 1999 Edition

CLIMATE

Average and Extreme Temperatures

Temperature	Jan	Feb	Mar	Apr	May	Jun	Jul	Aug	Sep	Oct	Nov	Dec	Yr.
Extreme High (°F)	67	77	89	97	98	105	110	107	103	95	80	69	110
Average High (°F)	31	37	48	64	74	84	88	85	77	66	49	36	62
Average Temp. (°F)	22	27	38	52	63	73	77	75	66	54	39	27	51
Average Low (°F)	11	17	27	40	52	61	66	64	54	42	29	17	40
Extreme Low (°F)	-23	-21	-16	5	27	38	44	43	25	13	-9	-23	-23

Note: Figures cover the years 1948-1992
Source: National Climatic Data Center, International Station Meteorological Climate Summary, 3/95

Average Precipitation/Snowfall/Humidity

Precip./Humidity	Jan	Feb	Mar	Apr	May	Jun	Jul	Aug	Sep	Oct	Nov	Dec	Yr.
Avg. Precip. (in.)	0.8	0.9	2.0	2.8	4.3	4.0	3.7	3.8	3.4	2.1	1.5	0.9	30.1
Avg. Snowfall (in.)	7	6	7	1	Tr	0	0	0	Tr	Tr	3	6	29
Avg. Rel. Hum. 6am (%)	78	80	79	77	80	82	84	86	85	81	79	80	81
Avg. Rel. Hum. 3pm (%)	61	59	54	46	49	50	51	53	51	47	55	61	53

Note: Figures cover the years 1948-1992; Tr = Trace amounts (<0.05 in. of rain; <0.5 in. of snow)
Source: National Climatic Data Center, International Station Meteorological Climate Summary, 3/95

Weather Conditions

Temperature			Daytime Sky			Precipitation		
5°F & below	32°F & below	90°F & above	Clear	Partly cloudy	Cloudy	0.01 inch or more precip.	0.1 inch or more snow/ice	Thunder-storms
23	139	35	100	142	123	97	20	46

Note: Figures are average number of days per year and covers the years 1948-1992
Source: National Climatic Data Center, International Station Meteorological Climate Summary, 3/95

AIR & WATER QUALITY

Maximum Pollutant Concentrations

	Particulate Matter (ug/m^3)	Carbon Monoxide (ppm)	Sulfur Dioxide (ppm)	Nitrogen Dioxide (ppm)	Ozone (ppm)	Lead (ug/m^3)
MSA[1] Level	98	5	0.050	n/a	0.08	0.12
NAAQS[2]	150	9	0.140	0.053	0.12	1.50
Met NAAQS?	Yes	Yes	Yes	n/a	Yes	Yes

Note: (1) Metropolitan Statistical Area - see Appendix A for areas included; (2) National Ambient Air Quality Standards; ppm = parts per million; ug/m^3 = micrograms per cubic meter; n/a not available
Source: EPA, National Air Quality and Emissions Trends Report, 1997

Pollutant Standards Index

In the Omaha MSA (see Appendix A for areas included), the Pollutant Standards Index (PSI) exceeded 100 on 0 days in 1997. A PSI value greater than 100 indicates that air quality would be in the unhealthful range on that day. *EPA, National Air Quality and Emissions Trends Report, 1997*

Drinking Water

Water System Name	Pop. Served	Primary Water Source Type	Number of Violations in 1998	Type of Violation/ Contaminants
Metropolitan Utilities District	506,420	Surface	None	None

Note: Data as of July 10, 1999
Source: EPA, Office of Ground Water and Drinking Water, Safe Drinking Water Information System

Omaha tap water is moderately alkaline, moderately soft, fluoridated.
Editor & Publisher Market Guide, 1999

Saint Louis, Missouri

Background

St. Louis, called the Gateway To The West, has experienced a series of ups and downs throughout its history. Fortunately today, the city is on an upswing.

St. Louis began as an inland river trading post for French settlers from New Orleans. Founder Pierre Laclède had been granted exclusive rights by the Louisiana government to trade with the tribes of the region. The site that he chose to name after Louis XV of France was rich with wildlife, including raccoon, beaver, muskrat, otter, and bear, making for an active fur trade. In 1827, John Jacob Astor started a very profitable fur business called the American Fur Company.

After the Civil War, St. Louis experienced an industrial and cultural boom. The city expanded in industries such as iron, steel, leather, and food, and became a center for Hegelian thought, thanks to the large influx of German immigrants who flavored the identity of St. Louis in many ways.

World War I, the Depression, and the Prohibition all contributed to St. Louis's economic decline, which persisted during the 1950s, 60s, and 70s. Since the 1980s, however, St. Louis has been on the upswing. Institutions and corporations such as the Federal Reserve Bank for the 8th District, Washington University, St. Louis University, Anheuser Busch, McDonnell Douglas, General Dynamics, Ralston Purina, and a number of automobile manufacturing plants such as Ford, General Motors, and Chrysler give St. Louis a strong and diversified economic base. St. Louis has recently been called the Silicon Valley of the Midwest, and is home to over 1,200 high-tech companies, representing a more than $2 billion investment and 150,000 jobs.

Saint Louis, situated at the confluence of the Missouri and Mississippi Rivers, is near the geographical center of the United States. It experiences the four seasons without the hardship of prolonged periods of extreme heat or high humidity. Winters are brisk, stimulating, and seldom severe. Thunderstorms which occur between 40-50 days a year are generally not severe. Tornadoes, on the other hand, have caused a great deal of destruction in the area.

General Rankings and Evaluative Comments

- Saint Louis was ranked #10 out of 11 large, midwestern metropolitan areas in *Money's* 1998 survey of "The Best Places to Live in America." The survey was conducted by first contacting 512 representative households nationwide and asking them to rank 37 quality-of-life factors on a scale of 1 to 10. Next, a demographic profile was compiled on the 300 largest metropolitan statistical areas in the U.S. The numbers were crunched together to arrive at an overall ranking (things Americans consider most important, like clean air and water, low crime and good schools, received extra weight). Unlike previous years, the 1998 rankings were broken down by region (northeast, midwest, south, west) and population size (100,000 to 249,999; 250,000 to 999,999; 1 million plus). The city had a nationwide ranking of #268 out of 300 in 1997 and #247 out of 300 in 1996. *Money, July 1998; Money, July 1997; Money, September 1996*

- *Ladies Home Journal* ranked America's 200 largest cities based on the qualities women care about most. Saint Louis ranked #186 out of 200. Criteria: low crime rate, well-paying jobs, quality health and child care, good public schools, the presence of women in government, size of the gender wage gap, number of sexual-harassment and discrimination complaints filed, unemployment and divorce rates, commute times, population density, number of houses of worship, parks and cultural offerings, number of women's health specialists, how well a community's women cared for themselves, complexion kindness index based on UV radiation levels, odds of finding affordable fashions, rental rates for romance movies, champagne sales and other matters of the heart. *Ladies Home Journal, November 1998*

- Zero Population Growth ranked 229 cities in terms of children's health, safety, and economic well-being. Saint Louis was ranked #24 out of 25 major cities (main city in a metro area with population of greater than 2 million) and was given a grade of F. Criteria: total population, percent of population under 18 years of age, household language, percent population change, percent of births to teens, infant mortality rate, percent of low birth weights, dropout rate, enrollment in preprimary school, violent and property crime rates, unemployment rate, percent of children in poverty, percent of owner occupied units, number of bad air days, percent of public transportation commuters, and average travel time to work. *Zero Population Growth, Children's Environmental Index, Fall 1999*

- Saint Louis was ranked #37 out of 59 metro areas in *The Regional Economist's* "Rational Livability Ranking of 59 Large Metro Areas." The rankings were based on the metro area's total population change over the period 1990-97 divided by the number of people moving in from elsewhere in the United States (net domestic in-migration). *St. Louis Federal Reserve Bank of St. Louis, The Regional Economist, April 1999*

- Saint Louis appeared on *Travel & Leisure's* list of the world's 100 best cities. It was ranked #43 in the U.S. Criteria: activities/attractions, culture/arts, people, restaurants/food, and value. *Travel & Leisure, 1998 World's Best Awards*

- Saint Louis was selected by *Yahoo! Internet Life* as one of "America's Most Wired Cities & Towns." The city ranked #42 out of 50. Criteria: home and work net use, domain density, hosts per capita, directory density and content quality. *Yahoo! Internet Life, March 1999*

- Cognetics studied 273 metro areas in the United States, ranking them by entrepreneurial activity. Saint Louis was ranked #23 out of the 50 largest metro areas. Criteria: Significant Starts (firms started in the last 10 years that still employ at least 5 people) and Young Growers (percent of firms 10 years old or less that grew significantly during the last 4 years). *Cognetics, "Entrepreneurial Hot Spots: The Best Places in America to Start and Grow a Company," 1998*

- Saint Louis was selected as one of the "Best American Cities to Start a Business" by *Point of View* magazine. Criteria: coolness, quality-of-life, and business concerns. The city was ranked #52 out of 75. *Point of View, November 1998*

- *Computerworld* selected the best markets for IT job seekers based on their annual salary, skills, and hiring surveys. Saint Louis ranked #9 out of 10. *Computerworld, January 11, 1999*

■ Reliastar Financial Corp. ranked the 125 largest metropolitan areas according to the general financial security of residents. Saint Louis was ranked #24 out of 125 with a score of 7.7. The score indicates the percentage a metropolitan area is above or below the metropolitan norm. A metro area with a score of 10.6 is 10.6% above the metro average. Criteria: Earnings and Wealth Potential (household income, education, net assets, cost of living); Safety Net (health insurance, retirement savings, life insurance, income support programs); Personal Threats (unemployment rate, low-income households, crime rate); Community Economic Vitality (cost of community services, job quality, job creation, housing costs).
Reliastar Financial Corp., "The Best Cities to Earn and Save Money," 1999 Edition

Business Environment

STATE ECONOMY

State Economic Profile

"St. Louis' weak economy and a slowdown in Kansas City are placing a drag on the Missouri economy. Gross State Product and job growth, after matching or surpassing the national for several years, has slowed. After strong home sales in 1998, MO's housing and construction markets will likely slow considerably in 1999.

Like most Plains states, MO's significant farm sector has been a drag on the economy. Farm income was down over 20% in 1998 as commodity prices and foreign demand remained weak. With overcapacity in MO's beef and grain sectors, a major restructing is in store. Even with a resurgence in Asian demand, the current trend in commodity prices is not likely to reverse.

Manufacturing employment shrank 0.5% in 1998. St. Louis witnessed an even greater decline of 0.9%. With the prospect of job cuts at Boeing's St. Louis facilities, Missouri will likely witness further contraction in manufacturing employment in 1999.

An increase in building activity in St. Louis, fueled by corporate relocations, helped to offset declining activity elsewhere in the state. Almost half of the new construction jobs created in MO were in St. Louis.

MO's relatively high unemployment rate has in some ways been a bonus, helping to attract some corporate relocations. MasterCard and Convergys, for instance, have moved operations to St. Louis to take advantage of the available labor. In spite of these moves, St. Louis should still add little to state GSP and job growth. Gains in Kansas City, Columbia and Springfield will help to offset the weakness in St. Louis and the soft farm economy." *National Association of Realtors, Economic Profiles: The Fifty States and the District of Columbia, http://nar.realtor.com/databank/profiles.htm*

IMPORTS/EXPORTS

Total Export Sales

Area	1994 ($000)	1995 ($000)	1996 ($000)	1997 ($000)	% Chg. 1994-97	% Chg. 1996-97
MSA[1]	3,673,337	3,997,678	4,497,447	4,711,500	28.3	4.8
U.S.	512,415,609	583,030,524	622,827,063	687,597,999	34.2	10.4

Note: (1) Metropolitan Statistical Area - see Appendix A for areas included
Source: U.S. Department of Commerce, International Trade Association, Metropolitan Area Exports: An Export Performance Report on Over 250 U.S. Cities, November 10, 1998

CITY FINANCES

City Government Finances

Component	FY92 ($000)	FY92 (per capita $)
Revenue	604,356	1,569.78
Expenditure	603,267	1,566.95
Debt Outstanding	766,899	1,991.97
Cash & Securities	1,446,300	3,756.67

Source: U.S. Bureau of the Census, City Government Finances: 1991-92

City Government Revenue by Source

Source	FY92 ($000)	FY92 (per capita $)	FY92 (%)
From Federal Government	32,477	84.36	5.4
From State Governments	37,849	98.31	6.3
From Local Governments	3,567	9.27	0.6
Property Taxes	36,894	95.83	6.1
General Sales Taxes	50,526	131.24	8.4
Selective Sales Taxes	58,460	151.85	9.7
Income Taxes	113,908	295.87	18.8
Current Charges	93,024	241.62	15.4
Utility/Liquor Store	30,186	78.41	5.0
Employee Retirement[1]	79,684	206.97	13.2
Other	67,781	176.06	11.2

Note: (1) Excludes "city contributions," classified as "nonrevenue," intragovernmental transfers.
Source: U.S. Bureau of the Census, City Government Finances: 1991-92

City Government Expenditures by Function

Function	FY92 ($000)	FY92 (per capita $)	FY92 (%)
Educational Services	3,359	8.72	0.6
Employee Retirement[1]	58,053	150.79	9.6
Environment/Housing	60,517	157.19	10.0
Government Administration	44,187	114.77	7.3
Interest on General Debt	66,304	172.22	11.0
Public Safety	139,776	363.06	23.2
Social Services	34,602	89.88	5.7
Transportation	128,168	332.91	21.2
Utility/Liquor Store	28,223	73.31	4.7
Other	40,078	104.10	6.6

Note: (1) Payments to beneficiaries including withdrawal of contributions.
Source: U.S. Bureau of the Census, City Government Finances: 1991-92

Municipal Bond Ratings

Area	Moody's	S & P
Saint Louis	Aaa	n/a

Note: n/a not available; n/r not rated
Source: Moody's Bond Record, 6/99

POPULATION

Population Growth

Area	1980	1990	% Chg. 1980-90	July 1998 Estimate	% Chg. 1990-98
City	453,085	396,685	-12.4	339,316	-14.5
MSA[1]	2,376,998	2,444,099	2.8	2,566,868	5.0
U.S.	226,545,805	248,765,170	9.8	270,299,000	8.7

Note: (1) Metropolitan Statistical Area - see Appendix A for areas included;
July 1998 MSA population estimate was calculated by the editors
Source: 1980/1990 Census of Housing and Population, Summary Tape File 3C;
Census Bureau Population Estimates 1998

Population Characteristics

Race	City 1980 Population	%	City 1990 Population	%	% Chg. 1980-90	MSA[1] 1990 Population	%
White	242,988	53.6	202,276	51.0	-16.8	1,986,599	81.3
Black	206,170	45.5	187,995	47.4	-8.8	422,234	17.3
Amer Indian/Esk/Aleut	679	0.1	1,331	0.3	96.0	5,726	0.2
Asian/Pacific Islander	2,214	0.5	3,566	0.9	61.1	22,808	0.9
Other	1,034	0.2	1,517	0.4	46.7	6,732	0.3
Hispanic Origin[2]	5,531	1.2	4,850	1.2	-12.3	25,036	1.0

Note: (1) Metropolitan Statistical Area - see Appendix A for areas included;
(2) people of Hispanic origin can be of any race
Source: 1980/1990 Census of Housing and Population, Summary Tape File 3C

Ancestry

Area	German	Irish	English	Italian	U.S.	French	Polish	Dutch
City	23.6	13.1	6.0	4.3	2.9	3.7	2.1	1.1
MSA[1]	41.2	19.3	12.2	4.6	3.7	6.1	3.0	2.0
U.S.	23.3	15.6	13.1	5.9	5.3	4.2	3.8	2.5

Note: Figures are percentages and include persons that reported multiple ancestry (eg. if a person reported being Irish and Italian, they were included in both columns); (1) Metropolitan Statistical Area - see Appendix A for areas included
Source: 1990 Census of Population and Housing, Summary Tape File 3C

Age

Area	Median Age (Years)	Age Distribution (%) Under 5	Under 18	18-24	25-44	45-64	65+	80+
City	32.7	8.0	25.2	10.3	31.2	16.6	16.7	4.7
MSA[1]	33.1	7.5	26.2	9.4	32.7	18.9	12.8	3.1
U.S.	32.9	7.3	25.6	10.5	32.6	18.7	12.5	2.8

Note: (1) Metropolitan Statistical Area - see Appendix A for areas included
Source: 1990 Census of Population and Housing, Summary Tape File 3C

Male/Female Ratio

Area	Number of males per 100 females (all ages)	Number of males per 100 females (18 years old+)
City	83.6	78.1
MSA[1]	91.6	87.3
U.S.	95.0	91.9

Note: (1) Metropolitan Statistical Area - see Appendix A for areas included
Source: 1990 Census of Population, General Population Characteristics

INCOME

Per Capita/Median/Average Income

Area	Per Capita ($)	Median Household ($)	Average Household ($)
City	10,798	19,458	25,605
MSA[1]	14,917	31,774	39,114
U.S.	14,420	30,056	38,453

Note: All figures are for 1989; (1) Metropolitan Statistical Area - see Appendix A for areas included
Source: 1990 Census of Population and Housing, Summary Tape File 3C

Household Income Distribution by Race

Income ($)	City (%)					U.S. (%)				
	Total	White	Black	Other	Hisp.[1]	Total	White	Black	Other	Hisp.[1]
Less than 5,000	12.5	6.9	20.6	15.7	8.9	6.2	4.8	15.2	8.6	8.8
5,000 - 9,999	15.3	13.3	18.3	14.6	11.5	9.3	8.6	14.2	9.9	11.1
10,000 - 14,999	12.3	11.3	13.9	9.3	12.4	8.8	8.5	11.0	9.8	11.0
15,000 - 24,999	20.7	21.9	19.0	19.1	25.0	17.5	17.3	18.9	18.5	20.5
25,000 - 34,999	14.8	16.8	11.8	18.3	16.6	15.8	16.1	14.2	15.4	16.4
35,000 - 49,999	12.6	14.9	9.2	13.5	12.0	17.9	18.6	13.3	16.1	16.0
50,000 - 74,999	8.4	10.5	5.4	5.9	8.4	15.0	15.8	9.3	13.4	11.1
75,000 - 99,999	2.0	2.7	1.0	2.3	3.0	5.1	5.5	2.6	4.7	3.1
100,000+	1.3	1.8	0.7	1.4	2.1	4.4	4.8	1.3	3.7	1.9

Note: All figures are for 1989; (1) people of Hispanic origin can be of any race
Source: 1990 Census of Population and Housing, Summary Tape File 3C

Effective Buying Income

Area	Per Capita ($)	Median Household ($)	Average Household ($)
City	13,477	24,588	32,252
MSA[1]	18,164	38,867	47,867
U.S.	16,803	34,536	45,243

Note: Data as of 1/1/99; (1) Metropolitan Statistical Area - see Appendix A for areas included
Source: Standard Rate & Data Service, Newspaper Advertising Source, 9/99

Effective Household Buying Income Distribution

Area	% of Households Earning						
	$10,000 -$19,999	$20,000 -$34,999	$35,000 -$49,999	$50,000 -$74,999	$75,000 -$99,000	$100,000 -$124,999	$125,000 and up
City	21.4	24.1	15.0	12.8	4.0	1.2	1.1
MSA[1]	13.9	21.1	19.4	21.8	8.5	2.7	2.7
U.S.	16.0	22.6	18.2	18.9	7.2	2.4	2.7

Note: Data as of 1/1/99; (1) Metropolitan Statistical Area - see Appendix A for areas included
Source: Standard Rate & Data Service, Newspaper Advertising Source, 9/99

Poverty Rates by Race and Age

Area	Total (%)	By Race (%)				By Age (%)		
		White	Black	Other	Hisp.[2]	Under 5 years old	Under 18 years old	65 years and over
City	24.6	12.6	37.4	26.0	23.5	41.4	39.7	18.7
MSA[1]	10.8	6.3	31.3	14.7	13.1	17.6	15.9	10.3
U.S.	13.1	9.8	29.5	23.1	25.3	20.1	18.3	12.8

Note: Figures show the percent of people living below the poverty line in 1989. The average poverty
threshold was $12,674 for a family of four in 1989; (1) Metropolitan Statistical Area - see Appendix A
for areas included; (2) people of Hispanic origin can be of any race
Source: 1990 Census of Population and Housing, Summary Tape File 3C

EMPLOYMENT

Labor Force and Employment

Area	Civilian Labor Force			Workers Employed		
	Jun. 1998	Jun. 1999	% Chg.	Jun. 1998	Jun. 1999	% Chg.
City	158,554	163,526	3.1	144,865	151,150	4.3
MSA[1]	1,331,964	1,374,693	3.2	1,268,230	1,316,070	3.8
U.S.	138,798,000	140,666,000	1.3	132,265,000	134,395,000	1.6

Note: Data is not seasonally adjusted and covers workers 16 years of age and older;
(1) Metropolitan Statistical Area - see Appendix A for areas included
Source: Bureau of Labor Statistics, http://stats.bls.gov

Unemployment Rate

Area	1998						1999					
	Jul.	Aug.	Sep.	Oct.	Nov.	Dec.	Jan.	Feb.	Mar.	Apr.	May.	Jun.
City	7.8	9.0	7.6	6.9	6.6	6.3	5.3	5.3	5.3	6.5	6.6	7.6
MSA[1]	5.1	4.6	3.9	3.6	3.5	3.4	3.5	3.3	3.1	3.4	3.6	4.3
U.S.	4.7	4.5	4.4	4.2	4.1	4.0	4.8	4.7	4.4	4.1	4.0	4.5

Note: Data is not seasonally adjusted and covers workers 16 years of age and older; all figures are percentages; (1) Metropolitan Statistical Area - see Appendix A for areas included
Source: Bureau of Labor Statistics, http://stats.bls.gov

Employment by Industry

Sector	MSA[1]		U.S.
	Number of Employees	Percent of Total	Percent of Total
Services	432,300	32.5	30.4
Retail Trade	239,300	18.0	17.7
Government	149,500	11.2	15.6
Manufacturing	192,900	14.5	14.3
Finance/Insurance/Real Estate	83,800	6.3	5.9
Wholesale Trade	75,700	5.7	5.4
Transportation/Public Utilities	83,300	6.3	5.3
Construction	n/a	n/a	5.0
Mining	n/a	n/a	0.4

Note: Figures cover non-farm employment as of 6/99 and are not seasonally adjusted;
(1) Metropolitan Statistical Area - see Appendix A for areas included; n/a not available
Source: Bureau of Labor Statistics, http://stats.bls.gov

Employment by Occupation

Occupation Category	City (%)	MSA[1] (%)	U.S. (%)
White Collar	55.9	61.6	58.1
Executive/Admin./Management	9.7	12.7	12.3
Professional	13.6	14.8	14.1
Technical & Related Support	4.0	4.0	3.7
Sales	9.6	12.2	11.8
Administrative Support/Clerical	19.0	17.8	16.3
Blue Collar	23.3	24.1	26.2
Precision Production/Craft/Repair	7.7	10.5	11.3
Machine Operators/Assem./Insp.	7.2	6.0	6.8
Transportation/Material Movers	3.8	3.8	4.1
Cleaners/Helpers/Laborers	4.6	3.8	3.9
Services	20.1	13.3	13.2
Farming/Forestry/Fishing	0.7	1.1	2.5

Note: Figures cover employed persons 16 years old and over;
(1) Metropolitan Statistical Area - see Appendix A for areas included
Source: 1990 Census of Population and Housing, Summary Tape File 3C

Occupational Employment Projections: 1996 - 2006

Occupations Expected to Have the Largest Job Growth (ranked by numerical growth)	Fast-Growing Occupations[1] (ranked by percent growth)
1. Salespersons, retail	1. Computer engineers
2. Teachers, secondary school	2. Systems analysts
3. Truck drivers, light	3. Desktop publishers
4. General managers & top executives	4. Home health aides
5. Cashiers	5. Teachers, special education
6. Nursing aides/orderlies/attendants	6. Personal and home care aides
7. Child care workers, private household	7. Speech-language pathologists/audiologists
8. Teachers aides, clerical & paraprofess.	8. Paralegals
9. Systems analysts	9. Occupational therapists
10. Marketing & sales, supervisors	10. Physical therapy assistants and aides

Note: Projections cover Missouri; (1) Excludes occupations with total job growth less than 300
Source: U.S. Department of Labor, Employment and Training Administration, America's Labor Market Information System (ALMIS)

TAXES

Major State and Local Tax Rates

State Corp. Income (%)	State Personal Income (%)	Residential Property (effective rate per $100)	Sales & Use State (%)	Sales & Use Local (%)	State Gasoline (cents/ gallon)	State Cigarette (cents/ pack)
6.25	1.5 - 6.0	n/a	4.225	2.625	17.05[a]	17.0[b]

Note: Personal/corporate income, sales, gasoline and cigarette tax rates as of January 1999. Property tax rates as of 1997; (a) Rate is comprised of 17 cents excise and 0.05 cents motor carrier tax; (b) Counties and cities may impose an additional tax of 4 - 7 cents per pack
Source: Federation of Tax Administrators, www.taxadmin.org; Washington D.C. Department of Finance and Revenue, Tax Rates and Tax Burdens in the District of Columbia: A Nationwide Comparison, July 1998; Chamber of Commerce, 1999

Total Taxes Per Capita and as a Percent of Income

Area	Per Capita Income ($)	Per Capita Taxes ($) Total	Federal	State/ Local	Percent of Income (%) Total	Federal	State/ Local
Missouri	26,334	9,207	6,136	3,072	35.0	23.3	11.7
U.S.	27,876	9,881	6,690	3,191	35.4	24.0	11.4

Note: Figures are for 1998
Source: Tax Foundation, www.taxfoundation.org

Estimated Tax Burden

Area	State Income	Local Income	Property	Sales	Total
Saint Louis	2,338	750	3,750	1,024	7,862

Note: The numbers are estimates of taxes paid by a married couple with two children and annual earnings of $75,000. Sales tax estimates assume they spend average amounts on food, clothing, household goods and gasoline. Property tax estimates assume they live in a $250,000 home.
Source: Kiplinger's Personal Finance Magazine, October 1998

**COMMERCIAL
REAL ESTATE**

Office Market

Class/ Location	Total Space (sq. ft.)	Vacant Space (sq. ft.)	Vac. Rate (%)	Under Constr. (sq. ft.)	Net Absorp. (sq. ft.)	Rental Rates ($/sq.ft./yr.)
Class A						
CBD	5,409,623	447,305	8.3	n/a	61,339	16.50-23.00
Outside CBD	10,337,109	520,792	5.0	1,264,993	959,084	18.00-27.50
Class B						
CBD	5,983,200	921,349	15.4	n/a	342,878	10.00-18.25
Outside CBD	14,183,292	1,502,867	10.6	91,477	292,531	12.00-25.00

Note: Data as of 10/98 and covers Saint Louis; CBD = Central Business District; n/a not available; Source: Society of Industrial and Office Realtors, 1999 Comparative Statistics of Industrial and Office Real Estate Markets

"The local economy is expected to remain strong and maintain its low unemployment rates. Within this, our SIOR reporter qualifies, there are some anticipated corporate cutbacks. Speculative development will be concentrated in the Clayton and Chesterfield sub-markets, with 800,000 sq. ft. proposed at this time. This may free up quality office space for absorption in the city itself. Conversions to residential lofts should have a long-term positive impact on the CBD, but the effect may not be felt this year. A plan for a new metro-area airport should also have a positive long-range impact on site prices, sales prices, and rental rates. Nevertheless, our local SIOR reporter forecasts a slight decrease in construction, which, with stable absorption, may result in increased rents." *Society of Industrial and Office Realtors, 1999 Comparative Statistics of Industrial and Office Real Estate Markets*

Industrial Market

Location	Total Space (sq. ft.)	Vacant Space (sq. ft.)	Vac. Rate (%)	Under Constr. (sq. ft.)	Net Absorp. (sq. ft.)	Gross Lease ($/sq.ft./yr.)
Central City	88,750,000	3,500,000	3.9	300,000	557,000	2.25-4.50
Suburban	117,585,000	2,500,000	2.1	2,500,000	3,130,000	4.00-6.50

Note: Data as of 10/98 and covers Saint Louis; n/a not available
Source: Society of Industrial and Office Realtors, 1999 Comparative Statistics of Industrial and Office Real Estate Markets

"As vacancy rates stayed at levels not seen since the early 1980s, Saint Louis will reap the benefits of a robust real estate market. Our local SIOR reporters indicate further growth for the market area. Sales prices of all industrial space are expected to increase at moderate to strong rates. Lease prices for warehouse and distribution space will rise between 11 and 15 percent above last year. Manufacturing and high-technology space will see lease prices escalate by as much as 10 percent. Overall, site prices should increase by at least six percent. Absorption will increase in warehouse/distribution space and High Tech/R&D space. Construction activity is expected to increase, reflecting the shortages of quality spaces available." *Society of Industrial and Office Realtors, 1999 Comparative Statistics of Industrial and Office Real Estate Markets*

Retail Market

Shopping Center Inventory (sq. ft.)	Shopping Center Construction (sq. ft.)	Construction as a Percent of Inventory (%)	Torto Wheaton Rent Index[1] ($/sq. ft.)
44,816,000	707,000	1.6	13.50

Note: Data as of 1997 and covers the Metropolitan Statistical Area - see Appendix A for areas included; (1) Index is based on a model that predicts what the average rent should be for leases with certain characteristics, in certain locations during certain years.
Source: National Association of Realtors, 1997-1998 Market Conditions Report

"In spite of slow population and income growth and a general strike at the McDonnell Douglas plant in 1996, St. Louis' retail market has fared relatively well. The area's rent index rose 9.2% in 1997 after a 2.9% drop in 1996. Rents remain above the Midwest average of

$12.27 per square foot. A large amount of retail space was vacated in 1996 due to the closing of Central Hardware, the Schnucks/National Markets merger and the reorganization of Phar-Mor. Much of that space has since been absorbed by retailers such as Value City, Baby Superstores, Ace Hardware and Bed, Bath & Beyond. The St. Louis retail market is expected to remain stable over the next three years." *National Association of Realtors, 1997-1998 Market Conditions Report*

COMMERCIAL UTILITIES

Typical Monthly Electric Bills

Area	Commercial Service ($/month)		Industrial Service ($/month)	
	12 kW demand 1,500 kWh	100 kW demand 30,000 kWh	1,000 kW demand 400,000 kWh	20,000 kW demand 10,000,000 kWh
City	109	1,703	18,544	297,344
U.S.	150	2,174	23,995	508,569

Note: Based on rates in effect January 1, 1999
Source: Edison Electric Institute, Typical Residential, Commercial and Industrial Bills, Winter 1999

TRANSPORTATION

Transportation Statistics

Average minutes to work	22.0
Interstate highways	I-44; I-55; I-64; I-70
Bus lines	
In-city	Bi-State Transit System, 578 vehicles
Inter-city	2
Passenger air service	
Airport	Lambert-St. Louis International
Airlines	15
Aircraft departures	229,259 (1996)
Enplaned passengers	13,546,822 (1996)
Rail service	Amtrak; MetroLink; Light Rail
Motor freight carriers	350
Major waterways/ports	Mississippi River; Port of St. Louis

Source: Editor & Publisher Market Guide, 1999; FAA Airport Activity Statistics, 1997; Amtrak National Time Table, Northeast Timetable, Spring/Summer 1999; 1990 Census of Population and Housing, STF 3C; Chamber of Commerce/Economic Development 1999; Jane's Urban Transport Systems 1999-2000

Means of Transportation to Work

Area	Car/Truck/Van		Public Transportation			Bicycle	Walked	Other Means	Worked at Home
	Drove Alone	Car-pooled	Bus	Subway	Railroad				
City	66.5	14.1	11.8	0.0	0.0	0.3	4.6	1.1	1.7
MSA[1]	79.7	12.0	2.8	0.0	0.0	0.1	2.1	0.7	2.4
U.S.	73.2	13.4	3.0	1.5	0.5	0.4	3.9	1.2	3.0

Note: Figures shown are percentages and only include workers 16 years old and over;
(1) Metropolitan Statistical Area - see Appendix A for areas included
Source: 1990 Census of Population and Housing, Summary Tape File 3C

BUSINESSES

Major Business Headquarters

Company Name	1999 Rankings	
	Fortune 500	Forbes 500
Alberici	-	431
Ameren	444	-
Anheuser-Busch	150	-
Clark USA	414	30
Edwards Jones	-	161
Emerson Electric	118	-
Enterprise Rent-A-Car	-	27
GenAmerica	392	-
Graybar Electric	404	35
HBE	-	487
May Department Stores	120	-
McCarthy	-	187
Mercantile Bancorp	496	-
Monsanto	187	-
Peabody Holding	-	63
Ralston Purina	293	-
Schnuck Markets	-	89
Siegel-Robert	-	481
Trans World Airlines	454	-

Note: Companies listed are located in the city; dashes indicate no ranking
Fortune 500: Companies that produce a 10-K are ranked 1 to 500 based on 1998 revenue
Forbes 500: Private companies are ranked 1 to 500 based on 1997 revenue
Source: Forbes, November 30, 1998; Fortune, April 26, 1999

Best Companies to Work For

Edward Jones (brokerage), A.G. Edwards (brokerage) and Enterprise Rent-A-Car, headquartered in Saint Louis, are among the "100 Best Companies to Work for in America." Criteria: trust in management, pride in work/company, camaraderie, company responses to the Hewitt People Practices Inventory, and employee responses to their Great Place to Work survey. The companies also had to be at least 10 years old and have a minimum of 500 employees. *Fortune, January 11, 1999*

Mercantile Bancorp (banking), headquartered in Saint Louis, is among the "100 Best Places to Work in IS." Criteria: compensation, turnover and training. *Computerworld, May 25, 1998*

Fast-Growing Businesses

According to *Inc.*, Saint Louis is home to one of America's 100 fastest-growing private companies: Charter Communications. Criteria for inclusion: must be an independent, privately-held, U.S. corporation, proprietorship or partnership; sales of at least $200,000 in 1995; five-year operating/sales history; increase in 1999 sales over 1998 sales; holding companies, regulated banks, and utilities were excluded. *Inc. 500, 1999*

Saint Louis is home to one of *Business Week's* "hot growth" companies: KV Pharmaceuticals. Criteria: increase in sales and profits, return on capital and stock price. *Business Week, 5/31/99*

According to Deloitte & Touche LLP, Saint Louis is home to one of America's 100 fastest-growing high-technology companies: Insight Technology Group. Companies are ranked by percentage growth in revenue over a five-year period. Criteria for inclusion: must be a U.S. company developing and/or providing technology products or services; company must have been in business for five years with 1993 revenues of at least $50,000. *Deloitte & Touche LLP, November 17, 1998*

Women-Owned Firms: Number, Employment and Sales

Area	Number of Firms	Employ-ment	Sales ($000)	Rank[2]
MSA[1]	78,100	244,200	30,848,700	24

Note: (1) Metropolitan Statistical Area - see Appendix A for areas included;
(2) Calculated on an averaging of the number of businesses, employment and sales
Source: The National Foundation for Women Business Owners, 1999 Facts on Women-Owned
Businesses: Trends in the Top 50 Metropolitan Areas

Women-Owned Firms: Growth

Area	% change from 1992 to 1999			Rank[2]
	Number of Firms	Employ-ment	Sales	
MSA[1]	36.2	106.1	140.7	36

Note: (1) Metropolitan Statistical Area - see Appendix A for areas included; (2) Calculated on an
averaging of the percent growth of number of businesses, employment and sales
Source: The National Foundation for Women Business Owners, 1999 Facts on Women-Owned
Businesses: Trends in the Top 50 Metropolitan Areas

Minority Business Opportunity

Saint Louis is home to one company which is on the Black Enterprise Industrial/Service 100 list (largest based on gross sales): World Wide Technology Inc. (distribution of information technology products and services) . Criteria: operational in previous calendar year, at least 51% black-owned and manufactures/owns the product it sells or provides industrial or consumer services. Brokerages, real estate firms and firms that provide professional services are not eligible. *Black Enterprise, www.blackenterprise.com*

One of the 500 largest Hispanic-owned companies in the U.S. are located in Saint Louis. *Hispanic Business, June 1999*

Small Business Opportunity

According to *Forbes*, Saint Louis is home to two of America's 200 best small companies: Jones Pharma and RehabCare Group. Criteria: companies included must be publicly traded since November 1997 with a stock price of at least $5 per share and an average daily float of 1,000 shares. The company's latest 12-month sales must be between $5 and $350 million, return on equity (ROE) must be a minimum of 12% for both the past 5 years and the most recent four quarters, and five-year sales and EPS growth must average at least 10%. Companies with declining sales or earnings during the past year were dropped as well as businesses with debt/equity ratios over 1.25. Companies with negative operating cash flow in each of the past two years were also excluded. *Forbes, November 2, 1998*

HOTELS & MOTELS

Hotels/Motels

Area	Hotels/Motels	Rooms	Luxury-Level Hotels/Motels		Average Minimum Rates ($)		
			♦♦♦♦	♦♦♦♦♦	♦♦	♦♦♦	♦♦♦♦
City	37	8,591	1	0	83	117	159
Airport	27	4,800	0	0	n/a	n/a	n/a
Suburbs	66	6,940	1	0	n/a	n/a	n/a
Total	130	20,331	2	0	n/a	n/a	n/a

Note: n/a not available; classifications range from one diamond (budget properties with basic amenities) to five diamond (luxury properties with the finest service, rooms and facilities).
Source: OAG, Business Travel Planner, Winter 1998-99

CONVENTION CENTERS

Major Convention Centers

Center Name	Meeting Rooms	Exhibit Space (sq. ft.)
Adam's Mark St. Louis	43	40,679
Cervantes Convention Center at America's Center	67	340,000
Frontenac Hilton	22	22,000
Henry VII Hotel	n/a	21,090
Hyatt Regency St. Louis at Union Station	24	24,300
Innsbrook Estates Executive Conference Center	9	n/a
Marriott's Pavillion Hotel	22	18,017
Regal Riverfront Hotel	24	30,855
St. Louis Airport Marriott	n/a	14,980
St. Louis Arena	n/a	18,896
St. Louis Executive Conference Ctr. at America's Center	3	20,000
St. Louis Soccer Park & Convention Center	3	2,784
The Ritz-Carlton, St. Louis	12	19,146

Note: n/a not available
Source: Trade Shows Worldwide, 1998; Meetings & Conventions, 4/15/99;
Sucessful Meetings, 3/31/98

Living Environment

COST OF LIVING

Cost of Living Index

Composite Index	Groceries	Housing	Utilities	Trans-portation	Health Care	Misc. Goods/ Services
96.9	100.7	96.0	101.2	93.0	106.8	94.5

Note: U.S. = 100; Figures are for the Metropolitan Statistical Area - see Appendix A for areas included
Source: ACCRA, Cost of Living Index, 1st Quarter 1999

HOUSING

Median Home Prices and Housing Affordability

Area	Median Price[2] 1st Qtr. 1999 ($)	HOI[3] 1st Qtr. 1999	Afford-ability Rank[4]
MSA[1]	120,000	71.3	109
U.S.	134,000	69.6	—

Note: (1) Metropolitan Statistical Area - see Appendix A for areas included; (2) U.S. figures calculated from the sales of 524,324 new and existing homes in 181 markets; (3) Housing Opportunity Index - percent of homes sold that were within the reach of the median income household at the prevailing mortgage interest rate; (4) Rank is from 1-181 with 1 being most affordable
Source: National Association of Home Builders, Housing Opportunity Index, 1st Quarter 1999

Median Home Price Projection

It is projected that the median price of existing single-family homes in the metro area will increase by 3.2% in 1999. Nationwide, home prices are projected to increase 3.8%.
Kiplinger's Personal Finance Magazine, January 1999

Average New Home Price

Area	Price ($)
MSA[1]	132,700
U.S.	142,735

Note: Figures are based on a new home with 1,800 sq. ft. of living area on an 8,000 sq. ft. lot; (1) Metropolitan Statistical Area - see Appendix A for areas included
Source: ACCRA, Cost of Living Index, 1st Quarter 1999

Average Apartment Rent

Area	Rent ($/mth)
MSA[1]	658
U.S.	601

Note: Figures are based on an unfurnished two bedroom, 1-1/2 or 2 bath apartment, approximately 950 sq. ft. in size, excluding all utilities except water; (1) Metropolitan Statistical Area - see Appendix A for areas included
Source: ACCRA, Cost of Living Index, 1st Quarter 1999

RESIDENTIAL UTILITIES

Average Residential Utility Costs

Area	All Electric ($/mth)	Part Electric ($/mth)	Other Energy ($/mth)	Phone ($/mth)
MSA[1]	—	58.91	41.86	19.69
U.S.	100.02	55.73	43.33	19.71

Note: (1) (1) Metropolitan Statistical Area - see Appendix A for areas included
Source: ACCRA, Cost of Living Index, 1st Quarter 1999

HEALTH CARE

Average Health Care Costs

Area	Hospital ($/day)	Doctor ($/visit)	Dentist ($/visit)
MSA[1]	472.50	61.20	64.00
U.S.	430.43	52.45	66.35

Note: Hospital—based on a semi-private room; Doctor—based on a general practitioner's routine exam of an established patient; Dentist—based on adult teeth cleaning and periodic oral exam; (1) Metropolitan Statistical Area - see Appendix A for areas included
Source: ACCRA, Cost of Living Index, 1st Quarter 1999

Distribution of Office-Based Physicians

Area	Family/Gen. Practitioners	Specialists		
		Medical	Surgical	Other
MSA[1]	313	1,852	1,273	1,326

Note: Data as of 12/31/97; (1) Metropolitan Statistical Area - see Appendix A for areas included
Source: American Medical Assn., Physician Characteristics & Distribution in the U.S., 1999

Hospitals

Saint Louis has 1 general medical and surgical hospital, 3 psychiatric, 1 rehabilitation, 1 children's general, 1 children's other specialty, 1 children's orthopedic. *AHA Guide to the Healthcare Field, 1998-99*

According to *U.S. News and World Report,* Saint Louis has 4 of the best hospitals in the U.S.: **Barnes-Jewish Hospital**, noted for cancer, cardiology, endocrinology, gastroenterology, geriatrics, gynecology, neurology, ophthalmology, orthopedics, otolaryngology, psychiatry, pulmonology, rheumatology, urology; **St. Louis University Hospital**, noted for cardiology, endocrinology, gastroenterology, geriatrics, neurology, orthopedics, otolaryngology, rheumatology, urology; **St. Anthony Medical Center**, noted for endocrinology; **St. John's Mercy Medical Center**, noted for geriatrics, gynecology, orthopedics. *U.S. News Online, "America's Best Hospitals," 10th Edition, www.usnews.com*

EDUCATION

Public School District Statistics

District Name	Num. Sch.	Enroll.	Classroom Teachers	Pupils per Teacher	Minority Pupils (%)	Current Exp.[1] ($/pupil)
Affton 101	4	2,636	152	17.3	n/a	n/a
Bayless	4	1,409	79	17.8	n/a	n/a
Hancock Place	3	1,725	94	18.4	n/a	n/a
Ladue	6	3,421	251	13.6	n/a	n/a
Lindbergh R-VIII	7	5,199	319	16.3	n/a	n/a
Mehlville R-IX	16	12,066	643	18.8	n/a	n/a
Normandy	14	5,715	321	17.8	n/a	n/a
Ritenour	9	6,369	335	19.0	n/a	n/a
Riverview Gardens	11	6,318	364	17.4	n/a	n/a
Spec. Sch. Dist. St. Louis Co.	14	7,454	n/a	n/a	n/a	n/a
St Louis Career Education	1	n/a	15	0.0	n/a	n/a
St. Louis City	113	46,235	3,131	14.8	82.2	n/a
University City	10	4,547	279	16.3	n/a	n/a
Wellston	4	719	53	13.6	n/a	n/a

Note: Data covers the 1997-1998 school year unless otherwise noted; (1) Data covers fiscal year 1996; SD = School District; ISD = Independent School District; n/a not available
Source: National Center for Education Statistics, Common Core of Data Public Education Agency Universe 1997-98; National Center for Education Statistics, Characteristics of the 100 Largest Public Elementary and Secondary School Districts in the United States: 1997-98, July 1999

Educational Quality

School District	Education Quotient[1]	Graduate Outcome[2]	Community Index[3]	Resource Index[4]
Saint Louis City	86.0	58.0	54.0	147.0

Note: Nearly 1,000 secondary school districts were rated in terms of educational quality. The scores range from a low of 50 to a high of 150; (1) Average of the Graduate Outcome, Community and Resource indexes; (2) Based on graduation rates and college board scores (SAT/ACT); (3) Based on the surrounding community's average level of education and the area's average income level; (4) Based on teacher salaries, per-pupil expenditures and student-teacher ratios.
Source: Expansion Management, Ratings Issue, 1998

Educational Attainment by Race

Area	High School Graduate (%)					Bachelor's Degree (%)				
	Total	White	Black	Other	Hisp.[2]	Total	White	Black	Other	Hisp.[2]
City	62.8	67.4	56.3	66.8	61.9	15.3	20.2	8.0	32.1	18.8
MSA[1]	76.0	78.1	64.1	79.9	75.2	20.7	22.1	11.4	40.5	24.3
U.S.	75.2	77.9	63.1	60.4	49.8	20.3	21.5	11.4	19.4	9.2

Note: Figures shown cover persons 25 years old and over; (1) Metropolitan Statistical Area - see Appendix A for areas included; (2) people of Hispanic origin can be of any race
Source: 1990 Census of Population and Housing, Summary Tape File 3C

School Enrollment by Type

Area	Preprimary				Elementary/High School			
	Public		Private		Public		Private	
	Enrollment	%	Enrollment	%	Enrollment	%	Enrollment	%
City	4,198	56.7	3,211	43.3	49,177	77.4	14,389	22.6
MSA[1]	26,907	50.2	26,648	49.8	337,304	80.6	81,322	19.4
U.S.	2,679,029	59.5	1,824,256	40.5	38,379,689	90.2	4,187,099	9.8

Note: Figures shown cover persons 3 years old and over;
(1) Metropolitan Statistical Area - see Appendix A for areas included
Source: 1990 Census of Population and Housing, Summary Tape File 3C

School Enrollment by Race

Area	Preprimary (%)				Elementary/High School (%)			
	White	Black	Other	Hisp.[1]	White	Black	Other	Hisp.[1]
City	44.4	53.6	2.0	1.2	33.2	65.2	1.6	1.4
MSA[2]	81.3	16.9	1.8	1.2	74.9	23.3	1.8	1.3
U.S.	80.4	12.5	7.1	7.8	74.1	15.6	10.3	12.5

Note: Figures shown cover persons 3 years old and over; (1) people of Hispanic origin can be of any race; (2) Metropolitan Statistical Area - see Appendix A for areas included
Source: 1990 Census of Population and Housing, Summary Tape File 3C

Classroom Teacher Salaries in Public Schools

District	B.A. Degree		M.A. Degree		Maximum	
	Min. ($)	Rank[1]	Max. ($)	Rank[1]	Max. ($)	Rank[1]
Saint Louis	25,288	61	43,714	61	46,958	77
Average	26,980	-	46,065	-	51,435	-

Note: Salaries are for 1997-1998; (1) Rank ranges from 1 to 100
Source: American Federation of Teachers, Survey & Analysis of Salary Trends, 1998

Higher Education

Two-Year Colleges		Four-Year Colleges		Medical Schools	Law Schools	Voc/ Tech
Public	Private	Public	Private			
2	3	2	10	2	2	20

Source: College Blue Book, Occupational Education, 1997; Medical School Admission Requirements, 1999-2000; Peterson's Guide to Two-Year Colleges, 1999; Peterson's Guide to Four-Year Colleges, 2000; Barron's Guide to Law Schools, 1999

MAJOR EMPLOYERS

Major Employers

AG Edwards & Sons (security brokers)	Monsanto Co.
Barnes-Jewish Hospital	Edison Brothers Stores (clothing)
Jones Financial Companies	Washington University
Ralston Purina	Southwestern Bell Telephone
St. John's Mercy Medical Center	St. Louis Children's Hospital

Note: Companies listed are located in the city
Source: Dun's Business Rankings, 1999; Ward's Business Directory, 1998

PUBLIC SAFETY

Crime Rate

Area	All Crimes	Violent Crimes				Property Crimes		
		Murder	Forcible Rape	Robbery	Aggrav. Assault	Burglary	Larceny -Theft	Motor Vehicle Theft
City	13,576.7	40.6	59.6	946.9	1,495.4	2,676.7	6,204.6	2,152.8
Suburbs[1]	n/a	n/a	n/a	n/a	n/a	n/a	n/a	n/a
MSA[2]	n/a	n/a	n/a	n/a	n/a	n/a	n/a	n/a
U.S.	4,922.7	6.8	35.9	186.1	382.0	919.6	2,886.5	505.8

Note: Crime rate is the number of crimes per 100,000 pop.; (1) defined as all areas within the MSA but located outside the central city; (2) Metropolitan Statistical Area - see Appendix A for areas incl.
Source: FBI Uniform Crime Reports, 1997

RECREATION

Culture and Recreation

Museums	Symphony Orchestras	Opera Companies	Dance Companies	Professional Theatres	Zoos	Pro Sports Teams
13	3	1	2	5	1	3

Source: International Directory of the Performing Arts, 1997; Official Museum Directory, 1999; Stern's Performing Arts Directory, 1997; USA Today Four Sport Stadium Guide, 1997; Chamber of Commerce/Economic Development, 1999

Library System

The St. Louis County Library has 18 branches, holdings of 2,316,166 volumes, and a budget of $21,363,500 (1997). *American Library Directory, 1998-1999*

MEDIA

Newspapers

Name	Type	Freq.	Distribution	Circulation
Central West End Journal	General	1x/wk	Local	6,849
Chesterfield Journal	General	2x/wk	Local	15,220
Citizen Journal	General	2x/wk	Local	22,550
County Star Journal	General	2x/wk	Local	39,536
Maryland Heights/Bridgeton Journal	General	2x/wk	Local	12,536
Mid-County Journal	General	2x/wk	Local	14,312
North County Journal East	n/a	2x/wk	Local	93,167
North County Journal West	General	2x/wk	Local	49,484
North Side Journal	General	2x/wk	Local	39,889
Noticias	n/a	1x/mo	Local	5,000
Oakville-Mehlville Journal	General	2x/wk	Local	19,975
Press Journal	General	2x/wk	Local	35,000
Saint Louis American	Black	1x/wk	Area	65,500
Saint Louis Argus	Black	1x/wk	Area	44,000
St. Louis Daily Record	Men/Women	5x/wk	Area	1,000
Saint Louis Jewish Light	Religious	1x/wk	Local	15,000
Saint Louis Sentinel	Black	1x/wk	Local	25,000
South City Journal	General	1x/wk	Local	23,215
South County Journal	General	2x/wk	Local	24,145
South Side Journal	General	2x/wk	Local	38,500
Southwest City Journal	General	2x/wk	Local	27,325
Southwest County Journal	General	2x/wk	Local	29,258
St. Louis Post-Dispatch	n/a	7x/wk	Area	338,793
Webster-Kirkwood Journal	General	2x/wk	Local	27,000
West County Journal	General	2x/wk	Local	28,844

Note: Includes newspapers with circulations of 1,000 or more located in the city; n/a not available
Source: Burrelle's Media Directory, 1999 Edition

Television Stations

Name	Ch.	Affiliation	Type	Owner
KTVI	n/a	FBC	Commercial	Fox Television Stations Inc.
KMOV	n/a	CBST	Commercial	n/a
KSDK	n/a	NBCT	Commercial	Gannett Company
KETC	n/a	PBS	Public	Saint Louis Regional Educational and Public Television Commission
KPLR	11	WB	Commercial	Acme Television Holdings
KAUO	19	n/a	n/a	Minority Broadcasters of Santa Fe Inc.
KNLC	24	n/a	Commercial	New Life Evangelistic Center Inc.
KDNL	30	ABCT	Commercial	Sinclair Communications Inc.
WHSL	46	n/a	Commercial	Roberts Broadcasting Inc.

Note: Stations included broadcast in the Saint Louis metro area; n/a not available
Source: Burrelle's Media Directory, 1999 Edition

AM Radio Stations

Call Letters	Freq. (kHz)	Target Audience	Station Format	Music Format
KTRS	550	General	N/S/T	n/a
KFNS	590	General	S	n/a
KJSL	630	Religious	T	n/a
KSTL	690	Religious	M/T	Christian
WEW	770	G/H	M/T	Adult Standards/Big Band/Jazz/Oldies/R&B
KFUO	850	General	M/T	Christian
WGNU	920	B/G	N/S/T	n/a
KMOX	1120	General	N/S/T	n/a
KGLX	1220	General	M/N	World Music
KSIV	1320	Religious	M/N	Christian
WRTH	1430	General	M/N/S	Easy Listening
KATZ	1600	General	M	Christian

Note: Stations included broadcast in the Saint Louis metro area; n/a not available
Target Audience: A=Asian; B=Black; C=Christian; E=Ethnic; F=French; G=General; H=Hispanic;
M=Men; N=Native American; R=Religious; S=Senior Citizen; W=Women; Y=Young Adult; Z=Children
Station Format: E=Educational; M=Music; N=News; S=Sports; T=Talk
Source: Burrelle's Media Directory, 1999 Edition

FM Radio Stations

Call Letters	Freq. (mHz)	Target Audience	Station Format	Music Format
KDHX	88.1	G/H	M	Jazz/Latin/R&B/Urban Contemporary
KCFV	89.5	General	E/M/N/S	Alternative
KRHS	90.1	General	E/M/T	Alternative/AOR/Classical/Country
KWUR	90.3	General	M/S/T	Alternative
KWMU	90.7	General	E/M/N/S/T	Classical/Jazz
KSIV	91.5	General	M/N/T	Christian
WIL	92.3	General	M/N/S	Country
KSD	93.7	General	M	Adult Contemporary/Classic Rock
KSHE	94.7	General	M/N/S	AOR
WFUN	95.5	n/a	n/a	n/a
KIHT	96.3	General	M/N	Oldies
KXOK	97.1	Black	Women	M/N/T
KYKY	98.1	General	M	Adult Contemporary
KFUO	99.1	General	M/N	Classical
KATZ	100.3	General	M	Adult Contemporary/Urban Contemporary
WVRV	101.1	General	M/N/T	Adult Contemporary/Modern Rock
KEZK	102.5	General	M	Adult Contemporary
KLOU	103.3	General	M	Oldies
WXTM	104.1	General	M	Classic Rock
KMJM	104.9	Black	M/N/S	Urban Contemporary
KPNT	105.7	General	M	Alternative
WKKX	106.5	General	M	Country
KSLZ	107.7	General	n/a	n/a

Note: Stations included broadcast in the Saint Louis metro area; n/a not available
Station Format: E=Educational; M=Music; N=News; S=Sports; T=Talk
Target Audience: A=Asian; B=Black; C=Christian; E=Ethnic; F=French; G=General; H=Hispanic;
M=Men; N=Native American; R=Religious; S=Senior Citizen; W=Women; Y=Young Adult; Z=Children
Music Format: AOR=Album Oriented Rock; MOR=Middle-of-the-Road
Source: Burrelle's Media Directory, 1999 Edition

CLIMATE

Average and Extreme Temperatures

Temperature	Jan	Feb	Mar	Apr	May	Jun	Jul	Aug	Sep	Oct	Nov	Dec	Yr.
Extreme High (°F)	77	83	89	93	98	105	115	107	104	94	85	76	115
Average High (°F)	39	43	54	67	76	85	89	87	80	69	54	42	66
Average Temp. (°F)	30	34	44	56	66	75	79	78	70	59	45	34	56
Average Low (°F)	21	25	34	46	55	65	69	67	59	48	36	26	46
Extreme Low (°F)	-18	-10	-5	22	31	43	51	47	36	23	1	-16	-18

Note: Figures cover the years 1945-1990
Source: National Climatic Data Center, International Station Meteorological Climate Summary, 3/95

Average Precipitation/Snowfall/Humidity

Precip./Humidity	Jan	Feb	Mar	Apr	May	Jun	Jul	Aug	Sep	Oct	Nov	Dec	Yr.
Avg. Precip. (in.)	1.9	2.2	3.4	3.4	3.8	4.0	3.8	2.9	2.9	2.8	3.0	2.6	36.8
Avg. Snowfall (in.)	6	4	4	Tr	0	0	0	0	0	Tr	1	4	20
Avg. Rel. Hum. 6am (%)	80	81	80	78	81	82	84	86	87	83	81	81	82
Avg. Rel. Hum. 3pm (%)	62	59	54	49	51	51	51	52	50	50	56	63	54

Note: Figures cover the years 1945-1990; Tr = Trace amounts (<0.05 in. of rain; <0.5 in. of snow)
Source: National Climatic Data Center, International Station Meteorological Climate Summary, 3/95

Weather Conditions

Temperature			Daytime Sky			Precipitation		
10°F & below	32°F & below	90°F & above	Clear	Partly cloudy	Cloudy	0.01 inch or more precip.	0.1 inch or more snow/ice	Thunder-storms
13	100	43	97	138	130	109	14	46

Note: Figures are average number of days per year and covers the years 1945-1990
Source: National Climatic Data Center, International Station Meteorological Climate Summary, 3/95

AIR & WATER QUALITY

Maximum Pollutant Concentrations

	Particulate Matter (ug/m^3)	Carbon Monoxide (ppm)	Sulfur Dioxide (ppm)	Nitrogen Dioxide (ppm)	Ozone (ppm)	Lead (ug/m^3)
MSA[1] Level	108	5	0.063	0.025	0.12	0.03
NAAQS[2]	150	9	0.140	0.053	0.12	1.50
Met NAAQS?	Yes	Yes	Yes	Yes	Yes	Yes

Note: (1) Metropolitan Statistical Area - see Appendix A for areas included; (2) National Ambient Air Quality Standards; ppm = parts per million; ug/m^3 = micrograms per cubic meter; n/a not available
Source: EPA, National Air Quality and Emissions Trends Report, 1997

Pollutant Standards Index

In the Saint Louis MSA (see Appendix A for areas included), the Pollutant Standards Index (PSI) exceeded 100 on 15 days in 1997. A PSI value greater than 100 indicates that air quality would be in the unhealthful range on that day. *EPA, National Air Quality and Emissions Trends Report, 1997*

Drinking Water

Water System Name	Pop. Served	Primary Water Source Type	Number of Violations in 1998	Type of Violation/ Contaminants
St. Louis City	370,000	Surface	None	None

Note: Data as of July 10, 1999
Source: EPA, Office of Ground Water and Drinking Water, Safe Drinking Water Information System

Saint Louis tap water is alkaline, moderately hard and fluoridated.
Editor & Publisher Market Guide, 1999

Springfield, Missouri

Background

At the edge of the Ozark Mountains, Springfield is the gateway to the scenic White River region in the Ozarks. The entire metro area consists of comparatively flat or very gently rolling tableland.

Settled in 1827, Springfield was incorporated as a town in 1838 and as a city in 1847. Throughout the Civil War, its location made it a military target for both Confederate and Union armies. On August 10, 1861 the Confederates took the city, but were permanently driven out a year later. Union forces held the area until the end of the war.

Today, Springfield is the center of an important food-processing area. Major economic activities include shipping, wholesaling, meat-packing, and dairy-product processing. As a regional agribusiness center, the Southwest Regional Stockyards is the sixth largest feeder cattle operation in the United States. The city also manufactures boats, auto trailers, railroad equipment, fabricated metals, prepressed concrete, paper products, chemical products, furniture, and clothing.

The city enjoys a plateau climate which is characterized by mild temperatures, low humidity, and plenty of sunshine. The air is remarkably free from industrial smoke and most fogs.

General Rankings and Evaluative Comments

■ Springfield was ranked #15 out of 24 mid-sized, midwestern metropolitan areas in *Money's* 1998 survey of "The Best Places to Live in America." The survey was conducted by first contacting 512 representative households nationwide and asking them to rank 37 quality-of-life factors on a scale of 1 to 10. Next, a demographic profile was compiled on the 300 largest metropolitan statistical areas in the U.S. The numbers were crunched together to arrive at an overall ranking (things Americans consider most important, like clean air and water, low crime and good schools, received extra weight). Unlike previous years, the 1998 rankings were broken down by region (northeast, midwest, south, west) and population size (100,000 to 249,999; 250,000 to 999,999; 1 million plus). The city had a nationwide ranking of #103 out of 300 in 1997 and #61 out of 300 in 1996. *Money, July 1998; Money, July 1997; Money, September 1996*

■ *Ladies Home Journal* ranked America's 200 largest cities based on the qualities women care about most. Springfield ranked #116 out of 200. Criteria: low crime rate, well-paying jobs, quality health and child care, good public schools, the presence of women in government, size of the gender wage gap, number of sexual-harassment and discrimination complaints filed, unemployment and divorce rates, commute times, population density, number of houses of worship, parks and cultural offerings, number of women's health specialists, how well a community's women cared for themselves, complexion kindness index based on UV radiation levels, odds of finding affordable fashions, rental rates for romance movies, champagne sales and other matters of the heart. *Ladies Home Journal, November 1998*

■ Zero Population Growth ranked 229 cities in terms of children's health, safety, and economic well-being. Springfield was ranked #26 out of 112 independent cities (cities with populations greater than 100,000 which were neither Major Cities nor Suburbs/Outer Cities) and was given a grade of B. Criteria: total population, percent of population under 18 years of age, household language, percent population change, percent of births to teens, infant mortality rate, percent of low birth weights, dropout rate, enrollment in preprimary school, violent and property crime rates, unemployment rate, percent of children in poverty, percent of owner occupied units, number of bad air days, percent of public transportation commuters, and average travel time to work. *Zero Population Growth, Children's Environmental Index, Fall 1999*

■ Cognetics studied 273 metro areas in the United States, ranking them by entrepreneurial activity. Springfield was ranked #20 out of 134 smaller metro areas. Criteria: Significant Starts (firms started in the last 10 years that still employ at least 5 people) and Young Growers (percent of firms 10 years old or less that grew significantly during the last 4 years). *Cognetics, "Entrepreneurial Hot Spots: The Best Places in America to Start and Grow a Company," 1998*

Business Environment

STATE ECONOMY

State Economic Profile

"St. Louis' weak economy and a slowdown in Kansas City are placing a drag on the Missouri economy. Gross State Product and job growth, after matching or surpassing the national for several years, has slowed. After strong home sales in 1998, MO's housing and construction markets will likely slow considerably in 1999.

Like most Plains states, MO's significant farm sector has been a drag on the economy. Farm income was down over 20% in 1998 as commodity prices and foreign demand remained weak. With overcapacity in MO's beef and grain sectors, a major restructing is in store. Even with a resurgence in Asian demand, the current trend in commodity prices is not likely to reverse.

Manufacturing employment shrank 0.5% in 1998. St. Louis witnessed an even greater decline of 0.9%. With the prospect of job cuts at Boeing's St. Louis facilities, Missouri will likely witness further contraction in manufacturing employment in 1999.

An increase in building activity in St. Louis, fueled by corporate relocations, helped to offset declining activity elsewhere in the state. Almost half of the new construction jobs created in MO were in St. Louis.

MO's relatively high unemployment rate has in some ways been a bonus, helping to attract some corporate relocations. MasterCard and Convergys, for instance, have moved operations to St. Louis to take advantage of the available labor. In spite of these moves, St. Louis should still add little to state GSP and job growth. Gains in Kansas City, Columbia and Springfield will help to offset the weakness in St. Louis and the soft farm economy." National Association of Realtors, Economic Profiles: The Fifty States and the District of Columbia, http://nar.realtor.com/databank/profiles.htm

IMPORTS/EXPORTS

Total Export Sales

Area	1994 ($000)	1995 ($000)	1996 ($000)	1997 ($000)	% Chg. 1994-97	% Chg. 1996-97
MSA[1]	103,823	120,178	120,349	141,448	36.2	17.5
U.S.	512,415,609	583,030,524	622,827,063	687,597,999	34.2	10.4

Note: (1) Metropolitan Statistical Area - see Appendix A for areas included
Source: U.S. Department of Commerce, International Trade Association, Metropolitan Area Exports: An Export Performance Report on Over 250 U.S. Cities, November 10, 1998

CITY FINANCES

City Government Finances

Component	FY92 ($000)	FY92 (per capita $)
Revenue	280,916	1,964.65
Expenditure	257,462	1,800.62
Debt Outstanding	296,583	2,074.22
Cash & Securities	286,736	2,005.36

Source: U.S. Bureau of the Census, City Government Finances: 1991-92

City Government Revenue by Source

Source	FY92 ($000)	FY92 (per capita $)	FY92 (%)
From Federal Government	5,152	36.03	1.8
From State Governments	13,849	96.86	4.9
From Local Governments	1,626	11.37	0.6
Property Taxes	6,026	42.14	2.1
General Sales Taxes	24,453	171.02	8.7
Selective Sales Taxes	8,094	56.61	2.9
Income Taxes	0	0.00	0.0
Current Charges	26,986	188.73	9.6
Utility/Liquor Store	161,235	1,127.64	57.4
Employee Retirement[1]	5,845	40.88	2.1
Other	27,650	193.38	9.8

Note: (1) Excludes "city contributions," classified as "nonrevenue," intragovernmental transfers.
Source: U.S. Bureau of the Census, City Government Finances: 1991-92

City Government Expenditures by Function

Function	FY92 ($000)	FY92 (per capita $)	FY92 (%)
Educational Services	0	0.00	0.0
Employee Retirement[1]	2,860	20.00	1.1
Environment/Housing	41,076	287.27	16.0
Government Administration	6,001	41.97	2.3
Interest on General Debt	7,594	53.11	2.9
Public Safety	22,240	155.54	8.6
Social Services	8,007	56.00	3.1
Transportation	27,998	195.81	10.9
Utility/Liquor Store	139,730	977.24	54.3
Other	1,956	13.68	0.8

Note: (1) Payments to beneficiaries including withdrawal of contributions.
Source: U.S. Bureau of the Census, City Government Finances: 1991-92

Municipal Bond Ratings

Area	Moody's	S & P
Springfield	Aa2	n/a

Note: n/a not available; n/r not rated
Source: Moody's Bond Record, 6/99

POPULATION

Population Growth

Area	1980	1990	% Chg. 1980-90	July 1998 Estimate	% Chg. 1990-98
City	133,116	140,494	5.5	142,898	1.7
MSA[1]	207,704	240,593	15.8	307,011	27.6
U.S.	226,545,805	248,765,170	9.8	270,299,000	8.7

Note: (1) Metropolitan Statistical Area - see Appendix A for areas included;
July 1998 MSA population estimate was calculated by the editors
Source: 1980/1990 Census of Housing and Population, Summary Tape File 3C;
Census Bureau Population Estimates 1998

Population Characteristics

Race	City 1980 Population	%	City 1990 Population	%	% Chg. 1980-90	MSA¹ 1990 Population	%
White	128,478	96.5	134,286	95.6	4.5	233,078	96.9
Black	2,900	2.2	3,373	2.4	16.3	3,626	1.5
Amer Indian/Esk/Aleut	733	0.6	1,116	0.8	52.3	1,816	0.8
Asian/Pacific Islander	686	0.5	1,328	0.9	93.6	1,578	0.7
Other	319	0.2	391	0.3	22.6	495	0.2
Hispanic Origin²	1,088	0.8	1,240	0.9	14.0	2,001	0.8

Note: (1) Metropolitan Statistical Area - see Appendix A for areas included;
(2) people of Hispanic origin can be of any race
Source: 1980/1990 Census of Housing and Population, Summary Tape File 3C

Ancestry

Area	German	Irish	English	Italian	U.S.	French	Polish	Dutch
City	30.7	21.6	20.3	2.0	5.9	5.0	1.3	4.0
MSA¹	31.4	22.0	20.1	2.0	6.5	4.9	1.2	4.0
U.S.	23.3	15.6	13.1	5.9	5.3	4.2	3.8	2.5

Note: Figures are percentages and include persons that reported multiple ancestry (eg. if a person reported being Irish and Italian, they were included in both columns); (1) Metropolitan Statistical Area - see Appendix A for areas included
Source: 1990 Census of Population and Housing, Summary Tape File 3C

Age

Area	Median Age (Years)	Under 5	Under 18	18-24	25-44	45-64	65+	80+
City	31.7	6.2	20.6	17.8	29.3	17.1	15.2	4.2
MSA¹	32.5	6.5	23.8	13.8	31.0	18.3	13.1	3.3
U.S.	32.9	7.3	25.6	10.5	32.6	18.7	12.5	2.8

Note: (1) Metropolitan Statistical Area - see Appendix A for areas included
Source: 1990 Census of Population and Housing, Summary Tape File 3C

Male/Female Ratio

Area	Number of males per 100 females (all ages)	Number of males per 100 females (18 years old+)
City	89.4	85.7
MSA¹	92.2	88.4
U.S.	95.0	91.9

Note: (1) Metropolitan Statistical Area - see Appendix A for areas included
Source: 1990 Census of Population, General Population Characteristics

INCOME

Per Capita/Median/Average Income

Area	Per Capita ($)	Median Household ($)	Average Household ($)
City	11,878	21,577	28,471
MSA¹	12,250	24,546	31,107
U.S.	14,420	30,056	38,453

Note: All figures are for 1989; (1) Metropolitan Statistical Area - see Appendix A for areas included
Source: 1990 Census of Population and Housing, Summary Tape File 3C

Household Income Distribution by Race

Income ($)	City (%)					U.S. (%)				
	Total	White	Black	Other	Hisp.[1]	Total	White	Black	Other	Hisp.[1]
Less than 5,000	8.3	8.2	10.0	15.8	8.5	6.2	4.8	15.2	8.6	8.8
5,000 - 9,999	13.1	13.0	16.9	17.6	17.9	9.3	8.6	14.2	9.9	11.1
10,000 - 14,999	12.9	12.9	17.4	12.0	17.6	8.8	8.5	11.0	9.8	11.0
15,000 - 24,999	22.8	22.9	26.1	14.8	21.2	17.5	17.3	18.9	18.5	20.5
25,000 - 34,999	17.1	17.1	16.0	16.0	18.5	15.8	16.1	14.2	15.4	16.4
35,000 - 49,999	13.7	13.9	6.4	11.9	8.5	17.9	18.6	13.3	16.1	16.0
50,000 - 74,999	7.9	8.0	5.4	8.0	5.8	15.0	15.8	9.3	13.4	11.1
75,000 - 99,999	1.8	1.9	1.0	0.0	0.0	5.1	5.5	2.6	4.7	3.1
100,000+	2.3	2.3	0.8	4.0	2.0	4.4	4.8	1.3	3.7	1.9

Note: All figures are for 1989; (1) people of Hispanic origin can be of any race
Source: 1990 Census of Population and Housing, Summary Tape File 3C

Effective Buying Income

Area	Per Capita ($)	Median Household ($)	Average Household ($)
City	15,139	28,016	36,927
MSA[1]	15,451	30,488	40,109
U.S.	16,803	34,536	45,243

Note: Data as of 1/1/99; (1) Metropolitan Statistical Area - see Appendix A for areas included
Source: Standard Rate & Data Service, Newspaper Advertising Source, 9/99

Effective Household Buying Income Distribution

Area	% of Households Earning						
	$10,000 -$19,999	$20,000 -$34,999	$35,000 -$49,999	$50,000 -$74,999	$75,000 -$99,000	$100,000 -$124,999	$125,000 and up
City	20.5	26.9	17.2	13.2	4.4	1.2	2.1
MSA[1]	18.8	25.9	18.9	15.6	4.8	1.3	2.0
U.S.	16.0	22.6	18.2	18.9	7.2	2.4	2.7

Note: Data as of 1/1/99; (1) Metropolitan Statistical Area - see Appendix A for areas included
Source: Standard Rate & Data Service, Newspaper Advertising Source, 9/99

Poverty Rates by Race and Age

Area	Total (%)	By Race (%)				By Age (%)		
		White	Black	Other	Hisp.[2]	Under 5 years old	Under 18 years old	65 years and over
City	17.8	17.0	30.7	42.2	30.1	26.4	21.2	13.4
MSA[1]	13.5	13.0	28.4	34.3	20.0	20.4	15.4	13.8
U.S.	13.1	9.8	29.5	23.1	25.3	20.1	18.3	12.8

Note: Figures show the percent of people living below the poverty line in 1989. The average poverty threshold was $12,674 for a family of four in 1989; (1) Metropolitan Statistical Area - see Appendix A for areas included; (2) people of Hispanic origin can be of any race
Source: 1990 Census of Population and Housing, Summary Tape File 3C

EMPLOYMENT

Labor Force and Employment

Area	Civilian Labor Force			Workers Employed		
	Jun. 1998	Jun. 1999	% Chg.	Jun. 1998	Jun. 1999	% Chg.
City	83,086	86,909	4.6	80,079	84,323	5.3
MSA[1]	164,356	171,988	4.6	158,817	167,233	5.3
U.S.	138,798,000	140,666,000	1.3	132,265,000	134,395,000	1.6

Note: Data is not seasonally adjusted and covers workers 16 years of age and older; (1) Metropolitan Statistical Area - see Appendix A for areas included
Source: Bureau of Labor Statistics, http://stats.bls.gov

Unemployment Rate

Area	1998						1999					
	Jul.	Aug.	Sep.	Oct.	Nov.	Dec.	Jan.	Feb.	Mar.	Apr.	May.	Jun.
City	3.1	3.5	3.0	2.6	2.6	2.4	2.3	2.1	2.1	2.3	2.4	3.0
MSA[1]	2.8	3.3	2.7	2.4	2.5	2.4	2.4	2.1	2.1	2.1	2.2	2.8
U.S.	4.7	4.5	4.4	4.2	4.1	4.0	4.8	4.7	4.4	4.1	4.0	4.5

Note: Data is not seasonally adjusted and covers workers 16 years of age and older; all figures are percentages; (1) Metropolitan Statistical Area - see Appendix A for areas included
Source: Bureau of Labor Statistics, http://stats.bls.gov

Employment by Industry

Sector	MSA[1]		U.S.
	Number of Employees	Percent of Total	Percent of Total
Services	49,900	29.9	30.4
Retail Trade	33,700	20.2	17.7
Government	20,100	12.1	15.6
Manufacturing	23,900	14.3	14.3
Finance/Insurance/Real Estate	7,700	4.6	5.9
Wholesale Trade	12,200	7.3	5.4
Transportation/Public Utilities	11,600	7.0	5.3
Construction	n/a	n/a	5.0
Mining	n/a	n/a	0.4

Note: Figures cover non-farm employment as of 6/99 and are not seasonally adjusted; (1) Metropolitan Statistical Area - see Appendix A for areas included; n/a not available
Source: Bureau of Labor Statistics, http://stats.bls.gov

Employment by Occupation

Occupation Category	City (%)	MSA[1] (%)	U.S. (%)
White Collar	58.6	56.7	58.1
Executive/Admin./Management	10.0	10.3	12.3
Professional	13.4	12.9	14.1
Technical & Related Support	3.6	3.4	3.7
Sales	15.3	14.5	11.8
Administrative Support/Clerical	16.3	15.6	16.3
Blue Collar	24.2	26.6	26.2
Precision Production/Craft/Repair	9.5	10.7	11.3
Machine Operators/Assem./Insp.	6.5	6.9	6.8
Transportation/Material Movers	4.1	4.8	4.1
Cleaners/Helpers/Laborers	4.1	4.3	3.9
Services	16.2	14.5	13.2
Farming/Forestry/Fishing	1.0	2.1	2.5

Note: Figures cover employed persons 16 years old and over; (1) Metropolitan Statistical Area - see Appendix A for areas included
Source: 1990 Census of Population and Housing, Summary Tape File 3C

Occupational Employment Projections: 1996 - 2006

Occupations Expected to Have the Largest Job Growth (ranked by numerical growth)	Fast-Growing Occupations[1] (ranked by percent growth)
1. Salespersons, retail	1. Computer engineers
2. Teachers, secondary school	2. Systems analysts
3. Truck drivers, light	3. Desktop publishers
4. General managers & top executives	4. Home health aides
5. Cashiers	5. Teachers, special education
6. Nursing aides/orderlies/attendants	6. Personal and home care aides
7. Child care workers, private household	7. Speech-language pathologists/audiologists
8. Teachers aides, clerical & paraprofess.	8. Paralegals
9. Systems analysts	9. Occupational therapists
10. Marketing & sales, supervisors	10. Physical therapy assistants and aides

Note: Projections cover Missouri; (1) Excludes occupations with total job growth less than 300
Source: U.S. Department of Labor, Employment and Training Administration, America's Labor Market Information System (ALMIS)

TAXES

Major State and Local Tax Rates

State Corp. Income (%)	State Personal Income (%)	Residential Property (effective rate per $100)	Sales & Use State (%)	Sales & Use Local (%)	State Gasoline (cents/ gallon)	State Cigarette (cents/ pack)
6.25	1.5 - 6.0	n/a	4.225	1.875	17.05[a]	17.0[b]

Note: Personal/corporate income, sales, gasoline and cigarette tax rates as of January 1999. Property tax rates as of 1997; (a) Rate is comprised of 17 cents excise and 0.05 cents motor carrier tax; (b) Counties and cities may impose an additional tax of 4 - 7 cents per pack
Source: Federation of Tax Administrators, www.taxadmin.org; Washington D.C. Department of Finance and Revenue, Tax Rates and Tax Burdens in the District of Columbia: A Nationwide Comparison, July 1998; Chamber of Commerce, 1999

Total Taxes Per Capita and as a Percent of Income

Area	Per Capita Income ($)	Per Capita Taxes ($) Total	Per Capita Taxes ($) Federal	Per Capita Taxes ($) State/ Local	Percent of Income (%) Total	Percent of Income (%) Federal	Percent of Income (%) State/ Local
Missouri	26,334	9,207	6,136	3,072	35.0	23.3	11.7
U.S.	27,876	9,881	6,690	3,191	35.4	24.0	11.4

Note: Figures are for 1998
Source: Tax Foundation, www.taxfoundation.org

COMMERCIAL REAL ESTATE

Data not available at time of publication.

COMMERCIAL UTILITIES

Typical Monthly Electric Bills

Area	Commercial Service ($/month) 12 kW demand 1,500 kWh	Commercial Service ($/month) 100 kW demand 30,000 kWh	Industrial Service ($/month) 1,000 kW demand 400,000 kWh	Industrial Service ($/month) 20,000 kW demand 10,000,000 kWh
City	n/a	n/a	n/a	n/a
U.S.	150	2,174	23,995	508,569

Note: Based on rates in effect January 1, 1999; n/a not available
Source: Edison Electric Institute, Typical Residential, Commercial and Industrial Bills, Winter 1999

TRANSPORTATION

Transportation Statistics

Average minutes to work	15.7
Interstate highways	I-44
Bus lines	
In-city	City Utilities
Inter-city	1
Passenger air service	
Airport	Springfield/Branson Regional Airport
Airlines	6
Aircraft departures	n/a
Enplaned passengers	n/a
Rail service	No Amtrak service
Motor freight carriers	22
Major waterways/ports	None

Source: Editor & Publisher Market Guide, 1999; FAA Airport Activity Statistics, 1997; Amtrak National Time Table, Northeast Timetable, Spring/Summer 1999; 1990 Census of Population and Housing, STF 3C; Chamber of Commerce/Economic Development 1999; Jane's Urban Transport Systems 1999-2000

Means of Transportation to Work

Area	Car/Truck/Van		Public Transportation			Bicycle	Walked	Other Means	Worked at Home
	Drove Alone	Car-pooled	Bus	Subway	Railroad				
City	80.4	11.0	0.9	0.0	0.0	0.3	4.2	0.8	2.4
MSA[1]	81.5	10.9	0.6	0.0	0.0	0.2	2.9	0.7	3.2
U.S.	73.2	13.4	3.0	1.5	0.5	0.4	3.9	1.2	3.0

Note: Figures shown are percentages and only include workers 16 years old and over;
(1) Metropolitan Statistical Area - see Appendix A for areas included
Source: 1990 Census of Population and Housing, Summary Tape File 3C

BUSINESSES

Major Business Headquarters

Company Name	1999 Rankings	
	Fortune 500	Forbes 500

No companies listed.

Note: Companies listed are located in the city; dashes indicate no ranking
Fortune 500: Companies that produce a 10-K are ranked 1 to 500 based on 1998 revenue
Forbes 500: Private companies are ranked 1 to 500 based on 1997 revenue
Source: Forbes, November 30, 1998; Fortune, April 26, 1999

HOTELS & MOTELS

Hotels/Motels

Area	Hotels/ Motels	Rooms	Luxury-Level Hotels/Motels		Average Minimum Rates ($)		
			♦♦♦♦	♦♦♦♦♦	♦♦	♦♦♦	♦♦♦♦
City	34	3,527	0	0	55	89	n/a

Note: n/a not available; classifications range from one diamond (budget properties with basic amenities) to five diamond (luxury properties with the finest service, rooms and facilities).
Source: OAG, Business Travel Planner, Winter 1998-99

CONVENTION CENTERS

Major Convention Centers

Center Name	Meeting Rooms	Exhibit Space (sq. ft.)
Hammons Student Center	3	35,000
University Plaza Trade Center	5	69,000
West Plains Civic Center	n/a	30,000

Note: n/a not available
Source: Trade Shows Worldwide, 1998; Meetings & Conventions, 4/15/99;
Sucessful Meetings, 3/31/98

Living Environment

COST OF LIVING

Cost of Living Index

Composite Index	Groceries	Housing	Utilities	Trans-portation	Health Care	Misc. Goods/ Services
92.1	96.2	89.1	73.6	98.2	95.2	94.8

Note: U.S. = 100
Source: ACCRA, Cost of Living Index, 1st Quarter 1999

HOUSING

Median Home Prices and Housing Affordability

Area	Median Price[2] 1st Qtr. 1999 ($)	HOI[3] 1st Qtr. 1999	Afford-ability Rank[4]
MSA[1]	n/a	n/a	n/a
U.S.	134,000	69.6	–

Note: (1) Metropolitan Statistical Area - see Appendix A for areas included; (2) U.S. figures calculated from the sales of 524,324 new and existing homes in 181 markets; (3) Housing Opportunity Index - percent of homes sold that were within the reach of the median income household at the prevailing mortgage interest rate; (4) Rank is from 1-181 with 1 being most affordable; n/a not available
Source: National Association of Home Builders, Housing Opportunity Index, 1st Quarter 1999

Median Home Price Projection

It is projected that the median price of existing single-family homes in the metro area will decrease by -1.0% in 1999. Nationwide, home prices are projected to increase 3.8%.
Kiplinger's Personal Finance Magazine, January 1999

Average New Home Price

Area	Price ($)
City	129,100
U.S.	142,735

Note: Figures are based on a new home with 1,800 sq. ft. of living area on an 8,000 sq. ft. lot.
Source: ACCRA, Cost of Living Index, 1st Quarter 1999

Average Apartment Rent

Area	Rent ($/mth)
City	506
U.S.	601

Note: Figures are based on an unfurnished two bedroom, 1-1/2 or 2 bath apartment, approximately 950 sq. ft. in size, excluding all utilities except water
Source: ACCRA, Cost of Living Index, 1st Quarter 1999

RESIDENTIAL UTILITIES

Average Residential Utility Costs

Area	All Electric ($/mth)	Part Electric ($/mth)	Other Energy ($/mth)	Phone ($/mth)
City	–	39.51	32.26	16.29
U.S.	100.02	55.73	43.33	19.71

Source: ACCRA, Cost of Living Index, 1st Quarter 1999

HEALTH CARE

Average Health Care Costs

Area	Hospital ($/day)	Doctor ($/visit)	Dentist ($/visit)
City	425.00	49.67	63.34
U.S.	430.43	52.45	66.35

Note: Hospital—based on a semi-private room; Doctor—based on a general practitioner's routine exam of an established patient; Dentist—based on adult teeth cleaning and periodic oral exam.
Source: ACCRA, Cost of Living Index, 1st Quarter 1999

Distribution of Office-Based Physicians

Area	Family/Gen. Practitioners	Specialists		
		Medical	Surgical	Other
MSA[1]	67	182	160	155

Note: Data as of 12/31/97; (1) Metropolitan Statistical Area - see Appendix A for areas included
Source: American Medical Assn., Physician Characteristics & Distribution in the U.S., 1999

Hospitals

Springfield has 4 general medical and surgical hospitals, 1 psychiatric. *AHA Guide to the Healthcare Field, 1998-99*

According to *U.S. News and World Report,* Springfield has 1 of the best hospitals in the U.S.: **St. John's Regional Health Center**, noted for urology. *U.S. News Online, "America's Best Hospitals," 10th Edition, www.usnews.com*

EDUCATION

Public School District Statistics

District Name	Num. Sch.	Enroll.	Classroom Teachers	Pupils per Teacher	Minority Pupils (%)	Current Exp.[1] ($/pupil)
Heart of the Ozarks Tech Comm	1	n/a	27	0.0	n/a	n/a
Springfield R-XII	56	25,386	1,518	16.7	n/a	n/a

Note: Data covers the 1997-1998 school year unless otherwise noted; (1) Data covers fiscal year 1996; SD = School District; ISD = Independent School District; n/a not available
Source: National Center for Education Statistics, Common Core of Data Public Education Agency Universe 1997-98; National Center for Education Statistics, Characteristics of the 100 Largest Public Elementary and Secondary School Districts in the United States: 1997-98, July 1999

Educational Quality

School District	Education Quotient[1]	Graduate Outcome[2]	Community Index[3]	Resource Index[4]
Springfield SD	122.0	119.0	97.0	132.0

Note: Nearly 1,000 secondary school districts were rated in terms of educational quality. The scores range from a low of 50 to a high of 150; (1) Average of the Graduate Outcome, Community and Resource indexes; (2) Based on graduation rates and college board scores (SAT/ACT); (3) Based on the surrounding community's average level of education and the area's average income level; (4) Based on teacher salaries, per-pupil expenditures and student-teacher ratios.
Source: Expansion Management, Ratings Issue, 1998

Educational Attainment by Race

Area	High School Graduate (%)					Bachelor's Degree (%)				
	Total	White	Black	Other	Hisp.[2]	Total	White	Black	Other	Hisp.[2]
City	77.0	77.3	70.6	68.9	77.0	20.7	20.9	12.4	20.1	27.6
MSA[1]	78.5	78.8	71.8	71.0	77.7	19.6	19.7	14.4	19.1	23.2
U.S.	75.2	77.9	63.1	60.4	49.8	20.3	21.5	11.4	19.4	9.2

Note: Figures shown cover persons 25 years old and over; (1) Metropolitan Statistical Area - see Appendix A for areas included; (2) people of Hispanic origin can be of any race
Source: 1990 Census of Population and Housing, Summary Tape File 3C

School Enrollment by Type

Area	Preprimary				Elementary/High School			
	Public		Private		Public		Private	
	Enrollment	%	Enrollment	%	Enrollment	%	Enrollment	%
City	1,135	62.4	683	37.6	16,946	92.8	1,316	7.2
MSA[1]	2,229	61.2	1,415	38.8	35,278	93.9	2,297	6.1
U.S.	2,679,029	59.5	1,824,256	40.5	38,379,689	90.2	4,187,099	9.8

Note: Figures shown cover persons 3 years old and over;
(1) Metropolitan Statistical Area - see Appendix A for areas included
Source: 1990 Census of Population and Housing, Summary Tape File 3C

School Enrollment by Race

Area	Preprimary (%)				Elementary/High School (%)			
	White	Black	Other	Hisp.[1]	White	Black	Other	Hisp.[1]
City	94.6	1.4	4.0	1.4	93.8	3.2	3.0	1.2
MSA[2]	96.5	0.9	2.6	1.1	96.1	1.8	2.0	1.0
U.S.	80.4	12.5	7.1	7.8	74.1	15.6	10.3	12.5

Note: Figures shown cover persons 3 years old and over; (1) people of Hispanic origin can be of any race; (2) Metropolitan Statistical Area - see Appendix A for areas included
Source: 1990 Census of Population and Housing, Summary Tape File 3C

Classroom Teacher Salaries in Public Schools

District	B.A. Degree		M.A. Degree		Maximum	
	Min. ($)	Rank[1]	Max. ($)	Rank[1]	Max. ($)	Rank[1]
	n/a	n/a	n/a	n/a	n/a	n/a
Average	26,980	-	46,065	-	51,435	-

Note: Salaries are for 1997-1998; (1) Rank ranges from 1 to 100; n/a not available
Source: American Federation of Teachers, Survey & Analysis of Salary Trends, 1998

Higher Education

Two-Year Colleges		Four-Year Colleges		Medical Schools	Law Schools	Voc/ Tech
Public	Private	Public	Private			
1	1	1	5	0	0	7

Source: College Blue Book, Occupational Education, 1997; Medical School Admission Requirements, 1999-2000; Peterson's Guide to Two-Year Colleges, 1999; Peterson's Guide to Four-Year Colleges, 2000; Barron's Guide to Law Schools, 1999

MAJOR EMPLOYERS

Major Employers

Bass Pro Shops (mail order)
Lester E. Cox Medical Center
Paul Mueller Co. (fabricated metal products)
Mid-America Dairymen
American National General Insurance
Cox Alternative Care of the Ozarks
New Prime Inc. (trucking)
St. John's Regional Health Center
Indiana Western Express (trucking)
Trailiner Corp (trucking)

Note: Companies listed are located in the city
Source: Dun's Business Rankings, 1999; Ward's Business Directory, 1998

PUBLIC SAFETY

Crime Rate

Area	All Crimes	Violent Crimes				Property Crimes		
		Murder	Forcible Rape	Robbery	Aggrav. Assault	Burglary	Larceny -Theft	Motor Vehicle Theft
City	6,977.8	4.6	41.1	103.1	323.7	1,317.5	4,740.8	447.0
Suburbs[1]	2,044.6	2.3	16.4	11.1	252.3	575.5	1,057.2	129.7
MSA[2]	4,380.1	3.4	28.1	54.7	286.1	926.8	2,801.1	279.9
U.S.	4,922.7	6.8	35.9	186.1	382.0	919.6	2,886.5	505.8

Note: Crime rate is the number of crimes per 100,000 pop.; (1) defined as all areas within the MSA but located outside the central city; (2) Metropolitan Statistical Area - see Appendix A for areas incl.
Source: FBI Uniform Crime Reports, 1997

RECREATION

Culture and Recreation

Museums	Symphony Orchestras	Opera Companies	Dance Companies	Professional Theatres	Zoos	Pro Sports Teams
2	1	1	0	0	1	0

Source: International Directory of the Performing Arts, 1997; Official Museum Directory, 1999; Stern's Performing Arts Directory, 1997; USA Today Four Sport Stadium Guide, 1997; Chamber of Commerce/Economic Development, 1999

Library System

The Springfield-Green County Library has seven branches, holdings of 469,856 volumes, and a budget of $5,396,347 (1996-1997). *American Library Directory, 1998-1999*

MEDIA

Newspapers

Name	Type	Freq.	Distribution	Circulation
The News-Leader	n/a	7x/wk	Area	62,808

Note: Includes newspapers with circulations of 500 or more located in the city; n/a not available
Source: Burrelle's Media Directory, 1999 Edition

Television Stations

Name	Ch.	Affiliation	Type	Owner
KYTV	n/a	NBCT	Commercial	Schurz Communications Inc.
KOLR	10	CBST	Commercial	Independent Broadcasting Company
KOZK	21	PBS	Public	Ozark Public Telecommunications Inc.
KDEB	27	FBC	Commercial	n/a
KSPR	33	ABCT	Commercial	Gocom Communications

Note: Stations included broadcast in the Springfield metro area; n/a not available
Source: Burrelle's Media Directory, 1999 Edition

AM Radio Stations

Call Letters	Freq. (kHz)	Target Audience	Station Format	Music Format
KWTO	560	General	N/S/T	n/a
KTOZ	1060	General	M/N	Adult Contemporary/Adult Standards/Big Band/Jazz/MOR/Oldies/R&B
KTTS	1260	General	M/N/S	Country
KGMY	1400	General	M/N	Adult Standards
KLFJ	1550	M/R/W	N/S	n/a

Note: Stations included broadcast in the Springfield metro area; n/a not available
Target Audience: A=Asian; B=Black; C=Christian; E=Ethnic; F=French; G=General; H=Hispanic; M=Men; N=Native American; R=Religious; S=Senior Citizen; W=Women; Y=Young Adult; Z=Children
Station Format: E=Educational; M=Music; N=News; S=Sports; T=Talk
Music Format: AOR=Album Oriented Rock; MOR=Middle-of-the-Road
Source: Burrelle's Media Directory, 1999 Edition

FM Radio Stations

Call Letters	Freq. (mHz)	Target Audience	Station Format	Music Format
KWFC	89.1	General	E/M/N/S	Christian/Gospel
KSMU	91.1	General	E/M/N	Classical/Jazz/R&B
KTTS	94.7	General	M/N/S	Country
KTOZ	95.5	General	M	Alternative
KXUS	97.3	General	M	AOR/Classic Rock
KWTO	98.7	General	M	Classic Rock
KADI	99.5	Religious	M/N/S	Christian
KGMY	100.5	General	M	Country
KTXR	101.3	General	M	Easy Listening
KZRQ	104.1	General	M	Modern Rock
KGBX	105.9	General	M	Adult Contemporary
KHTO	106.7	General	n/a	n/a

Note: Stations included broadcast in the Springfield metro area; n/a not available
Station Format: E=Educational; M=Music; N=News; S=Sports; T=Talk
Target Audience: A=Asian; B=Black; C=Christian; E=Ethnic; F=French; G=General; H=Hispanic; M=Men; N=Native American; R=Religious; S=Senior Citizen; W=Women; Y=Young Adult; Z=Children
Music Format: AOR=Album Oriented Rock; MOR=Middle-of-the-Road
Source: Burrelle's Media Directory, 1999 Edition

CLIMATE

Average and Extreme Temperatures

Temperature	Jan	Feb	Mar	Apr	May	Jun	Jul	Aug	Sep	Oct	Nov	Dec	Yr.
Extreme High (°F)	76	81	87	93	93	101	113	106	104	93	80	77	113
Average High (°F)	42	47	56	68	75	84	89	88	80	70	56	45	67
Average Temp. (°F)	32	37	45	56	65	74	78	77	69	59	46	36	56
Average Low (°F)	22	26	34	45	54	63	67	65	58	47	35	26	45
Extreme Low (°F)	-13	-17	-8	18	29	42	44	44	30	21	4	-16	-17

Note: Figures cover the years 1940-1990
Source: National Climatic Data Center, International Station Meteorological Climate Summary, 3/95

Average Precipitation/Snowfall/Humidity

Precip./Humidity	Jan	Feb	Mar	Apr	May	Jun	Jul	Aug	Sep	Oct	Nov	Dec	Yr.
Avg. Precip. (in.)	1.8	2.2	3.5	4.2	4.8	5.0	3.4	3.3	4.3	3.6	3.2	2.8	42.0
Avg. Snowfall (in.)	5	4	4	Tr	Tr	0	0	0	0	Tr	2	3	18
Avg. Rel. Hum. 6am (%)	78	80	79	79	85	86	87	88	87	82	80	79	82
Avg. Rel. Hum. 3pm (%)	58	56	52	50	55	55	53	50	52	50	54	59	54

Note: Figures cover the years 1940-1990; Tr = Trace amounts (<0.05 in. of rain; <0.5 in. of snow)
Source: National Climatic Data Center, International Station Meteorological Climate Summary, 3/95

Weather Conditions

Temperature			Daytime Sky			Precipitation		
10°F & below	32°F & below	90°F & above	Clear	Partly cloudy	Cloudy	0.01 inch or more precip.	0.1 inch or more snow/ice	Thunder-storms
12	102	42	113	119	133	109	14	55

Note: Figures are average number of days per year and covers the years 1940-1990
Source: National Climatic Data Center, International Station Meteorological Climate Summary, 3/95

AIR & WATER QUALITY

Maximum Pollutant Concentrations

	Particulate Matter (ug/m^3)	Carbon Monoxide (ppm)	Sulfur Dioxide (ppm)	Nitrogen Dioxide (ppm)	Ozone (ppm)	Lead (ug/m^3)
MSA[1] Level	95	5	0.054	0.011	0.08	n/a
NAAQS[2]	150	9	0.140	0.053	0.12	1.50
Met NAAQS?	Yes	Yes	Yes	Yes	Yes	n/a

Note: (1) Metropolitan Statistical Area - see Appendix A for areas included; (2) National Ambient Air Quality Standards; ppm = parts per million; ug/m^3 = micrograms per cubic meter; n/a not available
Source: EPA, National Air Quality and Emissions Trends Report, 1997

Drinking Water

Water System Name	Pop. Served	Primary Water Source Type	Number of Violations in 1998	Type of Violation/ Contaminants
Springfield	149,237	Surface	None	None

Note: Data as of July 10, 1999
Source: EPA, Office of Ground Water and Drinking Water, Safe Drinking Water Information System

Springfield tap water is alkaline, hard and fluoridated.
Editor & Publisher Market Guide, 1999

Wichita, Kansas

Background

Lying in the Southeastern Plains of Kansas, Wichita took its name from a local Indian tribe. Two white entrepreneurs, Jesse Chisholm and James R. Mead struck up a lively trade in the area with the native people starting in 1864. Shortly after the tribe was relocated to Indian Territory in Oklahoma in 1867, white settlers planted roots around Chisholm's and Mead's trading post. Chisholm laid out a trail from the post to Texas, from which cowboys drove longhorn cattle to the railhead of the Wichita and Southwestern Railroad, feeding the cows along the way on the prairie grass of Kansas.

In the 1880s, like many Plains's area cattle shipping points, Wichita became a wide-open town, with dance halls, gambling, and saloons. Wyatt Earp served there as lawman for a time. In 1886 the town officially became a city, having grown to over 20,000 in population, much of it due to eager speculation in prairie lands.

Other industries grew in the city. After the turn of the century, oil was discovered in the area, bringing more people. The city swelled to over 100,000 by 1930. Shortly after World War I, which saw great advancements in aviation, Wichita's first airplane factory was built. The city soon became the country's leading manufacturer of aircraft. Walter H. Beech, Clyde V. Cessna, and Lloyd C. Stearman were to become famous members of the community for their early leadership in the industry.

The oil rigs and aircraft factories kept the dire times of the Great Depression from Wichita, while much of the rest of the state was consumed by the Dust Bowl. During World War II, more airplanes rolled off the city's three assembly lines than in any other city in America. Growth continued in the aircraft industry until the 1980s, when there was a slump in sales. By the late 1990s, however, a revival of the industry was in full swing.

Wichita is the major industrial city in the state, with over 700 factories. It is a major manufacturer of private and military aircraft. Boeing, Cessna Aircraft Company, Bombardier Aerospace/Learjet Corporation, and Raytheon Aircraft Company all operate plants there. The city's renown in this industry has rightful earned it the nickname Air Capitol of the World. Another important company is Koch Industries, which originally began as an oil refinery business, and now also is involved in chemicals, chemical technology, gas liquids, and crude oil services, among others.

The city is also heavily involved in the food industry. It is one the country's major meat processors. Due to its location in the Wheat Belt, it is also much involved in the grinding of that grain.

The Wichita Area Chamber of Commerce launched, in the 1990s, a worker recruitment and job training program to assist local businesses. Area employers also receive help from Wichita State University's Center for Economic Development and Business Research, which analyzes data about the city's economy and makes projections on future conditions. Wichita State University is the third largest in Kansas.

The climate in Wichita is generally mild, punctuated occasionally by more intemperate weather conditions. Summers are warm, but the humidity is relatively low, with temperatures ranging from the upper fifties to the lower nineties. Winters are usually mild by comparison, with temperatures ranging from the upper teens to upper fifties. The city experiences on average 128 sunny days and ninety-seven partly sunny days. Tornadoes have been sighted in the metropolitan area and thunderstorms move through the area an average of fifty-six days a year. Wichita's mean annual precipitation is about thirty inches, most of it falling during the spring-through-fall growing season. Snowfall is usually around fifteen inches a year, with the ground rarely being covered for more than three days.

General Rankings and Evaluative Comments

■ Wichita was ranked #20 out of 24 mid-sized, midwestern metropolitan areas in *Money's* 1998 survey of "The Best Places to Live in America." The survey was conducted by first contacting 512 representative households nationwide and asking them to rank 37 quality-of-life factors on a scale of 1 to 10. Next, a demographic profile was compiled on the 300 largest metropolitan statistical areas in the U.S. The numbers were crunched together to arrive at an overall ranking (things Americans consider most important, like clean air and water, low crime and good schools, received extra weight). Unlike previous years, the 1998 rankings were broken down by region (northeast, midwest, south, west) and population size (100,000 to 249,999; 250,000 to 999,999; 1 million plus). The city had a nationwide ranking of #285 out of 300 in 1997 and #142 out of 300 in 1996. *Money, July 1998; Money, July 1997; Money, September 1996*

■ *Ladies Home Journal* ranked America's 200 largest cities based on the qualities women care about most. Wichita ranked #103 out of 200. Criteria: low crime rate, well-paying jobs, quality health and child care, good public schools, the presence of women in government, size of the gender wage gap, number of sexual-harassment and discrimination complaints filed, unemployment and divorce rates, commute times, population density, number of houses of worship, parks and cultural offerings, number of women's health specialists, how well a community's women cared for themselves, complexion kindness index based on UV radiation levels, odds of finding affordable fashions, rental rates for romance movies, champagne sales and other matters of the heart. *Ladies Home Journal, November 1998*

■ Zero Population Growth ranked 229 cities in terms of children's health, safety, and economic well-being. Wichita was ranked #32 out of 112 independent cities (cities with populations greater than 100,000 which were neither Major Cities nor Suburbs/Outer Cities) and was given a grade of B-. Criteria: total population, percent of population under 18 years of age, household language, percent population change, percent of births to teens, infant mortality rate, percent of low birth weights, dropout rate, enrollment in preprimary school, violent and property crime rates, unemployment rate, percent of children in poverty, percent of owner occupied units, number of bad air days, percent of public transportation commuters, and average travel time to work. *Zero Population Growth, Children's Environmental Index, Fall 1999*

■ Cognetics studied 273 metro areas in the United States, ranking them by entrepreneurial activity. Wichita was ranked #54 out of 134 smaller metro areas. Criteria: Significant Starts (firms started in the last 10 years that still employ at least 5 people) and Young Growers (percent of firms 10 years old or less that grew significantly during the last 4 years). *Cognetics, "Entrepreneurial Hot Spots: The Best Places in America to Start and Grow a Company," 1998*

■ Wichita was selected as one of the "Best American Cities to Start a Business" by *Point of View* magazine. Criteria: coolness, quality-of-life, and business concerns. The city was ranked #64 out of 75. *Point of View, November 1998*

■ Reliastar Financial Corp. ranked the 125 largest metropolitan areas according to the general financial security of residents. Wichita was ranked #32 out of 125 with a score of 6.1. The score indicates the percentage a metropolitan area is above or below the metropolitan norm. A metro area with a score of 10.6 is 10.6% above the metro average. Criteria: Earnings and Wealth Potential (household income, education, net assets, cost of living); Safety Net (health insurance, retirement savings, life insurance, income support programs); Personal Threats (unemployment rate, low-income households, crime rate); Community Economic Vitality (cost of community services, job quality, job creation, housing costs). *Reliastar Financial Corp., "The Best Cities to Earn and Save Money," 1999 Edition*

Business Environment

STATE ECONOMY

State Economic Profile

"The last few years, 1997 and 1998 in particular, have seen Kansas outpace the nation by a considerable gap. Record sales and price appreciation in the housing market matched the boom in jobs. Wichita's aircraft sectors and strong overall employment gains in Kansas City have driven growth. A slowdown in demand for aircraft will likely cool growth in Wichita, while the state posts only modest gains in the next few years.

Strong demand for aircraft has fueled a hiring binge by Boeing and affiliated firms in Wichita. Resulting employment gains spread to other sectors of the Wichita economy, bringing strong gains in services employment and a strong housing sector. However, projections for the aircraft sector have declined with potential layoffs on the part of Boeing in 1999. Wichita's heavy dependence on the aircraft sector will slow its economy considerably in 1999.

Soft foreign demand has also slowed Kansas City's employment growth in 1999. Its tight labor market and diverse economy will minimize this shock, although growth in 1999 will be considerably slower. Its transportation and telecommunications sectors will witness some growth in 1999. Almost 10% of 1998 employment gains were in KC's construction sector. Projected declines in permit activity translate into negative construction employment growth.

Weak population growth, especially among younger households, and a struggling farm economy will constrain growth in Kansas' non-metro areas, bringing considerable weakness to its rural economies. All of the state will see a flattening or decline in employment growth in 1999, with the exception of some moderate growth in the Kansas City area. Growth should trail the nation slightly." *National Association of Realtors, Economic Profiles: The Fifty States and the District of Columbia, http://nar.realtor.com/databank/profiles.htm*

IMPORTS/EXPORTS

Total Export Sales

Area	1994 ($000)	1995 ($000)	1996 ($000)	1997 ($000)	% Chg. 1994-97	% Chg. 1996-97
MSA[1]	1,540,558	1,727,720	1,916,812	2,273,438	47.6	18.6
U.S.	512,415,609	583,030,524	622,827,063	687,597,999	34.2	10.4

Note: (1) Metropolitan Statistical Area - see Appendix A for areas included
Source: U.S. Department of Commerce, International Trade Association, Metropolitan Area Exports: An Export Performance Report on Over 250 U.S. Cities, November 10, 1998

CITY FINANCES

City Government Finances

Component	FY92 ($000)	FY92 (per capita $)
Revenue	313,227	1,002.99
Expenditure	308,912	989.17
Debt Outstanding	538,808	1,725.33
Cash & Securities	680,919	2,180.39

Source: U.S. Bureau of the Census, City Government Finances: 1991-92

City Government Revenue by Source

Source	FY92 ($000)	FY92 (per capita $)	FY92 (%)
From Federal Government	10,137	32.46	3.2
From State Governments	32,745	104.85	10.5
From Local Governments	33,153	106.16	10.6
Property Taxes	51,667	165.44	16.5
General Sales Taxes	0	0.00	0.0
Selective Sales Taxes	24,849	79.57	7.9
Income Taxes	0	0.00	0.0
Current Charges	37,125	118.88	11.9
Utility/Liquor Store	24,768	79.31	7.9
Employee Retirement[1]	41,742	133.66	13.3
Other	57,041	182.65	18.2

Note: (1) Excludes "city contributions," classified as "nonrevenue," intragovernmental transfers.
Source: U.S. Bureau of the Census, City Government Finances: 1991-92

City Government Expenditures by Function

Function	FY92 ($000)	FY92 (per capita $)	FY92 (%)
Educational Services	4,759	15.24	1.5
Employee Retirement[1]	16,608	53.18	5.4
Environment/Housing	62,648	200.61	20.3
Government Administration	8,998	28.81	2.9
Interest on General Debt	29,757	95.29	9.6
Public Safety	47,455	151.96	15.4
Social Services	8,770	28.08	2.8
Transportation	80,221	256.88	26.0
Utility/Liquor Store	31,816	101.88	10.3
Other	17,880	57.25	5.8

Note: (1) Payments to beneficiaries including withdrawal of contributions.
Source: U.S. Bureau of the Census, City Government Finances: 1991-92

Municipal Bond Ratings

Area	Moody's	S & P
Wichita	Aa2	n/a

Note: n/a not available; n/r not rated
Source: Moody's Bond Record, 6/99

POPULATION

Population Growth

Area	1980	1990	% Chg. 1980-90	July 1998 Estimate	% Chg. 1990-98
City	279,272	304,011	8.9	329,211	8.3
MSA[1]	411,870	485,270	17.8	522,197	7.6
U.S.	226,545,805	248,765,170	9.8	270,299,000	8.7

Note: (1) Metropolitan Statistical Area - see Appendix A for areas included;
July 1998 MSA population estimate was calculated by the editors
Source: 1980/1990 Census of Housing and Population, Summary Tape File 3C;
Census Bureau Population Estimates 1998

Population Characteristics

Race	City 1980 Population	%	City 1990 Population	%	% Chg. 1980-90	MSA[1] 1990 Population	%
White	236,549	84.7	250,552	82.4	5.9	424,541	87.5
Black	30,263	10.8	34,161	11.2	12.9	36,558	7.5
Amer Indian/Esk/Aleut	2,942	1.1	3,724	1.2	26.6	5,508	1.1
Asian/Pacific Islander	4,525	1.6	7,612	2.5	68.2	8,914	1.8
Other	4,993	1.8	7,962	2.6	59.5	9,749	2.0
Hispanic Origin[2]	9,455	3.4	14,314	4.7	51.4	18,437	3.8

Note: (1) Metropolitan Statistical Area - see Appendix A for areas included;
(2) people of Hispanic origin can be of any race
Source: 1980/1990 Census of Housing and Population, Summary Tape File 3C

Ancestry

Area	German	Irish	English	Italian	U.S.	French	Polish	Dutch
City	34.2	17.5	15.7	1.5	4.7	4.4	1.0	3.7
MSA[1]	37.6	18.0	16.6	1.5	5.1	4.5	1.0	4.2
U.S.	23.3	15.6	13.1	5.9	5.3	4.2	3.8	2.5

Note: Figures are percentages and include persons that reported multiple ancestry (eg. if a person reported being Irish and Italian, they were included in both columns); (1) Metropolitan Statistical Area - see Appendix A for areas included
Source: 1990 Census of Population and Housing, Summary Tape File 3C

Age

Area	Median Age (Years)	Under 5	Under 18	18-24	25-44	45-64	65+	80+
City	31.7	8.6	26.6	10.2	34.1	16.7	12.4	2.7
MSA[1]	32.1	8.3	27.8	9.3	33.3	17.6	12.0	2.7
U.S.	32.9	7.3	25.6	10.5	32.6	18.7	12.5	2.8

Note: (1) Metropolitan Statistical Area - see Appendix A for areas included
Source: 1990 Census of Population and Housing, Summary Tape File 3C

Male/Female Ratio

Area	Number of males per 100 females (all ages)	Number of males per 100 females (18 years old+)
City	94.6	91.3
MSA[1]	96.0	92.8
U.S.	95.0	91.9

Note: (1) Metropolitan Statistical Area - see Appendix A for areas included
Source: 1990 Census of Population, General Population Characteristics

INCOME

Per Capita/Median/Average Income

Area	Per Capita ($)	Median Household ($)	Average Household ($)
City	14,516	28,024	35,453
MSA[1]	14,303	30,152	36,714
U.S.	14,420	30,056	38,453

Note: All figures are for 1989; (1) Metropolitan Statistical Area - see Appendix A for areas included
Source: 1990 Census of Population and Housing, Summary Tape File 3C

Household Income Distribution by Race

Income ($)	City (%)					U.S. (%)				
	Total	White	Black	Other	Hisp.[1]	Total	White	Black	Other	Hisp.[1]
Less than 5,000	6.3	4.7	17.4	11.4	7.0	6.2	4.8	15.2	8.6	8.8
5,000 - 9,999	8.9	8.0	15.4	11.0	8.6	9.3	8.6	14.2	9.9	11.1
10,000 - 14,999	9.4	9.0	11.9	12.1	13.0	8.8	8.5	11.0	9.8	11.0
15,000 - 24,999	19.5	19.6	18.7	20.4	21.9	17.5	17.3	18.9	18.5	20.5
25,000 - 34,999	17.7	17.9	14.4	19.2	21.5	15.8	16.1	14.2	15.4	16.4
35,000 - 49,999	18.3	19.3	12.3	12.7	16.8	17.9	18.6	13.3	16.1	16.0
50,000 - 74,999	13.6	14.5	7.4	9.5	8.2	15.0	15.8	9.3	13.4	11.1
75,000 - 99,999	3.5	3.8	2.2	1.4	1.8	5.1	5.5	2.6	4.7	3.1
100,000+	2.8	3.1	0.4	2.3	1.2	4.4	4.8	1.3	3.7	1.9

Note: All figures are for 1989; (1) people of Hispanic origin can be of any race
Source: 1990 Census of Population and Housing, Summary Tape File 3C

Effective Buying Income

Area	Per Capita ($)	Median Household ($)	Average Household ($)
City	16,985	33,613	41,786
MSA[1]	17,179	35,625	44,675
U.S.	16,803	34,536	45,243

Note: Data as of 1/1/99; (1) Metropolitan Statistical Area - see Appendix A for areas included
Source: Standard Rate & Data Service, Newspaper Advertising Source, 9/99

Effective Household Buying Income Distribution

Area	% of Households Earning						
	$10,000 -$19,999	$20,000 -$34,999	$35,000 -$49,999	$50,000 -$74,999	$75,000 -$99,000	$100,000 -$124,999	$125,000 and up
City	16.1	24.5	18.8	18.9	6.4	1.8	2.0
MSA[1]	15.2	23.6	19.8	20.5	6.7	1.8	2.0
U.S.	16.0	22.6	18.2	18.9	7.2	2.4	2.7

Note: Data as of 1/1/99; (1) Metropolitan Statistical Area - see Appendix A for areas included
Source: Standard Rate & Data Service, Newspaper Advertising Source, 9/99

Poverty Rates by Race and Age

Area	Total (%)	By Race (%)				By Age (%)		
		White	Black	Other	Hisp.[2]	Under 5 years old	Under 18 years old	65 years and over
City	12.5	8.7	34.4	23.3	19.0	21.0	17.8	9.6
MSA[1]	10.5	7.9	33.3	22.7	19.0	17.1	14.2	9.5
U.S.	13.1	9.8	29.5	23.1	25.3	20.1	18.3	12.8

Note: Figures show the percent of people living below the poverty line in 1989. The average poverty threshold was $12,674 for a family of four in 1989; (1) Metropolitan Statistical Area - see Appendix A for areas included; (2) people of Hispanic origin can be of any race
Source: 1990 Census of Population and Housing, Summary Tape File 3C

EMPLOYMENT

Labor Force and Employment

Area	Civilian Labor Force			Workers Employed		
	Jun. 1998	Jun. 1999	% Chg.	Jun. 1998	Jun. 1999	% Chg.
City	182,921	188,771	3.2	176,211	180,840	2.6
MSA[1]	290,507	299,332	3.0	280,666	288,039	2.6
U.S.	138,798,000	140,666,000	1.3	132,265,000	134,395,000	1.6

Note: Data is not seasonally adjusted and covers workers 16 years of age and older;
(1) Metropolitan Statistical Area - see Appendix A for areas included
Source: Bureau of Labor Statistics, http://stats.bls.gov

Unemployment Rate

Area	1998						1999					
	Jul.	Aug.	Sep.	Oct.	Nov.	Dec.	Jan.	Feb.	Mar.	Apr.	May.	Jun.
City	3.3	3.6	3.8	3.9	3.8	3.4	4.1	3.8	3.8	3.8	4.0	4.2
MSA[1]	3.0	3.4	3.4	3.5	3.5	3.1	3.7	3.5	3.4	3.4	3.5	3.8
U.S.	4.7	4.5	4.4	4.2	4.1	4.0	4.8	4.7	4.4	4.1	4.0	4.5

Note: Data is not seasonally adjusted and covers workers 16 years of age and older; all figures are percentages; (1) Metropolitan Statistical Area - see Appendix A for areas included
Source: Bureau of Labor Statistics, http://stats.bls.gov

Employment by Industry

Sector	MSA[1]		U.S.
	Number of Employees	Percent of Total	Percent of Total
Services	77,900	26.9	30.4
Retail Trade	48,900	16.9	17.7
Government	33,400	11.5	15.6
Manufacturing	74,000	25.5	14.3
Finance/Insurance/Real Estate	11,700	4.0	5.9
Wholesale Trade	15,900	5.5	5.4
Transportation/Public Utilities	10,800	3.7	5.3
Construction	15,900	5.5	5.0
Mining	1,200	0.4	0.4

Note: Figures cover non-farm employment as of 6/99 and are not seasonally adjusted;
(1) Metropolitan Statistical Area - see Appendix A for areas included
Source: Bureau of Labor Statistics, http://stats.bls.gov

Employment by Occupation

Occupation Category	City (%)	MSA[1] (%)	U.S. (%)
White Collar	61.5	59.2	58.1
Executive/Admin./Management	12.4	11.9	12.3
Professional	15.3	15.1	14.1
Technical & Related Support	4.0	3.8	3.7
Sales	12.3	11.4	11.8
Administrative Support/Clerical	17.5	17.0	16.3
Blue Collar	25.8	27.3	26.2
Precision Production/Craft/Repair	13.1	13.9	11.3
Machine Operators/Assem./Insp.	7.1	7.3	6.8
Transportation/Material Movers	2.7	3.1	4.1
Cleaners/Helpers/Laborers	2.9	3.0	3.9
Services	12.0	11.9	13.2
Farming/Forestry/Fishing	0.7	1.6	2.5

Note: Figures cover employed persons 16 years old and over;
(1) Metropolitan Statistical Area - see Appendix A for areas included
Source: 1990 Census of Population and Housing, Summary Tape File 3C

Occupational Employment Projections: 1996 - 2006

Occupations Expected to Have the Largest Job Growth (ranked by numerical growth)	Fast-Growing Occupations[1] (ranked by percent growth)
1. Salespersons, retail	1. Database administrators
2. Cashiers	2. Systems analysts
3. General managers & top executives	3. Paralegals
4. Truck drivers, light	4. Respiratory therapists
5. Registered nurses	5. Computer engineers
6. Nursing aides/orderlies/attendants	6. Medical records technicians
7. Food service workers	7. Home health aides
8. Marketing & sales, supervisors	8. Emergency medical technicians
9. General office clerks	9. Customer service representatives
10. Food preparation workers	10. Physical therapy assistants and aides

Note: Projections cover Kansas; (1) Excludes occupations with total job growth less than 300
Source: U.S. Department of Labor, Employment and Training Administration, America's Labor Market Information System (ALMIS)

TAXES

Major State and Local Tax Rates

State Corp. Income (%)	State Personal Income (%)	Residential Property (effective rate per $100)	Sales & Use State (%)	Local (%)	State Gasoline (cents/gallon)	State Cigarette (cents/pack)
4.0[a]	4.1 - 6.45	1.23	4.9	1.0	18.0	24.0

Note: Personal/corporate income, sales, gasoline and cigarette tax rates as of January 1999.
Property tax rates as of 1997; (a) Plus a 3.35% surtax on taxable income over $50,000. Banks 2.25% plus 2.125% surtax over $25,000
Source: Federation of Tax Administrators, www.taxadmin.org; Washington D.C. Department of Finance and Revenue, Tax Rates and Tax Burdens in the District of Columbia: A Nationwide Comparison, July 1998; Chamber of Commerce, 1999

Total Taxes Per Capita and as a Percent of Income

Area	Per Capita Income ($)	Per Capita Taxes ($) Total	Federal	State/Local	Percent of Income (%) Total	Federal	State/Local
Kansas	26,394	9,344	6,286	3,058	35.4	23.8	11.6
U.S.	27,876	9,881	6,690	3,191	35.4	24.0	11.4

Note: Figures are for 1998
Source: Tax Foundation, www.taxfoundation.org

Estimated Tax Burden

Area	State Income	Local Income	Property	Sales	Total
Wichita	2,612	0	3,000	882	6,494

Note: The numbers are estimates of taxes paid by a married couple with two children and annual earnings of $75,000. Sales tax estimates assume they spend average amounts on food, clothing, household goods and gasoline. Property tax estimates assume they live in a $250,000 home.
Source: Kiplinger's Personal Finance Magazine, October 1998

COMMERCIAL REAL ESTATE

Office Market

Class/ Location	Total Space (sq. ft.)	Vacant Space (sq. ft.)	Vac. Rate (%)	Under Constr. (sq. ft.)	Net Absorp. (sq. ft.)	Rental Rates ($/sq.ft./yr.)
Class A						
CBD	1,811,578	122,847	6.8	n/a	-44,575	5.00-15.85
Outside CBD	860,018	75,789	8.8	n/a	123,071	4.50-22.00
Class B						
CBD	1,967,728	586,679	29.8	n/a	-95,937	5.00-14.00
Outside CBD	1,361,637	211,825	15.6	n/a	41,200	4.50-23.00

Note: Data as of 10/98 and covers Wichita; CBD = Central Business District; n/a not available;
Source: Society of Industrial and Office Realtors, 1999 Comparative Statistics of Industrial and Office Real Estate Markets

"Wichita's economy remains strong and is growing at a solid but somewhat slower pace than in 1997. Demand has generated new construction in the suburbs; our SIOR reporter believes construction will continue to increase. There is an increased interest in Wichita's office market among investors. Vacant space in Class A buildings will be difficult to find in 1999, particularly in the suburbs. The outlook for 1999 includes a one to five percent increase in sales prices of Class A and Class B office space in the CBD. Sales prices for both classes of space located in the city's suburbs will increase by six to 10 percent. Absorption, construction, rental rates, and vacancy rates are expected to grow by six to 10 percent as well. Concessions by landlords may go up by one as much as five percent." *Society of Industrial and Office Realtors, 1999 Comparative Statistics of Industrial and Office Real Estate Markets*

Industrial Market

Location	Total Space (sq. ft.)	Vacant Space (sq. ft.)	Vac. Rate (%)	Under Constr. (sq. ft.)	Net Absorp. (sq. ft.)	Lease ($/sq.ft./yr.)
Central City	382,477	8,600	2.2	n/a	-128,500	2.00-5.50
Suburban	5,999,982	607,444	10.1	n/a	919,181	2.00-5.50

Note: Data as of 10/98 and covers Wichita; n/a not available
Source: Society of Industrial and Office Realtors, 1999 Comparative Statistics of Industrial and Office Real Estate Markets

"Wichita's economy is sound. Internally generated growth has been solid, and the area's vital aircraft industry is healthy. Sales prices for warehouse/distribution space are expected to increase by 11 to 15 percent in 1999. Leasing prices, absorption, and construction will also climb as much as 15 percent. Manufacturing and High-Tech/R&D construction, prices, and absorption are expected to increase up to five percent. Site prices are expected to rise six to 10 percent in 1999. At present, sales prices range from $15 to $35 per sq. ft. in both the suburbs and central city. High-Tech/R&D space is selling for roughly $30 per sq. ft. Lease prices have been $2.00 to $5.50 per sq. ft. both inside and outside Wichita High Tech/R&D commands $4.50 per sq. ft." *Society of Industrial and Office Realtors, 1999 Comparative Statistics of Industrial and Office Real Estate Markets*

COMMERCIAL UTILITIES

Typical Monthly Electric Bills

Area	Commercial Service ($/month)		Industrial Service ($/month)	
	12 kW demand 1,500 kWh	100 kW demand 30,000 kWh	1,000 kW demand 400,000 kWh	20,000 kW demand 10,000,000 kWh
City	173	2,198	21,900	386,400
U.S.	150	2,174	23,995	508,569

Note: Based on rates in effect January 1, 1999
Source: Edison Electric Institute, Typical Residential, Commercial and Industrial Bills, Winter 1999

TRANSPORTATION

Transportation Statistics

Average minutes to work	17.0
Interstate highways	I-135; I-35
Bus lines	
In-city	Wichita Metro TA
Inter-city	1
Passenger air service	
Airport	Wichita Midcontinent Airport
Airlines	8
Aircraft departures	17,217 (1996)
Enplaned passengers	678,337 (1996)
Rail service	No Amtrak Service
Motor freight carriers	34
Major waterways/ports	None

Source: Editor & Publisher Market Guide, 1999; FAA Airport Activity Statistics, 1997; Amtrak National Time Table, Northeast Timetable, Spring/Summer 1999; 1990 Census of Population and Housing, STF 3C; Chamber of Commerce/Economic Development 1999; Jane's Urban Transport Systems 1999-2000

Means of Transportation to Work

Area	Car/Truck/Van		Public Transportation			Bicycle	Walked	Other Means	Worked at Home
	Drove Alone	Car-pooled	Bus	Subway	Railroad				
City	82.6	10.6	1.1	0.0	0.0	0.3	2.3	1.0	2.2
MSA[1]	82.1	10.9	0.8	0.0	0.0	0.2	2.3	0.9	2.9
U.S.	73.2	13.4	3.0	1.5	0.5	0.4	3.9	1.2	3.0

Note: Figures shown are percentages and only include workers 16 years old and over;
(1) Metropolitan Statistical Area - see Appendix A for areas included
Source: 1990 Census of Population and Housing, Summary Tape File 3C

BUSINESSES

Major Business Headquarters

Company Name	1999 Rankings	
	Fortune 500	Forbes 500
Koch Industries	-	2

Note: Companies listed are located in the city; dashes indicate no ranking
Fortune 500: Companies that produce a 10-K are ranked 1 to 500 based on 1998 revenue
Forbes 500: Private companies are ranked 1 to 500 based on 1997 revenue
Source: Forbes, November 30, 1998; Fortune, April 26, 1999

Minority Business Opportunity

Two of the 500 largest Hispanic-owned companies in the U.S. are located in Wichita.
Hispanic Business, June 1999

HOTELS & MOTELS

Hotels/Motels

Area	Hotels/Motels	Rooms	Luxury-Level Hotels/Motels		Average Minimum Rates ($)		
			♦♦♦♦	♦♦♦♦♦	♦♦	♦♦♦	♦♦♦♦
City	33	3,311	0	0	67	92	n/a
Airport	9	1,088	0	0	n/a	n/a	n/a
Total	42	4,399	0	0	n/a	n/a	n/a

Note: n/a not available; classifications range from one diamond (budget properties with basic amenities) to five diamond (luxury properties with the finest service, rooms and facilities).
Source: OAG, Business Travel Planner, Winter 1998-99

CONVENTION CENTERS

Major Convention Centers

Center Name	Meeting Rooms	Exhibit Space (sq. ft.)
Century II Convention Center	20	198,500
Kansas Coliseum	1	n/a
The Cotillion Ballroom	n/a	28,500

Note: n/a not available
Source: Trade Shows Worldwide, 1998; Meetings & Conventions, 4/15/99;
Sucessful Meetings, 3/31/98

Living Environment

COST OF LIVING

Cost of Living Index

Composite Index	Groceries	Housing	Utilities	Trans-portation	Health Care	Misc. Goods/ Services
94.8	88.5	88.3	104.9	99.0	106.2	98.0

Note: U.S. = 100
Source: ACCRA, Cost of Living Index, 4th Quarter 1998

HOUSING

Median Home Prices and Housing Affordability

Area	Median Price[2] 1st Qtr. 1999 ($)	HOI[3] 1st Qtr. 1999	Afford-ability Rank[4]
MSA[1]	n/a	n/a	n/a
U.S.	134,000	69.6	–

Note: (1) Metropolitan Statistical Area - see Appendix A for areas included; (2) U.S. figures calculated from the sales of 524,324 new and existing homes in 181 markets; (3) Housing Opportunity Index - percent of homes sold that were within the reach of the median income household at the prevailing mortgage interest rate; (4) Rank is from 1-181 with 1 being most affordable; n/a not available
Source: National Association of Home Builders, Housing Opportunity Index, 1st Quarter 1999

Median Home Price Projection

It is projected that the median price of existing single-family homes in the metro area will increase by 4.7% in 1999. Nationwide, home prices are projected to increase 3.8%.
Kiplinger's Personal Finance Magazine, January 1999

Average New Home Price

Area	Price ($)
City	127,883
U.S.	141,438

Note: Figures are based on a new home with 1,800 sq. ft. of living area on an 8,000 sq. ft. lot.
Source: ACCRA, Cost of Living Index, 4th Quarter 1998

Average Apartment Rent

Area	Rent ($/mth)
City	508
U.S.	593

Note: Figures are based on an unfurnished two bedroom, 1-1/2 or 2 bath apartment, approximately 950 sq. ft. in size, excluding all utilities except water
Source: ACCRA, Cost of Living Index, 4th Quarter 1998

RESIDENTIAL UTILITIES

Average Residential Utility Costs

Area	All Electric ($/mth)	Part Electric ($/mth)	Other Energy ($/mth)	Phone ($/mth)
City	–	64.10	39.60	22.08
U.S.	101.64	55.45	43.56	19.81

Source: ACCRA, Cost of Living Index, 4th Quarter 1998

HEALTH CARE

Average Health Care Costs

Area	Hospital ($/day)	Doctor ($/visit)	Dentist ($/visit)
City	533.25	52.00	68.20
U.S.	417.46	51.94	64.89

Note: Hospital—based on a semi-private room; Doctor—based on a general practitioner's routine exam of an established patient; Dentist—based on adult teeth cleaning and periodic oral exam.
Source: ACCRA, Cost of Living Index, 4th Quarter 1998

Distribution of Office-Based Physicians

Area	Family/Gen. Practitioners	Specialists		
		Medical	Surgical	Other
MSA[1]	153	233	189	217

Note: Data as of 12/31/97; (1) Metropolitan Statistical Area - see Appendix A for areas included
Source: American Medical Assn., Physician Characteristics & Distribution in the U.S., 1999

Hospitals

Wichita has 4 general medical and surgical hospitals, 2 rehabilitation. *AHA Guide to the Healthcare Field, 1998-99*

EDUCATION

Public School District Statistics

District Name	Num. Sch.	Enroll.	Classroom Teachers	Pupils per Teacher	Minority Pupils (%)	Current Exp.[1] ($/pupil)
Wichita	95	46,859	2,715	17.3	42.9	5,654

Note: Data covers the 1997-1998 school year unless otherwise noted; (1) Data covers fiscal year 1996; SD = School District; ISD = Independent School District; n/a not available
Source: National Center for Education Statistics, Common Core of Data Public Education Agency Universe 1997-98; National Center for Education Statistics, Characteristics of the 100 Largest Public Elementary and Secondary School Districts in the United States: 1997-98, July 1999

Educational Quality

School District	Education Quotient[1]	Graduate Outcome[2]	Community Index[3]	Resource Index[4]
Wichita SD	95.0	89.0	128.0	100.0

Note: Nearly 1,000 secondary school districts were rated in terms of educational quality. The scores range from a low of 50 to a high of 150; (1) Average of the Graduate Outcome, Community and Resource indexes; (2) Based on graduation rates and college board scores (SAT/ACT); (3) Based on the surrounding community's average level of education and the area's average income level; (4) Based on teacher salaries, per-pupil expenditures and student-teacher ratios.
Source: Expansion Management, Ratings Issue, 1998

Educational Attainment by Race

Area	High School Graduate (%)					Bachelor's Degree (%)				
	Total	White	Black	Other	Hisp.[2]	Total	White	Black	Other	Hisp.[2]
City	81.9	84.7	67.3	60.1	58.0	22.7	24.4	10.6	16.9	11.3
MSA[1]	82.2	84.0	68.2	62.3	59.6	21.5	22.5	10.9	15.8	11.1
U.S.	75.2	77.9	63.1	60.4	49.8	20.3	21.5	11.4	19.4	9.2

Note: Figures shown cover persons 25 years old and over; (1) Metropolitan Statistical Area - see Appendix A for areas included; (2) people of Hispanic origin can be of any race
Source: 1990 Census of Population and Housing, Summary Tape File 3C

School Enrollment by Type

Area	Preprimary				Elementary/High School			
	Public		Private		Public		Private	
	Enrollment	%	Enrollment	%	Enrollment	%	Enrollment	%
City	3,357	58.0	2,428	42.0	43,283	86.8	6,572	13.2
MSA[1]	5,755	61.4	3,625	38.6	76,614	89.0	9,501	11.0
U.S.	2,679,029	59.5	1,824,256	40.5	38,379,689	90.2	4,187,099	9.8

Note: Figures shown cover persons 3 years old and over; (1) Metropolitan Statistical Area - see Appendix A for areas included
Source: 1990 Census of Population and Housing, Summary Tape File 3C

School Enrollment by Race

Area	Preprimary (%)				Elementary/High School (%)			
	White	Black	Other	Hisp.[1]	White	Black	Other	Hisp.[1]
City	82.6	12.2	5.3	5.4	74.4	16.0	9.6	7.3
MSA[2]	86.8	8.2	5.1	5.5	83.2	9.9	6.9	5.5
U.S.	80.4	12.5	7.1	7.8	74.1	15.6	10.3	12.5

Note: Figures shown cover persons 3 years old and over; (1) people of Hispanic origin can be of any race; (2) Metropolitan Statistical Area - see Appendix A for areas included
Source: 1990 Census of Population and Housing, Summary Tape File 3C

Classroom Teacher Salaries in Public Schools

District	B.A. Degree		M.A. Degree		Maximum	
	Min. ($)	Rank[1]	Max. ($)	Rank[1]	Max. ($)	Rank[1]
Wichita	24,494	76	34,629	96	38,620	98
Average	26,980	-	46,065	-	51,435	-

Note: Salaries are for 1997-1998; (1) Rank ranges from 1 to 100
Source: American Federation of Teachers, Survey & Analysis of Salary Trends, 1998

Higher Education

Two-Year Colleges		Four-Year Colleges		Medical Schools	Law Schools	Voc/ Tech
Public	Private	Public	Private			
0	0	1	2	0	0	16

Source: College Blue Book, Occupational Education, 1997; Medical School Admission Requirements, 1999-2000; Peterson's Guide to Two-Year Colleges, 1999; Peterson's Guide to Four-Year Colleges, 2000; Barron's Guide to Law Schools, 1999

MAJOR EMPLOYERS

Major Employers

Cessna Aircraft	Learjet
Via Christi Regional Medical Center	HCA Health Services of Kansas
Koch Industries (petroleum refining)	Martin K. Eby Construction
Evcon Industries (refrigeration equipment)	Intrust Bank
IFR Systems (measuring equipment)	Wichita Eagle & Beacon Publishing Co.

Note: Companies listed are located in the city
Source: Dun's Business Rankings, 1999; Ward's Business Directory, 1998

PUBLIC SAFETY

Crime Rate

Area	All Crimes	Violent Crimes				Property Crimes		
		Murder	Forcible Rape	Robbery	Aggrav. Assault	Burglary	Larceny -Theft	Motor Vehicle Theft
City	8,037.9	10.1	72.2	281.9	469.1	1,510.7	4,976.4	717.5
Suburbs[1]	n/a	n/a	n/a	n/a	n/a	n/a	n/a	n/a
MSA[2]	n/a	n/a	n/a	n/a	n/a	n/a	n/a	n/a
U.S.	4,922.7	6.8	35.9	186.1	382.0	919.6	2,886.5	505.8

Note: Crime rate is the number of crimes per 100,000 pop.; (1) defined as all areas within the MSA but located outside the central city; (2) Metropolitan Statistical Area - see Appendix A for areas incl.
Source: FBI Uniform Crime Reports, 1997

RECREATION

Culture and Recreation

Museums	Symphony Orchestras	Opera Companies	Dance Companies	Professional Theatres	Zoos	Pro Sports Teams
10	2	0	0	0	1	0

Source: International Directory of the Performing Arts, 1997; Official Museum Directory, 1999; Stern's Performing Arts Directory, 1997; USA Today Four Sport Stadium Guide, 1997; Chamber of Commerce/Economic Development, 1999

MEDIA

Library System

The Wichita Public Library has 11 branches, holdings of 616,364 volumes, and a budget of $5,290,298 (1997). *American Library Directory, 1998-1999*

Newspapers

Name	Type	Freq.	Distribution	Circulation
The Catholic Advance	Religious	1x/wk	Area	30,206
The Wichita Eagle	General	7x/wk	Area	90,060

Note: Includes newspapers with circulations of 1,000 or more located in the city;
Source: Burrelle's Media Directory, 1999 Edition

Television Stations

Name	Ch.	Affiliation	Type	Owner
KSNW	n/a	NBCT	Commercial	Lee Enterprises Inc.
KPTS	n/a	PBS	Public	Kansas Public Telecommunications Service Inc.
KAKE	10	ABCT	Commercial	Chronicle Broadcasting Inc.
KWCH	12	CBST	Commercial	Spartan Communications Inc.
KAAS	18	FBC	Commercial	Clear Channel Broadcasting Inc.
KSAS	24	FBC	Commercial	Clear Channel Broadcasting Inc.

Note: Stations included broadcast in the Wichita metro area; n/a not available
Source: Burrelle's Media Directory, 1999 Edition

AM Radio Stations

Call Letters	Freq. (kHz)	Target Audience	Station Format	Music Format
KSGL	900	General	E/M/N/S/T	Christian
KFDI	1070	General	M/N/S	Country
KNSS	1240	General	N/S/T	n/a
KFH	1330	General	N/T	n/a
KQAM	1480	General	S	n/a

Note: Stations included broadcast in the Wichita metro area; n/a not available
Target Audience: A=Asian; B=Black; C=Christian; E=Ethnic; F=French; G=General; H=Hispanic;
M=Men; N=Native American; R=Religious; S=Senior Citizen; W=Women; Y=Young Adult; Z=Children
Station Format: E=Educational; M=Music; N=News; S=Sports; T=Talk
Source: Burrelle's Media Directory, 1999 Edition

FM Radio Stations

Call Letters	Freq. (mHz)	Target Audience	Station Format	Music Format
KYFW	88.3	General	T	n/a
KMUW	89.1	G/H	M/N	Classical/Jazz
KCFN	91.1	General	M/N/S/T	Christian
KANR	92.7	General	N	n/a
KDGS	93.9	General	M	Urban Contemporary
KICT	95.1	General	M/N/S	Alternative
KRZZ	96.3	General	M/N/S	AOR/Classic Rock
KRBB	97.9	General	M	Adult Contemporary
KTLI	99.1	General	M	Christian
KFDI	101.3	General	M/N/S	Country
KZSN	102.1	General	M	Country
KEYN	103.7	General	M	Oldies
KWSJ	105.3	General	M	Jazz
KYQQ	106.5	General	M	Country
KKRD	107.3	General	M/N	n/a

Note: Stations included broadcast in the Wichita metro area; n/a not available
Station Format: E=Educational; M=Music; N=News; S=Sports; T=Talk
Target Audience: A=Asian; B=Black; C=Christian; E=Ethnic; F=French; G=General; H=Hispanic;
M=Men; N=Native American; R=Religious; S=Senior Citizen; W=Women; Y=Young Adult; Z=Children
Music Format: AOR=Album Oriented Rock; MOR=Middle-of-the-Road
Source: Burrelle's Media Directory, 1999 Edition

CLIMATE

Average and Extreme Temperatures

Temperature	Jan	Feb	Mar	Apr	May	Jun	Jul	Aug	Sep	Oct	Nov	Dec	Yr.
Extreme High (°F)	75	84	89	96	100	110	113	110	107	95	87	83	113
Average High (°F)	40	46	56	68	77	87	92	91	82	71	55	44	68
Average Temp. (°F)	30	35	45	57	66	76	81	80	71	59	45	34	57
Average Low (°F)	20	24	33	45	55	65	70	68	59	47	34	24	45
Extreme Low (°F)	-12	-21	-3	15	31	43	51	47	31	21	1	-16	-21

Note: Figures cover the years 1948-1990
Source: National Climatic Data Center, International Station Meteorological Climate Summary, 3/95

Average Precipitation/Snowfall/Humidity

Precip./Humidity	Jan	Feb	Mar	Apr	May	Jun	Jul	Aug	Sep	Oct	Nov	Dec	Yr.
Avg. Precip. (in.)	0.9	1.0	2.3	2.3	3.9	4.3	3.7	3.0	3.2	2.3	1.4	1.0	29.3
Avg. Snowfall (in.)	5	4	3	Tr	0	0	0	0	0	Tr	2	3	17
Avg. Rel. Hum. 6am (%)	78	79	77	78	83	83	78	79	82	80	79	79	80
Avg. Rel. Hum. 3pm (%)	56	54	48	46	51	47	42	43	47	47	51	56	49

Note: Figures cover the years 1948-1990; Tr = Trace amounts (<0.05 in. of rain; <0.5 in. of snow)
Source: National Climatic Data Center, International Station Meteorological Climate Summary, 3/95

Weather Conditions

Temperature			Daytime Sky			Precipitation		
10°F & below	32°F & below	90°F & above	Clear	Partly cloudy	Cloudy	0.01 inch or more precip.	0.1 inch or more snow/ice	Thunderstorms
13	110	63	117	132	116	87	13	54

Note: Figures are average number of days per year and covers the years 1948-1990
Source: National Climatic Data Center, International Station Meteorological Climate Summary, 3/95

AIR & WATER QUALITY

Maximum Pollutant Concentrations

	Particulate Matter (ug/m^3)	Carbon Monoxide (ppm)	Sulfur Dioxide (ppm)	Nitrogen Dioxide (ppm)	Ozone (ppm)	Lead (ug/m^3)
MSA[1] Level	57	5	0.007	n/a	0.09	0.01
NAAQS[2]	150	9	0.140	0.053	0.12	1.50
Met NAAQS?	Yes	Yes	Yes	n/a	Yes	Yes

Note: (1) Metropolitan Statistical Area - see Appendix A for areas included; (2) National Ambient Air Quality Standards; ppm = parts per million; ug/m^3 = micrograms per cubic meter; n/a not available
Source: EPA, National Air Quality and Emissions Trends Report, 1997

Drinking Water

Water System Name	Pop. Served	Primary Water Source Type	Number of Violations in 1998	Type of Violation/ Contaminants
City of Wichita	325,598	Surface	None	None

Note: Data as of July 10, 1999
Source: EPA, Office of Ground Water and Drinking Water, Safe Drinking Water Information System

Wichita tap water is soft.
Editor & Publisher Market Guide, 1999

Comparative Statistics

Population Growth: City

City	Population			% Change	
	1980	1990	1998[1]	1980-90	1990-98
Ann Arbor	107,960	109,592	109,967	1.5	0.3
Chicago	3,005,072	2,783,726	2,802,079	-7.4	0.7
Des Moines	191,003	193,187	191,293	1.1	-1.0
Detroit	1,203,339	1,027,974	970,196	-14.6	-5.6
Ft. Wayne	172,196	173,072	185,716	0.5	7.3
Gary	151,953	116,646	108,469	-23.2	-7.0
Grand Rapids	181,843	189,126	185,437	4.0	-2.0
Indianapolis	700,807	731,321	741,304	4.4	1.4
Kansas City	448,159	435,141	441,574	-2.9	1.5
Lansing	130,414	127,321	127,825	-2.4	0.4
Little Rock	158,461	175,781	175,303	10.9	-0.3
Madison	170,616	191,262	209,306	12.1	9.4
Milwaukee	636,212	628,088	578,364	-1.3	-7.9
Minneapolis	370,951	368,383	351,731	-0.7	-4.5
Oklahoma City	403,243	444,730	472,221	10.3	6.2
Omaha	314,267	335,795	371,291	6.9	10.6
St. Louis	453,085	396,685	339,316	-12.4	-14.5
Springfield	133,116	140,494	142,898	5.5	1.7
Wichita	279,272	304,011	329,211	8.9	8.3
U.S.	**226,545,805**	**248,765,170**	**270,299,000**	**9.8**	**8.7**

Note: (1) Census Bureau estimate as of 7/98
Source: 1980 Census; 1990 Census of Population and Housing, Summary Tape File 3C

Population Growth: Metro Area

MSA[1]	Population			% Change	
	1980	1990	1998[2]	1980-90	1990-98
Ann Arbor	264,740	282,937	543,178	6.9	92.0
Chicago	6,060,387	6,069,974	7,841,548	0.2	29.2
Des Moines	367,561	392,928	438,938	6.9	11.7
Detroit	4,488,072	4,382,299	4,335,309	-2.4	-1.1
Ft. Wayne	354,156	363,811	481,639	2.7	32.4
Gary	642,733	604,526	628,229	-5.9	3.9
Grand Rapids	601,680	688,399	1,040,835	14.4	51.2
Indianapolis	1,166,575	1,249,822	1,529,565	7.1	22.4
Kansas City	1,433,458	1,566,280	1,726,167	9.3	10.2
Lansing	419,750	432,674	452,490	3.1	4.6
Little Rock	474,464	513,117	560,128	8.1	9.2
Madison	323,545	367,085	404,794	13.5	10.3
Milwaukee	1,397,143	1,432,149	1,466,157	2.5	2.4
Minneapolis	2,137,133	2,464,124	2,840,562	15.3	15.3
Oklahoma City	860,969	958,839	1,049,263	11.4	9.4
Omaha	585,122	618,262	695,738	5.7	12.5
St. Louis	2,376,998	2,444,099	2,566,868	2.8	5.0
Springfield	207,704	240,593	307,011	15.8	27.6
Wichita	411,870	485,270	522,197	17.8	7.6
U.S.	**226,545,805**	**248,765,170**	**270,299,000**	**9.8**	**8.7**

Note: (1) Metropolitan Statistical Area - see Appendix A for areas included; (2) Pop. estimates calculated by the editors
Source: 1980 Census; 1990 Census of Population and Housing, Summary Tape File 3C

Population Characteristics: City

City	1990 Percent of Total (%)					
	White	Black	American Indian/ Esk./Aleut.	Asian/ Pacific Islander	Other	Hispanic Origin[1]
Ann Arbor	82.3	8.9	0.2	7.8	0.8	2.4
Chicago	45.5	39.0	0.2	3.7	11.5	19.2
Des Moines	89.3	7.1	0.4	2.3	1.0	2.4
Detroit	21.6	75.7	0.3	0.8	1.5	2.6
Ft. Wayne	80.3	16.7	0.4	1.0	1.6	2.5
Gary	16.3	80.6	0.2	0.1	2.8	5.4
Grand Rapids	76.7	18.6	0.8	1.0	2.9	4.5
Indianapolis	75.9	22.5	0.2	0.9	0.4	1.0
Kansas City	66.9	29.6	0.5	1.1	1.9	3.9
Lansing	74.0	18.6	1.3	1.7	4.5	8.0
Little Rock	64.7	34.1	0.3	0.8	0.1	0.8
Madison	90.8	4.1	0.4	3.9	0.8	1.9
Milwaukee	63.3	30.5	1.0	1.9	3.3	6.0
Minneapolis	78.5	13.0	3.3	4.3	0.8	2.0
Oklahoma City	74.9	15.9	4.3	2.3	2.6	4.8
Omaha	83.9	13.1	0.7	1.1	1.3	2.9
St. Louis	51.0	47.4	0.3	0.9	0.4	1.2
Springfield	95.6	2.4	0.8	0.9	0.3	0.9
Wichita	82.4	11.2	1.2	2.5	2.6	4.7
U.S.	**80.3**	**12.0**	**0.8**	**2.9**	**3.9**	**8.8**

Note: (1) People of Hispanic origin can be of any race
Source: 1990 Census of Population and Housing, Summary Tape File 3C

Population Characteristics: Metro Area

MSA[1]	1990 Percent of Total (%)					
	White	Black	American Indian/ Esk./Aleut.	Asian/ Pacific Islander	Other	Hispanic Origin[2]
Ann Arbor	83.8	11.1	0.3	4.2	0.6	2.0
Chicago	67.6	21.9	0.2	3.8	6.5	11.8
Des Moines	93.9	3.7	0.3	1.5	0.7	1.8
Detroit	76.1	21.5	0.4	1.3	0.7	1.8
Ft. Wayne	89.8	8.3	0.3	0.7	0.9	1.7
Gary	76.2	19.4	0.2	0.6	3.6	7.8
Grand Rapids	90.8	5.9	0.5	1.1	1.7	3.1
Indianapolis	85.0	13.7	0.2	0.8	0.3	0.9
Kansas City	84.4	12.8	0.5	1.0	1.3	2.9
Lansing	88.2	7.2	0.7	1.9	2.0	3.8
Little Rock	78.9	19.9	0.4	0.6	0.3	0.9
Madison	93.9	2.8	0.4	2.3	0.6	1.4
Milwaukee	82.7	13.8	0.6	1.3	1.7	3.4
Minneapolis	92.2	3.6	0.9	2.6	0.6	1.4
Oklahoma City	81.3	10.5	4.8	1.8	1.7	3.4
Omaha	89.1	8.3	0.5	1.1	1.0	2.5
St. Louis	81.3	17.3	0.2	0.9	0.3	1.0
Springfield	96.9	1.5	0.8	0.7	0.2	0.8
Wichita	87.5	7.5	1.1	1.8	2.0	3.8
U.S.	**80.3**	**12.0**	**0.8**	**2.9**	**3.9**	**8.8**

Note: (1) Metropolitan Statistical Area - see Appendix A for areas included;
(2) People of Hispanic origin can be of any race
Source: 1990 Census of Population and Housing, Summary Tape File 3C

Age: City

City	Median Age (Years)	Age Distribution (%)						
		Under 5	Under 18	18-24	25-44	45-64	65+	80+
Ann Arbor	27.1	5.7	17.1	27.1	35.7	12.8	7.3	1.8
Chicago	31.1	7.7	26.0	11.3	33.3	17.7	11.8	2.5
Des Moines	32.2	7.8	24.2	11.9	33.3	17.2	13.3	3.4
Detroit	30.7	9.0	29.4	11.0	30.7	16.7	12.1	2.5
Ft. Wayne	31.5	8.0	26.4	10.9	33.1	16.2	13.4	3.4
Gary	31.2	8.0	31.7	9.4	27.9	19.6	11.4	1.9
Grand Rapids	29.8	9.4	27.6	12.5	32.9	14.0	13.0	3.8
Indianapolis	31.6	8.0	25.6	10.4	34.9	17.6	11.4	2.6
Kansas City	32.7	7.7	24.7	9.8	34.2	18.4	12.9	3.2
Lansing	29.7	9.2	27.6	11.7	36.4	14.6	9.6	2.1
Little Rock	32.7	7.3	24.9	10.3	34.9	17.4	12.5	3.1
Madison	29.3	6.2	18.5	22.2	35.5	14.6	9.2	2.3
Milwaukee	30.3	8.6	27.5	12.0	32.6	15.5	12.4	3.1
Minneapolis	31.5	7.3	20.6	13.3	39.2	14.1	12.9	3.9
Oklahoma City	32.3	7.7	25.9	9.9	33.8	18.6	11.8	2.6
Omaha	32.1	7.6	25.5	10.9	32.7	18.1	12.9	3.2
St. Louis	32.7	8.0	25.2	10.3	31.2	16.6	16.7	4.7
Springfield	31.7	6.2	20.6	17.8	29.3	17.1	15.2	4.2
Wichita	31.7	8.6	26.6	10.2	34.1	16.7	12.4	2.7
U.S.	**32.9**	**7.3**	**25.6**	**10.5**	**32.6**	**18.7**	**12.5**	**2.8**

Source: 1990 Census of Population and Housing, Summary Tape File 3C

Age: Metro Area

MSA[1]	Median Age (Years)	Age Distribution (%)						
		Under 5	Under 18	18-24	25-44	45-64	65+	80+
Ann Arbor	29.2	6.7	21.5	19.4	36.1	15.5	7.5	1.7
Chicago	32.5	7.5	25.4	10.2	33.7	18.9	11.8	2.5
Des Moines	32.5	7.5	25.5	10.7	33.8	18.4	11.7	2.9
Detroit	33.0	7.6	26.1	9.8	33.0	19.2	11.8	2.4
Ft. Wayne	32.1	7.8	27.9	9.7	33.2	17.6	11.6	2.6
Gary	32.9	7.0	27.8	9.6	31.0	19.8	11.8	2.1
Grand Rapids	30.6	8.7	28.6	11.0	33.3	16.6	10.5	2.6
Indianapolis	32.3	7.7	26.4	9.8	34.4	18.4	11.1	2.5
Kansas City	32.9	7.7	26.4	9.1	34.2	18.7	11.6	2.8
Lansing	29.8	7.3	25.7	15.9	33.1	16.4	9.0	2.1
Little Rock	32.2	7.3	26.5	10.5	33.4	18.2	11.3	2.6
Madison	30.7	7.0	22.7	15.7	36.3	16.0	9.2	2.3
Milwaukee	32.7	7.7	26.3	9.9	32.9	18.4	12.5	3.0
Minneapolis	31.6	8.1	26.3	10.0	36.8	17.1	9.9	2.5
Oklahoma City	31.9	7.4	26.5	10.8	33.3	18.4	11.0	2.5
Omaha	31.4	8.1	27.9	10.0	34.1	17.5	10.6	2.5
St. Louis	33.1	7.5	26.2	9.4	32.7	18.9	12.8	3.1
Springfield	32.5	6.5	23.8	13.8	31.0	18.3	13.1	3.3
Wichita	32.1	8.3	27.8	9.3	33.3	17.6	12.0	2.7
U.S.	**32.9**	**7.3**	**25.6**	**10.5**	**32.6**	**18.7**	**12.5**	**2.8**

Note: (1) Metropolitan Statistical Area - see Appendix A for areas included
Source: 1990 Census of Population and Housing, Summary Tape File 3C

Male/Female Ratio: City

City	Number of males per 100 females (all ages)	Number of males per 100 females (18 years old+)
Ann Arbor	97.4	96.2
Chicago	91.8	88.4
Des Moines	89.0	85.0
Detroit	86.3	80.7
Ft. Wayne	91.2	86.3
Gary	84.4	78.3
Grand Rapids	90.2	85.6
Indianapolis	90.4	86.1
Kansas City	90.3	86.6
Lansing	90.0	86.1
Little Rock	85.3	81.6
Madison	96.5	92.9
Milwaukee	89.6	84.8
Minneapolis	94.1	92.2
Oklahoma City	93.3	89.5
Omaha	91.3	87.2
St. Louis	83.6	78.1
Springfield	89.4	85.7
Wichita	94.6	91.3
U.S.	**95.0**	**91.9**

Source: 1990 Census of Population, General Population Characteristics

Male/Female Ratio: Metro Area

MSA[1]	Number of males per 100 females (all ages)	Number of males per 100 females (18 years old+)
Ann Arbor	97.3	95.8
Chicago	93.3	89.9
Des Moines	91.7	87.4
Detroit	92.7	88.9
Ft. Wayne	94.6	90.7
Gary	92.8	88.9
Grand Rapids	94.8	91.1
Indianapolis	92.4	88.4
Kansas City	93.5	89.9
Lansing	93.6	90.6
Little Rock	92.0	88.2
Madison	97.4	94.4
Milwaukee	92.9	88.8
Minneapolis	95.5	92.6
Oklahoma City	95.0	91.3
Omaha	94.2	90.4
St. Louis	91.6	87.3
Springfield	92.2	88.4
Wichita	96.0	92.8
U.S.	**95.0**	**91.9**

Note: (1) Metropolitan Statistical Area - see Appendix A for areas included
Source: 1990 Census of Population, General Population Characteristics

Educational Attainment by Race: City

City	High School Graduate (%)					Bachelor's Degree (%)				
	Total	White	Black	Other	Hisp.[1]	Total	White	Black	Other	Hisp.[1]
Ann Arbor	93.9	95.4	77.6	95.2	94.1	64.2	65.9	33.4	78.7	74.0
Chicago	66.0	72.2	63.1	49.2	40.8	19.5	26.6	10.5	15.5	6.6
Des Moines	81.0	82.4	70.7	58.2	61.7	18.9	19.6	10.8	13.6	10.5
Detroit	62.1	61.3	62.6	55.8	45.3	9.6	12.1	8.4	18.7	7.2
Ft. Wayne	77.1	79.6	64.4	61.4	60.0	15.7	17.1	6.9	15.3	7.2
Gary	64.8	57.6	67.1	50.2	50.7	8.8	9.1	9.0	2.2	3.7
Grand Rapids	76.4	80.0	63.8	46.9	41.0	20.8	23.7	7.7	10.7	8.2
Indianapolis	76.4	79.2	65.2	79.8	75.2	21.7	24.5	9.6	39.4	20.2
Kansas City	78.8	82.9	68.5	68.6	62.4	22.0	26.5	10.0	18.5	11.4
Lansing	78.3	80.9	72.0	60.1	54.6	18.3	19.9	13.6	9.8	6.4
Little Rock	82.0	87.0	68.9	80.5	78.6	30.3	35.4	16.5	45.5	34.7
Madison	90.6	91.0	80.6	89.3	87.2	42.0	41.7	24.8	62.8	48.4
Milwaukee	71.5	76.3	60.2	54.0	46.9	14.8	17.6	6.9	13.2	6.2
Minneapolis	82.6	84.9	71.9	66.3	73.1	30.3	32.8	13.8	21.4	23.8
Oklahoma City	78.2	80.8	72.6	61.9	47.5	21.6	23.7	12.9	14.9	10.3
Omaha	82.6	84.5	69.0	72.8	61.5	23.1	24.7	9.4	24.5	11.1
St. Louis	62.8	67.4	56.3	66.8	61.9	15.3	20.2	8.0	32.1	18.8
Springfield	77.0	77.3	70.6	68.9	77.0	20.7	20.9	12.4	20.1	27.6
Wichita	81.9	84.7	67.3	60.1	58.0	22.7	24.4	10.6	16.9	11.3
U.S.	**75.2**	**77.9**	**63.1**	**60.4**	**49.8**	**20.3**	**21.5**	**11.4**	**19.4**	**9.2**

Note: Figures shown cover persons 25 years old and over; (1) people of Hispanic origin can be of any race
Source: 1990 Census of Population and Housing, Summary Tape File 3C

Educational Attainment by Race: Metro Area

MSA[1]	High School Graduate (%)					Bachelor's Degree (%)				
	Total	White	Black	Other	Hisp.[2]	Total	White	Black	Other	Hisp.[2]
Ann Arbor	87.2	88.5	74.3	92.1	82.0	41.9	43.0	21.5	67.0	44.9
Chicago	75.7	80.5	65.6	58.0	44.2	24.4	27.9	11.8	24.0	8.0
Des Moines	85.4	86.2	71.7	66.8	68.9	22.6	23.0	12.1	21.9	12.6
Detroit	75.7	78.5	64.4	73.2	62.9	17.7	19.2	9.9	34.1	13.1
Ft. Wayne	80.6	82.0	65.6	65.5	63.0	17.3	18.0	8.0	17.7	9.3
Gary	75.4	77.9	67.1	60.5	59.3	14.0	15.1	9.7	11.4	6.2
Grand Rapids	80.2	81.6	65.9	54.1	48.0	20.2	21.0	8.4	12.4	7.7
Indianapolis	78.6	80.4	65.6	79.9	76.3	21.1	22.4	9.9	37.9	21.6
Kansas City	82.3	84.2	70.3	71.8	67.3	23.4	24.9	11.7	22.0	13.3
Lansing	84.2	85.3	75.8	73.2	61.0	24.7	24.5	21.0	33.4	12.5
Little Rock	76.6	79.0	64.8	74.8	76.0	20.4	21.8	13.1	24.7	19.3
Madison	88.9	89.2	80.1	87.0	82.9	34.2	33.8	24.0	57.6	41.5
Milwaukee	79.7	82.5	60.7	60.5	51.7	21.3	23.0	7.6	19.4	8.5
Minneapolis	87.2	88.0	76.2	70.7	76.7	27.1	27.5	17.3	25.2	19.9
Oklahoma City	79.2	80.6	74.5	68.5	55.3	21.6	22.7	14.2	17.7	11.1
Omaha	84.4	85.5	72.7	75.3	68.7	22.8	23.6	12.0	24.5	13.9
St. Louis	76.0	78.1	64.1	79.9	75.2	20.7	22.1	11.4	40.5	24.3
Springfield	78.5	78.8	71.8	71.0	77.7	19.6	19.7	14.4	19.1	23.2
Wichita	82.2	84.0	68.2	62.3	59.6	21.5	22.5	10.9	15.8	11.1
U.S.	**75.2**	**77.9**	**63.1**	**60.4**	**49.8**	**20.3**	**21.5**	**11.4**	**19.4**	**9.2**

Note: Figures shown cover persons 25 years old and over; (1) Metropolitan Statistical Area - see Appendix A for areas included; (2) people of Hispanic origin can be of any race
Source: 1990 Census of Population and Housing, Summary Tape File 3C

Per Capita/Median/Average Income: City

City	Per Capita ($)	Median Household ($)	Average Household ($)
Ann Arbor	17,786	33,344	44,963
Chicago	12,899	26,301	34,682
Des Moines	13,710	26,703	33,199
Detroit	9,443	18,742	25,601
Ft. Wayne	12,726	26,344	31,336
Gary	8,994	19,390	25,447
Grand Rapids	12,070	26,809	32,106
Indianapolis	14,478	29,006	35,946
Kansas City	13,799	26,713	33,510
Lansing	12,232	26,398	30,458
Little Rock	15,307	26,889	36,897
Madison	15,143	29,420	36,977
Milwaukee	11,106	23,627	28,415
Minneapolis	14,830	25,324	33,245
Oklahoma City	13,528	25,741	33,258
Omaha	13,957	26,927	34,675
St. Louis	10,798	19,458	25,605
Springfield	11,878	21,577	28,471
Wichita	14,516	28,024	35,453
U.S.	**14,420**	**30,056**	**38,453**

Note: Figures are for 1989
Source: 1990 Census of Population and Housing, Summary Tape File 3C

Per Capita/Median/Average Income: Metro Area

MSA[1]	Per Capita ($)	Median Household ($)	Average Household ($)
Ann Arbor	17,115	36,307	45,105
Chicago	16,447	35,265	44,583
Des Moines	14,972	31,182	37,958
Detroit	15,694	34,612	42,218
Ft. Wayne	14,287	31,689	37,952
Gary	13,174	31,629	36,665
Grand Rapids	14,370	33,515	39,827
Indianapolis	15,159	31,655	39,103
Kansas City	15,067	31,613	38,701
Lansing	14,044	32,156	38,027
Little Rock	12,809	26,501	33,336
Madison	15,542	32,703	39,589
Milwaukee	14,785	32,316	38,958
Minneapolis	16,842	36,565	43,942
Oklahoma City	13,269	26,883	34,117
Omaha	13,989	30,323	36,870
St. Louis	14,917	31,774	39,114
Springfield	12,250	24,546	31,107
Wichita	14,303	30,152	36,714
U.S.	**14,420**	**30,056**	**38,453**

Note: Figures are for 1989; (1) Metropolitan Statistical Area - see Appendix A for areas included
Source: 1990 Census of Population and Housing, Summary Tape File 3C

Household Income Distribution: City

City	Less than $5,000	$5,000 -$9,999	$10,000 -$14,999	$15,000 -$24,999	$25,000 -$34,999	$35,000 -$49,999	$50,000 -$74,999	$75,000 -$99,999	$100,000 and up
				% of Households Earning					
Ann Arbor	5.6	7.9	8.4	15.7	14.6	15.3	17.3	7.5	7.8
Chicago	10.6	10.2	8.9	18.0	15.4	16.6	12.8	4.0	3.5
Des Moines	6.0	10.2	10.2	20.2	18.7	18.1	11.5	2.7	2.3
Detroit	16.1	16.2	10.9	16.5	13.0	13.6	9.7	2.8	1.2
Ft. Wayne	5.0	9.9	10.1	22.1	18.6	18.9	11.5	2.3	1.5
Gary	16.4	13.9	10.7	18.0	13.1	13.8	10.6	2.7	0.7
Grand Rapids	6.1	11.2	10.0	19.3	17.9	18.4	12.4	2.9	1.9
Indianapolis	5.9	8.6	9.0	19.1	17.0	18.8	14.4	4.0	3.2
Kansas City	8.4	9.5	9.5	19.2	16.8	17.3	12.9	3.5	2.9
Lansing	7.8	10.9	9.6	18.8	17.3	19.0	12.3	3.0	1.2
Little Rock	7.1	9.7	10.1	19.3	16.0	15.6	13.7	4.1	4.4
Madison	5.8	9.2	9.1	18.0	16.5	18.1	14.7	4.8	3.7
Milwaukee	6.3	14.9	11.2	20.0	16.6	17.5	10.6	2.1	1.0
Minneapolis	6.3	12.7	10.6	19.8	15.8	16.2	11.9	3.6	3.2
Oklahoma City	6.9	10.6	10.4	20.7	16.9	16.1	12.3	3.3	2.8
Omaha	6.2	9.8	10.0	20.2	17.0	17.6	12.5	3.3	3.3
St. Louis	12.5	15.3	12.3	20.7	14.8	12.6	8.4	2.0	1.3
Springfield	8.3	13.1	12.9	22.8	17.1	13.7	7.9	1.8	2.3
Wichita	6.3	8.9	9.4	19.5	17.7	18.3	13.6	3.5	2.8
U.S.	6.2	9.3	8.8	17.5	15.8	17.9	15.0	5.1	4.4

Note: Figures are for 1989
Source: 1990 Census of Population and Housing, Summary Tape File 3C

Household Income Distribution: Metro Area

MSA[1]	Less than $5,000	$5,000 -$9,999	$10,000 -$14,999	$15,000 -$24,999	$25,000 -$34,999	$35,000 -$49,999	$50,000 -$74,999	$75,000 -$99,999	$100,000 and up
				% of Households Earning					
Ann Arbor	4.7	6.7	7.4	14.9	14.5	17.9	19.7	7.7	6.6
Chicago	6.2	7.0	6.7	14.8	14.9	19.1	18.4	6.9	6.1
Des Moines	4.2	7.7	8.6	18.1	17.9	20.5	15.3	4.3	3.3
Detroit	6.3	8.6	7.3	14.2	14.1	18.7	18.7	7.1	5.1
Ft. Wayne	3.6	7.3	8.0	18.9	17.8	21.3	16.1	4.1	2.9
Gary	6.8	8.3	7.9	16.5	15.6	20.5	17.5	4.6	2.5
Grand Rapids	3.3	7.3	7.5	16.5	17.7	22.3	17.2	4.6	3.6
Indianapolis	4.7	7.5	8.2	18.0	16.7	19.7	16.5	4.9	3.8
Kansas City	5.3	7.6	8.1	17.4	16.9	19.5	16.4	4.9	3.8
Lansing	5.3	8.0	8.0	16.7	16.2	19.9	17.3	5.5	3.2
Little Rock	7.2	9.5	10.0	20.3	17.0	17.5	12.6	3.1	2.8
Madison	4.0	7.3	7.9	17.2	16.8	20.8	17.0	5.1	3.9
Milwaukee	3.8	9.5	8.2	16.5	15.9	20.7	17.1	4.8	3.6
Minneapolis	3.1	7.0	6.5	15.1	15.7	21.5	19.7	6.3	5.1
Oklahoma City	6.6	9.9	9.9	20.0	17.2	17.3	13.0	3.5	2.7
Omaha	4.8	8.1	8.5	19.2	17.5	19.8	14.9	4.0	3.2
St. Louis	5.6	8.2	8.2	16.8	16.1	19.6	16.7	5.0	4.0
Springfield	6.9	11.1	11.5	21.5	18.1	16.3	9.9	2.3	2.5
Wichita	5.4	8.2	8.6	18.7	17.6	19.7	15.0	3.9	2.9
U.S.	6.2	9.3	8.8	17.5	15.8	17.9	15.0	5.1	4.4

Note: Figures are for 1989; (1) Metropolitan Statistical Area - see Appendix A for areas included
Source: 1990 Census of Population and Housing, Summary Tape File 3C

Effective Buying Income: City

City	Per Capita ($)	Median Household ($)	Average Household ($)
Ann Arbor	20,629	39,589	53,397
Chicago	15,271	32,292	41,840
Des Moines	16,755	33,255	41,072
Detroit	10,539	21,290	28,770
Ft. Wayne	15,578	32,136	38,149
Gary	10,519	22,810	29,699
Grand Rapids	14,959	33,044	40,220
Indianapolis	17,522	35,279	43,100
Kansas City	16,316	32,318	39,976
Lansing	13,717	29,409	33,909
Little Rock	19,973	36,205	48,119
Madison	18,780	37,228	46,592
Milwaukee	13,219	28,470	34,271
Minneapolis	17,421	30,709	40,072
Oklahoma City	15,021	29,270	37,548
Omaha	20,477	40,682	51,388
St. Louis	13,477	24,588	32,252
Springfield	15,139	28,016	36,927
Wichita	16,985	33,613	41,786
U.S.	**16,803**	**34,536**	**45,243**

Note: Data as of 1/1/99
Source: Standard Rate & Data Service, Newspaper Advertising Source, 9/99

Effective Buying Income: Metro Area

MSA[1]	Per Capita ($)	Median Household ($)	Average Household ($)
Ann Arbor	19,305	43,600	53,479
Chicago	20,152	44,166	56,087
Des Moines	18,930	38,813	48,148
Detroit	17,649	38,496	46,990
Ft. Wayne	17,407	37,702	45,983
Gary	15,996	37,088	43,754
Grand Rapids	17,013	38,583	47,166
Indianapolis	19,042	38,764	48,792
Kansas City	18,388	38,137	47,475
Lansing	16,004	36,025	43,423
Little Rock	17,365	34,657	45,315
Madison	20,037	41,240	51,092
Milwaukee	17,808	38,781	47,035
Minneapolis	19,457	42,629	51,403
Oklahoma City	15,673	31,017	40,876
Omaha	20,761	43,263	55,345
St. Louis	18,164	38,867	47,867
Springfield	15,451	30,488	40,109
Wichita	17,179	35,625	44,675
U.S.	**16,803**	**34,536**	**45,243**

Note: Data as of 1/1/99; (1) Metropolitan Statistical Area - see Appendix A for areas included
Source: Standard Rate & Data Service, Newspaper Advertising Source, 9/99

Effective Household Buying Income Distribution: City

City	% of Households Earning						
	$10,000 -$19,999	$20,000 -$34,999	$35,000 -$49,999	$50,000 -$74,999	$75,000 -$99,000	$100,000 -$124,999	$125,000 and up
Ann Arbor	14.2	20.0	15.4	19.6	10.6	4.7	5.3
Chicago	15.5	21.8	17.0	17.4	7.0	2.4	2.7
Des Moines	16.7	25.1	20.1	18.1	5.5	1.6	1.8
Detroit	20.6	20.1	14.5	12.2	3.8	1.0	0.5
Ft. Wayne	17.3	26.8	20.3	17.7	5.1	1.1	1.1
Gary	19.8	21.0	14.3	13.9	4.5	0.7	0.4
Grand Rapids	17.0	24.1	19.4	18.7	5.8	1.7	1.4
Indianapolis	15.2	23.7	18.9	19.7	7.3	2.2	2.3
Kansas City	16.3	23.7	18.2	17.7	6.2	2.0	2.0
Lansing	18.2	25.0	19.6	16.2	4.0	1.0	0.4
Little Rock	15.1	22.3	17.0	18.6	8.6	3.1	4.2
Madison	14.6	22.3	17.8	20.6	8.5	3.0	2.9
Milwaukee	20.6	24.6	18.3	16.3	3.9	0.8	0.6
Minneapolis	18.9	24.5	16.9	16.7	5.7	2.1	2.1
Oklahoma City	19.1	25.8	17.4	15.5	5.0	1.5	1.7
Omaha	13.3	20.6	17.8	21.0	10.2	3.8	4.4
St. Louis	21.4	24.1	15.0	12.8	4.0	1.2	1.1
Springfield	20.5	26.9	17.2	13.2	4.4	1.2	2.1
Wichita	16.1	24.5	18.8	18.9	6.4	1.8	2.0
U.S.	**16.0**	**22.6**	**18.2**	**18.9**	**7.2**	**2.4**	**2.7**

Note: Data as of 1/1/99
Source: Standard Rate & Data Service, Newspaper Advertising Source, 9/99

Effective Household Buying Income Distribution: Metro Area

MSA[1]	% of Households Earning						
	$10,000 -$19,999	$20,000 -$34,999	$35,000 -$49,999	$50,000 -$74,999	$75,000 -$99,000	$100,000 -$124,999	$125,000 and up
Ann Arbor	12.2	19.2	18.1	23.8	11.2	3.8	3.6
Chicago	11.2	18.4	17.8	23.2	11.0	4.2	4.7
Des Moines	13.9	22.7	20.2	22.2	8.0	2.5	2.4
Detroit	13.9	19.4	18.1	21.6	9.0	2.8	2.7
Ft. Wayne	14.2	24.0	21.1	22.1	7.0	1.9	1.8
Gary	14.4	20.9	19.1	22.7	7.5	1.7	1.6
Grand Rapids	13.9	22.4	20.9	22.6	7.2	2.1	2.2
Indianapolis	14.0	22.2	18.8	21.9	8.7	2.7	2.7
Kansas City	13.9	22.3	19.5	21.4	8.2	2.6	2.7
Lansing	14.9	22.7	19.7	20.9	7.3	1.9	1.6
Little Rock	15.5	23.6	18.4	19.4	7.1	2.1	2.4
Madison	12.7	21.6	19.1	24.0	9.0	2.9	3.0
Milwaukee	14.6	21.3	19.6	22.8	7.8	2.2	2.4
Minneapolis	11.9	20.7	20.3	24.9	9.1	2.9	3.0
Oklahoma City	18.0	25.1	18.2	17.0	5.5	1.6	1.7
Omaha	11.8	20.4	18.6	23.0	11.2	3.8	3.8
St. Louis	13.9	21.1	19.4	21.8	8.5	2.7	2.7
Springfield	18.8	25.9	18.9	15.6	4.8	1.3	2.0
Wichita	15.2	23.6	19.8	20.5	6.7	1.8	2.0
U.S.	**16.0**	**22.6**	**18.2**	**18.9**	**7.2**	**2.4**	**2.7**

Note: Data as of 1/1/99; (1) Metropolitan Statistical Area - see Appendix A for areas included
Source: Standard Rate & Data Service, Newspaper Advertising Source, 9/99

Poverty Rates by Race and Age: City

City	Total (%)	By Race (%)				By Age (%)		
		White	Black	Other	Hisp.[1]	Under 5 years old	Under 18 years old	65 years and over
Ann Arbor	16.1	14.4	20.8	27.2	21.5	9.8	8.4	7.4
Chicago	21.6	11.0	33.2	23.7	24.2	35.6	33.9	15.9
Des Moines	12.9	11.0	30.8	23.5	18.3	21.8	19.3	9.1
Detroit	32.4	21.9	35.2	36.7	35.7	52.7	46.6	20.1
Ft. Wayne	11.5	8.4	25.8	16.4	11.9	18.6	16.5	9.0
Gary	29.4	16.4	32.0	32.2	27.9	49.1	43.0	19.1
Grand Rapids	16.1	10.8	33.8	31.1	33.3	24.6	23.2	10.0
Indianapolis	12.5	8.4	26.4	13.8	13.0	20.1	18.9	11.7
Kansas City	15.3	8.7	29.6	21.8	18.4	26.2	22.8	14.6
Lansing	19.4	14.2	33.6	35.5	31.1	30.8	28.5	11.4
Little Rock	14.6	7.2	28.9	12.4	19.8	23.6	21.7	13.5
Madison	16.1	13.8	35.2	42.2	22.9	15.7	13.2	4.8
Milwaukee	22.2	10.8	41.9	40.2	35.5	41.5	37.8	10.0
Minneapolis	18.5	11.7	40.5	47.4	28.9	33.1	30.6	11.0
Oklahoma City	15.9	11.2	32.4	25.6	30.7	27.4	22.9	13.1
Omaha	12.6	8.7	34.6	27.5	19.0	24.3	18.8	10.6
St. Louis	24.6	12.6	37.4	26.0	23.5	41.4	39.7	18.7
Springfield	17.8	17.0	30.7	42.2	30.1	26.4	21.2	13.4
Wichita	12.5	8.7	34.4	23.3	19.0	21.0	17.8	9.6
U.S.	**13.1**	**9.8**	**29.5**	**23.1**	**25.3**	**20.1**	**18.3**	**12.8**

Note: Figures show the percent of people living below the poverty line in 1989. The average poverty threshold was $12,674 for a family of four in 1989; (1) People of Hispanic origin can be of any race
Source: 1990 Census of Population and Housing, Summary Tape File 3C

Poverty Rates by Race and Age: Metro Area

MSA[1]	Total (%)	By Race (%)				By Age (%)		
		White	Black	Other	Hisp.[2]	Under 5 years old	Under 18 years old	65 years and over
Ann Arbor	12.2	10.0	23.0	25.8	18.9	12.6	10.8	8.0
Chicago	12.4	5.8	30.0	18.4	20.7	19.9	19.1	10.5
Des Moines	8.8	7.7	29.6	19.9	14.3	14.4	11.7	8.5
Detroit	12.9	7.1	33.0	17.7	20.6	22.9	19.6	10.5
Ft. Wayne	7.6	5.8	24.9	15.7	10.6	12.3	10.0	8.3
Gary	12.2	6.6	32.3	19.9	16.5	21.2	18.5	9.3
Grand Rapids	8.3	6.4	31.4	20.0	22.9	12.5	10.7	8.1
Indianapolis	9.6	6.9	26.2	12.1	11.5	15.1	13.7	10.3
Kansas City	9.8	6.9	28.1	16.1	14.9	15.9	13.7	11.2
Lansing	12.9	10.6	30.5	32.0	26.3	18.3	14.9	9.5
Little Rock	13.5	9.2	30.8	12.2	17.4	19.8	18.2	16.8
Madison	10.5	8.9	35.0	37.6	21.3	10.6	8.8	5.0
Milwaukee	11.6	5.8	41.3	32.8	30.3	22.5	19.4	7.1
Minneapolis	8.1	5.9	37.0	32.7	19.1	13.2	11.2	8.2
Oklahoma City	13.9	10.8	30.8	24.1	26.6	22.8	18.6	13.1
Omaha	9.6	7.3	30.8	20.8	14.8	16.9	13.1	9.8
St. Louis	10.8	6.3	31.3	14.7	13.1	17.6	15.9	10.3
Springfield	13.5	13.0	28.4	34.3	20.0	20.4	15.4	13.8
Wichita	10.5	7.9	33.3	22.7	19.0	17.1	14.2	9.5
U.S.	**13.1**	**9.8**	**29.5**	**23.1**	**25.3**	**20.1**	**18.3**	**12.8**

Note: Figures show the percent of people living below the poverty line in 1989. The average poverty threshold was $12,674 for a family of four in 1989; (1) Metropolitan Statistical Area - see Appendix A for areas included;
(2) People of Hispanic origin can be of any race
Source: 1990 Census of Population and Housing, Summary Tape File 3C

Major State and Local Tax Rates

City	State Corp. Income (%)	State Personal Income (%)	Residential Property (effective rate per $100)	Sales & Use		State Gasoline (cents/ gallon)	State Cigarette (cents/ pack)
				State (%)	Local (%)		
Ann Arbor	2.3[i]	4.4	n/a	6.0	None	19.0	75.0
Chicago	7.3[c]	3.0	1.92	6.25	2.5	19.3[d]	58.0[e]
Des Moines	6.0 - 12.0	0.36 - 8.98	2.36	5.0	None	20.0	36.0
Detroit	2.3[i]	4.4	2.58	6.0	None	19.0	75.0
Fort Wayne	7.9[f]	3.4	n/a	5.0	None	15.0[g]	15.5
Gary	7.9[f]	3.4	n/a	5.0	None	15.0[g]	15.5
Grand Rapids	2.3[i]	4.4	n/a	6.0	None	19.0	75.0
Indianapolis	7.9[f]	3.4	1.53	5.0	None	15.0[g]	15.5
Kansas City	6.25	1.5 - 6.0	1.20	4.225	2.375	17.05[k]	17.0[l]
Lansing	2.3[i]	4.4	n/a	6.0	None	19.0	75.0
Little Rock	1.0 - 6.5	1.0 - 7.0[a]	1.19	4.625	1.5	18.7[b]	31.5
Madison	7.9	4.77 - 6.77	n/a	5.0	0.5	25.4	59.0
Milwaukee	7.9	4.77 - 6.77	2.97	5.0	0.6	25.4	59.0
Minneapolis	9.8[j]	6.0 - 8.5	1.25	6.5	0.5	20.0	48.0
Oklahoma City	6.0	0.5 - 6.75[n]	1.13	4.5	3.875	17.0[o]	23.0
Omaha	5.58 - 7.81	2.62 - 6.99	n/a	5.0	1.5	24.4[m]	34.0
Saint Louis	6.25	1.5 - 6.0	n/a	4.225	2.625	17.05[k]	17.0[l]
Springfield	6.25	1.5 - 6.0	n/a	4.225	1.875	17.05[k]	17.0[l]
Wichita	4.0[h]	4.1 - 6.45	1.23	4.9	1.0	18.0	24.0

Note: (a) A special tax table is available for low income taxpayers reducing their tax payments; (b) Rate is comprised of 18.5 cents excise plus 0.2 cent motor carrier tax; (c) Includes a 2.5% personal property replacement tax; (d) Rate is comprised of 19 cents excise and 0.3 cent motor carrier tax. Carriers pay an additional surcharge of 6.3 cents. Rate does not include a 5 cent local option tax in Chicago.; (e) Counties and cities may impose an additional tax of 10 - 15 cents per pack; (f) Consists of 3.4% on income from sources within the state plus a 4.5% supplemental income tax; (g) Carriers pay an additional surcharge of 11 cents; (h) Plus a 3.35% surtax on taxable income over $50,000. Banks 2.25% plus 2.125% surtax over $25,000; (i) Value added tax imposed on the sum of federal taxable income of the business, compensation paid to employees, dividends, interest, royalties paid and other items; (j) Plus a 5.8% tax on any Alternative Minimum Taxable Income over the base tax; (k) Rate is comprised of 17 cents excise and 0.05 cents motor carrier tax; (l) Counties and cities may impose an additional tax of 4 - 7 cents per pack; (m) Rate is comprised of 23.5 cents excise and 0.9 cents motor carrier tax; (n) Range is for persons not deducting federal income tax. Separate schedules, with rates ranging from 0.5% to 10%, apply to taxpayers deducting federal income taxes; (o) Rate is comprised of 16 cents excise and 1 cent motor carrier tax

Source: Source: Federation of Tax Administrators, www.taxadmin.org; Washington D.C. Department of Finance and Revenue, Tax Rates and Tax Burdens in the District of Columbia: A Nationwide Comparison, July 1999; Chambers of Commerce, 1999

Employment by Industry

MSA[1]	Services	Retail	Gov't.	Manuf.	Finance/ Ins./R.E.	Whole- sale	Transp./ Utilities	Constr.	Mining
Ann Arbor	25.3	16.8	25.1	19.1	3.8	3.5	2.4	n/a	n/a
Chicago	32.6	16.0	11.5	15.4	7.6	6.5	6.1	4.2	<0.1
Des Moines	30.2	17.9	11.9	8.5	13.9	7.6	5.3	n/a	n/a
Detroit	31.2	17.4	11.0	20.3	5.2	6.1	4.5	4.3	<0.1
Ft. Wayne	25.0	17.1	9.1	27.2	5.5	6.1	4.8	n/a	n/a
Gary	27.3	19.1	14.0	18.2	3.4	4.1	5.4	n/a	n/a
Grand Rapids	25.3	18.3	9.4	27.4	4.3	6.8	3.4	n/a	n/a
Indianapolis	27.4	19.4	12.1	15.0	7.6	6.5	6.3	5.8	0.1
Kansas City	29.5	17.4	14.3	11.3	7.2	6.8	8.1	n/a	n/a
Lansing	25.4	19.1	26.3	12.3	6.4	3.7	2.6	n/a	n/a
Little Rock	29.4	17.4	19.0	10.8	5.8	5.9	7.0	n/a	n/a
Madison	26.0	16.8	25.6	10.6	8.0	4.6	3.4	n/a	n/a
Milwaukee	31.7	15.4	10.8	20.6	6.8	5.9	4.8	n/a	n/a
Minneapolis	29.4	17.5	13.0	16.5	7.5	6.1	5.6	4.4	n/a
Oklahoma City	30.8	18.6	19.5	10.4	5.9	4.9	4.7	3.9	1.3
Omaha	32.8	17.7	12.3	9.6	8.4	6.4	7.7	n/a	n/a
Springfield	29.9	20.2	12.1	14.3	4.6	7.3	7.0	n/a	n/a
St. Louis	32.5	18.0	11.2	14.5	6.3	5.7	6.3	n/a	n/a
Wichita	26.9	16.9	11.5	25.5	4.0	5.5	3.7	5.5	0.4
U.S.	**30.4**	**17.7**	**15.6**	**14.3**	**5.9**	**5.4**	**5.3**	**5.0**	**0.4**

Note: All figures are percentages covering non-farm employment as of 6/99 and are not seasonally adjusted; (1) Metropolitan Statistical Area - see Appendix A for areas included; n/a not available

Source: Bureau of Labor Statistics, http://stats.bls.gov

Labor Force, Employment and Job Growth: City

Area	Civilian Labor Force			Workers Employed		
	Jun. 1998	Jun. 1999	% Chg.	Jun. 1998	Jun. 1999	% Chg.
Ann Arbor	67,390	68,234	1.3	66,312	67,092	1.2
Chicago	1,322,758	1,360,840	2.9	1,241,949	1,278,196	2.9
Des Moines	122,089	125,470	2.8	118,904	122,294	2.9
Detroit	400,740	403,504	0.7	369,908	372,866	0.8
Ft. Wayne	99,785	100,427	0.6	96,836	96,677	-0.2
Gary	47,051	47,133	0.2	43,511	43,144	-0.8
Grand Rapids	114,362	117,902	3.1	109,258	111,925	2.4
Indianapolis	419,771	424,291	1.1	408,532	412,763	1.0
Kansas City	258,277	269,066	4.2	244,863	256,996	5.0
Lansing	65,832	65,702	-0.2	63,314	63,164	-0.2
Little Rock	100,745	105,148	4.4	96,556	101,464	5.1
Madison	132,796	134,318	1.1	130,334	132,147	1.4
Milwaukee	299,340	297,583	-0.6	282,160	281,729	-0.2
Minneapolis	211,608	214,370	1.3	204,556	207,440	1.4
Oklahoma City	245,638	250,635	2.0	235,425	242,981	3.2
Omaha	204,227	209,732	2.7	197,170	203,091	3.0
Springfield	83,086	86,909	4.6	80,079	84,323	5.3
St. Louis	158,554	163,526	3.1	144,865	151,150	4.3
Wichita	182,921	188,771	3.2	176,211	180,840	2.6
U.S.	**138,798,000**	**140,666,000**	**1.3**	**132,265,000**	**134,395,000**	**1.6**

Note: Data is not seasonally adjusted and covers workers 16 years of age and older
Source: Bureau of Labor Statistics, http://stats.bls.gov

Labor Force, Employment and Job Growth: Metro Area

Area	Civilian Labor Force			Workers Employed		
	Jun. '98	Jun. '99	% Chg.	Jun. '98	Jun. '99	% Chg.
Ann Arbor	296,042	299,888	1.3	289,780	293,190	1.2
Chicago	4,211,674	4,334,896	2.9	4,024,141	4,141,588	2.9
Des Moines	258,433	265,535	2.7	253,131	260,348	2.9
Detroit	2,288,959	2,304,934	0.7	2,201,080	2,218,676	0.8
Ft. Wayne	268,670	269,482	0.3	262,399	261,966	-0.2
Gary	309,637	308,679	-0.3	299,306	296,780	-0.8
Grand Rapids	603,513	620,984	2.9	584,012	598,270	2.4
Indianapolis	842,064	851,783	1.2	823,116	831,641	1.0
Kansas City	978,605	1,016,072	3.8	936,816	981,512	4.8
Lansing	240,498	240,072	-0.2	233,784	233,229	-0.2
Little Rock	298,209	310,958	4.3	286,072	300,613	5.1
Madison	264,691	267,827	1.2	260,364	263,987	1.4
Milwaukee	823,838	819,482	-0.5	793,434	792,220	-0.2
Minneapolis	1,692,549	1,719,174	1.6	1,653,173	1,676,687	1.4
Oklahoma City	533,628	544,617	2.1	512,767	529,228	3.2
Omaha	388,372	398,082	2.5	377,252	387,546	2.7
Springfield	164,356	171,988	4.6	158,817	167,233	5.3
St. Louis	1,331,964	1,374,693	3.2	1,268,230	1,316,070	3.8
Wichita	290,507	299,332	3.0	280,666	288,039	2.6
U.S.	**138,798,000**	**140,666,000**	**1.3**	**132,265,000**	**134,395,000**	**1.6**

Note: Data is not seasonally adjusted and covers workers 16 years of age and older;
(1) Metropolitan Statistical Area - see Appendix A for areas included
Source: Bureau of Labor Statistics, http://stats.bls.gov

Unemployment Rate: City

Area	1998						1999					
	Jul.	Aug.	Sep.	Oct.	Nov.	Dec.	Jan.	Feb.	Mar.	Apr.	May.	Jun.
Ann Arbor	2.2	1.4	1.9	1.4	1.3	1.3	1.8	1.9	1.7	1.5	1.6	1.7
Chicago	5.8	5.8	5.9	5.7	5.5	5.2	5.2	5.1	4.7	4.8	5.4	6.1
Des Moines	2.1	2.5	2.6	2.3	2.5	2.4	3.1	2.9	3.0	2.5	2.2	2.5
Detroit	9.8	6.6	7.8	6.8	6.2	5.9	7.7	8.0	7.3	6.7	6.8	7.6
Ft. Wayne	4.3	3.0	4.4	3.1	3.2	3.6	4.2	4.2	3.7	3.3	3.5	3.7
Gary	7.1	8.0	7.9	7.9	8.2	8.5	9.2	9.0	8.7	7.6	8.2	8.5
Grand Rapids	5.3	4.0	3.9	3.5	3.5	3.6	4.9	4.9	4.8	4.1	4.0	5.1
Indianapolis	2.8	2.8	2.8	2.6	2.8	2.8	3.0	2.8	2.6	2.4	2.6	2.7
Kansas City	5.6	5.0	4.2	3.7	3.7	3.5	3.1	3.4	3.4	3.4	3.5	4.5
Lansing	7.5	3.3	3.0	2.9	2.9	3.3	4.1	4.0	3.9	3.4	3.2	3.9
Little Rock	4.3	4.3	3.9	3.5	3.4	3.4	3.8	3.5	3.1	2.8	2.9	3.5
Madison	1.7	1.6	1.6	1.6	1.6	1.4	1.7	1.8	1.7	1.5	1.6	1.6
Milwaukee	6.0	6.0	5.4	5.6	5.3	4.6	5.3	5.5	5.3	5.2	5.4	5.3
Minneapolis	2.5	2.4	3.3	2.6	2.2	1.9	2.3	2.1	2.0	2.0	2.1	3.2
Oklahoma City	5.6	3.7	3.9	3.8	3.4	3.4	3.5	3.7	3.5	3.3	3.1	3.1
Omaha	3.3	2.9	2.8	2.9	2.5	2.2	3.2	2.9	2.7	2.2	2.7	3.2
Springfield	3.1	3.5	3.0	2.6	2.6	2.4	2.3	2.1	2.1	2.3	2.4	3.0
St. Louis	7.8	9.0	7.6	6.9	6.6	6.3	5.3	5.3	5.3	6.5	6.6	7.6
Wichita	3.3	3.6	3.8	3.9	3.8	3.4	4.1	3.8	3.8	3.8	4.0	4.2
U.S.	**4.7**	**4.5**	**4.4**	**4.2**	**4.1**	**4.0**	**4.8**	**4.7**	**4.4**	**4.1**	**4.0**	**4.5**

Note: All figures are percentages, are not seasonally adjusted and covers workers 16 years of age and older
Source: Bureau of Labor Statistics, http://stats.bls.gov

Unemployment Rate: Metro Area

Area	1998						1999					
	Jul.	Aug.	Sep.	Oct.	Nov.	Dec.	Jan.	Feb.	Mar.	Apr.	May.	Jun.
Ann Arbor	3.3	2.0	2.2	1.8	1.7	1.8	3.0	2.8	2.5	2.0	2.0	2.2
Chicago	4.2	4.2	4.2	4.0	4.0	4.0	4.3	4.2	3.8	3.6	3.9	4.5
Des Moines	1.6	1.9	2.0	1.8	1.9	1.9	2.4	2.3	2.3	1.9	1.7	2.0
Detroit	4.8	3.3	3.5	3.1	3.0	3.0	4.0	4.1	3.8	3.4	3.2	3.7
Ft. Wayne	3.5	2.4	3.3	2.4	2.5	2.7	3.2	3.2	2.8	2.4	2.6	2.8
Gary	3.1	3.6	3.6	3.5	3.7	3.9	4.2	4.2	4.0	3.4	3.7	3.9
Grand Rapids	3.7	2.9	2.7	2.6	2.7	2.7	3.7	3.7	3.6	3.0	2.9	3.7
Indianapolis	2.9	2.3	2.3	2.2	2.3	2.4	2.7	2.6	2.3	2.0	2.3	2.4
Kansas City	4.5	3.8	3.4	3.2	3.2	2.9	3.0	3.1	3.0	2.8	2.9	3.4
Lansing	6.4	2.4	2.2	2.1	2.2	2.5	3.2	3.1	3.0	2.5	2.4	2.9
Little Rock	4.2	4.1	3.8	3.5	3.4	3.4	3.8	3.5	3.0	2.8	2.8	3.3
Madison	1.6	1.4	1.4	1.4	1.4	1.3	1.8	1.9	1.7	1.4	1.4	1.4
Milwaukee	3.7	3.7	3.4	3.5	3.4	2.9	3.6	3.6	3.4	3.2	3.3	3.3
Minneapolis	1.7	1.7	2.7	1.8	1.7	1.6	2.3	2.0	1.9	1.6	1.6	2.5
Oklahoma City	5.2	3.5	3.7	3.6	3.2	3.2	3.3	3.4	3.2	3.0	2.8	2.8
Omaha	2.8	2.4	2.3	2.4	2.1	1.9	2.7	2.5	2.3	1.9	2.3	2.6
Springfield	2.8	3.3	2.7	2.4	2.5	2.4	2.4	2.1	2.1	2.1	2.2	2.8
St. Louis	5.1	4.6	3.9	3.6	3.5	3.4	3.5	3.3	3.1	3.4	3.6	4.3
Wichita	3.0	3.4	3.4	3.5	3.5	3.1	3.7	3.5	3.4	3.4	3.5	3.8
U.S.	**4.7**	**4.5**	**4.4**	**4.2**	**4.1**	**4.0**	**4.8**	**4.7**	**4.4**	**4.1**	**4.0**	**4.5**

Note: All figures are percentages, are not seasonally adjusted and covers workers 16 years of age and older
(1) Metropolitan Statistical Area - see Appendix A for areas included
Source: Bureau of Labor Statistics, http://stats.bls.gov

Average Hourly Wages: Occupations A - C

MSA[1]	Accountants/ Auditors	Assemblers/ Fabricators	Automotive Mechanics	Book- keepers	Carpenters	Cashiers	Clerks, Gen. Office
Ann Arbor	18.41	15.74	19.15	11.86	15.40	7.58	9.83
Chicago	19.36	10.18	14.95	12.20	22.47	7.16	10.49
Des Moines	17.59	9.59	12.31	10.62	14.43	6.94	9.33
Detroit	21.70	17.51	16.49	11.87	16.86	7.49	10.53
Ft. Wayne	18.10	13.35	14.06	10.68	13.04	6.70	9.10
Gary	17.27	10.00	15.01	9.86	17.90	6.23	8.69
Grand Rapids	17.31	10.46	14.60	11.15	14.04	7.55	9.77
Indianapolis	19.18	11.46	14.04	11.10	15.42	7.08	9.15
Kansas City	18.08	13.61	13.40	11.18	16.18	6.73	10.11
Lansing	22.88	9.62	14.69	11.56	15.60	6.79	10.29
Little Rock	18.11	9.62	12.99	10.30	11.31	6.71	8.96
Madison	18.54	8.77	14.08	11.17	14.52	7.31	10.05
Milwaukee	20.23	10.91	13.11	11.17	16.60	7.00	9.85
Minneapolis	19.29	11.97	14.62	12.34	17.03	7.44	10.43
Oklahoma City	17.29	14.43	13.43	10.05	11.28	6.50	9.11
Omaha	17.64	9.76	13.47	10.25	13.16	6.67	9.09
Springfield	16.55	8.38	11.48	9.14	10.91	6.65	8.06
St. Louis	18.69	14.99	14.19	10.84	18.42	6.78	9.61
Wichita	19.85	10.55	12.41	9.90	11.94	6.60	8.88

Notes: Wage data is for 1997 and covers the Metropolitan Statistical Area - see Appendix A for areas included; dashes indicate that data was not available
Source: Bureau of Labor Statistics, 1997 Metro Area Occupational Employment and Wage Estimates

Average Hourly Wages: Occupations C - F

MSA[1]	Clerks, Ship./Rec.	Computer Program.	Computer Support Specialists	Cooks, Restaurant	Electricians	Financial Managers	First-Line Supervisor/ Mgr., Sales
Ann Arbor	11.57	21.37	-	-	21.70	25.69	16.76
Chicago	12.13	24.28	19.79	8.24	23.77	29.70	18.68
Des Moines	12.92	20.49	16.18	7.65	16.86	26.72	15.86
Detroit	12.89	24.02	-	-	22.36	29.77	17.44
Ft. Wayne	10.30	17.22	16.78	7.62	15.61	23.53	15.02
Gary	11.88	23.91	14.64	7.66	20.45	21.28	12.62
Grand Rapids	11.52	21.14	-	-	17.51	27.04	18.13
Indianapolis	10.99	21.77	17.24	7.72	17.48	24.82	16.08
Kansas City	11.54	23.60	19.56	7.66	19.71	25.74	16.42
Lansing	12.78	21.43	-	-	17.62	26.35	14.92
Little Rock	9.99	21.26	16.45	8.22	11.87	23.04	15.23
Madison	11.77	21.38	18.51	7.55	17.31	24.12	15.97
Milwaukee	11.18	21.89	16.97	9.04	19.78	26.42	16.54
Minneapolis	12.19	22.86	17.80	8.73	22.55	29.55	18.18
Oklahoma City	10.09	20.49	14.55	7.43	15.49	24.80	13.85
Omaha	10.97	23.48	15.58	7.76	17.12	26.04	14.83
Springfield	11.19	19.62	14.95	7.53	15.23	20.44	13.79
St. Louis	11.41	23.66	19.25	7.71	21.20	27.23	16.49
Wichita	10.85	21.92	13.55	7.75	16.67	25.87	14.13

Notes: Wage data is for 1997 and covers the Metropolitan Statistical Area - see Appendix A for areas included; dashes indicate that data was not available
Source: Bureau of Labor Statistics, 1997 Metro Area Occupational Employment and Wage Estimates

Average Hourly Wages: Occupations F - L

MSA[1]	Food Preparation Worker	General Managers/ Top Exec.	Guards	Hand Packers	Janitors/ Cleaners	Laborers, Land-scaping	Lawyers
Ann Arbor	7.30	31.14	9.02	-	9.61	8.97	-
Chicago	6.59	32.29	8.46	8.01	8.79	11.02	33.96
Des Moines	7.33	28.25	8.43	7.40	8.35	8.89	31.56
Detroit	7.73	32.18	8.50	-	9.97	9.66	-
Ft. Wayne	6.82	27.78	8.88	8.17	8.16	8.06	28.78
Gary	6.17	27.54	7.63	7.27	7.80	8.67	33.51
Grand Rapids	7.06	30.20	7.71	-	9.90	8.50	-
Indianapolis	7.25	31.97	7.81	7.38	8.67	8.78	33.39
Kansas City	6.45	29.31	10.01	7.11	7.92	9.52	28.77
Lansing	7.25	27.71	8.59	-	9.42	9.16	-
Little Rock	6.70	26.49	6.86	7.19	6.65	7.92	31.62
Madison	7.05	28.39	7.80	8.30	8.67	9.21	32.45
Milwaukee	7.13	29.83	8.11	7.68	8.01	10.52	32.47
Minneapolis	7.80	32.32	8.93	7.96	8.81	10.28	33.97
Oklahoma City	6.28	24.08	7.60	7.29	7.28	7.45	35.43
Omaha	6.86	26.55	8.07	7.02	7.90	9.59	36.26
Springfield	7.05	23.84	11.48	5.97	7.85	9.94	38.74
St. Louis	7.33	29.35	8.78	7.81	7.63	10.48	33.09
Wichita	6.47	25.15	7.52	7.82	7.17	8.03	24.58

Notes: Wage data is for 1997 and covers the Metropolitan Statistical Area - see Appendix A for areas included; dashes indicate that data was not available
Source: Bureau of Labor Statistics, 1997 Metro Area Occupational Employment and Wage Estimates

Average Hourly Wages: Occupations M - P

MSA[1]	Maids/ House-keepers	Main-tenance Repairers	Marketing/ Advertising/ P.R. Mgrs.	Nurses, Licensed Practical	Nurses, Registered	Nursing Aides/ Orderlies/ Attendants	Physicians/ Surgeons
Ann Arbor	7.24	11.96	24.72	13.83	19.40	9.04	45.12
Chicago	7.33	13.35	27.83	13.64	19.97	8.12	49.00
Des Moines	7.27	10.75	26.07	-	-	8.64	-
Detroit	7.71	12.56	28.64	14.39	21.93	8.53	47.27
Ft. Wayne	6.80	11.33	28.30	12.21	16.66	7.49	55.90
Gary	7.31	12.36	20.53	12.19	19.05	7.63	55.18
Grand Rapids	6.82	11.92	26.06	12.69	17.46	8.32	56.82
Indianapolis	7.06	11.05	26.21	13.76	19.18	7.69	50.18
Kansas City	7.14	11.26	27.57	12.62	20.13	7.78	52.66
Lansing	6.15	11.07	30.02	13.49	18.51	8.63	52.83
Little Rock	6.30	9.94	25.64	11.30	19.54	7.45	36.64
Madison	7.64	11.56	23.85	12.38	19.53	9.09	-
Milwaukee	7.01	12.45	24.41	13.87	18.45	8.36	44.72
Minneapolis	8.04	12.76	30.87	13.62	21.79	9.64	51.97
Oklahoma City	6.27	10.10	23.22	11.52	17.39	6.87	50.52
Omaha	6.96	10.48	24.53	12.79	17.93	8.53	41.05
Springfield	6.12	9.91	21.71	10.88	17.40	7.38	53.77
St. Louis	7.04	11.26	26.13	12.69	17.60	7.43	51.01
Wichita	6.40	10.22	25.14	12.00	17.75	7.43	37.34

Notes: Wage data is for 1997 and covers the Metropolitan Statistical Area - see Appendix A for areas included; dashes indicate that data was not available
Source: Bureau of Labor Statistics, 1997 Metro Area Occupational Employment and Wage Estimates

Average Hourly Wages: Occupations R - S

MSA[1]	Receptionists/ Info. Clerks	Sales Reps., Except Scien./Retail	Sales Reps., Scientific/ Exc. Retail	Sales-persons, Retail	Secretaries, Except Leg./Med.	Stock Clerk, Sales Floor	Systems Analysts
Ann Arbor	8.91	18.99	25.44	9.51	11.52	7.77	23.12
Chicago	9.24	21.52	22.50	8.82	12.34	7.35	24.18
Des Moines	8.69	18.65	20.51	9.01	10.89	7.34	-
Detroit	8.99	21.35	26.53	9.07	12.13	8.23	22.50
Ft. Wayne	8.40	18.02	19.73	8.84	10.11	7.13	23.07
Gary	7.92	18.60	19.73	8.22	9.45	7.03	22.18
Grand Rapids	8.78	19.47	20.83	9.07	10.94	7.64	23.80
Indianapolis	8.64	20.63	20.68	8.86	10.80	7.59	24.42
Kansas City	8.78	20.36	24.90	8.82	11.12	6.84	23.66
Lansing	8.51	18.27	21.81	8.31	12.72	7.02	21.31
Little Rock	8.30	17.06	17.79	8.47	9.69	7.21	18.36
Madison	8.88	18.14	21.65	8.81	11.64	7.58	22.95
Milwaukee	8.82	20.57	22.64	9.21	11.46	7.01	23.63
Minneapolis	9.40	22.44	25.96	8.85	12.63	8.28	25.61
Oklahoma City	8.45	16.04	16.84	8.89	10.00	6.69	22.23
Omaha	8.18	18.33	19.88	8.44	10.03	7.50	21.08
Springfield	7.42	16.75	17.16	8.85	9.52	6.30	19.36
St. Louis	8.38	19.82	20.13	8.57	10.99	7.63	27.67
Wichita	8.21	17.21	21.51	7.88	9.51	7.30	20.71

Notes: Wage data is for 1997 and covers the Metropolitan Statistical Area - see Appendix A for areas included; dashes indicate that data was not available
Source: Bureau of Labor Statistics, 1997 Metro Area Occupational Employment and Wage Estimates

Average Hourly Wages: Occupations T - Z

MSA[1]	Teacher Aides	Teachers, Elementary School	Teachers, Secondary School	Telemar-keters	Truck Driv., Heavy/ Trac. Trail.	Truck Drivers, Light	Waiters/ Waitresses
Ann Arbor	-	22.82	25.85	12.92	16.05	9.64	5.86
Chicago	8.57	20.04	21.11	10.15	15.52	12.14	6.00
Des Moines	8.21	15.52	16.49	9.87	13.95	12.38	5.77
Detroit	-	18.60	22.28	10.35	15.62	11.30	5.89
Ft. Wayne	6.84	18.13	18.98	10.49	15.46	10.42	5.50
Gary	7.16	14.73	18.36	7.16	14.71	10.13	5.55
Grand Rapids	-	19.14	19.77	12.58	15.13	11.24	5.61
Indianapolis	8.57	18.62	19.87	9.17	15.22	9.77	5.72
Kansas City	7.95	15.46	15.06	8.71	15.36	9.40	5.82
Lansing	-	19.27	21.38	8.56	14.87	8.72	5.63
Little Rock	7.79	14.92	15.64	8.27	14.83	10.83	5.64
Madison	7.95	18.10	18.61	8.75	13.50	8.96	5.74
Milwaukee	9.88	17.88	21.20	9.89	14.87	9.79	5.63
Minneapolis	10.28	-	19.05	11.07	16.11	10.98	5.75
Oklahoma City	8.32	14.36	14.77	8.56	13.38	8.19	5.76
Omaha	7.46	15.25	15.92	7.66	12.35	9.54	5.89
Springfield	5.66	13.78	14.40	7.97	13.03	8.95	5.51
St. Louis	6.95	15.03	16.97	8.13	13.96	9.86	6.02
Wichita	7.52	15.25	15.41	7.69	11.87	8.47	5.45

Notes: Wage data is for 1997 and covers the Metropolitan Statistical Area - see Appendix A for areas included; hourly wages for elementary and secondary school teachers were calculated by the editors from annual wage data assuming a 40 hour work week; dashes indicate that data was not available
Source: Bureau of Labor Statistics, 1997 Metro Area Occupational Employment and Wage Estimates

Means of Transportation to Work: City

| City | Car/Truck/Van | | Public Transportation | | | Bicycle | Walked | Other Means | Worked at Home |
	Drove Alone	Car-pooled	Bus	Subway	Railroad				
Ann Arbor	61.8	9.2	5.4	0.0	0.0	2.1	17.1	0.5	3.9
Chicago	46.3	14.8	19.3	7.9	1.5	0.3	6.4	1.7	1.7
Des Moines	74.4	15.1	3.5	0.0	0.0	0.2	3.6	0.7	2.5
Detroit	67.8	16.1	10.2	0.0	0.0	0.1	3.4	1.3	1.1
Ft. Wayne	79.9	12.1	2.0	0.0	0.0	0.3	3.1	0.7	1.8
Gary	72.8	16.5	3.5	0.1	2.3	0.1	3.0	0.9	0.8
Grand Rapids	76.8	11.7	3.2	0.0	0.0	0.3	4.3	1.0	2.7
Indianapolis	78.0	13.4	3.1	0.0	0.0	0.2	2.4	0.8	2.0
Kansas City	74.7	13.6	5.6	0.0	0.0	0.1	2.8	1.0	2.2
Lansing	77.3	12.4	2.8	0.0	0.0	0.4	4.0	0.8	2.3
Little Rock	80.5	13.5	1.4	0.0	0.0	0.1	1.9	1.0	1.7
Madison	61.2	11.6	7.4	0.0	0.0	3.3	12.7	1.0	2.7
Milwaukee	67.2	13.2	10.8	0.0	0.0	0.3	6.0	0.8	1.6
Minneapolis	60.3	10.5	15.7	0.0	0.0	1.6	7.8	0.9	3.1
Oklahoma City	80.8	12.8	0.8	0.0	0.0	0.1	2.0	1.2	2.3
Omaha	78.0	12.2	3.1	0.0	0.0	0.1	3.3	0.8	2.5
St. Louis	66.5	14.1	11.8	0.0	0.0	0.3	4.6	1.1	1.7
Springfield	80.4	11.0	0.9	0.0	0.0	0.3	4.2	0.8	2.4
Wichita	82.6	10.6	1.1	0.0	0.0	0.3	2.3	1.0	2.2
U.S.	**73.2**	**13.4**	**3.0**	**1.5**	**0.5**	**0.4**	**3.9**	**1.2**	**3.0**

Note: Figures shown are percentages and only include workers 16 years old and over
Source: 1990 Census of Population and Housing, Summary Tape File 3C

Means of Transportation to Work: Metro Area

| MSA[1] | Car/Truck/Van | | Public Transportation | | | Bicycle | Walked | Other Means | Worked at Home |
	Drove Alone	Car-pooled	Bus	Subway	Railroad				
Ann Arbor	73.5	9.6	2.9	0.0	0.0	1.0	9.2	0.5	3.2
Chicago	63.8	12.0	8.7	4.1	3.9	0.2	4.2	1.1	2.0
Des Moines	77.3	13.7	2.1	0.0	0.0	0.1	2.9	0.6	3.4
Detroit	83.4	10.1	2.2	0.0	0.0	0.1	1.9	0.6	1.6
Ft. Wayne	82.3	11.0	1.1	0.0	0.0	0.2	2.3	0.6	2.5
Gary	79.9	12.0	1.3	0.1	1.8	0.1	2.7	0.6	1.6
Grand Rapids	82.7	9.8	1.1	0.0	0.0	0.2	2.8	0.6	2.8
Indianapolis	79.7	12.9	1.9	0.0	0.0	0.1	2.2	0.7	2.4
Kansas City	79.9	12.5	2.0	0.0	0.0	0.1	1.9	0.8	2.8
Lansing	77.0	11.3	1.5	0.0	0.0	0.8	5.7	0.7	3.0
Little Rock	79.8	14.4	0.8	0.0	0.0	0.1	1.9	1.0	2.0
Madison	68.5	12.5	4.4	0.0	0.0	1.9	8.2	0.8	3.6
Milwaukee	76.7	11.0	5.1	0.0	0.0	0.3	4.0	0.6	2.2
Minneapolis	76.0	11.2	5.2	0.0	0.0	0.4	3.2	0.6	3.4
Oklahoma City	80.3	13.3	0.5	0.0	0.0	0.2	2.1	1.0	2.5
Omaha	79.7	11.8	2.0	0.0	0.0	0.1	2.7	0.7	3.1
St. Louis	79.7	12.0	2.8	0.0	0.0	0.1	2.1	0.7	2.4
Springfield	81.5	10.9	0.6	0.0	0.0	0.2	2.9	0.7	3.2
Wichita	82.1	10.9	0.8	0.0	0.0	0.2	2.3	0.9	2.9
U.S.	**73.2**	**13.4**	**3.0**	**1.5**	**0.5**	**0.4**	**3.9**	**1.2**	**3.0**

Note: Figures shown are percentages and only include workers 16 years old and over;
(1) Metropolitan Statistical Area - see Appendix A for areas included
Source: 1990 Census of Population and Housing, Summary Tape File 3C

Cost of Living Index

Area	Composite	Groceries	Housing	Utilities	Transp.	Health	Misc.
Ann Arbor[7]	113.5	105.8	123.9	97.0	125.3	118.0	108.4
Chicago	n/a	n/a	n/a	n/a	n/a	n/a	n/a
Des Moines	97.3	95.6	90.2	104.4	96.8	100.8	101.9
Detroit	110.9	104.7	133.9	110.5	101.7	112.4	97.2
Fort Wayne[3]	94.3	101.3	90.5	100.7	91.7	89.9	93.9
Gary	n/a	n/a	n/a	n/a	n/a	n/a	n/a
Grand Rapids[5]	107.6	111.8	115.0	102.9	102.6	102.5	102.6
Indianapolis[2]	96.0	100.7	88.8	98.7	93.8	95.4	100.0
Kansas City[1]	98.2	95.5	90.4	102.0	94.3	107.0	105.0
Lansing	106.2	104.1	129.9	81.2	97.3	97.1	97.2
Little Rock[4]	95.5	106.7	83.1	116.2	103.6	98.7	92.6
Madison[6]	106.0	103.1	120.0	89.6	109.6	109.1	97.9
Milwaukee[1]	107.7	100.2	121.6	101.9	104.9	100.0	103.1
Minneapolis	103.5	98.1	96.0	107.1	116.9	115.3	105.8
Oklahoma City	92.2	94.5	80.0	98.2	94.2	92.3	99.4
Omaha	94.2	94.7	94.1	87.4	100.7	93.3	93.9
Saint Louis[1]	96.9	100.7	96.0	101.2	93.0	106.8	94.5
Springfield	92.1	96.2	89.1	73.6	98.2	95.2	94.8
Wichita[5]	94.8	88.5	88.3	104.9	99.0	106.2	98.0
U.S.	**100.0**	**100.0**	**100.0**	**100.0**	**100.0**	**100.0**	**100.0**

Note: n/a not available; (1) Metropolitan Statistical Area (MSA) - see Appendix A for areas included;
(2) Indianpolis/Marion County; (3) Ft. Wayne/Allen County; (4) Little Rock-North Little Rock; (5) 4th Quarter 1998; (6) 3rd
Quarter 1998; (7) 2nd Quarter 1996
Source: ACCRA, Cost of Living Index, 1st Quarter 1999 unless otherwise noted

Median Home Prices and Housing Affordability

MSA[1]	Median Price[2] 1st Qtr. 1999 ($)	HOI[3] 1st Qtr. 1999	Afford-ability Rank[4]
Ann Arbor	157,000	63.4	144
Chicago	153,000	70.1	117
Des Moines	94,000	90.6	4
Detroit	134,000	65.6	137
Ft. Wayne	n/a	n/a	n/a
Gary	n/a	n/a	n/a
Grand Rapids	100,000	80.2	55
Indianapolis	132,000	78.0	72
Kansas City	n/a	n/a	n/a
Lansing	101,000	75.6	90
Little Rock	n/a	n/a	n/a
Madison	n/a	n/a	n/a
Milwaukee	108,000	79.1	65
Minneapolis	129,000	82.8	32
Oklahoma City	85,000	81.0	44
Omaha	105,000	77.1	80
St. Louis	120,000	71.3	109
Springfield	n/a	n/a	n/a
Wichita	n/a	n/a	n/a
U.S.	**134,000**	**69.6**	–

Note: (1) Metropolitan Statistical Area - see Appendix A for areas included; (2) U.S. figures calculated from the sales of
524,324 new and existing homes in 181 markets; (3) Housing Opportunity Index - percent of homes sold that were within
the reach of the median income household at the prevailing mortgage interest rate; (4) Rank is from 1-181 with 1 being
most affordable; n/a not available
Source: National Association of Home Builders, Housing News Service, 1st Quarter 1999

Average Home Prices

Area	Price ($)
Ann Arbor[7]	155,000
Chicago	n/a
Des Moines	127,833
Detroit	199,140
Fort Wayne[3]	128,425
Gary	n/a
Grand Rapids[5]	163,663
Indianapolis[2]	125,307
Kansas City[1]	123,168
Lansing	189,500
Little Rock[4]	114,450
Madison[6]	166,687
Milwaukee[1]	171,978
Minneapolis	135,230
Oklahoma City	109,500
Omaha	132,129
Saint Louis[1]	132,700
Springfield	129,100
Wichita[5]	127,883
U.S.	**142,735**

Note: Figures are based on a new home with 1,800 sq. ft. of living area on an 8,000 sq. ft. lot; n/a not available; (1) Metropolitan Statistical Area (MSA) - see Appendix A for areas included; (2) Indianpolis/Marion County; (3) Ft. Wayne/Allen County; (4) Little Rock-North Little Rock; (5) 4th Quarter 1998; (6) 3rd Quarter 1998; (7) 2nd Quarter 1996
Source: ACCRA, Cost of Living Index, 1st Quarter 1999 unless otherwise noted

Average Apartment Rent

Area	Rent ($/mth)
Ann Arbor[7]	807
Chicago	n/a
Des Moines	557
Detroit	773
Fort Wayne[3]	523
Gary	n/a
Grand Rapids[5]	616
Indianapolis[2]	617
Kansas City[1]	566
Lansing	645
Little Rock[4]	588
Madison[6]	656
Milwaukee[1]	694
Minneapolis	621
Oklahoma City	537
Omaha	594
Saint Louis[1]	658
Springfield	506
Wichita[5]	508
U.S.	**601**

Note: Figures are based on an unfurnished two bedroom, 1-1/2 or 2 bath apartment, approximately 950 sq. ft. in size, excluding all utilities except water; n/a not available; (1) Metropolitan Statistical Area (MSA) - see Appendix A for areas included; (2) Indianpolis/Marion County; (3) Ft. Wayne/Allen County; (4) Little Rock-North Little Rock; (5) 4th Quarter 1998; (6) 3rd Quarter 1998; (7) 2nd Quarter 1996
Source: ACCRA, Cost of Living Index, 1st Quarter 1999 unless otherwise noted

Average Residential Utility Costs

Area	All Electric ($/mth)	Part Electric ($/mth)	Other Energy ($/mth)	Phone ($/mth)
Ann Arbor[7]	-	57.85	39.99	22.53
Chicago	n/a	n/a	n/a	n/a
Des Moines	-	48.84	55.50	19.76
Detroit	-	66.67	41.13	23.88
Fort Wayne[3]	-	49.04	47.87	23.83
Gary	n/a	n/a	n/a	n/a
Grand Rapids[5]	-	52.73	52.33	17.44
Indianapolis[2]	-	50.52	48.63	18.00
Kansas City[1]	-	55.17	43.06	24.04
Lansing	-	37.06	41.59	18.59
Little Rock[4]	-	75.02	36.30	28.10
Madison[6]	-	48.47	41.91	17.65
Milwaukee[1]	-	46.34	57.89	16.28
Minneapolis	-	50.76	54.68	22.28
Oklahoma City	-	60.79	35.77	20.58
Omaha	-	50.78	33.08	21.02
Saint Louis[1]	-	58.91	41.86	19.69
Springfield	-	39.51	32.26	16.29
Wichita[5]	-	64.10	39.60	22.08
U.S.	**100.02**	**55.73**	**43.33**	**19.71**

Note: Dashes indicate data not applicable; n/a not available;
(1) Metropolitan Statistical Area (MSA) - see Appendix A for areas included; (2) Indianpolis/Marion County; (3) Ft. Wayne/Allen County; (4) Little Rock-North Little Rock; (5) 4th Quarter 1998; (6) 3rd Quarter 1998; (7) 2nd Quarter 1996
Source: ACCRA, Cost of Living Index, 1st Quarter 1999 unless otherwise noted

Average Health Care Costs

Area	Hospital ($/day)	Doctor ($/visit)	Dentist ($/visit)
Ann Arbor[7]	535.00	48.80	71.00
Chicago	n/a	n/a	n/a
Des Moines	473.50	47.40	70.00
Detroit	550.41	52.80	81.90
Fort Wayne[3]	510.00	43.80	54.60
Gary	n/a	n/a	n/a
Grand Rapids[5]	449.50	55.00	62.80
Indianapolis[2]	427.19	49.10	62.50
Kansas City[1]	555.80	54.00	65.71
Lansing	479.00	42.75	71.33
Little Rock[4]	285.80	51.40	77.40
Madison[6]	314.75	67.50	66.50
Milwaukee[1]	411.50	55.80	65.40
Minneapolis	672.00	54.80	71.20
Oklahoma City	305.94	46.25	69.50
Omaha	355.00	46.00	66.80
Saint Louis[1]	472.50	61.20	64.00
Springfield	425.00	49.67	63.34
Wichita[5]	533.25	52.00	68.20
U.S.	**430.43**	**52.45**	**66.35**

Note: n/a not available; Hospital—based on a semi-private room; Doctor—based on a general practitioner's routine exam of an established patient; Dentist—based on adult teeth cleaning and periodic oral exam; (1) Metropolitan Statistical Area (MSA) - see Appendix A for areas included; (2) Indianpolis/Marion County; (3) Ft. Wayne/Allen County; (4) Little Rock-North Little Rock; (5) 4th Quarter 1998; (6) 3rd Quarter 1998; (7) 2nd Quarter 1996
Source: ACCRA, Cost of Living Index, 1st Quarter 1999 unless otherwise noted

Distribution of Office-Based Physicians

MSA[1]	General Practitioners	Specialists		
		Medical	Surgical	Other
Ann Arbor	111	545	354	541
Chicago	1,628	5,879	3,593	3,968
Des Moines	76	174	171	170
Detroit	601	2,688	1,751	1,797
Ft. Wayne	141	178	191	190
Gary	160	262	244	207
Grand Rapids	192	389	355	346
Indianapolis	458	968	772	866
Kansas City	162	510	428	351
Lansing	93	201	130	154
Little Rock	183	424	367	406
Madison	157	387	239	363
Milwaukee	364	1,061	740	953
Minneapolis	1,020	1,541	1,114	1,257
Oklahoma City	244	542	482	530
Omaha	218	429	373	396
St. Louis	313	1,852	1,273	1,326
Springfield	67	182	160	155
Wichita	153	233	189	217

Note: Data as of 12/31/97; (1) Metropolitan Statistical Area - see Appendix A for areas included
Source: Physician Characteristics & Distribution in the U.S., 1999

Educational Quality

City	School District	Education Quotient[1]	Graduate Outcome[2]	Community Index[3]	Resource Index[4]
Ann Arbor	Ann Arbor Public Schools	133.0	146.0	144.0	106.0
Chicago	City of Chicago	84.0	52.0	85.0	147.0
Des Moines	Des Moines Ind.	108.0	103.0	138.0	113.0
Detroit	Detroit City	54.0	50.0	63.0	60.0
Fort Wayne	Fort Wayne Community Sch.	88.0	89.0	129.0	79.0
Gary	Gary Community Sch.	62.0	54.0	82.0	74.0
Grand Rapids	Grand Rapids City	77.0	80.0	82.0	69.0
Indianapolis	Indianapolis Public Sch.	71.0	55.0	105.0	97.0
Kansas City	Kansas City SD	86.0	52.0	103.0	149.0
Lansing	Lansing Public	74.0	72.0	86.0	75.0
Little Rock	Little Rock SD	92.0	64.0	119.0	143.0
Madison	Madison Metropolitan	128.0	150.0	143.0	81.0
Milwaukee	Milwaukee SD	73.0	64.0	83.0	88.0
Minneapolis	Minneapolis SD	106.0	84.0	146.0	143.0
Oklahoma City	Oklahoma City SD	75.0	68.0	107.0	81.0
Omaha	Omaha Public Schools	122.0	118.0	136.0	128.0
Saint Louis	Saint Louis City	86.0	58.0	54.0	147.0
Springfield	Springfield SD	122.0	119.0	97.0	132.0
Wichita	Wichita SD	95.0	89.0	128.0	100.0

Note: Nearly 1,000 secondary school districts were rated in terms of educational quality. The scores range from a low of 50 to a high of 150; (1) Average of the Graduate Outcome, Community and Resource indexes; (2) Based on graduation rates and college board scores (SAT/ACT); (3) Based on the surrounding community's average level of education and the area's average income level; (4) Based on teacher salaries, per-pupil expenditures and student-teacher ratios.
Source: Expansion Management, Ratings Issue 1998

School Enrollment by Type: City

City	Preprimary				Elementary/High School			
	Public		Private		Public		Private	
	Enrollment	%	Enrollment	%	Enrollment	%	Enrollment	%
Ann Arbor	1,151	55.4	928	44.6	9,948	88.5	1,299	11.5
Chicago	27,249	61.1	17,333	38.9	391,046	79.5	101,138	20.5
Des Moines	2,441	67.2	1,194	32.8	26,321	91.6	2,402	8.4
Detroit	13,196	72.4	5,027	27.6	180,245	87.3	26,179	12.7
Ft. Wayne	1,880	53.2	1,652	46.8	24,519	83.7	4,783	16.3
Gary	1,560	79.8	396	20.2	25,315	93.7	1,700	6.3
Grand Rapids	3,105	60.8	2,004	39.2	24,319	76.0	7,660	24.0
Indianapolis	6,699	51.1	6,414	48.9	101,922	87.2	14,951	12.8
Kansas City	4,496	55.5	3,601	44.5	57,590	85.6	9,712	14.4
Lansing	1,707	65.2	911	34.8	20,001	90.4	2,118	9.6
Little Rock	1,427	40.4	2,108	59.6	22,873	79.7	5,818	20.3
Madison	2,039	54.5	1,705	45.5	19,043	90.4	2,023	9.6
Milwaukee	6,616	66.3	3,359	33.7	92,372	80.6	22,277	19.4
Minneapolis	3,848	59.9	2,577	40.1	38,107	84.8	6,823	15.2
Oklahoma City	4,639	60.5	3,033	39.5	66,351	90.3	7,166	9.7
Omaha	4,250	61.1	2,709	38.9	44,993	81.7	10,057	18.3
St. Louis	4,198	56.7	3,211	43.3	49,177	77.4	14,389	22.6
Springfield	1,135	62.4	683	37.6	16,946	92.8	1,316	7.2
Wichita	3,357	58.0	2,428	42.0	43,283	86.8	6,572	13.2
U.S.	**2,679,029**	**59.5**	**1,824,256**	**40.5**	**38,379,689**	**90.2**	**4,187,099**	**9.8**

Note: Figures shown cover persons 3 years old and over
Source: 1990 Census of Population and Housing, Summary Tape File 3C

School Enrollment by Type: Metro Area

MSA[1]	Preprimary				Elementary/High School			
	Public		Private		Public		Private	
	Enrollment	%	Enrollment	%	Enrollment	%	Enrollment	%
Ann Arbor	3,711	62.5	2,225	37.5	35,078	91.0	3,490	9.0
Chicago	70,174	57.4	52,166	42.6	837,481	82.5	178,237	17.5
Des Moines	5,840	67.4	2,829	32.6	59,903	93.4	4,230	6.6
Detroit	63,323	68.3	29,435	31.7	685,077	88.7	87,455	11.3
Ft. Wayne	4,397	54.1	3,726	45.9	56,218	84.7	10,137	15.3
Gary	6,173	58.8	4,317	41.2	106,474	89.5	12,519	10.5
Grand Rapids	12,129	66.4	6,136	33.6	103,726	81.8	23,081	18.2
Indianapolis	12,635	53.2	11,125	46.8	191,105	90.0	21,252	10.0
Kansas City	18,724	56.8	14,261	43.2	236,921	89.4	28,033	10.6
Lansing	5,761	67.9	2,718	32.1	68,193	91.6	6,215	8.4
Little Rock	4,862	53.5	4,231	46.5	80,860	88.7	10,321	11.3
Madison	4,454	59.1	3,077	40.9	47,805	92.0	4,184	8.0
Milwaukee	15,931	56.8	12,092	43.2	204,342	81.5	46,314	18.5
Minneapolis	35,492	63.1	20,730	36.9	359,955	89.1	44,235	10.9
Oklahoma City	10,338	60.2	6,849	39.8	156,353	92.8	12,146	7.2
Omaha	8,461	60.9	5,425	39.1	96,810	86.3	15,363	13.7
St. Louis	26,907	50.2	26,648	49.8	337,304	80.6	81,322	19.4
Springfield	2,229	61.2	1,415	38.8	35,278	93.9	2,297	6.1
Wichita	5,755	61.4	3,625	38.6	76,614	89.0	9,501	11.0
U.S.	**2,679,029**	**59.5**	**1,824,256**	**40.5**	**38,379,689**	**90.2**	**4,187,099**	**9.8**

Note: Figures shown cover persons 3 years old and over;
(1) Metropolitan Statistical Area - see Appendix A for areas included
Source: 1990 Census of Population and Housing, Summary Tape File 3C

School Enrollment by Race: City

City	Preprimary (%)				Elementary/High School (%)			
	White	Black	Other	Hisp.[1]	White	Black	Other	Hisp.[1]
Ann Arbor	82.9	9.4	7.7	3.6	72.4	17.0	10.6	2.5
Chicago	36.1	50.5	13.5	17.5	30.7	48.4	20.9	27.8
Des Moines	92.2	4.7	3.1	3.0	83.5	11.0	5.5	3.7
Detroit	18.1	78.5	3.4	3.5	13.5	83.3	3.1	3.3
Ft. Wayne	74.6	21.5	3.9	3.4	69.8	26.0	4.2	4.3
Gary	9.6	88.6	1.8	5.5	9.4	87.3	3.3	5.2
Grand Rapids	73.4	20.5	6.1	5.5	62.8	29.6	7.6	7.3
Indianapolis	76.0	22.5	1.5	1.2	67.8	30.4	1.8	1.3
Kansas City	65.3	31.4	3.3	4.2	55.4	40.0	4.6	5.5
Lansing	71.7	18.9	9.4	9.7	61.1	27.1	11.8	12.9
Little Rock	65.5	34.1	0.4	1.0	45.6	53.0	1.4	0.6
Madison	84.8	7.7	7.5	3.0	84.7	9.1	6.3	2.3
Milwaukee	54.3	38.4	7.3	7.2	43.2	47.0	9.8	10.0
Minneapolis	69.2	19.0	11.8	3.1	56.8	26.2	16.9	3.4
Oklahoma City	72.4	18.2	9.4	5.7	65.7	21.8	12.5	7.3
Omaha	80.7	15.0	4.3	3.2	76.9	19.1	4.0	4.2
St. Louis	44.4	53.6	2.0	1.2	33.2	65.2	1.6	1.4
Springfield	94.6	1.4	4.0	1.4	93.8	3.2	3.0	1.2
Wichita	82.6	12.2	5.3	5.4	74.4	16.0	9.6	7.3
U.S.	**80.4**	**12.5**	**7.1**	**7.8**	**74.1**	**15.6**	**10.3**	**12.5**

Note: Figures shown cover persons 3 years old and over; (1) People of Hispanic origin can be of any race
Source: 1990 Census of Population and Housing, Summary Tape File 3C

School Enrollment by Race: Metro Area

MSA[1]	Preprimary (%)				Elementary/High School (%)			
	White	Black	Other	Hisp.[2]	White	Black	Other	Hisp.[2]
Ann Arbor	83.4	12.4	4.1	1.9	78.3	16.6	5.1	2.4
Chicago	68.6	23.0	8.4	9.4	56.2	29.0	14.8	17.5
Des Moines	95.8	2.2	2.1	1.7	91.2	5.3	3.5	2.7
Detroit	77.6	19.5	2.9	2.3	69.8	26.9	3.3	2.6
Ft. Wayne	88.1	9.6	2.3	2.4	85.5	11.9	2.6	2.7
Gary	74.9	20.7	4.4	8.0	69.7	24.6	5.7	10.5
Grand Rapids	89.6	6.5	3.9	2.6	86.5	8.4	5.1	4.5
Indianapolis	85.9	12.8	1.4	1.1	81.0	17.5	1.5	1.2
Kansas City	85.4	12.3	2.3	3.3	80.0	16.3	3.7	4.0
Lansing	88.0	6.7	5.4	4.7	84.1	9.7	6.2	5.9
Little Rock	77.6	21.9	0.5	1.1	69.4	29.0	1.6	1.3
Madison	89.7	5.0	5.2	2.3	91.3	5.0	3.8	2.1
Milwaukee	82.1	14.0	3.9	3.9	72.3	22.0	5.6	5.7
Minneapolis	90.7	4.3	5.0	1.9	87.8	5.3	6.9	2.1
Oklahoma City	79.1	12.1	8.8	4.3	75.6	13.7	10.7	4.9
Omaha	87.5	9.1	3.4	2.7	85.7	11.0	3.3	3.2
St. Louis	81.3	16.9	1.8	1.2	74.9	23.3	1.8	1.3
Springfield	96.5	0.9	2.6	1.1	96.1	1.8	2.0	1.0
Wichita	86.8	8.2	5.1	5.5	83.2	9.9	6.9	5.5
U.S.	**80.4**	**12.5**	**7.1**	**7.8**	**74.1**	**15.6**	**10.3**	**12.5**

Note: Figures shown cover persons 3 years old and over; (1) Metropolitan Statistical Area - see Appendix A for areas included; (2) People of Hispanic origin can be of any race
Source: 1990 Census of Population and Housing, Summary Tape File 3C

Crime Rate: City

City	All Crimes	Violent Crimes				Property Crimes		
		Murder	Forcible Rape	Robbery	Aggrav. Assault	Burglary	Larceny -Theft	Motor Vehicle Theft
Ann Arbor	4,090.1	n/a	30.4	94.6	233.0	717.0	2,822.3	192.9
Chicago	n/a	27.4	n/a	914.3	1,320.4	1,469.1	4,324.5	1,215.1
Des Moines	8,627.6	6.1	43.5	192.4	251.2	1,257.6	6,167.7	709.1
Detroit	11,669.1	45.9	94.8	803.6	1,207.3	1,891.9	4,351.9	3,273.8
Ft. Wayne	8,199.4	19.3	60.5	268.6	194.2	1,312.8	5,544.9	799.2
Gary	8,703.6	84.1	137.4	635.3	797.6	2,394.4	2,664.0	1,990.9
Grand Rapids	7,182.4	12.8	20.9	294.9	841.5	1,440.0	3,988.4	583.8
Indianapolis	6,743.4	18.7	71.0	427.9	614.8	1,474.2	3,146.9	990.0
Kansas City	10,952.1	22.1	92.2	599.7	1,181.5	1,911.4	5,502.2	1,642.9
Lansing	7,713.3	13.0	130.0	215.3	804.3	1,379.5	4,760.1	411.1
Little Rock	11,865.8	18.5	89.8	471.6	705.5	2,224.2	7,516.3	839.9
Madison	4,460.6	1.5	40.9	171.8	218.7	705.7	2,991.6	330.4
Milwaukee	7,587.0	19.4	48.8	565.3	419.4	1,084.8	4,129.5	1,319.8
Minneapolis	11,439.5	15.9	147.3	909.0	777.9	2,263.3	5,730.7	1,595.4
Oklahoma City	11,655.6	12.5	86.6	295.9	677.9	2,071.4	7,547.6	963.7
Omaha	7,236.2	8.8	50.0	232.6	1,094.0	899.8	3,964.8	986.2
St. Louis	13,576.7	40.6	59.6	946.9	1,495.4	2,676.7	6,204.6	2,152.8
Springfield	6,977.8	4.6	41.1	103.1	323.7	1,317.5	4,740.8	447.0
Wichita	8,037.9	10.1	72.2	281.9	469.1	1,510.7	4,976.4	717.5
U.S.	**4,922.7**	**6.8**	**35.9**	**186.1**	**382.0**	**919.6**	**2,886.5**	**505.8**

Note: Crime rate is the number of crimes per 100,000 population; n/a not available;
Source: FBI Uniform Crime Reports 1997

Crime Rate: Suburbs

Suburbs[1]	All Crimes	Violent Crimes				Property Crimes		
		Murder	Forcible Rape	Robbery	Aggrav. Assault	Burglary	Larceny -Theft	Motor Vehicle Theft
Ann Arbor	3,566.2	3.9	44.1	70.4	207.7	603.3	2,363.7	273.2
Chicago	n/a	n/a	n/a	n/a	n/a	n/a	n/a	n/a
Des Moines	3,764.8	0.9	10.7	28.1	138.2	645.1	2,707.4	234.5
Detroit	4,215.1	2.5	31.3	78.0	264.0	541.1	2,819.8	478.4
Ft. Wayne	2,633.1	2.4	16.1	33.6	144.5	451.5	1,791.2	193.6
Gary	5,178.6	2.9	18.8	128.2	868.6	676.1	2,905.5	578.3
Grand Rapids	3,807.5	1.7	41.5	44.4	204.1	727.9	2,554.2	233.8
Indianapolis	3,630.7	3.4	22.1	68.9	188.0	588.0	2,455.8	304.6
Kansas City	n/a	n/a	n/a	n/a	n/a	n/a	n/a	n/a
Lansing	n/a	n/a	n/a	n/a	n/a	n/a	n/a	n/a
Little Rock	5,537.8	11.9	57.6	112.0	386.1	981.0	3,597.3	392.0
Madison	3,275.1	2.1	18.8	17.7	194.5	453.6	2,460.2	128.3
Milwaukee	3,012.6	0.9	6.8	42.8	73.9	386.5	2,339.0	162.6
Minneapolis	4,441.7	2.0	40.3	69.2	135.2	639.1	3,202.5	353.4
Oklahoma City	4,720.1	3.4	38.6	69.3	228.1	983.3	3,065.3	332.1
Omaha	3,033.3	1.5	14.2	48.9	147.2	539.7	2,031.9	249.9
St. Louis	n/a	n/a	n/a	n/a	n/a	n/a	n/a	n/a
Springfield	2,044.6	2.3	16.4	11.1	252.3	575.5	1,057.2	129.7
Wichita	n/a	n/a	n/a	n/a	n/a	n/a	n/a	n/a
U.S.	**4,922.7**	**6.8**	**35.9**	**186.1**	**382.0**	**919.6**	**2,886.5**	**505.8**

Note: Crime rate is the number of crimes per 100,000 population; n/a not available; (1) Defined as all areas within the MSA but located outside the central city
Source: FBI Uniform Crime Reports 1997

Crime Rate: Metro Area

MSA[1]	All Crimes	Violent Crimes				Property Crimes		
		Murder	Forcible Rape	Robbery	Aggrav. Assault	Burglary	Larceny -Theft	Motor Vehicle Theft
Ann Arbor	3,677.5	3.0	41.2	75.5	213.1	627.5	2,461.1	256.1
Chicago	n/a	n/a	n/a	n/a	n/a	n/a	n/a	n/a
Des Moines	6,029.0	3.3	26.0	104.6	190.8	930.3	4,318.6	455.5
Detroit	5,931.5	12.5	45.9	245.1	481.2	852.2	3,172.6	1,122.1
Ft. Wayne	4,809.1	9.0	33.5	125.5	164.0	788.2	3,258.6	430.4
Gary	5,828.3	17.9	40.7	221.7	855.5	992.9	2,861.0	838.7
Grand Rapids	4,459.9	3.8	37.5	92.8	327.3	865.6	2,831.4	301.4
Indianapolis	5,260.6	11.4	47.7	256.8	411.5	1,052.0	2,817.7	663.5
Kansas City	n/a	n/a	n/a	n/a	n/a	n/a	n/a	n/a
Lansing	n/a	n/a	n/a	n/a	n/a	n/a	n/a	n/a
Little Rock	7,639.7	14.1	68.3	231.4	492.2	1,393.9	4,899.0	540.8
Madison	3,877.2	1.8	30.0	96.0	206.8	581.6	2,730.1	230.9
Milwaukee	4,966.5	8.8	24.7	266.0	221.5	684.8	3,103.8	656.9
Minneapolis	5,364.5	3.8	54.4	179.9	220.0	853.3	3,535.9	517.2
Oklahoma City	7,910.7	7.6	60.7	173.6	435.0	1,483.8	5,127.3	622.6
Omaha	5,223.1	5.3	32.9	144.6	640.5	727.3	3,039.0	633.5
St. Louis	n/a	n/a	n/a	n/a	n/a	n/a	n/a	n/a
Springfield	4,380.1	3.4	28.1	54.7	286.1	926.8	2,801.1	279.9
Wichita	n/a	n/a	n/a	n/a	n/a	n/a	n/a	n/a
U.S.	**4,922.7**	**6.8**	**35.9**	**186.1**	**382.0**	**919.6**	**2,886.5**	**505.8**

Note: Crime rate is the number of crimes per 100,000 population; n/a not available;
(1) Metropolitan Statistical Area - see Appendix A for areas included
Source: FBI Uniform Crime Reports 1997

Temperature & Precipitation: Yearly Averages and Extremes

City	Extreme Low (°F)	Average Low (°F)	Average Temp. (°F)	Average High (°F)	Extreme High (°F)	Average Precip. (in.)	Average Snow (in.)
Ann Arbor	-21	39	49	58	104	32.4	41
Chicago	-27	40	49	59	104	35.4	39
Des Moines	-24	40	50	60	108	31.8	33
Detroit	-21	39	49	58	104	32.4	41
Ft. Wayne	-22	40	50	60	106	35.9	33
Gary	-27	40	49	59	104	35.4	39
Grand Rapids	-22	38	48	57	102	34.7	73
Indianapolis	-23	42	53	62	104	40.2	25
Kansas City	-23	44	54	64	109	38.1	21
Lansing	-24	37	48	57	100	30.6	51
Little Rock	-5	51	62	73	112	50.7	5
Madison	-37	35	46	57	104	31.1	42
Milwaukee	-26	38	47	55	103	32.0	49
Minneapolis	-34	35	45	54	105	27.1	52
Oklahoma City	-8	49	60	71	110	32.8	10
Omaha	-23	40	51	62	110	30.1	29
Springfield	-17	45	56	67	113	42.0	18
St. Louis	-18	46	56	66	115	36.8	20
Wichita	-21	45	57	68	113	29.3	17

Note: Tr = Trace
Source: National Climatic Data Center, International Station Meteorological Climate Summary, 3/95

Weather Conditions

City	Temperature			Daytime Sky			Precipitation		
	10°F & below	32°F & below	90°F & above	Clear	Partly cloudy	Cloudy	.01 inch or more precip.	1.0 inch or more snow/ice	Thunder-storms
Ann Arbor	(a)	136	12	74	134	157	135	38	32
Chicago	(a)	132	17	83	136	146	125	31	38
Des Moines	(a)	137	26	99	129	137	106	25	46
Detroit	(a)	136	12	74	134	157	135	38	32
Ft. Wayne	(a)	131	16	75	140	150	131	31	39
Gary	(a)	(b)	17	83	136	146	125	31	38
Grand Rapids	(a)	146	11	67	119	179	142	57	34
Indianapolis	19	119	19	83	128	154	127	24	43
Kansas City	22	110	39	112	134	119	103	17	51
Lansing	(a)	149	11	71	131	163	142	47	32
Little Rock	1	57	73	110	142	113	104	4	57
Madison	(a)	161	14	88	119	158	118	38	40
Milwaukee	(a)	141	10	90	118	157	126	38	35
Minneapolis	(a)	156	16	93	125	147	113	41	37
Oklahoma City	5	79	70	124	131	110	80	8	50
Omaha	(a)	139	35	100	142	123	97	20	46
Springfield	12	102	42	113	119	133	109	14	55
St. Louis	13	100	43	97	138	130	109	14	46
Wichita	13	110	63	117	132	116	87	13	54

Note: Figures are average number of days per year; (a) Figures for 10 degrees and below are not available; (b) Figures for 32 degrees and below are not available
Source: National Climatic Data Center, International Station Meteorological Climate Summary, 3/95

Air Quality

MSA[1]	PSI>100[2] (days)	Ozone (ppm)	Carbon Monoxide (ppm)	Sulfur Dioxide (ppm)	Nitrogen Dioxide (ppm)	Particulate Matter (ug/m3)	Lead (ug/m3)
Ann Arbor	n/a	0.09	n/a	n/a	n/a	n/a	n/a
Chicago	10	0.11	5	0.041	0.034	99	0.08
Des Moines	n/a	0.08	4	n/a	n/a	126	n/a
Detroit	12	0.12	5	0.044	0.026	106	0.09
Fort Wayne	n/a	0.10	6	n/a	n/a	77	0.03
Gary	12	0.12	4	0.032	n/a	138	0.04
Grand Rapids	10	0.12	2	0.008	n/a	60	0.01
Indianapolis	12	0.11	4	0.030	0.015	54	0.08
Kansas City	18	0.12	7	0.021	0.020	75	0.45
Lansing	n/a	0.09	n/a	n/a	n/a	n/a	n/a
Little Rock	1	0.10	5	0.006	0.010	61	n/a
Madison	n/a	0.09	4	0.017	n/a	42	n/a
Milwaukee	5	0.13	3	0.028	0.021	61	0.03
Minneapolis	0	0.09	5	0.027	0.023	77	0.01
Oklahoma City	4	0.10	5	n/a	0.015	58	0.00
Omaha	0	0.08	5	0.050	n/a	98	0.12
Saint Louis	15	0.12	5	0.063	0.025	108	0.03
Springfield	n/a	0.08	5	0.054	0.011	95	n/a
Wichita	n/a	0.09	5	0.007	n/a	57	0.01
NAAQS[3]	-	**0.12**	**9**	**0.140**	**0.053**	**150**	**1.50**

Note: (1) Metropolitan Statistical Area - see Appendix A for areas included; (2) Number of days the Pollutant Standards Index (PSI) exceeded 100 in 1997. A PSI value greater than 100 indicates that air quality would be in the unhealthful range on that day; (3) National Ambient Air Quality Standard; ppm = parts per million; ug/m³ = micrograms per cubic meter; n/a not available
Source: EPA, National Air Quality and Emissions Trends Report, 1997

Water Quality

City	Tap Water
Ann Arbor	Alkaline, soft and fluoridated
Chicago	Alkaline (Lake Michigan) and fluoridated
Des Moines	Alkaline, soft and fluoridated
Detroit	Alkaline, soft
Fort Wayne	Alkaline, soft and fluoridated
Gary	Soft, filtered and fluoridated
Grand Rapids	Alkaline, hard and fluoridated
Indianapolis	Alkaline, hard, fluoridated. Three separate systems with separate sources and purification plants.
Kansas City	Neutral, soft and fluoridated
Lansing	Alkaline, soft and fluoridated
Little Rock	Neutral, soft and fluoridated
Madison	Alkaline, hard and fluoridated
Milwaukee	Alkaline, medium hard and fluoridated
Minneapolis	Alkaline, soft and fluoridated. Water is hard in the suburbs.
Oklahoma City	Alkaline, soft and fluoridated
Omaha	Moderately alkaline, moderately soft, fluoridated
Saint Louis	Alkaline, moderately hard and fluoridated
Springfield	Alkaline, hard and fluoridated
Wichita	Soft

Source: Editor & Publisher Market Guide 1999

Appendix B

Metropolitan Statistical Areas

Ann Arbor, MI

Includes Lenawee, Livingston and Washtenaw Counties (as of 6/30/93)

Includes Washtenaw County (prior to 6/30/93)

Chicago, IL

Includes Cook, DeKalb, DuPage, Grundy, Kane, Kendall, Lake, McHenry and Will Counties (as of 6/30/93)

Includes Cook, DuPage and McHenry Counties (prior to 6/30/93)

Des Moines, IA

Includes Dallas, Polk and Warren Counties

Detroit, IL

Includes Lapper, Macomb, Monroe, Oakland, St. Clair and Wayne Counties

Ft. Wayne, IN

Includes Adams, Allen, DeKalb, Huntington, Wells and Whitley Counties (as of 6/30/93)

Includes Allen, DeKalb and Whitley Counties (prior to 6/30/93)

Gary, IN

Includes Lake and Porter Counties

Grand Rapids-Muskegon-Holland, MI

Includes Allegan, Kent, Muskegon and Ottawa Counties (as of 6/30/93)

Includes Kent and Ottawa Counties (prior to 6/30/93)

Indianapolis, IN

Includes Boone, Hamilton, Hancock, Hendricks, Johnson, Madison, Marion, M organ and Shelby Counties (as of 6/30/93)

Includes Boone, Hamilton, Hancock, Hendricks, Johnson, Marion, Morgan and Shelby Counties (prior to 6/30/93)

Kansas City, KS-MO

Includes Cass, Clay, Clinton, Jackson, Lafayette, Platte and Ray Counties, MO; Johnson, Leavenworth, Miami and Wyandotte Counties, KS (as of 6/30/93)

Includes Cass, Clay, Jackson, Lafayette, Platte and Ray Counties, MO; Johnson, Leavenworth, Miami and Wyandotte Counties, KS (prior to 6/30/93)

Lansing, MI

Includes Clinton, Eaton and Ingham Counties

Little Rock-North Little Rock, AR

Includes Faulkner, Lonoke, Pulaski and Saline Counties

Madison, WI

Includes Dane County

Milwaukee-Waukesha, WI

Includes Milwaukee, Ozaukee, Washington and Waukesha Counties

Minneapolis-St. Paul, MN-WI

Includes Anoka, Carver, Chicago, Dakota, Hennepin, Isanti, Ramsey, Scott, Sherburne, Washington, Wright and Pierce Counties, MN; St. Croix County, WI (as of 6/30/93)

Includes Anoka, Carver, Chicago, Dakota, Hennepin, Isanti, Ramsey, Scott, Washington and Wright Counties, MN; St. Croix County, WI (prior to 6/30/93)

Oklahoma City, OK

Includes Canadian, Cleveland, Logan, McClain, Oklahoma and Pottawatomie Counties

Omaha, NE

Includes Pottawattamie County, IA; Cass, Douglas, Sarpy and Washington Counties, NE

St. Louis, MO-IL

Includes St. Louis and Sullivan Counties; Crawford (part), Franklin, Jefferson, Lincoln, St. Charles, St. Louis and Warren Counties, MO; Clinton, Jersey, Madison, Monroe and St. Clair Counties, IL (as of 6/30/93)

Includes St. Louis and Sullivan Cities; Franklin, Jefferson, St. Charles and St. Louis Counties, MO; Clinton, Jersey, Madison, Monroe and St. Clair Counties, IL (prior to 6/30/93)

Springfield, MO

Includes Christian, Greene and Webster Counties (as of 6/30/93)

Includes Christian and Greene Counties (prior to 6/30/93)

Wichita, KS

Includes Butler, Harvey and Sedgwich Counties

Appendix C

Chambers of Commerce and Economic Development Organizations

Ann Arbor

Ann Arbor Area Chamber of Commerce
425 South Main
Suite 103
Ann Arbor, MI 48104
Phone: (734) 665-4433
Fax: (313) 665-4191

Chicago

Chicagoland Chamber of Commerce
330 North Wabash
Suite 2800
Chicago, IL 60611
Phone: (312) 494-6700
Fax: (312) 494-0196

City of Chicago
Department of Planning and Development
City Hall, Room 1000
121 North La Salle Street
Chicago, Il 60602
Phone: (312) 744-4190
Fax: (312) 744-2271

Des Moines

Greater Des Moines Chamber of Commerce
601 Locust Street
Suite 100
Des Moines, IA 50309
Phone: (515) 286-4950
Fax: (515) 286-4974

Detroit

Greater Detroit Chamber of Commerce
101 Woodward Street
Suite 1700
Detroit, MI 48226
Phone: (313) 964-4000
Fax: (313) 964-0183

Fort Wayne

City of Fort Wayne
Community of Economic Development Division
City-County Building
Room 800
1 Main Street
Fort Wayne, IN 46802
Phone: (219) 427-1140
Fax: (219) 426-7232

Greater Fort Wayne Chamber of Commerce
826 Ewing Street
Fort Wayne, IN 46802
Phone: (219) 424-1435
Fax: (219) 426-7232

Gary

Gary Chamber of Commerce
504 Broadway
Suite 328
Gary, IN 46402
Phone: (219) 885-7404
Fax: (219) 885-7408

Grand Rapids

Grand Rapids Area Chamber of Commerce
111 Pearl Street Northwest
Grand Rapids, Mi 49503
Phone: (616) 771-0300
Fax: (616) 771-0318

Indianapolis

Indianapolis Chamber of Commerce
320 North Meridian Street
Suite 200
Indianapolis, IN 46204-1777
Phone: (317) 464-2200
Fax: (317) 464-2217

Indianapolis Economic Development
Corporation
41 East Washington Street
Suite 310
Indianapolis, IN 46204
Phone: (317) 236-6262
Fax: (317) 236-6275

Kansas City

Greater Kansas City Chamber of Commerce
911 Main Street
2600 Commerce Tower
Kansas City, MO 64105
Phone: (816) 221-2424
Fax: (816) 221-7440

Kansas City Area Development Council
911 Main Street
Suite 2600
Kansas City, MO 64105
Phone: (816) 221-2121
Fax: (816) 842-2865

Lansing

Lansing Chamber of Commerce
300 East Michigan Avenue
Suite 300
Lansing, MI 48933
Phone: (517) 487-6340
Fax: (517) 484-6910

Little Rock

Greater Little Rock Chamber of Commerce
101 South Spring Street
Suite 200
Little Rock, AK 72201
Phone: (501) 374-4871
Fax: (501) 374-4883

Madison

Greater Madison Chamber of Commerce
P.O. Box 71
Madison, WI 53701-0071
Phone: (608) 256-8348
Fax: (608) 256-0333

Milwaukee

City of Milwaukee
Department of City Development
Economic Development Department
809 North Broadway
P.O. Box 324
Milwaukee, WI 53202
Phone: (414) 286-5840
Fax: (414) 286-5778

Metropolitan Milwaukee Association of Commerce
756 North Milwaukee Street
Milwaukee, WI 53202
Phone: (414) 287-4100
Fax: (414) 271-7753

Minneapolis

Greater Minneapolis Chamber of Commerce
81 South 9th Street
Suite 200
Minneapolis, MN 55402
Phone: (612) 370-9132
Fax: (612) 371-9195

Minneapolis Community Development Agency
105 5th Avenue South
Suite 200
Minneapolis, MN 55401
Phone: (612) 673-5085
Fax: (612) 673-5100

Minneapolis City Planning Department
350 South 5th Street
Room 210
Minneapolis, MN 55414
Phone: (612) 673-2597
Fax: (612) 673-2728

Oklahoma City

Greater Oklahoma City Chamber of Commerce
123 Park Avenue
Oklahoma City, OK 73102
Phone: (405) 297-8900
Fax: (405) 297-8916

Omaha

Omaha Chamber of Commerce
1301 Harney Street
Omaha, NE 68102
Phone: (402) 346-5000
Fax: (402) 346-7050

St. Louis

St. Louis Regional Commerce & Growth
Association
1 Metro Square
Suite 1300
St. Louis, MO 63102
Phone: (314) 231-5555
Fax: (314) 444-1122

Springfield

City of Springfield
Department of Planning & Development
840 Boonville Avenue
Springfield, MO 65802
Phone: (417) 862-5567
Fax: (417) 862-1611

Springfield Area Chamber of Commerce
P.O. Box 1687
Springfield, MO 65801-1687
Phone: (417) 862-5567
Fax: (417) 862-1611

Wichita

Wichita Chamber of Commerce
350 West Douglas
Wichita, KS 67202
Phone: (316) 265-7771
Fax: (316) 265-7502

City of Wichita
Economic Development Department
City Hall
12th Floor
455 North Main Street
Wichita, KS 67202
Phone: (316) 268-4502
Fax: (316) 268-4656

Appendix D

State Departments of Labor and Employment

Arkansas

Arkansas Department of Employment Security
P.O Box 2981
Little Rock, AR 72203-2981
Phone: (501) 862-1684

Illinois

Illinois Department of Employment Security
Occupational Employment Statistics
1657 South Blue Island Avenue
Chicago, Il 60608
Phone: (312) 243-5100

Indiana

Indiana Department of Workforce Development
10 North Senate Avenue
Indianapolis, IN 46204
Phone: (317) 232-6702

Iowa

Iowa Workforce Development
214 KEO
Suite 100
Des Moines, IA 50309
Phone: (515) 281-9619

Kansas

Kansas Department of Labor
401 Topeka Boulevard
Topeka, KS 66603
Phone: (785) 296-4161

Michigan

Michigan Employment Security Commission
7310 Woodard Avenue
Detroit, MI 48202
Phone: (313) 876-5000

Minnesota

Minnesota Department of Economic Security
390 North Robert Street
P.O. Box 550
Hutchinson, MN 55350
Phone: (320) 587-4740

Missouri

Missouri Department of Labor & Industrial
Relations
Division of Employment Security
P.O. Box 500
Jefferson City, MO 65102
Phone: (573) 751-2461

Nebraska

Department of Labor
1010 N Street
P.O. Box 95200
Lincoln, NE 68509-5200
Phone: (402) 471-2275

Oklahoma

Oklahoma Employment Security Commission
P.O. Box 52003
2401 North Lincoln Boulevard
Oklahoma City, OK 73152-2003
Phone: (405) 557-0200

Wisconsin

Wisconsin Department of Industry, Labor &
Human Relations
Bureau of Workforce Information
740 Regent Street
Suite 102
Madison, WI 53715-1233
Phone: (608) 264-5221